T0137643

IFIP Advances in Information and Communication Technology   **648**

Editor-in-Chief

Kai Rannenberg, Goethe University Frankfurt, Germany

IFIP – The International Federation for Information Processing

IFIP was founded in 1960 under the auspices of UNESCO, following the first World Computer Congress held in Paris the previous year. A federation for societies working in information processing, IFIP's aim is two-fold: to support information processing in the countries of its members and to encourage technology transfer to developing nations. As its mission statement clearly states:

> IFIP is the global non-profit federation of societies of ICT professionals that aims at achieving a worldwide professional and socially responsible development and application of information and communication technologies.

IFIP is a non-profit-making organization, run almost solely by 2500 volunteers. It operates through a number of technical committees and working groups, which organize events and publications. IFIP's events range from large international open conferences to working conferences and local seminars.

The flagship event is the IFIP World Computer Congress, at which both invited and contributed papers are presented. Contributed papers are rigorously refereed and the rejection rate is high.

As with the Congress, participation in the open conferences is open to all and papers may be invited or submitted. Again, submitted papers are stringently refereed.

The working conferences are structured differently. They are usually run by a working group and attendance is generally smaller and occasionally by invitation only. Their purpose is to create an atmosphere conducive to innovation and development. Refereeing is also rigorous and papers are subjected to extensive group discussion.

Publications arising from IFIP events vary. The papers presented at the IFIP World Computer Congress and at open conferences are published as conference proceedings, while the results of the working conferences are often published as collections of selected and edited papers.

IFIP distinguishes three types of institutional membership: Country Representative Members, Members at Large, and Associate Members. The type of organization that can apply for membership is a wide variety and includes national or international societies of individual computer scientists/ICT professionals, associations or federations of such societies, government institutions/government related organizations, national or international research institutes or consortia, universities, academies of sciences, companies, national or international associations or federations of companies.

More information about this series at https://link.springer.com/bookseries/6102

Weizhi Meng · Simone Fischer-Hübner ·
Christian D. Jensen (Eds.)

ICT Systems Security and Privacy Protection

37th IFIP TC 11 International Conference, SEC 2022
Copenhagen, Denmark, June 13–15, 2022
Proceedings

 Springer

Editors
Weizhi Meng 🆔
Technical University of Denmark
Lyngby, Denmark

Simone Fischer-Hübner 🆔
Karlstad University
Karlstad, Sweden

Christian D. Jensen 🆔
Technical University of Denmark
Lyngby, Denmark

ISSN 1868-4238   ISSN 1868-422X (electronic)
IFIP Advances in Information and Communication Technology
ISBN 978-3-031-07944-3   ISBN 978-3-031-06975-8 (eBook)
https://doi.org/10.1007/978-3-031-06975-8

This Springer imprint is published by the registered company Springer Nature Switzerland AG
The registered company address is: Gewerbestrasse 11, 6330 Cham, Switzerland

Preface

It is our pleasure to bring you this collection of papers selected for presentation at the 37th IFIP International Conference on ICT Systems Security and Privacy Protection, which was organized in a hybrid way from the Technical University of Denmark, Lyngby, Copenhagen, during 13–15 June, 2022. The IFIP SEC conferences are the flagship events of the International Federation for Information Processing (IFIP) Technical Committee 11 on Information Security and Privacy Protection in Information Processing Systems. The proceedings of IFIP SEC 2022 include 29 high-quality papers covering a wide range of research areas in the field of information security. The authors were from 18 different countries and regions.

The selection of papers was a highly challenging task: 127 received submissions were evaluated based on their significance, novelty, and technical quality. Each paper received at least three reviews, but most of them including all the accepted papers received four or more reviews by members of the Program Committee (PC). The PC members engaged in discussions over a three-week period, and the General and PC chairs held meetings electronically. With 29 selected out of 127 submitted papers, the acceptance rate was 22.8%.

We want to express our gratitude to all the contributors who helped to make IFIP SEC 2022 a success. There is a long list of people who volunteered their time and energy to put together the conference and who deserve acknowledgment. First of all, we want to thank all the authors of both the accepted and the rejected papers for trusting us by contributing their excellent work. We want to thank the members of the Program Committee and the sub-reviewers, who devoted significant hours of their time to evaluate all the submissions. We want to thank the Publication Chairs, Georgios Kambourakis and Wenjuan Li, the Local Organizing Chair, Ann-Cathrin Dunker, and the Web Chair, Wei-Yang Chiu, for the excellent job in promoting the conference, preparing logistics, and running the technical platforms in order for the hybrid conference to run smoothly. We also acknowledge the institutional support for IFIP SEC 2022, which came from the Technical University of Denmark, Cybersecurity Engineering Section. Without this support, it would not have been possible to organize the conference.

IFIP SEC 2022 is special because it is the first time since the outbreak of the SARS-CoV-2 (COVID-19) pandemic in 2019 that we have been able to bring researchers back together for a partially physical conference. We hope you find the proceedings of IFIP SEC 2022 interesting, stimulating, and inspiring for your future research regardless of the challenging times.

April 2022

Weizhi Meng
Simone Fischer-Hübner
Christian D. Jensen

Organization

General Chairs

Christian D. Jensen   Technical University of Denmark, Denmark
Simone Fischer-Hübner   Karlstad University, Sweden

Program Chair

Weizhi Meng   Technical University of Denmark, Denmark

Publicity Chairs

Georgios Kambourakis   University of the Aegean, Greece
Wenjuan Li   Hong Kong Polytechnic University, China

Web Chair

Wei-Yang Chiu   Technical University of Denmark, Denmark

Program Committee

Magnus Almgren	Chalmers University of Technology, Sweden
Claudio Ardagna	Università degli Studi di Milano, Italy
Joao Paulo Barraca	University of Aveiro, Portugal
Marcus Belder	Defence Science and Technology Group, Australia
Tamas Bisztray	University of Oslo, Norway
Ravishankar Borgaonkar	SINTEF, Norway
Jiageng Chen	CCNU, China
Robert Chetwyn	University of Oslo, Norway
Michal Choras	ITTI, Poland
K. P. Chow	University of Hong Kong, China
Nathan Clarke	University of Plymouth, UK
Miguel Correia	Universidade de Lisboa, Portugal
Nora Cuppens-Boulahia	Polytechnique Montréal, Canada
Paolo D'Arco	University di Salerno, Italy
Bernardo David	IT University of Copenhagen, Denmark
Ed Dawson	Queensland University of Technology, Australia
Sabrina De Capitani di Vimercati	Università degli Studi di Milano, Italy
Yvo Desmedt	University of Texas at Dallas, USA
Nicola Dragoni	Technical University of Denmark, Denmark
Givemore Dube	CSZ, Zimbabwe

Miguel Pardal	Universidade de Lisboa, Portugal
Gilbert Peterson	US Air Force Institute of Technology, USA
António Pinto	Politécnico do Porto, Portugal
Kai Rannenberg	Goethe University Frankfurt, Germany
Carlos Rieder	ISEC AG, Switzerland
Christophe Rosenberger	ENSICAEN, France
Juha Röning	University of Oulu, Norway
Reihaneh Safavi-Naini	University of Calgary, Canada
Pierangela Samarati	Università degli Studi di Milano, Italy
Ingrid Schaumüller-Bichl	FEMtech, Germany
Jürgen Schönwälder	Jacobs University Bremen, Germany
Jun Shao	Zhejiang Gongshang University, China
Paria Shirani	Ryerson University, USA
Nicolas Sklavos	University of Patras, Greece
Daniel Slamanig	AIT Austrian Institute of Technology, Austria
Kane Smith	University of North Carolina, USA
Agusti Solanas	Rovira i Virgili University, Spain
Chunhua Su	University of Aizu, Japan
Shamik Sural	IIT, Kharagpur, India
Neeraj Suri	Lancaster University, UK
Kerry-Lynn Thomson	Nelson Mandela Metropolitan University, South Africa
Bhavani Thuraisingham	University of Texas at Dallas, USA
Vicenc Torra	University of Skovde, Sweden
Lingyu Wang	Concordia University, Canada
Edgar Weippl	University of Vienna, Austria
Svetlana Yanushkevich	University of Calgary, Canada
Øyvind Ytrehus	University of Bergen, Norway
Vladimir Zadorozhny	University of Pittsburgh, USA
André Zúquete	University of Aveiro, Portugal
Rose-Mharie Åhlfeldt	University of Skovde, Sweden
Melek Önen	EURECOM, France

Additional Reviewers

Akand, Mamun	Chen, Yiqun
Aksoy, Alperen	Choudhary, Gaurav
Apolinário, Filipe	Christensen, Anton
Balestrucci, Alessandro	Cini, Valerio
Bena, Nicola	Cunha, Vitor
Berndt, Sebastian	Dushku, Edlira
Berto, Filippo	Dutta, Sabyasachi
Cabana, Olivier	Fdhila, Walid
Cabral Costa, Joana	Ferraris, Davide
Carpent, Xavier	Gernot, Tanguy
Chatzoglou, Efstratios	Giguet, Emmanuel

Gong, Yanan
Gouglidis, Antonios
Haffey, Preston
Harborth, David
Hoq, Md Nazmul
Johnstone, Mike
Judmayer, Aljosha
Kern, Andreas
Khodayarseresht, Ehsan
Kirsch, Andreas
Kouliaridis, Vasileios
Kävrestad, Joakim
Lai, Jianchang
Li, Wenjuan
Lian, Zhuotao
Lu, Yang
Löbner, Sascha
Ma, Jinhua
Manzoor, Salman
Martins, Ricardo
Matos Soares, João
Mayer, Wilfried
Mühlhauser, Michael
Nabi, Mahmudun
Niewolski, Wojciech
Niknia, Ahad
Ning, Jianting
Nitschke, Mirja
Nowak, Tomasz
Padyab, Ali
Pankova, Alisa
Perez Del Pozo, Angel L.
Pieper, Pascal

Pinto, Pedro
Pridöhl, Henning
Qin, Sz
Qiu, Chen
Ramacher, Sebastian
Reischuk, Ruediger
Roman, Rodrigo
Rosa, Pedro
Rossberger, Marc
Roxo, Tiago
Salvador, Paulo
Samaila, Musa
Schindler, Philipp
Sepczuk, Mariusz
Sequeiros, João Bernardo
Shaikh, Riaz Ahmed
Shen, Ao
Smolyakova, Sofya
Stifter, Nicolas
Sunar, Shiva
Söderström, Eva
Tange, Koen
Tiemann, Thore
Tronnier, Frederic
van der Zander, Benito
Wang, Terry
Wang, Ziyue
Wienöbst, Marcel
Wittig, Maximilian
Xu, Shengmin
Yang, S. J.
You, Weijing
Yu, Zhengxin

Contents

Blockchain

Mobile Security and Privacy

PETs and Crypto

Vulnerabilities

Privacy Models and Preferences

A Privacy Calculus Model for Contact Tracing Apps: Analyzing the German Corona-Warn-App

David Harborth$^{(\boxtimes)}$ (iD) and Sebastian Pape (iD)

Chair of Mobile Business and Multilateral Security,
Goethe University Frankfurt, Frankfurt, Germany
`david.harborth@m-chair.de`

Abstract. The SARS-CoV-2 pandemic is a pressing societal issue today. The German government promotes a contact tracing app named Corona-Warn-App (CWA), aiming to change citizens' health behavior during the pandemic by raising awareness about potential infections and enable infection chain tracking. Technical implementations, citizens' perceptions, and public debates around apps differ between countries, i.e., in Germany there has been a huge discussion on potential privacy issues of the app.

Thus, we analyze effects of privacy concerns regarding the CWA, perceived CWA benefits, and trust in the German healthcare system to answer why citizens use the CWA. We use a sample with 1,752 actual users and non-users and find support for the privacy calculus theory, i.e., individuals weigh privacy concerns and benefits in their use decision. Thus, citizens' privacy perceptions about health technologies (e.g., shaped by public debates) are crucial as they can hinder adoption and negatively affect future fights against pandemics.

Keywords: Covid-19 · Contact tracing apps · Information privacy

1 Introduction

With the global pandemic caused by the severe acute respiratory syndrome coronavirus 2 (SARS-CoV-2), digital proximity tracing systems to identify people who have been in contact with an infected person became a hot topic. Technical implementations, citizens' perceptions, and public debates around apps differ between countries, especially because of differences in the perceived importance of data protection. In particular in Germany, there have been many discussions on different implementations and their architecture [15], i.e., if the approach should be centralized or decentralized. As a result, the German contact tracing app named Corona-Warn-App (CWA) was build with a strong focus on privacy. It is based on the DP-3T protocol which ensures data minimization, prevents abuse of data and the tracking of users [14]. The German government along with its associated health institutes promote the use of the CWA, aiming to change

© IFIP International Federation for Information Processing 2022
Published by Springer Nature Switzerland AG 2022
W. Meng et al. (Eds.): SEC 2022, IFIP AICT 648, pp. 3–19, 2022.
https://doi.org/10.1007/978-3-031-06975-8_1

citizens' health behavior during the pandemic by raising awareness about potential infections and enable effective infection chain tracking.

While the discussion on the architecture and possible effects of it was mostly among experts, for a widespread use of the app, the app's acceptance by ordinary persons is of more importance [58]. Privacy concerns have been identified as one of the major barriers for the acceptance of contact tracing apps in prior work [4, 33]. The privacy calculus theory, in which individuals make their use decision by weighing privacy concerns and benefits is a suitable framework to explain the citizens' health behavior related to using the CWA [12,16,18,19,31,44,59]. The citizens' decision is of even more importance in countries like Germany where the use of the contact tracing app is voluntary and not enforced by the government. To the best of our knowledge, previous studies on contact tracing apps facilitating the privacy calculus are based on users' intentions rather than on their behavior. Therefore, we investigate the factors influencing the actual CWA use decisions on an individual level with a sample of 1,752 participants (896 CWA users/856 non-users) and address the question why citizens use contact tracing apps.

2   Privacy-Related Decision Making and Tracing Apps

The privacy-related decision making process of users is explained by several approaches and constructs in prior work [43,47,55,56]. The privacy calculus is one of the approaches aiming at explaining the role of privacy concerns in use behaviors, such as information disclosure or technology use. It represents a deliberate trade-off made by individuals weighing up benefits and costs [9,12,40]. The calculus assumes that if benefits outweigh the risks (i.e., privacy concerns [12]) users tend to engage in the privacy-related behavior. Empirical studies find that privacy risks negatively influence use intentions or behaviors and benefits positively influence the outcome variables [25,39]. The deliberate privacy-related decision making by users is questioned in more recent studies, e.g., by extending the original concepts of the privacy calculus with new factors [10,37] or by introducing behavioral biases influencing the trade-off [13,26].

Naturally, recent research on Covid-19 apps is sprouting up everywhere. A huge part consists of surveys on the users' adoption of one or more contact tracing apps, e.g., in Australia [16], China [38], France [1], Germany [1,4,38,44,48,50, 59], Ireland [18,49], Italy [1], Switzerland [4,59], Taiwan [19], the UK [1,34,42], and the US [1,31,38]. For example, Horstmann et al. found for a sample in Germany that the most common reasons for non-users were privacy concerns, lack of technical equipment, and doubts about the app's effectiveness [33]. Most of the other studies had similar results and identified privacy concerns as the or one of the main barriers to use contact tracing apps. In particular, people worried about corporate or government surveillance, potentially even after the pandemic [49], leakage of data to third parties [1], exposure of social interactions [4], and secondary use of the provided data [4]. However, misconceptions based on widespread knowledge gaps accompany the adoption of contact tracing apps [50].

Several of the mentioned studies on COVID-19 contact tracing apps have used the privacy calculus [4,16,18,19,31,44]. Some of them combined the privacy calculus with other constructs such as technology acceptance [16], social influence [16,18], or herding effects [59]. All studies found significant effects from benefits and privacy concerns on use intentions. However, all of them used self-reported download, install, and (continuous) use intentions as dependent variables. In contrast, our model relies on a quasi-observable factor (use of the CWA or not) which results from sampling participants, thereby, decreasing biases such as the social desirability bias. Furthermore, we refer to trust in the German healthcare system in contrast to trust in app developers [44] or service providers [42] since Horvath et al. found that users' trust in publicly-funded institutions, i.e., the British National Health Service can reduce privacy concerns [34]. For the sake of our cross-sectional online survey, we fall back on the original concepts of the privacy calculus – risks, benefits and CWA use – and nest it within the nomological net of the original "antecedents–privacy concerns–outcomes model" (APCO) [55]. We discuss the emerging research model and hypotheses in the next section.

3   Method

We present our questionnaire, data collection and research model in this section. We used the statistical software R (version 4.0.3) for the descriptive analyses and SmartPLS (version 3.3.2) [53] for the structural equation modeling.

3.1   Questionnaire and Data Collection

We adapted the constructs for privacy concerns (PC) and perceived benefits (PB) from prior literature [5,20] and applied it to the CWA. Trust in the German healthcare system is based on the construct by Pavlou [51]. The use of the CWA is measured with a binary variable indicating whether participants use the CWA (Use = 1) or not (Use = 0). We conducted a pretest in one class with graduate students and gathered qualitative feedback with respect to clarity of constructs and the questionnaire structure. After this pretest, we conducted the main study with a certified panel provider in Germany (ISO 20252 norm) which distributed the link to our survey in their panel from December 30, 2020 to January 14, 2021. The survey was implemented with LimeSurvey (version 2.72.6) [54] and hosted on a university server. We sampled the participants in a way to achieve a representative sample for Germany with approximately 50% females and 50% males as well as an age distribution following the EUROSTAT2018 census [17]. We also set a quota to end up with half of the sample using the CWA and the other half not using it. Our resulting sample consists of 1752 participants which is representative for Germany with respect to age and gender. The same diversity can be observed for income and education (see Table 1). 896 participants use the CWA (51.14%) and 856 do not (48.86%). 1299 use Android (74.14%), 436 use iOS (24.89%) and 17 stated to use smartphones with other mobile operating systems (OS) (0.97%).

Since we divided the sample into two approximately equal groups (CWA users and non-users), we check for statistically significant differences in the demographics between the groups. This is required to rule out confounding influences

Table 1. Participants' characteristics for age, gender, income and education

Demographics	N	%	Demographics	N	%
Age			**Gender**		
18-29 years	371	21.17%	Female	894	51.03%
30-39 years	316	18.04%	Males	853	48.69%
40-49 years	329	18.78%	Diverse	4	0.23%
50-59 years	431	24.60%	Prefer not to say	1	0.06%
60 years and older	305	17.41%	**Education**		
Net income			1 No degree	8	0.46%
500€- 1000€	160	9.13%	2 Secondary school	187	10.67%
1000€- 2000€	402	22.95%	3 Secondary school[+]	574	32.76%
2000€- 3000€	404	23.06%	4 A levels	430	24.54%
3000€- 4000€	314	17.92%	5 Bachelor's degree	240	13.70%
More than 4000€	292	16.67%	6 Master's degree	285	16.27%
Prefer not to say	180	10.27%	7 Doctorate	28	1.60%

[+]5 GCSEs at grade C and above

of these variables. All variables are non-normally distributed (based on Shapiro-Wilk tests for normality). Thus, we conducted Wilcoxon rank-sum tests to assess possible differences between CWA users and non-users.

Age and gender show no statistically significant differences since due to our sampling strategy. There are statistically significant differences between users and non-users of the CWA for the remaining demographics. Income is significantly higher for users compared to the non-users. However, the median is the same which is why we argue that the absolute difference is not having a substantial confounding effect on our analysis. The same argumentation holds for education with a median of 4 for users and 3.5 for non-users, smartphone experience in years with a mean 8.77 for users and 8.35 for non-users as well as experience in years with the respective smartphone OS (mean 7.85 for users and 7.46 for non-users). The used smartphone OS by participants in both groups is roughly similar with significantly more Android users in both groups (about three times more Android users compared to iOS). This distribution of operating systems is representative for Germany [57]. Thus, all differences between groups are – although statistically significant – negligible for our analysis since the absolute differences are relatively small. We also calculated mean sum scores for privacy concerns, perceived benefits and trust in the German healthcare system in order to check for differences between CWA users and non-users. We conducted Shapiro-Wilk tests for normality and Levene's tests of equal variances for the three constructs and find that they are not normally distributed and do not have equal variances

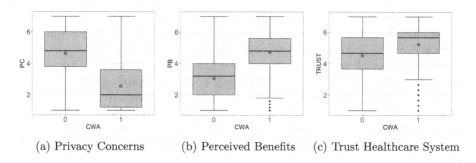

(a) Privacy Concerns   (b) Perceived Benefits   (c) Trust Healthcare System

Fig. 1. Boxplots for Privacy Concerns, Perceived Benefits and Trust in the German Healthcare System (CWA = 1: CWA users, CWA = 0: CWA non-users)

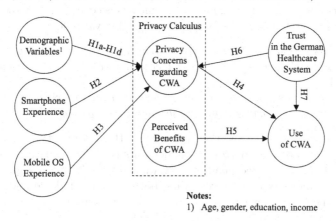

Notes:
1) Age, gender, education, income

Fig. 2. Research Model

between CWA users and non-users. Due to the non-parametric properties of our data we used the Wilcoxon rank-sum test. All variables are statistically significantly different between users and non-users with large to moderate effect sizes r for privacy concerns (r = −0.540, cf. Fig. 1a), perceived benefits (r = −0.553, cf. Fig. 1b), and trust (r = −0.258, cf. Fig. 1c).

3.2   Research Model and Hypotheses

We operationalize the "antecedents - privacy concerns - outcome" (APCO) model on an individual level, i.e., excluding factors such as cultural or organizational ones [55]. We focus on a narrow set of common antecedents on an individual level which are relevant for the case of the Corona-Warn-App. Privacy concerns are operationalized contextually, i.e., focusing on the specific perceptions of individuals related to the CWA. The outcome is the CWA use explained by the privacy calculus including trust in the German healthcare system as an additional antecedent of privacy concerns. Thus, this nomological net is mostly based on the original APCO model [55]. The resulting research model is shown in Fig. 2.

We include four demographic variables as antecedents (age, gender, income, education). The results for the effects of these antecedents in previous studies are inconclusive [27]. Prior work finds that older individuals and women are more concerned about their privacy [35,60]. We follow these findings and hypothesize that age has a positive effect on privacy concerns regarding the CWA and that females show higher levels of privacy concerns. Higher levels of education are usually associated with increasing privacy concerns [41]. However, since the German CWA was build based on privacy by design and can be considered to be privacy friendly, a better understanding of the CWA should reduce privacy concerns [50]. Thus, we hypothesize that there is a negative effect of education on privacy concerns (i.e., higher education levels correspond to lower privacy concerns). Similarly, a higher income is hypothesized to have a negative effect on privacy concerns as well (i.e., higher income levels correspond to lower privacy concerns) [55]. We hypothesize for the demographic variables:

1. (a) *Age has a positive effect on privacy concerns regarding the CWA.*
   (b) *Female participants show higher levels of privacy concerns regarding the CWA.*
   (c) *Education has a negative effect on privacy concerns regarding the CWA.*
   (d) *Income has a negative effect on privacy concerns regarding the CWA.*

Smartphone experience and the experience with the respective mobile operating system is included as control for participants technical experience by including these variables as antecedents of privacy concerns [29]. We argue that participants with more experience regarding both dimensions have higher privacy concerns as they might have witnessed more privacy-related breaches and attacks on smartphones [3,11]. Thus, we hypothesize:

2. *Smartphone experience has a positive effect on privacy concerns regarding the CWA.*
3. *Experience with the mobile OS has a positive effect on privacy concerns regarding the CWA.*

Individuals' privacy concerns are generally assumed to have a negative effect on the outcome variables [55]. In contrast to prior work on the CWA and privacy, we use the actual use decisions of participants instead of behavioral intentions. By that, we avoid biases in our results due to the behavioral-intention gap which is especially pronounced in privacy-related research [8]. Thus, we hypothesize:

4. *Privacy concerns regarding the CWA have a negative effect on the decision to use the app.*

Prior work finds that the relation between privacy concerns and behavior is also affected by other factors. The most common rationale is the privacy calculus which is also included in the APCO model. The privacy calculus states that individuals engage in a deliberate trade-off between benefits (of using a technology or disclosing information) and costs (privacy risks which are operationalized by privacy concerns) when making privacy-related decisions [12]. To account for this trade-off, we include the perceived benefits of using the CWA and hypothesize:

5. *The perceived benefits of using the CWA have a positive effect on the decision to use the app.*

Our last variable in the model is trust in the German healthcare system. We include this variable as trust in general is an important concept to explain privacy concerns and individual behavior [55]. In general, trust in certain entities alleviates privacy concerns related to these entities. In addition, trust has a direct positive effect on certain use or disclosure behaviors [23–25,28,30,36,43]. In the context of the pandemic and contact tracing apps, it can be seen that privacy concerns can be alleviated by users' trust in certain publicly-funded institutions, such as the British National Health Service (NHS) [34]. Our construct covers this partially as we include a more abstract notion of this idea in our model.

6. *Trust in the German healthcare system has a negative effect on the privacy concerns regarding the CWA.*
7. *Trust in the German healthcare system has a positive effect on the decision to use the app.*

4 Results

An analysis of the measurement model regarding reliability and validity is a precondition for interpreting the results of the structural model [22]. For the PLS algorithm, we chose the path weighting scheme with a maximum of 300 iterations and a stop criterion of 10^{-7}. For the bootstrapping procedure, we used 5000 bootstrap subsamples and no sign changes as the method for handling sign changes during the iterations of the bootstrapping procedure.

4.1 Assessment of the Measurement Model

Internal Consistency Reliability. Internal consistency reliability (ICR) measurements indicate how well certain indicators of a construct measure the same latent phenomenon. Two standard approaches for assessing ICR are Cronbach's α and the composite reliability. The values of both measures should be between 0.7 and 0.95 for research that builds upon accepted models [21]. Values for Cronbach's α (0.896, 0.960 and 0.867) and composite reliability (0.903, 0.965 and 0.895) for perceived benefits (PB), privacy concerns (PC) and trust in the healthcare system (TRUST), respectively, are within these suggested ranges.

Convergent Validity. We evaluate convergent validity based on the outer loadings of the indicators of the constructs (indicator reliability) and the average variance extracted (AVE) [22]. The lowest loading of the three constructs equals 0.796. Thus, indicator reliability is established as loadings above 0.7 imply that the indicators have much in common, which is desirable for reflective measurement models [21]. Convergent validity for the construct is assessed by the AVE (sum of the squared loadings divided by the number of indicators). The AVEs are 0.706 for PB, 0.864 for PC, and 0.790 for TRUST. This indicates that the constructs explain significantly more than half of the variance of the indicators, and thereby demonstrates convergent validity.

Table 2. Heterotrait-Monotrait ratio (HTMT)

	AGE	EDU	GDR	INCOME	Sp. Exp	MOS Exp.	PB	PC	USE
EDU	0.152								
GDR	0.012	0.045							
INCOME	0.048	0.243	0.088						
Smartphone Exp	0.148	0.052	0.044	0.123					
Mobile OS Exp	0.008	0.002	0.067	0.113	0.676				
Perc. Benefits	0.045	0.057	0.051	0.043	0.025	0.018			
Privacy Concerns	0.040	0.155	0.035	0.096	0.020	0.027	0.502		
USE	0.017	0.151	0.014	0.139	0.078	0.067	0.574	0.554	
TRUST	0.064	0.136	0.042	0.068	0.028	0.031	0.481	0.425	0.281

Discriminant Validity. We assess the degree of uniqueness of a construct compared to other constructs by investigating the cross-loadings for the single indicators. All outer loadings of a certain construct should be larger than its cross-loadings with other constructs [22] which is the case for our model. On a construct level, we compare the square root of the constructs' AVE with the correlations with other constructs. The square root of the AVE of a single construct should be larger than the correlation with other constructs (Fornell-Larcker criterion) [21]. All values are larger than correlations with other constructs, indicating discriminant validity. Prior work proposes the heterotrait-monotrait ratio (HTMT) as a superior approach for assessing discriminant validity [32]. Values close to 1 for HTMT indicate a lack of discriminant validity. A conservative threshold is 0.85 [32] and no value in our model is above the suggested threshold of 0.85 (Table 2). We assess if the HTMT statistics are significantly different from 1 with a bootstrapping procedure with 5,000 subsamples to get the confidence interval in which the true HTMT value lies with a 95% chance. The HTMT measure requires that no confidence interval contains the value 1. Our analysis shows that this is the case. Thus, discriminant validity is established.

Common Method Bias. The common method bias (CMB) can occur if data is gathered with a self-reported survey at one point in time in one questionnaire [52]. We need to test for the CMB since this is the case in our study. We perform a principal component factor analysis in R to conduct the Harman's single-factor test to address the issue of CMB [52]. The assumptions of the test are that CMB is not an issue if there is no single factor that results from the factor analysis or that the first factor does not account for the majority of the total variance [52]. The test shows that six factors have eigenvalues larger than 1 which account for 75.72% of the total variance. The first factor explains 34.65% of the total variance. Thus, we argue that CMB is not likely to be an issue in the data set.

Table 3. Path estimates and effect sizes f^2 and q^2 (only at least small effects sizes f^2 and q^2 shown)

Relation		Path estimate f^2	q^2	Result
H1a	Age → Privacy Concerns	−0.039		Not conf.
H1b	Gender → Privacy Concerns	−0.017		Not conf.
H1c	Education → Privacy Concerns	−0.097***		Confirmed
H1d	Income → Privacy Concerns	−0.045*		Confirmed
H2	Smartphone Exp. → Privacy Concerns	−0.050		Not conf.
H3	Mobile OS Exp. → Privacy Concerns	0.055		Not conf.
H4	Privacy Concerns → Use of CWA	−0.378*** 0.177	0.149	Confirmed
H5	Perceived Benefits → Use of CWA	0.395*** 0.185	0.181	Confirmed
H6	Trust in the German Healthcare System → Privacy Concerns	−0.374*** 0.164	0.137	Confirmed
H7	Trust in the German Healthcare System → Use of CWA	−0.054*		Rejected

4.2 Structural Model Assessment and Results

We assess collinearity, the level of R^2, the path coefficients, the effect size f^2, the predictive relevance Q^2, and the effect size q^2. We address these evaluation steps to ensure the predictive power of the model with regard to the target constructs privacy concerns and use.

Collinearity. Collinearity is present if two predictor variables are highly correlated with each other. To address this issue, we assess the inner variance inflation factor (VIF). All VIFs above 5 indicate that collinearity between constructs is present. For our model, the highest VIF is 1.939. Thus, collinearity is not an issue.

Significance and Relevance of Model Relationships. Values of adjusted R^2 are equal to 16.6% and 40.7% for privacy concerns and use, respectively. These values can be interpreted as weak and moderate for privacy concerns and use of the CWA [22]. The path estimates for our research model (see Fig. 2) are shown in Table 3. The sizes of significant path estimates are interpreted relative to each other in the model. Based on this, the effects of privacy concerns and perceived benefits on the use of the CWA (confirming H4 and H5) as well as of trust in the German healthcare system on privacy concerns (confirming H6) are strong. Education and income have statistically significant weak negative effects on privacy concerns (confirming H1c and H1d). However, both effect sizes are so small that they cannot be considered as relevant in the model (also visible in the f^2 effect sizes which are lower than the lowest suggested threshold of 0.02 [7]). Trust in the German healthcare system has a weak but negative effect on the use of the CWA (rejecting H7). None of the other hypotheses are significant.

Effect Sizes f^2. The f^2 effect size measures the impact of a construct on the endogenous variable by omitting it from the analysis and assessing the resulting change in the R^2 value [21]. The values are assessed based on thresholds by Cohen [7], who defines effects as small, medium and large for values of 0.02, 0.15 and 0.35, respectively. The effect sizes f^2 correspond to the path estimates with medium-sized effects of privacy concerns and perceived benefits on use of the CWA and trust in the healthcare system on privacy concerns (Table 3).

Predictive Relevance Q^2. The Q^2 measure indicates the out-of-sample predictive relevance of the structural model with regard to the endogenous latent variables based on a blindfolding procedure [21]. We used an omission distance d = 7 with recommended values between five and ten [22]. Furthermore, we report the Q^2 values of the construct cross-validated redundancy approach, since this approach is based on both the results of the measurement model as well as of the structural model [21]. Detailed information about the calculation cannot be provided due to space limitations. For further information see Chin [6]. Values above 0 indicate that the model has the property of predictive relevance. In our case, the Q^2 value is equal to 0.145 for PC and 0.404 for use. Since they are larger than zero, predictive relevance of the model is established.

Effect Sizes q^2. The assessment of q^2 follows the same logic as the one of f^2. It is based on the Q^2 values of the endogenous variables and calculates the individual predictive power of the exogenous variables by omitting them and comparing the change in Q^2 [21]. All individual values for q^2 are calculated with an omission distance d of seven. The thresholds for the f^2 interpretation can be applied, too [7]. The results show that the individual predictive power for hypotheses 4, 5 and 6 is given with medium-sized effects.

5   Discussion

We investigated the impact of privacy concerns related to the CWA, benefits of the CWA and trust in the German healthcare system on the CWA use decision. We used the APCO model [55] and the privacy calculus theory [12] for the hypothesis development and evaluated them with an online survey with 1,752 participants in Germany (896 users and 856 non-users).

Our results support the privacy calculus theory and that individuals weigh up risks and benefits as privacy concerns have a statistically significant negative effect and benefits have a statistically significant positive effect on use. We also find that trust in the German healthcare system is the important antecedent of privacy concerns by alleviating them. This confirms our hypothesis and indicates that participants associate trust in the healthcare system with the entities operating the CWA (Robert Koch Institute, part of the healthcare system as it is subordinated to the German Federal Ministry of Health). In this context, is it far more interesting that the direct positive effect of trust on the use cannot be found in the data. The effect is even negative (although the effect size is negligible). The hypotheses related to the antecedents education and income can be accepted, although the effect size for both effects is relatively small.

Related work on contact tracing app adoption in Germany based on the privacy calculus uses a different set of antecedents of privacy concerns, referred to trust to the app designers and the study used intentions to use the app as a target variable [44]. However, as in our work, they find statistically significant effects of benefits (positive) and concerns (negative) on intentions. Furthermore, trust has a negative effect on privacy concerns and a positive effect on intentions. Thus, our study with actual use decisions as dependent variable confirms that the privacy calculus is an appropriate tool to explain the CWA use.

5.1   Limitations

Our work has the following limitations. First, our study covers only the German Corona-Warn-App with all the respective characteristics of this app. Thus, the results are only generalizable to contact tracing apps in other countries to the extent that the population is comparable to the German population and that comparable apps have similar characteristics related to privacy and security aspects. However, even if apps in other countries are technically comparable, other influencing factors such as a positive or negative media coverage, failures in implementation efforts, etc., could still lead to different evaluations of individuals. Second, although we could minimize the effect of biases due to the study design (online questionnaire, self-reported measures) by having an observable dependent variable instead of reported use behaviors or intentions, we still had to rely on self-reported measures for the constructs in our model. Furthermore, our analysis closely followed the original APCO model with its focus on privacy concerns [55]. Thus, we did not consider interactions between antecedents or other potential relationships between other variables of the calculus such as effects of demographics on the perceived benefits of the CWA.

5.2   Future Work

The previously described effects could be considered in future work. For example, there were reports that more wealthy households were less affected by the pandemic not only from an economically but also in their daily lives, e.g., by having access to private transportation and enough living space [45]. We would assume that income has a negative effect on the perceived benefits as these households do not profit as much from technical solutions like the CWA. Similarly, the effect of trust in the healthcare system on use decisions could also be mediated by perceived benefits of the app as participants with higher trust in the medical care could be less cautious and do not see the benefits of such apps.

Besides interesting opportunities in extending the model and consider that there could be antecedents for the other variables in the APCO model and privacy calculus, we see the need for analyses of privacy and health behavior apps across countries alongside with analyses of causes for differences in potential privacy perceptions. Furthermore, it would be interesting to investigate to what extent contact tracing apps such as the CWA could induce a change in the health-related behaviors of individuals, e.g., did a notification about a past risk contact change the consequent behavior of individuals by making them more cautious?

Closely related is the question how individuals are influenced by politicians, the public debate, and others in their decision to adopt technologies like the CWA. We argued that these social influences could have been a major driver for the division of the German population into a group which does not believe that there are benefits of such apps and that privacy issues are too severe and into the group which uses the app. Thus, future work could analyze the influences in a more granular way in order to assess the reasons for this division. This is especially important since it has been shown that informative and motivational video messages have very limited effect, but even small monetary incentives can increase the app's adoption [46]. Thus, besides improving the citizens' knowledge and perception of privacy mechanisms and benefits of the app, future health behavior communication could make use of small monetary incentives, promote the app's benefits or even try to nudge citizens to use the app.

6   Conclusion

In summary, our work contributes to the current work on contact tracing apps in two ways. First, we provide – to the best of our knowledge – one of the first research findings which rely on an observable outcome variable measuring the actual contact tracing app use decisions of German citizens in a large-scale online survey; thus, avoiding certain biases (e.g., the intention-behavior gap [8]) and providing robust results to rely on for deriving practical recommendations.

Second, we practically recommend to consider the importance of appropriate communication strategies by policy makers when releasing health behavior apps, such as the CWA, to a large heterogeneous user base, especially when faced with crises such as a pandemics. We can see high levels of privacy concerns and significantly lower levels of perceived benefits in the group of non-users. In contrast, trust in the healthcare system is almost equal between groups. One possible explanation is that even though the CWA is developed in a privacy-friendly way politicians and media failed to properly explain the app's functions and data protection measures (e.g., decentralized approach) to the German citizens, and by that lost several millions of potential users. This is supported by a study on media coverage which found that governments or politicians were criticized for their lack of transparent communication [2]. In addition, the public debate around the German CWA was rather critical and the usefulness of the app was questioned on a daily basis [15,58]. This implies that there was no real strategy on how to introduce the app to the citizens and advocate it against expectable criticism which needs to be considered in future crises.

Acknowledgements. This work was supported by the Goethe-Corona-Fonds from Goethe University Frankfurt and the European Union's Horizon 2020 research and innovation program under grant agreement 830929 (CyberSecurity4Europe).

A   Questionnaire

Demographics

AGE in years

EDU Education (no degree, secondary school, secondary school (>5 GCSE), A levels, bachelor, master, doctorate)

GDR Gender (female, male, divers, prefer not to say)

INCOME of household (in €: 0.5k-1k, 1k-2k, 2k-3k, 3k-4k, >4k, prefer not to say)

Smartphone Experience in years

Mobile OS Experience in years

USE Corona-Warn-App user (yes/no)

Privacy concerns related to the Corona-Warn-App[1]

PC1 I think the Corona-Warn-App over-collects my personal information.

PC2 I worry that the Corona-Warn-App leaks my personal information to third-parties.

PC3 I am concerned that the Corona-Warn-App violates my privacy.

PC4 I am concerned that the Corona-Warn-App misuses my personal information.

PC5 I think that the Corona-Warn-App collects my location data.

Perceived benefits of the Corona-Warn-App (See footnote 1)

−**PB1** Using the Corona-Warn-App makes me feel safer.

−**PB2** I have a lot to gain by using the Corona-Warn-App.

−**PB3** The Corona-Warn-App can help me to identify contacts to infected individuals.

−**PB4** If I use the Corona-Warn-App I am able to warn others in case I am infected with Covid-19.

−**PB5** The spreading of Covid-19 in Germany can be decelerated by using the Corona-Warn-App.

Trust in the German healthcare system (See footnote 1)

−**TRUST1** The German healthcare system is trustworthy.

−**TRUST2** The players acting in the German healthcare system are trustworthy.

−**TRUST3** The German healthcare system can cope with the burden of Covid 19 infections.

References

1. Altmann, S., et al.: Acceptability of app-based contact tracing for Covid-19: cross-country survey evidence (2020)
2. Amann, J., Sleigh, J., Vayena, E.: Digital contact-tracing during the Covid-19 pandemic: an analysis of newspaper coverage in Germany, Austria, and Switzerland. PLoS ONE **16**(2), e0246524 (2021)

---

[1] Measured on a 7-point Likert scale ("strongly disagree" to "strongly agree").

3. Bellman, S., Johnson, E.J., Kobrin, S.J., Lohse, G.L.: International differences in information privacy concerns: a global survey of consumers. Inf. Soc. **20**(5), 313–324 (2004)

4. Bonner, M., Naous, D., Legner, C., Wagner, J.: The (lacking) user adoption of Covid-19 contact tracing apps-insights from Switzerland and Germany. In: Proceedings of the 15th Pre-ICIS Workshop on Information Security and Privacy, vol. 1 (2020)

5. Champion, V.L.: Instrument development for health belief model constructs. Adv. Nurs. Sci. (1984). https://doi.org/10.1097/00012272-198404000-00011

6. Chin, W.W.: The partial least squares approach to structural equation modeling. In: Marcoulides, G.A. (ed.) Modern Methods for Business Research, pp. 295–336. Lawrence Erlbaum, Mahwah (1998)

7. Cohen, J.: Statistical Power Analysis for the Behavioral Sciences. HillsDale (1988)

8. Crossler, R.E., Johnston, A.C., Lowry, P.B., Hu, Q., Warkentin, M., Baskerville, R.: Future directions for behavioral information security research. Comput. Secur. **32**, 90–101 (2013)

9. Culnan, M.J., Armstrong, P.K.: Information privacy concerns, procedural fairness, and impersonal trust: an empirical investigation. Organ. Sci. **10**(1), 104–115 (1999). https://doi.org/10.1287/orsc.10.1.104

10. Dienlin, T., Metzger, M.J.: An extended privacy calculus model for snss: analyzing self-disclosure and self-withdrawal in a representative U.S. sample. J. Comput.-Mediated Commun. **21**(5), 368–383 (2016). https://doi.org/10.1111/jcc4.12163

11. Dinev, T., Hart, P.: Internet privacy concerns and social awareness as determinants of intention to transact. Int. J. Electron. Commer. **10**(2), 7–29 (2005)

12. Dinev, T., Hart, P.: An extended privacy calculus model for e-commerce transactions. Inf. Syst. Res. **17**(1), 61–80 (2006). https://doi.org/10.1287/isre.1060.0080

13. Dinev, T., Mcconnell, A.R., Smith, H.J.: Informing privacy research through information systems, psychology, and behavioral economics: thinking outside the "APCO" box. Inf. Syst. Res. **26**(4), 639–655 (2015)

14. DP-3T Project: Decentralized privacy-preserving proximity tracing (2020). https://github.com/DP-3T/documents/blob/master/DP3T%20White%20Paper.pdf. Accessed 16 Dec 2021

15. DP-3T Project: Privacy and security risk evaluation of digital proximity tracing systems (2020). https://github.com/DP-3T/documents/blob/master/Security%20analysis/Privacy%20and%20Security%20Attacks%20on%20Digital%20Proximity%20Tracing%20Systems.pdf. Accessed 16 Dec 2021

16. Duan, S.X., Deng, H.: Hybrid analysis for understanding contact tracing apps adoption. Ind. Manag. Data Syst. (2021)

17. EUROSTAT: EUROSTAT 2018 (2021). https://ec.europa.eu/eurostat/de/home. Accessed 16 Dec 2021

18. Fox, G., Clohessy, T., van der Werff, L., Rosati, P., Lynn, T.: Exploring the competing influences of privacy concerns and positive beliefs on citizen acceptance of contact tracing mobile applications. Comput. Hum. Behav. **121**, 106806 (2021)

19. Garrett, P.M., et al.: Young adults view smartphone tracking technologies for Covid-19 as acceptable: the case of Taiwan. Int. J. Environ. Res. Public Health **18**(3), 1332 (2021)

20. Gu, J., Xu, Y.C., Xu, H., Zhang, C., Ling, H.: Privacy concerns for mobile app download: an elaboration likelihood model perspective. Decis. Support Syst. **94**, 19–28 (2017). https://doi.org/10.1016/j.dss.2016.10.002

21. Hair, J., Hult, G.T.M., Ringle, C.M., Sarstedt, M.: A Primer on Partial Least Squares Structural Equation Modeling (PLS-SEM). SAGE Publications (2017)

22. Hair, J., Ringle, C.M., Sarstedt, M.: PLS-SEM: indeed a silver bullet. J. Market. Theory Pract. **19**(2), 139–152 (2011)
23. Harborth, D., Pape, S.: Examining technology use factors of privacy-enhancing technologies: the role of perceived anonymity and trust. In: Twenty-fourth Americas Conference on Information Systems, New Orleans, USA, pp. 1–10 (2018)
24. Harborth, D., Pape, S.: JonDonym users' information privacy concerns. In: Janczewski, L.J., Kutyłowski, M. (eds.) SEC 2018. IAICT, vol. 529, pp. 170–184. Springer, Cham (2018). https://doi.org/10.1007/978-3-319-99828-2_13
25. Harborth, D., Pape, S.: Investigating privacy concerns related to mobile augmented reality applications. In: International Conference on Information Systems (ICIS), pp. 1–9 (2019)
26. Harborth, D., Pape, S.: Empirically investigating extraneous influences on the "APCO" model - childhood brand nostalgia and the positivity bias. Future Internet **12**(12), 1–16 (2020). https://doi.org/10.3390/fi12120220
27. Harborth, D., Pape, S.: Empirically investigating extraneous influences on the "APCO" model-childhood brand nostalgia and the positivity bias. Future Internet **12**(12), 220 (2020). https://doi.org/10.3390/fi12120220. https://www.mdpi.com/1999-5903/12/12/220. Accessed 16 Dec 2021
28. Harborth, D., Pape, S.: How privacy concerns, trust and risk beliefs, and privacy literacy influence users' intentions to use privacy-enhancing technologies: the case of Tor. ACM SIGMIS Data Base Adv. Inf. Syst. **51**(1), 51–69 (2020). https://doi.org/10.1145/3380799.3380805
29. Harborth, D., Pape, S.: Investigating privacy concerns related to mobile augmented reality applications - a vignette based online experiment. Comput. Hum. Behav. **122**, 106833 (2021). https://doi.org/10.1016/j.chb.2021.106833. https://linkinghub.elsevier.com/retrieve/pii/S0747563221001564. Accessed 16 Dec 2021
30. Harborth, D., Pape, S., Rannenberg, K.: Explaining the technology use behavior of privacy-enhancing technologies: the case of Tor and JonDonym. Proc. Priv. Enhancing Technol. (PoPETs) **2020**(2), 111–128 (2020). https://doi.org/10.2478/popets-2020-0020
31. Hassandoust, F., Akhlaghpour, S., Johnston, A.C.: Individuals' privacy concerns and adoption of contact tracing mobile applications in a pandemic: a situational privacy calculus perspective. J. Am. Med. Inform. Assoc. **28**(3), 463–471 (2021)
32. Henseler, J., Ringle, C.M., Sarstedt, M.: A new criterion for assessing discriminant validity in variance-based structural equation modeling. J. Acad. Mark. Sci. **43**(1), 115–135 (2014). https://doi.org/10.1007/s11747-014-0403-8
33. Horstmann, K.T., Buecker, S., Krasko, J., Kritzler, S., Terwiel, S.: Who does or does not use the 'corona-warn-app' and why? Eur. J. Pub. Health **31**(1), 49–51 (2021)
34. Horvath, L., Banducci, S., James, O.: Citizens' attitudes to contact tracing apps. J. Exp. Polit. Sci. 1–13 (2020)
35. Huang, Y., Liu, W.: The impact of privacy concern on users' usage intention of mobile payment. In: International Conference on Innovation Management and Industrial Engineering, vol. 3, pp. 90–93 (2012)
36. Karahanna, E., Gefen, D., Straub, D.W.: Trust and TAM in online shopping: an integrated model. MIS Q. **27**(1), 51–90 (2003)
37. Kehr, F., Kowatsch, T., Wentzel, D., Fleisch, E.: Blissfully ignorant: the effects of general privacy concerns, general institutional trust, and affect in the privacy calculus. Inf. Syst. J. **25**, 607–635 (2015). https://doi.org/10.1111/isj.12062

38. Kostka, G., Habich-Sobiegalla, S.: In times of crisis: public perceptions towards COVID-19 contact tracing apps in China, Germany and the US. Technical report, Social Science Research Network, Rochester, NY (2020). https://doi.org/10.2139/ssrn.3693783

39. Krasnova, H., Spiekermann, S., Koroleva, K., Hildebrand, T.: Online social networks: why we disclose. J. Inf. Technol. **25**(2), 109–125 (2010). https://doi.org/10.1057/jit.2010.6

40. Laufer, R.S., Wolfe, M.: Privacy as a concept and a social issue: a multidimensional developmental theory. J. Soc. Issues **33**(3), 22–42 (1977). https://doi.org/10.1111/j.1540-4560.1977.tb01880.x

41. Lee, H., Wong, S.F., Chang, Y.: Confirming the effect of demographic characteristics on information privacy concerns. In: PACIS 2016, p. 70 (2016)

42. Lewandowsky, S., et al.: Public acceptance of privacy-encroaching policies to address the Covid-19 pandemic in the United Kingdom. PLoS ONE **16**(1), e0245740 (2021)

43. Malhotra, N.K., Kim, S.S., Agarwal, J.: Internet users' information privacy concerns (IUIPC): the construct, the scale, and a causal model. Inf. Syst. Res. **15**(4), 336–355 (2004)

44. Meier, Y., Meinert, J., Krämer, N.: Investigating factors that affect the adoption of Covid-19 contact-tracing apps. A privacy calculus perspective (2021)

45. Miranda, L.: How the coronavirus has widened the chasm between rich and poor (2020). https://www.nbcnews.com/business/business-news/how-coronavirus-has-widened-chasm-between-rich-poor-n1240622. Accessed 16 Dec 2021

46. Munzert, S., Selb, P., Gohdes, A., Stoetzer, L.F., Lowe, W.: Tracking and promoting the usage of a Covid-19 contact tracing app. Nat. Hum. Behav. **5**(2), 247–255 (2021)

47. Norberg, P.A., Horne, D.R., Horne, D.A.: The privacy paradox: personal information disclosure intentions versus behaviors. J. Consum. Affairs **41**(1), 100–126 (2007)

48. Oldeweme, A., Märtins, J., Westmattelmann, D., Schewe, G.: The role of transparency, trust, and social influence on uncertainty reduction in times of pandemics: empirical study on the adoption of COVID-19 tracing apps. J. Med. Internet Res. **23**(2), 1–17 (2021). https://doi.org/10.2196/25893

49. O'Callaghan, M.E., et al.: A national survey of attitudes to Covid-19 digital contact tracing in the republic of Ireland. Irish J. Med. Sci. **190**, 863–887 (2020)

50. Pape, S., Harborth, D., Kröger, J.L.: Privacy concerns go hand in hand with lack of knowledge: the case of the German corona-warn-app. In: Jøsang, A., Futcher, L., Hagen, J. (eds.) SEC 2021. IAICT, vol. 625, pp. 256–269. Springer, Cham (2021). https://doi.org/10.1007/978-3-030-78120-0_17

51. Pavlou, P.A.: Consumer acceptance of electronic commerce: integrating trust and risk with the technology acceptance model. Int. J. Electron. Commer. **7**(3), 101–134 (2003). https://doi.org/10.1080/10864415.2003.11044275

52. Podsakoff, P.M., MacKenzie, S.B., Lee, J.Y., Podsakoff, N.P.: Common method biases in behavioral research: a critical review of the literature and recommended remedies. J. Appl. Psychol. **88**(5), 879–903 (2003)

53. Ringle, C.M., Wende, S., Becker, J.M.: SmartPLS 3 (2015). www.smartpls.com. Accessed 16 Dec 2021

54. Schmitz, C.: LimeSurvey Project Team (2015). http://www.limesurvey.org. Accessed 16 Dec 2021

55. Smith, H.J., Dinev, T., Xu, H.: Theory and review information privacy research: an interdisciplinary review. MIS Q. **35**(4), 989–1015 (2011)

56. Smith, H.J., Milberg, S.J., Burke, S.J.: Information privacy: measuring individuals concerns about organizational practices. MIS Q. **20**(2), 167–196 (1996)
57. Statista: Marktanteile der führenden mobilen Betriebssysteme an der Internetnutzung mit Mobiltelefonen in Deutschland von Januar 2009 bis September 2020. https://de.statista.com/statistik/daten/studie/184332/umfrage/marktanteil-der-mobilen-betriebssysteme-in-deutschland-seit-2009/. Accessed 16 Dec 2021
58. Voss, O.: Corona-App: Datenschutz-Debatte und offene Fragen (2020). https://background.tagesspiegel.de/digitalisierung/corona-app-datenschutz-debatte-und-offene-fragen. Accessed 16 Dec 2021
59. Wagner, A., Olt, C.M., Abramova, O.: Calculating versus herding in adoption and continuance use of a privacy-invasive information system: the case of Covid-19 tracing apps (2021)
60. Yang, H.C.: Young Chinese consumers' social media use, online privacy concerns, and behavioral intents of privacy protection. Int. J. China Market. **4**(1), 82–101 (2013)

Deriving and Using Synthetic Consequences for Privacy Risk Modeling

Stuart S. Shapiro$^{(\boxtimes)}$

MITRE Corporation, Bedford, MA 01730, USA
sshapiro@mitre.org

Abstract. Highly contextual socio-technical systems demand highly contextual risk models for relevant system properties, including privacy. Many privacy risk models revolve around adverse consequences, i.e., typologies of bad privacy outcomes. The attendant mirror issues of insufficient contextual nuance (too few/general consequences) versus problematic analytical manageability (too many/granular consequences) can be addressed through the development of synthetic consequences as part of privacy engineering risk management. The objective is to categorize the total set of consequences so as to produce a small number of categories that nonetheless manage to capture the full range of meaning of the original consequences. Those categories can then be tailored to better reflect the context of the socio-technical system being analyzed. Relevant theoretical foundations for the construction of synthetic consequences are discussed and a step-by-step methodology for deriving them is described. This methodology is then applied to the example of a smart TV.

Keywords: Privacy risk management · Risk modeling · Synthetic consequences

1 Introduction

Any risk assessment activity that is not ad hoc, in any domain, is based, either implicitly or explicitly, on a risk model that denotes some set of relevant dimensions and values and how they interact to generate risks. In the absence of a risk model, risk identification becomes essentially arbitrary. As a result, while privacy risk assessors may not be fully aware that they're employing a risk model, they almost invariably are, particularly when, as in many cases, legal compliance is an issue. This has typically translated into risk models grounded in Fair Information Practice Principles (FIPPs), as versions of these have tended to heavily inform privacy statutes and regulations. These include the federal Privacy Act in the US and the General Data Protection Regulation (GDPR) in the EU. Their grounding in FIPPs is reflected in associated privacy impact assessments (PIAs) and data protection impact assessments (DPIAs) respectively. However, additional privacy risk models are increasingly available.

Approved for public release. Distribution unlimited 21-01156-9.

W. Meng et al. (Eds.): SEC 2022, IFIP AICT 648, pp. 20–33, 2022.
https://doi.org/10.1007/978-3-031-06975-8_2

Many of these models, as well as FIPPs, revolve around adverse consequences. In other words, the models provide a typology of bad privacy outcomes. While useful, this can have drawbacks. Such typologies may be insufficiently comprehensive or nuanced for the relevant context. By the same token, though, a sufficiently broad set of consequences may, when combined with a variety of threats and vulnerabilities, create problems of analytical manageability, particularly under typical resource constraints. This dilemma can be partially addressed through the development of synthetic consequences as part of privacy engineering risk management.

This paper explores how project or assessment-specific consequences can be derived from existing privacy risk models and tailored to a specific socio-technical context. In doing so, it attempts to address a specific instance of a more general problem: as socio-technical systems become embedded in evermore complex contexts, risk models must become more contextual as well, while remaining analytically manageable. The remainder of the paper is organized as follows. Section 2 discusses the nature and role of risk models both generally and with respect to privacy specifically. Section 3 elaborates on the dilemma posed by trying to rely exclusively on the consequences of existing privacy risk models and the benefits of deriving synthetic consequences. Section 4 sets out some theoretical foundations for synthetic consequences in terms of cognitive categorization processes and mathematics and then defines a methodology for deriving them. Section 5 then illustrates the application of this methodology through the example of a smart TV. Finally, Sect. 6 offers some concluding thoughts and discusses the possible extension of this approach to vulnerability identification.

2 Privacy Risk Modeling

Risk models consist of some set of factors—threats, vulnerabilities, consequences, likelihoods, severities, etc.—and their relations to one another. The US National Institute of Standards and Technology (NIST) defines a risk model as "a fixed set of factors, a fixed assessment scale for each factor, and a fixed algorithm for combining factors" [1, p. 16]. It is generally understood that threats exploit vulnerabilities to produce (adverse) consequences as the principal factors while likelihoods and severities may attach to any or all of these. (The recently published ISO/IEC TR 27550 includes some privacy-specific discussion of risk modeling [2].) In some cases the models are wholly pre-constructed and utilized as-is while in other cases, at the other extreme, they are constructed from scratch to support a specific analysis. Many assessments, though, exhibit a combination of prior and in-situ risk model construction (the latter constituting the activity of risk modeling). This has certainly been the case for privacy, not least because existing privacy risk models are often sparse.

Existing privacy risk models tend to be sparse in the sense that they frequently address only a few potential model factors. By far, the most commonly addressed factor is consequences. This is not terribly surprising for a couple of reasons. The first is that risks are typically articulated in terms of consequences. Risk is not equivalent to consequence as it is normally associated with a quantitative or qualitative value denoting its level or degree. However, because the adverse consequence is the thing of concern, it is used to frame the risk. The second reason is that for risk models reflecting compliance obligations (which, for obvious reasons, are the most plentiful), their compliance imperatives are by definition the converse of adverse consequences. If, for example, a system is legally required to provide data subjects with access to their personal information, failure to provide that access would constitute an adverse consequence of the associated risk model. As a result of these two conditions, privacy risk models often focus on consequences, sometimes exclusively.

Due to their integration into legal compliance regimes, in which compliance violations are the adverse consequences, FIPPs are undoubtedly the most widely used privacy risk model. However, other models exist, partly as a result of the last decade of privacy scholarship. Of these, Solove's Taxonomy of Privacy [3] is probably the best known, describing 16 different types of adverse privacy consequence. Others include Calo's subjective and objective privacy harms (adverse consequences) [4] and Nissenbaum's contextual integrity heuristic [5], in which disruptions to informational norms can be considered vulnerabilities (creating the potential for adverse consequences). NIST's Privacy Risk Assessment Methodology (PRAM) [6] utilizes a risk model that addresses both vulnerabilities ("problematic data actions") and adverse consequences ("problems for individuals") that the vulnerabilities may make possible. However, it can be the case that models nominally consisting of a single factor can also implicate another factor. Thus, the descriptions in Solove's Taxonomy often imply the kinds of threats that could produce those consequences, while a vulnerability identified by the contextual integrity heuristic (i.e., a violation of informational norms) may imply the type of adverse consequence that could result from exploitation of that vulnerability. Similarly, a threat identified using the LINDDUN framework [7] will highlight the vulnerability it might exploit. Figure 1 shows these alignments, with dashed lines indicating implied factors.

While not all privacy risk models indirectly address factors beyond the ones they directly address, project or system-specific risk modeling can explicitly address some or all of the missing factors. This may also happen implicitly as a tacit aspect of the assessment process, a by-product of thinking through possible risk scenarios and, in effect, filling in the blanks. However, it is also possible to simply ignore factors completely unaddressed within a risk model. This introduces additional degrees of freedom into the model, which results in a broader set of identified risks with less definition.

3   Modeling Constraints and the Case for Synthetic Consequences

We start this discussion from a simple premise: FIPPs are often a necessary but always an insufficient basis for assessing privacy risk in modern socio-technical systems. Framing this in terms of the previous discussion, a privacy risk model based solely on FIPPs probably will not lead to the identification of all relevant privacy risks. FIPPs, while occupying a deservedly central place in the minds of privacy practitioners, nevertheless suffer from a number of problems. First and foremost, FIPPs are non-normative with respect to purpose, which is highly problematic given that many FIPPs are contingent on purpose. Second, a privacy risk model grounded exclusively in FIPPs by definition excludes consideration of privacy consequences that do not directly correspond to the violation of a Fair Information Practice Principle. Third, a FIPPs-based privacy risk model is inescapably parochial, in the sense that it focuses almost exclusively on the system or business process in question without explicitly considering the surrounding context.

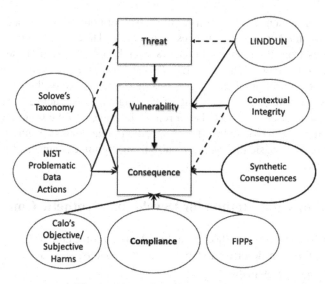

Fig. 1. Privacy risk model alignments

An obvious solution to these issues is to employ multiple privacy risk models when engaging in privacy risk assessment. One can, for example, combine FIPPs with Solove's Taxonomy to construct a broader privacy risk model. This would capture a variety of adverse privacy consequences beyond those consisting of FIPP violations. However, this would also approximately triple (depending on which version of FIPPs one used) the number of consequences to around two dozen. Given that any one consequence could potentially result from multiple vulnerabilities, each of which could potentially be exploited by multiple threats, combinatorial expansion can quickly afflict the privacy risk modeling process. While the expansion of the consequences in a hybrid privacy risk model clearly would be much less were FIPPs to be combined with, say, Calo's subjective/objective privacy harms (around 10 consequences), it could also be much greater were FIPPs to be combined with contextual integrity. As a point of comparison, the NIST Guide to Conducting Information Security Risk Assessments organizes consequences into just five "impact types" [1]. So FIPPs, even with their limited scope, actually already trend high in terms of number of consequences, creating a disincentive to expand the risk model.

Synthetic consequences, in contrast, offer a way of both achieving adequate scope and keeping the number of consequences manageable. They do this by systematically deriving subsets from the combined consequences based on which consequences are similar or related to others.[1] The objective is to categorize the total set of consequences so as to produce a small number of categories that, irrespective of their number, manage to capture the full range of meaning of the original consequences. Further, those categories can then be configured to better reflect the context of the socio-technical system, recognizing that they may take forms specific to that context. Both of these steps are grounded in some basic theory, principally from cognitive science, which is briefly discussed in the next section.

4 Foundations and Method for Developing Synthetic Consequences

We first describe some relevant theoretical foundations for the construction of synthetic consequences. We then describe a step-by-step methodology for deriving them from pre-existing sets of consequences.

4.1 Theoretical Foundations

Categories are not wholly products of either cognition or the environment [8]. Rather, they result from the interaction of the two. Domain knowledge helps us make sense of the environment through categorization while interaction with that environment shapes our domain knowledge. The properties of categories and their members and our contextual understanding both come into play when dealing with consequences as categories and as members of broader categories. While a comprehensive review of categorization processes is beyond the scope of this paper, it is worth briefly considering some of the basic aspects of these processes, including the nature of equivalence relations.

Typically, some members of a category are considered stronger or more representative examples of the category than other members [9]. These "central" members in turn are characterized by key (central) features. In their most basic form, central features are specific attribute-value pairs that exhibit immutability, i.e., resistance to change [10]. If those features are changed, category membership becomes more contestable. (For example, the central features of a member of the category US Social Security accounts would include a nine digit Social Security number.)

---

[1] Solove [3] actually divides the 16 consequences in his Taxonomy into four categories, however, only one of the categories—Invasions—actually relates to the nature of the constituent consequences. The other categories—Information Collection, Information Processing, Information Dissemination—convey only the nature of the relevant activity rather than the nature of the consequence.

Prior to contextualization, a synthetic consequence is a collection of other consequences. This is, then, a categorization exercise. (As such, it is fundamentally different from policy formalization [e.g., 11], with potential adverse privacy consequences from a risk assessment standpoint likely extending beyond pure policy violations in any case.) Individuals with little domain experience tend to perform initial categorization based on a single atomic feature or dimension, extending to multiple dimensions only for those items that could not be sorted using the initial dimension [12]. Experienced individuals, on the other hand, perform multi-dimensional sorting from the outset, leading to more nuanced categorization based on overall similarity.

Such similarity goes beyond atomic features and into structural alignment. Relations between features exist as well as relations between relations and so on [13]. (For example, a US Social Security number that starts within the range 545–573 tends to correspond to a place of birth in California, relating two features. New parents with a California address would request a Social Security number for that child, implying that the number starts within the range 545–573, associating the two relations.) The more feature structure that members of a category share, the greater the category's coherence, i.e., the greater the overall strength or soundness of the category [14]. Some of this structure may involve dependency relations, such that particular features are contingent on other features to degrees ranging from correlation all the way to causation.

This is taken a step further in categories characterized by some higher-order relation (i.e., a relation exhibiting or implying significant semantic structure) that logically connects all their members. This is the case, for example, with goal-oriented categories in which the category members all contribute to achieving an objective, such as the set of specific organizational requirements that achieve compliance with the GDPR. The existence of an invariant higher-order relation is, it has been argued, what renders probabilistic categories—those characterized by family resemblance, where members exhibit different subsets of a larger set of features—learnable [15]. While different members may exhibit different feature combinations, those combinations all reflect an overarching definable commonality. Indeed, Solove explicitly argues that privacy is a category whose members are characterized by family resemblance [3]. From Solove's perspective, the invariant higher-order relation that supplies the category's coherence revolves around the concept of privacy problems, i.e., problems falling under the rubric of privacy that "have achieved a significant degree of social recognition" and have been seen as warranting legal attention [3]. All the members of the category participate in this relation.

We are not just assigning consequences to categories, though, we are partitioning consequences into subsets in which, for the purpose of synthesis, we will claim that each member is equivalent to every other member. In other words, we assert a relevant equivalence relation among all the members of each subset such that each consequence in a subset is considered approximately identical in its effect. Each of these subsets, therefore, is deemed an equivalence class and all equivalence classes within a given set are disjoint.

This returns us to the concept of category coherence. To achieve coherent categories, we must identify combinations of central features and relational structures that can form their bases. This does not imply that all members of each equivalence class necessarily will exhibit all central features and relational structures relevant to that class, but rather that each member will exhibit enough of these to distinguish it from other equivalence classes.

How, then, do we identify these multiple sets of central features and relational structures for any given case? While it is unlikely that such a process can be deterministic, it can't be completely arbitrary. Therefore, we posit three heuristics to guide identification of central features and relational structures and subsequent identification of the resultant equivalence classes. We have both induced them from existing synthetic consequences we have developed [e.g., 16] and deduced them from categorization theory. These heuristics are described in the next section.

Note that multiple attempts or permutations may be required to achieve a satisfactorily defined set of equivalence classes. However, the objective is not to iterate across all possible combinations in pursuit of a theoretical minimum, but rather to reduce the number of consequences to a more manageable figure. Ultimately, the adequacy decision belongs to the risk assessment practitioner.

There is a validation heuristic, though, arising out of the need to assign contextual equivalence class designations, i.e., category labels and descriptions. While one can, in principle, employ completely generic labels (e.g., EC_1, EC_2, EC_3, etc.), usability dictates the need for meaningful labels and definitions of each equivalence class. Through this, the equivalence classes become synthetic consequences and therefore members of a larger category of adverse privacy consequences. If that category is lent coherence by an invariant higher-order relation, we posit that meaningful labels are likely to connect with the contextual higher-order relation in which the members participate. Another way of thinking about this is that the higher-order relation reflects the equivalence of the members of each class, an equivalence grounded in the nature of their participation in the higher-order relation. If we cannot find a label and description that captures this participation, reconsideration of the equivalence class memberships may be in order. However, note that, as is the case with Solove's approach, this relation need not be formally defined; an informal description can provide sufficient analytical traction.

4.2 Methodology

We can now enumerate the steps required to derive a synthetic consequence set from a set of consequences. Note that this is a generic methodology that potentially can be applied to system properties beyond privacy. We will illustrate the application of the methodology in the next section by applying it to an example involving a smart TV.

1. Construct the union of the original consequences.
2. Analyze the consequences using the following heuristics in this order:

   a. Independent features, actions, and absent actions in particular;
   b. Feature relations, e.g., correlated features, dependent features, causal features;
   c. Higher-order relations, goals in particular.

3. Group consequences with significant intersections—taking into account feature relations and higher-order relations as well as atomic features—into provisional equivalence classes with the objective of minimizing the number of classes. Multiple iterations may be required to achieve a likely minimum, initially selecting elements with higher cardinalities and, if the results are problematic (e.g., yielding multiple orphan consequences), sorting on elements with lower cardinalities. Some interpretation may be required due to differences in wording.
4. Identify the contextual higher-order relation in which the equivalence classes participate and use the nature of that participation as the basis of the equivalence class labels and descriptions. Because the equivalence classes represent adverse consequences, this higher-order relation will resemble an anti-goal [17]. If one or more labels or descriptions do not exhibit a clear link with the higher-order relation, revise the higher-order relation. If problems persist, revisit Step 3.

We will now demonstrate these steps in the context of a smart TV as described below.

5 Smart TV Example

In the US, the smart TV will collect and store a record of the programs watched by individual users who each have their own profile on the device, including via streaming services such as Netflix. This viewing data will consist of entries that include the date and time (timestamp), the channel and/or service provider, and the program name. This viewing data will be regularly transmitted to the TV manufacturer, who will combine it with demographic data (based on IP address) and maintain the combined data, including IP address, in a repository. The data will be used to support behavioral advertising through the TV. Users must opt-in to the collection and use of viewing data by the manufacturer, as governed by the privacy policy associated with the TV.

5.1 Step 1: Construct the Union of the Consequences

The TV manufacturer, also in the US, has decided to consider privacy consequences from three different sources: the Video Privacy Protection Act of 1988, a US Federal Trade Commission (FTC) version of FIPPs, and Calo's privacy harms. These are paraphrased and itemized below, along with designations to enable convenient referencing.

Video Privacy Protection Act of 1988 [18].

- VPPA1: Disclosure of personal rental information without consent.
- VPPA2: Disclosure to police without a valid warrant or court order.
- VPPA3: Disclosure of "genre preferences" along with names and addresses for marketing despite consumer opt out.

FTC report on privacy online [19].

- FTC1: Failure to disclose information practices before collecting personal information (PI).

- FTC2: PI used without consent for purposes beyond those for which the information was provided.
- FTC3: Inability to view and contest the accuracy and completeness of PI.
- FTC4: PI is inaccurate.
- FTC5: PI is subject to unauthorized use.

Note that FTC4 and FTC5 are derived from what was originally a compound imperative in the source report.

Calo's privacy harms [4].

- Calo1: Perception of unwanted surveillance (subjective privacy harm).
- Calo2: Forced or unanticipated use of PI (objective privacy harm).

In those cases in which items were originally structured as imperatives or prohibitions, we have reframed them as adverse consequences. None of the consequences are clearly duplicative, therefore, their union is all of them combined.

5.2 Step 2: Analyze Consequences

The results of this step are presented in Table 1. Relations between features are *italicized*. Note that we have expressed the opt out in VPPA3 in terms of consent, since it is the denial of consent, while we have not expressed the unauthorized use in FTC5 in terms of consent as the source document makes clear that this is a security issue.

5.3 Step 3: Group into Provisional Equivalence Classes

Tables 2 and 3 convey alternative possible sets of equivalence classes resulting from the stepwise grouping process, **bolding** the bases for the grouping decisions and underlining inferred higher-order relations. Table 2 reflects an initial focus on "no consent," given its relatively high cardinality across features and relational structures, as a basis for establishing the first equivalence class. An additional class can then be formed on the basis of inaccurate PI and the inability to contest it. However, there is no clear basis for any other equivalence classes, leaving the remaining 4 original consequences as orphans (whose presence in Table 2 is left implicit). The end result, then, is a total of six classes, of which four consist of orphan consequences. While this is not an intolerable result, neither is it a particularly satisfying one.

Table 3 reflects an alternative emphasis on "disclosure," with lower cardinality, for defining the initial class. While this produces a smaller first class, it enables the formation of additional multi-member classes based on the usage of personal information without consent, inaccurate PI (as before), and the inferred relation between unexplained practices and perceived surveillance. This produces a smaller set of four equivalence classes with no orphan consequences and highlights the importance of considering multiple grouping approaches. While this does not preclude the possibility of producing an even smaller number of equivalence classes, the resulting 60% reduction in consequences is significant enough to justify proceeding to the next step.

Table 1. Consequence analysis

Consequence	Independent features	Feature relations	Higher-order relations
VPPA1	PI disclosure No consent	PI disclosure *despite* no consent	
VPPA2	PI disclosure Disclosure to police No valid warrant or court order	PI disclosure *to* police	(PI disclosure *to* police) *despite* no warrant or court order
VPPA3	PI disclosure Disclosure for marketing No consent	PI disclosure *for* marketing	(PI disclosure *for* marketing) *despite* no consent
FTC1	PI collection No practices communicated	PI collection *despite* no practices communicated	
FTC2	PI usage No consent	PI usage *despite* no consent	
FTC3	No PI viewing No contesting PI accuracy	No PI viewing *implies* no contesting PI accuracy	
FTC4	PI inaccurate		
FTC5	PI usage No authorization	PI usage *despite* no authorization	
Calo1	Perceived surveillance Unwanted surveillance	Perceived surveillance *and* unwanted surveillance	
Calo2	PI usage No consent	PI usage *despite* no consent PI usage *not* anticipated	

Table 2. Grouping starting from "No Consent"

Consequence	Independent features	Feature relations	Higher-order relations
VPPA1, VPPA3, FTC2, Calo2	PI disclosure **No consent** PI disclosure Disclosure for marketing **No consent** PI usage **No consent** PI usage **No consent**	PI disclosure *despite* **no consent** PI usage *despite* **no consent** PI usage *despite* **no consent** PI usage *not* anticipated	(PI disclosure *for* marketing) *despite* **no consent** **Information life** **cycle action *despite* no consent**
FTC3, FTC4	No PI viewing No contesting **PI accuracy** **PI inaccurate**	No PI viewing *implies* **no contesting PI accuracy** **No contesting PI accuracy** *despite* **PI inaccurate**	

5.4 Step 4: Contextualize the Consequences

The final step involves developing a contextualized label and description for each of the derived equivalence classes. However, we must first identify an invariant contextual higher-order relation that will establish a basis for this activity. For this, it is useful to revisit the description of the smart TV scenario at the beginning of this section. Based on this, we will assert that the higher-order relation in which the consequences participate involves improper profiling.

Having identified this relation, we can now develop appropriately contextualized labels and descriptions for the synthetic consequences. Difficulty doing so would suggest that either the higher-order relation is inappropriate or that the consequence groupings are less coherent than originally believed, either one raising questions regarding the validity of the resulting synthetic consequences. These questions would prompt revision of the higher-order relation or reconsideration of the groupings, respectively. However, neither of these appears to be an issue and the resulting labels and descriptions are shown in Table 4. This set of four synthetic consequences can now be employed for privacy risk assessment of the smart TV.

Table 3. Grouping starting from "Disclosure"

Consequence	Independent features	Feature relations	Higher-order relations
VPPA1, VPPA2, VPPA3	PI **disclosure** No consent PI **disclosure** **Disclosure** to police No valid warrant or court order PI **disclosure** **Disclosure** for marketing No consent	PI **disclosure** *despite* no consent	(PI **disclosure** *to* police) *despite* no warrant or court order (PI **disclosure** *for* marketing) *despite* no consent
FTC2, FTC5, Calo2	**PI usage** No consent **PI usage** No consent	**PI usage** *despite* **no consent** **PI usage** *despite* no authorization **PI usage** *despite* **no consent** **PI usage** *not* anticipated	
FTC3, FTC4	No PI viewing No contesting **PI accuracy** **PI inaccurate**	No PI viewing *implies* **no contesting PI accuracy** **No contesting PI accuracy** *despite* **PI inaccurate**	
FTC1, Calo1	PI collection No practices communicated Perceived surveillance Unwanted surveillance	PI collection *despite* no practices communicated Perceived surveillance *and* unwanted surveillance	**(PI collection** *despite* **no practices communicated)** *implies* **perceived surveillance**

Table 4. Synthetic consequences resulting from contextualization

Constituent consequences	Synthetic consequence	Description
VPPA1, VPPA2, VPPA3	Involuntary Profile Availability	Program-based profiles of individuals are made available to unknown entities without permission
FTC2, FTC5, Calo2	Involuntary Profile Exploitation	Program-based profiles of individuals are used for unknown purposes without permission
FTC3, FTC4	Blackbox Profiling	Individuals have no insight into the state of their PI as maintained by the TV, TV manufacturer, or others, and/or they have no ability to manipulate it
FTC1, Calo1	Ambiguous Profiling	Uncertainty regarding PI processing engenders surveillance concerns

6   Conclusions and Future Directions

By synthesizing four consequence equivalence classes from the original ten consequences, we have made privacy risk assessment more manageable in a number of ways. The reduction in the number of consequences simplifies the risk model that is being employed. (Recall that there is *always* a risk model being used in any non-arbitrary privacy risk assessment, though it may not be explicitly defined.) The concomitant reduction in model complexity will reduce the level of effort required to perform any privacy risk assessment. Further, the contextual tailoring of the synthetic consequences will also make for more efficient assessment by alleviating the analyst of the necessity of bridging between the specifics of the socio-technical system being assessed and abstract privacy consequences, an advantage that is qualitative and goes beyond a quantitative improvement that is, in this example, modest in absolute terms. (One can easily imagine, though, the potential for more profound quantitative improvements in cases that start with many more consequences.) While one could simply bank that saved effort, one could also redeploy it to support the application of more sophisticated forms of privacy risk analysis, such as System-Theoretic Process Analysis for Privacy (STPA-Priv) [20].

There is, of course, a trade-off involved given that the process of deriving synthetic consequences itself entails significant effort. For a one-off privacy risk assessment, a judgement will be required as to whether this trade-off is worthwhile. However, if the risk assessment is likely to undergo future updates in response to system or environmental changes, the effort of deriving synthetic consequences can be amortized over multiple assessments. Further, if the synthetic consequences are domain rather than system-specific and therefore reusable, the expected amortization across different assessments would make the case for them even more compelling.

Judgement is also very relevant when executing the synthesis process. As a result, different people may arrive at somewhat different sets of consequences derived from the same initial set. However, a similar observation could be made of any of the existing consequence-oriented privacy risk models. Someone else employing an approach like that which produced any of these could be reasonably expected to produce a set of non-identical consequences, but this hardly de-legitimizes either set. Rather, we simply acknowledge that each may exhibit particular strengths and weaknesses, but that they are all likely to prove useful even if non-definitive. Ultimately, they are a means, not an end.

While synthesizing consequences will certainly mitigate the combinatorial expansion inherent in the privacy risk model for any complex socio-technical system, it only addresses one facet of the expansion problem. Even allowing for the fact that this expansion is seldom unconstrained (i.e., not every possible threat will exploit every possible vulnerability which will lead to every possible type of consequence), it likely will remain problematic, particularly given the general desire/insistence for low-overhead privacy risk assessment. This raises the natural question of whether a similar process can be applied to the other risk model factors. Coming before consequences in the modeling chain, vulnerabilities may be the logical next step in leveraging synthesis as a technique.

While not as numerous among established privacy risk models as sets of consequences, sets of vulnerabilities have been described (irrespective of whether they are identified as such) as part of the PRAM [6] and LINDDUN [7] assessment techniques.

Contextual integrity [5], moreover, amounts to a method of identifying context-specific privacy vulnerabilities. However, given the scope of the technique, these could prove numerous in any given case. Synthesizing vulnerability equivalence classes, then, could greatly mitigate the resultant complexity. Further, because vulnerabilities identified through application of the contextual integrity heuristic would be intrinsically contextual, this would streamline the final step of the synthesis process.

Acknowledgements. Thanks to MITRE colleague Julie Snyder and to discussants at the Privacy Law Scholars Conference for comments on an earlier version of this paper.

References

1. US National Institute of Standards and Technology (NIST): Guide for Conducting Risk Assessments, NIST Special Publication 800-37, Revision 1. NIST, Gaithersburg, MD (2012)
2. International Organization for Standardization (ISO), Privacy Engineering for System Life Cycle Processes, ISO/IEC TR 27550:2019. ISO, Geneva, Switzerland (2019)
3. Solove, D.: Understanding Privacy. Harvard University Press, Cambridge (2010)
4. Calo, M.R.: The boundaries of privacy harm. Indiana Law J. **86**(3), 1131 (2011)
5. Nissenbaum, H.: Privacy in Context: Technology, Policy, and the Integrity of Social Life. Stanford Law Books, Palo Alto (2009)
6. NIST Privacy Engineering Program Resources. https://www.nist.gov/itl/applied-cybersecurity/privacy-engineering/resources. Accessed 14 July 2021
7. Deng, M., Wuyts, K., Scandariato, R., Preneel, B., Joosen, W.: A privacy threat analysis framework: supporting the elicitation and fulfillment of privacy requirements. Requirements Eng. **16**(1), 3–32 (2011). https://doi.org/10.1007/s00766-010-0115-7
8. Malt, B.C.: Category coherence in cross-cultural perspective. Cogn. Psychol. **29**(2), 85–148 (1995). https://doi.org/10.1006/cogp.1995.1013
9. Lakoff, G.: Women, Fire, and Dangerous Things: What Categories Reveal About the Mind. University of Chicago Press, Chicago (1987)
10. Sloman, S.A., Love, B.C., Ahn, W.-K.: Feature centrality and conceptual coherence. Cogn. Sci. **22**(2), 189–228 (1998). https://doi.org/10.1207/s15516709cog2202_2
11. Pardo, R., Le Métayer, D.: Analysis of privacy policies to enhance informed consent. In: Foley, S.N. (ed.) DBSec 2019. LNCS, vol. 11559, pp. 177–198. Springer, Cham (2019). https://doi.org/10.1007/978-3-030-22479-0_10
12. Johansen, M.K., Palmeri, T.J.: Are there representational shifts during category learning? Cogn. Psychol. **45**(4), 482–553 (2002). https://doi.org/10.1016/S0010-0285(02)00505-4
13. Gentner, D.: Structure-mapping: a theoretical framework for analogy. Cogn. Sci. **7**(2), 155–170 (1983). https://doi.org/10.1207/s15516709cog0702_3
14. Rehder, B., Burnett, R.C.: Feature inference and the causal structure of categories. Cogn. Psychol. **50**(3), 264–314 (2005). https://doi.org/10.1016/j.cogpsych.2004.09.002
15. Jung, W., Hummel, J.: Making probabilistic relational categories learnable. Cogn. Sci. **39**(6), 1259–1291 (2015)
16. US Department of Transportation (USDOT): Privacy Issues for Consideration by USDOT Based on Review of Preliminary Technical Framework (Final – Rev A), Report Number FHWA-JPO-15-236. USDOT, Washington, DC (2016). https://www.regulations.gov/document?D=NHTSA-2016-0126-0003
17. van Lamsweerde, A.: Requirements Engineering: From System Goals to UML Models to Software Specifications. Wiley, Chichester (2009)

18. Video Privacy Protection Act of 1988, 18 U.S.C. § 2710 (2002)
19. US Federal Trade Commission (FTC): Privacy Online: Fair Information Practices in the Electronic Marketplace. FTC, Washington, DC (2000)
20. Shapiro, S.: Privacy risk analysis based on system control structures: adapting system-theoretic process analysis for privacy engineering. In: 2016 IEEE Security and Privacy Workshops (SPW), San Jose, CA, pp. 17–24 (2016)

Enhanced Privacy in Smart Workplaces: Employees' Preferences for Transparency Indicators and Control Interactions in the Case of Data Collection with Smart Watches

Alexander Richter[1]([✉]), Patrick Kühtreiber[1], and Delphine Reinhardt[1,2]

[1] Computer Security and Privacy, University of Göttingen,
Goldschmidtstr. 7, 37073 Göttingen, Germany
{richter,kuhtreiber,reinhardt}@cs.uni-goettingen.de
[2] Campus Institute Data Science, Goldschmidtstr. 1, 37073 Göttingen, Germany

Abstract. Employees are increasingly wearing smart watches for their work duties. While these devices can support employees in their tasks, they can also collect sensitive information like health or location data about them, thus endangering their privacy. Even when collective agreements, allowing employers to collect such data have been signed, we argue that employees should be aware of the data collection and be able to control it. Therefore, we propose different indicators that aim at enhancing employees' awareness about the current data collection as well as interactions to allow them to stop and resume it according to their preferences. To compare them, we have conducted an online questionnaire-based study with 1,033 participants. The results indicate that our participants wish to have such indicators to raise their awareness and further wish to control the data collection.

Keywords: Smart workplaces · Smart watches · Privacy awareness · Privacy indicators · Control mechanisms · Preferences

1 Introduction

More and more smart watches are sold worldwide [15,19]. In addition to be used for private purposes, companies also recognize their potential and increasingly equip their employees with such devices [21,42]. For example, they are used for allowing faster access to information [28,36], improving well-being [16], or enhance occupational safety [4]. As these devices collect various data about their wearers, they pose potential risks to the wearer's privacy. Such risks may reduce the employees' acceptance. Therefore, it is recommended that companies record only work-related data and establish transparent processes to optimize the balance between advantages and associated risks [38]. Such transparency is

© IFIP International Federation for Information Processing 2022
Published by Springer Nature Switzerland AG 2022
W. Meng et al. (Eds.): SEC 2022, IFIP AICT 648, pp. 34–50, 2022.
https://doi.org/10.1007/978-3-031-06975-8_3

also enforced in the General Data Protection Regulation (GDPR), especially in Art. 5 (1) and Recitals 58 and 60. Although previous research on transparency mechanisms to increase privacy awareness exists [1,3,8,17], none covers this aspect in the work-context, especially when considering data collection on smart watches. Thus, it is still unclear how transparency on smart watches should be implemented by employers in a work-context. Apart from this aspect, based on the GDPR, data subjects have also the right to control their data (e.g.,GDPR, Art. 19). They have the right to revoke their consent to the processing at any time. This allows control over the data as soon as it has been collected. However, the GDPR does not provide any reference to the possibility of temporarily interrupting data collection. While research on control mechanisms is done in private domains to control data collection [9,20,24,37], none contributed insights about interrupting smart watch data collection when used in workplaces. As a result, we herein propose privacy-enhancing solutions tailored to employees using smart watches for working tasks. More precisely, we have designed three different transparency indicators showing when and which data collection occurs (see Fig. 1) and considered six different control interactions (see Fig. 2), which allow users to temporally interrupt the data collection. We have further explored the preferences of potential users for our proposed solutions using an online questionnaire. 1,033 participants contributed to our study. The key insights are as follows. Our participants prefer a splash-screen design to raise their awareness about actual data processing. The splash-screen design (see Fig. 1(a)) is like a notification on the smart watch screen, which requires the user's active involvement. Moreover, they want to be able to stop the data collection by preferably using a button in the menu of the work application running on the smart watch. Our results contribute to the privacy research regarding transparency and control in a work-context to enhance employees' privacy. Moreover, our findings could result in practical implications as employers can develop our findings in future smart watch applications used in smart workplaces to enhance employee transparency and control.

The remainder of the paper is structured as follows: In Sect. 2, we review related work. We present our research goals in Sect. 3. We detail our decision drivers in Sect. 4 and 5. We present our methodology in Sect. 6 and our results in Sect. 7, which we discuss in Sect. 8, and make concluding remarks in Sect. 9.

2   Related Work

Related research can be classified into three categories: (1) privacy concerns, (2) raising privacy awareness, and (3) control mechanisms. The first category includes existing work on privacy concerns related to wearable devices. According to [32], privacy concerns are related to embedded sensors, which can measure, collect, and store data. Thereby, most concerns are indicated about revealing conversations, commuting, or stress [32]. Moreover, they found that users do not understand the implications of potential threats of collected data unless they have a personal connection to the data [32]. However, in the context of smart watches, privacy concerns can arise in many ways [12,27], as individuals may have misconceptions or even false beliefs about these devices [39]. Regarding privacy concerns in the context of workplace environments, previous work highlights employees' concerns, including the fear of surveillance or tracking by the employer, or that the devices record sensitive information [6,12,34]. As a result, this can negatively impact workers' job satisfaction and stress levels, leading to productivity declines [23,38].

In the second category, previous studies are dedicated to raising privacy awareness by nudging through visual indicators [17], warning messages [1,3,8,35] or encouraging privacy-protective behavior [41]. However, the scope of these studies is limited to the private domain. The authors in [17] presented three approaches to raise user awareness when a front-face camera is accessed by an application. Their three approaches included designs using notification, frame, and camera preview and were evaluated by participants in a user study. The authors in [8] proposed a solution to increase users' privacy awareness about threats in participatory sensing applications based on picture-based warnings. This empowers users to be informed about potential risks without having to read long texts. Other smartphone-based solutions are presented by [1,3]. Both approaches provide detailed privacy information about the applications' behavior. However, they are designed for smartphones and not watches with different design constraints. Another work is the PATCOM project by [35]. They developed a smart watch application prototype, which can inform users when entering privacy-compromising environments. Hence, they provide some level of transparency by notifying users about the potential data collection, which can help strengthen trust in the environment. Finally, the approach in [41] raises privacy awareness with a game encouraging privacy-protective behavior for smart watch users but for private usages.

The third and last category deals with mechanisms to control data collection. Data control can be applied at different levels including stopping data collection, correcting and deleting data. Stopping sensors from collecting data usually leads to a disruption of the underlying service. Instead, users should be able to restrict sensor readings and still benefit from limited functions [7]. For example, smart speakers provide mute buttons to stop the microphone functions [20,24]. However, the speakers can still be used for playing music. Another privacy-enhancing interaction is the privacy hat designed by [37], which has to be placed physically on top of the smart speaker to mute it. A more granular approach is proposed in [9] for smartphones with which users can separately control the collection of different sensor modalities.

To the best of our knowledge no previous work exists, which investigates employees' preferences regarding both (1) privacy indicators visualizing data collection on smart watches to increase employees' privacy awareness and (2) control interactions to interrupt data collection when equipped with a smart watch at work.

3 Research Goals

Once employees themselves or the works council have consented to the collection of data through a collective agreement, employers can collect data about employees with the help of the smart watch according to the signed agreement. In this case, a one-time consent can generate a continuous data collection. Nevertheless, in accordance with the GDPR, employers must process personal data lawfully and transparently (GDPR, Art. 5 (1) a)), even though the GDPR leaves the regulations on the handling of employee data to the member states (GDPR, Art. 88). In general, the principle of Fair and Transparent Processing requires that the data subject is informed about the collection of personal data (GDPR, Recital 60). In detail, the principle of transparency requires that information about the processing should not only be easily accessible but also understandable (GDPR, Recital 39, 58). This can be supported by comprehensible visual elements, such as standardized symbols, which can provide an understandable overview of the processing (GDPR, Recital 60). To ensure that users are aware of the processing of personal data, we argue that privacy indicators can be used. Privacy indicators aim to provide individuals with meaningful information about how their privacy is being handled [33]. Such indicators may be textual, graphic, or audible [33]. Meanwhile, many IoT devices including smart speakers [10,18,20] are equipped with an LED that indicates data collection [31]. Motivated by the previously mentioned GDPR requirements and existing indicators, the question arises how employers can provide transparency about data collection for their employees by using similar indicators tailored to smart watches. This leads to our first research question (RQ):

▶ RQ1: Which transparency indicator visualization(s) do employees perceive as sufficient and useful to be informed about the current data collection?

Transparency is often associated to the control over personal data by the data subjects themselves. Based on the GDPR, data subjects have the right to rectification (GDPR, Art. 16), erasure (GDPR, Art. 17), and restriction of processing (GDPR, Art. 19) of their data. In addition, a data subject has the right to object (GDPR, Art. 21). This allows the data subject to revoke their consent to the processing at any time. These rights allow control over the data as soon as it has been collected. Nevertheless, the GDPR does not provide any reference to the possibility of temporarily interrupting data collection. We argue that users should, however, be able to do so. This should also apply if a previously concluded company agreement allows the employers to collect data about their employees. The resulting self-determination of the employees to interrupt data collection can contribute in increasing their trust in the employers. However, such temporary interruptions in data collection can result in employers mistrusting employees using them. To prevent this scenario, additional mechanisms should be added to protect the employees. Nevertheless, in our scenario, the conditions of the interruptions are defined by the employers who provide the underlying application running on the smart watch. Therefore, we aim at addressing the following research question:

▶ RQ2: Which interaction(s) is/are perceived by the employees as appropriate to control the data collection?

4   Privacy Indicators

Our first objective is to indicate data collection with privacy indicators to provide transparency about it. In what follows, we motivate our design decisions based on an analysis of existing drivers and detail our resulting designs.

4.1   Design Drivers

To design our privacy indicator, we consider two factors: (1) notification of the data collection and (2) the display of the related information that affect the design of the subsequent layout on smart watches. Firstly, notifications are visual, auditory, or haptic stimuli triggered by applications or services to relay information that are outside of the scope of users' attention. Auditory or haptic stimuli are especially efficient in interrupting users activities to gain their attention [5]. These interruptions can be perceived as intrusive and annoying, especially when the wearer receives numerous notifications [26,29,40]. For example, results in [40] indicate that notifications of a messenger application were perceived as less annoying than the notifications of a music application because these notifications were of lesser interest. Therefore, the notifications should be of interest, i.e., perceived as useful to the user. Moreover, they should be used with care to avoid habituation effects.

Secondly, smart watches are constrained by size and shape. Compared to smartphones, their screen is even smaller. Since smart watch wearers only briefly check the screen [30], the provided information should be as brief as possible to accommodate the screen size and not to appear cluttered, while providing concise and understandable information about ongoing data collection. Moreover, it should cater to existing smart watch forms including round or square screens.

Thirdly, in the context of smart workplaces, the collection of activity, health, and location data are possible. An indication of such data collection needs to be easy to understand and fast to distinguish. Therefore, the presentation of the ongoing data collection of the different data types should differ at least in color. A double coding should be introduced to cater for color-blind users.

4.2   Resulting Designs

We present our privacy indicators which were created based on the aforementioned design drivers. Hereby, the currently available smart watch operating systems serve as basis for our design decisions.

Design A: Splash-Screen. The first design shown in Fig. 1(a) is the most common and known as a notification. It is motivated by [17,35] and represents a normal notification, which the wearer must actively close. The used color depends on the collected data type(s). We have attributed blue to activity data, red to health

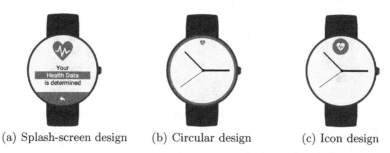

(a) Splash-screen design   (b) Circular design   (c) Icon design

Fig. 1. Examples of proposed indicators to visualize the collection of health data on a smart watch (Clolor figure online)

data, and yellow to location data. In addition to color, the splash-screen design offers an icon and an additional text to further inform the wearers. In addition, it can be supported by an auditory or haptic signal. Possible limitation of this indicator are that (1) it prevent users from seeing anything else on the screen and (2) requires an explicit interaction to close it. As a result, the wearers' attention may be improved but at the cost of more efforts.

Design B: Circle. The second design shown in Fig. 1(b) and motivated by [17] is a circle that surrounds the watch face and differs in color based on the data type following the same color scheme as above. In addition, a supportive icon is added. The circle indicator is displayed for a few seconds and can also be supported by an auditory or haptic signal. During data collection, the circle appears around the watch face and disappears when the data collection stops. This means that the wearers are constantly informed about the current data collection. If neither an auditory signal nor vibration is added, this indicator is a very reduced and simple way to notify the wearer about data collection when the wearer is looking at the watch face. Its advantage is that it uses the watch face and does not cover it or require any action from the wearer as compared to the previous design. However, its simplicity may negatively affect the wearer's understanding at the beginning, as the color is only mapped with an icon and no additional information.

Design C: Icon. Our last design shown in Fig. 1(c) and motivated by [2] is a bigger visual cue on the watch face at the top of the smart watch screen. It consists of a bigger colored icon. Auditory or haptic stimuli can also extend the design. As with the previous design, the respective indicator is visible for a few seconds. As soon as data collection is active, the indicator on the watch face appears. As compared to design B, the circle with the small icon is replaced by a bigger icon on the watch face. A bigger size could mitigate the mentioned weakness of design B. However, the indicator is only visible when the wearer actively looks at the smart watch in contrast to design A.

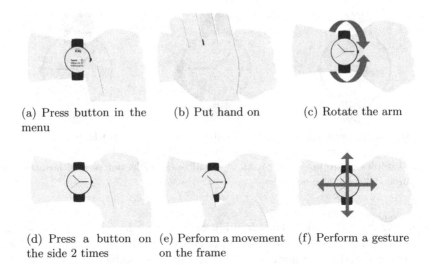

(a) Press button in the menu

(b) Put hand on

(c) Rotate the arm

(d) Press a button on the side 2 times

(e) Perform a movement on the frame

(f) Perform a gesture

Fig. 2. Proposed mechanisms to interrupt personal data collection on a smart watch

5   Control Interactions

Our second objective is to allow users to control the data collection by temporarily interrupting it. This objective aims to support employees in controlling their personal information and refers to the right to restrict personal information processing (GDPR, Art. 18).

5.1   Design Drivers

To allow such control, the corresponding interactions should be easy to understand and executable by the wearers in different situations. The chosen interactions should also take into about the wearers' physical capabilities and be reliably recognized by the smart watch. The possible interaction options are via touchscreen, buttons, frame, and sensors that detect arm movement.

5.2   Selected Control Interactions

In the following, we describe the selected control interactions illustrated in Fig. 2, which enable the user to interrupt the data collection.

Interaction A: Press a Button in the Menu. Figure 2(a) represents a manual interaction, as the wearer needs to open the respective application, go through the settings and deactivate the data collection using a button. This is advantageous as users are usually familiar with the use of menus. However, the interaction requires different steps.

Interaction B: Put Hand on. Figure 2(b) presents an interaction leveraging the ambient light sensor of the smart watch. Every time the wearer covers this sensor with the palm, the data collection stops. For this interaction, no further steps are needed. This interaction is easy to perform, but could foster many false interruptions depending on the deployment scenarios.

Interaction C: Rotate the Arm. Figure 2(c) shows an interaction based on a hand gesture by rotating the arm with the smart watch in a specific manner. As soon as the smart watch sensors detect the movement, the data collection is interrupted. Although this interaction only requires an easy arm rotation, it causes the screen to be out of the wearers' view. Furthermore, this interaction can be triggered unintentionally.

Interaction D: Press a Button on the Side. Figure 2(d) shows the easiest to understand interaction after the menu interaction. The smart watch wearer presses the mechanical button at the side of the watch to stop the collection. This interaction is easy to perform and easy to remember. To avoid false positive interruptions, the button needs to be pressed two times.

Interaction E: Perform a Movement on the Frame. Figure 2(e) presents a finger gesture performed on the smart watch frame. The wearer has to touch the frame and swipe down, for example. This interaction is easy to remember as it needs to be performed at the smart watch's frame. However, wearing gloves can hinder performing it as the device could not recognize the finger, for instance.

Interaction F: Perform a Gesture. Figure 2(f) shows our second real gesture. Similar to the gesture in Fig. 2(c), the wearer has to perform a hand movement. Here, the hand movement is a movement in the air using a special pattern.

In summary, we consider three designs for the privacy indicators and six different interactions to control the data collection in what follows.

6 Methodology

6.1 Survey Distribution

To answer our research questions, we have conducted an online questionnaire conforming to the GDPR and approved by the Data Protection Officer of our university. While we do not have a formal IRB process at our university, we have taken particular care to minimize potential harms to the participants, by, e.g., reducing the number of questions to the minimum to avoid fatigue. Participants have been informed that they could leave the questionnaire at any time. The questionnaire has been distributed by a panel certified ISO 26362 and the participants have been financially rewarded. Our inclusion criteria were that our participants had to be between 18 and 67 years old, living and working full-time in Germany. Participants were chosen based on quotas, i.e., the distribution in terms of age and gender is representative of the German population [13]. In total, 1,033 participants answered our questionnaire in August 2021.

6.2   Survey Design

Our questionnaire is articulated around a smart workplace scenario, in which the participants have to imagine that they are equipped with smart watches when performing their jobs. After starting with demographics questions to fulfill the survey quotas, the main questionnaire starts. In the first part, we analyze their preferences for three different smart watch indicators introduced in Sect. 4.2 displayed on the smart watch when data is collected. For each indicator we propose an alternative in color and related icon for different collected data types: Activity, health, and location. For example, Fig. 1 shows the three different alternatives for health data. Based on these alternatives, we ask the participants different questions to elicit their preferences on a 5-point Likert scale from "strongly disagree" to "strongly agree". Then, in the second part, we investigate the scenarios in which they would like to control the data collection and propose different interactions for each data type (see Fig. 2). Each interaction is illustrated by an animation, so that our participants could understand the interactions more easily. Later in the questionnaire, we ask our participants questions regarding their smart watch ownership, usage, and main purpose. To elaborate on our participants' technical affinity, we ask nine questions with a 6-point Likert scale from "completely disagree" to "completely agree" proposed by [14]. At the end of the questionnaire, we finally ask our participants to provide work-related information, including the sector, work function, work environment, and work conditions based on predefined choices. The questionnaire is available online (https://owncloud.gwdg.de/index.php/s/YGW2QXRHsJ5y8Nv).

7   Results

7.1   Demographics

Among our 1,033 participants, 48% are women and 52% are men. Their age distribution matches the current population of Germany [13]. A majority of our participants work in health and social care (15%) followed by industry (14%), public service (7%), and IT/telecom (6%). Their working conditions are as follows: 90% work inside, 64% in quiet environments, and 63% walk rather little during work. Interestingly, 43% already own a smart watch. Overall, more females (47%) than males (40%) stated that they own a smart watch. A Mann-Whitney U test indicates that gender is a significant influence ($p = .013$). Likewise, age ($p < .001$, Kruskal-Wallis test). Especially younger participants own a smart watch. A pairwise comparison (Bonferoni-Correction) reveals significant differences between the age categories 18–24 and 45–54 ($p < .001$), 18–24 and 55–67 ($p < .001$), 25–34 and 45–54, ($p < .01$), 25–34 and 55–67 ($p = .01$), 35–44 and 45–54, ($p < .01$), as well as 35–44 and 55–67 ($p = .01$). The majority (70%) use their smart watch daily. Although about 79% use their smart watch mainly for private purposes (79%), some indicated that they use it also for work (19%) or even exclusively for work (2%). Regarding the results based on the technical affinity score proposed by [14], we assume that our participants are rather tech-savvy. Overall, all participants reach a mean score of 3.94 ($SD = 0.96$) on a scale from one to six. A closer look reveals that males ($M = 4.18, SD = 0.92$) reach significantly ($p = .05$) higher scores than females ($M = 3.68, SD = 0.93$). While gender has an impact, age does not.

7.2   Preferences for Privacy Indicators

When considering our three privacy indicators (see Fig. 1), the results indicate that our participants prefer the splash-screen design (38%) followed by the icon design (34%) and the circle design (28%). A closer look at our results regarding the seven sub-questions (see Fig. 3) about how the data collection is presented shows a similar picture. The seven questions reach a Cronbach's Alpha of 0.86, indicating acceptable reliability [11]. In all sub-questions, except sub-question three, the splash-screen design reaches higher means, shown in Fig. 3. Our participants think that the splash-screen design would better raise their general awareness about privacy issues ($M = 3.45, SD = 1.2$) and increase their awareness about the data collection ($M = 3.68, SD = 1.0$) than the other two indicators in both cases. However, they are rated similarly in terms of acceptance. Although the notification presented in the splash-screen design is not new, our participants find it on average more intuitive ($M = 3.87, SD = 1.0$) than the circle ($M = 3.41, SD = 1.2$) or icon ($M = 3.58, SD = 1.1$) design. In general, the results indicate that the splash-screen design, on average, is the easiest to understand for our participants. However, this indicator is estimated to be the most disturbing in comparison to the other two.

Additional Feedback. Regarding additional signals such as vibration or sound, the results show that 48% of our participants would like to have auditory feedback. A qualitative content analysis [22] shows that the open answers from proponents of auditory feedback most frequently relate to *awareness, informed, or remembered*, while those from opponents frequently relate to the categories *disturbing, annoying, or distracting* instead. In contrast, 58% would wish for a complementary haptic feedback. The most frequent categories based on the proponents' answers are *less disturbing, awareness, remembered, informed, more discrete*, while the opponents' answer categories are similar to those from the auditory opponents. While a χ^2-test reveals, that only gender ($\chi^2_{(1)} = 7.34, p = .007$) has a significant relationship with participants' decision on additional sound, gender ($\chi^2_{(1)} = 4.29, p < .04$), age ($\chi^2_{(4)} = 20.15, p < .001$), and smartwatch ownership ($\chi^2_{(1)} = 37.26, p < .001$) significantly relate to additional vibrations.

Deactivation Option. When it comes to the question to deactivate such an indicator, their answers reveal that 32% would rather deactivate such privacy indicators. Statements include *"I don't think it's essential to know when it's being recorded"* (participant 289) or *"may be disruptive in meetings"* (participant 69). A χ^2-test reveals, a significant relationship with gender ($\chi^2_{(1)} = 5.64, p = .02$), age ($\chi^2_{(4)} = 18.22, p = .001$), and ownership ($\chi^2_{(1)} = 15.67, p < .001$).

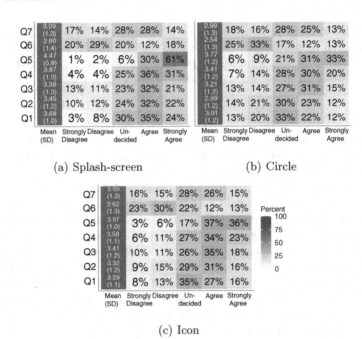

	Mean (SD)	Strongly Disagree	Disagree	Un-decided	Agree	Strongly Agree		Mean (SD)	Strongly Disagree	Disagree	Un-decided	Agree	Strongly Agree
Q7	3.09 (1.3)	17%	14%	28%	28%	14%		2.99 (1.3)	18%	16%	28%	25%	13%
Q6	2.80 (1.4)	20%	29%	20%	12%	18%		2.54 (1.3)	25%	33%	17%	12%	13%
Q5	4.47 (0.8)	1%	2%	6%	30%	61%		3.77 (1.2)	6%	9%	21%	31%	33%
Q4	3.87 (1.0)	4%	4%	25%	36%	31%		3.41 (1.2)	7%	14%	28%	30%	20%
Q3	3.38 (1.3)	13%	11%	23%	32%	21%		3.21 (1.2)	13%	14%	27%	31%	15%
Q2	3.45 (1.2)	10%	12%	24%	32%	22%		2.99 (1.2)	14%	21%	30%	23%	12%
Q1	3.68 (1.0)	3%	8%	30%	35%	24%		3.01 (1.2)	13%	20%	33%	22%	12%

(a) Splash-screen   (b) Circle

	Mean (SD)	Strongly Disagree	Disagree	Un-decided	Agree	Strongly Agree
Q7	3.09 (1.3)	16%	15%	28%	26%	15%
Q6	2.62 (1.3)	23%	30%	22%	12%	13%
Q5	3.97 (1.0)	3%	6%	17%	37%	36%
Q4	3.58 (1.1)	6%	11%	27%	34%	23%
Q3	3.41 (1.2)	10%	11%	26%	35%	18%
Q2	3.32 (1.2)	9%	15%	29%	31%	16%
Q1	3.29 (1.1)	8%	13%	35%	27%	16%

Percent: 100, 75, 50, 25, 0

(c) Icon

Fig. 3. Results of proposed privacy indicators. Attitude on "This privacy indicator... (Q1) would reinforce my perception about data collection. (Q2) would catch my general attention. (Q3) seems to me to be useful for the purpose. (Q4) is intuitive. (Q5) is easy to understand. (Q6) is disturbing. (Q7) is acceptable in order to visualize the data collection."

7.3 Preferences for Control Interactions

Concerning the interruption of data collection, 67% of our participants "strongly agree" (48%) or "agree" (19%) that they would like to have this opportunity. Overall, our participants indicated they would like to interrupt data collection in private scenarios for all data types (i.e., activity, health, location) and during the walk to the toilet (67%), or when having breaks (65%) when, e.g., the location would be collected. The detailed results are shown in Table 1 and suggest similar results among the different data types. When considering the different proposed mechanisms to interrupt data collection, a majority (51%) would prefer to press a button in the menu. In comparison, arm movements like arm rotation or another arm gesture are less desired. Figure 4 show the results for each interaction option on the scale from "strongly not suitable" to "strongly suitable" for all data types. Along all data types, our participants do not differ much between the presented interactions.

Table 1. Employees' selection of situations to interrupt data collection

Case	Activity	Health	Location	Private Context
During concentration periods	21%	21%	21%	
During a private conversation	40%	42%	42%	✓
During professional meeting	23%	26%	23%	
While smoking	24%	23%	29%	✓
While eating	52%	56%	52%	✓
During the break	61%	62%	65%	✓
During the walk to the toilet	61%	65%	67%	✓

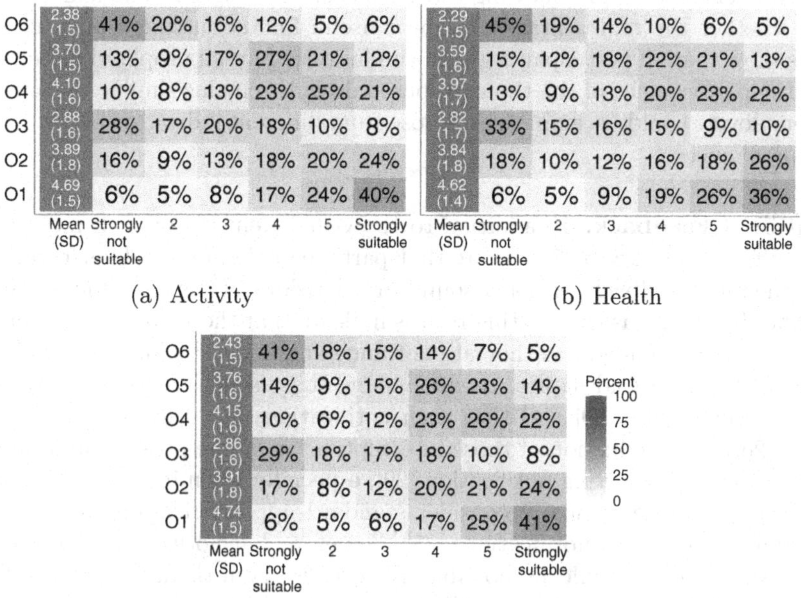

(a) Activity

(b) Health

(c) Location

Fig. 4. Results of employees' attitude on the suitability of smart watch interactions: (O1) Press a button in the menu, (O2) Put your hand on, (O3) Rotate the arm, (O4) Press a button on the side 2 times, (O5) Perform a movement on the frame, (O6) Perform a gesture

8   Discussion

We next discuss the results obtained for the privacy indicators followed by those for the control interactions. We finally address the limitations of this work.

8.1   Privacy Indicators

Our first research question (see Sect. 3) focuses on analyzing which privacy indicators are perceived by employees as sufficient and useful to visualize data collection. The results described in Sect. 7 reveal that our participants prefer the splash-screen design. This is surprising as this design requires an additional and active action from the users to be able to access the main screen of the watch. In contrast, both other designs do not require a dedicated interaction from the users. One of the reasons to explain this result might be that our participants are already familiar with notifications from other applications or smart devices based on a similar interaction. However, the differences in terms of preferences between the splash-screen design and the other designs remain low. The icon design is the next preferred design following the splash-screen design. In particular, when asked whether the representations appear useful for the intended purpose, the results show that all participants gave a similar rating for all proposed indicators. Since the performance of the three proposed designs remains similar, we suggest that employers could let employees choose from different indicators according to their preferences.

Additional Feedback. In addition to the visual elements of such indicators, the results shown in Sect. 7 indicate that participants' opinions differ regarding supplementary feedback, either a sound or vibrations. Thus, the findings from [25] differ from ours as the existing results indicate that those participants prefer soundless privacy nudges, as they are not annoying, intrusive, or interruptive in a private context. Besides, prior research found that users have to deal with tons of notifications daily [29] and that such notifications are disruptive on smartphones [26, 29]. A reduction of those interruptions could be possible in a professional context by deferring notification [29], especially when it comes to privacy notifications, as users usually consider standard app notifications to be more important than privacy notifications [25]. Therefore, less noticeable notifications such as silent mode should be possible [25] because even then, privacy notifications would be read according to [25]. Employers should therefore consider this aspect when informing their employees about current data collection. Again, existing work extended by our gained insights suggest that employers should support individuals' preferences and offer different options regarding privacy indicators. We however recommend that they should also consider the working environments of their employees to take into account potential safety issues that might arise if employees would be distracted by a acoustic or haptic notification during their tasks.

Deactivation Option. Our results indicate that one-third of our participants would like to disable these indicators. However, most would not. This highlights that employees would like to know when data collection arises. However, we recommend employers to let the last decision from the employees' perspective so that they can disable it when they want to, as it was not intended to be distracting.

8.2   Control Interactions

Overall, our results presented in Sect. 7, indicate that our participants want to have the control to interrupt employers' data collection when working with a smart watch. This possibility is especially wished for in situations considered as private by our participants. Such situations include private conversations, breaks, or going to the toilet. From the obtained results, employers should hence provide such an option. The realization of this function can be done by different control interactions. Considering our second research question (see Sect. 3), our results indicate that our participants prefer to (1) press a button in the menu or (2) interact with a physical button on the smart watch to stop the data collection. As a result, they potentially chose an interaction that may be more familiar to them. Other interactions may not have been imaginable in their working environments. For example, raising an arm and making arm gestures seems inappropriate when sitting in an office in front of a colleague, while it could be imaginable in an industrial scenario. Hence, this confirms that employees would like to have more discrete interactions. Note that the participants' preferences only slightly differ for the different considered data types (i.e., health, location, and activity).

8.3   Limitations

Since the conducted study is based on an online questionnaire, the answers provided by our participants reflect their claimed opinions and not necessarily their actual behavior. Moreover, we have submitted them a scenario that they should imagine. As a result, what they imagined may differ between participants. This is beneficial as the participants may have adapted their thoughts to their own working context, which is not possible to do with our questionnaire. However, we cannot be sure that this is the case. As a result, the exploration conducted in this study should be confirmed by future real-world experiments in context.

Some of our participants did not own a smartwatch yet. As a result, they needed to imagine how it would be and their answers are likely influenced by previous experiences with other devices. However, we have decided to also ask them about their preferences, as we have assumed that they could be more reluctant about data collection than actual users. Such differences could however not be observed. We have finally focused in our study on German employees over 18. Our results may hence differ with younger working participants or other cultures. This cross-cultural aspect will be considered in future work when conducting our next study in context. Our results may finally not be applicable in other application areas due to the known dependency of privacy-related decisions on context.

9   Conclusions

We have investigated employees' preferences for different proposed privacy indicators to raise awareness about data collection and control interactions to stop this collection. To this end, we have conducted an online questionnaire-based study with 1,033 full-time employed participants to get first insights about their preferences. Our results indicate that our participants prefer the splash-screen indicator (Fig. 1(a)) to visualize data collection followed by the icon (Fig. 1(c)) and the circle indicator (Fig. 1(b)). The participants are, however, split about their preferences to have an additional haptic or auditory feedback. Being able to interrupt data collection is important for our participants, especially in more private situations. Their willingness to do so does not significantly vary with the collected data types. Similarly to the privacy indicators, our participants tend to prefer the interaction they are familiar with. The majority prefers doing it via a menu interaction with virtual buttons. While our results provide a first exploration of employees' preferences, more efforts including real-wold studies in context are needed to be able to provide usable transparency and control to employees in smart workplaces. Such provision could be beneficial for both employees and employers. The former would benefit from more transparency and control that could increase their trust in the latter, thus fostering their acceptance of smart workplaces.

Acknowledgments. We would like thank our participants and our group members for their feedback on the questionnaire.

References

1. Almuhimedi, H., et al.: Your location has been shared 5,398 times! a field study on mobile app privacy nudging. In: Proceedings of the 33rd Annual ACM Conference on Human Factors in Computing Systems (2015)
2. Apple Inc.: About the orange and green indicators in your iPhone status bar (2017). https://support.apple.com/en-us/HT211876. Accessed 09 Sept 2021
3. Bal, G., Rannenberg, K., Hong, J.: Styx: design and evaluation of a new privacy risk communication method for smartphones. In: Cuppens-Boulahia, N., Cuppens, F., Jajodia, S., Abou El Kalam, A., Sans, T. (eds.) SEC 2014. IAICT, vol. 428, pp. 113–126. Springer, Heidelberg (2014). https://doi.org/10.1007/978-3-642-55415-5_10
4. Barata, J., da Cunha, P.R.: Safety is the new black: the increasing role of wearables in occupational health and safety in construction. In: Abramowicz, W., Corchuelo, R. (eds.) BIS 2019. LNBIP, vol. 353, pp. 526–537. Springer, Cham (2019). https://doi.org/10.1007/978-3-030-20485-3_41
5. Bovard, P.P., et al.: Multi-modal interruptions on primary task performance. In: Schmorrow, D.D., Fidopiastis, C.M. (eds.) AC 2018. LNCS (LNAI), vol. 10916, pp. 3–14. Springer, Cham (2018). https://doi.org/10.1007/978-3-319-91467-1_1
6. Choi, B., Hwang, S., Lee, S.H.: What drives construction workers' acceptance of wearable technologies in the workplace?: indoor localization and wearable health devices for occupational safety and health. Autom. Constr. **84**(1), 31–41 (2017)
7. Christin, D., Engelmann, F., Hollick, M.: Usable privacy for mobile sensing applications. In: Naccache, D., Sauveron, D. (eds.) WISTP 2014. LNCS, vol. 8501, pp. 92–107. Springer, Heidelberg (2014). https://doi.org/10.1007/978-3-662-43826-8_7
8. Christin, D., Michalak, M., Hollick, M.: Raising user awareness about privacy threats in participatory sensing applications through graphical warnings. In: Proceedings of the 11th International Conference on Advances in Mobile Computing & Multimedia (MoMM) (2013)

9. Christin, D., Reinhardt, A., Hollick, M., Trumpold, K.: Exploring user preferences for privacy interfaces in mobile sensing applications. In: Proceedings of 11th ACM International Conference on Mobile and Ubiquitous Multimedia (MUM) (2012)
10. Chung, H., Iorga, M., Voas, J.M., Lee, S.: Alexa, Can I Trust You? Computer **50**(9), 100–104 (2017)
11. Cortina, J.M.: What is coefficient alpha? An examination of theory and applications. J. Appl. Psychol. **78**(1), 98 (1993)
12. Datta, P., Namin, A.S., Chatterjee, M.: A survey of privacy concerns in wearable devices. In: Proceedings of the 2018 IEEE International Conference on Big Data (Big Data) (2018)
13. S.B. (Destatis): 12111–0004: Bevölkerung (Zensus): Deutschland, Stichtag, Geschlecht, Altersgruppen (2021). https://www-genesis.destatis.de/genesis/online
14. Franke, T., Attig, C., Wessel, D.: A personal resource for technology interaction: development and validation of the affinity for technology interaction (ATI) scale. Int. J. Hum.-Comput. Interact. **35**(6), 456–467 (2019)
15. Gartner Inc.: Gartner Forecasts Global Spending on Wearable Devices to Total $81.5 Billion in 2021 (2021). https://www.gartner.com/en/newsroom/press-releases/2021-01-11-gartner-forecasts-global-spending-on-wearable-devices-to-total-81-5-billion-in-2021. Accessed 14 Feb 2021
16. Glance, D.G., Ooi, E., Berman, Y., Glance, C.F., Barrett, H.R.: Impact of a digital activity tracker-based workplace activity program on health and wellbeing. In: Proceedings of the 6th International Conference on Digital Health Conference (DH) (2016)
17. Hassib, M., Abdelmoteleb, H., Khamis, M.: Are my Apps Peeking? Comparing nudging mechanisms to raise awareness of access to mobile front-facing camera. In: Proceedings of the 19th International Conference on Mobile and Ubiquitous Multimedia (MUM) (2020)
18. Hernández Acosta, L., Reinhardt, D.: A survey on privacy issues and solutions for voice-controlled digital assistants. Pervasive Mob. Comput. (2021)
19. CCS Insight: Healthy Outlook for Wearables As Users Focus on Fitness and Well-Being (2021). https://www.ccsinsight.com/press/company-news/healthy-outlook-for-wearables-as-users-focus-on-fitness-and-well-being/. Accessed 21 Sept 2021
20. Lau, J., Zimmerman, B., Schaub, F.: Alexa, are you listening?: privacy perceptions, concerns and privacy-seeking behaviors with smart speakers. ACM Hum.-Comput. Interact. **2**(CSCW), 1–31 (2018)
21. Maltseva, K.: Wearables in the workplace: the brave new world of employee engagement. Bus. Horiz. **63**, 493–505 (2020)
22. Mayring, P.: Qualitative content analysis. Companion Qual. Res. **1**(2), 159–176 (2004)
23. Meyers, N.: Employee privacy in the electronic workplace: current issues for IT professionals. In: Proceedings of the 14th Australasian Conference on Information Systems (ACIS) (2003)
24. Mhaidli, A.H., Venkatesh, M.K., Zou, Y., Schaub, F.: Listen only when spoken to: interpersonal communication cues as smart speaker privacy controls. In: Proceedings of the 20st Privacy Enhancing Technologies Symposium (PoPETs) (2020)
25. Micallef, N., Just, M., Baillie, L., Alharby, M.: Stop annoying me! an empirical investigation of the usability of app privacy notifications. In: Proceedings of the 29th Australian Conference on Computer-Human Interaction (OZCHI) (2017)
26. Mirzamohammadi, S., Sani, A.A.: Viola: trustworthy sensor notifications for enhanced privacy on mobile systems. IEEE Trans. Mob. Comput. **17**(11), 2689–2702 (2018)

27. Motti, V.G., Caine, K.: Users' privacy concerns about wearables. In: Brenner, M., Christin, N., Johnson, B., Rohloff, K. (eds.) FC 2015. LNCS, vol. 8976, pp. 231–244. Springer, Heidelberg (2015). https://doi.org/10.1007/978-3-662-48051-9_17
28. Peissner, M., Hipp, C.: Potenziale der Mensch-Technik-Interaktion für die effiziente und vernetzte Produktion von morgen. Fraunhofer-Verlag Stuttgart (2013)
29. Pielot, M., Church, K., de Oliveira, R.: An in-situ study of mobile phone notifications. In: Proceedings of the 16th International Conference on Human-Computer Interaction with Mobile Devices & Services (MobileHCI) (2014)
30. Pizza, S., Brown, B., McMillan, D., Lampinen, A.: Smartwatch in Vivo. In: Proceedings of the 34th Conference on Human Factors in Computing Systems (CHI) (2016)
31. Prange, S., Shams, A., Piening, R., Abdelrahman, Y., Alt, F.: PriView-exploring visualisations to support users' privacy awareness. In: Proceedings of the ACM Conference on Human Factors in Computing Systems (CHI) (2021)
32. Raij, A., Ghosh, A., Kumar, S., Srivastava, M.: Privacy risks emerging from the adoption of innocuous wearable sensors in the mobile environment. In: Proceedings of the 29th ACM Conference on Human Factors in Computing Systems (SIGCHI) (2011)
33. Reidenberg, J.R., Russell, N.C., Herta, V., Sierra-Rocafort, W., Norton, T.B.: Trustworthy privacy indicators: grades, labels, certifications, and dashboards. Wash. UL Rev. **96**, 1409 (2018)
34. Schall, M.C.J., Sesek, R.F., Cavuoto, L.A.: Barriers to the adoption of wearable sensors in the workplace: a survey of occupational safety and health professionals. Hum. Factors **60**(3), 351–362 (2018)
35. Shaw, P.A., Mikusz, M.A., Davies, N.A.J., Clinch, S.E.: Using smartwatches for privacy awareness in pervasive environments. Poster at the 18th International Workshop on Mobile Computing Systems and Applications (HotMobile) (2017)
36. Stocker, A., Brandl, P., Michalczuk, R., Rosenberger, M.: Mensch-zentrierte IKT-Lösungen in einer Smart Factory. e & i Elektrotechnik und Informationstechnik **131**(7) (2014)
37. Tiefenau, C., Häring, M., Gerlitz, E., von Zezschwitz, E.: Making privacy graspable: can we nudge users to use privacy enhancing techniques? CoRR (2019)
38. Tomczak, D.L., Lanzo, L.A., Aguinis, H.: Evidence-based recommendations for employee performance monitoring. Bus. Horiz. **61**(2), 251–259 (2018)
39. Udoh, E.S., Alkharashi, A.: Privacy risk awareness and the behavior of smartwatch users: a case study of Indiana University students. In: Proceedings of the 2016 Future Technologies Conference (FTC) (2016)
40. Weber, D., Voit, A., Le, H.V., Henze, N.: Notification dashboard: enabling reflection on mobile notifications. In: Proceedings of the 18th International Conference on Human-Computer Interaction with Mobile Devices and Services Adjunct (MobileHCI). ACM (2016)
41. Williams, M., Nurse, J.R., Creese, S.: (smart) watch out! encouraging privacy-protective behavior through interactive games. Int. J. Hum.-Comput. Stud. **132**, 121–137 (2019)
42. Zebra Technologies: Quality Drives a Smarter Plant Floor: Manufacturing Vision Study (2017)

Network Security and IDS

DAEMON: Dynamic Auto-encoders for Contextualised Anomaly Detection Applied to Security MONitoring

Alexandre Dey[1,3]([✉]), Eric Totel[2], and Benjamin Costé[3]

[1] IRISA, Rennes, France
alexandre.dey@irisa.fr
[2] SAMOVAR, Telecom Sud-Paris, Institut Polytechnique de Paris,
Palaiseau, France
eric.totel@telecom-sudparis.eu
[3] Airbus Cyber Security, Saint-Jacques-de-la-Lande, France
benjamin.b.coste@airbus.com

Abstract. The slow adoption rate of machine learning-based methods for novel attack detection by Security Operation Centers (SOC) analysts can be partly explained by their lack of data science expertise and the insufficient explainability of the results provided by these approaches. In this paper, we present an anomaly-based detection method that fuses events coming from heterogeneous sources into sets describing the same phenomenons and relies on a deep auto-encoder model to highlight anomalies and their context. To implicate security analysts and benefit from their expertise, we focus on limiting the need of data science knowledge during the configuration phase. Results on a lab environment, monitored using off-the-shelf tools, show good detection performances on several attack scenarios (F1 score ≈0.9), and eases the investigation of anomalies by quickly finding similar anomalies through clustering.

Keywords: Anomaly detection · Heterogeneous log analysis · Human-automation cooperation · Intrusion detection · Machine learning

1 Introduction

Security monitoring of large information systems is often entrusted to Security Operation Centres (SOC). Within a SOC, the activity of the monitored system is recorded in the form of security events. These events can come from various sources, including endpoint monitoring (e.g., process auditing, anti-viruses, file integrity monitoring, etc.), network layer monitoring (e.g., network flow, network intrusion detection system or NIDS, etc.), as well as application logs (e.g., web server logs, authentication logs, etc.). Security Information and Event Management (SIEM) systems are often used to collect and analyse these events.

W. Meng et al. (Eds.): SEC 2022, IFIP AICT 648, pp. 53–69, 2022.
https://doi.org/10.1007/978-3-031-06975-8_4

SOC analysts perform intrusion detection of monitored systems thanks to automated real-time detection systems that recognize known attacks often relying on sets of correlation rules. Moreover, the threat hunting analysts uncover unknown attack methodologies by exploring events in the search of potentially suspicious activities. The number of false alarms raised by the real-time detection systems should be kept to a strict minimum in order to react as quickly as possible to known attacks and give threat hunters time to perform more thorough analysis. However, due to the huge amount of data that needs to be analyzed and pieced together to investigate anomalous (and potentially malicious) patterns, the threat hunting process greatly benefits from automation tools.

In recent years, multiple anomaly detection methods have been applied to security monitoring. One approach consists in prioritizing events so that the most anomalous ones are presented first to the analysts. However, multiple limitations still slows the adoption of these methods that are mainly based on machine learning. First, most machine learning based methods require extracting numerical metrics from the security events [6,19]. This step can be tedious, especially for security analysts that often lack the required data science knowledge. While novel deep learning advances can partially alleviate this limitation by being more flexible regarding the input data [7], the results they provide may still be hard to interpret. This lack of explainability can be lowered by presenting contextualized events to the analysts [16]. Recently, multiple approaches have been applied to endpoint monitoring with interesting results such as information flow tracking [2,10] and event causality [29]. However, in the context of a SOC, it is unlikely to have access to the level of detail necessary to find causal links between events, and we need to rely on approximations instead.

In this paper, we propose a method to detect traces of anomalous and potentially malicious activity by analysing security events coming from multiple sources (e.g., process auditing, network probes, web proxies, etc.). Our method does not require specific information from logs, and can therefore be configured for various monitoring strategies (i.e., ability to configure it for various sources of events, and various levels of visibility). The first step of this method is to regroup events into sets that describe the same action (e.g., a network connection seen as an opened socket by the endpoint monitoring tool, and as a network flow by network probes). To analyse these sets, we use an auto-encoder model, a specific type of deep neural network that is particularly suited for anomaly detection. We design the model so that it can analyse any attribute contained in security events, and link information from all the events within each set to detect anomalies based on the context (e.g., reading /etc./password at startup is normal for a web server, but reading the same file when answering a request might not be). The model can learn incrementally to adapt to the evolution of the normal behaviour of a system. To account for changes in the monitoring strategy, the structure of the model can be updated without requiring a complete retraining (which is computationally intensive). Due to the large volumes of events that needs to be analysed, whenever possible, we choose algorithms that can benefit from parallel and distributed computing. We give a particular attention to integrate easily into SOC analysts habits and capabilities. Specifically, the configuration step do not require advanced knowledge in data science, and instead focuses on available expertise from SOC analysts. The first contribution of our work is an event fusion method that can benefit from parallel and distributed computing. The second is a neural network auto-encoder with dynamic structure that can be trained continuously, can be adapted based on the monitoring strategy of the system and can highlight anomalous behaviours based on the sets of events that describe them.

In Sect. 2, we present security monitoring related work. The method used to regroup events into sets is explained in Sect. 3, and the neural network that is used to analyse these sets is described in Sect. 4. We assess our method and present results in Sect. 5.

2   Related Work

2.1   Anomaly Detection and Security Log Analysis

Security event analysis can be seen as a special case of log analysis. He et al. [11] recently provided a comprehensive review of anomaly detection in logs. Essentially, the anomalous activity identification process can be decomposed in three major steps, namely, parsing the logs (i.e., going from unstructured logs to structured events), extracting interesting features and finally using an anomaly detection algorithm. Most machine learning algorithms require these features to be numerical [15,30]. Authors have applied these methods to security log analysis [6,17,27] but the quality of the results are in these cases more dependant on the quality of the feature extraction and transformation (for non numerical features) processes, which can be hard to define for a security analyst with no background in data science. Recently, Dey et al. [5] proposed methods that ease these processes by using deep learning method to be more flexible regarding the input data. However this method lacks the context that is valuable for investigating the alerts. Bertero et al. [1] and Du et al. [7] drew inspiration from natural language processing to take into account the context of the events. Debnath et al. [4] proposed a generic framework to automate the parsing phase of log analysis. However, both approaches fail to analyze the attributes of the events which make them less effective for security logs. For example, they would not detect a connection to an automatically generated command and control domain because they would see a normal Domain Name System (DNS) request followed by an HyperText Transfer Protocol (HTTP) connection and would not see that the domain name looks weird. Pei et al. [21] proposed to represent security events as a graph and identifies communities as potential attacks. The features they use to weigh the edges between the events are learned in a supervised manner from examples of attacks, and is therefore not applicable in our unsupervised context. Liu et al. [14] chose to model users interactions by using a complex set of rules. While the approach is relevant for the author's use-case (insider threat scenario), it is difficult to adapt for a SOC which monitors multiple systems and where human resource is too scarce to fine-tune such a method specifically for each of these systems.

We want to model all the relevant information contained in security events as in [5], while taking the context of the log into consideration as in [1,4,7].

2.2   Alert Correlation

Alert correlation methods are already part of SOC tools. Valeur [26]
described extensively the correlation process, which can be decomposed into four major steps, the **normalization**, the **enrichment** and the **aggregation** of events, which consists in fusing similar alerts and correlating multiple steps of the attack to detect known patterns. The last step is a **global analysis** of these events.

In our context, we analyze both events and alerts (i.e., every behaviour, not only suspicious ones). This allows the detection of novel attacks, but also implies that the volume of information to process is greatly more consequent than what is processed by an alert correlation system. In this paper we do not focus on the normalization and enrichment of events as these are already part of SOC processes, and extensive public resources are already available for these (e.g., the Elastic Common Schema [8] and MITRE ATT&CK® data sources [18]). Instead we focus on the fusion part of the aggregation process to propose a solution that can process the high volume of events in parallel. Solutions for automatically identifying which events should be aggregated has already been studied in previous work [24,28]. In our case, we adapt a model that is already common for alert fusion, by aggregating events that are close in time and using simple logic rules to separate unrelated events within these time windows.

3   Fusion of Events in Sets of Meta-events

3.1   Events for Security Monitoring

The Notion of Data Source. From one IT system to another, the sensors that are deployed are likely to be different. In fact, each system has its own set of application (and the associated logs), its specific antivirus, NIDS, firewalls, etc. This can prove to be challenging when adapting a monitoring tool to a new IT system. However from the functionality point of view, there is often a significant overlap between two different systems. For example, two different Intrusion Detection Systems (IDS) still serve the same purpose, major Operating Systems (OS) rely on a similar definition of a process, etc. The normalization process is supported by distribution of events into data sources. Data sources are categories of events often associated with a non-exhaustive list of valuable pieces of information called attributes that can be extracted from these events. Famous framework MITRE ATT&CK® proposes a few examples of data sources [18]. In our case, each data source is associated with a list of normalized attributes that are relevant for anomaly detection.

Definition of an Event. In an information system, activity is recorded by sensors inside logs. Each action is recorded differently by the various sensors (e.g., IDS will focus on information relevant for security, while application logs aim at facilitating diagnosis) in the form of events, with the aim of providing an audit trail that can be used by human analysts to better understand the activity of the system. An event can be decomposed into attributes (e.g., an antivirus log will contain information about the machine, the suspected file, the rule that triggered the event, etc.), among which only a subset may have value for security monitoring. In essence, events can be seen as sets of key-value pairs that can be understood by humans. Normalization of events attributes is performed thanks to data sources attributes defined above.

Definition of a Meta-event. Among the events collected when monitoring an information system, finding duplicated events is highly probable. This can be attributed mostly to four facts. **(1)** The same action being performed several times in a short period of time (e.g., a process spawning a pool of child processes). Due to the asynchronous nature of modern computing, it is unlikely to have the exact time-stamp of each events. **(2)** The sensor that registers the events or the chosen attributes of these events might not provide enough information to distinguish two similar but different actions (e.g., multiple threads connecting to the same service in parallel will generate socket events that can be hard to distinguish if the source port of the connection is not considered). **(3)** Redundant sensors or multiple implementations of these sensors (e.g., two different IDSes) for high availability. **(4)** For performance reason, the log shipping method of a lot of modern monitoring solutions often follow the "at least once" delivery policy by default rather than the "exactly once" policy.

For this reason, we chose to consider a meta-event as a group of events pertaining to the same data source during a predefined period of time and with equal attributes[1]. As explained in Introduction, the proposed system aims to leverage knowledge of SOC analysts. The definition of a meta-event therefore depends on three choices, namely, the data sources, the size of the time window inside which events can be grouped together, and the list of attributes that needs to be equal for events to be grouped. As long as these choices remains in the hands of analysts, the performance of our system depends on assignments made. For the sake of this work, we define time window, data sources and event attributes based on expert knowledge provided by SOC analysts.

3.2   Linking Meta-events

When monitoring an information system, the various sensors will record events differently (e.g., an endpoint audit mechanism may attribute network socket opening to processes, while network probes will focus on analyzing the network protocol). To extract as much information as possible from available logs, we regroup all the events related to the same action and jointly analyze them. This is known as the alert fusion step of the correlation process [26], and we extend it to take both audit events and IDS alerts as inputs (instead of only alerts).

To leverage the available knowledge of current SOC analysts, we chose an approach that is similar to what is actually done for alert fusion: slicing the time

---

[1] Timestamp excepted.

into small windows, and then using logic in the form of rules to separate events describing different actions. Figure 1 gives an overview of the complete process.

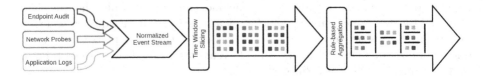

Fig. 1. Overview of the fusion steps

Group by Time Proximity. While the asynchronous nature of modern computing may render the strict ordering of the events via their time-stamps highly improbable, the various sensors deployed inside the monitored system are likely to react to the same action within a short period of time (at least if the whole system is synchronized using the same time server, or if the log shipping system is in charge of setting the time-stamps). Therefore, the first step we perform is to regroup events appearing inside the same time window. The size of the window is configurable as, depending on the tools available, the time between the first event and the last event matching the same action can vary from milliseconds to a few minutes (e.g., for NIDS that trigger alerts at the end of the connections). Each slice of time can be handled completely in parallel.

Correlation of Meta-events. Linking security events based on causal dependencies can ease the investigation process [29]. Indeed, each action inside an IS, such as attacks, is observed from various sensors. Each one records different pieces of information about the root action. We hence aim to uncover the root action through event correlation (cf. Sect. 2.2) of given groups of events. This correlation is based on two assumptions: **(1)** Regardless of the data source, two events coming from the same origin (e.g., same process, same host, same user, etc.) and within a short period of time are more likely to share a common cause. Indeed two correlated events can be either causally linked, caused by the same cause or a coincidence. The probability of a coincidence is lower when analyzing finer grained events (e.g., endpoint monitoring, syscall auditing, etc.). **(2)** Some event attributes are common to multiple data sources [13,21], which enables us to regroup events from heterogeneous sensors. For instance, an endpoint auditing mechanism can log sockets opened by processes which can be linked with NIDS logs using the source IP address, and other endpoint logs using the process identifier. For some tools, some attributes are specifically designed to link events together (e.g., the zeek network probe [20] events have attributes that are meant to link each analyzers results to the original network flow). Meta-events with attributes indicating the same origin are therefore pieced together. The list of such attributes is called a correlation rule. This regrouping operation is designed to be both associative and commutative (i.e., the processing order do not impact the result) and can therefore be considered as a reduction operator, which can be handled in parallel.

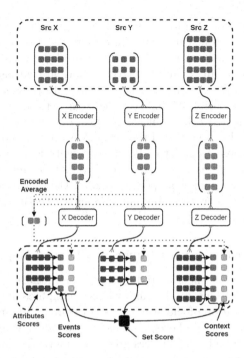

Fig. 2. Overview of the anomaly scoring for a set of meta-events

4 Anomaly Score Computation Using Dynamic Auto-encoders

Grouping together events in sets of meta-events offer a better understanding of observed phenomenon. We go further by prioritizing sets of meta-events with neural network-based anomaly detection system by computing an anomaly score for each set and the meta-events that compose it. Figure 2 provides a functional overview of the model, which is described in the following section.

4.1 Basics on Neural Networks and Auto-encoders

A neural network is a composition of functions with trainable parameters. These functions are called the neurons of the network. A neural network is trained to minimize an objective function, which often contains at least a measure of the divergence between the expected output and the one effectively predicted by the network. To solve this minimisation problem, the most used algorithms derives from the gradient back-propagation method [23], which requires the gradient of the objective function for each parameter of the network. Therefore, in this paper, we generalize the neural network definition to a composition of differentiable functions, where parameters are trained using any variant of the gradient back-propagation method. Historically, neural networks auto-encoders have been used to map vectors from high-dimensional space (e.g., the pixels of an image, complex set of extracted features, etc.) into more easily comprehensible values (e.g., a class, a small vector, etc.). With the rise of deep learning, researchers moved from using only fully connected layers of formal neurons to incorporating layers specifically adapted to the structure of the data provided as input to the model (e.g., 2-D convolution for images, recurrent networks for text, etc.). For tasks that require the network to output in a high dimensional space (e.g., image or text generation), the structure of the network is often organised in two parts, an encoder which maps inputs into a latent representation, and a decoder which takes the latent representation as input and outputs value into the expected vector space. The auto-encoder is a special Encoder-Decoder model for which the output space is the same as the input space. Such a structure can be adapted to detect anomalies in security events [5].

4.2 Dynamic Structure with Coherent Encoded Representation

For each data source, an encoder and a decoder is initialized at the beginning of the training phase. One of the limitations highlighted in [5] was that the compressed representation of the events was not comparable from one source to another. Besides, each source of events needs its own model, which can be difficult to manage once the number of sources grows too high. We propose to alleviate these limitations using a dynamic network structure combined with a penalty added to the objective function. It encourages the encoder to encode meta-events appearing frequently in the same sets into close vectors in the encoded space.

For each set of meta-events, we select the encoder-decoder pairs corresponding to each data source in the set and build an auto-encoder out of them. In addition to the reconstruction error (i.e., the difference between the original input and the output of the network), we compute the distance between the encoded representation of each meta-event of the set and the average value of these encoded representations for the whole set. We derive the **context score** from this distance, and minimizing it is added as an objective for the encoder, which encourages it to compute an encoded representation that is close for meta-events that frequently happen in the same context (e.g., an HTTP request is often accompanied by a DNS query).

4.3 Computing Anomaly Score

Attribute Score. The reproduction error of the auto-encoder (difference between the input and the output) will be higher for anomalous data. To guide the investigation of anomalies, it is interesting to determine which attributes are likely to be the cause of the anomaly. However, the reproduction error from one attribute to another cannot be trivially compared. In [5] a Gaussian Mixture Model (GMM) was used as an approximation of the distribution of the loss. The Cumulative Distribution Function (CDF) of the Gaussian with the highest mean value was then used to compute an anomaly score between 0 and 1 for every attribute. However, in cases where the variance of the loss is close to 0, this method provides unsatisfactory results (i.e., high score for all events or low score even for anomalies). Besides, the GMM parameters cannot be approximated accurately within the network (i.e., using gradient descent), which forces a calibration phase after training the auto-encoder, and to maintain an additional model. In our case, we propose to use a logistic distribution instead of the Gaussian mixture. The objective is to have a score that is close to 0 for most of the normal events, while still being close to 1 when the attribute is anomalous. To do so, we train the parameters of the distribution accordingly, directly within the network, by adding terms to the loss function (Fig. 3). The CDF equation for the logistic regression is given in Eq. 2, with λ that controls the steepness of the curve and μ the symmetry point $f(\mu) = 0.5$. One possibility would be to set μ (the point at which the logistic CDF is 0.5) to be the highest value on the (supposedly normal) data. To do so, we constraint the parameters of the logistic distribution (Eq. 4). Specifically, a constraint is added to the μ parameter of the attribute scoring function (Eq. 3). For this constraint, the lower α is, the closer to the maximal input value μ will be, and $\overline{X}$ is the average value of the reproduction error for a batch of data. In addition to the constraint on μ, another one is added to avoid λ being negative (which would cause the score to be higher for normal values than anomalous ones).

$$f_{\lambda,\mu}(x) = \frac{1}{1 + e^{-\lambda(x-\mu)}} \quad (2)$$

$$g(x) = \begin{cases} x & \text{if } x \geq 0 \\ 0 & \text{otherwise} \end{cases} \quad (1)$$

$$E_\mu(X) = \alpha * g\left(\mu - \overline{X}\right) + g\left(\overline{X} - \mu\right) \quad (3)$$

$$E(X) = E_\mu(X) + \overline{f_{\lambda,\mu}(X)} + g(-\lambda) \quad (4)$$

Fig. 3. Constraints for the scoring function

Meta-event Score. The score of a meta-event is the weighted mean of the score of all its attributes. The weight w_i of each attribute x_i is computed by a small neural network that takes as input the average value of the encoded representation for a set of meta-event. Minimizing the standard deviation of the weight vector is added as an objective to discourage the weighting neural network to amplify or attenuate excessively some attributes.

Set Score. The score of a set is the weighted mean of the scores of all the meta-events that constitutes it. The weight q_i for a meta-event is $q_i = \frac{s_i}{\sum_j s_j}$ with s_i the score of the ith meta-event in the set.

4.4 Handling Concept Drift

Normal behavior of an IT system is bound to evolve with time, as new behaviours appear and old one cease to manifest. Indeed, new users are added, old ones are removed, software are updated, etc. In data science, this phenomenon is called concept drift and is handled by updating the model. In the context of security monitoring this phenomenon can manifest in different ways. First, correlations between variables evolves (e.g., a known user started using a known command) and/or the correlation rules used for regrouping events into sets of meta-events (data sources do not change, only the composition of the sets) need to be changed. In this case, only the model weights needs to be updated, and as neural networks learn incrementally by nature, it is only a matter of performing a few training steps on data containing the new behaviors. The second manifestation of concept drift is a modification of the input space which requires a modification of the pre-processing functions parameters (e.g., a new user, a new software deployed, etc.). Finally, in some cases the data sources schema must be updated (e.g., new type of sensor deployed, modification of the analyzed attributes, etc.). By combining the neural networks capacity to learn incrementally and the design in functional blocks (for each attribute of each datasource), we can handle concept drift without requiring a costly complete retraining of the model. Kirkpatrick et al. [12] proposed the Elastic Weight Consolidation (EWC) algorithm in order to attenuate catastrophic forgetting of neural networks, i.e., the network completely forgets older normal behaviors too quickly. EWC consists in adding penalties and constraints on the network's weight during training to avoid modifying weights that are essential to solve the previously learned tasks. Authors have also proposed the use of small sample of previous data either as a small knowledge base constituted during training and used during inference (episodic memory) [3,25], or simply by selecting a sample of past experiences when training on new data (experience replay) [22]. We chose this second approach as it is simpler (computationally speaking) than episodic memory, and it also applicable to the adjusting of the transformation function parameters (EWC is only useful for network weights).

5 Approach Assessment

5.1 The Evaluation Dataset

Assessing the performance of an anomaly-based security log analysis method requires the collection of enough logs to model the normal behaviour of the experimental monitored system. For confidentiality reasons, it is not possible to use production data, so the data needs to be collected from a lab environment and user interaction with this environment must be simulated. As accounting for every possible cases of a real IT system is impossible, this simulation is bound to be biased. However, considering that each user action is done by human operators as it would be done on a production environment, the collected logs will be similar to the ones collected on a production system.

In order to increase signification of collected events (e.g., admin tasks should not be performed from user workstations), the monitored system's architecture is intended to be reasonably secure (well separated infrastructure, administrator and user zones, controlled outgoing and incoming traffic, updated software and antivirus, etc.). Six simulated users perform various office tasks (documents writing, mail, web browsing, etc.) across Linux and Windows workstations while an administrator maintains the infrastructure of the system and sometimes connects to the users endpoints to install software or update configurations.

The first two days of the dataset serves as a baseline of "normality" (i.e., without any attack traces) that is required for anomaly detection system training. The presence of attack traces inside the training data would prevent detection of said attack, but attacks employing different techniques would still be detected. The first attack scenario (day 3) emulates an attacker with custom tooling (to avoid detection by antivirus), but is noisy (multiple IDS alerts, a few antivirus alerts, more trial and errors, etc.). The day after (day 4), a new software is deployed on a Centos machine. The second scenario (day 5) reemploys the same tooling as the first scenario, but is more subtle (generates less IDS alerts, no antivirus alerts, actions are more precise, etc.). During the attack, the administrator diagnoses a problem on windows machines (and therefore generate unusual activity). After this (day 6), a new sensor (Sysmon) is enabled on the user endpoints, and is expected to generate a large amount of false positives. The last scenario (day 7) is much more discreet than the previous ones and relies on new tools. The attacker limits its activity to a minimum to avoid generating too much events. This scenario aims at emulating a more advanced threat actor.

The dataset contains 4.2 million events, over a period of 7 working day. These events come from typical monitoring tools commonly found inside IT systems (i.e., Sysmon, Auditd, Windows Audit Logs, Windows Defender, Zeek IDS, Suricata IDS and Squid HTTP Proxy). We configure these tools to record a higher volume of information than what is usually deployed on IT systems (e.g., all available IDS rules, process monitoring with windows audit, socket monitoring with Sysmon and auditd, etc.). This enables us to test various levels of verbosity for assessing our method without regenerating a datasets.

5.2 Defining the Assessment Strategy

Commonly used quantitative metrics (e.g., False/True Positives Rates, F1 score, etc.) can provide valuable information regarding the performance of a detection method, but they only give a partial view of the usefulness of the detection system. For instance, missing 50 out of 100 connection attempts to a service in a brute force attack would not prevent analysts from finding out the source and the target of the attack, while increasing the False Negative Rate (FNR). However, missing a single event that characterizes an attack would not have a major impact on the FNR, while greatly reducing the quality of the detection.

We alleviate this limitation with an alternative definition of a False Negative that is more inline with analysts practices. In fact, we know every actions that are performed by the attacker, but annotating individually the thousands of events that can be attributed to these actions would be time consuming and error prone. Instead, we start from a high threshold above which we consider a set of meta-events as an anomaly, and we lower it until we can find anomalies characterising every step of the attack (i.e., what is the machine impacted, the technique employed, etc.). Any set below this threshold that is a consequence of malicious activity will not be considered as a False Negative, as it will not add useful information to characterise the attack. Empirically, we find that a threshold of 0.4 is a good choice for the three scenario we have. However, this threshold is not optimal as multiple legitimate actions can have a score higher than it. Therefore, we gradually increase this threshold and we compute the precision (proportion of True Positive in all the anomalies), recall (proportion of the attack accurately detected) and F1 score (harmonic mean of precision and recall) to quantify the performance. For all these metrics, a value close to 0 implies a useless anomaly detection while a score of 1 is synonym of a good one. We consider the optimal threshold to be the one that maximizes the F1 score.

We mitigate the impact of a lucky (or unlucky) initialisation of the model by training 10 models with different initialisation of the parameters on the first two days of normal data. This data is randomly splitted for each model, with 90% used for training the model and 10% to control that the model is not over-fitting the training data (often called validation set). We test the performance of each of these models on the first scenario. After that, we keep only one model and use it as the base for incremental learning and evaluating the performance on the other two scenarios.

5.3   Results

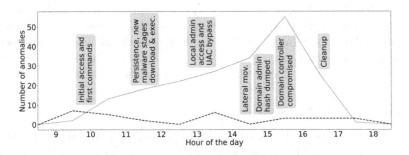

Fig. 4. Aggregated number of meta-event sets with a score above 0.5 per hour for scenario 1.

For each of the 10 randomly initialized models, we record the best F1 score on the first attack scenario. The average value of this score is 0.88 with the lowest value at 0.85 and highest at 0.91. The Fig. 4 has been generated using the best model (F1: 0.91, recall: 0.93 and precision: 0.88). The dashed black line shows the number of anomalies per hour detected during a single day without attack. On the opposite, red line shows number of anomalies per hour produced when an attack occurred. As expected, we can see that the number of anomalies increases as the attack progresses. The maximum number of anomalies is reached when most of the machines are compromised, and especially the domain controller. The cleanup phase is accompanied by a decreasing number of anomalies as machines progressively stop exhibiting attack behaviours. This scenario shows that our system can be used as intrusion detection system as it detects attack-related events and because it does not report more than fifty anomalies per hour from an initial number of events of approximately 20000 per hour.

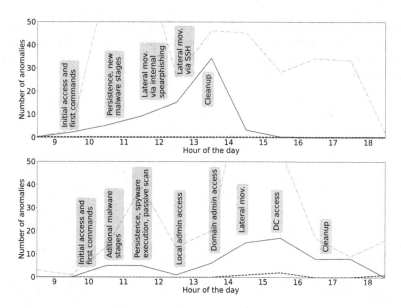

Fig. 5. Aggregated number of meta-event sets with a score above 0.5 per hour, for scenario 2 (top) and 3 (bottom)

For the second scenario, we use the false positives from the first scenario and the fourth day of the collected dataset as the input to incrementally update the anomaly detection model. We reach a F1 score of 0.97 with a recall of 0.99 and a precision of 0.95. Similarly, for the third scenario, we reach an F1 score of 0.92 with a precision of 0.86 and a recall of 0.98. Without retraining (i.e., using the same model used for scenario 1), the best F1 score drops below 0.3 for both scenarios. To highlight the effectiveness of the retraining, in Fig. 5, we add the plot (orange dot-dashed line) of the same normal day than the black dashed plot, but this time analysed by the outdated model.

Similarly to the first scenario, there is an increasing number of anomalies reported during the attack process of the scenario 2. We see lower numbers of anomalies, which is expected considering the attack a bit less noisy. As the third scenario is designed to be as discreet as possible, we see far less anomalies. Nevertheless, meta-events raised by our system are sufficient for an analyst in order to recognize the attack pattern. The orange line shows the necessity of the incremental learning process for our anomaly based detection system.

The latent representation provided by the model enables the use of standard clustering algorithms to cluster meta-event groups. Most of the time, new behaviours reappear regularly. Thus, the manifestation of these new behaviours in the log should form clusters of similar activity. In our case, we use the DBSCAN algorithm [9] to perform this clustering and we find that the discovered cluster permits to reduce the annotation time. Figure 6 shows two anomalous meta-event groups that are found to be similar. The first one corresponds to the events generated when the attacker enumerated local users and groups and the second to the enumeration of domain users and groups. Preliminary results are encouraging, but a more in depth evaluation of the clustering performance is still required.

win_process_audit	win_process_sysmor						
timestamp	score	agent.name	process.parent.command_line	process.parent.executable	process.executable	process.command_line
2021-06-23 08:22:00.956000000	0.505922	WIN-2	cmd.exe	C:\WINDOWS\SYSWOW64 \CMD.EXE	C:\WINDOWS \SYSWOW64 \WHOAMI.EXE	whoami /all
2021-06-23 08:22:09.728999936	0.506463	WIN-2	cmd.exe	C:\WINDOWS\SYSWOW64 \CMD.EXE	C:\WINDOWS \SYSWOW64 \NET.EXE	net localgroup
2021-06-23 08:22:09.763000064	0.520170	WIN-2	net localgroup	C:\WINDOWS\SYSWOW64 \NET.EXE	C:\WINDOWS \SYSWOW64 \NET1.EXE	C:\Windows \system32\net1 localgroup

win_process_audit	win_process_sysmor						
timestamp	score	agent.name	process.parent.command_line	process.parent.executable	process.executable	process.command_line
2021-06-23 11:39:09.503000064	0.506828	WIN-2	cmd.exe	C:\WINDOWS\SYSWOW64 \CMD.EXE	C:\WINDOWS \SYSWOW64 \NET.EXE	net user /domain
2021-06-23 11:39:09.548999936	0.520004	WIN-2	net user /domain	C:\WINDOWS\SYSWOW64 \NET.EXE	C:\WINDOWS \SYSWOW64 \NET1.EXE	C:\Windows \system32\net1 user /domain
2021-06-23 11:39:16.097999872	0.507229	WIN-2	cmd.exe	C:\WINDOWS\SYSWOW64 \CMD.EXE	C:\WINDOWS \SYSWOW64 \NET.EXE	net group /domain
2021-06-23 11:39:16.116000000	0.524452	WIN-2	net group /domain	C:\WINDOWS\SYSWOW64 \NET.EXE	C:\WINDOWS \SYSWOW64 \NET1.EXE	C:\Windows \system32\net1 group /domain

Fig. 6. These two anomalous meta-event groups belong to the same cluster in the latent space.

5.4 Discussion

Even though these results are promising, some limitations can be highlighted. In fact, it still relies on parameters that needs to be defined by an expert. More precisely, an inadequate choice of attributes for the datasources, i.e., missing important attributes or adding useless ones, can lead to unsatisfactory results. For instance, with the current scoring system, a datasource with more than 10 attributes will rarely cause alerts because most of the attributes would seem normal and dilute the score of anomalous attributes. Besides, the chosen time-window can have an impact on the quality of the fusion step. Indeed, during testing, we realised that a time-window below 120 s often fail can lead to a significant amount of missed fusion opportunity between datasources that have different ways of setting the timestamp (e.g., a network probe often emits an event at the end of a connection, while an endpoint monitoring would do so at its beginning). Symmetrically, we found that a time-window above 300 s would lead spurious correlations between meta-events.

It was demonstrated in previous section that the proposed system is able to monitor the attackers in detail and offer a reduced set of anomalies that needs to be investigated by the analyst. While our system has solely been tested in a simulated environment, multiple real-life applications have been envisioned.

First, it can be used to analyze events coming from *detection labs*, i.e., controlled systems specifically designed to analyze attackers, where user activity is simulated to fool attackers. Second, large SOCs which can receive 10M to 20M of events per hour (compared to ≈20000 for our dataset). Using the proposed method would not alleviate alert fatigue. However, it can be integrated in current SOC practices which consist in analyzing fine-grained events (e.g., Sysmon, netflow, etc.) only for reduced perimeters. Specifically, for known suspicious behaviours, analysts often design scripts meant to automatically retrieve the context surrounding the detected behaviour. Incorporating our method in these scripts could allow faster handling of these investigations, which can reduce alert fatigue, and/or permit the use of wider spectrum detection rules (which can catch more advanced attacks). It is also possible to restrict our method to specific assets of the monitored environments (e.g., domain controllers, servers, etc.).

6 Conclusion

Modern SOCs handle alerts based on attack patterns or signatures in order to perform intrusion detection. However, to detect unknown threats, gaining a deeper visibility of the system is required. This is done by analysing both events and alerts (and not only alerts), in search for anomalies. Consequently, a significant growth in the volume of information that needs to be analysed and the number of false positives occurs. While machine learning based approaches can help analysts detect novel attacks, their adoptions into SOC have been slow. Part of the explanation for this is the lack of explainability and the need for data science expertise (that is scarce in SOC teams).

We therefore proposed a new anomaly detection approach that takes advantage from available security analysts expertise to highlight and contextualise anomalies in security logs. This approach is based on the fusion of fine-grained events into sets of meta-events, and on an autoencoder neural network with dynamic structure to compute an anomaly score for each of these sets. Our system is designed to adapt to new behaviours (concept drift) by learning incrementally while not forgetting old behaviours too quickly. For validation purpose, we performed several scenario-based evaluations on a lab environment monitored using tools often deployed on production systems. The results show that our system reports a low number of anomalies per hour and that this number is correlated with the progress of the attack scenarios. For all of our evaluation scenario, the system reports enough information to completely reconstruct the attack.

Future work includes publishing the dataset used for experimentation alongside additional results, as well as correcting some identified limitations of the method. Specifically, while the involvement of security experts in the configuration of the system allows for results that are more understandable to them, it also exposes the system to human error which could degrade its performance. Our focus will be on diminishing the impact of these errors and reinforcing the transparency of the system for human operators. We also plan to adapt the method to use-cases that are suitable for testing in a SOC (e.g., monitoring specific servers, reducing noise of wide-spectrum detection rules, etc.).

References

1. Bertero, C., Roy, M., Sauvanaud, C., Trédan, G.: Experience report: log mining using natural language processing and application to anomaly detection. In: 2017 IEEE 28th International Symposium on Software Reliability Engineering (ISSRE), pp. 351–360. IEEE (2017)
2. Brogi, G., Tong, V.V.T.: TerminAPTor: highlighting advanced persistent threats through information flow tracking. In: 2016 8th IFIP International Conference on New Technologies, Mobility and Security (NTMS), pp. 1–5. IEEE (2016)
3. de Masson d'Autume, C., Ruder, S., Kong, L., Yogatama, D.: Episodic memory in lifelong language learning. CoRR abs/1906.01076 (2019)
4. Debnath, B., et al.: LogLens: a real-time log analysis system. In: 2018 IEEE 38th International Conference on Distributed Computing Systems (ICDCS), pp. 1052–1062. IEEE (2018)
5. Dey, A., Totel, E., Navers, S.: Heterogeneous security events prioritization using auto-encoders. In: Garcia-Alfaro, J., Leneutre, J., Cuppens, N., Yaich, R. (eds.) CRiSIS 2020. LNCS, vol. 12528, pp. 164–180. Springer, Cham (2021). https://doi.org/10.1007/978-3-030-68887-5_10
6. Ding, Z., Fei, M.: An anomaly detection approach based on isolation forest algorithm for streaming data using sliding window. IFAC Proceedings Volumes **46**, 12–17 (2013)
7. Du, M., Li, F., Zheng, G., Srikumar, V.: DeepLog: anomaly detection and diagnosis from system logs through deep learning. In: Proceedings of the 2017 ACM SIGSAC Conference on Computer and Communications Security, pp. 1285–1298. ACM (2017)
8. Elastic. Elastic common schema. https://github.com/elastic/ecs. Accessed 25 Mar 2021
9. Ester, M., Kriegel, H.-P., Sander, J., Xu, X., et al.: A density-based algorithm for discovering clusters in large spatial databases with noise. In: KDD, vol. 96, pp. 226–231 (1996)
10. Hassan, W.U., Bates, A., Marino, D.: Tactical provenance analysis for endpoint detection and response systems. In: 2020 IEEE Symposium on Security and Privacy (SP), pp. 1172–1189. IEEE (2020)
11. He, S., Zhu, J., He, P., Lyu, M.R.: Experience report: system log analysis for anomaly detection. In: 2016 IEEE 27th International Symposium on Software Reliability Engineering (ISSRE), pp. 207–218. IEEE (2016)
12. Kirkpatrick, J., et al.: Overcoming catastrophic forgetting in neural networks. Proc. Natl. Acad. Sci. **114**, 3521–3526 (2017)
13. Leichtnam, L., Totel, E., Prigent, N., Mé, L.: Forensic analysis of network attacks: restructuring security events as graphs and identifying strongly connected subgraphs. In: 2020 IEEE European Symposium on Security and Privacy Workshops (EuroS&PW), pp. 565–573. IEEE (2020)
14. Liu, F., Wen, Y., Zhang, D., Jiang, X., Xing, X., Meng, D.: Log2vec: a heterogeneous graph embedding based approach for detecting cyber threats within enterprise. In: Proceedings of the 2019 ACM SIGSAC Conference on Computer and Communications Security, pp. 1777–1794 (2019)

15. Liu, F.T., Ting, K.M., Zhou, Z.-H.: Isolation forest. In: 2008 Eighth IEEE International Conference on Data Mining, pp. 413–422. IEEE (2008)
16. Milajerdi, S.M., Gjomemo, R., Eshete, B., Sekar, R., Venkatakrishnan, V.: HOLMES: real-time apt detection through correlation of suspicious information flows. In: 2019 IEEE Symposium on Security and Privacy (SP), pp. 1137–1152. IEEE (2019)
17. Mirsky, Y., Doitshman, T., Elovici, Y., Shabtai, A.: Kitsune: an ensemble of autoencoders for online network intrusion detection. arXiv preprint arXiv:1802.09089 (2018)
18. MITRE. Att&ck data sources. https://github.com/mitre-attack/attack-datasources. Accessed 16 Mar 2021
19. Pascoal, C., De Oliveira, M.R., Valadas, R., Filzmoser, P., Salvador, P., Pacheco, A.: Robust feature selection and robust PCA for internet traffic anomaly detection. In: 2012 Proceedings IEEE INFOCOM, pp. 1755–1763. IEEE (2012)
20. Paxson, V.: Bro: a system for detecting network intruders in real-time. Comput. Netw. **31**, 2435–2463 (1999)
21. Pei, K., et al.: HERCULE: attack story reconstruction via community discovery on correlated log graph. In: Proceedings of the Annual Computer Security Applications Conference (ACSAC). ACM (2016)
22. Rolnick, D., Ahuja, A., Schwarz, J., Lillicrap, T.P., Wayne, G.: Experience replay for continual learning. CoRR abs/1811.11682 (2018)
23. Rumelhart, D.E., Hinton, G.E., Williams, R.J.: Learning internal representations by error propagation. Technical report, California Univ San Diego La Jolla Inst for Cognitive Science (1985)
24. Sadoddin, R., Ghorbani, A.A.: An incremental frequent structure mining framework for real-time alert correlation. Comput. Secur. **28**, 153–173 (2009)
25. Sprechmann, P., et al.: Memory-based parameter adaptation (2018)
26. Valeur, F.: Real-time intrusion detection alert correlation. Citeseer (2006)
27. Veeramachaneni, K., Arnaldo, I., Korrapati, V., Bassias, C., Li, K.: Ai2: training a big data machine to defend. In: 2016 IEEE 2nd International Conference on Big Data Security on Cloud (BigDataSecurity), IEEE International Conference on High Performance and Smart Computing (HPSC), and IEEE International Conference on Intelligent Data and Security (IDS), pp. 49–54. IEEE (2016)
28. Viinikka, J., Debar, H., Mé, L., Lehikoinen, A., Tarvainen, M.: Processing intrusion detection alert aggregates with time series modeling. Inf. Fusion **10**, 312–324 (2009)
29. Xosanavongsa, C., Totel, E., Bettan, O.: Discovering correlations: a formal definition of causal dependency among heterogeneous events. In: 2019 IEEE European Symposium on Security and Privacy (EuroS P), pp. 340–355 (2019)
30. Zhou, C., Paffenroth, R.C.: Anomaly detection with robust deep autoencoders. In: Proceedings of the 23rd ACM SIGKDD International Conference on Knowledge Discovery and Data Mining, pp. 665–674. ACM (2017)

FOCUS: Frequency Based Detection of Covert Ultrasonic Signals

Wouter Hellemans[1,2(✉)], Md Masoom Rabbani[3(✉)], Jo Vliegen[3], and Nele Mentens[3,4]

[1] KU Leuven, Leuven, Belgium
wouter.hellemans@student.uhasselt.be
[2] University of Hasselt, Hasselt, Belgium
[3] ES&S, imec-COSIC, ESAT, KU Leuven, Leuven, Belgium
{mdmasoom.rabbani,jo.vliegen,nele.mentens}@kuleuven.be
[4] LIACS, Leiden University, Leiden, The Netherlands
n.mentens@liacs.leidenuniv.nl

Abstract. Today's evolving and inventive attacks allow an adversary to embed tracking identifiers or malicious triggers in ultrasonic sound and covertly transmit them between devices without the users' knowledge. An adversary can exploit an electronic device by manipulating the microphone, gyroscope or speaker using ultrasonic sound. Almost all types of electronic devices are vulnerable to this type of attack. Indeed, some preventive measures are in place to counter ultrasonic invasion. However, they are primitive and often are not capable of detecting the attacks.

To this end, we propose FOCUS: Frequency based detection of Covert Ultrasonic Signals. In particular, FOCUS displays a low-end, low-cost ultrasonic detection mechanism that can be employed anywhere. We validate FOCUS through two proof-of-concept (PoC) implementations utilizing Raspberry Pi and Arduino based hardware modules, respectively. The results demonstrate that FOCUS can detect ultrasonic sound and alert users of possible ultrasonic invasion.

Keywords: Embedded system · Ultrasonic sound invasion · Network security & privacy

1 Introduction

Collecting information about users is becoming an ever more important part of the business strategy of various companies. The increasingly stringent regulations (e.g., the European GDPR[1]), have caused companies to use new and controversial strategies to collect this information about the user. One of these emerging

---

[1] https://ec.europa.eu/info/law/law-topic/data-protection/data-protection-eu_nl.

© IFIP International Federation for Information Processing 2022
Published by Springer Nature Switzerland AG 2022
W. Meng et al. (Eds.): SEC 2022, IFIP AICT 648, pp. 70–86, 2022.
https://doi.org/10.1007/978-3-031-06975-8_5

technologies is ultrasonic invasion (UI). This technology uses ultrasonic beacons (UB) that are imperceptible to humans[2], but are sensed by mobile devices.

The main application of UB lies in cross-device tracking (xDT). The purpose of xDT is to establish a profile of the user across different devices. Typically, xDT is done by exchanging unique identifiers between different devices (e.g., an advertising identifier). This poses a serious privacy threat since, by targeting different devices, a much more detailed profile can be created than with traditional tracking technologies (e.g., Cookies). For example, with the use of xDT by means of UB, it becomes possible to link a work phone with a personal phone when they are on the same desk. In addition, since the entire process of receiving the signals emitted from the beacons by electronic devices usually happens in the background, the users are often unaware of the profile that is being created.

Since API level 26, Android has placed several restrictions[3] on background services, which make the unnoticed processing of UB signals more challenging. Because these background services consume device resources without the user being aware, they could result in a deteriorated user experience. Therefore, they are killed by the Android operating system after 1 min. For long running services, the concept of a foreground service was introduced. All this makes receiving UB signals more difficult, yet not impossible. After all, it is possible to do the receiving of the signals emitted from the beacons with a background service within the 1 min timeframe. Further, the receiving of UB signals can also be built into an unsuspicious foreground service of an application (e.g., a music application).

Another measure that makes the sensing of UB signals less stealthy on an Android mobile device, is the run-time permission required to record audio. Since API level 23, the RECORD_AUDIO permission of the MediaRecorder API is considered a 'dangerous' permission[4]. Whereas normal permissions are validated at application installation, the Android operating system forces dangerous permissions to be validated at-run time. However, when UB sensing is for example built into an application that supports voice messaging, the users are most likely unaware that permitting the audio record poses a threat to their privacy. Similar concepts apply to iOS, but are not discussed further in this paper.

What makes this research even more urgent, is the fact that ultrasonic technology is already being actively deployed. Lisnr [4] is a company, with over 250'000 customers, that offers services using UB (e.g., for contactless transactions using UB between mobile wallets and vendors). Another example is the company Shopkick, where users can collect points for vouchers by walking into participating stores that have ultrasonic transmitters installed. Since the previous two companies only do beacon sensing while their application or website is open on the user's mobile device, the users are aware that their microphone

---

[2] The upper hearing threshold in practice is around 17 kHz. Thus the near-ultrasonic range is 17–20 kHz.

[3] https://developer.android.com/about/versions/oreo/background.

[4] https://developer.android.com/guide/topics/media/mediarecorder.

is being used. However, there are also companies that run the entire process in the background. Silverpush is a company that has developed services to embed UB sensing as third-party content in, for example, a website or application. In this way, a user only needs to have an application with a Silverpush component installed on his device and the personal information, coming from UB embedded in TV streams, websites or even billboards is completely collected and processed in the background. In 2017, researchers discovered 234 apps with Shopkick components listening to UB in the background [1]. In this paper, we introduce and compare three different ways to detect sounds in the near-ultrasonic range and alert the user of the presence of these signals. We call our solution 'Frequency-based detection of Covert Ultrasonic Channels (FOCUS)'.

Our solution provides the following contributions:

1. To the best of our knowledge, FOCUS is the first work to consider the external detection of signals in the near-ultrasonic range. This external detection intercepts the signal, allowing users to detect the attack, even before it reaches their device. This opens up the path to external mitigation mechanisms that prevent the ultrasonic signals from reaching or influencing the victim device.
2. FOCUS runs completely in the background of the user's device, allowing the detection of ultrasonic sound without any interaction.
3. FOCUS operates completely wireless, allowing the detector to be installed in hard-to-reach places.
4. We present two PoC implementations, based on Arduino and Raspberry Pi hardware modules, and we show that the results are promising. Because of the limited resources in the Arduino module, standard frequency analysis methods cannot be deployed. Therefore, we propose and implement an lightweight solution for detecting ultrasound signals on low-cost platforms.

The remainder of this article is organized in the following manner. We discuss the state-of-the-art on acoustic air-gapped covert channels in Sect. 2 and provide a background overview in Sect. 3. In Sect. 4, we give the problem setting and in Sect. 5, we discuss the system model and adversarial assumptions. Sections 6 and 7 discuss the protocol and the results obtained. In Sects. 8 and 9, we discuss the advantages and disadvantages of our solution and give a security analysis. Finally, the paper is concluded in Sect. 10, where we also discuss the possibility of future research.

2   Related Work

A covert channel is a means of communication between two entities that was not anticipated by the designer of the entities. The concept of a covert channel was first formulated by Lampson in 1973 [11]. Since this type of communication is not intended to happen, covert channels can pose a serious privacy threat by bypassing existing communication protocols (e.g., for the purpose of data exfiltration). A special type of covert channels are air-gapped covert channels. What makes this type of covert channel more dangerous than other types, is the fact that it can occur between entities that are physically and logically disconnected from each other. The classification proposed by [8] divides air-gapped covert channels into five main categories: electromagnetic, magnetic, optical, thermal, and acoustic. However, in FOCUS, the main emphasis lies on the acoustic channel. Thus we discuss acoustic in the below section.

2.1 Acoustic

The covert channel that this paper focuses on, is the acoustic covert channel. This type of channel uses sound waves to exchange information between two computers. Depending on the type of sound used, two main categories can be distinguished: audible and ultrasonic acoustic covert channels.

Audible. This acoustic method uses a sound with a frequency that can be perceived by the human hearing (smaller than about 17 kHz). The concept was first explored by Madhavapeddy et al. [12], who conducted a comparative study between different modulation schemes to establish a speaker-to-microphone communication between two computers. Since this approach requires the transmitter to be equipped with a speaker, speakerless audible acoustic covert channels were later introduced by Guri et al.: Fansmitter uses noise from the fans of a PC for the transmitter [7]. DiskFiltration, as an alternative, uses noise coming from the actuator arm of a hard disk drive [9]. The main drawback that all these audible methods share is the fact that the noise can be perceived by the victim.

(Near)-Ultrasonic. This type of covert-channel, which uses signals in the 17–20 kHz range, is the main subject of this paper. Near-ultrasonic signals have the advantage that they are imperceptible to human hearing, yet can be generated and sensed by commodity hardware. This is because commodity microphones typically have a sampling frequency of 44.1 kHz. A first speaker-to-microphone implementation of this type of covert channel between computers was realized by Madhavapeddy et al. in 2005 [12] and could achieve speeds of 8 bps over a distance of 3.4 m. Later work by Carrara et al. achieved speeds of 230 bps, over a distance of 11 m, with a speaker-to-microphone implementation [5]. In 2015, Deshotels et al. accomplished a speaker-to-microphone ultrasonic covert channel between smartphones that could achieve a bit rate of 345 bps over a distance of 30 m [6]. All of these implementations share the disadvantage of requiring a microphone for detection. However, in secure environments, microphones are often not available due to security reasons. Therefore, Guri et al. proposed a microphoneless approach, in which a passive speaker is reversed by means of jack retasking and can therefore serve as a receiver [8]. Another microphoneless approach was presented in 2018 by Matyunin et al. Their research demonstrated that it is possible to use a MEMS gyroscope as a receiver for ultrasonic signals near the resonant frequency of the gyroscope (19–29 kHz) [13].

2.2 Differences with Previous Research

Whereas previous research has focused on developing a complete communication protocol (i.e. transmitter and receiver), this research focuses on the external detection of ultrasonic covert channels using a microphone. The main difference is that this research tries to intercept the ultrasonic signal with an external device, rather than having the detection happen on the victim's device, like in [5,6,8,12,13]). In this way, it is possible to intercept the sound before the victim has a chance to process it, opening up the path to external prevention mechanisms. In addition, developing both a transmitter and receiver has the convenience that the receiver can already have information about the transmitted signal in advance (e.g., the frequency in [6]), which makes the sensing much easier but not applicable to any other general ultrasonic signal. Another point in which this study differs from previous ones is the fact that earlier research used spectral analysis for detection, whereas in this paper, a novel approach is proposed that does not require a high-end analog-to-digital converter (ADC). For example, [13] uses a fast Fourier transform (FFT) on the acquired data from the gyroscope. Similarly, [8] uses spectral analysis for detection (Praat tool[5]). On top of that, [8] requires the use of an invasive kernel driver to remap the audio jack to an input, while this paper focuses on minimal invasive approaches. Our proof-of-concept implementation on a low-end Arduino platform shows that the detection can successfully be done without the use of traditional frequency analysis mechanisms.

3   Background

This section provides background information on various types of modulation schemes that can be used in a near-ultrasonic communication protocols. Then, an overview is given of the algorithms typically used to decode the received ultrasonic signal on the victim's device. Finally, this section highlights an important limitation to the use of spectral analysis for the detection of ultrasound.

3.1   Possible Modulation Schemes

For the transmission of ultrasonic signals, several modulation schemes have been proposed. On-off keying (OOK) uses the presence or absence of a sine wave signal to encode a 1 or a 0, respectively. Although this approach is the simplest, in most cases OOK has a lower data rate than the other modulation schemes. Another modulation scheme is phase-shift keying (PSK), in which data are encoded by varying the phase of a signal of constant frequency. This scheme, however, has the disadvantage that discontinuities can occur in the ultrasonic signal, which can still produce an audible click [2] from the speakers. A final modulation scheme, that is used in practice by SilverPush and Lisnr [2], is frequency-shift keying (FSK). FSK encodes bits by changing the frequency of a carrier signal. The number of frequencies that can be used, and associated the data rate, are determined by the allowed frequency range and by noise. Like PSK, discontinuities can occur in the signal with this modulation scheme, resulting in audible

---

[5] https://www.fon.hum.uva.nl/praat/.

clicks from the speakers. One solution to these clicks, which was proposed by Deshotels, is to gradually decrease the amplitude of the signal at the beginning and end of each transmitted character [6]. Since the modulation scheme employed depends on the attacker, this study considers any signal in the near-ultrasonic range as a potential covert channel. In addition, it is not known in advance which frequencies are used by the attacker, so the full range of 17–20 kHz is to be considered. However, if the frequencies are known in advance, more efficient detection is possible.

3.2 Algorithms Used for Decoding Ultrasound

Previous research indicated that Fast Fourier Transform (FFT) and Goertzel are the main algorithms for the detection of UB [2]. Both FFT and Goertzel are algorithms for efficiently computing the Discrete Fourier Transform (DFT) of a digital signal, whose output can be regarded as samples of the Discrete Time Fourier Transform (DTFT) of a digital signal. That is, the DTFT, which is a subcategory of the Z-transform, converts an input sequence in the time domain into an output sequence in the frequency domain. In general, the DTFT of an infinitely long sequence is given by:

$$H(\omega) = \sum_{n=-\infty}^{\infty} h(n)e^{-j\omega n}$$

where $H(\omega)$ in general, is a complex number function of the angular frequency ω. For the detection of ultrasonic signals, only the magnitude of the complex number is of interest and the phase can be disregarded. As a result, the magnitude can be computed directly without separately calculating the real and imaginary parts. In this way, the computational efficiency of the algorithm is improved.

In practice, SilverPush would use only Goertzel and Shopkick would use only FFT. In addition, Lisnr would use both Goertzel and FFT. Whereas FFT has a lower time complexity to compute a range of frequencies, Goertzel has the advantage of detecting a single frequency with little computational effort. The latter is mainly important in mobile applications, where battery consumption plays an important role. In addition, a recent comparison of Goertzel and FFT for dual Tone Multi-Frequency (DTMF) detection showed that for smaller bin sizes, Goertzel gives more accurate results [10]. In this study, FFT failed to detect DTMF tones correctly for a bin size smaller than 128, while Goertzel's algorithm was successful. In this regard, Goertzel solves the reliability problem of external detection, which was mentioned by [8] as the main limitation of this approach.

3.3 Limitation of Spectral Analysis

The main disadvantage of the FFT and Goertzel algorithms for the detection of UB, is that they require a high-end analog-to-digital converter (ADC) according to the Nyquist theorem. To address this problem, this paper also proposes a simpler approach that does not require this ADC and uses of a digital counter.

4   Problem Setting

Wherever we go and whatever we might be doing, as long as we have an electronic device with a microphone, speakers or gyroscope, that device might be listening. All types of electronic smart devices (e.g., laptops, tablets, headphones, smartwatches, IoT home appliances) are working with the most clandestine and unavoidable methods for tracking our locations and behaviour.

Ad-tracking audio signals are used by mobile apps, which our phone can detect but we cannot. For example, we watch television as regular viewers and we have our phone(s) nearby or with us in the TV room. Presently, TVs are working as beacons that emit ultrasound and our phone(s) are working as receivers. Beacons emit high frequency sounds and receivers listen to them.

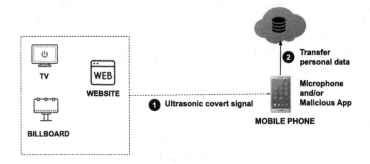

Fig. 1. Ultrasonic invasion through TV, websites, advertising boards

As shown in Fig. 1, TVs, ultrasonic beacon embedded websites or ultrasound emitting ad boards will emit ultrasound during commercial breaks that we will not notice, but our phones and IoT appliances with microphones will. Our phones can create an identifier with details about us watching a specific show at a specific time after receiving signals from the TV. Our phone can save these details and share with various applications, which will then give it to third-party users. The core idea is to link several devices we own in order to locate us and gather information about us. Beacons may be incorporated into tablets, phones, websites, and even billboards. This whole process takes place in the background and does not require user permission.

5   System Details

In this section we describe our system model and adversarial assumptions.

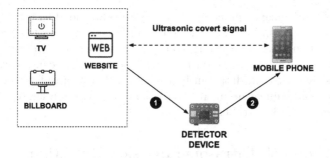

Fig. 2. System model

System Model. We consider a typical setting where a user has a mobile phone, laptop or desktop and TV or has access to an advertising billboard. In designing the ultrasonic detection scheme of such a system, we consider the presence of three main entities as shown in Fig. 2.

- Ultrasound emitter: As shown in Fig. 2, TVs, websites, billboards etc. are ultrasound emitters. Using the embedded ultrasound beacon, these devices emit ultrasound to gather information about users.
- Detector device: This device operates externally from the attacker and the victim, and detects the ultrasound emitted by the attacker. Furthermore, it alerts the victim of the malicious activity happening. In our PoC implementation we use Arduino and Raspberry Pi platforms as detector devices.
- Mobile device: The mobile device shown in Fig. 2 serves a dual function. On the one hand, this device is the victim, and will transmit various personal data to a database upon detection of ultrasonic signals emitted by the attacker. On the other hand, the mobile device also constitutes a part of the proposed solution, in the sense that it communicates with the detector device to alert the user.

Adversarial Assumptions. We presume for our adversarial ability analysis that a victim (user) frequently uses a mobile phone, watches TV, and surfs the Internet. In terms of attacker capabilities, we look at previous research [3,15] as well as commercial implementations (Shopkick, Lisnr, Signal360, and Silverpush) that use microphones as receivers that can be exploited to track a victim's location or gain private information from the victim's mobile. Thus for attackers capabilities we assume three main attack scenarios:

- Web tracking: Ultrasonic beacons embedded in websites can emit ultrasound which can be received by the microphone of a victim's mobile.
- Commercial advertisement tracking: The adversarial media (e.g., TV or Billboard) provider uses the ultrasonic beacons with encoded tracking IDs that are embedded in broadcast content. The adversary can monitor what and when users watch by capturing these IDs with an application installed on the user's mobile device.

– Data theft: Adversary app components can be embedded as third party content in ignorant applications installed on different devices of the victim. We assume that there is at least one device with an infected app that can transmit, and at least one device with an infected app that can receive. In this way, sensitive personal data can be exchanged between different devices via ultrasonic communication in the background, and thus an aggregated profile of the victim can be established.

6   Our Protocol: Ultrasonic Invasion Detection

FOCUS is comprised of three different detection mechanisms, respectively utilizing low-end, mid-end, and high-end hardware. First, a low-end approach is presented that uses a digital counter as a software-based high-frequency detector implemented on an Arduino. Next, the mid-end approach is discussed that uses the Goertzel algorithm on a Raspberry Pi. Although it was not implemented, an ESP32 or ARM Cortex-M could also be used for this purpose. A third high-end approach, employs the Goertzel algorithm on a smartphone and is provided for reference purposes only. After all, detection with a smartphone (victim's device) is essentially no longer external detection, as it will not help to prevent the ultrasonic invasion. Nevertheless, this detector is useful to indicate whether the ultrasounds detected by one of the other approaches can be effectively used as a covert channel. In case the FOCUS implementation on the smartphone does not detect ultrasound, a malicious application on the smartphone probably cannot either and no privacy threat is present. Finally, a smartphone app is proposed that integrates the low-end and high-end approaches, alerting the user of the presence of malicious activity.

6.1   Low-End: Arduino

For this implementation, an Iduino 1485297 microphone volume sensor with an operating range 50 Hz to 20 kHz is used. The digital output of this microphone is connected to the interrupt pin of an Arduino Uno Rev 3 that uses an ATmega328P microprocessor running at a clock frequency of 16 MHz. The sampling rate of the ADC of this Arduino model 9600 Hz and is therefore insufficient to utilize Goertzel or FFT algorithms. The digital output of the sound sensor produces a high signal if the intensity of the detected sound is above a certain threshold and a low signal below this threshold. This threshold is adjustable with a potentiometer and, for this research, was experimentally set to the lowest possible value at which ambient noise does not produce a high signal. In this way, the highest possible sensitivity can be obtained. For the supply voltage we use 5 V, which ensures that the high output is also 5 V.

A program was subsequently written in the Arduino IDE that, using the Arduino's built-in hardware interrupts, counts the number of edge transitions of the microphone pulses over a 100 ms period. Each period of a sine wave causes four transitions from high to low or from low to high by intersecting the upper or lower threshold. From this, it can be concluded that if more than 6800 transitions are detected during a 100 ms period, sound with a frequency higher than 17 kHz is present. However, in order to account for deviations of pulses that are not detected (e.g., due to ambient noise), the lower threshold is set in practice at 6750 transitions. Because the sensitivity of the microphone for frequencies higher than 20 kHz is too low, no pulses will be generated for these frequencies and consequently an upper threshold is irrelevant. The pseudo-code of the algorithm for the digital counter software high-frequency detector is given in Algorithm 1.

Algorithm 1. Software high-frequency detector

1: **if** $first\_measurement$ **then**
2:     $timestamp \leftarrow millis\,()$
3:     $first\_measurement \leftarrow false$
4: **else**
5:     **if** $millis\,() - timestamp >= 100$ **then**
6:         **if** $number\_of\_pulses >= 6750 \ \{17kHz\}$ **then**
7:             $detected \leftarrow true$
8:         **end if**
9:         $first\_measurement \leftarrow true$
10:         $number\_of\_pulses \leftarrow 0$
11:     **end if**
12: **end if**

6.2   Mid-End: Raspberry Pi

For the mid-end implementation, a Lioncast Universal USB microphone is used, connected to a Raspberry Pi model 3 v1.2. This Raspberry Pi runs on a quad-core Broadcom BCM2837 CPU with a clock speed of 1.2 GHz. The digital data measured by the microphone are read out in Python using the PyAudio library. A sampling rate of 44.1 kHz and a chunk size of 8192 are used for this purpose. Next, for each chunk, it is determined whether ultrasound is present. Depending on whether this sound is present or not, a message is displayed or the next chunk is taken in, respectively. The detection of ultrasound in a given chunk is done by applying the Goertzel algorithm[6] from Algorithm 2 to the chunk for each frequency between 17 and 20 kHz in steps 10 Hz. Subsequently, the calculated magnitude is compared to a threshold to determine the presence of ultrasound signals. This threshold is empirically set at the lowest possible value at which no false positives are detected, which is 50'000. The variable "coeff" in the algorithm is a constant determined by the sampling frequency, the target frequency and the chunk size.

---

[6] https://www.embedded.com/the-goertzel-algorithm/.

Algorithm 2. Goertzel algorithm for 1 considered frequency

1: **for** every sample **do**
2: $\quad Q_0 \leftarrow coeff * Q_1 - Q_2 + sample$
3: $\quad Q_2 \leftarrow Q_1$
4: $\quad Q_1 \leftarrow Q_0$
5: **end for**
6: magnitudeSquared $\leftarrow Q_1^2 + Q_2^2 - Q_1 * Q_2 * coeff$

6.3 High-End: Smartphone

The high-end implementation uses the built-in microphone of a Samsung Galaxy S8+, which runs on an octa-core Exynos 8895 CPU with a clock speed of 2.3 GHz. The detection of ultrasonic signals is done in an analogous way for this implementation as for the mid-end approach. However, an application developed via Android Studio in Java is used here, rather than a Python script. The measured digital data from the microphone are read out in this application using the AudioRecord API at a sampling rate of 44.1 kHz. For the chunk size, we opt to take the minimum size supported by the device. Specifically for the Samsung Galaxy S8+, the chunk size is 3528. For this implementation, the threshold for the magnitude calculated with the Goertzel algorithm is set at 100'000.

When an ultrasound signal is detected, the International Mobile Equipment Identity (IMEI) number, phone number and software version of the device are automatically sent to a Cloud Firestore NoSQL database. The IMEI number, which usually consists of 15 digits, is a unique identifier for each cell phone. Since this number could, for example, be used to track a stolen device or to unlock a device, it could, coupled with the information from the ultrasonic signal, pose a serious privacy threat for the victim. In addition to sending personal data to the database, the FOCUS application alerts the user of the malicious activity by means of a notification, indicating the frequency at which ultrasound has been detected.

7 Evaluation

In this section, we discuss the performance evaluation of FOCUS in terms of detection distance and frequency sensitivity, based on our proof-of-concept implementation described in Sect. 6.

7.1 Detection Distance

First of all, the maximum distance at which a reliable detection is possible is determined for the various detection methods. For this purpose, the transmitter uses a sine wave of 17 kHz emitted by the built-in speakers of a MacBook Pro A1989 at different volume levels. These speakers are calibrated using the Audio/Musical Instrument Digital Interface (MIDI) settings to operate at 44.1 kHz, in order to match the sampling rate of the mid-end and high-end detection methods and in order to consider the lowest quality transmitter capable of generating UB signal. To generate the sine signals, the Szynalski[7] Online Tone Generator is used. For the mid-end and high-end FOCUS implementation, three different positions relative to the speakers are verified: above the laptop, next to the laptop, and in front of the laptop. Where the first position is more focused on detecting commercial advertisement tracking, the last two positions are more tailored to simulate a typical desk environment (e.g., for web tracking). For the low-end implementation, however, only the position above the laptop is considered in the measurements. This is because the other positions do not give a sufficiently reliable result, with in many cases even no detection possible. For each position, three volume levels are considered based on the MacBook Pro's volume settings: maximum volume, half volume, and quarter volume. Measured with the Decibel X app[8] directly above the speakers, for a frequency of 17 kHz, these levels correspond to 92 dB, 84 dB and 67 dB, respectively. For the high-end approach, an additional fourth level is considered, corresponding to a setting of 1/16 volume and 57 dB. All measurements are performed in a 450 cm by 350 cm room with a normal level of background noise (e.g., people talking). Due to the dimensions of the room, and because of their limited relevance, the exact distance is not determined for distances greater than 200 cm and less than 1 cm.

Since the low-end detection mechanism operates in a different manner than the mid-end and high-end mechanisms, different criteria are imposed to determine when reliable detection occurs. For the Arduino, we look at a status LED that turned on for 100 ms with each detection. If this LED remains permanently high, it can be concluded that the considered distance can be reliably detected. For the Raspberry Pi and the smartphone we look at whether detection is possible for the considered distance three times in a row within the three iterations of the Goertzel algorithm.

Table 1. Detectable distances with a 17 kHz signal

Volume level (dB)	Low-end			Mid-end			High-end		
	Position (cm)			Position (cm)			Position (cm)		
	1	2	3	1	2	3	1	2	3
95	40			>200	140	160	>200	>200	>200
84	30			160	25	90	>200	>200	>200
67	10			60	10	50	>200	>200	>200
57							>200	80	175

Table 1 shows the resulting distances for the different detection scenarios for a frequency of 17 kHz. One can see that all of the FOCUS implementations are capable of detecting the 17 kHz signal under every circumstance. Moreover,

---

[7] https://www.szynalski.com/tone-generator/.
[8] https://play.google.com/store/apps/details?id=com.skypaw.decibel&hl=nl&gl=US.

the high-end method can detect further than the mid-end approach and the latter further than the low-end approach. In addition, it can be stated that for position 1, further distances can be achieved than for positions 2 and 3. This can be explained by the orientation of the laptop speakers.

7.2 Frequency Sensitivity

To verify the frequency sensitivity of the different FOCUS implementations, the different measurements are replicated with the same criteria at a frequency of 20 kHz. In this way, we consider both the lowest and the highest frequency of the UB, in order to allow for a reliable detection. The same volume levels are considered for this experiment, but for 20 kHz this correspond to 84 dB, 72 dB, 63 dB and 45 dB, respectively.

Table 2. Detectable distances with a 20 kHz signal

Volume level (dB)	Low-end			Mid-end			High-end		
	Position (cm)			Position (cm)			Position (cm)		
	1	2	3	1	2	3	1	2	3
84	60			>200	50	130	>200	>200	>200
72	20			50	<1	10	>200	>200	>200
63	<1			20	<1	<1	>200	80	110
45							35	5	10

Table 2 shows the resulting distances for the different detection scenarios for a frequency of 20 kHz. One can see that, again, all of the implementations are capable of detecting the signal under every circumstance. In general, it can be concluded that for a 20 kHz signal, lower detection distances can be realized than for a 17 kHz sine wave. This is because the sensitivity of a typical consumer microphone drops as the signal approaches 20 kHz. An exception to this observation is position 1 for the low-end detection method, where for the 20 kHz signal a greater distance was established. Possibly this can be explained by deviations in the signal caused by the acoustics, resulting in insufficient transitions being detected to reach the lower threshold.

7.3 Real-World Performance

To demonstrate the real-world implications of FOCUS, 30 international websites were evaluated for ultrasonic beacons through FOCUS. Each of these websites was visited, using a VPN, from India and the USA. For each website, the scenario of an everyday user was assumed (e.g., adding an item to the shopping basket) and, where possible, a number of videos on the site were also evaluated. In this process, in one video[9], ultrasound was detected by both the smartphone and the Raspberry Pi implementation of FOCUS. However, due to the lack of data, it cannot be stated with certainty whether this is effectively a beacon. Moreover, as previously mentioned by [2], who monitored the audio output of the top 500 Alexa websites, finding beacons is a time-consuming process that can be compared to looking for a needle in a haystack. All this suggests that larger-scale research is needed.

8 Security Analysis

Our main goal is to detect ultrasonic sound in the victim's vicinity and inform the victim about the ultrasound detection. Although we can not prevent the ultrasonic invasion yet, detecting the signal and notifying the user will still help to raise awareness in order to take precautions.

For the three attack scenarios from the adversarial model, as described in Sect. 5, it is known that commercial advertisement tracking is already actively employed by commercial companies (e.g., Shopkick, Lisnr, Signal360). Also, previous research has already shown that web tracking is possible by de-anonymizing a session in the Tor browser [14]. By intercepting the ultrasound signals between the attacker and the victim, FOCUS is able to detect both attack scenarios. In addition, FOCUS also demonstrates the danger of a data-theft scenario. In the high-end detection method, personal information is sent to a database upon detection. By implementing this approach across different apps with different privileges on different devices, it is possible to establish an aggregated profile of the victim. For this scenario as well, by intercepting the ultrasonic signals, FOCUS can demonstrate that a malicious activity is happening.

9 Discussion

In this article, our main objective is to detect UB signals and to alert the user of this clandestine practice. Particularly, we verify different possible detection methods against different positions and sound levels. Nevertheless, in addition to the advantages, each mechanism has specific disadvantages.

For the Arduino approach, it is not possible to determine at which exact frequency the detected sound was located, only whether ultrasound was present or not. Although the software high-frequency detector employed should theoretically be able to determine the frequency, it yields inconsistent results during measurements. In addition, for this approach, reliable detection is only possible in the extension of the speakers and the maximum detection distance is small compared to the other FOCUS implementations. However, since this implementation would be mounted directly against the speaker being monitored, this does not pose a threat to the effectiveness of this solution.

---

[9] https://www.instructure.com/en-au/canvas/resources/higher-education/canvas-learning-management-platform-across-globe-higher-education-students-leaders.

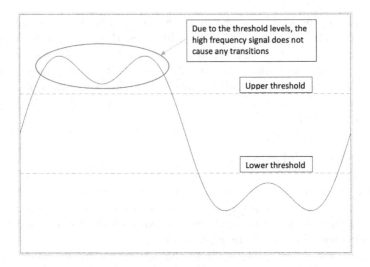

Fig. 3. Transition between high and low states of microphone volume sensor

Another disadvantage of the low-end approach is the fact that detection is not possible under the presence of strong noise at lower audible frequencies. The main reason for this lies in the fact that the microphone used (as well as most consumer microphones) has a higher sensitivity for signals with a frequency lower than 17 kHz than for ultrasonic signals. As a result, the superposition of the audible signals and the ultrasonic signals does not produce sufficient transitions to reach the threshold of the digital counter. This is also shown in Fig. 3, where only the signal with the lower frequency is able to cause transitions.

One solution, which was also verified in Simulation Program with Integrated Circuit Emphasis (SPICE), would be to use the analog output instead of the digital output of the microphone. This output can then be filtered using a high-pass filter (e.g., a second-order Butterworth high-pass filter) so that only the ultrasonic signals are passed through. By subsequently comparing the resulting signal to an adjustable reference voltage via an operational amplifier comparator, it is possible to detect whether ultrasonic beacons are present in the measured signal. To make this method less sensitive to high-frequency noise, the comparator can be a Schmitt trigger that provides hysteresis.

The smartphone FOCUS implementation on the other hand has the advantage that it can achieve the most accurate detection of the three approaches. However, this approach carries the disadvantage of high battery consumption on the detecting device, due to constant resource consumption of the Goertzel algorithm. For practical applications, it is therefore unlikely that it will be used for long periods of time. However, if it is known in advance which frequencies are being exploited by the attacker, the Goertzel algorithm can only be executed on these frequencies and low-power detection is possible.

As for the FOCUS smartphone application, we are aware that the Android Operating System requires permission to access the microphone and the phone, the former to detect the ultrasound and the latter to access the IMEI number and the phone number, which are sent to the Cloud Firestore Database upon detection. This paper assumes that the malicious app components are embedded in an app for which the user would unsuspectingly accept these permissions (e.g., apps that enable phone calls).

Since FOCUS focusses on the presence or absence of a sine wave, it is capable of detecting both FSK and OOK modulation schemes. These are the only schemes used in practice, because PSK causes phase discontinuities resulting in audible clicks. In addition, as the Arduino implementation of FOCUS relies on the zero crossing rate, it could theoretically be generalized to detect DolphinAttack as well when paired with an ultrasonic microphone. Indeed, DolphinAttack is based on double-sideband transmitted-carrier amplitude modulation (AM-DSB-TC). By using the zero crossing rate, it should be possible to detect the carrier and therefore the presence of the attack signal.

10   Conclusion and Future Work

This paper presents FOCUS, an environment for the detection of ultrasonic invasion. We develop three different approaches for ultrasound detection: low-end, mid-end and high-end. The low-end approach employs a novel low-cost software high-frequency detector that utilizes a digital counter. While in the measurements, the high-end method serves as a reference, the mid-end and low-end approaches are compared in terms of detection distance and frequency sensitivity. We demonstrate the performance of FOCUS through two proof-of-concept implementations based on a Raspberry-Pi and an Arduino, respectively. The results confirm both the practicality and efficiency of FOCUS.

In future work we will, in addition to the detection, develop a means of preventing the attacks. Further, we will explore the practical applications of ultrasonic invasion (e.g., the exploitation of electronic voting machines).

Acknowledgement. This work is supported by the ESCALATE project, funded by FWO and SNSF (G0E0719N), and by Cybersecurity Initiative Flanders (VR20192203).

References

1. Arp, D., Quiring, E., Wressnegger, C., Rieck, K.: Privacy threats through ultrasonic side channels on mobile devices. In: 2017 IEEE European Symposium on Security and Privacy (EuroS P), pp. 35–47 (2017). https://doi.org/10.1109/EuroSP.2017. 33
2. Arp, D., Quiring, E., Wressnegger, C., Rieck, K.: Bat in the Mobile: A Study on Ultrasonic Device Tracking (2016). https://www.sec.cs.tu-bs.de/pubs/2016-batmobile.pdf

3. Arp, D., Quiring, E., Wressnegger, C., Rieck, K.: Privacy threats through ultrasonic side channels on mobile devices. In: 2017 IEEE European Symposium on Security and Privacy (EuroS & P), pp. 35–47 (2017). https://doi.org/10.1109/EuroSP.2017. 33

4. Butler, C.: Visa makes strategic investment in LISNR, a start-up that wants to rival technology used by Apple Pay, November 2019. https://www.cnbc.com/ 2019/11/05/visa-invests-in-lisnr-a-start-up-that-wants-to-rival-apple-pay.html. Accessed 01 May 2021

5. Carrara, B., Adams, C.: On acoustic covert channels between air-gapped systems. In: Cuppens, F., Garcia-Alfaro, J., Zincir Heywood, N., Fong, P.W.L. (eds.) FPS 2014. LNCS, vol. 8930, pp. 3–16. Springer, Cham (2015). https://doi.org/10.1007/ 978-3-319-17040-4_1

6. Deshotels, L.: Inaudible sound as a covert channel in mobile devices. In: 8th USENIX Workshop on Offensive Technologies (WOOT 14). USENIX Association, San Diego, August 2014. https://www.usenix.org/conference/woot14/workshop-program/presentation/deshotels

7. Guri, M., Solewicz, Y., Elovici, Y.: Fansmitter: acoustic data exfiltration from air-gapped computers via fans noise. Comput. Secur. **91**, 101721 (2020). https://doi.org/10.1016/j.cose.2020.101721. https://www.sciencedirect. com/science/article/pii/S0167404820300080

8. Guri, M., Solewicz, Y., Elovici, Y.: Speaker-to-speaker covert ultrasonic communication. J. Inf. Secur. Appl. **51**, 102458 (2020). https://doi.org/10.1016/j.jisa.2020. 102458. https://www.sciencedirect.com/science/article/pii/S2214212619304697

9. Guri, M., Solewicz, Y.A., Daidakulov, A., Elovici, Y.: DiskFiltration: data exfiltration from speakerless air-gapped computers via covert hard drive noise. CoRR abs/1608.03431 (2016). http://arxiv.org/abs/1608.03431

10. Joseph, T., Tyagi, K., Kumbhare, D.R.: Quantitative analysis of DTMF tone detection using DFT, FFT and Goertzel algorithm. In: 2019 Global Conference for Advancement in Technology (GCAT), pp. 1–4 (2019). https://doi.org/10.1109/ GCAT47503.2019.8978284

11. Lampson, B.W.: A note on the confinement problem. Commun. ACM **16**(10), 613–615 (1973). https://doi.org/10.1145/362375.362389. https://doi.org/10.1145/ 362375.362389

12. Madhavapeddy, A., Sharp, R., Scott, D., Tse, A.: Audio networking: the forgotten wireless technology. IEEE Pervasive Comput. **4**(3), 55–60 (2005). https://doi.org/ 10.1109/MPRV.2005.50

13. Matyunin, N., Szefer, J., Katzenbeisser, S.: Zero-permission acoustic cross-device tracking. In: 2018 IEEE International Symposium on Hardware Oriented Security and Trust (HOST), pp. 25–32 (2018). https://doi.org/10.1109/HST.2018.8383887

14. Mavroudis, V., Hao, S., Fratantonio, Y., Maggi, F., Kruegel, C., Vigna, G.: On the privacy and security of the ultrasound ecosystem. In: Proceedings on Privacy Enhancing Technologies, pp. 95–112 (2017). https://doi.org/10.1515/popets-2017-0018

15. Mavroudis, V., Hao, S., Fratantonio, Y., Maggi, F., Kruegel, C., Vigna, G.: On the privacy and security of the ultrasound ecosystem. In: Proceedings of the 17th Privacy Enhancing Technologies Symposium, PETS 2017, pp. 95–112. DE GRUYTER (2017). https://doi.org/10.1515/popets-2017-0018

Passive, Transparent, and Selective TLS Decryption for Network Security Monitoring

Florian Wilkens[1](✉), Steffen Haas[1], Johanna Amann[2], and Mathias Fischer[1]

[1] Universität Hamburg, Hamburg, Germany
{florian.wilkens,steffen.haas,mathias.fischer}@uni-hamburg.de
[2] International Computer Science Institute (ICSI), Berkeley, USA
johanna@icir.org

Abstract. More and more Internet traffic is encrypted. While this protects the confidentiality and integrity of communication, it prevents network monitoring systems (NMS) from effectively analyzing the now encrypted payloads. Many enterprise networks have deployed man-in-the-middle (MitM) proxies that intercept TLS connections at the network border to examine packet payloads and to regain visibility. However, TLS interception via MitM proxies often reduces connection security and potentially introduces additional attack vectors.

In this paper, we present a cooperative approach in which endpoints selectively send TLS keys to the NMS for decrypting TLS connections. This enables hosts to control which TLS connections an NMS can decrypt and lets users retain privacy for chosen connections. We implement a prototype based on the Zeek NMS that is able to receive key material from hosts, decrypt TLS connections, and analyze the cleartext. Meanwhile, our patch was merged into Zeek upstream and will be part of Zeek v4.3.0. In our evaluation, we initially compare our approach to MitM proxies and can deduce that it significantly reduces the computational overhead. Furthermore, our experimental results on real-world traffic indicate that our TLS decryption adds a runtime overhead of 2.5 times compared to the analysis of cleartext. Additionally, our results indicate that when buffering traffic for only short amounts of time at the NMS, all keys from the hosts arrive in time to completely decrypt 99,99% of all observed TLS connections.

Keywords: TLS · NMS · MitM · Network security monitoring · Man-in-the-middle

1 Introduction

Nowadays, the majority of Internet traffic is encrypted, and the biggest share of it by Transport Layer Security (TLS). For example, Google reports that about 90% of all websites visited by their Chrome browser use HTTPS[1]. However, TLS

---

[1] https://transparencyreport.google.com/https/overview.

© IFIP International Federation for Information Processing 2022
Published by Springer Nature Switzerland AG 2022
W. Meng et al. (Eds.): SEC 2022, IFIP AICT 648, pp. 87–105, 2022.
https://doi.org/10.1007/978-3-031-06975-8_6

prevents the analysis of packet payloads by network monitoring systems (NMS) and restrict them to connection metadata. While some of these systems can work with metadata only [1], most NMSs require the cleartext payload, i.e., deep packet inspection [2]. Especially in the context of security monitoring, access to cleartext payloads is essential for real-time intrusion detection and for forensic analysis as part of incident response. While metadata can help to identify simple attacks in the network, payload data is required to identify the attack vector and tools the attacker used throughout the incident. In enterprise network administrators often deploy mandatory man-in-the-middle (MitM) proxy servers that terminate TLS at the organization boundary to enable effective security monitoring. These proxies then forward decrypted traffic to an NMS for cleartext payload analysis. However, terminating TLS connections raises several concerns:

1. MitM proxies raise privacy concerns for users as all traffic is intercepted without exception. While this is reasonable in high-security environments, a regular enterprise network should let users retain privacy for domains unlikely to endanger the network.
2. The integrity of the TLS connection is not guaranteed to be end-to-end (with regards to the client and server endpoints), as the MitM proxy essentially maintains two separate TLS connections to client and server and relays messages between them. Thus, a compromised MitM proxy is able to transparently forge packets that both endpoints will treat as valid from the respective counterparty.
3. MitM proxies add a potential attack vector to the network that needs to be maintained. This is especially important as the proxy has complete access to the traffic and could arbitrarily modify it. Recent studies have confirmed, that this setup often weakens the overall connection security [4,6,9,15,16,18].

The main contribution of this paper is a generic system for the passive inspection of TLS encrypted traffic without the need for a MitM proxy. Instead, we suggest that endpoints *selectively* forward TLS key material to an NMS, so that it can directly decrypt and analyze packets in TLS connections without intercepting or otherwise modifying the connections. In contrast to other state-of-the-art solutions like MitM proxies or TLS extensions for multi-entity support [3], our approach:

- works without modifications of the TLS protocol,
- adds no additional latency to TLS session establishment,
- enables only trusted observers to inspect cleartext payloads of TLS connections,
- supports policy-based, partial traffic inspection, that is enforced directly on endpoints,
- and preserves the end-to-end integrity of the TLS session for non-authenticated encryption with associated data (AEAD) cipher suites as the NMS only receives decryption keys but no integrity keys.

We implement our approach as a proof-of-concept (PoC) module for the open-source NMS Zeek [17] that can receive key material from endpoints and use it to decrypt TLS connections. The resulting payloads are transparently passed to Zeek's builtin analyzers for inspection. Our patch is available on GitHub[2] and already has been merged into Zeek mainline. We evaluate our prototype in two different dimensions: *(i)* We measure the *decryption overhead* by comparing the computational overhead for processing encrypted and cleartext traffic. *(ii)* We estimate the *impact of key transfer latency* between client and NMS on the number of decrypted packets, bytes, and connections. Our results indicate that decryption imposes a 2.5 times computational overhead compared to the processing of equivalent not encrypted traffic. The latency for key transfer is rather low and requires only a small traffic buffer (of about 40 ms) infront of the NMS to decrypt 99.99% of observed TLS connections in small deployments.

The remainder of the paper is structured as follows: Sect. 2 states objectives for our approach and reviews the state of the art. Section 3 introduces our approach on passive and transparent TLS decryption. Section 4 discusses the computational complexity of our approach compared to MitM proxies, describes our prototype, and summarizes our performance evaluation based on the Alexa Top 1000 websites. Section 5 concludes the paper.

2   Objectives and State of the Art

In this section, we describe objectives for passive and transparent TLS decryption on an NMS. Additionally, we summarize and discuss the state of the art in the areas of MitM proxies, and TLS protocol modifications along our objectives.

2.1   Objectives for Passive TLS Decryption

Before we summarize state of the art in the next section, we briefly describe objectives for the goal of passive TLS decryption already outlined in Sect. 1. These objectives are used to evaluate both related work and our own concept and prototype described later. To regain visibility into encrypted TLS traffic on a trusted NMS, a well-designed solution should exhibit the following properties:

- **No interception:** TLS is a well-designed protocol to ensure end-to-end data confidentiality and integrity between two endpoints. Additional entities, that intercept this connection, represent new and unwanted attack vectors that may weaken the security of the connection and break mutual authentication [4,6,9,15,16,18].
- **No protocol modification:** TLS is deployed widespread across a wide variety of devices and networks. Thus, changes on the protocol-level are unlikely to gain enough traction for widespread adoption.
- **No additional latency:** While security and network monitoring is an important topic in any enterprise network, it should not deter the user experience by introducing additional latency to the connection.

---

[2] https://github.com/zeek/zeek/pull/1814.

- **End-to-end data integrity:** The NMS needs to break end-to-end confidentiality between client and server to perform analysis tasks on the cleartext. However, it does not require integrity violation as application data only needs to be read.
- **Selective decryption:** Endpoints should be able selectively influence which connections are allowed to be decrypted by the NMS to let users retain some privacy for sensitive data. While high-security environments might require inspection of all network traffic, there are also scenarios in which total visibility is not feasible, e. g., for legal or compliance reasons.
- **Low maintenance effort:** Security monitoring is an essential service in an enterprise network and as such should require low maintenance for regular operations. This is both relevant for client machines and any middleboxes deployed in the network.

2.2 State of the Art

In this section, we review MitM proxies as current state-of-the-art for TLS visibility in enterprise networks as well as research in the areas of TLS protocol modifications and trusted execution environments. We compare all approaches with our objectives and which areas leave room for improvement.

TLS Interception via MitM. The most popular way to decrypt TLS traffic is to use a man-in-the-middle (MitM) proxy that terminates all connections and thus can access cleartext data. As industry best-practice this approach is often deployed in enterprise networks. Many implementations are available depending on the use-case and inner protocol that should be analyzed including open-source tools such as *mitmproxy* [5]. Commercial offerings for network security also often include a component that intercepts TLS either as a separate application or directly integrated into the NMS. Due to its popularity, TLS interception has been discussed broadly in recent years with the overwhelming consensus that it significantly weakens the security properties of intercepted connections [4,6, 9,15,16,18]. In [9] Jarmoc et al. discuss the security of intercepting end-to-end encryption in general. They state, that there is no implementation solely for the purpose of only intercepting TLS connections, but rather multiple classes of applications such as web proxies, data loss prevention system or network IDSs sometimes include an integrated feature for this. According to the authors all of them introduce potential risk into the environment they protect including legal peril, an increase in the overall threat surface by having a single point of decryption and a possible decreased cipher strength among others. More recently, Durumeric et al. [6] also confirm that intercepting proxies and the corresponding security degradation for clients are still prevalent. They find that there is an order of magnitude more interception than previously estimated. Additionally, they evaluate multiple middleboxes and conclude that nearly all reduce overall connection security and many introduce severe vulnerabilities.

Modifications of the TLS Protocol. TLS is designed to support end-to-end encryption between exactly two entities. However, there are proposals to add multi-entity support that would enable previously defined forwarding endpoints to decrypt the payload as well. In [13] the authors propose Multi-Context TLS (mcTLS) that extends the TLS header by multiple so-called contexts that act as a permission system and enable the client to allow selected middleboxes to read and write the TLS payload. However, mcTLS has two major downsides: *(i)* the additional contexts require additional computation on the client and add additional latency during connection establishment. *(ii)* the modified TLS header with contexts is incompatible to standard TLS and thus forces all nodes on the path to support mcTLS. The second downside is partially addressed in Middlebox TLS (mbTLS) also by Naylor et al. [12]. mbTLS extends the standard TLS handshake with a custom extension that middleboxes on the path can use to inject themselves into the connection with the client's consent. The endpoints then establish secondary TLS sessions with each of their respective middleboxes. To establish trust in the middleboxes, remote attestation via an enclave is used. Overall, this improves on mcTLS but *(i)* further complicates deployment and maintenance as middleboxes now require a hardware enclave and *(ii)* add additional latency through the secondary TLS sessions. Middlebox-aware TLS (maTLS) [10] modifies TLS, such that all middleboxes on the communication path explicitly forward security parameters to the client. This is implemented via a combination of Split TLS with added support of entity checks in a new TLS protocol. It ensures explicit authentication, security parameter validation to ensure confidentiality and modification validity checks for integrity. Like mcTLC, this also is incompatible to standard TLS with all the downsides. Similar to mcTLS and mbTLS the connection establishment requires additional computation time and delay is caused by the multiple entities that potentially perform computations on the connection. Legislators have also pushed to modify TLS encryption in a way that would allow access for law enforcement. Enterprise TLS (ETLS) [7] as proposed by the European Telecommunications Standards Institute (ETSI) adapts TLS 1.3 to make forward secrecy optional and keep the outdated RSA mode available. In practice service providers could then always use the same key and thus leave access to authorities, even at some point in the future.

Table 1. Objectives & state of the art. – not achieved (✓) partially achieved ✓ achieved

Objective	MitM proxy	mbTLS/mcTLS [12,13]	maTLS [10]	ETLS [7]
No interception	–	–	–	✓
No protocol modification	✓	–	–	(✓)
No additional latency	–	–	–	✓
Selective decryption	–	(✓)	(✓)	(✓)
Low maintenance effort	(✓)	–	–	✓
E2E data integrity	–	(✓)	(✓)	–

Summary. Table 1 shoes the state of the art and marks which of our objectives are met by the respective approach. MitM proxies offer the advantage, that the TLS protocol does not need to be modified and maintenance effort is relatively low as only the proxy itself needs to be maintained and the CA needs to be deployed to clients. However, the proxy breaks the E2E data integrity, adds additional latency and comceptually cannot guarantee selective decryption. mcTLS and mbTLS modify the TLS protocol to support middleboxes through a permission system. Maintenance effort is high, as middleboxes and endpoints need to be kept in sync due to the protocol. maTLS checks the same of our objectives. Selective decryption and E2E integrity could potentially be implemented but are not the focus. ETLS checks most of our objectives but has a major flaw: perfect forward secrecy is intentionally disabled to allow external audits through a shared private key. This does not retain the user in control of which connections are decryptable and adds another attack vector as the shared key could be compromised. In summary, no approach fulfills all our objectives. We also note, that true selective decryption can only be achieved, if the client retains control over the TLS key material.

3   Passive TLS Decryption at an NMS

In this chapter, we describe the concept of passively decrypting TLS connections at a network monitoring system (NMS). We assume that hosts in a network protected by an NMS are also equipped with a privileged endpoint protection daemon. Figure 1 gives an overview about the complete process and components involved. First, the local daemon obtain TLS session keys. Second, it filters the key for sensitive connections according to policy. Third, they transfer the keys to the NMS. Fourth, the NMS matches the keys to connections and starts passive decryption and further analysis. Steps 1–3 are executed directly on the endpoint and do not require direct user interaction.

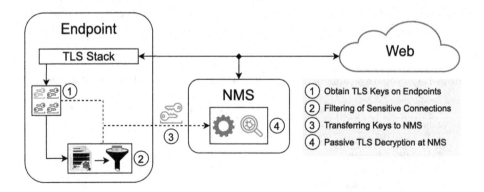

Fig. 1. Overview on passive TLS Decryption via cooperative endpoints

Keeping authority over keys on the endpoints and performing the decryption directly at the NMS offers increased flexibility. *(i)* The endpoint can enforce policy-based control about which connections are allowed to be decrypted by the NMS by withholding keys for sensitive connections. *(ii)* The NMS can opt to skip decryption for performance reasons, e. g., for video conferencing or streaming content. Both use-cases are not easily possible with current state-of-the-art MitM proxies. A concern compared to enterprise MitM deployments might be that visibility could be lost if an attacker should manage to disable the endpoint protection daemon thus disabling key transfer and preventing decryption. However, such an incident would already be detected and flagged even in legacy deployments, as the endpoint protection daemon is already monitored for liveness. Our approach might seem straight-forward on first sight. However, the individual steps encompass conceptual and technical challenges that we describe in greater detail in the following sections.

3.1 Obtaining TLS Keys on Endpoints

In the first step, TLS keys need to be obtained from the client machines as they represent the cryptographic endpoint. This is done in the context of the privileged endpoint protection daemon that has access to the network stack. A typical TLS connection, uses multiple secrets as well as session keys for different purposes. The simplest solution would be to obtain the pre-master secret and forward it to the NMS with the client random as the connection identifier. The NMS would then perform key derivation and obtain all session keys (and IVs if an AEAD cipher suite is used) to decrypt the encrypted application data packets. However, this enables the NMS to derive all session keys including the integrity keys. This would allow a compromised NMS to forge packets on behalf of both endpoints and thus introduce an additional attack vector to the network. For non-AEAD ciphers, we can mitigate this by only forwarding encryption keys to the NMS and keeping the integrity keys used by the HMAC on the client. Unfortunately, AEAD ciphers require both encryption keys and IVs to decrypt the data even if no integrity checks need to be performed by the NMS. From now on, we use the term *keys* synonymously with either just the encryption keys (if the cipher suite allows for that) or encryption keys and associated IVs. The keys can be obtained in multiple ways depending on operating system, cryptographic library, and application. There may even be a daemon collecting key material on the host already, e. g., osquery[3] as part of a zeek-osquery deployment [8] or a Zeek Agent instance[4]. If keys need to be newly obtained, the simplest way is the **SSL keylog interface** supported by widely used cryptographic libraries such as openSSL and NSS [11]. If enabled, the libraries write TLS pre-master secrets and the corresponding client randoms to the file specified in an environment variable. While this approach is easy to deploy, it might introduce some problems: *(i)* The logfile is readable by the user, as the browser process is running with user

---

[3] https://www.osquery.io/.
[4] https://github.com/zeek/zeek-agent-v2.

permissions. *(ii)* Writing secrets to a file and reading them in the aftermath via an application adds additional latency. While this can be partially addressed by using a RAM disk, the NMS might receive keys too late and the first few packets of a TLS connection cannot be decrypted. The **kernel TLS (kTLS)** interface [19] offers another way to obtain the desired keys. kTLS was introduced to the Linux kernel in version 4.13 and moves the TLS packet handling to kernel space. At the time of writing only a limited subset of AEAD cipher suites is supported. To use it, an application opens a regular socket and performs a normal TLS setup via key exchange and derivation. Next, it configures the encryption key as well as IV for the socket via a `setsockopt` system call. From that point on, regular `send` and `receive` operations can be used with the kernel performing encryption and integrity checks. A process with elevated permissions can monitor this system call for keys, extract and forward them to the NMS.

3.2   Client-Side Filtering of Sensitive Connections

Once the keys have been obtained by the daemon on the endpoint, it has to decide if the keys should be forwarded to the NMS to enable decryption of the associated connection. This filtering process considers connections attributed like IP addresses, hostnames and domains name to mark a connection as sensitive according to both network and user policy. For sensitive connections, the daemon does not transfer the keys to the NMS, forcing it to fall back to metadata-only analysis. Overall the decision to mark connections as sensitive is governed by:

- The **network policy** establishes the baseline for which connections must be decrypted and thus which keys need to be always forwarded. This will often be a "forward-by-default" policy, as the organization wants as much visibility as possible. However, there are cases where full visibility must not be required, e. g., legal or compliance scenarios in which certain information is not allowed to be decrypted. An example would be medical data in the health-care sector. Such scenarios require a more sensible network policy, that enforces visibility for selected services only and cannot use existing MitM proxies that decrypt all TLS traffic.
- **User policy:** It compliments the network policy by allowing the user to opt-out of decryption for selected services that are not covered by the network policy already. The user policy can be implemented via a self-serve portal where users can submit opt-out requests for certain domains (or in special cases IP addresses/hostnames). After review the updated policy is installed on the endpoint. Naturally, the user policy has to be sanctioned by security personnel and thus will likely not allow the user to retain privacy for all desired services. In these cases the network policy would likely overrule the user choice. However, the conceptual mechanism to include user choices itself already offers a large advantage compared to MitM proxies that decrypt all communication without any direct user involvement.

The concrete filtering process can be implemented via cryptographically signed policy lists that are validated via an internal public key infrastructure (PKI). Each connections' attributes are matched to these lists and marked accordingly. The daemon then transfers keys for non-sensitive connections to the NMS. Validation failure of the list integrity implicates unauthorized modification and could be used as an additional indicator of compromise (IoC). In this case, the daemon would fall back to forwarding all keys to the NMS to aid incident response. Overall, we recognize that selective decryption is *(i)* not feasible in all scenarios (especially high-security environments) and *(ii)* may impose additional challenges on security personnel. However, it enables organizations to support users in retaining some privacy which is not possible with MitM proxies. Moreover, we believe, that improved user privacy can outweigh the disadvantages in many scenarios or even enable the use of NMS in settings that have previously not been possible because of legal or compliance reasons, e.g., medical institutions. Finally, the lines between private and work activity are blurred and crossed. In such cases, users have legitimate reasons to conceal certain private connections from the organization's NMS which is enabled by our approach.

3.3   Transferring Keys to the NMS

After the filtering process is completed or skipped, the key material is forwarded to the NMS. The actual transmission method used is dependent on the NMS in question and conceptually trivial. However, the transport channel should be chosen carefully, as the key material is highly sensitive. Mutually authenticated TLS connections also based on the internal PKI between endpoints and NMS are a solid choice. The transmission should be direct without additional intermediaries to minimize the threat surface and prevent unauthorized decryption outside of the NMS. However, if the network policy requires it, keys could be also stored to a secured database to perform authorized offline decryption of dumped traffic at a later point in time.

3.4   Passive TLS Decryption at the NMS

Once the NMS receives TLS key material, it needs to identify the connection the key material belongs to. This identifier differs for TLS versions and different implementations of session resumption. To identify a connection that was established via a full TLS 1.2 handshake, the *client random* that is sent with the *ClientHello* is unique and thus can be used to match key material. For subsequent resumed connections, the NMS needs to associate the key material with the session identifier. This is either *session ID*, *session ticket* or *TLS 1.3 PSK* depending on TLS version and implementation. If the session identifier is then encountered in a later handshake, the NMS matches the key material as for full handshakes. In TLS 1.2 this process is trivial as both session ID and session ticket are sent in cleartext. The TLS 1.3 PSK approach is slightly more complicated as the PSK is already encrypted when sent from the server in the first connection and additionally exchanged after the first use in the resumed connection. However, this does not pose a problem to our approach as the NMS can already decrypt the first connection with key material from the client and thus store the decrypted PSK.

Once the connection has been identified, the NMS uses the obtained secrets to decrypt TLS application data in the connection. This poses two major challenges: First, the *cipher diversity* across different versions of TLS forces the NMS to implement many decryption algorithms. This can be mitigated by reusing popular cryptographic libraries such as OpenSSL or NSS. An incremental approach with a subset of supported cipher suites is also possible starting with popular ciphers. Second, *missing key material* at arrival time of the first encrypted packet needs to be addressed. This can happen either because the endpoint withheld the key material due to selective decryption or because the key material is still in transit to the NMS. In the first case, the NMS should simply skip decryption, while the second case would require the NMS to buffer packets until the key material arrives. However, this might introduce a denial of service attack vector if the NMS needs to buffer too many packets for connections especially as the NMS cannot know in advance if key material will arrive at some point in the future. To solve this problem, a traffic buffer in front of the NMS should be deployed that delays only the encrypted traffic for a short time before it is forwarded to the NMS. We quantify the impact of the key transfer latency on the decryption and recommend a buffer size in our evaluation (c.f. Sect. 4.4).

4   Evaluation

In this section, we first discuss the computational complexity our approach induces and compare it with the commonly deployed MitM proxy setup. Next, we describe the features and limitations of our PoC that we implemented to evaluate our concept. Finally, we describe the results from two experiments in which we measured the *decryption overhead* and the impact of key transmission latency on the *decryption success rate*.

4.1   Computational Complexity

We compare the computational overhead of our approach with MitM proxies on a conceptual level. TLS adds non-negligible computation overhead to every connection and the proxy has to set up and maintain two TLS connections per endpoint connection. A decrypting NMS remains passive and thus does not directly initiate TLS connections. Instead, it only decrypts the encrypted payloads to gain access to cleartext data.

Table 2. Simplified computational complexity for typical TLS connections

Approach	CV	KE	E_{sym}	D_{sym}
TLS client	1	1	s	r
TLS server	0	1	r	s
Intercepting proxy	1	2	$s + r$	$s + r$
Decrypting & passive NMS	0	0	–	$s + r$

Table 2 summarizes the simplified computational costs of establishing TLS connections for TLS client and server respectively, a MitM proxy, and a passive NMS. We assume the default behavior of HTTPS where the client authenticates the server only. The TLS client performs a *certificate validation* (CV) for the server certificate and a *key exchange* (KE) to establish session keys. The exact number of cryptographic operations here differs based on the cipher suite used, but usually involves CPU-intensive asymmetric cryptography. Once the key material is established, the client encrypts s bytes of its request via the symmetric cipher E_{sym} that was agreed upon and sends them to the server. After a response is received, r number of bytes are decrypted. The TLS server performs a similar number of operations, but usually without certificate validation as clients rarely use certificates in HTTPS. The number of encrypted and decrypted bytes are swapped as request bytes from clients s have to be decrypted and response bytes r encrypted. However, the overall computation effort should be nearly identical as symmetric ciphers require the same amount of computation for encryption and decryption.

The MitM proxy acts as TLS server to the client and as the client for the TLS server and thus performs the combined computations of both endpoints. While the KE results in a predictable amount of computation, s and r vary in different scenarios. For small connections such as simple websites, the doubled amount of symmetric cryptography is less impactful, while large connections such as large file downloads require significant amounts of additional computation on the proxy. The decrypting NMS has one large conceptual advantage to the proxy: due to its passive analysis, it only needs to decrypt all bytes $s + r$ of connection once to achieve cleartext access to the payloads. As no TLS connection is established, no KE needs to be performed and even validation of the server certificate is not required as the client would reject the connection in case of failure. However, analysis of the server certificate might be part of regular NMS tasks. Additionally, our approach offers some further potential performance gains compared to MitM as the NMS can decide to skip decryption on-demand if cleartext data is not needed. This is useful for common use-cases such as video-conferencing or streaming services which are notorious for their high bandwidth demands and thus comparatively high decryption cost. While a MitM proxy in theory could skip decryption of the connections, e. g., by detecting the domain and forwarding the *ClientHello* instead of terminating it, the NMS can simply discard the bytes it is only a passive part of the connection. This can help to reduce D_{sym} below the maximum of $s + r$. Furthermore, our approach offers yet again greater flexibility, as the NMS can adapt this decision based on the current threat level or other intelligence, e. g., by enabling decryption of all connections if a current attack is taking place or imminent threats are expected.

In summary, our approach conceptually requires less computational resources compared to TLS intercepting MitM proxies. While symmetric cryptography is continuously becoming faster to execute on modern hardware, it still represents the largest share of computation in a proxy and thus dictates how machine resources need to be reserved. Our approach requires significantly less computation and offers greater flexibility about which connections to decrypt while still enabling the NMS to perform analysis on cleartext payloads. However, the lowered computational load is shifted from proxy machines to NMS machines that have to be scaled up. Thus, in our first experiment, we aim to quantify this impact of added decryption on NMS performance to estimate the required changes for real-world deployments.

4.2 Implementation of Our Zeek Prototype

We implement our approach for passive and transparent TLS decryption as a proof-of-concept (PoC) prototype for the Zeek NMS [17]. While some features were intentionally left out to reduce complexity, our prototype is able to successfully decrypt TLS connections and perform analysis tasks on the cleartext application data payloads in real-world scenarios. Our prototype currently consists of a patched Zeek version based on v3.2.3 and a simple Python daemon that runs on endpoints and forwards key material. Both TLS key derivation and the actual decryption is performed by openSSL, as Zeek already links to this library. At the time of publishing our patch has been merged into Zeek mainline[5].

Obtaining TLS Keys on Endpoints: For simplicity, we *obtain key material* via the SSL keylog interface as described in Sect. 3.1. We instrument Firefox to write TLS pre-master secrets and client randoms to a file monitored by our Python daemon which are then forwarded to Zeek. While we opted for Firefox, our setup it not limited to this browser, as all popular browsers can be configured to dump TLS pre-master secrets in the same format.

Client-Side Filtering of Sensitive Connections: The daemon currently does not perform any filtering and thus does not support *selective decryption*. Instead all client randoms and pre-master secrets are forwarded to Zeek independent of the domains involved. A complete implementation would need to match connections identifiers and secrets to domains as this information is not directly present in the SSL keylog file alone.

Transferring Keys to the NMS: The Python daemon maintains a connection to the Zeek instance via *broker*, Zeek's default communication library, and *transfers new secrets to Zeek* once they appear in the file.

---

[5] see: https://github.com/zeek/zeek/pull/1814.

Passive TLS Decryption at the NMS: Our patched Zeek version is able to receive both pre-master secrets or derived TLS session keys. In the first case, the TLS key derivation is performed once the first packet of the matching connection is encountered and the resulting session keys are cached for later use. Once session keys are available, Zeek *decrypts the TLS application data* and forwards the cleartext to its internal protocol detection engine and subsequent analyzers.

Current Limitations: Our prototype was explicitly built as a PoC. It is capable to passively decrypt real-world TLS traffic without actively intercepting the connection. However, it currently exhibits some limitations that prevent complete real-world deployments: *(i)* Our prototype only supports a single, but one of the most popular, cipher suite, namely `TLS_ECDHE_RSA_WITH_AES_256_GCM_SHA384`. This cipher suite was chosen as it is commonly used in TLS 1.2 and exhibits several features of a modern cipher suite like perfect forward secrecy. Galois/Counter Mode (GCM) is favorably to our prototype as it was designed with parallel processing in mind and allows each block to be decrypted separately. Thus, our prototype is in worst-case also able to start the decryption in the middle of the connection if some initial packets could not be decrypted. *(ii)* Our prototype does not perform any *traffic buffering* and thus may encounter an encrypted packet before the respective keys are received. If this happens, it prints a debug message and skips decryption for this packet. This results in partial decryption of the overall connection. Usually, this means that the contained HTTP1/2 data cannot be fully parsed and analyzed. This limitation is however not directly tied to our implementation, as a real-world deployment likely would not buffer packets in the NMS itself anyway (as this opens up a potential DoS vector) but rather by a dedicated hardware or software appliance. The required size of this network buffer is an important question and we estimate it for small networks in second experiment in Sect. 4.4. *(iii)* Support for *TLS session resumption* is currently left out of scope to reduce complexity, but can be added by linking the respective connection identifier to the received key material. This is trivially possible as the NMS retains visibility into the complete payload.

4.3   Experiment I: Decryption Overhead

In this first experiment, we evaluate the central performance metric for our prototype implementation: *decryption overhead*, i.e., the additional runtime added by performing TLS decryption. This metric is important when deploying TLS decryption, as NMS resources need to be scaled up to accommodate for the additional computation requirements. There are two interesting scenarios to consider:

1. An organization is currently not deploying MitM proxies to terminate and decrypt TLS connections. Instead, a regular NMS is used to analyze encrypted traffic at the network boundary. Due to the encryption, the NMS is only able to analyze connection meta-data resulting in a comparatively low resource utilization.

2. The organization follows industry best-practices and deploys a MitM proxy that forward payloads from terminated TLS connection to an NMS. In this case, the NMS has full cleartext access to all connections and can perform a more sophisticated analysis, which results in higher resource utilization.

In both scenarios the NMS machines need to be scaled up, as more computation will be performed. However, in the second scenario, MitM proxies are no longer required and their previously allocated resources can be used for monitoring. To evaluate the decryption overhead for both scenarios, we design a capture environment that simulates both deployments.

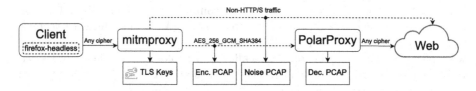

Fig. 2. Setup to capture the data set to evaluate decryption overhead

Setup and Data Set. Figure 2 shows the setup to capture the data set for this experiment. The client machine runs Firefox in headless mode that visits all Alexa top 1000 websites in order. The traffic is transparently routed through mitmproxy [5] to extract the TLS pre-master secrets and force the cipher suite that our prototype implements. The outgoing traffic from this machine is then routed differently based on the destination port. Web traffic destined for the ports 80/443 is forwarded to another host running PolarProxy [14], while all remaining non-HTTP/S traffic is routed directly to the Internet. We use PolarProxy as it can export decrypted HTTP/2 traffic directly to a pcap file, a feature that mitmproxy does not support. This pcap represents the commonly deployed second scenario described above in which the NMS receives decrypted traffic from a TLS intercepting proxy. The encrypted traffic and noise traffic is also captured and stored in different pcap files. These pcaps represent the aforementioned first scenario in which the NMS analyzes encrypted traffic only.

The resulting data set captured from our deployment comprises the *TLS pre-master secrets* extracted from mitmproxy and pcaps for *encrypted web traffic*, *other noise traffic* as well as the *decrypted HTTP/2 payloads*. All pcaps and the captures TLS pre-master secrets are freely available online [20]. Please note that this first experiment focuses on decryption performance and overhead alone. As such, we configure Zeek to load all TLS pre-master secrets from disk at the start of the experiment and let it analyze the respective scenario pcaps. This results in all keys being instantly available, which is not comparable to real-world deployments. To address this, we analyze the impact of real-time transmission of TLS keys and their delayed arrival at the NMS in the second experiment (c.f. Sect. 4.4).

Results. Figure 3a shows the decryption overhead by comparing the runtime of the unmodified Zeek version and our PoC for three different traffic profiles. Each traffic profile is defined in both *decrypted* and *encrypted* fashion as follows: *(i)* **https** contains only traffic that was originally sent via HTTPS. This includes most websites from Alexa top 1000 minus a few that did not support TLS at all. The decrypted variant is built from the decrypted pcap written by PolarProxy while the encrypted variants derives from the pcap captures between mitmproxy and PolarProxy. For HTTPS both pcaps are filtered by destination port 443. *(ii)* **web** consists of the same pcaps but removes the port filter and consists of all HTTP and HTTPS traffic. *(iii)* **all** extends the previous traffic profile by adding non-HTTP/S noise traffic and effectively contains all captured traffic.

The first two bars per traffic type show the runtime for the cleartext traffic for both the unmodified Zeek and our prototype. For all three traffic types, the runtime is nearly identical. This is expected as no decryption has to be performed and both version perform identical analysis tasks on cleartext data. These measurements thus resemble the NMS runtime in a typical MitM proxy deployment without including the runtime of the proxy itself. The third bar shows the runtime of the unmodified Zeek version analyzing encrypted traffic. The runtime is smaller than for the cleartext traffic, as this Zeek version cannot decrypt the payloads and thus falls back to metadata only analysis. This difference is most visible from the HTTPS only data set as no noise or HTTP data is present, which would be in cleartext and thus potentially triggering complex analysis scripts. This measurement also establishes a baseline for the first scenario described in the introduction of this section: an NMS processes encrypted network traffic and no MitM proxy is deployed. The fourth bar shows the runtime of our prototype that decrypts the TLS connections and analyzes the contained payloads. The added decryption results in a comparatively large runtime overhead as expected. Compared to the MitM baseline (cleartext traffic), we see an

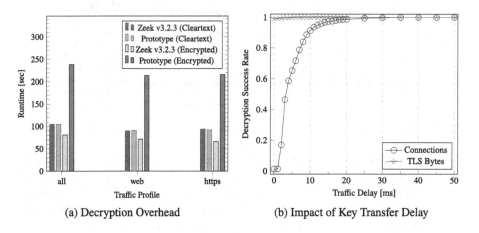

(a) Decryption Overhead   (b) Impact of Key Transfer Delay

Fig. 3. Experimental results

increase by a factor of 2.5. An administrator should scale the resources of NMS machines by this factor when switching from a MitM proxy deployment to our approach. As MitM proxies are no longer needed in this scenario their resources could be repurposed. Compared to the first scenario (encrypted traffic), the overhead grows to about 3 times. However, this is reasonable, as no decryption was performed previously (neither by a MitM proxy nor the NMS). The previous comparison and our discussion in Sect. 4.1 show that deploying a MitM proxy would likely result in higher overall resource usage.

Note: While this experiment can be considered a micro-benchmark the results should give a good estimation of the expected decryption overhead in typical scenarios. The missing features, such as support for more ciphers, are not expected to negatively impact performance. Combined with the complexity discussion, we are confident that our approach reduces overall computation efforts compared to a MitM proxy deployment.

4.4   Experiment II: Key Transmission Latency

In the second experiment, we evaluate the real-world viability of our approach by examining the delay between the key material being made available on the client machine and the arrival at the NMS after transmission through the network. This is especially relevant, when considering cipher suites that require the cleartext of the previous packet for decryption a newly arriving packets. For these ciphers either the key material needs to be available once the first encrypted packet arrives, the NMS needs to buffer packets, or the network traffic needs to be delayed before being passed to the NMS.

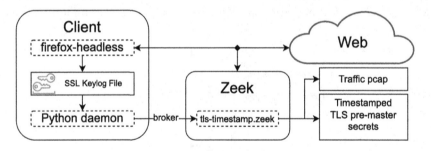

Fig. 4. Setup to capture the data set to evaluate the impact of key transmission latency

Setup and Data Set. We design a setup to capture timestamped TLS premaster secrets as seen in Fig. 4. The client again runs Firefox in headless mode and is configured to only offer the prototype's supported cipher. It then browses Alexa top 1000 websites and write the SSL keylog file. Our python daemon also runs on the client machine and watches this file for changes. New pre-master secrets are immediately forwarded to Zeek via its Broker communication library. On arrival, Zeek timestamps the key material to document the arrival time and stores the traffic as pcap. The resulting data set comprises the *traffic pcap* as well as the *timestamped TLS pre-master secrets* and is freely available online [20]. The timestamped TLS pre-master secrets are pre-loaded in our prototype that then analyzes the captured pcap file. However, the timestamp now dictates when Zeek starts to actually use the key. It only starts decryption once the network timestamp in the pcap is larger than the timestamp of the corresponding pre-master secret. This resembles a real-world deployment without any traffic buffering. For simulating this buffering, we use the pcap as is and simply add the desired delay time to the current network time in the comparison operation in Zeek. This enables us to quickly simulate multiple different deplays without altering the pcap.

Results. In this experiment, we count the number of TLS payload bytes that could be decrypted. As our supported cipher suite can start decryption from any packet in the connection, this can be anything between 0 (if the key arrives after the connection is already finished) or the full amount of payload bytes in the connection. We consider a connection *completely decryptable* if the key is available before the first encrypted payload packet is encountered. This is important for two reasons: *(i)* some cipher suites can only decrypt complete connections as part of the decrypted payload is used as IV for the next packet. *(ii)* especially for HTTP the first bytes of the connection are important for the NMS as they contain the client request. If they are missed, the NMS cannot analyze the protocol level. The *decryption success rate* is then calculated as the ratio of decrypted bytes/connections and total bytes/connections respectively.

Our results are shown in Fig. 3b. The x-axis shows the simulated traffic delay in ms and the y-axis the decryption success rate. In regular deployments without any delay only 1.3% of all connections are completely decryptable. This is expected as the key transfer latency prevents the first packets from being decrypted. However, 98.9% of all TLS payload bytes can already be decrypted. This indicates that only few of the first bytes are missed. This is further supported by the sharply increasing success rate in the first few ms. At 10ms traffic delay already 91.3% of all connections can be decrypted and the success rate steadily increases until at 40 ms effectively 100% of both bytes and connections can be decrypted. In summary, our results indicate, that only a small delay (in our setting 40 ms) is sufficient to achieve near-complete decryption. Depending on the utilization of the tapped network link, this results in a buffer size of up to 400M for a typical 10G uplink in a medium sized network. It is important to note that this small delay is only required before passing traffic to the NMS and thus does not impact other hosts in the network.

5   Conclusion

In this paper, we present an approach to passively decrypt TLS traffic on a trusted network monitoring system (NMS) that is based on client machines selectively forwarding TLS key material to a trusted NMS to enable decryption without intercepting the TLS connection. This provides several advantages compared to man-in-the-middle (MitM) proxies which are commonly deployed: *(i)* No latency is added, as no additional communication partner is involved *(ii)* Endpoints retain control about which connections can be decrypted by the NMS *(iii)* End-to-end data integrity is preserved if non-AEAD ciphers are used, as the NMS only receives encryption keys.

We implement our approach as a PoC for the Zeek NMS. While our implementation currently has some limitations, it shows promising results in both decryption overhead and real-world applicability. Our evaluation indicates, that TLS decryption increases the runtime by a 2.5 when compared to analyzing cleartexts only. It is important to consider that our approach does not require a MitM proxy to extract cleartext traffic. Our complexity analysis reveals that our approach requires significantly less computational resources than MitM proxies. Furthermore, we evaluate how the transfer of TLS key material impacts the decryption. Our results indicate, that adding a marginal delay infront of the NMS (in our setting as low as 40 ms) is enough to fully decrypt 99.99% of all observed TLS connections. This is easily realized via existing hardware or software appliances. Overall, we are confident that our approach and PoC are usable for real-world analysis tasks which is reinforced by the accepted pull request to Zeek mainline (See footnote 5).

References

1. Anderson, B., McGrew, D.: Identifying encrypted malware traffic with contextual flow data. In: Proceedings of the 2016 ACM Workshop on Artificial Intelligence and Security (2016). https://doi.org/10.1145/2996758.2996768
2. Antonello, R., et al.: Deep packet inspection tools and techniques in commodity platforms: challenges and Trends. J. Netw. Comput. Appl. (2012). https://doi.org/10.1016/j.jnca.2012.07.010
3. Badra, M.: Securing communications between multiple entities using a single TLS session. In: 2011 4th IFIP International Conference on New Technologies, Mobility and Security (2011). https://doi.org/10.1109/NTMS.2011.5721148
4. de Carné de Carnavalet, X., Mannan, M.: Killed by proxy: analyzing client-end TLS interception software. In: Proceedings 2016 Network and Distributed System Security Symposium (2016). https://doi.org/10.14722/ndss.2016.23374
5. Cortesi, A., Hils, M., Kriechbaumer, T.: Mitmproxy - an interactive HTTPS proxy (2022). https://mitmproxy.org. Accessed 31 Mar 2022
6. Durumeric, Z., et al.: The security impact of HTTPS interception. In: Proceedings 2017 Network and Distributed System Security Symposium (2017). https://doi.org/10.14722/ndss.2017.23456
7. ETSI Technical Committee Cyber Security (CYBER): ETSI TS103523-3 v1.1.1: Middlebox Security Protocol, Part3: Enterprise Transport Security (2018). Technical Specification
8. Haas, S., Sommer, R., Fischer, M.: Zeek-Osquery: host-Network Correlation for advanced monitoring and intrusion detection. In: ICT Systems Security and Privacy Protection (2020). https://doi.org/10.1007/978-3-030-58201-2_17

9. Jarmoc, J.: SSL/TLS interception proxies and transitive trust. In: Black Hat Europe 2012 (2012)
10. Lee, H., et al.: maTLS: how to Make TLS middlebox-aware? In: Proceedings 2019 Network and Distributed System Security Symposium (2019). https://doi.org/10.14722/ndss.2019.23547
11. MDN Contributors: Firefox Source Docs: NSS Key Log Format (2022). https://firefox-source-docs.mozilla.org/security/nss/legacy/key_log_format/index.html. Aaccessed 31 Mar 2022
12. Naylor, D., Li, R., Gkantsidis, C., Karagiannis, T., Steenkiste, P.: And then there were more: secure communication for more than two parties. In: Proceedings of the 13th International Conference on Emerging Networking EXperiments and Technologies (2017)
13. Naylor, D., et al.: Multi-context TLS (mcTLS): enabling secure in-network functionality in TLS. ACM SIGCOMM Comput. Commun. Rev. **45**, 199–212 (2015). https://doi.org/10.1145/2829988.2787482
14. NETRESEC AB: PolarProxy TLS proxy (2022). https://www.netresec.com/?page=PolarProxy. Accessed 31 Mar 2022
15. O'Neill, M., Ruoti, S., Seamons, K., Zappala, D.: TLS proxies: friend or foe? In: Proceedings of the 2016 Internet Measurement Conference (2016). https://doi.org/10.1145/2987443.2987488
16. O'Neill, M., Ruoti, S., Seamons, K., Zappala, D.: TLS inspection: how often and who cares? IEEE Internet Comput. **21**, 22–29 (2017). https://doi.org/10.1109/MIC.2017.58
17. Paxson, V.: Bro: A system for detecting network intruders in real-time. In: 7th USENIX Security Symposium (USENIX Security 99) (1999). https://doi.org/10.1016/S1389-1286(99)00112-7
18. Waked, L., Mannan, M., Youssef, A.: To intercept or not to intercept: analyzing TLS interception in network appliances. In: Proceedings of the 2018 on Asia Conference on Computer and Communications Security (2018). https://doi.org/10.1145/3196494.3196528
19. Watson, D.: KTLS: linux kernel transport layer security. In: Netdev 1.2 (2016). https://netdevconf.org/1.2/papers/ktls.pdf
20. Wilkens, F., Haas, S., Fischer, M.: Evaluation dataset: cooperative TLS-decryption via Zeek (2022). https://doi.org/10.25592/uhhfdm.10116

Network Security and Privacy

A Study on the Use of 3rd Party DNS Resolvers for Malware Filtering or Censorship Circumvention

Martin Fejrskov[1]([✉]), Emmanouil Vasilomanolakis[2], and Jens Myrup Pedersen[2]

[1] Telenor A/S, Aalborg, Denmark
mfea@telenor.dk
[2] Cyber Security Group, Aalborg University, Copenhagen, Denmark
{emv,jens}@es.aau.dk

Abstract. DNS resolvers perform the essential role of translating domain names into IP addresses. The default DNS resolver offered by an Internet Service Provider (ISP) can be undesirable for a number of reasons such as censorship, lack of malware filtering options and low service quality. In this paper, we propose a novel method for estimating the amount of DNS traffic directed at non-ISP resolvers by using DNS and NetFlow data from an ISP. This method is extended to also estimate the amount of DNS traffic towards resolvers that offer malware filtering or parental control functionality. Finally, we propose a novel method for estimating the amount of DNS traffic at non-ISP resolvers that would have been censored by ISP resolvers. The results of applying these methods on an ISP dataset shows to which extent 3rd party resolvers are chosen by users for either malware filtering or censorship circumvention purposes.

Keywords: DNS · NetFlow · Resolver · ISP · Filtering · Censorship

1 Introduction

The DNS resolver service has traditionally been provided to customers by Internet Service Providers (ISPs). Recently, providers of public DNS resolver services, such as Google and Cloudflare, have gained popularity, and are estimated by Radu et al. to handle more than 50% of all DNS resolutions globally [17]. Although Radu et al. discuss the possible reasons users can have for choosing public DNS services, the authors remain at speculations on this topic.

Some equipment vendors (e.g. webcams) use 3rd party DNS resolvers as a default setting in products. Three main reasons for a user to *actively* choose a 3rd party DNS resolver are presented by web pages containing security advice:

– Service quality: Speed, reliability, and basic security features such as DNS-over-TLS (DoT), DNS-over-HTTPs (DoH) and DNSSEC validation.

Funded by Telenor A/S and Innovation Fund Denmark, 2022.

- Privacy: Adherence to more strict privacy principles and no modification of the responses, for example to inject ads in NXDOMAIN responses [23].
- Filtering/censoring: The 3rd party provider does not follow government orders to censor responses. Conversely, the 3rd party provider may offer filtering of domains related to malware, porn, drugs, etc. as an add-on service.

As ISPs can deploy resolvers topologically closer to the end users than any 3rd party resolver, an ISP will always be able to offer a faster resolver service than any 3rd party resolver. As a fast DNS resolution can make an Internet connection appear faster, this represents a competitive advantage to an ISP. A competitive ISP can therefore be assumed to offer DNS resolvers with good service quality (although examples of ISPs not having this focus do exist [1]). European Union legislation forbids ISPs to collect personal information, and forbids ISPs to modify DNS responses for ad injection. Therefore a rational customer at a competitive, European ISP should not be inclined to use service quality or privacy as the main reason for choosing a 3rd party DNS resolver.

Following the arguments presented above, and assuming a rational customer and a competitive, European ISP, only the third category, filtering/censoring, is relevant, which will therefore be the focus of this paper. We recognize that there can be a difference between perceived privacy and actual privacy, as well as a difference between perceived and actual service quality, however we consider this topic out of scope of our paper. The contribution of the paper is the methods and measurements needed to answer the following research questions:

- RQ1: To which extent are 3rd party resolvers used compared to the default ISP resolvers?
- RQ2: To which extent are 3rd party resolvers that offer malware filtering or parental control used?
- RQ3: To which extent are 3rd party resolvers used to circumvent censorship?

These methods and associated results can be relevant for ISPs to assess the business case for offering DNS based filtering services. The results can also be relevant to regulatory bodies to assess the effect of DNS based censorship.

Section 2 introduces related work and other background information. The three following Sects. (3, 4 and 5) each answer one of the research questions outlined above. Section 6 summarizes the answers and concludes the paper.

2   Background and Related Work

2.1   Data Availability

The simplest way to examine how much and which DNS traffic is directed at 3rd party resolvers is to ask the operators of those services. The privacy policies of the five major public DNS resolver providers (according to Radu et al.) reveal that the providers store data that could answer the question in either anonymized or non-anonymized form, however, they are generally not willing to share the data [4,5,11,16,25]. Another approach is to collect data by interacting with user equipment. One example is the use of apps as probes by the Open Observatory of Network Interference (OONI) project. A second example is the use of advertisement campaigns (or similar mechanisms) that trigger a resolver to query observer-controlled authoritative servers [3]. These approaches can measure which resolvers are used relative to other resolvers, but do not quantify the amount of traffic from each client towards each resolver, which is the purpose of our paper.

Although ISPs are not legally allowed to inspect the DNS traffic to 3rd party resolvers, Fejrskov et al. describe that DNS data from the ISPs own resolvers as well as sampled NetFlow data (that includes 3rd party resolver traffic) can be used in anonymized form even when considering European Union legislation [9]. In our paper the ISP approach is adopted, and data from Telenor Denmark, a national ISP in Europe with 1,5M mobile and 100k broadband subscriptions, is used. Their DNS resolvers adhere to the service quality and privacy criteria mentioned in the introduction, and provide no add-on block offerings.

2.2   Estimating DNS Traffic Based on NetFlow Data

Konopa et al. suggest a method to detect DoH traffic based on NetFlow records [14]. However, the method relies on access to unsampled NetFlow records which is not available in our paper. Although some papers discuss using NetFlow to identify specific applications, we are not aware of any other papers that directly focus on estimating the amount of DNS traffic. An intermediate step is to use the NetFlow records to estimate the actual number of UDP or TCP flows, a technique often referred to as flow inversion. Several papers, most recently [2], estimate the flow size distribution using various sampling methods, different traffic models, and uses different information from the sampled packets, such as the presence of TCP SYN packets and sequence numbers. Duffield et al. describe and validate a simpler technique that estimates the actual amount of TCP flows as the multiplication of the sample rate and the observed number of flows for which the initial SYN packet was observed [7]. Neither paper present any methods that are applicable to this paper for estimating the amount of UDP flows.

2.3   DNS Response Manipulation

Several studies characterize the use of response manipulation in resolvers [13, 15,24] , including both filtering, censoring, injection, etc. Most papers consider response manipulation as an undesired feature as opposed to something positive that the user has actively chosen to gain features such as malware protection. In all papers, the characterization of servers is based on whether or not the server actually performs response manipulation, independently of whether it is advertised or not. In our paper, we therefore find it interesting to characterize resolvers based on whether they advertise themselves as filtering or not, in order to investigate to which extent such functionality is desirable by users.

2.4 Censorship and Circumvention Detection

The legislation in Denmark requires ISPs to perform DNS based blocking of certain domains in 7 different categories [21]. In our paper, all categories are included with no distinction between them, giving a total of approximately 800 domains that have a DNS A record. The legislation (and following public discussion) is about blocking web pages, and DNS is seen as the tool that can implement this [6].

Related work on censorship fall in four categories: Techniques for implementing censorship, detecting censorship, circumventing censorship, and measure circumvention attempts. Only the last category is relevant to this paper, and this seems to be the topic of only a few papers. Three of these focus on the use of specific tools or apps like TOR [19], an app for changing DNS resolver [10], and on the use of DNS servers owned by VPN providers [8]. Our focus is only on circumvention that involves the use of 3rd party resolvers, not on specific tools.

The Danish Rights Alliance, an organisation focusing on copyright and other conditions for content creators, measures the effect of DNS based blocking by analysing web site visits [22]. They concluded that the effect of blocking a specific site through DNS blocking reduces the number of visits to the specific site by up to 75% after 4–5 months. In our paper, it is not a requirement that the censored sites consent to embedding code in their web page that measure usage statistics, and the focus is not limited to copyright.

Callejo et al. conclude that 13% of the global DNS queries are resolved by 3rd party rather than by ISP-provided DNS resolvers [3]. They also conclude that the use of 3rd party providers is more frequent in countries with a high level of censorship (a poor rating by the Reporters Without Borders' (RWB) World Press Freedom Index). Their approach relies on serving ads through browsers, and for the reasons mentioned initially in this section, the approach is not applicable for our paper. However, they conclude that the use of 3rd party resolvers in countries rated as Good by RWB is around 7–11% of the total traffic, which is an interesting figure to compare to our results.

3 Prevalence of 3rd Party Resolvers

This section presents a method for estimating the number of DNS responses represented by a set of sampled NetFlow records towards 3rd party DNS resolvers. The method consists of three steps that are described in more detail in the following three subsections. The number of 3rd party DNS responses is compared to the number of responses served by Telenor Denmark's DNS resolvers to answer the first question (RQ1) posed in the introduction.

Four different DNS traffic types are considered in this section: DNS over UDP and TCP, DNS-over-TLS (DoT) and DNS-over-HTTPS (DoH). As DNS requests can potentially be malformed, and as only requests that result in a response are relevant from a user perspective, this study will focus on the number of responses rather than the number of requests.

3.1 Identifying Relevant Netflow Records

The first step is to identify the NetFlow records that represent 3rd party DNS resolver traffic. In this paper, it is a precondition that the available NetFlow records represent a view of all flows crossing a well-defined network boundary. Users and the default DNS resolvers are defined to be on the internal of the network boundary, 3rd party resolvers and other servers are defined to be on the external side. The NetFlows are considered sampled with a rate of 1:Q.

For an external IP address to be considered a potential 3rd party DNS resolver, and to filter away irregular and irrelevant traffic such as that originating from DDoS attacks and port scanning, some TCP or UDP traffic must be observed on port 53 or 853 in both directions, that is both to and from the server. However, due to the use of sampled NetFlow, observing records that form a bidirectional flow is not required, as both directions of the same flow will rarely be sampled given a high sample rate. TCP and DoT records originating from the potential resolver IP must report a packet size of at least 54 bytes to ensure that the response is at least large enough to contain a valid IP, TCP and DNS header. Therefore, packets only containing, for example, a TCP Reset flag indicating that no service is available do not qualify. This packet size criterion is not necessary for UDP based flows, as a server with no UDP service will respond with an ICMP packet instead of a UDP packet.

TCP port 443 traffic towards the resolvers outlined above is considered DoH traffic. We recognize that operators could run both DoH and Web services on the same IP address, and therefore the amount of DoH traffic estimated using this method should be considered as an upper bound rather than an exact number.

Traffic towards authoritative servers also satisfies the aforementioned criteria for a potential resolver, and these flows must be disregarded. Any of the following criteria are used to identify authoritative server IPs:

- The server returns an error code when resolving a well-known domain name, but answers succesfully when resolving the domain name found in the server's reverse/pointer (PTR) record.
- The IP address of the server is identical to any IP address with which the default resolvers communicate.
- The PTR record of the server IP reveals that the server is a well-known authoritative server, such as the DNS root servers or the authoritative servers of major commercial DNS providers.

As a result of the selection process described above, N NetFlow records are considered to represent user-initiated traffic to/from 3rd party resolvers, and only these records are considered for further analysis.

3.2 Average Number of Flows per Netflow Record

Having identified a number of NetFlow records that represent a number of observed flows towards 3rd party resolvers, the next step is to estimate the number of actual flows. This requires different approaches for TCP and UDP traffic.

As outlined in Sect. 2, the estimated number of actual TCP flows, $\hat{F}_{TCP}$, can be found by multiplying the NetFlow sample rate with the number of flows in which a SYN packet is observed, $\hat{F}_{TCP} = Q \cdot F_{SYN}$. The number of observed SYN flows, F_{SYN}, is determined by aggregating the observed response SYN records, N_{SYN}, by the 6-tuple of observed flow start time, source and destination IP address, source and destination port number and protocol. For a Q much larger than the expected number of packets in a TCP flow, it is only expected that each TCP flow is sampled once, and in that case $\hat{F}_{SYN} = N_{SYN}$, which is demonstrated as a valid practice in Sect. 3.5.

To estimate the number of actual UDP flows, we use the property that a DNS request or response is always contained within a single UDP packet, and the property that a new UDP flow is made for each request due to the prevalence of source port randomization [12]. In other words, one UDP NetFlow record represents one flow and one DNS response. Therefore, the estimated number of UDP flows, $\hat{F}_{UDP}$, is given by the number of observed UDP response records multiplied by the NetFlow sample rate, $\hat{F}_{UDP} = Q \cdot N_{UDP}$. Note that although a response is always contained within a single UDP packet, this packet may be split into several IP packets due to fragmentation. In this case, only the first IP packet will contain UDP headers, and therefore only the first packet will be considered a UDP packet by the NetFlow emitting router. Therefore, the assumption of a one-to-one relation between DNS responses and UDP packets should be considered valid when using NetFlow as measurement method.

3.3   Average Number of DNS Responses per Flow

Having estimated the number of actual TCP/UDP flows represented by NetFlow records, the next step is to identify the number of DNS responses per flow. For this purpose, it is assumed that the average number of responses per TCP flow for 3rd party resolvers and for the default resolvers are similar, that the average number of responses per DoT flow for 3rd party resolvers and for the default resolvers are similar, and that these numbers can be calculated from the collected data from the default resolvers. Different collection methods will allow for different methods for calculating the numbers, and the method described below reflects an approach applicable to our data set.

To estimate the average number of responses per TCP/DoT/DoH session, DNS response data from the default resolvers that include the ports of the response is used. The minimum time between flow closure and the allowed reuse of the related source port from the same request source IP address is denoted $t_{graceperiod}$. The longest allowed time for a TCP session to be open is denoted $t_{maxsessionlength}$, and therefore should be true that $t_{maxsessionlength} > t_{graceperiod}$. A response, c is considered belonging to the same flow as another response b, if the two responses are less than $t_{graceperiod}$ apart ($t_b + t_{graceperiod} > t_c$), and if the response c and the first response in the flow, a, are less than $t_{maxsessionlength}$ apart ($t_a + t_{maxsessionlength} > t_c$).

It should be noted that the specific values of both $t_{maxsessionlength}$ and $t_{graceperiod}$ can differ among clients and servers, as such settings can be either operating system, application or deployment specific. The choice of values for these will therefore depend on the specific DNS server software settings.

Using this method to estimate which DNS responses belong to the same flow makes it possible to calculate an estimated, average number of responses per TCP flow, $\hat{R}_{TCP}$, and an estimated, average number of responses per DoT flow, $\hat{R}_{DoT}$. Notice that the similar number for UDP flows, $\hat{R}_{UDP}$, is always 1 for the reasons outlined in Sect. 3.2.

3.4 Method Summary

The number of DNS responses from 3rd party DNS resolvers, $\hat{D}$, is estimated using NetFlow records as

$$
\begin{aligned}
\hat{D} &= \hat{D}_{UDP} + \hat{D}_{TCP} + \hat{D}_{DoT} + \hat{D}_{DoH} \\
&= \hat{F}_{UDP} \cdot \hat{R}_{UDP} + \hat{F}_{TCP} \cdot \hat{R}_{TCP} + \hat{F}_{DoT} \cdot \hat{R}_{DoT} + \hat{F}_{DoH} \cdot \hat{R}_{DoH} \\
&= Q(N_{UDP} + N_{TCP,SYN} \cdot \hat{R}_{TCP} + N_{DoT,SYN} \cdot \hat{R}_{DoT} + N_{DoH,SYN} \cdot \hat{R}_{DoH})
\end{aligned}
$$

for a large NetFlow sample rate Q, the number of relevant UDP NetFlow records, N_{UDP}, the number of relevant NetFlow records observing a SYN packet, $N_{TCP,SYN}$, $N_{DoT,SYN}$ and $N_{DoH,SYN}$, and the estimated, average number of DNS responses per TCP/DoT/DoH flow, $\hat{R}_{TCP}$, $\hat{R}_{DoT}$ and $\hat{R}_{DoH}$.

3.5 Measurements and Discussion

Anonymized DNS and NetFlow data collected over a period of 4 days (covering both weekdays and weekend) from 2021-08-08 to 2021-08-11 from Telenor Denmark's network is used to demonstrate the use of the estimation method elaborated in the previous section. The DNS data is derived from the response packets for all DNS queries towards the default DNS resolvers. The NetFlow data is derived from traffic passing the BGP AS border with sample rate $Q = 512$. Metrics are summarized in Table 1. Although the data set only contains 4 days of data, we consider it to be representative, as DNS services are used on a daily basis, and as the amount of users is large (1,6M). The internal IP addresses in the data are anonymized by truncation to a /24 prefix, and the AM/PM information of the timestamps is truncated as suggested by Fejrskov et al. [9].

The NetFlow sample rate, $Q = 512$, is higher than the expected number of packets in a DNS TCP flow. Therefore the number of observed flows is almost identical to the number of NetFlow records ($\hat{F}_{TCP,SYN} \approx N_{TCP,SYN}$ and $\hat{F}_{DoT,SYN} \approx N_{DoT,SYN}$) as anticipated in Sect. 3.2.

232 NetFlow records relating to UDP traffic on port 853 were observed. This could represent DNS-over-DTLS (DNSoD) traffic [18]. Due to the small amount and the experimental status of the DNSoD standard, we disregard these records.

Table 1. Metrics for 3rd party DNS resolver traffic estimation.

Metric	Symbol	Count
Total NetFlow records	n	$2,75 \cdot 10^9$
Relevant NetFlow records	N	$3,32 \cdot 10^6$
NetFlow UDP records	N_{UDP}	$2,85 \cdot 10^6$
NetFlow TCP SYN records	$N_{TCP,SYN}$	$98,9 \cdot 10^3$
NetFlow TCP SYN flow	$\hat{F}_{TCP,SYN}$	$98,5 \cdot 10^3$
NetFlow DoT SYN records	$N_{DoT,SYN}$	$12,6 \cdot 10^3$
NetFlow DoT SYN flow	$\hat{F}_{DoT,SYN}$	$12,6 \cdot 10^3$
NetFlow DoH SYN records	$N_{DoH,SYN}$	$15,9 \cdot 10^3$
NetFlow DoH SYN flow	$\hat{F}_{DoH,SYN}$	$15,9 \cdot 10^3$
Max TCP session length	$t_{maxsessionlength}$	$100\,\mathrm{s}$
TCP source port grace period	$t_{graceperiod}$	$30\,\mathrm{s}$
DNS responses per TCP flow	$\hat{R}_{TCP}$	1,19
DNS responses per DoT flow	$\hat{R}_{DoT}$	11,3

Moreover, $43,2 \cdot 10^3$ NetFlow records relating to UDP traffic (from port 53) report more than one packet per flow, which seems to contradict the assumption of one UDP packet per flow made in Sect. 3.2. Although an experimental IETF RFC from 2016 [20] describes the use of multiple UDP packets for responses, it seems unlikely that this should be implemented in several 3rd party resolvers. We therefore believe that a more plausible explanation is that this is caused by re-transmission of requests and responses. As re-transmissions are of no interest to this paper, a UDP NetFlow record (from port 53) reporting more than one packet will only be counted as one packet, and therefore as one request or response.

The value of $t_{graceperiod} = 30\,\mathrm{s}$ is chosen to match the default tcp-idle-timeout value of the Bind software running on the default DNS resolvers. The value of $t_{maxsessionlength} = 100\,\mathrm{s}$ is chosen arbitrarily to a value larger than $t_{graceperiod}$. Experiments show that choosing a significantly higher value, $t_{maxsessionlength} = 1000\,\mathrm{s}$, does not change the estimated average number of requests per flow significantly.

Table 2. Number of responses observed on the default resolvers and estimated from 3rd party resolvers. Notice that the DoH number should be considered an upper bound.

	UDP	TCP	DoT	DoH	Sum
Default	$15,2 \cdot 10^9$	$10,9 \cdot 10^6$	$446 \cdot 10^6$	0	
	87,67%	0,06%	2,57%	0%	90,31%
3rd party	$1,46 \cdot 10^9$	$60,3 \cdot 10^6$	$73,2 \cdot 10^6$	$92,3 \cdot 10^6$	
	8,39%	0,35%	0,42%	0,53%	9,69%

The estimated 3rd party DNS resolver traffic is summarized in Table 2 in comparison to the amount of traffic at Telenor Denmark's default DNS resolvers. As Telenor Denmark's default DNS resolvers do not offer DoH service, the 3rd party DoH number is calculated by assuming that $\hat{R}_{DoH} = \hat{R}_{DoT}$.

Note that the estimated number of DNS responses from 3rd party resolvers listed in Table 2 also include responses for servers that could not be explicitly identified as either authoritative or resolving. This is applicable to approximately 0,79% of the listed responses from 3rd party resolvers.

Some customers use VPN services for connecting to their employer's VPN gateway or for keeping the traffic private. We consider it most likely that such traffic will use the 3rd party resolvers operated by the VPN gateway operator, that this operator is located outside Telenor Denmark's network, and that the DNS traffic is therefore not visible in the data set used for this study. Although a study of how widespread the use of VPN services is could be interesting, we consider it complementary to the scope of this paper.

The first question posed in the introduction (RQ1) asks to which extent the DNS traffic is directed at 3rd party resolvers. In Table 2 it can be seen that the fraction of the total DNS traffic that is directed at 3rd party resolvers is estimated to be between $9,69 - 0,79 = 8,90\%$ and $9,69\%$. These results are in line with the 7–11% measured by Callejo et al. [3].

4 Prevalence of Filtering 3rd Party Resolvers

The second research question (RQ2) asks to which extent 3rd party resolvers that offer desirable filtering services (such as malware filtering or parental control features) are used. In this section, the data presented in Sect. 3.5 is further enriched by adding information about which organisation runs the resolver, whether the resolver is public or private, and whether or not the resolvers are advertised by the owners as filtering.

4.1 Method

To identify if a 3rd party resolver is private or public, two methods are used:

- The resolver is queried with a popular domain name. If this query returns the correct result, the resolver is considered public. If no response is received, the server is considered private.
- If the owner of the resolver is known to only run private resolvers, the resolver is marked as private. These include the resolvers of other ISPs, some VPN services, as well as commercial DNS resolver companies known for only providing private services.

To identify the owner of a resolver, simple methods such as resolving the PTR record of the server, performing a Google or Whois search, are used. The owner's web page is then used to determine if the resolver offers filtering functionality.

Some DNS resolvers exist with the purpose of enabling the user to circumvent some restrictions put in place by web site owners, such as enabling the user to view TV shows that are only broadcasted in some countries due to copyright restrictions. Some, but not all, of these resolvers are associated with VPN services. For the purpose of this paper, we consider these as non-filtering resolvers, as actively choosing these resolvers is conceptually more similar to trying to avoid censorship, than to desire additional filtering.

Another category of resolvers are those that are associated with DNS hijacking malware that changes the DNS resolver settings on a device to point to a resolver under control of a malicious party. This resolver will then most likely manipulate the DNS response to achieve the purpose of the malicious actor. For the purpose of this paper, we consider these resolvers non-filtering, as they are unlikely to perform any kind of filtering that is considered desirable by the user.

4.2   Measurements and Discussion

The result of identifying server owner, advertised filtering features and private/public category is summarized in Table 3. Unknown filtering status represents that we were not able to identify the owner/operator of the resolver. Unknown public/private status is typically caused by the server sending back a wrong answer or an error, such as REFUSED, NXDOMAIN or SERVFAIL.

Table 3. Categorization of 3rd party DNS responses.

	Public	Private	Unknown	Sum
Filtering	$202 \cdot 10^6$	$6,41 \cdot 10^6$	$101 \cdot 10^3$	
	12,02%	0,38%	0,01%	12,41%
Non-filtering	$1,37 \cdot 10^9$	$53,5 \cdot 10^6$	$204 \cdot 10^3$	
	81,11%	3,18%	0,01%	84,30%
Unknown	$16,0 \cdot 10^6$	$26,4 \cdot 10^6$	$12,9 \cdot 10^6$	
	0,95%	1,57%	0,77%	3,29%

A key finding is that between 12,41% and 12,41,3,29 = 15,70% of traffic for 3rd party resolvers is for filtering resolvers. This suggests that malware filtering, etc., is not likely to be the primary motivation for using 3rd party resolvers.

In Sect. 3.5, it was concluded that the amount of 3rd party resolver responses is between 8,90% and 9,69% of all responses. In other words, the total fraction of responses that originate from filtering DNS resolvers is between $8,90\% \cdot 12,41\% = 1,10\%$ and $9,69\% \cdot 15,70\% = 1,52\%$, which answers the second research question. This shows that the use of filtering resolvers is not prevalent among Telenor Denmark's customers.

5   Censorship Avoidance Detection

The third question posed in the introduction (RQ3) asks if 3rd party resolvers are used to circumvent censorship. It is a prerequisite that the ISP's default DNS servers censor some domains based on national legal requirements, and that these are not censored by 3rd party resolvers. This section presents a method that uses ISP data to estimate how many DNS responses for censored domains are sent by 3rd party resolvers, and the results obtained by applying the method.

5.1   Method

As elaborated in Sect. 2, the censorship focuses on web domain names, and in contrast to the two previous sections that considered flows related to DNS servers, this section focuses on flows related to web servers only.

The core idea of the estimation method is to categorize the web flows seen in NetFlow records, use this categorization to estimate the fraction of the web flows that are towards censored sites, and then use this number of web flows to estimate the number of related DNS queries at 3rd party resolvers for censored domains. The categorization of flows is illustrated in Table 4 and elaborated in the following paragraphs. The lowercase w_1 to w_{12} represent the count of the flows within each category, and the uppercase W_1 to W_{12} represents the sets of flows within each category.

Table 4. Categorization of the set of all web flows, W.

				Default	3rd par.	None
W	Tainted	Shared	Censored dom.	$W_1 = \emptyset$	W_5	$W_9 = \emptyset$
			Non-censored dom.	W_2	W_6	W_{10}
		Non-Shared	Censored dom.	$W_3 = \emptyset$	W_7	$W_{11} = \emptyset$
	Non-Tainted		(Non-censored dom.)	W_4	W_8	W_{12}

The (uncensored) A records of all the censored domains contain a number of IP addresses, which will be referred to as tainted IP addresses. Some of the tainted IP addresses are assigned to servers that serve both censored and non-censored domains, and these addresses will be referred to as shared IP addresses. Flows relating to these servers are in categories W_1, W_2, W_5, W_6, W_9 and W_{10}). Conversely, some servers with tainted IP addresses only serve censored domains (no non-censored domains), and the IP addresses of these servers are referred to as non-shared IPs. Flows relating to these servers are in categories W_3, W_7 and W_{11}. Finally, the web flows that do not relate to any server IP found in the A record of any censored domain are referred to as non-tainted (categories W_4, W_8 and W_{18}). Some web flows are created following a DNS lookup at the default resolver (categories W_1 to W_4 in Table 4), some web flows are created following a DNS lookup at a 3rd party resolver (W_5 to W_8), and some web flows are created without any preceding DNS lookup (W_9 to W_{12}).

As queries for censored domains towards the default DNS server result in a censored response, such queries will not cause a subsequent flow to be created to the web server, therefore by definition $W_1 = \emptyset$ and $W_3 = \emptyset$. As the censoring is based on domain names only, we find it reasonable to assume that flows towards censored sites must be preceded by a DNS lookup, therefore in addition $W_9 = \emptyset$ and $W_{11} = \emptyset$. The number of flows towards censored sites created after a DNS lookup to a 3rd party resolver would be $w_5 + w_7$, and this is the interesting number to estimate.

By definition all web servers are located on the outside of the NetFlow boundary, and all clients on the inside of the NetFlow boundary. The set of relevant flows, W, is found using two criteria: First, only records relating to server TCP/UDP port 80 or 443 are considered. Second, only servers for which traffic both from and to the server is observed are considered, although the to/from traffic can relate to different flows to mitigate the effects of NetFlow sampling, following the same arguments as for DNS flows in Sect. 3.1. Flows are thereafter defined by aggregating NetFlow records by 5-tuple on a daily basis, and timestamped with the earliest timestamp on that day.

To estimate $w_5 + w_7$, the following steps are needed. Please refer to Table 4 for an overview of the different flow categories. An initial step is to identify the set of tainted and the set of shared IP addresses:

- T_{ip}: Let T_{ip}, the set of tainted IPs, be the set of DNS A record IPs returned by doing a DNS lookup towards a non-censoring DNS resolver of all the censored domains.
- S_{ip}: Let R_{ip} denote the set of IP addresses found in the Rdata field of A records of all responses from the default resolvers. As this because of the censoring will not include any non-shared IPs, R_{ip} thus contains all the non-tainted and all the shared IP addresses. The set of shared IP addresses, S_{ip}, can then be found as the subset of the tainted addresses, T_{ip}, that are also found in R_{ip}, $S_{ip} = T_{ip} \ltimes R_{ip}$.

These two IP address sets are then used split the full set of web flows W into sets of tainted, non-tainted, shared and non-shared flows corresponding to the four main categories (T, NT, S, NS) in Table 4:

- T and NT: Split the full set of flows, W, into the set of tainted flows $T = W_1 \cup W_2 \cup W_3 \cup W_5 \cup W_6 \cup W_7 \cup W_9 \cup W_{10} \cup W_{11}$ and the set of non-tainted flows $NT = W_4 \cup W_8 \cup W_{12}$. These can be determined based on whether or not one of the flow IP addresses can be found in T_{ip} such that $T = W \ltimes T_{ip}, NT = W \triangleright T_{ip}$.
- S: Find the set of shared flows, $S = w_1 \cup w_2 \cup w_5 \cup w_6 \cup w_9 \cup w_{10}$. This can be found using T as a tainted flow address is shared, if the server IP can be found in the default DNS responses, $S = T \ltimes S_{ip}$.
- $NS = W_7$: Find the number of non-shared (and by definition, censored) flows preceded by a 3rd party DNS lookup, W_7, by finding the total number of non-shared flows, NS, and exploiting that $W_3 = \emptyset$ and $W_{11} = \emptyset$. $NS = W_7$ can be found using T as a tainted flow address is non-shared, if the server IP can not be found in the default DNS responses, $W_7 = NS = T \triangleright S_{ip} = T - S$.

The set of shared flows, S, consists of two subsets of flows, related to censored domains, $W5$, and non-censored domains, $W_2 \cup W_6 \cup W_{10}$. The next steps of the method focus on identifying which flows belong to which of these two subsets by various means. For this purpose, the concept of flow renaming will be used several times to determine which web flows are associated with which DNS responses. In our paper, flows and DNS responses are considered associated, if a flow is created no longer than θ minutes after the DNS lookup, if the client IP addresses match, and if the server IP of the flow is the IP found in the Rdata record of the DNS response. The effect of DNS caching at the user is assumed to be mitigated by the aggregation of flow records to the earliest timestamp during a specific day as mentioned above.

- W_2: Find the set of tainted, shared, non-censored flows preceded by a DNS lookup at the default servers, W_2. As $W_1 = \emptyset$ and $W_3 = \emptyset$ this can be found by renaming the flows of S by using all entries in the DNS response log, D, such that $W_2 = S \ltimes_\theta D$. The same method can in theory be applied to the set of non-tainted flows, NT, to find the untainted set W_4. However, the amount of data can be large, and the following steps therefore do not depend on the feasibility in practice of using renaming to distinguish between W_4 and $W_8 \cup W_{12}$.
- $w_6 + w_{10}$: The fraction of re-nameable flows within the non-tainted flow set and within the non-censored flow set is assumed to be the same, as none of these flows are censored. Therefore, $\frac{w_6+w_{10}}{w_2} = \frac{w_8+w_{12}}{w_4}$, where $w_6 + w_{10}$ is then easily found as w_2 is already known. Although W_4, W_8 and W_{12} cannot be identified (as elaborated above), the ratio $\frac{w_8+w_{12}}{w_4}$ can be found by renaming a sampled set of non-tainted flows, $\frac{w_8+w_{12}}{w_4} = \frac{w_{8_s}+w_{12_s}}{w_{4_s}} = \frac{nt_s-w_{4_s}}{w_{4_s}}$ where $sample(NT) = NT_s = W_{4_s} \cup W_{8_s} \cup W_{12_s}$, $W_{4_s} = NT_s \ltimes_\theta D$.
- w_5: Find the number of shared, censored flows preceded by a 3rd party DNS lookup, w_5, by subtraction: $w_5 = s - (w_2 + w_6 + w_{10})$.

These steps provide the necessary values to calculate $w_5 + w_7$ which is the estimated number of flows towards censored sites that are associated with a DNS lookup to a 3rd party resolver.

Flow renaming is performed in the steps for finding W_2 and $w_6 + w_{10}$, and we consider this mechanism to be the largest cause of uncertainty to the result. The method as used in this paper is greedy in the sense that too many flows will be considered re-nameable and therefore as non-censored, both because flows and DNS responses are considered related based on a time interval (larger time interval is more greedy), but also because user IP addresses are anonymized by truncation. Therefore, the estimated value of $w_5 + w_7$ should be considered as the lower boundary of the real value. As shown in a later subsection, the estimation of the lower boundary instead of the actual value turns out to be a sufficient metric to support our conclusions.

The next step is to calculate the number of estimated, actual DNS responses, $\hat{p}$, that relate to the estimated, observed, flows $w_5 + w_7$. The techniques described in Sect. 2 for estimating the actual number of flows based on the observed number of flows are not applicable in this case, as they depend on the availability of NetFlow records and not just the availability of an estimated flow count. Instead, we propose to identify all servers for which only port 80/443 flows are observed, let w_{web} denote the number of flows towards these servers and let p_{web} denote the count of DNS responses with an A record containing the IP addresses of these servers. Then we will estimate the number of DNS responses related to the censored flows as $\hat{p} = \frac{p_{web}}{w_{web}}(w_5 + w_7)$. As the value of $w_5 + w_7$ is considered a lower boundary, the value of $\hat{p}$ should also be considered a lower boundary.

5.2 Measurements and Discussion

The estimation method detailed above is applied to DNS and NetFlow data from Telenor Denmark's network collected over a period of 4 days from 2021-09-23 to 2021-09-26. The most interesting metrics are summarized in Table 5. 1:1000 of the non-tainted flows are used to estimate $w_6 + w_{10}$. Results for two different values, $\theta = 1$ min and $\theta = 60$ min, of the time interval allowed in the renaming process are presented in order to illustrate the importance of this parameter as discussed above. A $\theta > 60$ min does not give significantly different results.

In summary, we estimate that at least $\hat{p} = 477 \cdot 10^3$ DNS responses for censored domains have been answered by 3rd party DNS resolvers. This number can be compared to the number of censored DNS responses served by the default resolvers, $44,6 \cdot 10^3$, and the ratio between these numbers is $r = 10,7$.

Table 5. Metrics for censorship evasion estimation.

Metric	Symbol	Count	
Relevant flows	w	$1,03 \cdot 10^9$	
Shared flows	s	$196 \cdot 10^3$	
Non-shared flows	$ns = w_7$	$7,40 \cdot 10^3$	
Ratio of responses and flows	$\frac{p_{web}}{w_{web}}$	$18,1$	
Censored responses at default DNS resolvers	$d_{censored}$	$44,6 \cdot 10^3$	
Renaming interval	θ	1 min	60 min
Shared, non-censored flows preceded by default lookup	w_2	$103 \cdot 10^3$	$166 \cdot 10^3$
Shared, non-cens. flows not preceded by def. lookup	$w_6 + w_{10}$	$28,0 \cdot 10^3$	$11,1 \cdot 10^3$
Shared, censored flows preceded by 3rd party lookup	w_5	$65,5 \cdot 10^3$	$19,0 \cdot 10^3$
Estimated DNS responses related to censored flows	$\hat{p}$	$1,32 \cdot 10^6$	$477 \cdot 10^3$
Ratio of censored responses at default and 3rd party	r	$29,6$	$10,7$

Section 3.5 concluded that approximately 9% of the total DNS traffic was from 3rd party resolvers. If 3rd party resolvers were not used to circumvent censorship, it would be expected that $r \approx 0,09$. Censored 3rd party resolver responses are therefore at least two orders of magnitude more prevalent than expected, which suggests that 3rd party DNS resolvers are chosen to circumvent censorship. It is more challenging to consider if censorship circumvention is the *primary* reason for a user to choose a 3rd party resolver. Hypothetically, even if this was the only reason for choosing 3rd party resolvers, the number of censored domains would still only be a small fraction of the total responses, as individual users will then also use the 3rd party resolver for non-censored domains.

As the number of censored responses from 3rd party servers is only an estimated number, it is not possible to assess how many users resolve censored domains using this method either. Even if this was possible, it would not be meaningful to compare this number of users to the number of users receiving censored responses from the default resolvers, without knowing more about the intentions of these users. One may argue that all of the responses from the default servers are caused by unintentional web page visits that will not be repeated by a user, whereas all the responses from the 3rd party servers could be caused by deliberate web page visits that will most likely be repeated by the user.

Although the results in this paper are based on only a single dataset, we find that the methods are independent of the dataset, and that the temporal length of the dataset is sufficient to present valid results for Telenor Denmark. We fully recognize that using the dataset of another ISP in another country could yield different results, both for technical reasons (such as differences in default DNS resolver setup) and cultural reasons (desire to circumvent censorship etc.).

6 Conclusion

In this paper we propose a method for estimating the amount of TCP/UDP/ DoT/DoH DNS responses by using information from NetFlow records. This method is applied to estimate how much of the DNS traffic in an ISP is from 3rd party resolvers instead of the ISP's default resolvers. Using data from Telenor Denmark it is concluded that 8,9–9,7% of the total DNS traffic is from 3rd party resolvers (RQ1). This result supports and is supported by the most recent related work that uses a completely different method for obtaining the results [3]. Also, it is concluded that 1,1–1,5% of the total DNS traffic is from filtering resolvers (RQ2). Although it is expected that some traffic is from filtering resolvers, the specific number is not quantified by any existing research that we are aware of. The low number suggests that filtering resolvers are not commonly used by Telenor's customers, and this could represent an unexploited business opportunity to promote the use of such services.

Furthermore, we propose a NetFlow based method for estimating the amount of DNS responses from 3rd party resolvers that would have been censored by the ISP's default DNS resolvers. Using data from Telenor Denmark, it is concluded that DNS responses for censored domains are at least two orders of magnitude more prevalent at 3rd party resolvers than at the ISP's default resolvers (RQ3). We are not aware of any related work quantifying this number on an ISP scale. The high number suggests that 3rd party resolvers are actively chosen in order to circumvent censorship, which should be considered when the censorship legislation is up for evaluation.

It is correct that we only rely on a single dataset, however, we believe that the methods are independent of the dataset, and that the single dataset used is sufficiently large to present valid results for the specific ISP. We fully recognize that using the dataset of another ISP in another country could yield different results. This is, however, more likely attributed to cultural differences (knowledge about cyber security in the population, the desire/need to circumvent censorship in a particular country, etc.) rather than the merits of the presented method.

The focus of this paper is purely technical, however for future work it could be interesting to compare the obtained results with a user questionnaire asking for the user's primary motivation for actively choosing 3rd party servers.

Although the specific results presented in this paper applies only to Telenor Denmark's customers, the methods are general, and it is our hope that they will be used by other ISPs and organisations to identify both business opportunities and regulatory challenges.

References

1. Ager, B., Mühlbauer, W., Smaragdakis, G., Uhlig, S.: Comparing DNS resolvers in the wild. IMC: ACM SIGCOMM conference on Internet measurement (2010). http://dx.doi.org/10.1145/1879141.1879144
2. Antunes, N., Pipiras, V., Jacinto, G.: Regularized inversion of flow size distribution. INFOCOM: IEEE Conference on Computer Communications (2019). https://doi.org/10.1109/INFOCOM.2019.8737406
3. Callejo, P., Cuevas, R., Vallina-Rodriguez, N., Rumin, Á.C.: Measuring the global recursive DNS infrastructure: a view from the edge. IEEE Access **7**, 168020–168028 (2019). https://doi.org/10.1109/ACCESS.2019.2950325
4. Cisco: Cisco Umbrella Privacy data sheet (2021). https://trustportal.cisco.com/c/dam/r/ctp/docs/privacydatasheet/security/umbrella-privacy-data-sheet.pdf
5. Cloudflare: 1.1.1.1 Public DNS Resolver (2020). https://developers.cloudflare.com/1.1.1.1/privacy/public-dns-resolver
6. Danish Ministry of Justice: Lov om ændring af retsplejeloven og forskellige andre love (2017). https://www.retsinformation.dk/eli/ft/201612L00192
7. Duffield, N., Lund, C., Thorup, M.: Properties and prediction of flow statistics from sampled packet streams. IMW: ACM SIGCOMM Internet Measurement Workshop (2002). https://doi.org/10.1145/637201.637225
8. Farnan, O., Darer, A., Wright, J.: Analysing censorship circumvention with VPNs via DNS cache snooping. In: IEEE Security and Privacy Workshops (SPW) (2019). http://dx.doi.org/10.1109/SPW.2019.00046
9. Fejrskov, M., Pedersen, J.M., Vasilomanolakis, E.: Cyber-security research by ISPs: a NetFlow and DNS anonymization policy. In: International Conference on Cyber Security And Protection Of Digital Services (2020). https://doi.org/10.1109/CyberSecurity49315.2020.9138869

10. Florio, A.D., Verde, N.V., Villani, A., Vitali, D., Mancini, L.V.: Bypassing censorship: a proven tool against the recent Internet censorship in Turkey. In: IEEE International Symposium on Software Reliability Engineering Workshops (2014). https://doi.org/10.1109/ISSREW.2014.93
11. Google: Your privacy (2021). https://developers.google.com/speed/public-dns/privacy
12. Hubert, A., van Mook, R.: RFC 5452: measures for making DNS more resilient against forged answers (2009). https://datatracker.ietf.org/doc/html/rfc5452
13. Khormali, A., Park, J., Alasmary, H., Anwar, A., Mohaisen, D.: Domain name system security and privacy: a contemporary survey. Comput. Netw. **185**, 107699 (2021). https://doi.org/10.1016/j.comnet.2020.107699
14. Konopa, M., et al.: Using machine learning for DNS over HTTPS detection. In: European Conference on Cyber Warfare and Security (2020). http://dx.doi.org/10.34190/EWS.20.001
15. Pearce, P., et al.: Global measurement of DNS manipulation. In: USENIX Security Symposium (2017). https://www.usenix.org/system/files/conference/usenixsecurity17/sec17-pearce.pdf
16. Quad9: Data Privacy Policy (2021). https://www.quad9.net/privacy/policy/
17. Radu, R., Hausding, M.: Consolidation in the DNS resolver market - how much, how fast, how dangerous? J. Cyber Policy (2019). https://doi.org/10.1080/23738871.2020.1722191
18. Reddy.K, T., Wing, D., Patil, P.: RFC 8094: DNS over datagram transport layer security (DTLS) (2017). https://www.rfc-editor.org/rfc/rfc8094.html
19. Roberts, H., Zuckerman, E., York, J., Faris, R., Palfrey, J.: 2010 circumvention tool usage report. The Berkman Center for Internet & Society (2010). https://cyber.harvard.edu/sites/cyber.harvard.edu/files/2010_Circumvention_Tool_Usage_Report.pdf
20. Sivaraman, M., Kerr, S., Song, L.: DNS message fragments (2016). https://www.ietf.org/staging/draft-muks-dnsop-dns-message-fragments-00.txt
21. Telecom Industry Association Denmark: Blokeringer (2021). https://www.teleindu.dk/brancheholdninger/blokeringer-pa-nettet/
22. The Danish Rights Alliance: Report On Share With Care 2 (2020). https://rettighedsalliancen.dk/wp-content/uploads/2020/06/Report-On-Share-With-Care-2_Final.pdf
23. The ICANN Security and Stability Advisory Committee (SSAC): SAC 032 - Preliminary Report on DNS Response Modification (2008). https://www.icann.org/en/system/files/files/sac-032-en.pdf
24. Trevisan, M., Drago, I., Mellia, M., Munafò, M.M.: Automatic detection of DNS manipulations. In: IEEE International Conference on Big Data (2017). https://doi.org/10.1109/BigData.2017.8258415
25. Yandex: Terms of use of the Yandex.DNS service (2021). https://yandex.com/legal/dns_termsofuse/

RAAM: A Restricted Adversarial Attack Model with Adding Perturbations to Traffic Features

Peishuai Sun[1,2], Shuhao Li[1,2(✉)], Jiang Xie[1,2], Hongbo Xu[1,2], Zhenyu Cheng[1,2], and Rui Qin[1,2]

[1] Institute of Information Engineering, Chinese Academy of Sciences, Beijing, China
{sunpeishuai,lishuhao,xiejiang,xuhongbo,chengzhenyu,qinrui}@iie.ac.cn
[2] School of Cyber Security, University of Chinese Academy of Sciences, Beijing, China

Abstract. In recent years, intrusion detection system (IDS) based on machine learning (ML) algorithms has developed rapidly. However, ML algorithms are easily attacked by adversarial examples, and many attackers add perturbations to features of malicious traffic to escape ML-based IDSs. Unfortunately, most attack methods add perturbations without sufficient restrictions, generating unpractical adversarial examples. In this paper, we propose *RAAM*, a restricted adversarial attack model with adding perturbations to traffic features, which escapes ML-based IDSs. *RAAM* employs the improved loss to enhance the adversarial effect uses regularizer and masking vectors to restrict perturbations. Compared with previous work, *RAAM* can generate adversarial examples with superior characteristics: regularization, maliciousness and small perturbation. We conduct experiments on the well-known NSL-KDD dataset, and test on nine different ML-based IDSs. Experimental results show that the mean evasion increase rate (*EIR*) of *RAAM* is 94.1% in multiple attacks, which is 9.2% higher than the best of related methods, *DIGFuPAS*. Especially, adversarial examples generated by *RAAM* have lower perturbations, and the mean distance of perturbations (L_2) is 1.79, which is 0.81 lower than *DIGFuPAS*. In addition, we retrain IDSs with adversarial examples to improve their robustness. Experimental results show that retrained IDSs not only maintain the ability of detection for original examples, but also are hard to be attacked again.

Keywords: Adversarial attack · Machine learning · Intrusion detection system

1 Introduction

An Intrusion Detection System (IDS) is typically placed in a network to monitor traffic and detect malicious activity. It classifies traffic into different categories based on features, and reports malicious results to the network administrator. Traditional IDSs use rules to detect malicious traffic, but their efficiency

© IFIP International Federation for Information Processing 2022
Published by Springer Nature Switzerland AG 2022
W. Meng et al. (Eds.): SEC 2022, IFIP AICT 648, pp. 126–141, 2022.
https://doi.org/10.1007/978-3-031-06975-8_8

and generalization cannot adapt to constantly changing attack patterns. Fortunately, with the development of artificial intelligence, many machine learning (ML) algorithms have been proposed for IDSs. Usually, features of network traffic are extracted, and models are trained offline based on ML algorithms. Then the trained models are deployed on IDSs for online detection. Researches show that ML-based IDSs have stronger generalization and accuracy.

Although ML algorithms are widely used in various fields, some researchers find that ML algorithms have low robustness. In computer vision, Szegedy et al. [1] firstly propose the concept of adversarial examples. They find that only small perturbations on original images can mislead the ML system to wrongly classify images that humans easily classify correctly. Since then, lots of adversarial attack methods have been proposed in various fields [13,14,16–18]. However, these methods are not applicable for network traffic analysis. The traffic is composed of a discrete bytes stream. Compared with images, traffic is not differentiable. In addition, network protocols have very complex rules, and minor traffic changes can easily cause a protocol session to fail. Therefore, researchers focus on features of traffic, and generate adversarial features rather than actual traffic.

Generative Adversarial Network (GAN) [20] is trained through the adversarial game of the generator and the discriminator to generate more realistic and credible examples. The goal of the generator is to learn generating examples that can escape the detection of the discriminator. On the contrary, the discriminator is to distinguish between examples from original and generated data. Many researchers apply it to the generation of adversarial examples due to the strong ability of generation. Lin et al. [4] first use GAN to generate adversarial features of traffic for attacking IDSs, and get a high evasion increase rate (EIR). However, like most adversarial attacks methods, they do not restrict attacks insufficiently. This can make adversarial examples ineffective and unpractical.

In the paper, we employ GAN to generate perturbations. Different from previous work, we do not directly add perturbations to traffic features as adversarial examples. In particular, we have strict restrictions on adversarial attacks to ensure the authenticity of adversarial examples. Our main contributions are as follows:

- We propose a restricted adversarial attack model called *RAAM*. It mainly includes the following parts: (1) WGAN [19] for generating perturbations, (2) masking vectors for keeping the functional features unchanged, (3) regularizer R for controlling the distance of perturbations. Experimental results show that adversarial examples generated by *RAAM* have small perturbations due to the constraints it imposes on attack traffic.
- We employ the improved loss for WGAN. In particular, it does not simply imitate features of benign traffic, but search blind spots and boundary of ML-based IDSs. Experimental results show that generated adversarial examples by *RAAM* can attack ML-based IDSs better than previous methods.
- We design a prototype system based on *RAAM*, and conduct adversarial attack experiments on the well-known NSL-KDD dataset [21]. *RAAM* attacks

nine ML-based IDSs (MLP, RNN, SVM *et al.*), and the mean *EIR* is 94.10%, which is 9.2% higher than the advanced attack method, *DIGFuPAS* [6]. The mean L_2 is 1.79, which is 0.81 lower than *DIGFuPAS*. In addition, we use *RAAM* to enhance the robustness of IDSs. Simply put, *RAAM* generates adversarial examples to retrain IDSs for defending adversarial attacks. Experiments show that the retrained IDSs not only maintain the ability to detect the original examples but also are hard to be attacked.

The remainder of this paper is organized as follows. Section 2 introduces the related work. In Sect. 3, we analyze scene and motivation of adversarial attacks. Methodology is proposed in Sect. 4. Subsequently, in Sect. 5, we evaluate our method and show the relevant experimental results. Finally, we discuss and summarize in Sect. 6 and Sect. 7, respectively.

2   Related Work

In the field of network traffic, IDSs are always a hot issue because of the complexity and variability of attack and defense adversary. In recent years, IDSs based on ML algorithms emerge gradually [9–12]. Their performance is recognized by academia and industry. However, some researchers find that ML algorithms have low robustness and are easily confused by adversarial attacks. Based on different scenes, we divide adversarial attacks into white-box and black-box.

2.1   White-Box Adversarial Attack

A white-box adversarial attack means that attackers know all the parameters and structures of ML models, and can attack pointedly. Aiken and Scott-Hayward [2] propose a method to escape the detection of ML algorithms in distributed denial of service (DDoS). They select three features to add perturbations, and successfully reduce the detection rate of IDSs from 100% to 0%. However, their method only focuses on DDoS attacks without discussing other classes of attacks, and the selected features are relatively single.

Huang *et al.* [3] conduct adversarial experiments on three deep learning (DL) algorithms. They mainly use three measures: fast gradient sign method (FGSM), jacobian-based saliency map attack (JSMA), and JSMA reverse (JSMA-RE) [14, 15]. The generated scanning traffic is highly adversarial to IDSs. However, they do not restrict adversarial examples, which means that the generated examples are illegal.

Hashemi *et al.* [8] generate adversarial features and then transform them into actual traffic space. It is the first time that they legally modify network traffic to escape IDSs.

However, it is difficult to realize in practice, since attackers cannot completely know the information of model. Corresponding to the white-box, the black-box attack is more realistic.

2.2   Black-Box Adversarial Attack

A black-box adversarial attack means that attackers know nothing about structures of ML model, including training parameters, and defense methods, *etc.* Attackers can only interact with the target model through output results. Han *et al.* [7] generate practical adversarial traffic in the black-box scene. They consider the cost of attacks and use adversarial machine learning techniques to search for features located at the decision boundary of the ML model. However, they only use GAN to select features instead of generating, and the adversarial performance is relatively weak.

Recently, GAN is a popular method for adversarial attacks. Lin *et al.* [4] are the first to propose an adversarial model based on GAN to attack IDSs, called *IDSGAN*. *IDSGAN* is divided into three parts: an IDS as the attacked black-box model, a discriminator as a classification model to learn the black-box model, and a generator as the generation model to generate adversarial malicious examples. Experiments show that adversarial examples generated by *IDSGAN* can significantly reduce the detection rate of IDSs.

However, Usama *et al.* [5] point out that *IDSGAN* modifies two functional features of network traffic, which makes the generated traffic invalid. They make improvements on the basis of *IDSGAN* to ensure that all modified features are nonfunctional, and functional features remain the same. However, the original GAN used by Usama *et al.* has no obvious effect on IDSs, and the detection rate of IDSs does not drop significantly.

Duy *et al.* [6] propose an improved framework based on WGAN, called *DIG-FuPAS*. They also modify the nonfunctional features for malicious traffic, and use three different inputs to compare the performance of generating examples. In addition, they conduct experiments on multiple datasets to prove the versatility and generalization of the *DIGFuPAS*. At the end of the paper, IDSs and adversarial models are repeatedly trained to achieve a dynamic balance between attack and defense. However, they do not consider the attack cost, which means that adversarial examples are restricted.

In general, adversarial attacks achieve excellent attack effects, but they lack enough restriction on adversarial attack models, which can cause invalid. In addition, the black-box scene is more generic than the white-box. Therefore, we propose a restricted adversarial attack model in the black-box scene.

3   Scene and Motivation

3.1   The Adversarial Attack Scene

In this paper, we focus on generating adversarial examples to escape IDSs. We attack ML-based IDSs in the black-box scene by adding perturbations to traffic features.

Targeting ML-Based IDSs: IDSs do not detect the actual traffic because the traffic data is very complex with unstructured data. Usually, ML-based IDSs extract features of traffic to classify. The target of attacks is ML models. Specially, we will visually describe in Sect. 3.2 how attackers exploit flaws of ML models to attack.

Perturbations in Traffic Features: In the network traffic field, the adversarial attack is a difficult task. Different from other fields such as computer vision, images are continuously differentiable data and can be tampered with arbitrarily. However, traffic data is a discrete byte stream and is not differentiable. It is not feasible to directly use a gradient-based attack method on network traffic. Therefore, we attack based on the features of traffic. More precisely, we add perturbations to the features extracted from malicious traffic. If the adversarial features can attack ML models successfully, traffic with these features can also escape IDSs.

In Black-Box Scene: As mentioned in Sect. 2, we conduct adversarial attacks in the black-box scene. It is plug-and-play to attack any ML-based IDS.

3.2   Visual Description

We explain this process of attacks for a more visual description in Fig. 1. As shown in Fig. 1(a), triangles represent malicious examples, crosses represent benign examples, and two types of examples are separated by the line, which represents the decision boundary of a ML-based IDS. Attackers can add perturbations to malicious examples to escape the IDS.

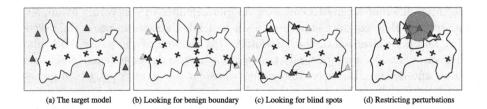

(a) The target model   (b) Looking for benign boundary   (c) Looking for blind spots   (d) Restricting perturbations

Fig. 1. Adversarial attack scene.

Looking for Benign Boundary: Obviously, mapping malicious examples completely into benign feature space is definitely able to attack any model. However, malicious and benign examples are fundamentally different, so they cannot have exactly the same features. As shown in Fig. 1(b), attackers can make it imitate benign examples and find the boundary of the ML-based IDS.

Looking for Blind Spots: In general, ML-based IDSs have weak robustness. Specifically, only part of high probability regions of examples are sufficiently trained, but low probability regions of examples are ignored. We call low probability regions blind spots of ML models, as shown in Fig. 1(c). Attackers can generate adversarial examples by exploring these blind spots of the model.

Restricting Perturbations: Attacks can not be unrestricted to avoid destroying the characteristic of malicious examples. Therefore, the perturbations of adversarial examples should be as small as possible, as shown in Fig. 1(d). It is necessary to keep adversarial examples within a small range.

In summary, attackers look for the boundary and blind spots of ML-based IDSs on a small scale, and generate adversarial examples to escape detection.

3.3 Motivation

In the previous related work, adversarial examples can usually achieve a high *EIR*. However, most adversarial examples lack sufficient restrictions. In particular, we summarize three following important characteristics of adversarial examples.

Regularization: Regularization means that adversarial examples should not violate rules of network protocols. For example, the length of traffic packets cannot exceed the maximum range specified by the protocol specification, and the protocol type of traffic packets is unchangeable.

Maliciousness: Maliciousness means that adversarial examples cannot destroy their functional features. For instance, for DoS attack traffic, the number of downstream bytes (from destination to source) should be much larger than the number of upstream bytes. If the preceding features are not met, DoS attack traffic losses maliciousness. Therefore, these functional features should remain the same.

Small Perturbation: Small perturbation means that adversarial examples should be sufficiently similar compared with original malicious examples. Features can not be modified without restriction. For example, attackers modify the packet sending frequency and packet lengths to attack. However, excessive perturbation can result in traffic packets being invalid.

In light of this, we restrict adversarial attacks so that adversarial examples not only have a high *EIR*, but also keep regularization, maliciousness and small perturbation.

4 Methodology

In this section, we describe the adversarial attacks with formula. Then the restricted adversarial attack model *RAAM* is introduced.

4.1 Math Description

As we describe in Sect. 3.3, attackers should keep adversarial examples regularization, maliciousness and small perturbation. Specifically, the ML model is defined as f, the input as x, and the output as $f(x)$. As shown in Eq. 1, for an adversarial attack, results of the model $f(x)$ should be misled by adding perturbations δ as small as possible. R represents the restriction for adversarial examples to ensure matching actual traffic features.

$$argmin_\delta \ f(R(x + \delta)) \neq f(x) \qquad (1)$$

4.2   Model Architecture

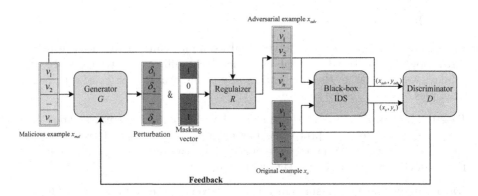

Fig. 2. The architecture of $RAAM$ based on WGAN.

Overview. We briefly introduce our restricted adversarial attack model, $RAAM$, which is based on WGAN to solve the problem of unstable GAN training. As shown in Fig. 2, $RAAM$ is mainly consisted of three components: a generator G, a discriminator D and a black-box IDS. First, the input of G is the original malicious example x_{mal} which is consisted of feature vector v_i, and the output is the perturbation δ. Then, δ is added to x_{mal} for generating the adversarial example x_{adv}. Specially, we come up with the masking vector and regularizer R to restrict δ and keep regularization, maliciousness and small perturbation. What's more, x_{adv} and the original example x_o including the original benign example and the original malicious example is input into the black-box IDS to get the label y. Finally, the example and the label are input to D for training. D imitates the detection ability of the IDS, while games with G through feedback.

Generator G. The generator G is a neural network for generation. It generates the perturbation δ with the same dimensions of the original example. However, as we discussed in Sect. 3.3, not all features of the example can be changed, and functional features should keep the same to maintain maliciousness. Therefore, the perturbation δ is multiplied by the masking vector composed of 0 and 1 as shown in Eq. 2, so that perturbation vectors δ_i of functional features are zeros.

$$\delta_i' = \begin{cases} 0, & \delta_i \in functional \ features, \\ \delta_i, & \delta_i \notin functional \ features. \end{cases} \qquad (2)$$

Regularizer *R*. The regularizer R is to keep x_{adv} regularization and small perturbation. As shown in Fig. 1(d), perturbations δ should be in a restricted range. Specifically, a perturbation threshold ε is set to control the perturbation distance, as shown in Eq. 3. In addition, any feature vector of adversarial examples v_i can not exceed the range of actual traffic features as shown in Eq. 4.

$$\delta' = \begin{cases} \delta, & |\delta| \leq \varepsilon, \\ \dfrac{\varepsilon}{|\delta|} * \delta, & |\delta| > \varepsilon. \end{cases} \tag{3}$$

$$(\delta_i + v_i) \in [Min(v_i), Max(v_i)] \quad (i = 1 \sim n) \tag{4}$$

Black-box IDS. The black-box IDS is the target model of adversarial attack, which can be any trained ML model. The structure and parameters of the model do not need to be known, and only the output result is needed. Its input is adversarial examples x_{adv} and original examples x_o, and the output is y_{mal} and y_{ben}. The output is used as labels for motivational D training.

Discriminator *D*. The discriminator D is used to identify whether the example is malicious or benign. Different from the traditional WGAN model, it mainly includes three types of inputs, which are benign, malicious, and adversarial examples. D get their labels from the black-box IDS to train for distilling learning [23]. The output of D is a one-dimensional score, which is low for malicious and high for benign examples. Then it is feed back to G and D to train accordingly. G is motivated to generate highly adversarial examples to confuse D.

Improved Loss. WGAN mainly relies on the loss L_G and L_D of the generator G and the discriminator D to carry out iterative training. In L_G back propagation, parameters of D are frozen, while in L_D back propagation, parameters of G are frozen. G is trained by updating in weight corresponding to gradient information from scores of D. As shown in Eq. 5, scores of D are the L_G, which represents the difference between adversarial examples with original benign examples.

$$L_G = - \mathop{\mathbb{E}}_{\tilde{x} \in x_{adv}} [D(\tilde{x})] \tag{5}$$

For the discriminator D, on the one hand, L_D is calculated by the evaluation scores of D for adversarial examples x_{adv} and original benign examples x_o. On the other hand, D imitates detection capabilities of the black-box IDS to classify between original malicious examples x_{mal} and original benign example x_{ben}. Therefore, as shown in Eq. 6, we propose the improved loss so that D not only generates adversarial examples with G game, but also imitates the IDS better.

$$L_D = \underbrace{\mathop{\mathbb{E}}_{\tilde{x} \in x_{adv}} [D(\tilde{x})] - \mathop{\mathbb{E}}_{x \in x_{ben}} [D(x)]}_{\text{Original loss}} + \underbrace{\mathop{\mathbb{E}}_{\tilde{x} \in x_{mal}} [D(\tilde{x})]}_{\text{Improved loss}} \tag{6}$$

In general, the generator G and the discriminator D are balanced in the game. G tries to confuse D which has a similar detection ability to the black-box IDS by distilling learning. This indirectly implements adversarial attacks against the black-box IDS.

5   Experiment and Evaluation

In this section, we introduce the preparation of the adversarial attack experiment, including the data, training of black-box IDSs, and the implementation of *RAAM*. Then we define evaluation metrics and verify the performance of *RAAM* for generating adversarial examples against IDSs. Finally, we retrain IDSs by adversarial examples to resist adversarial attacks.

5.1   Dataset

Dataset Selection. We select the well-known NSL-KDD dataset to train and evaluate the performance of *RAAM*. NSL-KDD is an improved version of KDD-99 and has become the benchmark dataset of IDSs based on ML algorithms. As shown in Table 1, there are two separate subsets of NSL-KDD that can be used to train and test ML models, called KDDTrain+ and KDDTest+, respectively. In addition, NSL-KDD consists of five traffic categories, including Probe, DoS, U2R, R2L and benign traffic.

Table 1. The data sampling result of NSL-KDD.

Dataset	Total	Benign	DoS	Probe	U2R	R2L
KDDTrain+	125973	67343	45927	11656	52	995
KDDTest+	22544	9711	7458	2421	200	2654

Features Selection. NSL-KDD is extracted from real network traffic and has different categories of features. From the perspective of attributes, features can be divided into four categories: Intrinsic, Content, Time-based traffic and Host-based traffic [22]. As presented in Sect. 3.3, each category of attack traffic has unchangeable functional features, as shown in Table 2. *RAAM* can only change the nonfunctional features in order to avoid destroying the maliciousness.

Dataset Preprocessing. SMOTE sampling method is used to enhance the data and solve the problem of data imbalance. We also normalize data with Max-Min normalization. In addition, the training sets are divided into two parts: 50% is used for the training of IDSs, and the other is used for the training of *RAAM*.

Table 2. Functional features of attack categories in NSL-KDD dataset.

Attack	Intrinsic	Content	Time-based traffic	Host-based traffic
Probe	✓		✓	✓
DoS	✓		✓	
U2R	✓	✓		
R2L	✓	✓		

5.2   Evaluation Methods and Experimental Configurations

Evaluation Metrics. For the evaluation metrics, we use the method proposed by *IDSGAN*, which measures the detection rate (DR) and the evasion increase rate (EIR). As shown in Eq. 7, DR refers to the proportion of malicious traffic records $N_{detected}$ correctly detected by black-box IDSs to all attack records N, which directly reflects the escape ability of examples and the robustness of black-box IDSs. As shown in Eq. 8, EIR is the rate of the increase in the detection rate DR_{adv} for adversarial examples compared with the detection DR_o for original malicious examples to measure the evasive attack of *RAAM*.

$$DR = \frac{N_{detected}}{N} \tag{7}$$

$$EIR = 1 - \frac{DR_{adv}}{DR_o} \tag{8}$$

A lower DR represents that more malicious or adversarial examples can escape black-box IDSs. Conversely, a higher EIR represents that more adversarial examples can escape black-box IDSs than original malicious examples. Thus, the motivation for *RAAM* is to achieve a lower DR_{adv} and a higher EIR. In addition, we set *F1* score to measure the ability of black-box IDSs to detect malicious and benign traffic. What's more, the restriction of adversarial examples should also be considered besides adversarial performance. We represent the distance of perturbations by measuring the Euclidean distance (L_2) between the adversarial examples x_{adv} and the original malicious examples x_{mal} in Eq. 9.

$$L_2 = \sqrt{\sum_{i=1}^{n} \left| x_{adv}^i - x_{mal}^i \right|^2} \tag{9}$$

Hyper-parameters. Based on experience and previous experiments, we determined some basic parameters of the model. For WGAN, the epoch size is 50, the batch size is 128, and the learning rate of both discriminator and generator is 0.0001. The perturbation threshold ε is 4, and the cutting weight threshold of discriminator training is 0.01. Like the most basic GANs, the generator and the discriminator of *RAAM* are both multi-layer neural networks.

Experiment Setting. *RAAM* is implemented in Python3.7 based on Scikit-learn and Pytorch. The system is Ubuntu 16.04. All software applications are deployed on a server machine with 64 cores and 128GB memory. To further speed up matrix calculations, three NVIDIA TITAN XPs are deployed.

In order to detect the adversarial performance of *RAAM* in a more comprehensive way, nine current mainstream ML models are selected as black-box IDSs, including Logistic Regression (LR), Support Vector Machine (SVM), Naive Bayes (NB), Decision Tree (DT), Random Forest (RF), K-NearestNeighbor (KNN), Multilayer Perceptron (MLP), Convolutional Neural Network (CNN), Recurrent Neural Network (RNN) models. LR, SVM, NB, DT, RF, KNN and MLP are based on Scikit-learn, while CNN, RNN and WGAN are based on PyTorch.

5.3   Escape Detection

We present our experimental results and evaluate the performance of *RAAM*. There are two external contrast experiments and one self-contrast experiment. The baseline experiment is that adversarial examples are added with blind random perturbations, called *Random* attack. The next contrast experiment is an advanced adversarial attack architecture, called *DIGFuPAS* [6]. In addition, the improved loss is used or removed to verify its effect. We select the same attack types to compare with *DIGFuPAS* expediently, including DoS, U2R and R2L attacks, respectively. In particular, U2R and R2L attacks are classified into one type U2R & R2L attack because they are similar and in small quantities. Table 3 shows the detection ability of different ML-based IDSs for original examples. Table 4 shows the results of adversarial attacks in the DoS attack, and the results of the U2R & R2L attack are shown in Table 5. Finally, we detect different adversarial performances by changing the perturbation threshold ε in Fig. 3.

Table 3. The detection results of original examples in NSL-KDD.

Attack	Metric	LR	SVM	NB	DT	RF	KNN	MLP	CNN	RNN	Mean
DoS	$F1$ (%)	86.58	89.62	86.50	88.55	90.90	93.04	91.16	93.40	90.05	89.97
	DR (%)	85.03	82.99	86.70	94.13	95.09	94.90	95.40	98.39	98.14	92.30
U2R & R2L	$F1$ (%)	80.71	71.60	80.17	77.41	78.18	80.41	79.27	78.76	82.28	78.75
	DR (%)	59.50	44.28	69.91	57.69	64.47	69.16	65.62	56.21	66.31	61.46

Original Detection. First, we evaluate the detection ability of the nine ML-based IDSs. As shown in the Table 3, in the DoS attack, the *F1* score of test sets can reach 86%–93%, and the detection rate *DR* can reach 82%–98% on various models. In the U2R & R2L attack, the *F1* score achieves 71%–82%, and the detection rate *DR* achieves 44%–69% because the number of the U2R & R2L attack is low. On the whole, ML-based IDSs can well identify malicious traffic and benign traffic.

Table 4. Compared performance of adversarial methods in the DoS attack.

Method	Metric	LR	SVM	NB	DT	RF	KNN	MLP	CNN	RNN	Mean
Random	*DR* (%)	86.07	87.81	13.49	30.36	30.20	80.56	84.36	75.52	90.34	64.30
	EIR (%)	−1.22	−5.80	84.44	67.74	68.24	15.11	11.57	23.24	7.94	30.14
	L_2	2.37	2.37	2.38	2.36	2.38	2.38	2.37	2.38	2.37	2.37
DIGFuPAS	DR (%)	0	0.61	0	18.35	9.54	4.94	1.14	0.55	74.56	12.18
	EIR (%)	100	99.2	100	77.50	88.02	93.81	98.62	99.33	9.52	85.11
	L_2	2.71	2.56	2.05	2.67	2.60	3.33	3.35	3.06	1.74	2.67
RAAM (Base)	*DR* (%)	30.16	0	68.45	9.78	18.86	27.02	14.32	0.37	18.06	20.78
	EIR (%)	64.53	100	21.04	89.61	80.16	71.52	84.98	99.62	81.59	77.00
	L_2	1.48	2.05	1.93	2.06	2.25	2.20	1.51	1.76	1.91	**1.90**
RAAM (Improved)	*DR* (%)	11.07	0.07	0.64	9.48	9.47	0.75	0.06	0.12	7.11	**4.30**
	EIR (%)	86.98	99.91	99.26	89.92	90.03	99.20	99.94	99.88	92.75	**95.31**
	L_2	1.99	1.83	2.03	1.43	2.20	2.05	2.29	1.93	2.05	1.97

Comparison of Adversarial Effects. As shown in Table 4, all attack methods except *Random* can interfere with the detection of IDSs in the *DoS* attack. This shows that ML-based IDSs are easily attacked by adversarial attacks. In various IDSs, the mean *DR* of *RAAM* is 4.30% which is 60% lower than *Random* and 7.88% lower than *DIGFuPAS*, and the mean *EIR* is 95.31% which is 64.91% higher than *Random* and 10.2% higher than *DIGFuPAS*. Compared with the other two methods, *RAAM* has stronger adversarial effects. We think this is mainly because *RAAM* uses the improved loss so that the discriminator D can better imitate black-box IDSs. We will prove its effect through the comparison experiment in later. In addition, the mean distance of perturbations L_2 of *RAAM* is 1.97, which is 0.4 lower than *Random* and 0.7 lower than *DIGFuPAS*. This shows that the restriction of *RAAM* is effective and adversarial examples have lower perturbations.

For the U2R & R2L attack, *DIGFuPAS* does not use SMOTE sampling in the original paper, so its black-box IDSs are poor in detecting these types of attacks with a small number of examples. Therefore, we use the results reproduced by ourselves instead of the results in their paper. As shown in Table 5, the mean *DR* and *EIR* of *RAAM* are 4.76% and 92.88% respectively, which are also lower and higher than the other two methods. For the perturbations, the mean L_2 of *RAAM* is 1.61, which is also the lowest.

It is worth mentioning that we find that the RF model and the DT model are the least affected by adversarial attacks. What they have in common is that they are all tree models. We think this is because the tree models are least sensitive to irrelevant data, and some researchers have also proved that tree models have stronger stability [24].

Improved Loss. We research the impact of improved loss by removing it. As shown in Table 4 and Table 5, when improved loss is removed, *EIR* decreased significantly in multiple black-box IDSs such as SVM, NB, KNN, *etc.* We believe that this is because the discriminator D with the base loss cannot transfer the ability to learn black-box IDSs, so that the generator G has no motivation to generate more deceptive adversarial examples for black-box IDSs.

Table 5. Compared performance of adversarial methods in the U2R & R2L attack.

Method	Metric	LR	SVM	NB	DT	RF	KNN	MLP	CNN	RNN	Mean
Random	DR (%)	58.53	49.62	92.68	35.53	25.27	57.48	51.99	73.71	70.83	57.29
	EIR (%)	1.63	−12.0	80.66	−32.5	60.8	16.87	20.75	−31.1	−6.80	10.92
	L_2	2.49	2.49	2.50	2.49	2.48	2.49	2.49	2.50	2.48	2.49
DIGFuPAS	DR (%)	0	0	0.74	15.45	14.10	25.21	0.48	0	19.27	8.36
	EIR (%)	100	100	98.94	73.21	78.12	63.56	99.26	100	70.93	87.11
	L_2	2.34	2.73	2.46	2.90	2.33	2.07	2.33	3.06	2.42	2.51
RAAM (Base)	DR (%)	1.05	0	17.58	63.88	0.13	55.38	0.27	99.42	0.47	26.46
	EIR (%)	98.23	100	74.85	−10.7	99.78	19.92	99.58	−76.8	99.28	56.01
	L_2	1.27	2.50	1.81	1.36	1.83	2.11	1.89	1.36	1.27	1.71
RAAM (Improved)	DR (%)	1.65	0	17.58	6.23	0.23	16.86	0	0	0.33	**4.76**
	EIR (%)	97.21	100	74.85	89.19	99.63	75.60	100	100	99.49	**92.88**
	L_2	0.89	1.56	1.18	1.31	1.73	2.29	1.74	2.25	1.51	**1.60**

Effect of Different Perturbations. We observe adversarial performance by changing the perturbation threshold ε. In this way, the robustness of different ML models are evaluated in Fig. 3 shows experimental results with different threshold ε in the DoS attack NSL-KDD. Even if perturbation threshold ε reaches an extremely low value of 1, DR can remain 30%–50% in most black-box IDSs. In addition, KNN and LR models perform well under sufficiently small perturbations, while the RNN and RF models perform weakly. In general, the more complex the model can be attacked by the lower perturbations.

5.4   Detection Effect of Enhanced IDSs

In this subsection, we research how IDSs defend against attackers through adversarial training. Specifically, we use generated adversarial examples to retrain IDSs for enhancement. Then we attack the retrained IDSs again to detect their robustness. Note that the previous adversarial examples are not used, but the new generation for attacking the retrained IDSs again in the black-box scene.

In the experiment, we use adversarial examples generated by *RAAM* to retrain, and use different adversarial methods to attack the enhanced IDSs. We mainly consider two points of the enhanced IDSs, (1) it has stronger robustness for adversarial examples; (2) it does not interfere with the detection of original examples. Therefore, we observe two main metrics, DR of adversarial examples and *F1* score of original examples.

We conduct experiments in the DoS attack as an illustration. As shown in Table 6, the first two lines represent the comparison results for the detection of the original examples, and the other lines represent the detection of the three attacks. After retraining, *F1* score does not decrease significantly and even rises slightly in several ML-based IDSs. This shows that enhanced IDSs still have a good ability to detect original examples. DR increases by 36.89% on average against *DIGFuPAS*, and DR increases by 25.72% on average against *RAAM*. In general, the enhanced IDSs are more robust for adversarial attacks without affecting the detection of original examples.

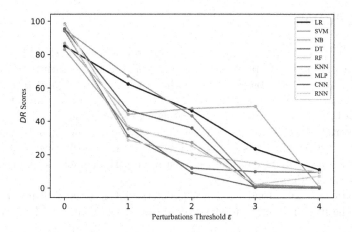

Fig. 3. DR of different perturbation threshold ε in the DoS attack.

Table 6. The comparative results of previous and retrained IDSs in the DoS attack of NSL-KDD.

Method	Metric	LR	SVM	NB	DT	RF	KNN	MLP	CNN	RNN	Mean
Original	$F1$ (%)	86.58	89.62	86.50	88.55	90.90	93.04	91.16	93.40	90.05	**89.97**
+Retrained	$F1$ (%)	85.01	86.67	82.57	88.42	91.03	91.80	92.36	90.93	89.83	88.73
Random	DR (%)	86.07	87.81	13.49	30.36	30.20	80.56	84.36	75.52	90.34	64.30
+Retrained	DR (%)	86.54	87.83	25.60	39.85	28.71	81.47	82.77	88.54	91.05	**68.04**
DIGFuPAS	DR (%)	0	0.61	0	18.35	9.54	4.94	1.14	0.55	74.56	12.18
+Retrained	DR (%)	85.22	56.01	0.10	9.67	20.21	31.27	72.05	94.50	72.74	**49.08**
RAAM	DR (%)	11.07	0.07	0.64	9.48	9.47	0.75	0.06	0.12	7.11	4.30
+Retrained	DR (%)	58.79	13.85	57.20	19.09	19.10	35.15	22.94	25.92	18.24	**30.03**

6   Discussion

In this paper, we propose a restricted adversarial attack with adding smaller perturbations distance. We think that the fewer number of perturbation features is also important for restricted adversarial attack. We intend to modify only one or several nonfunctional features for attacks. This can better preserve the nature of the original malicious traffic.

In addition, our work only conducts adversarial attacks against binary-classification models. In other fields, there are some adversarial attacks against multi-classification models, call targeted attacks. Attackers can misidentify a example from one category to a particular category. In the network traffic detection field, multi-classification tasks are increasingly common. Therefore, it is meaningful to conduct targeted attacks against multi-classification models.

7   Conclusion

In this paper, we focus on issues that adversarial attacks should have more sufficient restrictions. We propose $RAAM$, a restricted adversarial attack model. We attack different ML-based IDSs in the black-box scene, and test with the NSL-KDD dataset. WGAN with the improved loss is used for imitating IDSs, and gets a higher mean EIR 94.1%. Regularizer R and the masking vector are used to restrict attacks, and get a lower mean distance of perturbations L_2 1.79. In addition, we retrain IDSs to improve their robustness. Experimental results show that retrained IDSs can weaken most adversarial attacks without affecting the detection of original examples.

In the future, we intend to conduct adversarial attacks with fewer features for multi-classification, and target more advanced and complex ML-based IDSs.

Acknowledgement. This work is supported by the National Key Research and Development Program of China (Grant No. 2018YFB0804704).

References

1. Szegedy, C., et al.: Intriguing properties of neural networks. arXiv preprint arXiv:1312.6199 (2013)
2. Aiken, J., Scott-Hayward, S.: Investigating adversarial attacks against network intrusion detection systems in SDNs. In: IEEE Conference on Network Function Virtualization and Software Defined Networks (NFV-SDN), pp. 1–7 (2019)
3. Huang, C.-H., Lee, T.-H., Chang, L., Lin, J.-R., Horng, G.: Adversarial attacks on SDN-Based deep learning IDS system. In: Kim, K.J., Kim, H. (eds.) ICMWT 2018. LNEE, vol. 513, pp. 181–191. Springer, Singapore (2019). https://doi.org/10.1007/978-981-13-1059-1_17
4. Lin, Z., Shi, Y., Xue, Z.: IDSGAN: generative adversarial networks for attack generation against intrusion detection. arXiv preprint arXiv:1809.02077 (2018)
5. Usama, M., Asim, M., Latif, S., et al.: Generative adversarial networks for launching and thwarting adversarial attacks on network intrusion detection systems. In: 2019 15th international Wireless Communications & Mobile Computing Conference (IWCMC), pp. 78–83 (2019)
6. Duy, P.T., Khoa, N.H., Nguyen, A.G.T., et al.: DIGFuPAS: deceive IDS with GAN and function-preserving on adversarial examples in SDN-enabled networks. Comput. Secur. **109**, 102367 (2021)
7. Han, D., Wang, Z., Zhong, Y., et al.: Evaluating and improving adversarial robustness of machine learning-based network intrusion detectors. IEEE J. Sel. Areas Commun. **39**, 2632–2647 (2021)
8. Hashemi, M.J., Cusack, G., Keller, E.: Towards evaluation of NIDSs in adversarial setting. In: Proceedings of the 3rd ACM CoNEXT Workshop on Big DAta, Machine Learning and Artificial Intelligence for Data Communication Networks, pp. 14–21 (2019)
9. Xie, J., Li, S., Yun, X., et al.: HSTF-model: an HTTP-based Trojan detection model via the hierarchical spatio-temporal features of traffics. Comput. Secur. **96**, 101923 (2020)

10. van Ede, T., Bortolameotti, R., Continella, A., et al.: FlowPrint: semi-supervised mobile-app fingerprinting on encrypted network traffic. In: Network and Distributed System Security Symposium (NDSS), vol. 27 (2020)

11. Han, D., Wang, Z., Chen, W., et al.: DeepAID: interpreting and improving deep learning-based anomaly detection in security applications. In: Proceedings of the 2021 ACM SIGSAC Conference on Computer and Communications Security, pp. 3197–3217 (2021)

12. Xie, G., Li, Q., Jiang, Y.: Self-attentive deep learning method for online traffic classification and its interpretability. Comput. Netw. **196**, 108267 (2021)

13. Hu, W., Tan, Y.: Generating adversarial malware examples for black-box attacks based on GAN. arXiv preprint arXiv:1702.05983 (2017)

14. Goodfellow, I.J., Shlens, J., Szegedy, C.: Explaining and harnessing adversarial examples. arXiv preprint arXiv:1412.6572 (2014)

15. Papernot, N., McDaniel, P., Jha, S., et al.: The limitations of deep learning in adversarial settings. In: IEEE European Symposium on Security and Privacy (EuroS&P), pp. 372–387 (2016)

16. Liu, C., Ding, W., Hu, Y., et al.: Rectified binary convolutional networks with generative adversarial learning. Int. J. Comput. Vis. **129**(4), 998–1012 (2021)

17. Demetrio, L., Biggio, B., Lagorio, G., et al.: Functionality-preserving black-box optimization of adversarial windows malware. In: IEEE Transactions on Information Forensics and Security, pp. 3469–3478 (2021)

18. Rahman, M.S., Imani, M., Mathews, N., et al.: Mockingbird: defending against deep-learning-based website fingerprinting attacks with adversarial traces. IEEE Trans. Inf. Forensics Secur. **16**, 1594–1609 (2020)

19. Gulrajani, I., Ahmed, F., Arjovsky, M., et al.: Improved training of Wasserstein GANs. arXiv preprint arXiv:1704.00028 (2017)

20. Goodfellow, I., Pouget-Abadie, J., Mirza, M., et al.: Generative adversarial nets. Adv. Neural Inf. Process. Syst. **27** (2014)

21. Tavallaee, M., Bagheri, E., Lu, W., Ghorbani, A.: A detailed analysis of the KDD CUP 99 data set. In: Submitted to Second IEEE Symposium on Computational Intelligence for Security and Defense Applications (2009)

22. Davis, J.J., Clark, A.J., et al.: Data preprocessing for anomaly based network intrusion detection: a review. Comput. Secur. **30**, 353–375 (2011)

23. Hinton, G., Vinyals, O., Dean, J.: Distilling the Knowledge in a neural network. Stat 1050–1058 (2015)

24. Shwartz-Ziv, R., Armon, A.: Tabular data: deep learning is not all you need. arXiv preprint arXiv:2106.03253 (2021)

Evaluation of Circuit Lifetimes in Tor

Kevin Köster$^{(\boxtimes)}$, Matthias Marx, Anne Kunstmann, and Hannes Federrath

Universität Hamburg, Hamburg, Germany
{kevin.koester,matthias.marx,anne.kunstmann,
hannes.federrath}@uni-hamburg.de

Abstract. Tor is a popular anonymity network which achieves its anonymity by constructing paths over three Tor relays, so-called circuits. Multiple streams that correspond to TCP connections can be multiplexed over a single circuit. By default, circuits are used for about ten minutes before switching to new circuits. Once that time limit is reached the circuit cannot be used for any new streams. This time-window is called the maximum circuit dirtiness (MCD). This paper analyzes the consequences of changing the MCD for all clients in the network and provides data on how changing the MCD affects various metrics of the Tor network. Our analysis shows that reducing the MCD to a sane value has almost no impact on the clients. Neither performance nor anonymity of the clients are significantly affected by the MCD. On the relays however halving the default MCD reduces the memory usage by about 20% while maintaining the original throughput and no measurable increase in CPU usage. Raising the MCD shows the opposite effect and increases memory usage. By drastically reducing the MCD, a significant number of extra circuits are created. From a performance point of view, the MCD should be reduced. Building on this work, side effects on specific attacks on Tor should be investigated in future work.

Keywords: Tor · Circuit · Dirtiness · Privacy · Anonymity

1 Introduction

Tor [28] is a popular anonymity network with a large user base. It has about eight million daily [19] and about two million concurrent users [29]. The network itself consists of about 7 000 relays with a bandwidth of about 500 GiB/s [29]. It aims to provide low latency communication to enable Internet browsing and using real time applications such as voice chats. If a client wants to route data through the Tor network to a given target, it selects three relays and establishes an encrypted connection through them. This is called a *circuit* and the three chosen relays are known as the *guard*, the *middle* and the *exit*. For each hop the data is encrypted once and every relay decrypts one of the encryption layers. Finally the *exit* relay completely decrypts the data and sends it to the target. By using this method no relay ever knows the client and the target of a given connection at the same time. The target sees only the IP address of the *exit* relay, the IP address of the client

© IFIP International Federation for Information Processing 2022
Published by Springer Nature Switzerland AG 2022
W. Meng et al. (Eds.): SEC 2022, IFIP AICT 648, pp. 142–157, 2022.
https://doi.org/10.1007/978-3-031-06975-8_9

is concealed. Each circuit can handle multiple streams. When the client want to establish a connection to a target, Tor then tries to find a suitable existing *circuit* to use. If none is found a new *circuit* gets constructed. Since creating a new circuit involves establishing various connections and cryptographic handshakes which might induce a considerable delay, Tor prepares some open circuits in advance to keep the delay to a minimum.

When the age of a circuit exceeds a certain lifetime, no new streams can use this circuit and only already established streams are allowed to use it. The circuit is marked for closure as soon as all attached connections are closed. The circuit's lifetime is referred to as the maximum circuit dirtiness (MCD) and is, by default, 10 min. The MCD was last changed in 2005, where it was increased from 30 s to 10 min for performance reasons (commit `d2400a5afd`). In this paper, we evaluate different MCDs and their impact on performance and privacy.

The higher the MCD, the less frequently a client changes circuits. It might cause circuits to stay open even if they never see any user data again. With a lower MCD, those circuits would be closed earlier. A too low MCD, however, might result in an increased number of circuits which put additional strain on the Tor network. Furthermore, creating more circuits increases the number of opportunities to choose a malicious relay.

We use the *Shadow* discrete-event network simulator to run simulated Tor networks with different settings for the MCDs. Since the main motivation for changing the default MCDs in the first place was the relays' performance, we put a focus on evaluating the performance implications.

Our key findings are as follows:

1. Decreasing the default MCD on all Tor clients from 10 min to 5 min reduces memory usage of the relays by about 20%.
2. An MCD within a range of 30 s to 60 min has a small impact the CPU usage of relays and no impact on the total throughput of the Tor network. By halving the default MCD to 5 min no measurable difference can be found.
3. Changing the MCD has a small influence on the total number of circuits created over time and the average amount of data transmitted per circuit. Reducing the MCD from 10 min to 5 min increases the number of circuits created by only about 3%.

The remainder of this paper is structured as follows: In Sect. 2, we present related work. In Sect. 3, we present our methodology and experimental setup, followed by Sect. 4 where we present our findings. Finally, we discuss unanswered questions and conclude our paper in Sect. 5.

2   Related Work

In this section, we present previous research related to Tor's MCD. First, we present prior work where the MCD was modified to control the creation of new circuits. Then, we describe approaches to formalize anonymity. Lastly, we provide a brief background on running realistic and reproducible simulations of the Tor network.

2.1 Modifying the Maximum Circuit Dirtiness

In the literature, the MCD has been modified to control creation of new circuits. However, to the best of our knowledge, it has not been studied how the MCD affects Tor's performance and users' privacy.

Wacek et al. [31] changed the MCD to increase the frequency at which new circuits are requested in order to study relay selection algorithms. The same approach was used by Wang and Goldberg [32], Kim et al. [16] and Shen et al. [26] who changed the MCD to enforce the usage of a new circuit for every visited website or conversely to prevent the generation of new circuits. The overall performance of the Tor network was not studied in these works.

Koch et al. [18] analyzed the reliability of circuits with respect to geographic locations of the exit nodes. They identified that circuits ending in Germany or the Netherlands usually are pretty stable and last the default MCD of ten minutes unless being closed before. Circuits ending in France, however, were quite unstable and had a higher number of timeouts. They observed an average circuit usage time of 7.5 min which is lower than the default MCD.

2.2 Assessing Anonymity, Privacy, and Security

By changing the MCD in Tor, we expect that the number of generated circuits increases which may influence the distribution of selected circuits. In order to show if changing the MCD affects the circuits Tor selects and thus might influence the anonymity of the clients, a metric is required. Furthermore an evaluation is needed if an adversary is able to gather more data due to a different MCD.

Serjantov et al. [24] and Díaz et al. [2,3] both independently proposed an anonymity metric based on the Shannon entropy [25]. The Shannon entropy can be calculated as follows

$$H(X) = -\sum_{i=1}^{n} p_i log_2(p_i) \tag{1}$$

where n is the number of total events and p_i the probability of a specific event. The maximum entropy can be calculated with

$$H_{max} = log_2(n) \tag{2}$$

which is the case if $p_i = \frac{1}{n} \forall \in 1, .., n$. To calculate a normalized entropy we just have to divide by the maximum entropy of the system

$$H_{norm}(X) = \frac{H(X)}{H_{max}} = -\sum_{i=1}^{n} p_i log_n(p_i) \tag{3}$$

In the context of Tor, n might be set to the number of possible entry-exit-combinations and p_i the probability a certain combination of relays is used to build a circuit. This can be used as a metric which shows the quality of circuit selection algorithms. The normalized entropy can then be used to compare systems with different amounts of users and selected circuit combinations.

In addition to measuring the entropy of the circuit selection, we take an adversary into account who controls part of the Tor network and aims to deanonymize the users. Tor is known to be susceptible to traffic correlation attacks [27]. Adversaries that are able to read a portion of incoming and outgoing traffic to and from the Tor network could link incoming traffic to outgoing traffic and thus deanonymize Tor users. To conduct such attacks, adversaries need control of some Tor guards and exits by either running them themselves or by hijacking existing relays. Alternatively, they could control an autonomous system (AS) or an Internet exchange point.

2.3   Simulation of Tor Networks

Since we cannot simply change the MCD (in a part) of the live Tor network, we evaluate different settings in a simulated Tor network. A variety of programs can be used for this. Moreover, simulating has the advantage that third parties can reproduce our results more easily.

Shadow [11] runs programs in an environment with a simulated network topology and time. Thus, the result of the simulation is not impacted by the speed of the simulating machine or other running tasks. This significantly improves the reproducibility of the simulations. *Shadow* is able to simulate an arbitrary amount of different hosts which is only limited by the available memory of the simulating host. The available processing power is also relevant as it speeds up the simulation but, with enough time, a slow CPU does not prevent the execution of a given simulation and leads to the same results as a fast CPU would do. As the simulation is a closed system, all encryption functions from *Tor* are disabled as they do not serve any purpose and only slow down the simulation. Since all calculations are done instantaneously for the simulated programs, this does not influence the results of the simulation but shows one major weakness of *Shadow*: Any CPU intensive calculation will not impact the network performance at all.

To measure the network performance some kind of traffic is needed. In prior experiments [5,8,17,19] a static recurring transfer with a size of 320 KiB was used to represent the download of a website. This approach dates back to 2010 and is based on the average size of a website [4]. However, this approach is outdated as the number of requests and data transmitted is far higher today. According to the HTTP Archive [7] the average size of a website in 2021 was about 2 MiB and consists of about 70 different requests. This clearly shows the need for newer and more accurate traffic models.

With *Privcount*, Jansen et al. [12] developed a program to measure Tor without compromising the anonymity of Tor users. They published a traffic model that is based on data captured in 2018 [14]. The model covers streams as well as packets based on real users behavior. To use that model in a simulation the application *tornettools* [10] is provided, which allows the generation of a realistic Tor network scaled to any size. To significantly reduce the run time of the simulation, 100 simulated clients use a common simulated Tor instance. This reduces the accuracy of the simulation, but also allows for a much larger simulation.

With *Chutney* [30] an alternative to *Shadow* exists which is able to simulate Tor networks. In contrast to *Shadow* it runs the networks in real-time and will not guarantee reproducibility as the environment does not provide a simulated time. Therefore the size of the simulated networks is heavily limited and we will use Chutney to confirm a part of our results.

3   Methodology

This section presents the simulation that was set up in order to evaluate different MCDs on the Tor network. Since the Tor specification does not precisely tell how to use every feature, e.g. repurposing existing circuits, Tor might behave unexpectedly at times. A purely theoretical evaluation approach is therefore not sufficient. Consequently, we simulate merely a fraction of the Tor network in order to modify the MCD and focus on its impact on the network performance.

The aforementioned *Shadow* simulator [11] combined with *tornettools* will be used to run the simulation and generate a realistic network along with realistic traffic. Since simulating the entire Tor network requires about 4 TiB of memory [13], we only simulate a fraction of the Tor network.

Additionally, we make use of *Shadow*'s memory tracking functionality to determine the resource consumption of each simulated node. Since its memory tracking is not well-tested, we verify our results by adding the same functionality provided by *Chutney* [30]. Realistic client traffic is simulated with the help of *tgen* [23] and added to *Chutney* with the priorly mentioned traffic model. To track the memory consumption, we used *Heaptrack* [6] by integrating it into *Chutney*. *Heaptrack* provides insight into memory usage while inducing little CPU and memory overhead.

3.1   Adversary Model

To evaluate how changing MCD affects the client's security, we consider an adversary who is able to control a fraction of the Tor network. Following previous works [1,8], our adversary controls 10% of Tor's entry and exit bandwidth. Should a client choose a compromised entry and exit relay for a circuit, the circuit is considered compromised. The adversary is able to observe the traffic along that circuit and deanonymize the user. To simulate this adversary, relays were chosen randomly and added to the set of compromised nodes until the threshold of 10% for entry and exit bandwidth was reached. We kept track of the amount of traffic sent over those compromised relays and repeated the procedure ten times in order to calculate an average over the obtained results.

3.2   Simulation Parameters

Our hardware operates with 350 GiB of memory and is able to simulate a fraction of approximately 8% of the entire Tor network for one hour with unmodified Tor software. A modification of the MCD might cause the memory usage to increase and subsequently decrease the largest possible network size that can be simulated. Due to this increase of memory usage, we first simulated a network fraction of 3% which allowed us to test a wider set of MCDs. We chose values ranging from 30 s, 50 s, 100 s, 200 s, 5 min, 400 s, 500 s, 10 min (default) to longer time periods of 20 min, 40 min, and 60 min.

During the evaluation of aforementioned MCDs, the value of 5 min stood out positively with regard to decreasing memory usage. A larger network fraction of 8% was simulated in order to evaluate the network's behavior with an MCD of 5 min at larger scale. For the simulation, four different snapshots of the Tor network from different months displayed in Table 1 were used three times and provided with an initial seed to avoid outliers and biases in our data. We only use one single traffic model and, thus, the number of clients does not change with the date and is fixed at 63 355 users for every simulation.

Table 1. Time windows used for Tor snapshots and their simulated network size scaled to 8% of the Tor network

Month	Relays	Guards	Exits
2021-01	553	263	123
2021-02	538	261	112
2021-03	537	271	102
2021-04	528	272	91

To generate the required files, we first select the respective snapshot of the Tor network. Then, we set the seed to "1" and increase it by 1 for every repeated simulation for a specific snapshot. The resulting configuration files are then copied, so even the used cryptographic keys are identical to the reference version. In these copies only the Setting "MaxCircuitDirtiness" is changed for all clients. The circuit renewal process was not modified and follows the Tor protocol.

3.3   Changes to the Simulation Software

To evaluate the simulation, several changes were made to the existing software stack. None of these changes should affect the result of the simulation and only provide additional data.

To quantify the CPU time of each host, we added an additional field to the *Shadow* heartbeat message which keeps track of the required CPU time. This CPU time period is quantified by measuring the time period between a timer before handing over the control to the process next in line. The timer is stopped after the process returns. Every interruption of the current process, e.g. writing to a socket or accessing the disk, is omitted from the measuring process by handing the control back to *Shadow* and in order to avoid skewing the obtained results. In this way, the actual CPU time only includes a small overhead for

Table 2. Used software versions

Name	Commit	Based on version
Tor	tor-0.3.5.7	0.3.5.7
Tornettools [10]	fd2f8d1	1.10
Oniontrace [22]	e9a9dd3	1.0.0
Shadow [9]	67c1f19f	1.15.0
Tgen [23]	47d5eb3	1.0.0

handing back the control as well as the timer start and stop. *Shadow* itself does not simulate the required CPU time and a high CPU usage does not impact the performance of the simulated program. We can only measure whether Tor uses more CPU but we cannot measure the impact the CPU usage has on other metrics.

By default, *Shadow* merely monitors the memory usage of the entire simulation. By enabling the "ram" option, this functionality can be extended to single hosts participating in the network. As *Shadow* catches every call for memory allocation and deallocation, it is possible to monitor all used memory on the heap for each simulated process. The impact of the stack on the total memory consumption on Linux systems is by default limited to 8 MiB [21] and thus negligible. No further changes were made to *Shadow*.

Circuit Statistics To evaluate how different MCDs affect the circuit generation, we expanded the plot scripts to include the number of active circuits for a given time. Additionally we observed all circuits generated by all clients to calculate the entropy of the circuit-selection. Since we are modifying the closing time of circuits it is reasonable to believe that we create more circuits which may impact the circuit selection algorithm. Therefore we calculate the Shannon entropy [25] as described in Sect. 2. As the n we are using all possible combinations of entry- and exit-nodes a client could choose. $p_i, i \in 1, .., n$ is the number of times the combination i was used by the clients divided by n. This metric shows the uniformity of the selection of entry and exit nodes. The middle nodes are not considered.

3.4   Reproducing Our Results

To make our results reproducible, all used software versions are provided in Table 2. The simulation with *tornettools* requires a bunch of preparation steps in order to simulate the Tor network. This includes, e.g., downloading the server descriptors as well as the consensus, *onionperf*, and bandwidth data for a specific time range. To facilitate the reproducibility of our evaluation, we provide an automation for these manual steps.[1]

---

[1] Available at https://github.com/kevinkoester/tornettools_manager.

3.5 Limitations

Even though we are able to simulate many different states of the Tor network and use different seeds for the traffic generation, we are still limited to the single traffic model. The traffic model only generates active circuits which the clients actually use to send data, inactive circuits are not covered by the model.

As already mentioned, each calculation done in the simulation is done instantaneously from the perspective of the simulated program. Therefore an overload of the relays cannot be simulated using the default settings. *Shadow* offers the functionality to simulate those, but loses its determinism by doing that. Therefore we are able to measure the used CPU time while missing reproducibility of our measures.

4 Analysis

As described in Sect. 3, each simulation of the Tor network was set up based on the entirety of monthly Tor consensus documents and then provided with a seed. These simulations were then used to demonstrate how changing the MCD impacts the network performance. Among each simulation set, the results did not show any significant differences. For that reason, we selected one simulation from each set to represent the overall results. For simulations modeling a 3% fraction of the network size, we selected the Tor snapshot of May 2021. The larger simulations of 8% are built after the snapshot of March 2021. Both simulations use a seed of "1" as described in Sect. 4.

In the following subsections, the simulation results will be analyzed and the effects of raising and lowering the MCD will be discussed for each metric along with their impact on the Tor network. From our range of tested MCDs, we select two opposite values, 30 s (the previous default) and 60 min, to demonstrate the influence of extremes on both ends. Afterwards, we demonstrate how doubling and reducing the default MCD by half affects the network. Additionally, we show how the Tor network is affected by an MCD of 5 min with simulations that model a network fraction of 8%.

We first address the performance aspects in Subsect. 4.1 and eventually discuss some privacy implications in Subsect. 4.2.

4.1 Performance

The simulations show that decreasing the MCD reduces the Tor relays' memory usage while the clients stay mostly unaffected by this modification.

The simulations also show a slight trend towards lower CPU usage. However, those differences are within the margin of error and can show the opposite effect in other simulations. Thus, these results are not conclusive. Moreover, we could not observe any significant change in throughput or overhead in the network traffic for all tested MCDs.

Circuit Generation. Figure 1 shows the number of concurrently open circuits and the total number of created circuits for different numbers of MCDs on the Y-axis. The X-axis shows the simulated time.

In Fig. 1a, it can be seen that the number of concurrently open circuits stabilizes after a while. An exception is a MCD of 60 min which effectively disables the MCD functionality and thus circuits are never being closed due to their lifetime. This causes the number of concurrently open circuits and total created circuits to be almost identical.

Doubling the MCD from 10 min to 20 min increases the number of concurrently open circuits by about 73%. The difference between the default MCD of 10 min and 5 min is about 40%. The difference between 5 min and 30 s is relatively small at about 3%.

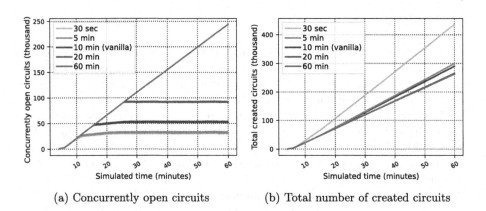

(a) Concurrently open circuits   (b) Total number of created circuits

Fig. 1. Number of open circuits for different numbers of the MCD

Lowering the MCD causes unused circuits to be closed sooner and thus we see a lower number of concurrently open circuits. Increasing the MCD causes the circuits to stay open longer even if they are never used again and thus results in an increased number of concurrently open circuits. One can also see that doubling the default MCD has a larger impact on the absolute number of concurrently open circuits than halving it. Reducing the MCD beyond 5 min only has diminishing returns. Overall the number of concurrently open circuits correlates with the MCD. The lower the MCD, the lower the number of concurrently open circuits.

Figure 1b shows that the higher the MCD is set, the lower the total amount of created circuits is. With a MCD of 30 s the total number of created circuits is increased by about 50% compared to the default MCD. Halving the MCD results in about 3% more circuits and doubling it in about 8% less circuits created.

With a lower MCD, circuits are closed sooner. Therefore the Tor client might need to create extra circuits for some streams if no suitable circuits are available, whereas with a higher MCD an already existing circuit could have been used.

If we run the same simulation with a larger network, we see similar results. Vanilla Tor creates about 142 600 concurrently open circuits as seen in Fig. 2a. Lowering the MCD to half of the original value causes the number of concurrently active circuits to be reduced to about 88 000, which is a reduction of about 38%. For the total number of created circuits we do see a difference, but it is rather small with a 3% increase.

Overall lowering the MCD leads to a decrease of concurrently open circuits while slightly increasing the total number of created circuits. Raising the MCD shows the opposite effect. The scale of the simulation doesn't influence this result.

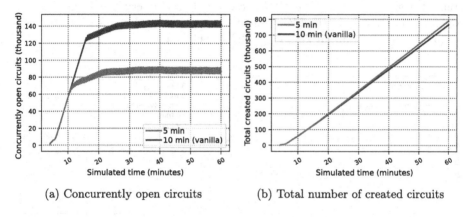

(a) Concurrently open circuits   (b) Total number of created circuits

Fig. 2. Number of open circuits with half the MCD

CPU Usage. We note that the used CPU time is the only value that significantly changed throughout the experiments. In our smaller simulation (scaled to 3% of the Tor network), we observed a measurable difference for MCDs of 30 s and 60 min for a single configuration. This leads to an increase of about 10% for 30 s and a decrease of about 4.5% for an MCD of 60 min for the used CPU time. However, this is only the case for this specific configuration and other simulations didn't show this behavior. All other measurements were within the margin of error and showed a slightly lower, yet not conclusive, CPU usage for an MCD of 30 s. In the simulations scaled to 8% the size of the live Tor network, halving the MCD shows no significant difference throughout the simulation.

Overall, we see that measuring the CPU time in *Shadow* is not very reliable. But if it does show a significant difference it correlates with the number of total created circuits. The more circuits are built, the higher the used CPU time. Even when enabling CPU delays and encryption in *Shadow* we were not able to observe any significant difference. Due to the unreliable nature of measuring the CPU time, using the total number of created circuits as a measure is preferred. Still, only very small MCDs like 30 s show an increased CPU usage. Therefore, halving the default MCD does not result in a degradation of performance.

Memory Usage. In Fig. 3, the total memory consumption in GiB of all guards and clients can be seen on the Y-axis. It is clearly visible that decreasing the MCD leads to an overall lower memory consumption while increasing the MCD shows the opposite effect and all guards have an increased memory usage. We see the same trend for the exit and middle relays. Halving the MCD leads to a decrease of about 22%, while doubling the MCD leads to an increase of about 59%. If we compare the amount of memory used in Fig. 3a and the number of concurrently active circuits in Fig. 1, we can see that those graphs are almost identical and there seems to be a correlation between those two metrics.

The same effect is also present for the client as seen in Fig. 3b albeit considerable lower. By reducing the MCD we can only see a very small difference of roughly 3%. By raising the MCD however, a noticeable difference can be seen up to an increase of about 23% for a MCD of 60 min.

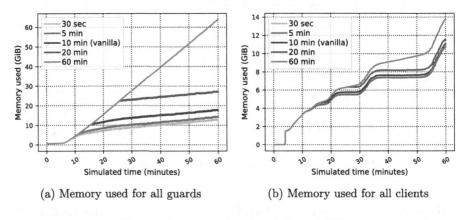

(a) Memory used for all guards   (b) Memory used for all clients

Fig. 3. Memory used with a different MCD

Scaling the simulation size to 8% of the Tor network yields the same results. Figure 4a shows the memory usage of all guards in the simulation with an unmodified and a halved default MCD. It can clearly be seen that the reduced MCD has a lower memory consumption of about 21%. The clients are affected as well but only show an increase in used memory by about 4%. Considering we simulate 63 355 clients the difference can be neglected. To verify these results we simulated a small network in *Chutney* with 10 clients and 18 relays, which shows the same trend. A reduced MCD leads to an overall decrease in memory usage. Since lowering the MCD leads to less concurrently active circuits, the amount of data that needs to be hold in memory is also reduced and thus the results are as expected.

Since the memory is constantly rising for both the entire simulation and for each simulated entity, which is especially visible for the client, we investigated whether we could reproduce those findings. We used a small network with one authority node, one exit, one guard, one node with guard and exit capabilities

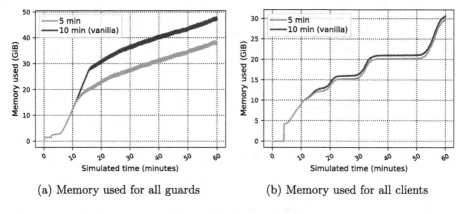

(a) Memory used for all guards   (b) Memory used for all clients

Fig. 4. Memory used with half the MCD

and one middle node. 20 clients with access to 10 server were used in a simulation of 72 h. The memory consumption rises for all nodes in the network without showing a significant decrease. One might think we just missed the *free* calls or *Tor* might free memory in a different way. However, fluctuations can be seen during the whole operation. Additionally, the memory usage of the whole simulation rises constantly which is measured using a different method and independent of the memory allocation in the simulated application. Following the same trend as the graphs for the memory consumption of the clients (Fig. 3b, Fig. 4b), this simulation showed noticeable jumps in memory consumption throughout the entirety of the simulation. We were not able to reproduce these results using *Chutney* which hint towards the possibility of a memory leak in *Shadow*. This behavior can still be seen using *Shadow* version "2" and *Tor* version "0.4.6.8".

4.2   Privacy

To evaluate the risks of changing the MCD, we measure the Shannon entropy of Tor's circuit selection and simulate an adversary that is capable of end-to-end correlation attacks. Furthermore, we discuss the implications of a changed MCD with respect to other attacks on Tor. We note that small changes to the MCD do not compromise privacy, larger changes need to be investigated further.

First, we review the impact on circuit selection. To compute the Shannon entropy in our simulations, all combinations of selected input and output combinations were used as input. After about 10 min of simulated time, the entropy stabilizes and stays constant throughout the remaining simulation. For all evaluated values of the MCD and without changing the circuit selection mechanism, a maximum deviation of about 0.2% is observed and, thus, falls within the margin of error.

While simulating an adversary who controls 10% of Tor's guard and exit bandwidth with an unmodified entropy for circuit selection, we could not determine a significant difference in the total amount of compromised traffic for any

MCD. However, the number of compromised circuits scales with the total amount of created circuits. An MCD of 5 min results in 3% more circuits only while an MCD of 30 s results in 50% more circuits. The rate of compromise does not change.

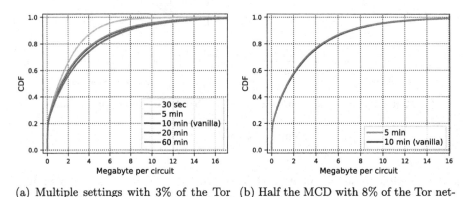

(a) Multiple settings with 3% of the Tor network

(b) Half the MCD with 8% of the Tor network

Fig. 5. Megabytes transferred per circuit with different MCD settings

Figure 5 shows the cumulative distribution fraction for transferred megabytes per circuit. Figure 5a shows that the lower the MCD, the less data is transferred per circuit. If we focus on the MCD of 5 min we see practically no difference to the default MCD (Fig. 5b). These results are in line with the total amount of created circuits, where we could only observe a significant difference for a low MCDs of 30 s. For higher MCDs, the data transferred per circuit is roughly the same.

Overall, changing the MCD does not affect the amount of compromised data. However, a reduction to 30 s results in 50% more circuits and the time to first compromise in end-to-end correlation attacks is reduced. The actual effects of more generated circuits on different attacks needs to be investigated in future work. The impact of halving the default MCD from 10 min to 5 min could be acceptable, as this results in only 3% more circuits.

4.3   Impact on Other Attacks

Results show that with lower MCDs, the number of created circuits increases. Each newly created circuit also increases the probability of selecting a compromised relay. This results in a higher risk of traffic correlation attacks [15]. An increase of circuits might reduce the time of first compromise. Whether and to what extent this is the case could be subject of further research.

The impact of different MCDs on attacks, such as circuit or website fingerprinting, depends on the aspects of the actual attack, underlying adversary model and user behavior. By decreasing the MCD, circuits are generally closed earlier.

Consequently, they are used for fewer connections which facilitates the distinction of different contexts for an adversary [32]. For users of the Tor Browser, this circumstance does not pose a significant additional threat as the browser isolates circuits to the URL bar domain [20]. The adversary would therefore gain little additional knowledge. However, there is no solution for Tor users that do not rely on the Tor browser yet. The specific effects of very short MCD, have yet to be studied.

5   Conclusion

After evaluating different MCDs, our results show that lowering the MCD from a default of 10 min to 5 min greatly reduces the memory usage of Tor relays. The initial concern that low MCDs might negatively impact the CPU usage or throughput proved to be mostly unfounded. Only for the original MCD of 30 s a degradation could be observed and leads to a significant increase of generated circuits. This did not, however, apply to any other tested MCDs. In fact, lowering the MCD to 5 min only results in a slight increase of circuits but reduces the memory consumption by 20%.

With a reduced MCD, alternative circuit selection strategies, that would usually be impractical due to high memory usage or large number of concurrently open circuits, could now become a feasible option. This includes, e.g., isolating streams based on their target, which was analyzed by Kiran et al. [17].

During the evaluation, we noticed a memory leak caused by either *Tor* or *Shadow*. We were not able to reproduce the issue neither outside the simulation nor to find the cause of that leak. Fixing the issue might allow for larger simulation setups or to even free additional memory of Tor relays.

While we simulated the Tor network during different time periods and used different seeds for the simulation, the underlying traffic model did not change. Our results are therefore dependent on the accuracy of this particular traffic model. Moreover, the model is based on a default MCD of 10 min which might impact the obtained results. Tests with other traffic models could help to clarify whether this might have introduced a bias or skewed the data otherwise.

Finally, the evaluation focused specifically on performance aspects of our simulation. Future work should also pay attention to the possible impact on security aspects, i.e., how changes to the MCD might influence traffic correlation and circuit or website fingerprinting attacks.

References

1. AlSabah, M., Bauer, K., Elahi, T., Goldberg, I.: The path less travelled: overcoming tor's bottlenecks with traffic splitting. In: De Cristofaro, E., Wright, M. (eds.) PETS 2013. LNCS, vol. 7981, pp. 143–163. Springer, Heidelberg (2013). https://doi.org/10.1007/978-3-642-39077-7_8

2. Diaz, C.: Anonymity metrics revisited. In: Dagstuhl Seminar Proceedings. Schloss Dagstuhl-Leibniz-Zentrum für Informatik (2006)

3. Díaz, C., Seys, S., Claessens, J., Preneel, B.: Towards measuring anonymity. In: Dingledine, R., Syverson, P. (eds.) PET 2002. LNCS, vol. 2482, pp. 54–68. Springer, Heidelberg (2003). https://doi.org/10.1007/3-540-36467-6_5

4. Google Inc., Let's Make the Web Faster - Google Code, 26 May 2010. https:// web.archive.org/web/20120324082535/https://code.google.com/speed/articles/ web-metrics.html. Accessed 13 Jan 2022

5. Hanley, H., et al.: DPSelect: a differential privacy based guard relay selection algorithm for Tor. In: PoPETs 2019, no. 2 (2019)

6. Heaptrack. KDE Applications. https://apps.kde.org/heaptrack/. Accessed 13 Jan 2022

7. HTTP Archive: Page Weight (2021). https://archive.org/reports/page-weight. Accessed 06 Jan 2022

8. Imani, M., Amirabadi, M., Wright, M.: Modified relay selection and circuit selection for faster tor. IET Commun. **13**(17), 2723–2734 (2019)

9. Jansen, R.: Shadow - the shadow simulator. https://shadow.github.io/. Accessed 13 Jan 2022

10. Jansen, R.: Shadow/Tornettools. shadow, 10 July 2021. https://github.com/ shadow/tornettools. Accessed 13 Jan 2022

11. Jansen, R., Hopper, N.: Shadow: running tor in a box for accurate and efficient experimentation (2012)

12. Jansen, R., Johnson, A.: Safely measuring tor. In: CCS, pp. 1553–1567. ACM (2016)

13. Jansen, R., Tracey, J., Goldberg, I.: Once is never enough: foundations for sound statistical inference in tor network experimentation. arXiv preprint arXiv:2102.05196 (2021)

14. Jansen, R., Traudt, M., Hopper, N.: Privacy-preserving dynamic learning of tor network traffic. In: CCS, pp. 1944–1961. ACM (2018). https://doi.org/10.1145/ 3243734.3243815

15. Johnson, A., et al.: Users get routed: traffic correlation on tor by realistic adversaries. In: CCS, pp. 337–348. ACM (2013)

16. Kim, H., Lee, S., Kim, J.: Inferring browser activity and status through remote monitoring of storage usage. In: ACSAC, pp. 410–421. ACM (2016). https://doi. org/10.1145/2991079.2991080

17. Kiran, K., et al.: Anonymity and performance analysis of stream isolation in tor network. In: ICCCNT, pp. 1–6. IEEE (2019)

18. Koch, R., Golling, M., Rodosek, G.D.: Disequilibrium: tor's exit node selection under the stereoscope. In: Trustcom/BigDataSE/ISPA, vol. 1, pp. 942–949. IEEE (2015)

19. Mani, A., et al.: Understanding tor usage with privacy-preserving measurement. In: IMC, pp. 175–187 (2018)

20. Perry, M., et al.: The design and implementation of the tor browser [DRAFT]. 15 June 2018. https://2019.www.torproject.org/projects/torbrowser/ design/. Accessed 13 Jan 2022

21. Resource.h « Linux « Uapi « Include - Kernel/Git/Torvalds/Linux.Git - Linux Kernel Source Tree. https://git.kernel.org/pub/scm/linux/kernel/git/torvalds/linux. git/tree/include/uapi/linux/resource.h#n66. Accessed 13 Jan 2022

22. Jansen, R.: OnionTrace. shadow, 6 October 2020. https://github.com/shadow/ oniontrace. Accessed 13 Jan 2022

23. Jansen, R.: TGen. shadow, 6 October 2020. https://github.com/shadow/tgen. Accessed 13 Jan 2022

24. Serjantov, A., Danezis, G.: Towards an information theoretic metric for anonymity. In: Dingledine, R., Syverson, P. (eds.) PET 2002. LNCS, vol. 2482, pp. 41–53. Springer, Heidelberg (2003). https://doi.org/10.1007/3-540-36467-6_4
25. Shannon, C.E.: A mathematical theory of communication. Bell Syst. Tech. J. **27**(3), 379–423 (1948)
26. Shen, S., Gao, J., Wu, A.: Weakness identification and flow analysis based on tor network. In: CNS, pp. 90–94. IEEE (2018)
27. Sun, Y., et al.: RAPTOR: routing attacks on privacy in tor. In: Usenix Security, pp. 271–286 (2015)
28. Syverson, P., Dingledine, R., Mathewson, N.: Tor: the second-generation onion router, pp. 303–320 (2004)
29. The Tor Project. Welcome to Tor Metrics. https://metrics.torproject.org/. Accessed 13 Jan 2022
30. Tor Project. Chutney - The Chutney Tool for Testing and Automating Tor Network Setup. https://gitweb.torproject.org/chutney.git. Accessed 13 Jan 2022
31. Wacek, C., et al.: An empirical evaluation of relay selection in tor. In: NDSS (2013)
32. Wang, T., Goldberg, I.: Improved website fingerprinting on tor. In: WPES, pp. 201–212. ACM (2013)

Forensics

D-Cloud-Collector: Admissible Forensic Evidence from Mobile Cloud Storage

Mark Vella$^{(\boxtimes)}$ⓘ and Christian Colombo$^{(\boxtimes)}$ⓘ

Department of Computer Science, University of Malta, Msida, Malta
{mark.vella,christian.colombo}@um.edu.mt

Abstract. Difficulties with accessing device content or even the device itself can seriously hamper smartphone forensics. Mobile cloud storage, which extends on-device capacity, provides an avenue for a forensic collection process that does not require physical access to the device. Rather, it is possible to remotely retrieve credentials from a device of interest through undercover operations, followed by live cloud forensics. While technologically appealing, this approach raises concerns with evidence preservation, ranging from the use of malware-like operations, to linking the collected evidence with the physically absent smartphone, and possible mass surveillance accusations. In this paper, we propose a solution to ease these concerns by employing hardware security modules to provide for controlled live cloud forensics and tamper-evident access logs. A Google Drive-based proof of concept, using the SEcube hardware security module, demonstrates that *D-Cloud-Collector* is feasible whenever the performance penalty incurred is affordable.

Keywords: Cloud storage forensics · Digital evidence preservation · Right to privacy · Hardware security modules · Tamper-evident logs

1 Introduction

Nowadays, smartphones store sufficient data about their owners to the extent that they can provide a single source of digital forensic evidence to solve incidents involving criminal behaviour [19]. On the flip side, the same sophisticated technology that comes in handy for investigators can also be used to block access to digital evidence [5]. Locked/encrypted or even missing/damaged devices are a case in point. Firmware manipulation combined with device rooting, or else hardware-level acquisition, provide some options to investigators. Yet these tend to be very intrusive or else cannot fully solve the encrypted content problem respectively [15]. In the case of the San Bernardino terror attack[1], a spectacular stand-off between law enforcement and technology vendors ensued. While in

---

[1] https://www.insidescience.org/news/looming-end-smartphone-company-law-enforcement-standoff.

This work is supported by the LOCARD Project under Grant H2020-SU-SEC-2018-832735.

W. Meng et al. (Eds.): SEC 2022, IFIP AICT 648, pp. 161–178, 2022.
https://doi.org/10.1007/978-3-031-06975-8_10

this case a third party forensics tool vendor came to the rescue, such solutions remain largely specific to device models and operating system versions [13,17], and taken out by security updates.

In recent years the mobile security landscape has witnessed a significant increase in malware exploiting social engineering tactics [25], as well as advanced software exploitation able to pull off successful credentials attacks of sorts [17]. Once deployed in a sufficiently controlled manner, the same malware techniques could offer a remote solution that does not even require physical access to smartphones. The key enablers of this approach comprise mobile cloud storage services and the application programmer interfaces (APIs) exposed by them (e.g. Google Drive for Developers[2] and the CloudKit framework for Apple iCloud[3]). To compensate for physical storage constraints, smartphone vendors offer cloud storage services (for file storage and app data backups) that integrate seamlessly with the mobile operating system (OS) along with a storage quota for free.

Once retrieved stealthily during an undercover operation, credentials can be used by a cloud forensics tool that consumes cloud storage APIs. Akin to the classic telephone tapping context, investigators can present a probable cause to believe that a remote undercover operation could help in solving a serious crime, such as drug trafficking, money laundering, or terrorism [21]. In this case, the arrangement executes a remote credentials theft attack on the target device. Similar to the classic phone context, however, law enforcement agencies are held to a higher standard of operational integrity due to the intrusive nature of such operations. Recent accusations of mass surveillance by governments using the Pegasus spyware have caused an uproar[4], invoking a breach of the right to privacy as described by the Universal Declaration of Human Rights Article 12 [20], and associated laws, e.g. GDPR in the EU.

1.1 Research Problem

A universally accepted mechanism to preserve evidence, thereby helping in having it admissible for court proceedings, is the forensic chain of custody (CoC) [4]. A comprehensive CoC involving digital investigation is required, such that for any given evidence, the following is included with proper authentication using digitally signed hashes [6]: i. the custodian (e.g. first responders, case investigators), ii. details of the evidence itself with proper identification (e.g. phone IMEI or storage image checksum), iii. relevant case details, iv. the temporal information associated with the evidence and custody, as well as v. the spatial data related to the evidence location. Overall, the CoC should be suitable to track the entire lifecycle of evidence as proof of its integrity.

In our case (see Fig. 1), the CoC is also burdened with demonstrating proper usage of the remotely retrieved credentials. In particular, investigators need support in establishing that credentials usage falls within the parameters of not

---

[2] https://developers.google.com/drive.

[3] https://developer.apple.com/documentation/cloudkit/.

[4] https://theconversation.com/spyware-why-the-booming-surveillance-tech-industry-is-vulnerable-to-corruption-and-abuse-164917.

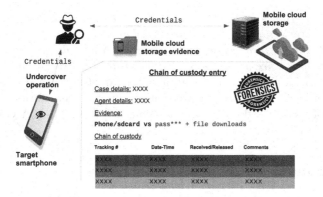

Fig. 1. *D-Cloud-Collector*: reconciling mobile cloud storage evidence obtained via remote undercover operations with forensic chains of custody.

impinging on the target's right to privacy. One further issue concerns compatibility with existing CoC. In the case of mobile forensics, typical CoC entries correspond to a physical device or part thereof, e.g. sd card. In this manner, the CoC entry for the device links it to the digital image, while any extracted evidence relates to the authenticated digital image. However, the stolen credentials approach does not fit this generally accepted procedure. Instead, in this case, the credentials do not immediately associate with the device in question. Digital evidence is collected through live forensics rather than forensic imaging of device storage. Device confiscation is not even required.

1.2 Contributions

In this paper, we propose *D-Cloud-Collector* (DCC), a live forensics solution for mobile cloud storage that reconciles with CoC requirements: 1a. Credentials are obtained through an undercover operation only after approval by the relevant authorities. 1b. All access to cloud evidence is fully authenticated and logged through the use of a removable Hardware Security Module (HSM), e.g. a USB token, which also provides 1c. A one-to-one mapping between the acquired evidence and the absent mobile device. All this whilst ensuring 2. Security and 3. Practicality in terms of performance, although at the cost of additional evidence collection time.

The scope of work presented in this paper is to validate the HSM's central role in DCC. This hardware component provides secure storage and usage of the authorization tokens and symmetric keys needed for the secure access of cloud APIs. Additionally, a secure hash-based primitive implemented inside the HSM enables tamper-evident cloud API access to logs. Ancillary features already widely used in security solutions complete the full DCC picture. Specifically, the HSM's tamper-evident features, CPU protection rings, and anti-code injection module loaded by the forensic collection tool on the investigator's workstation protect the security of the HSM itself. We defer their in-depth treatment to subsequent work.

The key contributions of this work, therefore, aim to answer the following research question: *"How can HSMs be utilised as a basis to collect evidence from mobile cloud storage, through stealthily-retrieved credentials, in a manner that is consistent with evidence preservation and the right to protect personal data?"* To this end we provide: 1. A characterization of the target use case and a conceptual description of DCC (Sect. 4). 2. A proof-of-concept implementation of the HSM component of DCC based on the SEcube chip [26] (Sect. 5). 3. A Google Drive case study (Sect. 6).

2   Background

Credentials Theft Vectors on Smartphones. Spyware targeting Android [25] and iOS [11] smartphones alike propagate in the form of trojan/infected versions of legitimate apps. Statistics show that detection mechanisms employed by app stores let through a significant number of spyware samples [9]. While tech-savvy users may get suspicious by the sheer amount of permissions required by these rogue apps during the installation process, a good number of users do fall prey to their deceptive tactics [27]. Even more so, certain threat vectors allow trojan apps not to look overly suspicious [22], bypassing the need for sensitive permissions or requiring any device rooting/jailbreaking. The result is highly stealthy malware that goes unnoticed by victims for long periods.

OAuth2. DCC relies on cloud service providers supporting an authorization mechanism that allows account owners to delegate privileges to third party apps. While not tied to a specific mechanism, OAuth2 is a widely adopted standard framework [7], and our DCC implementation assumes it. It presupposes HTTPS and the consequently derived security services from the underpinning TLS1.3. The critical step in OAuth2 is app-flow redirection through a web browser requesting user content for the third-party app, which is granted access to the user's cloud service account. Following successful third-party application and user permission granting, the application receives an access token to be presented by all subsequent access requests. A refresh token is also obtained and is used whenever a new access token is needed following its expiration.

Hardware Security Modules. Hardware security modules aim to make up for the limitations faced by software-only protection mechanisms. While secure elements, trusted platform modules (TPM) and Trusted Execution Environments (TEE) are bound to specific hardware, HSMs offer a more flexible solution [8]. These devices typically take the form of high-performance plugin cards[5] or removable external devices[6]; their primary application being secure cryptography implementation (standard PKCS#11 [24] is dedicated for this purpose).

---

[5] https://cpl.thalesgroup.com/encryption/hardware-security-modules/general-purpose-hsms.

[6] https://www.secube.blu5group.com/products/usecube-bundle-including-5-usecube-tokens-and-1-devkit/.

3   Related Work

Along with the analysis of messaging apps, the importance of mobile forensics in criminal investigations involving the use of cloud storage services has already been acknowledged [3]. While cloud storage forensics has been explored from multiple aspects, to the best of our knowledge, our work is the first to focus specifically on mobile cloud storage forensics, where the collection process leverages stealthily obtaining credentials. This collection method effectively replaces the conventional confiscate-unlock-image-collect-analyze procedure [15]. DCC's role is restricted to the collection phase, replacing phone storage imaging with cloud storage collection using the obtained credentials. The need for device confiscation and unlocking is replaced by remote installation of undercover investigation software. Evidence examination and the associated CoC can proceed similarly to any phone-present approach, possibly even through a distributed CoC based on a distributed ledger [12,14].

DCC could also extend the role of the undercover operation software beyond credentials retrieval and make it collect evidence from cloud storage. This approach would avoid the need for an HSM to protect the retrieved credentials from dishonest investigators. Instead, the cloud storage evidence could be registered directly into a CoC by the undercover tool, with the integrity of this operation safeguarded by blockchain-backed evidence storage [10]. However, this approach entails a significant extension of the covert operation. When considering the computationally intensive evidence collection operation, this approach could severely increase the chance of giving away the entire operation.

The Cloud-Forensics-as-a-Service model (CFaaS) [18] is a cloud forensic process model that requires a prior agreement between the cloud service providers and consumers. The model expects both parties to synchronise on both sides' forensic data collection process, with the correlation of evidence collected on each side carried out during a subsequent analysis stage. The bilateral agreement is finalised during a cloud forensic readiness stage. A similar approach [1] that focuses on cyberattacks targeting mobile cloud apps goes as far as requiring the synchronisation of client and server-side forensic readiness. With cloud service providers' provision of log services for forensic investigation purposes, concerns related to the possibility of malicious behaviour also abound. In this regard, logging services must be hardened against dishonest cloud users, providers, and investigators [28]. Threats to secure logging comprise scenarios where the three entities are individually malicious or collude. Public key cryptography ensures confidentiality, while chained hashes of log entries along with proofs of past logs ensure integrity. On its part, DCC employs a similar log hashing scheme in the HSM to ensure tamper-evident logs. On the other hand, OAuth2 tokens for evidence retrieval ensure that cloud storage from other accounts remains inaccessible. Furthermore, read-only tokens should be prioritized whenever provided, thus protecting evidence integrity.

In contrast, the approach taken in DCC reflects the most likely scenario occurring during a criminal investigation, where no prior agreements exist, nor is any collaboration sought from the cloud provider. This scenario is not unique

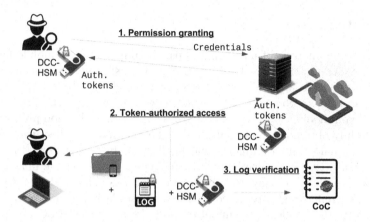

Fig. 2. A HSM-centric approach to DCC.

to DCC, and in fact, some consumer-driven cloud forensic solutions that address different settings than the one studied in this work have already been explored [16]. The motivating factors are several. Besides the organisational challenge otherwise entailed, legal obstacles also loom [22]. Existing mutual legal assistance treaties are considered inadequate for the cross-border sharing of cloud evidence. Legal frameworks proposed to address this scenario have been widely criticised for violations of international law and for not being sufficiently sensitive to human rights. DCC focuses on the technical aspects of cloud forensics, providing means through which investigators can demonstrate the case-relevant usage of the stealthily obtained credentials.

4   Use Case and Conceptual Design

The assumed context within which DCC-based tools are to operate is as follows:

1. A bilateral agreement between the cloud service provider and the investigators is unavailable or perhaps not even possible.
2. An undercover investigation software has been implanted onto the target's smartphone using social engineering or software exploitation for delivery. Subsequently, it obtains the cloud credentials (user & password) while suppressing any alerts related to their usage by investigators.
3. A proxy server placed between the investigator's workstation and the cloud service provider, which doubles as a log management server, might offer a solution. Yet this arrangement is not deemed fully compatible with CoC practices unless sufficient resources are available to dedicate servers per case, only releasing them on case closure.

This last assumption merits further elaboration. In this hypothetical setup, during an initialisation stage, the cloud credentials are supplied directly to the proxy server and subsequently exchanged for authorization tokens. From this point onward, an investigator workstation collects the related cloud evidence, performing all API requests through this proxy server, with the server adding the authorization tokens and performing de/encryption. Responses take the reverse route with the authorization tokens stripped from responses after decryption and ultimately delivering collected evidence to the investigator. The credentials are only used directly for a very brief period, after which they can be disposed of for further integrity. If the authorization tokens never leave the proxy server in plaintext form, there is no other way to make use of them. Similarly, access request logs are managed solely by the proxy server and are considered tamper-proof. The digitally signed access logs are to be registered with the CoC, thereby considered authentic and comprehensive of all cloud storage accesses.

However, the proxy server approach is difficult to reconcile with CoC requirements concerning linking the access logs and associated mobile cloud evidence with the absent smartphone. Suppose it was possible to dedicate a physical proxy server per case. In that scenario, it could be considered a replacement of the physically missing smartphone, with the collected cloud evidence and access logs replacing the phone's storage forensic image. Yet this comes across as an expensive proposition, especially for long-running cases. The idea of a proxy device that replaces the smartphone under custody is a concept we would like to stick to, but at the same time, it also has to be cost-effective. DCC proposes to use a dedicated HSM, referred to here as the *DCC-HSM*, as a much cheaper option than a dedicated proxy server. The tamper-evident features expected of any HSM combined with local-only access present the restricted attack surface.

As shown in Fig. 2, the first two DCC stages, *permission granting* and *token-authorized access* mirror the proxy server-based approach. The DCC-HSM is attached locally to the investigator workstation, at the expense of offering reduced computational power compared to a fully-fledged server. Access logs also become prone to tampering prior to digitally signing them. An additional secure hash-based operation is therefore required and is employed during an additional *log verification* stage. The collected evidence, along with tamper-evident access logs, offer a replacement for forensic smartphone storage images. Thereby, the DCC-HSM provides a physical substitute for the missing phone.

5 Proposed Approach—D-Cloud-Collector (DCC)

D-Cloud-Collector (DCC) is a live forensics solution for mobile cloud storage obtained through the undercover retrieval of credentials from smartphones.

5.1 DCC Architecture

Figure 3 presents how DCC's main components are used during the first two stages of operation. The start of the 'permission granting' stage assumes that a session key has already been negotiated over TLS and is solely stored inside the HSM, referred to as *DCC-HSM*. Once the 'permission granting' procedures

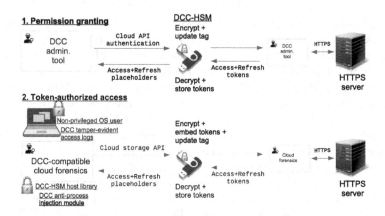

Fig. 3. The *D-Cloud-Collector* (DCC) components and their involvement in the first two stages of operation. The central role of the hardware security module (DCC-HSM) is noteworthy.

begin, the *DCC administration tool* forwards a cloud API authentication request to the DCC-HSM. The request is first encrypted with the stored symmetric key and returned to the administration tool. Subsequently, it is forwarded to the cloud web server as HTTPS traffic, causing the previously discussed OAuth2 flow redirection and is the only point in time at which the investigator provides the stolen user/password. The corresponding encrypted response is sent back to the DCC administration tool (through an embedded web server) containing the OAuth2 refresh/access tokens. It is the DCC-HSMs responsibility to decrypt the response, extract the tokens and store them on the HSM, while at the same time replacing them with placeholder tokens inside the plaintext response. The availability of the OAuth2 tokens—which never leave the DCC-HSM in plaintext—is the key prerequisite for the second stage.

The token-authorized access stage represents all file download requests made to the cloud API server using the previously obtained OAuth2 tokens, renegotiating further TLS session keys as required. All API requests pass through the DCC-HSM for replacing the placeholder tokens with the actual ones, with subsequent encryption. Most responses will contain the downloaded evidence and which ones are to be decrypted again by DCC-HSM. During this second stage, any *cloud forensics tool* which is *compatible with DCC* instantiates the administration tool, i.e. a tool that can implement the flows shown in Fig. 3, with DCC-HSM integration through a *host library* being a key requirement. Throughout both stages, all encryption requests also result in the computation of an authentication tag that depends on all previous encrypted requests. In this manner, the authenticity of the cloud access log, external to the HSM, can be verified.

DCC also carries several security requirements to protect the OAuth2 tokens inside the DCC-HSM, i.e. beyond the fact that the HSM needs to be tamper-evident. The key requirement comprises TLS session keys to be immediately scrubbed from memory by the DCC administration and DCC-compatible cloud

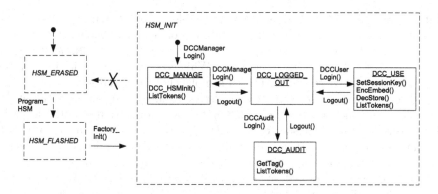

Fig. 4. DCC-HSM's lifecycle.

forensics tool. By doing so, a malicious DCC end-user never gets the opportunity to decrypt ciphertext containing the access tokens. Besides requiring tool conformity, this requirement also entails tool hardening to protect from tool tampering, thereby fending off any future accusations that some form of foul-play was ever involved when handling cloud storage credentials. The first ancillary component comprises operating system (OS)-level access controls that prohibit *non-privileged OS users* from debugging program memory, or else to carry out process injection to leak session keys. Since process-injection can also happen through software bug exploitation, an additional *anti-process injection module* is also needed. Given that all the ancillary components secure the DCC-HSM, we choose to focus on describing this central component first for the scope of this paper. An in-depth treatment of the ancillary components makes sense only once the design of the DCC-HSM is thoroughly explored. We, therefore, start by delving deeper into the DCC-HSM's functionality.

5.2 The DCC-HSM Component

Figure 4 illustrates the DCC-HSM's lifecycle as a state machine. The top-level states correspond to the state transitions that take an HSM without any firmware to an operational state that is flashed with a binary image. Initially, the DCC-HSM is operated upon by the DCC administration tool. Specifically, starting with an empty device in the HSM_ERASED state, the HSM is flashed with software and transitions to HSM_FLASHED. At this point, the DCC-HSM device exposes its services through the host library. Factory_Init() is always the first service to be called where it initialises device parameters not strictly related to DCC functionality, e.g. device PINs and serial numbers. Once called, the DCC-HSM transitions into HSM_INIT. This top-level state is programmatically irreversible, implying DCC-HSM's strict association with a specific case, effectively replacing the physically missing device.

Once in HSM_INIT the DCC-HSM is ready to take part in the three DCC stages, providing access to its services depending on the current HSM_INIT sub-state.

Initially, only the DCC_MANAGE state is accessible via DCC_ManagerLogin(). Still within the context of the DCC administration tool, once supplied with the correct device administrator PIN, this operation takes the device to the HSM_MANAGE state, thereby setting DCC-specific parameters. While logged in this device in manager mode, it is possible to set the OAuth2 token placeholders and reserve space for the actual token strings on the device's persistent memory. Furthermore, the initial authentication tag value is set. HSM_HSMInit() is the operation responsible for all these tasks. On a newly flashed device, this operation is called automatically with default values, i.e. besides the possibility of being called explicitly with specific values. This means that from the point of calling Logout() onward, the device is ready for DCC participation (see Fig. 3). The DCC_USE state requires a normal user login (DCCUserLogin()). In this state, TLS-negotiated session keys are provided through SetSessionKey(). API request/response en/decryption, and the associated access token storage and placeholder replacement services are provided by EncEmbed() and DecStore(). Both the 'permission granting' and the 'token-authorized access' DCC stages operate in the DCC_USE state. On completion of the first stage, the DCC-HSM stores the OAuth2 refresh and access token strings. These tokens are used by both the EncEmbed() and DecStore() operations to replace, or be replaced by, the placeholder tokens respectively. Assuming that the stealthily obtained passwords are safely disposed of, in this configuration, the DCC-HSM becomes the only medium through which the mobile cloud storage can be accessed.

Loaded with a refresh/access token pair, whose presence (not values) is verifiable through ListTokens(), the device is now ready to be operated upon by the DCC-compatible cloud forensics tool. The next time that a cloud evidence search-and-download procedure is needed, a call to DCCUserLogin() takes the DCC-HSM back to the DCC_USE state, and following calls to SetSessionKey() as necessary, a sequence of EncEmbed() and DecStore() operations are invoked to securely perform authorized requests followed by file downloads. The last two operations are also responsible for updating the internally-stored authentication tag. Each tag is computed out of the sequence of web API requests, comprising the entire plaintext HTTP request headers and any payload data. Whenever requests contain OAuth2 tokens, the tag is computed using the placeholder tokens rather than the actual token strings. Otherwise, it wouldn't be possible to verify the externally-stored logs, which should not have access to the token strings but only the placeholders. For this reason, the external log verification procedure must adhere to the following constraints: i. It synchronises the initial authentication tag with DCC-HSM, and ii. It processes an access log corresponding to the concatenation of plaintext requests as sent to the DCC-HSM for encryption. Tag computation is based on the hash extend algorithm, universally employed by TPMs [2], where for the next access log entry, a new tag t' is computed out of the previous tag t as: $t' \leftarrow hash(t \,\|\, \text{log entry})$.

Whenever access log verification is required (DCC stage 3), DCC_AuditLogin() has to be called by the DCC administration tool to transition the DCC-HSM to the DCC_AUDIT state. This transition represents an auditor login.

In this state, it becomes possible to call the `GetTag()` service, which retrieves the last computed tag. Likewise, the access log generated by the cloud forensics tool is passed on to the DCC administration tool. It computes an external tag starting with the same initial tag. Only a pair of matching DCC-HSM/external tags constitutes proof of authenticity. On the other hand, a non-match event indicates a tampered-with log. Furthermore, since a successful 'permission granting' DCC stage leaves the DCC-HSM the only way to access the corresponding mobile cloud storage, the access log is also deemed comprehensive.

6 DCC-HSM Proof of Concept Evaluation

6.1 SEcube HSM

We prototyped DCC-HSM on the SEcube chip [26]. We chose this chip due to the tamper-evident features of its embedded STM32F4 microcontroller, a very low power ARM Cortex M4 RISC 180 MHz CPU, with on-chip 256 KB SRAM and 2 MB flash. Importantly, any firmware developed on its corresponding developer board is immediately transferable to the USEcube™ USB Token[7] priced approximately just over €100. Furthermore, this multi-chip module also stacks a Lattice MachXO2-7000 device and an EAL5+ certified secure element. The two components carry potential for future enhancements for hardware acceleration and authenticated firmware updates and private-key binding, respectively. The DCC-HSM firmware is developed on top of the OpenSDK software libraries[8], comprising a device-side firmware and host-device libraries that communicate over the USB mass storage device class. WolfCrypt's ChaCha20/Poly1305 authenticated stream cipher was integrated with the firmware using STM32CubeMX to provide TLS1.3-compatible authenticated encryption. This cipher offers a popular option for hardware lacking AES acceleration. The complete DCC-HSM services (Fig. 4) implemented in the SEcube's firmware are exposed as additions to the OpenSDK's host libraries. Logic related to the DCC administration and cloud forensics tools uses the Python bindings for the Drive API (V3). All sources experiment (discussed next) files are available for download[9].

6.2 Google Drive Case Study

The Google Drive app is available for both Android and iOS devices, providing 15 GB of storage[10]. Aspects of the three DCC stages (Fig. 2) follow.

---

[7] https://www.secube.blu5group.com/products/usecube-bundle-including-5-usecube-tokens-and-1-devkit/.

[8] https://github.com/SEcube-Project/SEcube-SDK.

[9] https://github.com/mmarrkv/DCC.

[10] https://play.google.com/store/apps/details?id=com.google.android.apps.docs.

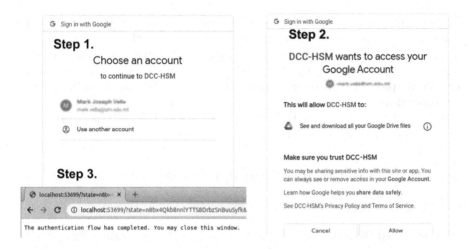

Fig. 5. DCC's permission granting stage with a Google OAuth 2.0 endpoint.

Stage 1: Permission Granting. The following snippet shows the (redacted) JSON store associated with the DCC administration and cloud forensics tools.

```
{"installed":
{"client_id":"<snip...>",
 "project_id":"dcc-hsm",
 "auth_uri":"https://accounts.google.com/o/oauth2/auth",
 "token_uri":"https://oauth2.googleapis.com/token",
 "auth_provider_x509_cert_url":"https://www.googleapis.com/oauth2/v1/
       certs",
 "client_secret":"<snip...>",
 "redirect_uris":["urn:ietf:wg:oauth:2.0:oob", "http://localhost"]}}
```

In particular, the application is registered to use the native application OAuth2 flow (`installed`), application name (`project_id`) and credentials (`client_id`, `client_secret`), the authorization service to which they are to be sent (`auth_uri`), and `http://localhost`, specifying that the access tokens will be sent to a local web server. Figure 5 includes screen captures from the permission granting process, involving flow redirection to a web browser (step 1) where the stolen password will have to be used, granting access to DCC-HSM (step 2), and receipt of an authorization code by the locally spawned web server (step 3).

The authorization code is intended for the OAuth2 token service (`token_uri`), with the following request/response snippets showing the receipt of both refresh and access tokens. Following response decryption, actual token strings remain on the HSM with the administration/forensics applications only getting access to the placeholder strings `PLC_ACC*` and `PLC_RFSH*`[11]. The `scope` of the tokens was chosen to provide read-only access to the Google Drive account concerned, further strengthening evidence preservation.

---

[11] Stale Google tokens are actually used in the implementation.

```
POST https://oauth2.googleapis.com/token HTTP/1.1
Host: oauth2.googleapis.com <snip...>
HTTP/1.1 200 OK<snip...>
{ "access_token": "PLC_ACC<snip...>",
  "expires_in": 3599,
  "refresh_token": "PLC_RFRSH<snip...>",
  "scope": "https://www.googleapis.com/auth/drive.readonly",
  "token_type": "Bearer"
```

Stage 2: Token-Authorized Access. The second stage involves the bulk of
the evidence collection process, yet it is the most straightforward stage
from a DCC point-of-view. Web API endpoints corresponding to stored files
(drive/v3/files/*) are accessed with the placeholder tokens placed inside the
authorization HTTP header. Once forwarded to the DCC-HSM, actual token
strings replace placeholders followed by encryption as per the following request
snippet, with the ensuing encrypted responses undergoing the reverse process.

```
GET https://www.googleapis.com/drive/v3/files/1
    Xay4B_uRSdxpmDJypmYwJi8gro1bR7B1?alt=media HTTP/1.1
Host: www.googleapis.com
x-goog-api-client: gdcl/2.28.0 gl-python/3.8.5
range: bytes=0-104857600
authorization: Bearer PLC_ACC<...snip...>
```

Stage 3: Log Verification. The last stage of DCC needs to compare the currently
stored authentication tag with an external recomputation of the tag over the
access log. The key requirement is that the external computation synchronizes
its initial tag with the HSM's. The log itself comprises the exact same sequence
of plaintext HTTP requests sent to the HSM, i.e. containing the placeholder
tokens instead of actual strings, as follows:

```
POST https://oauth2.googleapis.com/token HTTP/1.1
Host: oauth2.googleapis.com<snip...>
GET https://www.googleapis.com/drive/v3/files?q=mimeType%3D%27
    application%2Fvnd.google-apps.folder%27+and+name+%3D+%27
    file_collection%27&pageSize=10&fields=nextPageToken%2C+files%28id
    %2C+name%29&alt=json HTTP/1.1
Host: www.googleapis.com<snip...>
authorization: Bearer PLC_ACC<snip...>
GET https://www.googleapis.com/drive/v3/files/1
    Xay4B_uRSdxpmDJypmYwJi8gro1bR7B1?alt=media<snip...>
authorization: Bearer PLC_ACC<snip...>
```

If the access log is in order, log verification returns a matching authentication tag. However, by property of cryptographic hashes, even a single character
modification would result in a completely different tag, exposing tampering.
Therefore, it is also essential that the external verification procedure uses the
same hash while ensuring no discrepancies between the implementations. For
our case study, both the SEcube firmware and the log verification routine make
use of WolfCrypt's SHA3-256, resulting in a matching tag for intact logs as per
the following:

```
>>: Device audit in progress
>>: Tag value: 8d 88 42 1f e4 9e <snip...>
>>>>>Compute Tag value outside DCC–HSM

Tag value: 8d 88 42 1f e4 9e <snip...>
>>>>>Comparison + verdict: MATCH
```

6.3 Security Analysis

Besides the tamper-evident registers supported by the chosen HSM and the additionally required DCC modules needed to protect session keys from malicious users (see Sect. 5.1), the firmware itself may still introduce security holes. A case in point concerns our first attempt at optimizing the implementation of DecStore(). This version assumed that token replacement is only needed for JSON-formatted payloads returned by calls to https://oauth2.googleapis.com/token. Yet this approach opened up the possibility for an attack that re-injects an HSM-encrypted request, now containing the actual token string, back to the HSM and have it decrypted, as shown by the following listing:

```
>>: Decryption in progress
GET https://www.googleapis.com/drive/v3/files?q=mimeType%3D%27
    application%2Fvnd.google-apps.folder%27+and+name+%3D+%27
    file_collection%27&pageSize=10&fields=nextPageToken%2C+files%28id
    %2C+name%29&alt=json HTTP/1.1<snip...>
authorization: Bearer ya29.a0ARrd<snip...>
```

Removal of this optimisation fixed the issue even though this cat-and-mouse scenario, to which every software is prone, is far from closed.

6.4 Performance Analysis

Our proposal trades a fully-fledged proxy server for a low-cost removable HSM, which incurs a performance penalty. Yet, here we are speaking about a collection process carrying no real-time requirements, i.e. besides completing evidence collection within a reasonable time frame. We measured the processing time required by the HSM to process all necessary requests involving evidence ranging from 1.5–15 GB, thus covering Google Drive's free storage capacity in 10 steps. For experiment repeatability, we obtained a packet capture of the traffic through a web proxy and conducted all measures in an offline manner. This web proxy setup entailed patching Python's httplib2 and requests modules to deactivate X.509 certificate verification. Figure 6 shows a plot of the measurements, including both un/patched versions of the firmware, as well as a baseline comprising the hpenc[12] fast encryption tool and which maximises the utilisation of the 8-core Intel© Core™ i7-10700 CPU @ 2.90 GHz used for experimentation.

Measurements show a quasi-linear increase in processing times for both firmware versions, ranging 0.9/1.2–7.4/8.1 h for un/patched versions. Repeated runs

---

[12] https://github.com/vstakhov/hpenc.

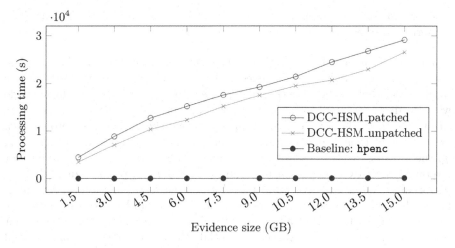

Fig. 6. DCC-HSM processing times for the 1.5–15 GB evidence range.

registered very little dispersion, with $\sigma = 19.1/28.9$ s, for un/patched versions with 1.5 GB evidence. The baseline's impressive handling of the increase in computation load is a stark reminder of the cost of security, providing controlled cloud storage access and log integrity with CoC compatibility.

7   Conclusions and Future Work

This paper proposed DCC: a live forensics solution for mobile cloud storage obtained through the undercover retrieval of smartphone credentials. In what follows, we revisit the aims and outline future directions.

CoC Requirements. DCC needs to provide evidence preservation and address mass surveillance concerns through compatibility with CoC requirements. The SEcube proof of concept for Google Drive emphasises the central role of the HSM in being a physical replacement for the missing smartphone. The HSM links directly to the stealthily retrieved passwords by securely storing the corresponding OAuth2 tokens. Being the only source for these tokens also provides controlled access to cloud storage. Therefore, the computed authentication tags go beyond detecting access log tampering to prove comprehensiveness. CoC entries can therefore proceed with a DCC-HSM-centric approach.

Security. Having validated the functionality aspect of the DCC-HSM through the Google Drive case study, the focus must now shift to security. Besides further security analysis of the current DCC-HSM, the missing DCC components that provide session key protection must be looked into. In this regard, a tamper-evident approach to system logs [23], along with a seamless process to harden stock cloud forensics tools against loading of additional code widely used by modern web browsers[13] are both in the pipeline.

Practicality. Our first DCC-HSM prototype demonstrates that DCC is practical even though the additional evidence collection time is a factor. Performance results show that the SEcube HSM can process 15 GB of evidence within a single working day. Yet provisions may be necessary in case of evidence tampering suspicions from the device owner's end, e.g. use the stolen password to lock owners out of their account through a password change. Avenues for speeding up the process are still available. For example, in SEcube's case, we still haven't leveraged the FPGA, while an upgrade to USB 3.0 can provide an immediate performance gain. Another issue may be posed by two-factor authentication (2FA) that would block DCC in its first stage. DCC can be updated to directly retrieve the OAuth2 tokens, although this enhancement mainly depends on what is possible in terms of undercover credentials theft. Alternatively, an extended permanence of the undercover operation tool can hijack all 2FA operations.

Final Remark. Besides the evidence preservation role, CoC compatibility is also needed for the 'right to protect personal data' purposes. From a technical perspective, the DCC proposition includes tamper-evident log controls, specifically to allow investigators to demonstrate the case-relevant usage of the stealthily obtained credentials. However, this aspect goes beyond the technical means of CoC compatibility. Once the security-related components of DCC are also in place, the focus can shift to legal matters, with field studies becoming necessary.

References

1. Ab Rahman, N.H., Cahyani, N.D.W., Choo, K.K.R.: Cloud incident handling and forensic-by-design: cloud storage as a case study. Concurr. Comput.: Pract. Exp. **29**(14), e3868 (2017)
2. Arthur, W., Challener, D., Goldman, K.: A Practical Guide to TPM 2.0: Using the New Trusted Platform Module in the New Age of Security. Springer, Heidelberg (2015). https://doi.org/10.1007/978-1-4302-6584-9
3. Cahyani, N.D.W., Ab Rahman, N.H., Glisson, W.B., Choo, K.K.R.: The role of mobile forensics in terrorism investigations involving the use of cloud storage service and communication apps. Mob. Netw. Appl. **22**(2), 240–254 (2017)
4. Casey, E.: Handbook of Digital Forensics and Investigation. Academic Press (2009)
5. Chernyshev, M., Zeadally, S., Baig, Z., Woodward, A.: Mobile forensics: advances, challenges, and research opportunities. IEEE Secur. Priv. **15**(6), 42–51 (2017)
6. Cosic, J., Baca, M.: A framework to (im) prove "chain of custody" in digital investigation process. In: Central European Conference on Information and Intelligent Systems, p. 435. Faculty of Organization and Informatics Varazdin (2010)
7. Hardt, D., et al.: The OAuth 2.0 authorization framework (2012)
8. Jauernig, P., Sadeghi, A.R., Stapf, E.: Trusted execution environments: properties, applications, and challenges. IEEE Secur. Priv. **18**(2), 56–60 (2020)

---

[13] https://blogs.windows.com/msedgedev/2017/02/23/mitigating-arbitrary-native-code-execution/.

9. Kotzias, P., Caballero, J., Bilge, L.: How did that get in my phone? Unwanted app distribution on Android devices. In: 2021 IEEE Symposium on Security and Privacy (SP), pp. 53–69. IEEE (2021)

10. Kumar, G., Saha, R., Lal, C., Conti, M.: Internet-of-Forensic (IoF): a blockchain based digital forensics framework for IoT applications. Futur. Gener. Comput. Syst. **120**, 13–25 (2021)

11. La Porta, L.: Trojan malware infecting 17 apps on the app store (2019). https://www.jamf.com/blog/ios-trojan-malware/. Accessed January 2022

12. Li, M., Lal, C., Conti, M., Hu, D.: LEChain: a blockchain-based lawful evidence management scheme for digital forensics. Futur. Gener. Comput. Syst. **115**, 406–420 (2021)

13. Liu, F., Liu, K.S., Chang, C., Wang, Y.: Research on the technology of iOS jailbreak. In: 2016 Sixth International Conference on Instrumentation & Measurement, Computer, Communication and Control (IMCCC), pp. 644–647. IEEE (2016)

14. Lone, A.H., Mir, R.N.: Forensic-chain: blockchain based digital forensics chain of custody with PoC in hyperledger composer. Digit. Investig. **28**, 44–55 (2019)

15. Mahalik, H., Tamma, R., Bommisetty, S.: Practical Mobile Forensics. Packt Publishing Ltd. (2016)

16. Manral, B., Somani, G., Choo, K.K.R., Conti, M., Gaur, M.S.: A systematic survey on cloud forensics challenges, solutions, and future directions. ACM Comput. Surv. (CSUR) **52**(6), 1–38 (2019)

17. Meng, H., Thing, V.L., Cheng, Y., Dai, Z., Zhang, L.: A survey of Android exploits in the wild. Comput. Secur. **76**, 71–91 (2018)

18. Moussa, A.N., Ithnin, N., Zainal, A.: CFaaS: bilaterally agreed evidence collection. J. Cloud Comput. **7**(1), 1–19 (2018). https://doi.org/10.1186/s13677-017-0102-3

19. Mylonas, A., Meletiadis, V., Tsoumas, B., Mitrou, L., Gritzalis, D.: Smartphone forensics: a proactive investigation scheme for evidence acquisition. In: Gritzalis, D., Furnell, S., Theoharidou, M. (eds.) SEC 2012. IAICT, vol. 376, pp. 249–260. Springer, Heidelberg (2012). https://doi.org/10.1007/978-3-642-30436-1_21

20. Nieto, A., et al.: Privacy-aware digital forensics (2019)

21. Sherr, M., Shah, G., Cronin, E., Clark, S., Blaze, M.: Can they hear me now? A security analysis of law enforcement wiretaps. In: Proceedings of the 16th ACM Conference on Computer and Communications Security, pp. 512–523 (2009)

22. Siry, L.: Cloudy days ahead: cross-border evidence collection and its impact on the rights of EU citizens. New J. Eur. Crim. Law **10**(3), 227–250 (2019)

23. Soriano-Salvador, E., Guardiola-Múzquiz, G.: SealFS: storage-based tamper-evident logging. Comput. Secur. **108**, 102325 (2021)

24. Standard, O.: PKCS# 11 cryptographic token interface base specification version 2.40 (2015)

25. Stefanko, L.: Android trojan steals money from PayPal accounts even with 2FA on (2018). https://www.welivesecurity.com/2018/12/11/android-trojan-steals-money-paypal-accounts-2fa/. Accessed January 2022

26. Varriale, A., Vatajelu, E.I., Di Natale, G., Prinetto, P., Trotta, P., Margaria, T.: SEcube™: an open-source security platform in a single SoC. In: 2016 International Conference on Design and Technology of Integrated Systems in Nanoscale Era (DTIS), pp. 1–6. IEEE (2016)

27. Yaswant, A.: GriftHorse Android trojan steals millions from over 10 million victims globally (2021). https://blog.zimperium.com/grifthorse-android-trojan-steals-millions-from-over-10-million-victims-globally/. Accessed January 2022

28. Zawoad, S., Dutta, A.K., Hasan, R.: Towards building forensics enabled cloud through secure logging-as-a-service. IEEE Trans. Dependable Secure Comput. **13**(2), 148–162 (2015)

Robust PDF Files Forensics Using Coding Style

Supriya Adhatarao and Cédric Lauradoux[✉]

Univ. Grenoble Alpes, Inria, Lyon, France
{supriya.adhatarao,cedric.lauradoux}@inria.fr

Abstract. Identifying how a file has been created is often interesting in security. It could be used by both attackers and defenders. Attackers can exploit this information to tune their attacks and defenders can understand how a malicious file has been created after an incident. As malicious PDF files are commonly used by attackers, in this work, we want to identify how a PDF file has been created. This problem is important because PDF files are extremely popular and widely used.

Our approach to detect which software has been used to produce a PDF file is based on the coding style: given patterns that are only created by certain PDF producers. We have analysed the coding style of 900 PDF files produced using 11 PDF producer tools on 3 different Operating Systems. We have obtained a set of 192 rules which can be used to identify 11 PDF producers. We have tested our detection tool on 508836 PDF files published on scientific preprint servers. Our tool can detect certain producers with an accuracy of 100%. Its overall detection is still high (74%).

Keywords: Forensics · Coding style · PDF file

1 Introduction

The Portable Document Format (PDF) is a very popular file format used online and created by Adobe Systems. To improve the content and the user experience, the format has evolved over time and supports more features such as security, searchability, or description by metadata. It is standardised as an open format ISO since 2008 and the latest version of the standard is PDF 2.0 [10]. This popularity of PDF files has two side effects: (i) PDF files are a popular attack vector and (ii) they contain hidden information that can expose authors' sensitive data. Hackers are embedding malicious content to penetrate systems. This is possible because the file format is getting more and more complex. Hackers can also use the PDF files published by an organisation to tune their attacks. Many works [2,4,9,11,14,20–23] in the past have been dedicated to PDF files security and privacy.

© IFIP International Federation for Information Processing 2022
Published by Springer Nature Switzerland AG 2022
W. Meng et al. (Eds.): SEC 2022, IFIP AICT 648, pp. 179–195, 2022.
https://doi.org/10.1007/978-3-031-06975-8_11

In this paper, we focus on the following forensics problem: *is it possible to determine how a PDF file has been created using the file itself?* A detector to determine the PDF producing tool has applications both in offensive security and incident response. In offensive security, it can be used to determine which software is used to create and view PDF files by an author or by an organisation. The attackers can find vulnerabilities[1] corresponding to the PDF viewer identified. Then, the attacker can craft and send malicious PDF files to the organisation thanks to the knowledge obtained from PDF files. During an incident response, a PDF producing tool detector is valuable to understand how a malicious PDF file has been created. It is a useful step towards an attack attribution.

Simplest approach to design a PDF producing tool detector consists of looking at the file's metadata. By default, PDF producer tools put a lot of information in the field `Creator` and `Producer` of the file's metadata. It is possible to find the name of the producer tool and its version as well as details on the Operating System. Unfortunately, metadata are not a reliable source of information: they can be easily modified/removed using tools like `exiftool`[2] or using sanitization tools like `Adobe Acrobat`.

The PDF standard [10] defines the language that is supported by PDF viewers. Developers of PDF producer tools have their own interpretation of the PDF language. Therefore, it is likely that their coding style is reflected on the output of their PDF producer tool. We have designed a robust PDF producing tool detector based on the coding style of the file. We found that there are coding style elements [13] in PDF files which can be used to identify the producer tool.

To observe the coding style of PDF files, firstly we have created a dataset of 900 PDF files using 11 popular PDF producer tools. We then compared different files to identify the pattern in each section of the PDF files. We created 192 rules in the regular expression engine to identify these patterns and detect the PDF producer tools. Finally, to test the efficiency of our detection tool, we have gathered 508836 PDF files downloaded from scientific preprints. We are able to detect PDF files created by `LibreOffice` and `PDFLaTeX` tools with an accuracy of 100%. PDF files created by `Microsoft Office Word` and `Mac OS X Quartz` were detected with an accuracy greater than 90%. In general, our tool correctly detected the producer tool of 74% of the PDF files in our dataset.

This paper is organised as follows. In Sect. 2 we describe the internal structure of a PDF file. In Sect. 3 we describe the PDF ecosystem and the tools we have chosen for our analysis. We give examples of coding style and programming patterns found in PDF files in Sect. 4. We present and test our detector in Sect. 5. Finally, we position our results to the related work done on PDF files in Sect. 6 and our comparison includes the reverse engineering of arXiv's PDF detector tool.

---

[1] Many vulnerabilities have been found in the past in PDF viewers: 1090 vulnerabilities have been reported in December 2020 according to https://cve.mitre.org.

[2] https://exiftool.org/.

2   Background on PDF Standard

Portable Document Format (PDF) is based on the Postscript language. It has been standardised as ISO 32000 and was developed by Adobe in 1993 to present documents. This document is independent of application software, hardware, and Operating Systems used and hence it is widely used. Apart from text, a PDF includes information such as fonts, hyperlinks, instructions for printing, images, keywords for search and indexing etc. Since 2008, PDF is standardised as an open format ISO and the latest version of the standard is PDF 2.0 [10]. In this section, we will outline the structure of a PDF file and how metadata information is stored within the file. The PDF document has a specific file structure, Fig. 1 describes the basic structure [1]. It is organised into four parts: `header`, `body`, `cross reference table` and `trailer`.

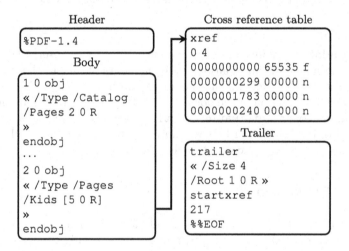

Fig. 1. PDF in a nutshell.

Header: Every PDF document starts with the same magic number %PDF (0 × 25504446) with % being the comment symbol. The version of specification used to encode the file is then appended: -m.n where m is the major number and n is the minor number (Fig. 1). The header can be composed of a second comment line if the file contains some binary data which is often the case. It consists of at least four binary characters [1].

Body: The body is a collection of indirect objects. It is the actual content of the document as viewed by the user. These objects represent the fonts, pages, sampled images and object streams of the PDF document. There are eight objects: boolean, numbers, strings, names, arrays, dictionaries, streams and the null object. All the objects in the document are labeled so that they can be referred to by other objects and the label is unique for each of these objects in the PDF document.

Cross Reference Table: This section consistsThe body is a collection of a collection of entries which gives the byte offsets for each indirect object in the document. This table is essentially used for quick and random access to objects. Cross reference table starts with the keyword `xref` and hence it is also called `xref table`.

Trailer: The trailer part of the PDF document is used for quick access to find the cross reference table and certain special objects in the document. The last line of a PDF document is an end-of-file marker `%%EOF`. This marker is preceded by a byte offset and the `startxref` keyword which indicates the first entry of the cross reference table (Fig. 1).

There are several PDF producer tools to create a PDF document and these PDF producer tools use these 4 sections as the basis for creation of a PDF document.

PDF Metadata: In addition to the content viewed by the user, PDF files also include some metadata information. PDF metadata stores all the information related to the PDF document. This metadata information is usually stored in an object in the body section of the document. PDF producer tools store metadata either in a `document information dictionary` or in a `metadata stream`. It is a special object which can be easily altered or removed without having any influence on the rest of the content of the document.

3   PDF Ecosystem

Writing directly PDF commands is difficult for a human, there exist several options to create a PDF file using different file formats (Fig. 2). There is a large ecosystem of PDF creation tools, converters and optimizers which are available online or locally. Many editors also propose in their software the option to convert certain file formats into PDF. Most people are accustomed to convert user-friendly (rich text) documents (doc/docx, ppt) into PDF files. These conversions can be straight-forward, for instance, they are integrated in word processing applications such as `Microsoft Office` and `LibreOffice` which transform the doc/docx files into PDF files. Intermediary conversions maybe needed for some file formats, like for the LATEX chain `tex` → `dvi` → `ps` → `PDF`. Popular Operating Systems (OS) and even browsers commonly provide support to print content (html pages, images etc.) into PDF files. There are several online tools which convert different file formats into PDF files.

We broadly classify PDF producer tools into five categories: OS-based tools, word processors, LATEX processors, browsers and optimizer/transformation tools (Fig. 2). We expected that each PDF producer tool has its own way to create the PDF code. To verify our guess, we chose 11 PDF producer tools (`Acrobat Distiller, Microsoft Office Word, LibreOffice, Ghostscript, Mac OS X Quartz, PdfTeX, SKia/PDF, Cairo, xdviPDFmx,`

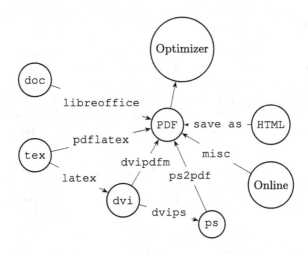

Fig. 2. Different options available to create a PDF file.

LuaTeX and PDFLaTeX) which represent the different categories in Fig. 2. We used these 11 PDF producer tools on three different Operating Systems: Microsoft Windows (Windows 10) , MAC OS (10.15.7) and Linux (Ubuntu 18.04.4 LTS), whenever it was possible.

In order to create PDF files, we first created source files, our dataset includes 25 source documents for Microsoft Word compatible software and 30 source documents for LaTeX compilation chains. These source documents include many different elements like text, images, tables, equations etc. to be representative of the usual content found in a PDF file. Then, we apply the 11 producer tools on our source documents to create PDF files. Finally using these PDF files, we observed the differences and patterns between the PDF files produced from the same source files. Our goal was to create a unique producer signature or fingerprint.

It is important to notice that PdfTeX tool name used in this paper is the label of LaTeX software whereas PDFLaTeX is a standard label used by open archive HAL[3] as its PDF producer tool. We could not create a dataset of PDF files for the PDFLaTeX tool. Since we did not want to pollute the website of HAL with our test files, we only downloaded some random PDF files created by HAL for our analysis.

4   Elements of Coding Style

We have analysed the elements of coding style in each section of a PDF file: header, body, cross reference table and trailer.

---

[3] https://hal.archives-ouvertes.fr/?lang=en.

4.1 Header

The header section of PDF files always has the same organisation across all the producer tools. It consists of two comment lines: the first comment line always starts with the same magic number %PDF (Fig. 1) and is often followed by another comment if the file contains some binary data. This comment in the second line is left undefined by the specification. During our analysis, we observed that it is often present and producer tools leave different values in the file.

Table 1. Header- producer magic number and the associated producer tools.

Unique binary data (in hexadecimal)	PDF producer tools	OS Windows, Linux, Mac OS X	Distribution TeXLive/MikTeX
0xE2E3CFD3	Acrobat distiller	3 OSs	–
0xB5B5B5B5	Microsoft office word	Windows	–
0xD0D4C5D8	pdfTeX	3 OSs	TeXLive & MikTeX
0xD0D4C5D8	**LuaTeX**	**Linux**	**TeXLive**
0xCCD5C1D4C5D8D0C4C6	**LuaTeX**	**Linux**	**MikTeX**
0xCCD5C1D4C5D8D0C4C6	**LuaTeX**	**Mac OS X & Windows**	**TeXLive & MikTeX**
0xE4F0EDF8	xdvipdfm	3 OSs	TeXLive & MikTeX
0xc7ec8fa2	GhostScript	3 OSs	TeXLive & MikTeX
0xc3a4c3bcc3b6c39f	LibreOffice	Linux	–
0xC4E5F2E5EBA7F3A0D0C4C6	Mac Os X	Mac OS X	–
0xB5EDAEFB	Cairo	3 OSs	–
0xD3EBE9E1	Skia	3 OSs	–
0xF6E4FCDF	PdfLaTeX	Online	–

Table 1 shows different binary data associated with the 11 producer tools and the associated Operating System, for LaTeX tools, it also shows the distribution. Some values are shared by different tools and some are specific to a distribution and Operating System. For instance, 0xE2E3CFD3 is the binary value associated with the tool `Acrobat Distiller` and it is unique. Our analysis also showed that it is possible that one tool uses several values across different Operating Systems. In our analysis, LuaTeX uses 2 different values (0xD0D4C5D8 and 0xCCD5C1D4C5D8D0C4C6). It depends on the LaTeX distribution and the OS used. 0xD0D4C5D8 value is shared by two producer tools `pdfTeX, LuaTeX`. It is interesting to note that when this value is used by `LuaTeX`, it is specifically associated with `Texlive` distribution on Linux systems only. This value could be used in the detection of the OS used to create the PDF file.

Nine producer tools in our evaluation have unique values and this value can be used to directly reveal the PDF producer tool. This value can be considered as `producer magic number`. Removing the `producer magic number` or even altering it does not have any influence on the display of a PDF file. Therefore it is not necessarily a very robust method to identify a PDF producer tool because it can be easily modified. Nonetheless, the `producer magic number` can significantly help in the detection of the PDF producer tool or at least narrow down the identification to a small set of tools.

4.2 Body

The body section of a PDF file is a collection of indirect objects. It is the actual content of the document as viewed by the user. These objects represent the fonts, pages, sampled images and object streams of the PDF file. There are eight types of objects: *boolean, numbers, strings, names, arrays, dictionaries, streams* and *the null object*. All the objects in the document are labelled so that they can be referred to by other objects. The label is unique for each object in the PDF file.

Potential differences across producer tools include the way objects are created, stored, ordered, identified and its contents (metadata information coding, length of the encoded text, images and different fonts).

Listing 1.1 and 1.2 shows examples of the same stream object created by **pdfTeX** and **LuaTeX** tools. The way they are encoded is different but PDF viewers will display the same output. Even if the object ID and all the keys (Length, Filter, FlateDecode etc.) used look alike for these two tools, it is possible to distinguish them using the order of arrangement of keys and the use of escape sequences (newline and spaces). Such differences across different objects encoded in the PDF files can be used in the detection of producer tools.

```
1  4 0 obj
2  <</Length 2413         /Filter/FlateDecode>>
3  stream
4  .....
5  endstream
6  endobj
```

Listing 1.1. Object encoding using pdfTeX tool

```
1  4 0 obj
2  <<
3  /Length 2006
4  /Filter  /FlateDecode
5  >>
6  stream
7  .....
8  endstream
9  endobj
```

Listing 1.2. Object encoding using LuaTeX tool.

4.3 Cross Reference Table

Cross reference table or the xref table gives the offsets (in bytes) for each indirect object which is used for quick and random access to objects in the body section (Fig. 1). This section of a PDF file is optional and many producer tools do not include it. Some producer tools use linearization or incremental saves and the information related to this table is encoded in the trailer object. Cross reference table is always coded in the same way across all the different tools (when it is present).

As shown in Fig. 1, the cross reference table starts with the keyword xref followed by two numbers separated by a space. The first number indicates the object number of the first object in the subsection. The second number indicates the total number of entries in the subsection.

Each cross reference entries (one per line) is associated to exactly one object and it is 20 bytes long and has the format "nnnnnnnnnn ggggg n/f eol", where the first 10 bytes are nnnnnnnnnn, indicating the byte offset of the referenced entry, followed by a space and then by 5 digits entry ggggg, which is a generation number of the object followed by a space and then a n, where n is a literal keyword to indicate that the object is in use while f is used to indicate that an object is free and this is followed by a space and last 2 bytes constituting the end-of-line.

Since this section of PDF file is optional and fewer tools include it, its presence or absence can narrow down the detection of PDF producer tools to a smaller set of candidate tools. We found only nine tools among 11 that include the cross reference table (Acrobat Distiller and xdviPDFmx do not include this table). We also observed that pdfTeX tool includes this table only in MikTeX distribution for all three OSs whereas the table has been removed for TexLive distributions.

4.4   Trailer

The trailer part is used for quick access to find the cross reference table and certain special objects in the document. The last object present in this part includes Root information and some other keys-values. The trailer part is very interesting to detect the producer tool used as it is possible to distinguish producer tools based on the keys used to describe this object.

In Table 2 we have listed all the different keys used in the trailer object for 11 producer tools. Tools like LibreOffice, Acrobat Distiller and Microsoft Office Word have their own keys that are distinguishable from any other tools and hence are unique and tool specific. Whereas tools like LuaTeX, pdfTeX, Ghostscript and Mac OS X Quartz share the same set of keys, but the order of arrangement of these keys is different. It is also interesting to note that for LuaTeX and pdfTeX, the keys differ across LaTeX distribution. All these differences potentially can lead to the detection of the producer tool.

It is important to notice that we have excluded the elements containing the metadata in the creation of our rules. Metadata information is stored in an object within the body section of the file. Removing the metadata object or even altering the values present in it has no effect on the functioning of the PDF files.

Table 2. Trailer - different trailer keys used by PDF producer tools (all the keys are same across 3 Operating Systems: Windows, Linux and Mac OS X).

Producer tool	Key strings in trailer section
Acrobat distiller	/DecodeParms /Columns /Predictor /Filter /FlateDecode /ID /Info /Length /Root /Size /Type /XRef /W
TexLive LuaTeX	**/Type /XRef /Index /Size /W /Root /Info /ID /Length /Filter /FlateDecode**
TexLive pdfTeX	**/Type /XRef /Index /Size /W /Root /Info /ID /Length /Filter /FlateDecode**
MikTeX LuaTeX	**trailer /Size /Root /Info /ID**
MikTeX pdfTeX	**trailer /Size /Root /Info /ID**
Ghostscript	trailer /Size /Root /Info /ID
xdvipdfm	/Type /XRef /Root /Info /ID /Size /W /Filter /FlateDecode /Length
Microsoft office word	trailer /Size /Root /Info /ID /Prev /XRefStm
LibreOffice	trailer /Size /Root /Info /ID /DocChecksum
Mac OS × Quartz	trailer /Size /Root /Info /ID
Cairo	trailer /Size /Root /Info
Skia/PDF	trailer /Size /Root /Info
PDFLaTeX	trailer /Root /info /ID /Size

Rules for Detection Tool: We used different patterns observed for each section of the PDF file and exploited them to detect the PDF producer tools. We have used regular expressions and expressed them using YARA[4] rules. Listing 1.3 shows an example of a YARA rule written to match one of the text patterns generated by the `Microsoft Office Word` tool only. We observed that this object is present in every PDF file created using `Microsoft Office Word` tool.

```
string:
    $rule= /4 0 obj\r\n<<\/Filter\/FlateDecode\/Length
    [0-9]*>>\r\nstream\r\n/
condition:
    $rule
```

Listing 1.3. Example of one YARA rule for an object present in the body part of a PDF file created using Microsoft Office Word tool.

Earlier in this section we have seen that, for the same content of PDF files, the number of objects and the way objects are created differs. Since the coding style is different across tools, the number of YARA rules are also different across tools. Table 3 shows the number of rules we have written for each producer tool.

Patterns to Detect Operating System: In the header section, we have already provided an example that helps in the detection of OS and the LaTeX distribution used (LuaTeX tool). During our analysis of 11 producer tools, for two LaTeX chain of tools (pdfTeX and LuaTeX), we observed that some object's

---

[4] https://github.com/virustotal/yara.

Table 3. Rules for each PDF producer tool.

Producer tool	#rules	Producer tool	#rules	Producer tool	#rules
Acrobat distiller	13	Microsoft office word	16	PDFLaTeX	9
LibreOffice	15	Ghostscript	15	SKia/PDF	12
Mac OS X Quartz	30	xdviPDFmx	13	Cairo	16
PdfTeX	31	LuaTeX	22		

coding style in the body section of the PDF are specific to the OS used and hence few of our rules can be used to detect the OS. Figure 3 provides an example of all the rules associated with the tool pdfTeX, including a number of rules specific across different OSs. In the Fig. 3, we can observe that there are 18 common rules across all the three OSs and 3 rules specific to Windows OS, 4 to MAC OS and 2 to Linux. When one of these OS specific objects is present within the PDF file, we use our OS specific rules for the detection of OS used to create the PDF file.

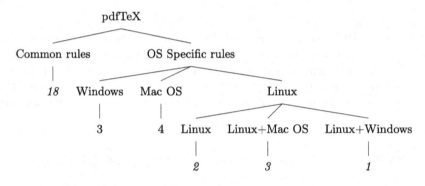

Fig. 3. Number of YARA rules across three Operating Systems for *pdfTeX* tool.

To conclude, the patterns found in different sections of the PDF file can be exploited to detect the PDF producer tools and sometimes the OS used.

5   Results and Observation

In this section we first describe the dataset used to test the accuracy of our methodology of coding style. Then we show the results for the detection of 11 popular PDF producer tools.

5.1   Dataset

Conference proceedings and preprints are clearly the best options to obtain a large number of PDF files. We have downloaded PDF files from the preprints of the scientific community. Our first dataset was downloaded from the Cryptology ePrint Archive[5], it includes 11405 PDF documents from 2004 to 2018. We observed that all the PDF documents were originally compiled by the authors using a PDF producer tool of their choice. Open archive HAL[6] administrators provided us with access to a second set of dataset of PDF files. It consists of 544460 PDF files from 1996 to 2019. HAL provides options to either directly submit a PDF file or submit source files and create a PDF file using HAL's pdf producer tool `PdfLaTeX`. We observed that around 47% of the PDF files in the HAL dataset were compiled by HAL while the remaining 53% were originally compiled by the author(s) using a PDF producer tool of their choice. All the PDF files submitted to HAL are concatenated with a cover page using Apache PDFBOX. Hence all the PDF files published on HAL are modified. We observed that the metadata of 53% of the PDF files in HAL dataset are likely to be original values of authors PDF producer tools. For the rest of the HAL's PDF files, we have clues that metadata were altered by HAL and still we have considered all these PDF files in HAL dataset for our experiments.

Our dataset is respectively called IACR dataset and HAL dataset throughout the paper for convenience. We have tested our rules on the PDF files of both IACR and HAL dataset. We applied our rules to detect the PDF producer tool and then the results obtained using our tool are validated using the PDF producer tool name found in the metadata field `producer`. *We would like to clarify that, during the PDF producer tool detection, we have not considered the metadata object present in the PDF file. Our rules are used on the rest of the PDF file. Metadata field producer was used only to validate our results.*

Cleaning the Dataset: Based on the values found in metadata field producer, IACR dataset includes 10892 (96%) PDF files from the 11 tools we are inspecting and 497944 (91%) from HAL dataset. We applied our rules on these sets of PDF files and findings are described below.

5.2 Detection of 11 PDF Producer Tools

We first attempted to use the patterns found in each section separately and the results are given in Table 4. It shows when the producer detected by our tool is correct, wrong or when it is unable to detect a producer tool. Table 4 shows that detection of the producer tool based only on the header and xref table is not efficient for IACR dataset. The results for these two sections are improved for the HAL dataset. Body and trailer sections offer better perspective for both the dataset. However, the results are not conclusive.

For each individual section, our tool can sometimes detect two producer tools. This case is considered as a wrong prediction in Table 4. We have evaluated the frequency of this event in Table 5. Two cases are possible. The detection can be *confused*: for the same PDF file, our tool detects the correct producer and

[5] https://eprint.iacr.org/.

[6] https://hal.archives-ouvertes.fr/.

Table 4. Detection of PDF producer tools for header, body, xref and trailer section.

IACR (10892 PDF files)				
Detection	Header	Body	Xref table	Trailer
Correct	1676 (15%)	7302 (67%)	898 (8%)	8641 (79.3%)
Wrong	8325 (76.4%)	1839 (17%)	1277 (12%)	141 (1.3%)
No result	891 (8%)	1751 (16%)	8717 (80%)	2110 (19.3%)
HAL (497944 PDF files)				
Detection	Header	Body	Xref table	Trailer
Correct	235859 (47%)	197069 (40%)	232540 (46.7%)	229060 (46%)
Wrong	204214(41%)	241101 (48%)	232104 (46.6%)	259988 (52.2%)
No result	57871 (12%)	59774 (12%)	33300 (6.7%)	8896 (1.8%)

another one (incorrect). We have an error when the two tools detected are incorrect. The results in Table 5 shows that the detection based on a single section of the PDF file has too much uncertainty. For instance the header section for IACR dataset resulted in 66% of confused detection, since pdfTeX and LuaTeX use the same producer magic number. Our tool often detects 2 tools for PDF files produced by either pdfTeX and LuaTeX.

Table 5. Frequency of detection of 2 PDF producer tools.

IACR (10892 PDF files)				
Detection	Header	Body	Xref table	Trailer
Confused	7213 (66.2%)	433 (4%)	1228 (11.2%)	130 (1.2%)
Error	1112 (10.2%)	1406 (13%)	49 (0.5%)	11 (0.1%)
HAL (497944 PDF files)				
Detection	Header	Body	Xref table	Trailer
Confused	19673 (4%)	44751 (9%)	16028 (3.2%)	153 (0.03%)
Error	184541 (37%)	196350 (39%)	216076 (43.4%)	259835 (52%)

To tackle the confused detection and improve our tool, we have combined the results of each section using a majority vote. In case of equality, *i.e.* two producers have received two votes, we have considered that our tool makes a wrong decision. Table 6 shows results for the detection of producer tools for combination of all the sections using majority votes. Our tool finds the correct PDF producer tool 74% of the time for IACR dataset and 48% for HAL dataset.

PDF files in the HAL dataset are modified using the PDFLaTeX tool. These modified PDF files include the coding style of both PDFLaTeX and the original tool initially used to create the PDF file. We noticed mainly that when HAL modifies a PDF file, the header is changed, a cross reference table is either inserted or updated and a trailer object is added. Therefore using the majority votes, the detection of the producer tool is PDFLaTeX tool but the metadata field producer includes the original producer tool information and hence the results are considered wrong. Just like PDF producer tools, PDF modification tools also have their specific style for modification. Currently our tool does not apply to the detection of modified/concatenated PDF files and hence the results obtained for HAL dataset are less impressive.

Table 6. Detection of PDF producer tool and OS using combination of different sections.

Detection	IACR (10892)	HAL (497944)
Producer tool	8018 (74%)	239967 (48%)
OS	3344 (29%)	105930 (19%)

OS Detection: Along with detection of the PDF producer tool used, coding style can also reveal the OS. Table 6 shows corresponding results obtained for the detection of OS. Header, trailer and xref section's coding style does not vary much across different Operating Systems and hence predicting the OS using these sections is harder and sometimes impossible. But using the body section's coding style it is possible to detect the OS for some producer tools. During the analysis of coding style we observed that body section coding style includes one or two objects that can be used to detect the Operating System. For instance, pdfTeX (MikTeX distribution) uses some keys across Microsoft Windows, Linux and Mac OS that are distinguishable from one another and leads to the detection of OS. Even though we could identify OS for a smaller number of PDF files (Table 6), these results are not conclusive for the majority of the files in our dataset.

5.3 Results for Each Producer Tool

Our tool is more efficient for the detection of certain producer tools. Table 7 shows the differences between the different tools evaluated. The detection is still done using a majority vote over all the parts of the PDF file. PDF files produced by Microsoft Office Word, Mac OS X Quartz, PDFLaTeX and LibreOffice are detected with higher accuracy (more than 90%). As previously explained the PDF files in HAL dataset are modified, some parts of the PDF files are replaced by the coding style of PDFLaTeX tool. Since we use the majority votes, the results for tools other than PDFLaTeX (91%) lead to wrong detection. If the PDF file is not modified, our rules detects the PDF producer tool with higher accuracy and results obtained for detection of producer tools in IACR dataset supports it.

Table 7. Detection of individual PDF producer tool.

Producer tool	#PDF IACR	#detection	#PDF HAL	#detection
Acrobat distiller	369	269 (73%)	96157	3497 (4%)
Microsoft office word	147	141 (96%)	15995	4388 (28%)
LibreOffice	4	4 (100%)	464	451 (95%)
Ghostscript	1200	993 (83%)	115948	1940 (2%)
Mac OS × Quartz	62	61 (98%)	7767	2111 (27%)
SKia/PDF	0	0	88	67 (76%)
Cairo	0	0	1100	357 (32%)
PdfTeX	7745	6001 (77%)	10375	743 (7%)
xdviPDFmx	1347	536 (40%)	836	102 (12%)
LuaTeX	17	12 (71%)	67	4 (6%)
PDFLaTeX	1	1 (100%)	249147	226255 (91%)

The results obtained in this section shows that it is possible to detect the PDF producer tool of a PDF file using its coding style. Therefore, creating PDF files without metadata or altering metadata is not enough to hide information.

6   Related Works

Many works have been devoted to PDF malware detection [4–6,14–16] and to privacy issues related to hidden data [3,7,9,17].

ArXiv hosts around 1.6 million e-prints in different science fields. ArXiv administrators (https://arxiv.org) have designed a tool. All the submissions are controlled to check that the material provided is appropriate, topical and meets arXiv's guidelines. LaTeX, AMSLaTeX, PDFLaTeX sources, PDF and HTML with JPEG/PNG/GIF images formats are accepted by arXiv. ArXiv accepts only PDF files that are produced by Microsoft Word compatible software. PDF files created using LaTeX software are not accepted. The sources must be submitted and arXiv's server produces the PDF file directly from the source. Using a guess and determine approach, we were able to reverse-engineer arXiv PDF detection tool. It appears that arXiv detector first tests if the metadata of the PDF file submitted matches those of a LaTeX file. If this test is not conclusive, it checks if LaTeX fonts have been used. If both tests failed, arXiv detector considers that the file has been produced by Microsoft Word compatible software. We have created a PDF file using LaTeX software and using other fonts (Listing 1.4) and it was accepted by ArXiv. So far we have found that only the ArXiv detector is very similar to our tool. However, it only detects if a PDF file has been produced using LaTeX software using metadata and LaTeX fonts. Whereas, our tool can identify 11 PDF producer tools by analysing the PDF coding style even when the metadata has been removed and the PDF file is sanitised.

Our PDF producer detector shares similar ideas with BinComp [18], a tool designed to detect which compiler has been used to create a binary. This tool has been designed to perform code authorship attribution. The overall goal of such a software is to help to identify the authors of malicious software. This domain has been very active in the last few years [8,12,19]. Our tool is designed to identify coding style patterns used by PDF producer tools to detect PDF producer tools.

```latex
\documentclass{article}
\usepackage[T1]{fontenc}
\usepackage{newtxmath,newtxtext}
\usepackage{lipsum}
% just to generate dummy text
\begin{document}
\lipsum
\end{document}
```

Listing 1.4. PDF compiled using **pdfLaTeX** With MS Word-style font.

7 Conclusion

Our work shows that coding style can be exploited to identify which software has been used to create a PDF file. Our tool has applications both in offensive security and in incident response. It is not only useful to detect the PDF producer tool but it can also be very useful to analyse how a malicious file has been created. It is more robust than just looking at the metadata fields of the PDF file, which is highly unreliable (it can be altered or removed from the file). The results obtained with our tool show that it is working with high accuracy (74%). In our work, we exploit patterns in all the four sections of PDF files and hence it is much harder for an adversary to manipulate the content of a PDF file to fool our tool.

An interesting question to consider in our future work would be, is it possible to extend our tool to other PDF producer tools? In other words, is it possible to automate the creation of Yara rules to identify a producer tool? An exhaustive approach would consist in taking a string of a fixed length in a PDF file. This string can be included in a regular expression and the new rule can be tested to check if it is accurate or not. If it is not, the strings can be extended until it is accurate. Unfortunately, this approach is time consuming: the complexity depends on the file size. Applying machine learning techniques could be a promising future work.

References

1. PDF Reference: Adobe Portable Document Format Version 1.4 with Cdrom. Addison-Wesley Longman Publishing Co., Inc, Boston, MA, USA, 3rd edn. (2001)
2. Adhatarao, S., Lauradoux, C.: Exploitation and Sanitization of Hidden Data in PDF Files. CoRR abs/2103.02707 (2021). https://arxiv.org/abs/2103.02707

3. Aura, T., Kuhn, T.A., Roe, M.: Scanning electronic documents for personally identifiable information. In: Juels, A., Winslett, M. (eds.) Proceedings of the 2006 ACM Workshop on Privacy in the Electronic Society, WPES 2006, pp. 41–50. ACM (2006)
4. Carmony, C., Hu, X., Yin, H., Bhaskar, A.V., Zhang, M.: Extract me if you can: abusing PDF parsers in malware detectors. In: 23rd Annual Network and Distributed System Security Symposium, NDSS 2016. The Internet Society (2016)
5. Castiglione, A., Santis, A.D., Soriente, C.: Security and privacy issues in the Portable Document Format. J. Syst. Softw. **83**(10), 1813–1822 (2010)
6. Chen, Y., Wang, S., She, D., Jana, S.: On training robust pdf malware classifiers. In: 29th USENIX Security Symposium, USENIX Security 2020, pp. 2343–2360. USENIX Association (2020)
7. Feng, Y., Liu, B., Cui, X., Liu, C., Kang, X., Su, J.: A systematic method on PDF privacy leakage issues. In: 17th IEEE International Conference on Trust, Security and Privacy in Computing and Communications/12th IEEE International Conference on Big Data Science And Engineering, TrustCom/BigDataSE 2018, pp. 1020–1029. IEEE (2018)
8. Ferreira, A., et al.: Data-driven feature characterization techniques for laser printer attribution. IEEE Trans. Inf. For. Secur. **12**(8), 1860–1873 (2017)
9. Garfinkel, S.L.: Leaking sensitive information in complex document files-and how to prevent it. IEEE Secur. Priv. **12**(1), 20–27 (2014)
10. ISO: Document management–Portable document format–Part 2: PDF 2.0. ISO ISO 32000–2:2017, International Organization for Standardization, Geneva, Switzerland (2008)
11. Martin, D., Wu, H., Alsaid, A.: Hidden surveillance by web sites: web bugs in contemporary use. Commun. ACM **46**(12), 258–264 (2003)
12. Kalgutkar, V., Kaur, R., Gonzalez, H., Stakhanova, N., Matyukhina, A.: Code authorship attribution: methods and challenges. ACM Comput. Surv. **52**(1), 3:1–3:36 (2019)
13. Kernighan, B.W., Plauger, P.J.: The Elements of Programming Style, 2nd edn. McGraw-Hill, New York (1978)
14. Maiorca, D., Biggio, B.: Digital investigation of PDF files: unveiling traces of embedded malware. IEEE Secur. Priv. **17**(1), 63–71 (2019)
15. Maiorca, D., Biggio, B., Giacinto, G.: Towards adversarial malware detection: lessons learned from PDF-based attacks. ACM Comput. Surv. **52**(4), 78:1–78:36 (2019)
16. Markwood, I.D., Shen, D., Liu, Y., Lu, Z.: PDF mirage: content masking attack against information-based online services. In: 26th USENIX Security Symposium, USENIX Security 2017, pp. 833–847. USENIX Association (2017)
17. Mendelman, K.: Fingerprinting an Organization Using Metadata of Public Documents. Master's thesis, University of Tartu, Estonia (2018)
18. Rahimian, A., Shirani, P., Alrbaee, S., Wang, L., Debbabi, M.: BinComp: a stratified approach to compiler provenance Attribution. Dig. Invest. **14**, S146–S155 (2015)
19. Simko, L., Zettlemoyer, L., Kohno, T.: Recognizing and imitating programmer style: adversaries in program authorship attribution. PoPETs **2018**(1), 127–144 (2018)
20. Smith, R.M.: Microsoft Word Documents that Phone Home (2000). Retrieve on Internet Archive: Wayback Machine https://web.archive.org/web/20010203194100, http://www.privacyfoundation.org/advisories/advWordBugs.html

21. Smutz, C., Stavrou, A.: Malicious PDF detection using metadata and structural features. In: 28th Annual Computer Security Applications Conference, ACSAC 2012, pp. 239–248. ACM (2012)
22. Stevens, D.: Malicious PDF documents explained. IEEE Secur. Priv. **9**(1), 80–82 (2011)
23. Xu, W., Qi, Y., Evans, D.: Automatically evading classifiers: a case study on PDF malware classifiers. In: 23rd Annual Network and Distributed System Security Symposium, NDSS 2016. The Internet Society (2016)

Light-Weight File Fragments Classification Using Depthwise Separable Convolutions

Kunwar Muhammed Saaim[1], Muhamad Felemban[2,3(✉)], Saleh Alsaleh[2,3], and Ahmad Almulhem[2,3]

[1] Aligrah Muslim University, Aligarh, Uttar Pradesh, India
kmsaaim@zhcet.ac.in
[2] Computer Engineering Department, KFUPM, Dhahran, Saudi Arabia
[3] Interdisciplinary Research Center for Intelligent Secure Systems, KFUPM, Dhahran, Saudi Arabia
{mfelemban,salehs,ahmadsm}@kfupm.edu.sa

Abstract. In digital forensics, classification of file fragments is an important step to complete the file carving process. There exist several approaches to identify the type of file fragments without relying on meta-data. Examples of such approaches are using features like header/footer and N-gram to identify the fragment type. Recently, deep learning models have been successfully used to build classification models to achieve this task. In this paper, we propose a light-weight file fragment classification using depthwise separable convolutional neural network model. We show that our proposed model does not only yield faster inference time, but also provide higher accuracy as compared to the state-of-art convolutional neural network based models. In particular, our model achieves an accuracy of 78.45% on the FFT-75 dataset with 100K parameters and 167M FLOPs, which is 24× faster and 4–5× smaller than the state-of-the-art classifier in the literature.

Keywords: Digital forensics · File carving · File fragments classification · Deep learning · Depthwise separable convolution

1 Introduction

Digital forensics is the science of collecting digital evidence to investigate cyber-crimes and cyberattack scenarios. The process of digital forensics include preservation, identification, and extraction of data and computer files. There are several digital forensics tools and techniques that facilitate this process [27,32]. Often, attackers attempt to wipe out any evidence that incriminates them, for example, by formatting the hard disk [6]. In such scenarios, traditional recovery methods based on file system meta-data are deemed to be ineffective.

To overcome this challenge, digital investigators use file carving to reconstruct files based on their contents [15,24,26]. In other words, file carving process recovers files from blocks of binary data without using any information available in

© IFIP International Federation for Information Processing 2022
Published by Springer Nature Switzerland AG 2022
W. Meng et al. (Eds.): SEC 2022, IFIP AICT 648, pp. 196–211, 2022.
https://doi.org/10.1007/978-3-031-06975-8_12

the file system structure. Researchers have attempted to reconstruct files entirely or partially using a variety of techniques including header/footer matching [33], probabilistic measures [3], and n-gram analysis [41]. With the absence of meta-data, it is challenging to identify the type of a carved file. The problem is even more challenging when file carving is carried out on fragmented files. File fragmentation is used when there is not enough contiguous space to write a file on the hard disk. In general, two tasks can be recognized in fragmented file carving: selecting a candidate sequence of file blocks and classifying the type of the fragment [26].

There exist several approaches for file fragments classification in the literature [1,4,5,8,12,16,25,29,33,39,41–43]. For example, *Sceadan* tool determines the type of bulk data based file content [5]. Recently, deep learning has been used to identify the type of file fragments. For example, Gray-scale [8] and FiFTy [29] tools illustrate how Convolutional Neural Networks (CNNs) can be efficiently used for file fragments classification. Although CNN is the most used deep learning model for classification, we argue that existing solutions can be further improved in terms of performance and accuracy by modifying the architecture of the neural network.

To illustrate, the convolution layer in CNNs can be either 2D convolution layer [8] or 1D convolution layer [29]. One drawback of CNNs is the exponential increase in number of parameters as the number of layers increase, i.e., the model depth increases. Such increase in the number of parameters increases the complexity of the model and, consequently, increases the training and inference time. On the other hand, deep CNN models provides better accuracy. Therefore, it is utterly important to find a balance between the speed and accuracy in terms of the number of layers. To over come this challenge, researchers proposed a computationally cheaper model called depthwise separable convolution [21,36, 37]. Depthwise separable convolution is cheap because it dramatically reduces the required number of parameters in the model.

In this paper, we propose a light-weight file fragment classification based on depthwise separable convolutional neural network. The rationale behind designing a light-weight classification model is to provide the ability to process huge volume of data without requiring significant computational resources. Therefore, the process of file fragment classification can be feasible without specialized hardware, e.g., GPUs and TPUs. To evaluate the performance of our model, we compared our results with FiFTy [29] and a baseline Recurrent Neural Networks (RNN) [19]. We have trained 12 different models using various file types and different fragment sizes using FFT-75 dataset [28]. The results show that our model achieves an accuracy similar to FiFTy using 6.3× less floating-point operations (FLOPs) on 4096 bytes fragment and 85× less FLOPs on 512 bytes fragment as compared to FiFTy. Furthermore, our model achieves 78.45% accuracy with 100K parameters and 167M FLOPs, while FiFTy achieves 77.04% accuracy with 449K parameters and 1047M FLOPs. Finally, our model outperforms the previous best classifier by being 24× faster on GPU than FiFTy and 650× faster than baseline RNN.

The rest of this paper is organized as follows. In Sect. 2, we provide necessary background for this work. In Sect. 3, we discuss the state-of-the-art of file fragment classification. In Sect. 4, we present our model. In Sect. 5, we discuss the experiments and evaluation results. Finally, conclusions and future work are presented in Sect. 6.

2   Preliminaries

2.1   Convolution Neural Network

CNN is a type of artificial neural network that is widely used for image and object recognition and classification. CNN contains one or many convolution layers that can extract features from the inputs and predict an output based on the extracted features [13]. A convolution layer can be considered as a 2D matrix (kernel) that performs the convolution operation. Mathematically, convolution operation is the dot product between the kernel and the input of the layer. Different kernels can be used to give importance to the input data points whose output is stacked in depth. The kernel filters are smaller than the layer's input so that kernel weights can be shared across input dimensions.

In the context of file fragment classification, the input to CNN consists of a vector of 4096 or 512 dimensions, which corresponds to 4 KB or 512 bytes fragments, respectively. Then, the input is fed to an embedding layer that transforms the input vector into a continuous (4096,32) or (512,32) dimensional vector, based on the size of the fragments. The embedding layer can be thought of as a preprocessing step to prepare input vectors for the subsequent CNN layers. The output of the embedding layer is fed into a convolution layer with kernels of any size. Several convolution layers can be stacked [29]. As a result of stacking standard convolution layers when developing a deep neural network (DNN), the model can have a large number of parameters.

2.2   Depthwise Separable Convolution

The separable convolution model was first introduced by Sifre and Mallat [34]. Since then, several models have been proposed based on the idea of separable convolution, including Xception-net [9] and Mobilenets [21]. The automatic feature extraction behaviour of standard convolution can be achieved by smaller and faster depthwise separable convolution. Depthwise separable convolution is a form of factorized convolutions in which the normal convolution kernel is split into two parts: one depthwise convolution and a 1×1 convolution, called pointwise convolution. The splitting of convolution into two layers has a drastic effect on reducing the number of parameters and computation time required for training and inference. The depthwise convolution applies a single filter to each input channel. The pointwise convolution then applies a 1×1 convolution to combine the outputs of the depthwise convolution [21].

Figure 1a depicts a standard one-dimensional convolution operation that takes $D_F \times 1 \times M$ feature maps as input and produces $D_F \times 1 \times N$ feature

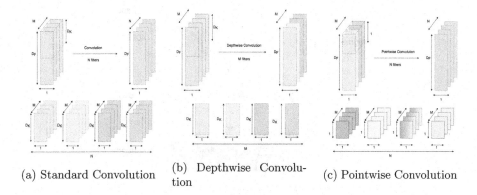

(a) Standard Convolution   (b) Depthwise Convolution   (c) Pointwise Convolution

Fig. 1. Standard convolution in (a) is factorized into two layers: Depthwise Convolution in (b) and pointwise in (c).

maps, where D_F is length of the input feature, M is the number of input channels, and N is the number of output channels. In convolutional network, the number of parameters with kernel size K is $D_K \times 1 \times N \times M$. Subsequently, the total computation cost is

$$D_F \cdot N \cdot M \cdot D_K \tag{1}$$

Unlike CNNs, depthwise separable convolution factorizes the convolution layer into two layers: depthwise convolution depicted in Fig. 1b and pointwise convolution shown in Fig. 1c. The depthwise convolution layer with one filter per input channel has $D_K \times 1 \times M$ parameters with K sized kernel and M number of channels. Therefore, depthwise convolution has a computation cost of:

$$D_F \cdot M \cdot D_K \tag{2}$$

On the other hand, pointwise convolution uses a linear combination of filtered feature maps with the help of 1×1 convolution. The cost of 1×1 convolution is the same as standard convolution having a kernel size of 1, i.e., $D_F \times N \times M$. Consequently, the total computation cost of depthwise separable convolution is:

$$D_F \cdot M \cdot D_K + D_F \cdot N \cdot M \tag{3}$$

As a result, the total reduction in the computation cost when using depthwise separable convolution is:

$$\frac{D_F \cdot M \cdot D_K + D_F \cdot N \cdot M}{D_F \cdot N \cdot M \cdot D_K} \tag{4}$$

$$= \frac{1}{N} + \frac{1}{D_K} \tag{5}$$

The value of N ranges from 32 to 1024 and D_K for one-dimensional convolution can be between 9 and 27. Therefore, the reduction in computation cost is between 85% and 95%.

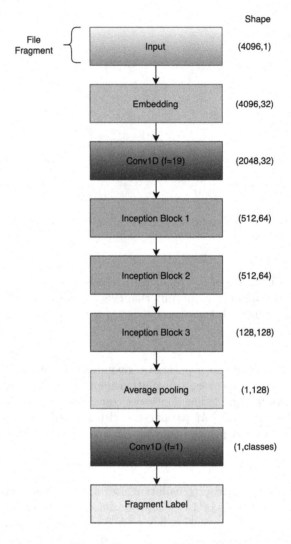

Fig. 2. Network architecture

3 Depthwise Separable Convolutional Model for File Fragments Classification

In this section, we describe our depthwise separable convolutional architecture for file fragment classification. The objective is to reduce the inference time of file fragment classification while maintaining high accuracy. Figure 2 shows the overall architecture of the model. It consists of an embedding layer, a standard convolution block, and depthwise separable inception blocks. A file fragment byte ranging from 0 to 255 is transformed into a dense continuous vector of 32 dimensions by a learnable embedding layer. In order to extract essential fea-

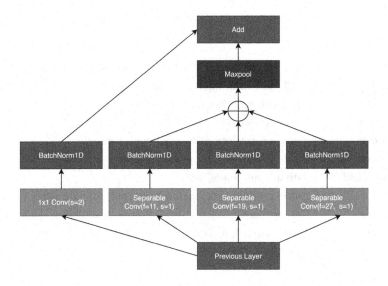

Fig. 3. Depthwise separable convolution inception block

tures automatically for classification, the dense vector representation is passed through a standard convolution block and multiple depthwise separable inception blocks. To get the final features for classification, the output of the last depthwise separable convolution block is averaged along the spatial dimension. The class probabilities are determined from feature vectors using 1×1 convolution followed by *softmax* activation function [11]. A Hardswish function [20] is used to activate all the blocks in the network.

$$Hardswish(x) = \begin{cases} 0 & if\, x \leq -3, \\ x & if\, x \geq +3, \\ \frac{x \cdot (x+3)}{6} & otherwise \end{cases} \tag{6}$$

In general, the embedding layer maps every file fragment byte value to a 32-dimensional continuous vector learned at training time. It is used to compress the input feature dimension into a smaller and more realistic space. Each single byte value would be represented by a 256-dimensional sparse vector in the absence of the embedding layer. With multiple layers of standard and depthwise separable convolutions, features are automatically derived by non-linearly transforming inputs.

3.1 Inception Block

Figure 3 depicts the architecture of the inception block. The previous layer's output is passed to three parallel depthwise separable convolutions and one 1×1 convolution. Typically, the kernel size can have any value. However, we use kernels of sizes of 11, 19, and 27, with strides of 1, 1, 1, and 4, respectively.

Table 1. Grouping of different file types

Grouping	Files
Archive	apk, jar, msi, dmg, 7z, bz2, deb, gz, pkg, rar, rpm, xz, zip
Audio	aiff, flac, m4a, mp3, ogg, wav, wma
Bitmap	jpg, tiff, heic, bmp, gif, png
Executable	exe, mach-o, elf, dll
Human-readable	md, rtf, txt, tex, json, html, xml, log, csv
Office	doc, docx, key, ppt, pptx, xls, xlsx
Published	djvu, epub, mobi, pdf
Raw	arw, cr2, dng, gpr, nef, nrw, orf, pef, raf, rw2, 3fr
Vector	ai, eps, psd
Video	mov, mp4, 3gp, avi, mkv, ogv, webm
Miscellaneous	pcap, ttf, dwg, sqlite

Kernel sizes were chosen because they performed well in the previous state-of-the-art network [29] and were not large enough to significantly increase that model parameters. A batch normalization layer follows the convolution layers. All the depthwise separable convolution layer output are added and max-pooled with a pool size of 4. The 1×1 convolution branch is added to the max-pooled output. If the input and output have same number of channel, then the 1×1 convolution layer is replaced by the direct addition of the previous layer output to the max-pooled output as a skip connection.

4   Performance Evaluation

In this section, we present the results of our experimentation. We first describe the dataset used in our experimentation. Then, we give a brief description of a baseline model based on RNN. Finally, we provide an in-depth comparison of our proposed architecture with the baseline model, and FiFTy [29].

4.1   Dataset

To evaluate the performance of our model, we used the dataset provided by Mittal et al. in [28], which contains a balanced number of files per class. Other datasets, e.g., [14], are highly imbalanced with 20 files-types comprising 99.3% of the dataset and remaining 0.7% belonging to 43 file types. The dataset used is composed of 75 types of files that are organized into 6 different scenarios. The Scenarios are described as follows in [29]:

1. (All; 75 classes): All file types are separate classes; this is the most generic case and can be aggregated into more specialized use-cases.

Table 2. Comparison of results of three models on all 75 file types

Model	Neural network	Block size	# Params	Accuracy	Speed [ms/block][†]	Speed [min/GB][†]
Our model	Depthwise separable CNN	4096	**103,083**	**78.45**	**2.65**	**0.055**
		512	**103,083**	**65.89**	**2.78**	**0.382**
FiFTy	1-D CNN	4096	449,867	77.04	38.189	1.366
		512	289,995	65.66	38.67	3.052
Baseline RNN	LSTM	4096	717,643	70.51	268.58	36.375
		512	379,851	**67.5**	126.54	33.431

[†] Computed on Nvidia Titan X

2. (Use-specific; 11 classes): File types are grouped into 11 classes according to their use; this information may be useful for elaborate, hierarchical classification or for determining the primary use of an unknown device.
3. (Media Carver - Photos & Videos; 25 classes): Every file type tagged as a bitmap (6), RAW photo (11) or video (7) is considered as a separate class; all remaining types are grouped into one other class.
4. (Coarse Photo Carver; 5 classes): Separate classes for different photographic types: JPEG, 11 RAW images, 7 videos, 5 remaining bitmaps are grouped into one separate class per category; all remaining types are grouped into one other class.
5. (Specialized JPEG Carver; 2 classes): JPEG is a separate class, and the remaining 74 file types are grouped into one other class; scenario intended for analyzing disk images from generic devices.
6. (Camera-Specialized JPEG Carver; 2 classes): JPEG is a separate class, and the remaining photographic/video types (11 RAW images, 3GP, MOV, MKV, TIFF and HEIC) are grouped into one other class; scenario intended for analyzing SD cards from digital cameras.

4.2   Baseline Model

As a baseline model for performance comparison, we implemented a Long Short Term Memory (LSTM) based model. Prior research using LSTMs to classify file fragments had been published [16]. Nevertheless, the low number of learnable parameters hindered their effectiveness in classifying 75 types of files. Further, the model fed raw bytes directly to the LSTM layers in a one-hot representation. We implemented LSTM models with an embedding layer. The model specifications are as follows. File fragment byte sequences were fed into a 32-dimensional embedding layer, followed by bidirectional and unidirectional LSTM layers. The LSTM layer has 128 neurons in each of its two layers for 512-byte fragments and 128 and 256 neurons in its bidirectional and unidirectional layers for 4 KB fragments, respectively. A softmax dense layer produced the output labels.

4.3   Experimental Setup

We used automated hyper-parameter tuning for learning rate, optimizer choice, and activation function using TPE [7] implemented through Optuna [2]. We

Table 3. Comparison between fifty and our model in terms of inference time and model parameters

Scenario	Fragment size	#param (Ours)	#param (FiFTy)	Inf. time (ours) (CPU)	Inf. time (FiFTy) [ms/block]	Inf. time (ours) (GPU)	Inf. time (FiFTy) [ms/block]
1	4096	**103,083**	449,867	**56.502**	121.476	**2.656**	38.189
	512	**103,083**	289,995	**35.691**	75.551	**2.782**	38.673
2	4096	**94,827**	597,259	**50.067**	92.324	**2.720**	29.826
	512	**94,827**	269,323	**38.888**	89.344	**2.795**	29.809
3	4096	**96,633**	453,529	**48.24**	102.808	**2.646**	37.286
	512	**96,633**	690,073	**34.654**	99.710	**2.903**	35.361
4	4096	**94,053**	684,485	**49.341**	100.117	**2.775**	40.176
	512	**94,053**	474,885	**34.121**	79.346	**2.751**	35.965
5	4096	**93,666**	138,386	**49.124**	99.855	**2.878**	39.262
	512	**93,666**	336,770	**35.236**	79.831	**2.725**	42.413
6	4096	**93,666**	666,242	**49.35**	98.536	**2.689**	34.931
	512	**93,666**	242,114	**34.403**	89.104	**2.807**	38.982

found out that Adam optimizer [23] and Hardswish [20] are the best optimizer and activation function, respectively. We did not perform tuning of convolution kernel size; we used the kernel sizes from previous work [29] that proved to be effective. The kernel sizes for different branches of the inception block were taken as 11,19, and 27.

The accuracy for different networks was calculated as follows:

$$Accuracy = \frac{TP + TN}{TP + TN + FP + FN} \tag{7}$$

where TP is True Positive, TN is True Negative, FP is False Positive, and FN is False Negative.

To achieve higher accuracy from smaller models, we pretrained our network on corresponding fragment size dataset. We tried to leverage the performance of transfer learning in gaining higher accuracy [31]. In particular, to develop a 4096-byte fragment, the model was pretrained on 512-byte fragment dataset and vice-versa. We found that 6–8% accuracy was increased when pretraining was done using 512-byte fragment data for developing the 4096-byte fragment model. However, similar performance was not achieved when pretraining was done 4096-byte fragment data for the 512-byte fragment model.

All of our experiments were run on a machine with dual Intel Xeon CPU E5-2620 CPUs at 2.40 GHz (12 physical cores, 24 logical cores), 192 GB RAM, and a single Nvidia Titan X GPU, running on Ubuntu 20.04 Operating System. Pytorch 1.5.0 was used for neural network design.

4.4   Results

We observe that our models, in general, perform better than FiFTy models in inference time with no significant loss of accuracy. The results are summarised in Table 2. Moreover, we observe our model is superior to both FiFTy and RNN in terms of accuracy and inference time for scenario 1 (75 file types). In other words, when run on 1 GB data of 4096-byte fragments, FiFTy and RNN model

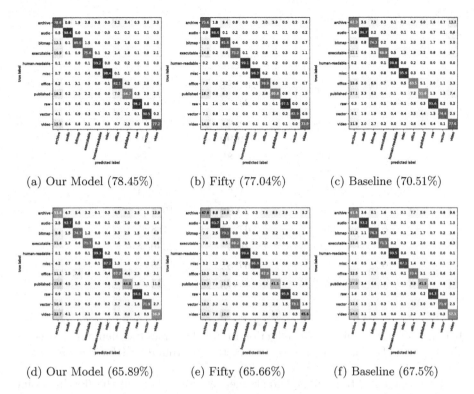

(a) Our Model (78.45%)   (b) Fifty (77.04%)   (c) Baseline (70.51%)

(d) Our Model (65.89%)   (e) Fifty (65.66%)   (f) Baseline (67.5%)

Fig. 4. Confusion matrices for Our model, FiFTy [29] and Baseline RNN model on 4 KB fragments in (a)–(c) and 512 bytes in (d)–(f). Due to large number of classes(75), classes belonging to same super class were clustered into one.

are 24× and 650× slower than our proposed model, respectively. Using 512-byte fragments, FiFTy is 8× slower, and RNNs is 86× slower than our model when run on 1 GB of data. RNN models perform well with 512-byte fragments due to their ability to handle short sequences. In contrast, when the fragment size increases to 4096-bytes, the performance deteriorates due to the vanishing gradient problem of RNNs [18]. While RNNs has higher accuracy on the 512-byte fragments, the model is not practical because it takes a long time for inference.

In view of a large number of file types, plotting a confusion matrix of all file types was not feasible, so we plotted the confusion matrix of file types grouped by use-cases in Fig. 4. The grouping is shown in Table 1. Most of the misclassification is happening in Archive file group due to other file types embedded in them.

The Table 3 summarizes the number of neural network parameters in our proposed model and the FiFTy model. For all six scenarios and both fragment sizes, our models have far fewer parameters than FiFTy. Additionally, the table compares the inference times for each of the six scenarios on both the GPU and CPU. Our model outperforms FiFTy by a wide margin on GPU and CPU inference time for all six scenarios. There is a 50% reduction in time for 4096-

Table 4. Comparison between fifty and our model for floating point operations (Mega FLOPs)

Scenario	Fragment size	FLOPs (ours)	FLOPs (FiFTy)
1	4096	**167.83**	1047.59
	512	**21.00**	1801.71
2	4096	**167.82**	1327.90
	512	**20.99**	918.06
3	4096	**167.82**	647.78
	512	**20.99**	3579.57
4	4096	**167.81**	2378.51
	512	**20.98**	1576.71
5	4096	**167.81**	488.37
	512	**20.98**	2330.48
6	4096	**167.81**	1126.00
	512	**20.98**	611.30

byte file fragments and a 58% reduction for 512-byte files fragments compared to FiFTy on CPU. For GPU, the time reduction is around 92% for both fragment types.

To provide hardware-independent metrics, we calculated the floating-point operations (FLOPs) in our models and FiFTy. Table 4 provides the FLOPs comparison for FiFTy and our models. Comparatively to FiFTy, our models have 81% fewer floating-point operations for 4096-byte fragments and 97% fewer for 512-byte fragments.

Our proposed models and FiFTy's accuracy is compared in Table 5. The accuracy of our models is comparable with that of FiFTy, although our models have a faster inference time. Using the main scenario of 75 files, our model achieves a higher accuracy with a significantly shorter inference time. Other scenarios have comparable accuracy to corresponding FiFTy models with a much faster run time. Overall, we achieve far better inference time while maintaining similar accuracy.

4.5   Discussion

Our models lag in the same area as previous work in the literature, e.g., [8,29]. In particular, we observe that high entropy files are difficult to classify because there is no statistical trace that the convolutional kernel can extract. Moreover, many files are container types that have another type of object embedded in them, e.g., *pdf* files that can contain embedded *jpg* images. As a result, classifiers behave erratically. Moreover, our model does not perform well for similar file types with different format, e.g., *ppt*, *pptx*, and *key*. However, other file types, e.g., *doc* and *docx.* are not affected by this as *docx* are zip file containing all the associated

Table 5. Comparison between fifty and our model in terms of accuracy

Scenario	#of files	Fragment size	Acc (Ours)	Acc (FiFTy)
1	75	4096	**78.45**	77.04
		512	**65.89**	65.66
2	11	4096	85.7	**89.91**
		512	75.84	**78.97**
3	25	4096	93.06	**94.64**
		512	80.79	**87.97**
4	5	4096	**94.17**	94.03
		512	87.14	**90.30**
5	2	4096	**99.28**	99.12
		512	98.94	**99.07**
6	2	4096	**99.59**	99.59
		512	98.76	**99.23**

XML files whereas *doc* is stored as binary. Finally, the feasibility of using our model to classify encrypted file fragments will be investigated in the future.

5   Related Work

Several techniques have been proposed for file fragments identification and classification. The techniques range from basic methods like using magic numbers, and file headers [10] to more advanced methods using machine learning and deep learning [5,29]. Generally, file carving methods can be classified into 1) statistical methods, 2) machine learning methods, and 3) deep learning methods.

Statistical Methods. Karresand et al. [22] proposed *Oscar*, for determining the probable file type of binary data fragment. *Oscar* uses Byte Frequency Distribution of 4096-byte-sized fragments of different file types for the construction of vector models based on mean and standard deviation, called centroids. A vector distance between the mean and standard deviation of the segment to be classified and the centroids is calculated; if it is lower than a certain threshold value, the segment is classified as a modeling file. Binary classification was done by combining 49 file types into one class and JPEG into another. JPEG achieved a detection rate of 97.90, which was mainly due to byte-stuffing [40].

Machine Learning Methods. In [25], Li et al. proposed a Support Vector Machine (SVM) model that is trained using the histogram of the data bytes as a feature vector. The SVM is used for binary classification with one class fixed as JPEG and the other class varying as DLL, EXE, PDF, and MP3. Similarly,

Fitzgerald et al. [12] proposed an SVM model for the classification of file fragments. The file fragments were presented as a bag of words (bag of bytes) with feature vector consisting of uni-gram and bi-gram counts and other statistical measures such as entropy. Zheng et al. [43] proposed a similar approach of using byte frequency distribution (BFD) or histogram and entropy as a feature vector for SVM.

An prominant tool in file carving is *Sceadan*, which is an open-source tool developed by Beebe et al. [5] used various statistical features such as uni-gram, bi-gram, entropy, mean byte value, longest streak, etc. Ten separate input vectors were prepared out of the statistical features; the vectors were grouped into four sets: uni-grams, bi-grams, all global features except n-grams, a subset of global features. These sets were fed to SVMs of linear and radial basis function (RBM) for classification into 38 diverse file types. They reported an accuracy of 73.4%. Increasing the number of features(in terms of the type, not number) that are input to the SVM harmed the accuracy. The best accuracy was achieved by concatenation of uni-gram and bi-gram.

Deep Learning Methods. Wang et al. [42] used one layer convolution with multiple kernel sizes. The raw byte values were converted to their corresponding binary representation and fed to the embedding layer to convert the binary value to a continuous dense vector. They studied 20 file types from the *GovDocs1* dataset. Chen et al. [8] took a different approach and converted the 4096-byte file fragment to a 64×63 gray-scale image. Their intuition was that data fragments from different files would have different texture features, reflected in the gray-scale image. The gray-scale images were fed to a deep CNN network like VGG [35] with many convolutions and max-pool layers followed by dense classification. Hiester [16] compared feed-forward, recurrent and convolutional neural networks with input fragments in the form of binary representation (fragment bits). The studied file types were JPEG, GIF, XML and CSV. On these easily distinguishable file types, only recurrent networks gave satisfactory results. They emphasized lossless representation for achieving high accuracy, but this binary representation increases the input's dimensionality. Mittal et al. [29] developed *FiFTy*, an open-source convolutional neural network for file fragment type identification. An open-source dataset was also developed by them, which is reported to be the largest open source dataset for file fragment classification. A compact neural network was developed that used trainable embedding space and convolutional neural networks.

When compared with neural network-based classifier [8,29,42] our model achieves better accuracy on largest number of file types. We have only compared our models with deep learning based methods as they can be accelerated using GPUs. Our models far exceed recurrent neural network based classifier [16] by being 650× faster. Compared to machine learning based classifier [5], which takes 9 min/GB, our model takes 0.05 min/GB.

6   Conclusion

File fragments classification is an essential task in digital forensics. In this paper, we proposed an efficient file fragments classification model. Our primary focus is to develop a faster model than the current best model without compromising on accuracy. We designed a classification model for different scenarios with all having parameters less than 100K. Our model is based on depthwise separable convolution layers that are connected in inception-like fashion. The evaluation results show that depthwise separable convolutions perform fast file fragments classification with reasonable accuracy.

Several improvements can be made to increase the classification accuracy for classes with high misclassification rate. Without hardware constraints, neural architecture search [30, 44] is the best method to design an architecture for data-specific models. Moreover, for simple scenarios like classifying JPEGs against other file types, redundant connections in the neural network can be removed using in-network distillation [17, 38].

Acknowledgement. The authors would like to acknowledge the Interdisciplinary Research Center for Intelligent Secure Systems at KFUPM.

References

1. Ahmed, I., Lhee, K.-S., Shin, H.-J., Hong, M.-P.: Fast content-based file type identification. In: Peterson, G., Shenoi, S. (eds.) DigitalForensics 2011. IAICT, vol. 361, pp. 65–75. Springer, Heidelberg (2011). https://doi.org/10.1007/978-3-642-24212-0_5

2. Akiba, T., Sano, S., Yanase, T., Ohta, T., Koyama, M.: Optuna: a next-generation hyperparameter optimization framework. In: Proceedings of the 25rd ACM SIGKDD International Conference on Knowledge Discovery and Data Mining (2019)

3. Alghafli, K., Yeun, C.Y., Damiani, E.: Techniques for measuring the probability of adjacency between carved video fragments: the vidcarve approach. IEEE Trans. Sustain. Comput. **6**, 131–143 (2019)

4. Amirani, M.C., Toorani, M., Mihandoost, S.: Feature-based type identification of file fragments. Secur. Commun. Netw. **6**, 115–128 (2013)

5. Beebe, N.L., Maddox, L.A., Liu, L., Sun, M.: Sceadan: using concatenated n-gram vectors for improved file and data type classification. IEEE Trans. Inf. Forensics Secur. **8**(9), 1519–1530 (2013)

6. Bennett, D.: The challenges facing computer forensics investigators in obtaining information from mobile devices for use in criminal investigations. Inf. Secur. J. Global Perspect. **21**(3), 159–168 (2012)

7. Bergstra, J.S., Bardenet, R., Bengio, Y., Kégl, B.: Algorithms for hyper-parameter optimization. In: Shawe-Taylor, J., Zemel, R.S., Bartlett, P.L., Pereira, F., Weinberger, K.Q. (eds.) Advances in Neural Information Processing Systems, vol. 24, pp. 2546–2554. Curran Associates, Inc. (2011). http://papers.nips.cc/paper/4443-algorithms-for-hyper-parameter-optimization.pdf

8. Chen, Q., et al.: File fragment classification using grayscale image conversion and deep learning in digital forensics. In: 2018 IEEE Security and Privacy Workshops (SPW) (2018). https://doi.org/10.1109/spw.2018.00029

9. Chollet, F.: Xception: deep learning with depthwise separable convolutions, pp. 1800–1807 (2017). https://doi.org/10.1109/CVPR.2017.195

10. Darwin, I.F.: Libmagic (2008). ftp://ftp.astron.com/pub/file

11. Dunne, R.A., Campbell, N.A.: On the pairing of the softmax activation and cross-entropy penalty functions and the derivation of the softmax activation function. In: Proceedings of 8th Australian Conference on the Neural Networks, Melbourne, vol. 181, p. 185. Citeseer (1997)

12. Fitzgerald, S., Mathews, G., Morris, C., Zhulyn, O.: Using nlp techniques for file fragment classification. Digital Invest. **9** (2012). https://doi.org/10.1016/j.diin.2012.05.008

13. Fukushima, K.: A self-organizing neural network model for a mechanism of pattern recognition unaffected by shift in position. Biol. Cybern. **36**, 193–202 (1980)

14. Garfinkel, S., Farrell, P., Roussev, V., Dinolt, G.: Bringing science to digital forensics with standardized forensic corpora. Digital Invest. **6** (2009). https://doi.org/10.1016/j.diin.2009.06.016

15. Garfinkel, S.L.: Carving contiguous and fragmented files with fast object validation. Digital Invest. **4**, 2–12 (2007)

16. Hiester, L.: File fragment classification using neural networks with lossless representations (2018)

17. Hinton, G., Vinyals, O., Dean, J.: Distilling the knowledge in a neural network. arXiv preprint arXiv:1503.02531 (2015)

18. Hochreiter, S.: The vanishing gradient problem during learning recurrent neural nets and problem solutions. Int. J. Uncertainty Fuzz. Knowl.-Based Syst. **6**(02), 107–116 (1998)

19. Hochreiter, S., Schmidhuber, J.: Long short-term memory. Neural Comput. **9**(8), 1735–1780 (1997)

20. Howard, A., et al.: Searching for mobilenetv3. In: Proceedings of the IEEE International Conference on Computer Vision, pp. 1314–1324 (2019)

21. Howard, A., et al.: Mobilenets: efficient convolutional neural networks for mobile vision applications (2017)

22. Karresand, M., Shahmehri, N.: Oscar - file type identification of binary data in disk clusters and ram pages. In: SEC (2006)

23. Kingma, D.P., Ba, J.: Adam: a method for stochastic optimization. arXiv preprint arXiv:1412.6980 (2014)

24. Lei, Z.: Forensic analysis of unallocated space. Ph.D. thesis, UOIT (2011)

25. Li, Q., Ong, A., Suganthan, P., Thing, V.: A novel support vector machine approach to high entropy data fragment classification (2010)

26. Lin, X.: File carving. In: Introductory Computer Forensics, pp. 211–233. Springer, Cham (2018). https://doi.org/10.1007/978-3-030-00581-8_9

27. Marziale, L., Richard, G.G., III., Roussev, V.: Massive threading: using gpus to increase the performance of digital forensics tools. Digital Invest. **4**, 73–81 (2007)

28. Memon, G.M.P.K.N.: File fragment type (fft) - 75 dataset (2019). https://doi.org/10.21227/kfxw-8084

29. Mittal, G., Korus, P., Memon, N.: Fifty: large-scale file fragment type identification using convolutional neural networks. IEEE Trans. Inf. Forensics Secur. **16**, 28–41 (2020)

30. Pham, H., Guan, M.Y., Zoph, B., Le, Q.V., Dean, J.: Efficient neural architecture search via parameter sharing. arXiv preprint arXiv:1802.03268 (2018)

31. Pratt, L.Y.: Discriminability-based transfer between neural networks. In: Advances in Neural Information Processing Systems, pp. 204–211 (1993)
32. Rafique, M., Khan, M.: Exploring static and live digital forensics: methods, practices and tools. Int. J. Sci. Eng. Res. 4(10), 1048–1056 (2013)
33. Richard III, G.G., Roussev, V.: Scalpel: A frugal, high performance file carver. In: DFRWS. Citeseer (2005)
34. SIfre, L., Mallat, S.: Rigid-motion scattering for texture classification (2014)
35. Simonyan, K., Zisserman, A.: Very deep convolutional networks for large-scale image recognition. CoRR abs/1409.1556 (2014). http://arxiv.org/abs/1409.1556
36. Szegedy, C., et al.: Going deeper with convolutions. In: Computer Vision and Pattern Recognition (CVPR) (2015). http://arxiv.org/abs/1409.4842
37. Tan, M., Le, Q.V.: Efficientnet: rethinking model scaling for convolutional neural networks. arXiv preprint arXiv:1905.11946 (2019)
38. Tian, Y., Krishnan, D., Isola, P.: Contrastive representation distillation. arXiv preprint arXiv:1910.10699 (2019)
39. Vulinović, K., Ivković, L., Petrović, J., Skračić, K., Pale, P.: Neural networks for file fragment classification. In: 2019 42nd International Convention on Information and Communication Technology, Electronics and Microelectronics (MIPRO), pp. 1194–1198. IEEE (2019)
40. Wallace, G.K.: The jpeg still picture compression standard. Commun. ACM 34(4), 30–44 (1991). https://doi.org/10.1145/103085.103089
41. Wang, F., Quach, T.T., Wheeler, J., Aimone, J.B., James, C.D.: Sparse coding for n-gram feature extraction and training for file fragment classification. IEEE Trans. Inf. Forensics Secur. 13(10), 2553–2562 (2018)
42. Wang, Y., Su, Z., Song, D.: File fragment type identification with convolutional neural networks. Proceedings of the 2018 International Conference on Machine Learning Technologies - ICMLT 18 (2018). https://doi.org/10.1145/3231884.3231889
43. Zheng, N., Wang, J., Wu, T., Xu, M.: A fragment classification method depending on data type. 2015 IEEE International Conference on Computer and Information Technology; Ubiquitous Computing and Communications; Dependable, Autonomic and Secure Computing; Pervasive Intelligence and Computing, pp. 1948–1953 (2015)
44. Zoph, B., Vasudevan, V., Shlens, J., Le, Q.V.: Learning transferable architectures for scalable image recognition. In: Proceedings of the IEEE Conference on Computer Vision and Pattern Recognition, pp. 8697–8710 (2018)

Trust and PETs

Novel Approaches for the Development of Trusted IoT Entities

Davide Ferraris[1(✉)], Carmen Fernandez-Gago[2], and Javier Lopez[1]

[1] Department of Computer Science, University of Malaga, Malaga, Spain
{ferraris,jlm}@lcc.uma.es
[2] Department of Applied Mathematics, Malaga, Spain
mcgago@lcc.uma.es

Abstract. The Internet of Things (IoT) is a paradigm allowing humans and smart entities to be interconnected anyhow and anywhere. Trust is fundamental in order to allow communication among these actors. In order to guarantee trust in an IoT entity, we believe that it must be considered during the whole System Development Life Cycle (SDLC). Anyhow, we think that usual development techniques are not effective for the IoT. For this reason, in this paper, we describe a methodology to develop an IoT entity by proposing a holistic approach implementing three different techniques: a bottom-up approach, a top-down approach and a trusted block development. Firstly, the top-down approach will start from the general IoT entity going down to its specific functionalities. Secondly, the bottom-up approach will focus on the contexts related to the IoT entity. It starts from basic ones, going up aggregating them to the composition of the IoT entity as a whole. Finally, the trusted block development will define different blocks of code related to functionalities and contexts. Every block can be considered a *trust island* where the contexts and functionalities are specified only for a particular block.

Keywords: Trust · SysML · UML · Internet of Things (IoT) · System Development Life Cycle (SDLC)

1 Introduction

The Internet of Things (IoT) is composed of two words: Internet and things. With these two words, we can understand the scope of this technology allowing the connection of things among them through the internet [19]. The word "thing" is generic and it can represent either humans or objects. In fact, through IoT, we can connect different types of things and how to connect them in a protected and trusted way is one of the main challenges in this field. In this paper, we will use the terms things, devices or entities for the same purpose.

Statista has predicted that 75.4 billions of devices would be connected by 2025[1]. This prediction is helpful to understand that the IoT paradigm will grow

---

[1] https://www.statista.com/statistics/471264/iot-number-of-connected-devices-worldwide/.

W. Meng et al. (Eds.): SEC 2022, IFIP AICT 648, pp. 215–230, 2022.
https://doi.org/10.1007/978-3-031-06975-8_13

up to define how the world will be connected in the next years. For this reason, many opportunities will arise, but also many problems, especially related to trust and security [2]. A way to mitigate them is offered by security and trust.

Trust is difficult to define because it can be related to many different topics, from Psychology to Computer Science [5]. Moreover, trust is strongly connected to the context. In fact it "means many things to many people" [3]. In a trust relationship, there are basically two actors involved: the trustor and the trustee. The trustor is the one who needs a favor or a service, but he/she cannot fulfill it alone. For this reason, the trustor needs the trustee, which is the one keeping the trust. The level of trust between trustor and trustee can change over time positively or negatively due to the good or bad behavior of the trustee and on the outcome of the trust relationship. Moreover, it is strongly dependent on a particular context (i.e., a trustor can trust a trustee as a driver, but not as a cook).

Anyhow, the development of trust models for an IoT entity is a task that needs to be tackled. We believe that the usual System and Software Development Life Cycle (SDLC) approaches might be of help. For this reason, in this paper, we will focus on an important phase of the SDLC considering the central phase of the K-Model proposed in [8]: the development phase.

During the development of an IoT entity, the developers can consider several approaches in order to perform this crucial task. A widely used approach is the so-called top-down. It is basically a way to consider the problem starting from a general perspective to a specific one. Moreover, the top-down approach can be used even for software development through a Functional Breakdown Structure (FBS) or a Work Breakdown Structure (WBS) [13]. However, in our case, it is important to consider not only the functionalities but also their connections to the domains such as trust and security in order to divide and perform the analysis according to their scope.

On the contrary, the bottom-up approach starts from a specific viewpoint to a generic overview of the system. It is a method used particularly in software engineering [10,13], but it can also be used to develop IoT infrastructures [18]. In our paper, we move forward and consider it according to the different contexts and domains of the IoT entities.

However, in our opinion, these two approaches alone are not enough for the development of a trusted IoT entity. In fact, it is important to highlight that an IoT entity is composed of software and an effective way to develop the code is following a finite state approach as stated by [22] and [1] creating trusted block of codes. This approach is even more important in an environment such as the IoT, where usually all the functionalities are performed separately and following a step-by-step process.

Nevertheless, top-down and bottom-up approaches have always been considered separately, such as the block or finite-state approach. In this work, we will extend these approaches by developing the block approach and implementing it to balance and connect top-down and bottom-up approaches among them. Moreover, the utilization of the block approaches will allow the developers to focus separately on the different contexts and functionalities according to the domain and their composition.

The structure of the paper is as follows. In Sect. 2, we describe the related work and the background of this paper. Then, the approaches designed for the development phase are presented in Sect. 3. In Sect. 4, we show how these approaches must be implemented in a use case. Finally, in Sect. 5, we conclude the paper and discuss the future work.

2   Related Work

In this section, we firstly discuss about IoT, trust and development techniques. Finally, we discuss about our previous work, showing why it is necessary to propose new development approaches in order to guide developers through the SDLC.

2.1   Trust, IoT and Development

In Information Technology, trust is strongly dependent on other domains such as security and privacy [12,17]. Moreover, Ferraris et al. [8] stated that these relations are even more important for the IoT.

The IoT allows smart entities to be controlled anywhere and anyhow [19]. However, they must be secured through the Internet and it is essential to guarantee trust during the communication among smart entities [24]. In fact, we consider trust as "the personal, unique and temporal expectation that a trustor places on a trustee regarding the outcome of an interaction between them" [15]. According to this definition, we understand that there are at least two actors in a trust relationship: a trustor and a trustee. For this reason, we can state that there must be at least a trustor and a trustee in any trusted IoT communication.

Moreover, the IoT is a heterogeneous and dynamic field. In order to implement trust and its related domain in the IoT, it is necessary to consider it through the whole SDLC [8].

However, in the IoT the usual development techniques could not work properly also because of the actual network infrastructure, which was not built precisely for the IoT [23]. Solutions similar to the Software-Defined Networking (SDN) [4] can help to solve this problem allowing the development of new applications and techniques for the IoT [20]. Anyhow, if we can state that SDN is related to the network infrastructure, Software Defined Perimeter (SDP)[2] is related to the services and applications running on it. They can be used together to improve the functionalities of the IoT technology[3]. Thus, during the development of an IoT entity, it is helpful to take these infrastructures into consideration

---

[2] https://cloudsecurityalliance.org/working-groups/software-defined-perimeter.
[3] http://www.waverleylabs.com/software-defined-network-sdn-or-software-defined-perimeter-sdp-whats-the-difference/.

and to use development techniques that help to separate services, functionalities and contexts. These techniques can be represented by known development approaches such as the top-down and bottom-up approaches.

Ganchev et al. [11] proposed a top-down approach to create an IoT architecture for smart cities. Patel et al. [16] introduced a general approach that can be used to reunite the physical and the digital world belonging to the IoT paradigm. On the contrary, Reaidy et al. proposed a bottom-up approach to develop IoT infrastructures [18].

These works are interesting, but we need something more specific for a general IoT environment that also considers trust and related domains. In fact, as stated by [14] "an important question is what consequences a bottom-up and top-down construction of the IoT infrastructure has for the security, privacy and trust". Moreover, according to [21], it is important to find a balance between top-down planning and bottom-up innovation. We believe that in order to perform this task, it is necessary to implement a third approach that can consider both the approaches highlighting their points of strength and establishing a balance among them: a trusted block development. Thus, for these reasons, we develop the approaches that we will show in Sect. 3, considering them together to provide developers with a trusted block development technique based on the idea stated in [1, 22].

2.2   Background

In our previous works, we have developed a framework that holistically considers trust during the whole SDLC of a smart IoT entity [8]. The framework is composed of a K-Model and several transversal activities (i.e., Traceability, Risk Analysis). In addition, it is fundamental to take the context into consideration during each phase of the SDLC. This aspect is very important for IoT due to the dynamicity and heterogeneity of this paradigm. The context depends on several aspects such as the environment, the functionalities of an entity or the rules of the company developing the IoT entity.

In the K-Model that is shown in Fig. 1, we can see different phases covering all the SDLC of the IoT entity under development: from cradle to grave. The first phase is related to the needs phase, where the purpose of the IoT entity to be developed is proposed the purpose of the IoT entity to be developed. In this phase, all the stakeholders related to the IoT device have a key role. The second phase considers the requirements elicitation process. In this phase, the developers must elicit the requirements according to the needs considered in the previous one. We have described this phase in [7]. Then, the third phase considers the model specification. We have developed a model-driven approach to ensure trust in the modeling phase of the K-Model proposing several diagrams (i.e., requirement diagram, context diagram) to cover all the crucial aspects of the modeling phase [9]. The output of this phase is the input of the following and central phase of the K-Model. In this paper, we will consider, explore and expand it: the development phase.

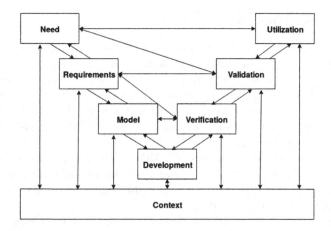

Fig. 1. K-Model: with the *Transversal Activities* it compounds the framework [8]

3 Development

The development is the core phase of the K-Model presented in Sect. 2.2. This phase transforms the needs, requirements and models in the product that will be verified and validated in order to be distributed to the customers. In the IoT, the challenges are numerous because of the dynamicity and heterogeneity of this technology. The SDN could solve problems related to the old infrastructure and also using the SDP technology it is possible to create separated contexts to make the IoT entities communicate in a trusted and secure way. Ferraris et al. [6] proposed an architecture similar to the SDP technique that is useful to define the boundaries in a Smart home environment guaranteeing a trusted interaction among IoT entities. We will follow this idea and consider the possible contexts in which the IoT entity will be involved in order to develop it properly.

We believe that in order to holistically consider all the information collected in the previous phases of the K-Model, the developers must organize their work in a schematic way. Our proposed approaches help them fulfilling this goal. In fact, the top-down approach presented in Sect. 3.1 allows developers to consider functionalities firstly from a generic perspective and then in a specific way. On the contrary, the bottom-up approach discussed in Sect. 3.2 considers contexts from a specif point of view to a more generic one. The utilization of both approaches helps developers to better consider all the fundamental aspects of the IoT entity. Finally, both the approaches are considered during the trusted block development proposed in Sect. 3.3.

In order to show the steps of the development phase, in Sect. 3.4, we will present the order of utilization of our proposed approaches.

3.1   Top-Down Approach

During the development of an IoT entity, a useful methodology is to analyze the IoT entity under development following a top-down approach.

In Sect. 2, we mentioned several methodologies implementing this approach (i.e., WBS or FBS). Moreover, in the previous phases of the K-Model, we have focused on how important it is to consider the domains related to trust. For this reason, we think that it is useful to mix the FBS considering also the related domains of each functionality.

We named this top-down approach FDBS (Functional Domain Breakdown Structure). In this approach, it is fundamental to highlight each functionality according to its domain. However, it is possible that a particular functionality could belong to more than one domain.

According to the original FBS structure, we create a descending tree where the root is related to the IoT entity and the children define its functionalities. The final leaves of the FDBS tree will contain basic functionalities. For the FDBS, we create another parameter denoting which domain is considered for the proper functionality or sub-functionality (i.e., trust and privacy). As it is possible that two or more requirements could be the same and belong to different domains [7], thus, it is possible that a single functionality belongs to different domains. However, in this case we will not have two or more functionalities, but we will have a single functionality belonging to more than one domain.

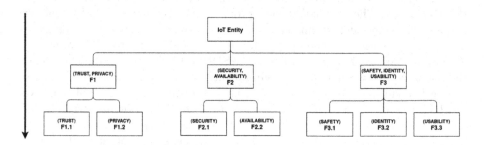

Fig. 2. Functional Domain Breakdown Structure (FDBS)

Figure 2 shows an example of FDBS. There are three levels. The IoT entity is set at the top level. Then its main functionalities are set at the medium level, splitting them into sub-functionalities at the bottom level. As we can see, the domains are represented at the top of the box containing the functionalities. About this point, we want to remark for the reader that the IoT entity is composed of all the domains, but the functionalities can belong to a subset of domains.

However, in order to show how to implement our top-down approach in a use case scenario, we will present a specific example in Sect. 4.

3.2 Bottom-Up Approach

For the bottom-up approach, the basic elements of a system are firstly analyzed and implemented. Then, the developer analyzes composed elements in order to proceed from a specific to a general view of the entity.

As we explained in Sect. 2.2, it is very important to take context into consideration during the SDLC of an IoT entity. Therefore, we will use this approach to model all the contexts belonging to the IoT entity under development. In fact, the IoT entities can participate in different contexts and some of them shall be separated from the others. Strongly related to the contexts, we also consider the domains (i.e., trust and security). However, there is the possibility that some contexts share functionalities and they can be considered together under a super-context. This super-context will include the single domains belonging to the contexts in the lower layer.

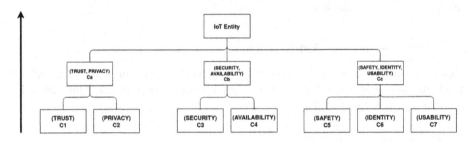

Fig. 3. Bottom-up approach (context)

The bottom-up approach is presented in Fig. 3. It starts from the single contexts considering the ones at the bottom level and their domains. Then, the contexts having commonalities can be considered together under a super-context. In this general representation, we have three levels and the top level belongs to the IoT entity in its whole.

3.3 Trusted Block Development

In order to consider and develop software that is fundamental for any IoT entities, we propose a trusted block development.

This approach helps developers to delimit the software according to the contexts and functionalities highlighted in the bottom-up and top-down approaches. This development style is fundamental to keep separated the different codes.

In Fig. 4, we can see that the blocks are separated and they can contain several sub-blocks of code. They can be sequential or not, but it is important that they are separated. This is fundamental in order to preserve the separation among functionalities and contexts. This programming technique allows developers to create boundaries related to trust, creating *"trust islands"*. In fact, if

Fig. 4. Trusted block development: each block is a *trust island*

we consider variables existing only in a particular block, we can create trust operations according to the users or functionalities belonging only to that particular block. In fact, this design is helpful to keep the roles of a user separated according to a particular context. For example, a user can be considered and trusted in a block A, but it cannot be considered or not trusted in a block B. We will show an example of this part in Sect. 4.3.

3.4 Implementation Approaches

These approaches must follow a step-by-step methodology in order to be effectively implemented according to the K-Model proposed in Sect. 2.2. This methodology is presented in Fig. 5.

The steps are the following:

1. The first step corresponds to the output of the previous phases of the K-Model (i.e., Need, Requirements and Model). In fact, all the tasks performed up to this step must be taken into consideration in order to develop the IoT entity. The needs specify the intended IoT entity, the requirements have been elicited according to them and the implemented models create useful guidelines to develop the IoT device in this central phase of the K-Model.
2. Then, in Sects. 3.1 and 3.2 the proposed approaches are implemented in the second step. A context diagram will be very useful in the bottom-up approach. On the other hand, the other diagrams will be fundamentals during the implementation of the top-down approach.
3. Thirdly, as we specified in Sect. 3.3, according to both the approaches, we need to implement the trusted block development.
4. The fourth step of the methodology corresponds to the final developed entity that will be verified and validated in the following phases of the K-Model. Anyhow, it is possible to come back to step number one in the case some modifications are needed.

In the next section, we provide a use case scenario that realizes the implementation approaches presented in Sect. 3.

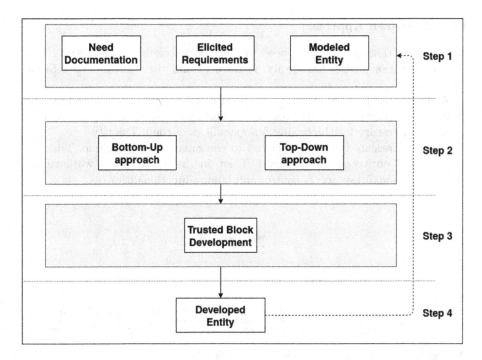

Fig. 5. Step-by-step methodology

4   Use Case Scenario

As a use case scenario, we will expand the one presented in [7] implementing the approaches proposed in Sect. 3.

In this scenario, the IoT entity under development is a Smart Cake Machine needed to bake cakes and interfacing with other IoT entities: a smart fridge that is in the same smart home and smart super-markets belonging to the smart city environment. These connections are useful in order to check and order a particular ingredient, in the case it was needed for a recipe. Moreover, the IoT entity must allow trusted users to interact with it and deny the interaction for untrusted users.

In this section, we show how it is possible to apply the aforementioned approaches in order to develop the desired IoT entity. Anyhow, we will focus only on particular aspects also highlighted in [7]. In any case, it will be the developer the one in charge to choose which contexts and functionalities must be considered in order to develop the IoT entity according to the previous phases of the K-Model.

4.1 Top-Down Approach

According to this approach, we need to follow a descending path starting from the consideration of the IoT entity as a whole and then going deep into the functionalities.

Analysing our previous work [7], we can state that some of the elicited requirements were related to the access control mechanisms. Furthermore, other requirements are necessary for the baking functionalities of the IoT entity.

Figure 6 presents the FDBS related to the Smart Cake Machine. Thus, we have the IoT entity on the top level. Then, in the second level, we have two general functionalities: access control and baking functionalities.

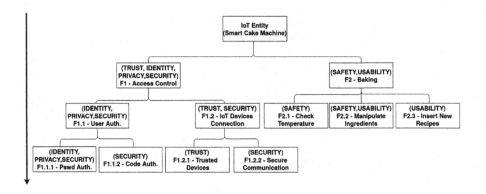

Fig. 6. FDBS - use case: smart cake machine

Considering access control, the related functionalities are divided into two fundamental parts: user authentication and IoT devices connections. In fact, the Smart Cake Machine can interact with trusted users and IoT devices. Concerning the users and according to our previous paper [7], we can consider two types of authentication: password and code authentication. The first one is related to the domains of identity, security and privacy. In fact, a password is related to a single user and it must be stored securely. Moreover, the data of the users must be collected and kept private. On the other hand, the code authentication can be considered without storing user information and it can be shared with other users whom the owner of the IoT device trusts. Moreover, this code must be securely provided.

About the connections between the Smart Cake Machine and the other devices, we need to consider the trusted devices guaranteeing that the communication among them is secure. So, the functionalities needed to create trust models for the devices will belong to the trust domain. The communication among these devices will belong to the security domain.

It is important to note that any functionalities belonging to this part of the "tree" is connected to the main functionality "Access Control". They are fundamentals to grant device access only to whom is trusted and can provide the credentials in order to interact with the device.

In Fig. 6, we can see that the right part of the tree is related to the baking functionalities. In order to bake a cake, there are three fundamental functionalities. The first one is to check the temperature. It is a safety function for the correct preparation of the cake and for the safety of users and the device. The second one is related to the manipulation of the ingredients. This functionality is related to the safety and usability domain. In fact, safety is due to the health aspect. The usability and safety domains is related to the correct utilization of the machine manipulating the ingredients. Finally, the third functionality is related to the possibility of inserting new recipes. In this case, the usability domain is important because the interface must be user-friendly. As we can see, the domains are collected and separated according to the different functionalities.

4.2 Bottom-Up Approach

This approach is useful to define the different contexts according to the Smart Cake Machine use case.

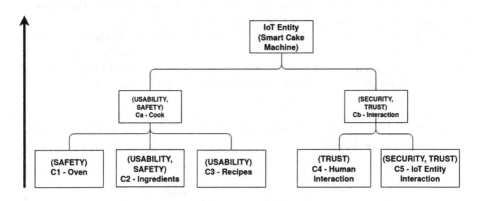

Fig. 7. Bottom-up approach - use case: smart cake machine

We can see the proposed contexts in Fig. 7. We describe the contexts from right to left.

One context is related to the interaction among smart entities (i.e., smart super-market, smart fridge). Then, another context is related to the utilization of the device by human users. These two contexts can be considered together in a super-context related to the interactions. Trust and security are fundamental for these interactions and they are properly considered the main domains for these contexts. Then, we have a third context related to the recipes, another one about the ingredients and a fifth context related to the oven. These three contexts can be summarized into a super-context named cook context, where the considered domains are usability and safety. The two super-context are fundamentals for the trusted IoT Entity.

4.3   Trusted Block Development

After the utilization of bottom-up and top-down approaches, the developer must create the code according to them and to the previous phases of the K-Model. We present two different blocks in order to explain the different aspects of this approach and the differences among domains. The first block we present is *cook*, the second is related to *authentication*.

Block Cook. In this case, we start from the definitions of the contexts and functionalities creating separate code blocks according to them. We can see that contexts C1, C2 and C3 proposed in the bottom-up approach are also covered in the top-down approach with the functionalities F2.1, F2.2 and F2.3. In fact, it is possible to consider the same or similar aspects in both approaches.

Thus, we will present the code block containing these highlighted aspects. For the first context and functionality related to the oven and the temperature, we need to set temperature attributes in order to fix predetermined levels related to different states during the cooking process. Then, for the ingredients, we need to consider them in order to be cataloged and inserted by the users. Finally, there are the recipes. We assume that they must be uploaded by the users or they can be memorized in the device by the vendors.

The domains are the same considered in the previous approaches (i.e., safety, usability) and they are declared at the start of the code blocks. We want to remind to the reader, that these domains are strongly connected to trust and their consideration allow developers to implement trust in the IoT entity.

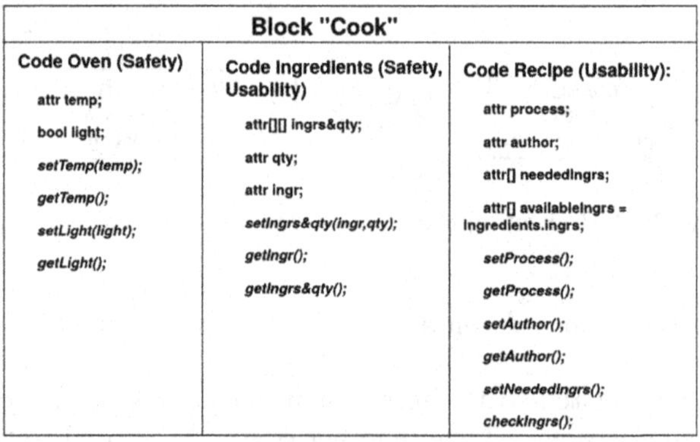

Block "Cook"		
Code Oven (Safety)	**Code Ingredients (Safety, Usability)**	**Code Recipe (Usability):**
attr temp;	attr[][] ingrs&qty;	attr process;
bool light;	attr qty;	attr author;
setTemp(temp);	attr ingr;	attr[] neededingrs;
getTemp();	setIngrs&qty(ingr,qty);	attr[] availableingrs = ingredients.ingrs;
setLight(light);	getIngr();	setProcess();
getLight();	getIngrs&qty();	getProcess();
		setAuthor();
		getAuthor();
		setNeededingrs();
		checkIngrs();

Fig. 8. Trusted block development - block cook

In our example, we can see in Fig. 8 that the block named *Cook* is composed of three parts: Oven, Ingredients and Recipe. We use the generic terminology attr (i.e., attribute) to consider characters, strings or numbers (i.e., integers, doubles, floats). Moreover, we use a Boolean variable and arrays of attributes. Then, we create methods useful to manipulate and check the attributes. For example, the attribute *setIngrs&qty(ingr, qty)* is fundamental to set which ingredient and its amount is considered. Another interesting method is *checkIngrs()*. It can be used to compare if the needed ingredients are available. We do not deeply specify the methods, we only declare them.

Block Authentication. Also in this case, we can start from the definitions of the contexts and functionalities by developing separate code blocks. In this case, we consider C4 (i.e., Human Interaction) and the functionalities related to code and password authentication (i.e., F1.1, F1.1.1 and F1.1.2), In fact, in order to create and use a code or a password, the IoT entity must interact with the users. The example is narrow and we just want to give a hint on how to consider the steps in order to create separate code blocks.

Thus, for the first code named *Code*, we can see that it is connected to security and not to identity for example. This is because, in this use case, the code is unique and it can be used by different users in order to interact with the IoT device. On the other hand, we set different passwords according to the users in the second part of the block called *authentication*. In this case, each user has a password. We do not show exactly the procedure to create it, it depends on the user interface and the protocols that can be implemented. In this case, we want only to show how to distinguish between the different cases.

Therefore, we can see in Fig. 9 that the block named *Authentication* is composed of two attributes: the code that can be generated and the expiration date. Then, according to the password code, we can see that we have to parameters: user and password. They are related and for another user it should not be possible to use the password of another. In this case, it is possible to separate the tasks related to a particular user, but this is another level of implementation that we do not discuss here. We wanted to present how the blocks must be implemented without going deeply with the specifications that are strictly connected to the use cases that will be considered.

```
Block
"Authentication"

Code Code (Security):
    attr code;
    attr expiration;
    getCode();
    createCode(code);
    setDate(expiration);
    getDate();
Code Password (Identity, Privacy, Security):
    attr user;
    attr password;
    setPassword(user,password);
    getPassword(user);
    storePassword();
```

Fig. 9. Trusted block development - block authentication

5 Conclusion and Future Work

We have presented three approaches for the development of a trusted smart IoT entity during the core phase of the K-Model. These approaches allow developers to follow a schematic methodology in order to implement contexts and functionalities. Firstly, we have presented a top-down approach (FDBS) that is useful to specify domains and functionalities belonging to the IoT entity under development. Secondly, we have presented a bottom-up approach to implementing the domains and contexts belonging to the IoT entity under development. In this part, we need to start from the single contexts and aggregate them according to their scope under super-contexts. Finally, all the contexts will compound the IoT entity as its whole. As for the top-down approach, it is represented as a tree. Thirdly, we present a trusted block development considering the previous approaches. This development style is useful for the developers in order to consider all particularities of contexts and functionalities in single blocks of code according to contexts and functionalities. These three approaches are useful to develop the trusted IoT entity according to all the phases of the K-Model.

In future work, we will apply these approaches to a real use case scenario in order to validate them. Moreover, we will follow all the phases of the K-Model in order to provide the development phase with all the needed input and create the fundamental outputs for the following phases of the SDLC.

Acknowledgment. This work has been supported by the Spanish project SecureEDGE (PID2019-110565RB-I00), by the EU project H2020-MSCA-RISE-2017 under grant agreement No. 777996 (Sealed-GRID) and the EU H2020-SU-ICT-03-2018 Project No. 830929 CyberSec4Europe (cybersec4europe.eu). Moreover, we thank Huawei Technologies for their support.

This work reflects only the authors view and the Research Executive Agency is not responsible for any use that may be made of the information it contains.

References

1. Carmely, T.: Using finite state machines to design software. EE Times (2009)
2. Čolaković, A., Hadžialić, M.: Internet of Things (IoT): a review of enabling technologies, challenges, and open research issues. Comput. Netw. **144**, 17–39 (2018)
3. Erickson, J.: Trust metrics. In: International Symposium on Collaborative Technologies and Systems, CTS 2009, pp. 93–97. IEEE (2009)
4. Feamster, N., Rexford, J., Zegura, E.: The road to SDN: an intellectual history of programmable networks. ACM SIGCOMM Comput. Commun. Rev. **44**(2), 87–98 (2014)
5. Fernandez-Gago, C., Moyano, F., Lopez, J.: Modelling trust dynamics in the internet of things. Inf. Sci. **396**, 72–82 (2017)
6. Ferraris, D., Daniel, J., Fernandez-Gago, C., Lopez, J.: A segregated architecture for a trust-based network of internet of things. In: 2019 16th IEEE Annual Consumer Communications & Networking Conference (CCNC) (CCNC 2019), Las Vegas, USA (2019)
7. Ferraris, D., Fernandez-Gago, C.: Trustapis: a trust requirements elicitation method for IoT. In: International Journal of Information Security, pp. 1–17 (2019)
8. Ferraris, D., Fernandez-Gago, C., Lopez, J.: A trust by design framework for the internet of things. In: NTMS 2018 - Security Track (NTMS 2018 Security Track), Paris, France (2018)
9. Ferraris, D., Fernandez-Gago, C., Lopez, J.: A model-driven approach to ensure trust in the IoT. Human-Centric Comput. Inf. Sci. **10**(1), 1–33 (2020)
10. Fraser, C.W., Henry, R.R.: Hard-coding bottom-up code generation tables to save time and space. Softw. Pract. Exp. **21**(1), 1–12 (1991)
11. Ganchev, I., Ji, Z., O'Droma, M.: A generic iot architecture for smart cities (2014)
12. Hoffman, L.J., Lawson-Jenkins, K., Blum, J.: Trust beyond security: an expanded trust model. Commun. ACM **49**(7), 94–101 (2006)
13. Jørgensen, M.: Top-down and bottom-up expert estimation of software development effort. Inf. Softw. Technol. **46**(1), 3–16 (2004)
14. Kozlov, D., Veijalainen, J., Ali, Y.: Security and privacy threats in IoT architectures. In: BODYNETS, pp. 256–262 (2012)

15. Moyano, F., Fernandez-Gago, C., Lopez, J.: A conceptual framework for trust models. In: Fischer-Hübner, S., Katsikas, S., Quirchmayr, G. (eds.) TrustBus 2012. LNCS, vol. 7449, pp. 93–104. Springer, Heidelberg (2012). https://doi.org/10.1007/978-3-642-32287-7_8

16. Patel, P., Pathak, A., Teixeira, T., Issarny, V.: Towards application development for the internet of things. In: Proceedings of the 8th Middleware Doctoral Symposium, p. 5. ACM (2011)

17. Pavlidis, M.: Designing for trust. In: CAiSE (Doctoral Consortium), pp. 3–14 (2011)

18. Reaidy, P.J., Gunasekaran, A., Spalanzani, A.: Bottom-up approach based on internet of things for order fulfillment in a collaborative warehousing environment. Int. J. Prod. Econ. **159**, 29–40 (2015)

19. Roman, R., Najera, P., Lopez, J.: Securing the internet of things. Computer **44**(9), 51–58 (2011)

20. Valdivieso Caraguay, A.L., Benito Peral, A., Barona Lopez, L.I., Garcia Villalba, L.J.: SDN: evolution and opportunities in the development IoT applications. Int. J. Distrib. Sensor Netw. **10**(5), 735142 (2014)

21. Van Kranenburg, R., Bassi, A.: IoT challenges. Commun. Mobile Comput. **1**(1), 9 (2012)

22. Wagner, F., Schmuki, R., Wagner, T., Wolstenholme, P.: Modeling Software with Finite State Machines: A Practical Approach. Auerbach Publications, Boca Raton (2006)

23. Xu, T., Wendt, J.B., Potkonjak, M.: Security of IoT systems: design challenges and opportunities. In: 2014 IEEE/ACM International Conference on Computer-Aided Design (ICCAD), pp. 417–423. IEEE (2014)

24. Yan, Z., Zhang, P., Vasilakos, A.V.: A survey on trust management for internet of things. J. Netw. Comput. Appl. **42**, 120–134 (2014)

Requirements and Secure Serialization for Selective Disclosure Verifiable Credentials

Vasilis Kalos$^{(\boxtimes)}$ and George C. Polyzos

Mobile Multimedia Laboratory, Department of Informatics,
School of Information Sciences and Technology,
Athens University of Economics and Business, 104 34 Athens, Greece
{kalos20,polyzos}@aueb.gr

Abstract. The emergence of the Verifiable Credentials recommendation from W3C allows the adoption of credential systems in a much wider range of user-centric applications and use cases. With this shift to user-centric credential systems, Selective Disclosure has been proposed and used to cryptographically secure user privacy. Although much work has been undertaken in creating selective disclosure supporting cryptographic protocols, those schemas are not directly applicable for credentials. Implementations rely on canonicalization algorithms to transform a credential to the necessary data format, which will be used by the cryptographic layer. Those algorithms are often used without the necessary cryptographic and security considerations, leading to insecure implementations. In this work we define three necessary security properties for the canonicalization algorithms. We also propose a mathematical model for JSON credentials, which we use to prove the security of a proposed canonicalization algorithm.

Keywords: Self-Sovereign Identity (SSI) · Privacy · JSON · Canonicalization · Linked data · JSON LD · Anonymous credentials

1 Introduction

Credentials systems play a key role in the management of user identities on the Internet, with systems like Open ID Connect (OIDC) [16] widely used to this day.[1] In the credentials ecosystem, there are three main entities: the Issuer that creates and signs the credential (e.g., an airline company that issues a ticket), the Holder that controls the credential (e.g., a traveller that bought the ticket) and the Verifier that checks the validity of that credential (e.g., the airport agent that validates the ticket). A limitation of existing credentials systems, like OIDC, is that the issuing and verification procedures are tightly coupled, which allows for the tracking of the user by the identity provider (Idp) [4]. Furthermore, the Idp must always be online for the process to be successful.

---

[1] OpenID. Market Share & Web Usage Statistics: https://www.similartech.com/technologies/openid.

© IFIP International Federation for Information Processing 2022
Published by Springer Nature Switzerland AG 2022
W. Meng et al. (Eds.): SEC 2022, IFIP AICT 648, pp. 231–247, 2022.
https://doi.org/10.1007/978-3-031-06975-8_14

As an answer to the above limitations, anonymous credentials [5,13,15,19] have been proposed, which decouple the "identity issuance" procedure from the verification process, with W3C's Verifiable Credentials (VCs) standard [17] being the first step towards a standardized data model. In general, a VC is a data structure, usually either in JSON or JSON Linked Data (JSON-LD) [18] format, containing various metadata and claims as key-value pairs. The W3C specification allows, and many of the envisioned use cases [12,14] expect, the creation and usage of long-lived credentials, which in many cases would contain the user's personal information (e.g., age and address, medical records, security information like passwords, bank account numbers etc.).

An important problem that rises as a result, concerns the disclosure of the user's private data. If the included cryptographic proofs are created with "traditional" digital signatures (like RSA etc.), the entire credential must be presented to the Verifier for the proof to be validated. As a result, anyone could gain access to all the information in that VC, something that can be proven to reduce the usability and flexibility of VCs at best or be quite dangerous at worst. Furthermore, not all the information in a VC will be always needed by all the potential Verifiers. From these, and many other use cases[2], emerges the need to hide personal or sensitive information from the VC and still be able to convince a Verifier regarding the ownership, correctness, and integrity of the revealed information.

To meet those requirements, the use of cryptographic protocols supporting "selective disclosure" has been proposed [1,3,6,15]. Selective disclosure protocols work by signing a list of messages and giving the Holder the ability to choose what messages they want to reveal in each interaction with a Verifier. In this work, we will consider selective disclosure as being comprised of two different properties. Firstly, the "selective showing" part, which allows the Holder to prove the integrity, ownership, and authenticity of any subset from a set of signed messages, and secondly, the "zero-knowledge" part [9], that protects against any information about the un-disclosed messages being leaked. As we mentioned though, in practice a credential will be in some structured data format (e.g., JSON, JSON-LD etc.). Turning these formats to a list of messages, to be signed by a selective disclosure supporting cryptographic protocol, is not trivial. In consequence, many implementations and standards will use over-complicated or insecure "data canonicalization" algorithms, or make some over-simplifications [11]. Most importantly however, those algorithms might be overlooked during security analysis as a potential point of exploit, with some being used without the necessary security audits.

In this work we draw attention to the need for rigorous security assessments of the canonicalization algorithms when used to enable the selective disclosure of a Verifiable Credential. To achieve that, we first present a threat model for those algorithms. Then, we introduce a novel modelling of a JSON credential that we use to give an example of a canonicalization algorithm and demonstrate its security in the context of the presented threat model. Finally, we evaluate the performance of our canonicalization algorithm.

---

[2] Further cases: https://identity.foundation/bbs-signature/draft-bbs-signatures.html.

2   Related Work

There is a long line of work around anonymous credentials [3,6,10,15,19], first envisioned by Chaum [8]. Different proposals introduce different properties for a wide range of use-cases. For example, proposals like Microsoft's U-Prove [15] offer the ability to efficiently revoke a credential at any time, but to do so, inserts correlatable elements to the credential. On the other hand, El-Passo [19] offers two factor authentication and correlation protection, but does not support credential revocation (it can optionally support anonymity revocation, though in this case, the user will be correlatable by the same Verifier). Those systems apply various cryptographic protocols ([5,7,9]) to achieve anonymity and user privacy. Those cryptographic protocols offer a vast range of features like range proofs, delegating signatures etc. Almost all the anonymous credentials proposals though use selective disclosure to protect the user's privacy. For this reason, in our work we are mainly focusing on the selective showing and zero-knowledge (of the undisclosed credential) properties, although our results are generic enough that may also apply to other properties as well (like range proofs etc.).

For canonicalization algorithms, perhaps the most notable example is the URDNA algorithm [2], mainly used in the case of JSON-LD credentials (but could also be applied to a JSON format). URDNA works by modelling a credential as a graph. Then it creates labels for each node and edge of that graph. It then returns the edges of the knowledge graph as the messages corresponding to the credential. That said, URDNA does suffer from the third vulnerability defined in our threat model (Definition 6, in Sect. 3), i.e., it compromises the zero-knowledge of the underlying cryptographic protocol's selective disclosure property [11]. Note that we have presented that result to the relevant W3C working group and an efficient solution has already been derived. Other canonicalization algorithms like JSON Web Proofs[3] and Termwise Canonicalization[4] (of which the first version also suffered from the second vulnerability of our threat model but has been patched since then) have been proposed and are currently developed.

3   Background and Definitions

3.1   Credentials

For simplicity, in this work we define a credential to be any JSON or JSON-LD data structure (unless otherwise stated), containing attributes and metadata as key-value pairs (for example credentials that are compliant with W3C's Verifiable Credential Data Model specification). Let $\mathcal{CR}[K, V]$ be the space of all credentials with keys from K and values from V. Let also $C \xleftarrow{R} \mathcal{CR}[K, V]$ denote a randomly sampled credential from the $\mathcal{CR}[K, V]$ space.

---

[3] https://github.com/json-web-proofs/json-web-proofs.
[4] https://github.com/yamdan/jsonld-signatures-bbs.

Before continuing, we will need to define the equality between two credentials. We will also need to define when a credential C_1 is a "sub-credential" to another credential C_2, meaning that every key and value of C_1 is also present in C_2 and with the same structure. The two definitions follow,

Definition 1 (Sub-Credentials). *Let S and C be two credentials. S is a sub-credential of C iff Algorithm 1 on input (S, C) returns true. In that case we write that $S \lhd C$. We also define $\mathcal{UP}(S) = \{C \in \mathcal{CR}[K, V] : S \lhd C\}$ and $\mathcal{SU}(C) = \{S \in \mathcal{CR}[K, V] : S \lhd C\}$.*

Definition 2 (Credentials Equality). *Let C_1 and C_2 be two credentials. If both C_1 and C_2 are in JSON-LD format, then $C_1 = C_2$ iff $URDNA(C_1) = URDNA(C_2)$. If the credentials are in JSON format, then $C_1 = C_2$ iff $C_1 \lhd C_2$ and $C_2 \lhd C_1$.*

Algorithm 1. Recursive algorithm that checks if a credential is contained by another credential

---

procedure SUB-CREDENTIAL(C_1, C_2)
    for *key* $\in C_1$ **do**
        if *key* $\notin C_2$ **then**
            return false
        else if $C_1(key)$ is a JSON object **then**
            SUB-CREDENTIAL($C_1(key), C_2(key)$)
        else
            if $C_1(key) \neq C_2(key)$ **then**
                return false
    return true

3.2 Selective Disclosure and Canonicalization Algorithms

As a canonicalization algorithm we define any algorithm that on input of a credential, returns a list of messages (or claims, or attributes as they have been often called in research). Note that we don't restrict the nature of those messages and don't request anything about their semantic meaning, though most applications will use canonicalization algorithms that map to messages conveying similar information with the credential. More formally, we give the following definition.

Definition 3 (Canonicalization Algorithm). *Let M be the space of messages and $\mathbb{P}(M)$ the space of all the finite sets with elements from M. Given a credential $C \in CR[K, V]$ we define the canonicalization algorithm, indexed by C as,*

$$Can_C : CR[K, V] \to \mathbb{P}(M)$$

We also define $\mathcal{O}^{Can}(\cdot, \cdot)$ to be an Oracle that on query (C, S) will answer with,

$$\mathcal{O}^{Can}(C, S) = \begin{cases} Can_C(S) \; if \; S \lhd C \\ null \qquad otherwise \end{cases}$$

We define canonicalization algorithms to be indexed by a credential for a multiple of reasons. Consider the case where an Issuer canonicalizes a credential C to create a signature, which it sends, along with C, to a Holder. Let the Holder choose a sub credential S of C to present to the Verifier, along with a proof of knowledge of the signature (which they create by also canonicalizing S). Depending on the credential that was originally signed (i.e., C), the canonicalization's algorithms result on S may need to differ, for the proof generation and verification process to succeed. That said, the Holder cannot just send C to the Verifier, resulting to the need to send $Can_C(\cdot)$ instead. We stress that this is just a convention to simplify notation. In practice instead of $Can_C(\cdot)$, the Holder will send the necessary information (that is still depended on the original credential, i.e., C), encoded in an appropriate format. The Verifier will use that information to canonicalize the presented credential correctly. For an example of this procedure, see Sect. 4.3.

The general structure of the cryptographic protocols, for which the canonicalization algorithms are intended can be seen in Fig. 1. We stress that the Verifier will not get a list of messages from the Holder but a credential (a sub credential of the original, that contains only the information the Holder wants to disclose). The reason being, that the Verifier will be interested in the semantic and structural information that this credential provides, which may not translate exactly to the messages corresponding to the canonicalized result (aside from the fact that this is the way that has been standardized by W3C). That said, the cryptographic layer awaits a list of messages. It is this mismatch that enables the possible exploits, defined in the next section.

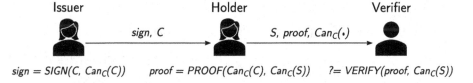

Fig. 1. The general structure of a credentials system using selective disclosure. The $SIGN, PROOF$ and $VERIFY$ functions are generalisations of the signing, proof generation and verification functions, of the selective disclosure cryptographic protocols.

3.3   Threat Model

In this section we formally define the considered threat model. Usual security properties (e.g., unforgeability of a signature, security of a private key etc.) are not considered, as we assume that the underlying cryptographic protocols are secure. We are mainly considering threats that could lead to the malicious miss-use of the canonicalization algorithm by the Holder or the Verifier.

To that end, we define two properties (Definitions 4 and 5) that if not met, could allow the Holder to find a different credential (or sub-credential for when they don't disclose part of their VC) than the one created and signed by the Issuer, that after canonicalized, results to the same messages (or subset of those messages) with the ones that the Issuer signed, effectively allowing the Holder to cheat the Verifier. The definitions follow,

Definition 4 (Collision resistant). *For credentials C and canonicalization algorithm Can_C, $\nexists$ different credentials S_1 and S_2, so that $Can_C(S_1) = Can_C(S_2)$.*

Definition 5 (Forgery resistant). *For credential C and canonicalization algorithm Can_C $\nexists$ subset $m \subset Can_C(C)$ so that there is credential S' with $S' \ntriangleleft C$ and $Can_C(S) = m$.*

Note that we don't consider the case where $\exists C_1, C_2, S$ with $C_1 \neq C_2$, $S \triangleleft C_i$, $i = 1, 2$ and $Can_{C_1}(S) = Can_{C_2}(S)$. Although the Holder could technically "cheat" by revealing $Can_{C_2}(\cdot)$ instead of $Can_{C_1}(\cdot)$, they don't actually reveal any information that is not signed by the Issuer (they only reveal S).

To protect the zero-knowledge property of the underlying selective disclosure capable system, we need the output of $Can_C(S)$ to not reveal information about the not disclosed part of C to the Verifier. Following we formalize that requirement in two different levels.

Definition 6 (Hiding). *Let adversary $\mathcal{A}^{\mathcal{O}^{Can}}$ be a probabilistic polynomial time (PPT) running algorithm $\mathcal{A}$ with access to the $\mathcal{O}^{Can}(\cdot, \cdot)$ oracle.*

- *we will denote the canonicalization algorithm as being "total hiding" if the advantage $Adv(S)$ of $\mathcal{A}^{\mathcal{O}^{Can}}$ for credential S defined as,*

$$Adv(S) = \left| Pr(\mathcal{A}^{\mathcal{O}^{Can}}(C, S, Can_C(S)) = 1 : C \in \mathcal{UP}(\mathcal{S})) \right.$$
$$\left. - Pr\left(\mathcal{A}^{\mathcal{O}^{Can}}(C', S, Can_C(S)) = 1 : \begin{array}{l} C \in \mathcal{UP}(S), C' \neq C \\ C' \xleftarrow{R} \mathcal{UP}(S), \end{array} \right) \right|,$$

is negligibly above semantic interpretation $\forall S \in \mathcal{CR}[K, V]$.
- *we will denote the canonicalization algorithm as being "values hiding" if the advantage $Adv(S)$ of $\mathcal{A}^{\mathcal{O}^{Can}}$ for credential S defined as,*

$$Adv(S) = \left| Pr(\mathcal{A}^{\mathcal{O}^{Can}}(C, S, Can_C(S)) = 1 : C \in \mathcal{UP}(\mathcal{S})) \right.$$
$$\left. - Pr\left(\mathcal{A}^{\mathcal{O}^{Can}}(C', S, Can_C(S)) = 1 : \begin{array}{l} C \in \mathcal{UP}(S), C' \neq C \\ C' \xleftarrow{R_{val}} C/S, \end{array} \right) \right|, \tag{1}$$

is negligible above semantic interpretation $\forall S \in \mathcal{CR}[K, V]$.

All probabilities are defined over the coin flips of Can_C and $\mathcal{A}^{\mathcal{O}^{Can}}$ as well as the choices of C and C'.

By $C' \xleftarrow{R_{val}} C/S$ we define a credential C' that is the same as C with all the values that don't also belong to the sub-credential S of C being random. By "negligible above semantic interpretation" we define a PPT algorithm $\mathcal{A}$ that has no more advantage in distinguishing the two distributions, than it would have by just semantically examining the credentials (note that all our proofs are in the standard model). Formally, $\mathcal{A}$ will have "negligible above semantic interpretation" advantage if given $Can_C(S)$ and access to the oracle $\mathcal{O}^{Can}(\cdot, \cdot)$, it results to a negligible rise in the advantage it would have, if it was only given the two credentials (i.e., (C, S) and (C', S)). Intuitively, consider the following example. Let the Holder having a credential $C = \{age : 25, profession : JuniorDev\}$, presenting the sub-credential $S = \{profession : JuniorDev\}$ $(S \triangleleft C)$. An adversary $\mathcal{A}$ that sees S, after semantically examining the credentials, may be able to deduce that the Holder is more likely to possess C rather, for example, the credential $C' = \{age : 90, profession : JuniorDev\}$.

As a result, the "total hiding" property defines that given credential $S \triangleleft C$, the output of the canonicalization algorithm $Can_C(S)$ will not give any additional advantage, to an adversary trying to extract information about the rest of the credential that is not part of S (i.e., C). On the other hand, the "values hiding" property defines that the adversary will not gain any additional advantage, when trying to extract any information regarding the values of C not in S (but they may get some information on the keys or the structure of C, that does not appear in S).

The reason we define a stronger ("total hiding") and a weaker ("values hiding") version of the same property, is that for many implementations the weaker level of security will be enough, while leading to simpler and more efficient algorithms. Furthermore, in many applications, information regarding the structure of the credential will be either publicly available, as to enable certain protocols (e.g., Holder, Verifier VC negotiations etc.) or will be leaked through some other way (perhaps through some requirement of the cryptographic protocol). Those applications could use faster algorithms, by opting for the weaker hiding property.

We can easily show now that given the output of a "values hiding" canonicalization algorithm $Can_C(S)$, C cannot be retrieved and that different outputs of Can_C cannot be linked together. Obviously, the same result holds for "total hiding" algorithms.

Theorem 1. *Let a "values hiding" canonicalization algorithm Can.*

- *there is no PPT algorithm $\mathcal{A}_1$ that given $Can_C(S)$ will return C with non-negligible probability.*
- *there is no PPT algorithm $\mathcal{A}_2$ that given, $Can_{C_i}(S_i)$ for $C_i \in \mathcal{CR}[K, V]$ and $S_i \triangleleft C_i$, $i = 1, 2$, can decide with non-negligible advantage if $C_1 = C_2$.*

Proof. For the first property, let $\mathcal{A}$ be a PPT that on input $(C', Can_C(S))$, for $S \in \mathcal{CR}[K, V]$ and $C, C' \in \mathcal{UP}(S)$ returns 1 if $\mathcal{A}_1(Can_C(S)) = C'$ and 0 otherwise. Obviously $\mathcal{A}$, will be able to distinguish between the distributions $\{(C, Can_C(S)) : C \in \mathcal{UP}(S)\}$ and $\{(C', Can_C(S)) : C', C \in \mathcal{UP}(S), C \neq C'\}$ with non-negligible advantage, breaking the "values hiding" property.

For the second property we will take advantage that we allow $\mathcal{A}$ in Definition 6 to call the $\mathcal{O}^{Can}(\cdot, \cdot)$ oracle. As such, we define a PPT algorithm $\mathcal{A}^{\mathcal{O}^{Can}}$ that on input $(C_2, Can_{C_1}(S_1))$ query's the oracle to get $z = \mathcal{O}^{Can}(C_2, S_2)$. It holds, $S_2 \lhd C_2 \Rightarrow z \neq null$. Let $\mathcal{A}^{\mathcal{O}^{Can}}(C_2, Can_{C_1}(S_1))$ return J with $J = \mathcal{A}_2(Can_{C_1}(S_1), z) = \mathcal{A}_2(Can_{C_1}(S_1), Can_{C_2}(S_2))$. If $C_1 = C_2$, then $J = 1$ with non-negligible advantage (equivalently $J = 0$ if $C_1 \neq C_2$). It is trivial to see that $\mathcal{A}^{\mathcal{O}^{Can}}$ breaks the "values hiding" property.

We also define an canonicalization algorithm to be pregnable against "vulnerabilities 1, 2" and "3" if it is not "collision resistant", "forgery resistant" or "hiding" correspondingly.

4   Proposed Algorithm and Security Analysis

4.1   JSON Modelling

When considering JSON-LD or JSON credentials, the modelling was mainly done using graphs and more specifically, the knowledge graph representing the claims of the VC. That modelling, although flexible, requires complicated, not intuitive canonicalization algorithms. As a novelty of our paper, we propose an alternative modelling, that will represent the credential in a way closer to the one required by the cryptographic algorithms, i.e., as a set of bit-arrays. To do that, we will use finite functions, that can be naturally (i.e., by definition) transformed into a set. We will then demonstrate how to use our modelling to prove the security properties of a proposed canonicalization algorithm. Our hope is that this representation of a credential, will make it easier for other algorithms to be proven secure, and make the security analysis of credential systems supporting selective disclosure more formal.

The basic observation is that a JSON representation is comprised from two things: the **Structure** and the **Values**. We will model those two separately and consider a JSON data-structure to be a combination of both. We first define a non-zero positive integer $n \in \mathbb{N}$. Let $[n] = \{1, 2, ..., n\}$.

Structure:
Let K be the set of all possible "keys" that can appear in the JSON and K^* be the set of finite tuples with elements from K. We define the **structure** of a JSON to be K along with an injective function ϕ,

$$\phi : [n] \to K^* \tag{2}$$

Values:
Similarly, we define the **values** of a credential as a set V of all the possible literal values that can appear in the JSON, along with a function g,

$$g : [n] \to V \tag{3}$$

Note that we make no assumptions for g, in contrast with ϕ that we define to be injective. We now end up on the following definition for a JSON data-structure.

Definition 7. *We define a JSON data-structure J to be $J = (K, V, n, \phi, g)$, or since K and V can be as extensive as we want, for simplicity we will define a JSON structure as $J = (n, \phi, g)$.*

The intuition behind the proposed modelling is that $[n]$ will map each place in the JSON data-structure where a literal value could appear to an integer. Then ϕ will use those integers to map each position in the JSON with a literal value to the set of keys that will lead to that literal value and g will map each literal value position to the corresponding actual literal value.

As an example of our modelling, consider the credential of Fig. 2, with each place that a literal value can go mapped to an integer in $[6] = \{1, 2, ..., 6\}$.

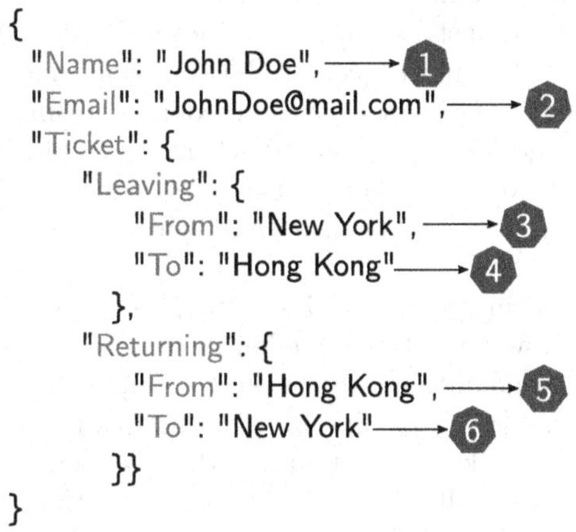

```
{
    "Name": "John Doe", ─────▶ 1
    "Email": "JohnDoe@mail.com", ─────▶ 2
    "Ticket": {
        "Leaving": {
            "From": "New York", ─────▶ 3
            "To": "Hong Kong" ─────▶ 4
        },
        "Returning": {
            "From": "Hong Kong", ─────▶ 5
            "To": "New York" ─────▶ 6
        }}
}
```

Fig. 2. modelling a JSON data-structure example.

The values of the ϕ and g functions can be seen at Table 1. Note that $\forall\, i_0, i_1 \in [6]$, with $i_0 \neq i_1 \Rightarrow \phi(i_0) \neq \phi(i_1)$, while $g(3) = g(6)$ and $g(4) = g(5)$.

Table 1. Values of the ϕ and g functions of the Credential on Fig. 2.

n	ϕ	g
1	(name)	John Doe
2	(email)	JohnDoe@bestMail.com
3	(Ticket, Leaving, From)	New York
4	(Ticket, Leaving, To)	Hong Kong
5	(Ticket, Returning, From)	Hong Kong
6	(Ticket, Returning, To)	New York

From the above example it can be seen that the order with which we map each literal value position in the JSON to an integer, should not matter, hence the following definition of JSON equality,

Definition 8. *Let $J_1 = (n_1, \phi_1, g_1)$ and $J_2 = (n_2, \phi_2, g_2)$ be two JSON data-structures. We define that $J_1 = J_2$ iff $n_1 = n_2 = n$ and there is a permutation σ of $[n]$, such that $\phi_1 = \phi_2(\sigma)$ and $g_1 = g_2(\sigma)$.*

Similarly, we get the following definition for when a JSON credential is a sub-credential to another credential,

Definition 9. *Let $J_1 = (n_1, \phi_1, g_1)$ and $J_2 = (n_2, \phi_2, g_2)$ be two JSON data-structures. We define that $J_1 \lhd J_2$ iff $n_1 \leq n_2$ and there is a permutation σ of $[n_2]$, such that $\forall i \in [n_1]$, $\phi_1(i) = \phi_2(\sigma(i))$ and $g_1(i) = g_2(\sigma(i))$*

It is easy to see that Definitions 8 and 9 are consistent with Definitions 2 and 1 respectively. As an example, if C_1 and C_2 credentials with $C_1 \ntriangleleft C_2$, then from Definition 1, there must be either a value in C_1 that does not appear in C_2 or a key in C_1 (or a nested object of C_1) that does not appear in C_2 (or a nested object of C_2). If we represent those credentials using our modeling, i.e., as $C_1 = (n_1, \phi_1, g_1)$ and $C_2 = (n_2, \phi_2, g_2)$ where ϕ_1, ϕ_2, g_1, g_2 as in Table 1 for the example of Fig. 2, we can conclude that, for some $i \in [n_1]$ either $\phi_1(i) \notin [\phi_2(1), ..., \phi_2(n_2)]$ or $g_1(i) \notin [g_2(1), ..., g_2(n_2)]$ which means that $C_1 \ntriangleleft C_2$ per Definition 9 as well.

An important part in Definition 7 of JSON structures is that the function ϕ is injective. However, if the credential contains a list, that may not be the case, given the definitions above. For example, consider the credential $C = \{\text{"key"} : [\text{"v}_1\text{"}, \text{"v}_2\text{"}]\}$. Using the same method as in the example of Fig. 2, we will get $\phi(1) = \phi(2) = \text{"key"}$. To eliminate that problem, we consider a subset of $\mathcal{CR}[K, V]$ which we will call "simple credentials" and that will not contain any lists. We will denote the set of those credentials as $\mathcal{SCR}[K, V]$. We stress that our definition is not as restrictive as it may seem, since there is a simple mapping between any credential from $\mathcal{CR}[K, V]$ to a credential in $\mathcal{SCR}[K, V]$, using the following transformation; $\psi([a_1, a_2, ..., a_L]) = \{I_1 : a_1, I_2 : a_2, ..., I_L : a_L\}$ where $I_i, i \in \mathbb{N}$ is an index reserved for this use (for example "_lid#i"). By applying the transformation ψ to all the lists of a credential (i.e., transforming a list to a mapping between the index of the list element and that element) in $\mathcal{CR}[K, V]$ we get a credential in $\mathcal{SCR}[K, V]$. This will allow us to define the proposed canonicalization algorithm (see Sect. 4.2) for any credential in $\mathcal{CR}[K, V]$.

Let credential $C \in \mathcal{CR}[K, V]$ and $C' \in \mathcal{SCR}[K, V]$ with C' be the credential C after ψ is applied to all its lists. We define a mapping $\psi_C : SC[C] \rightarrow SC(C')$ such that, on input $S \lhd C$, $\psi_C(S)$ will be the credential S after all lists of S are transformed the same way the lists of C did (note that since $S \lhd C$, for every list L of S, there will be a list L' of C with $L \subseteq L'$). As an example,

$$C = \{\text{"key"} : [\text{"v}_1\text{"}, \text{"v}_2\text{"}]\} \rightarrow \psi_C(C) = \{\text{"key"} : \{I_1 : \text{"v}_1\text{"}, I_2 : \text{"v}_2\text{"}\}\}$$
$$S = \{\text{"key"} : [\text{"v}_2\text{"}]\} \rightarrow \psi_C(S) = \{\text{"key"} : \{I_2 : \text{"v}_2\text{"}\}\}$$

It is trivial to show that $\psi_{C_1}(S_1) = \psi_{C_2}(S_2) \Rightarrow S_1 = S_2$ and that if $S_1 \lhd S_2 \Leftrightarrow \psi_C(S_1) \lhd \psi_C(S_2)$ (note that the transformation ψ is injective). A drawback of our modelling is that, following Definitions 7 and 8, if the JSON contains a list and we change the order of the elements in that list we will get a different JSON (per the Definition 8 of equality). Although that caveat does not seem to have any significance in practice, especially for cryptographic applications where the signed data should not be able to change in any way, additional work could be done to extend the above modelling to also account for that case (defining broader classes of equality etc.). For the intended applications however, those definitions will suffice.

4.2 Canonicalization Algorithm

Let credential $C = (n, \phi, g) \in \mathcal{CR}[K, V]$. The proposed canonicalization algorithm $JCan_C$ (Algorithm 2) on input S, transforms S to a simple credential $S_C = (n_S, \phi_{S_C}, g_{S_C})$ using the mapping ψ_C and returns $\{\phi_{S_C}(i), g_{S_C}(i)\}_{i \in [n_S]}$.

Algorithm 2. Canonicalize a JSON credential

---

function $JCan_C(S)$
  $S_C \leftarrow \psi_C(S)$
  $Messages \leftarrow []$
  $Claim \leftarrow None$
  procedure RECURSE(S_C)
    for $key \in S_C$ **do**
      if typeof $S_C[key] = JSONobject$ **then**
        $Claim \leftarrow Claim + key + "."$
        RECURSE($S_C[key]$)
      else
        $Claim \leftarrow Claim + " : " + S_C[key]$
        $Messages.push(Claim)$
        $Claim \leftarrow None$
  return Messages

The following 2 Lemmas will be used for the security proofs of the $JCan$ algorithm. Lemma 1 provides a natural way to check equality between credentials using our Definition 7.

Lemma 1. Let $J_1 = (n_1, \phi_1, g_1)$ and $J_2 = (n_2, \phi_2, g_2)$. Then $J_1 = J_2$ iff $n_1 = n_2 = n$ and $\{(\phi_1(i), g_1(i))\}_{i \in [n]} = \{(\phi_2(i), g_2(i))\}_{i \in [n]}$.

Proof. We will first prove the ($\Rightarrow$) direction. Lets assume that $n_1 = n_2 = n$ and that $\{(\phi_1(i), g_1(i))\}_{i \in [n]} = \{(\phi_2(i), g_2(i))\}_{i \in [n]}$. Then $\forall \, i \in [n]$, $\exists \, i' \in [n]$ so that $(\phi_1(i), g_1(i)) = (\phi_2(i'), g_2(i'))$. We define σ as,

$$\sigma : [n] \rightarrow [n]$$
$$\sigma(i) = i' \Leftrightarrow (\phi_1(i), g_1(i)) = (\phi_2(i'), g_2(i'))$$

We will show that σ is a permutation.

1) Let $i_0, i_1 \in [n]$ and $i'_0, i'_1 \in [n]$ with $\phi_1(i_0) = \phi_2(i'_0)$ and $\phi_1(i_1) = \phi_2(i'_1)$. If $i_0 = i_1 \Rightarrow \phi_1(i_0) = \phi_1(i_1) \Rightarrow \phi_2(i'_0) = \phi_2(i'_1) \Rightarrow i'_0 = i'_1$ since ϕ_2 injective. As a result σ is a function.

2) Let now $i_0 \neq i_1$. Lets assume $\sigma(i_0) = \sigma(i_1) \Rightarrow i'_0 = i'_1$ meaning that $\phi_2(i'_0) = \phi_2(i'_1) \Rightarrow \phi_1(i_0) = \phi_1(i_1) \Rightarrow i_0 = i_1$ since ϕ_1 is injective. We arrived in a contradiction and as a result, σ is injective.

3) Let an $i \in [n]$. Since $\{(\phi_1(i), g_1(i))\}_{i \in [n]} = \{(\phi_2(i), g_2(i))\}_{i \in [n]}$ we can conclude that $\exists i' \in [n]$ so that $(\phi_2(i), g_2(i)) = (\phi_1(i'), g_1(i'))$ and as a result $\phi_1(i') = \phi_2(i) \Rightarrow \sigma(i') = i$. As a result, the σ function is also bijective. We conclude then that σ is a permutation.

From the definition of the σ permutation it is easy to see that $\phi_1(i) = \phi_2(\sigma(i))$ and that $g_1(i) = g_2(\sigma(i))$ which means that $J_1 = J_2$.

The opposite ($\Leftarrow$) direction, meaning that if $J_1 = J_2$ then $n_1 = n_2 = n$ and $\{(\phi_1(i), g_1(i))\}_{i \in [n]} = \{(\phi_2(i), g_2(i))\}_{i \in [n]}$ is trivial.

Lemma 2. *Given* $J = (n, \phi, g)$ *and* $S \subset \{\phi(i), g(i)\}_{i \in [n]}$, $\nexists J' = (n', \phi', g')$, *with* $J' \ntriangleleft J$ *and* $\{\phi'(i), g'(i)\}_{i \in [n']} = S$

Proof. Let $J' = (n', \phi', g')$, where ϕ', g' as in the example of Fig. 2, with $J' \ntriangleleft J$ and $\{\phi'(i), g'(i)\}_{i \in [n']} = S$. This is with no loss of generality since, given Definition 8 of equality between two JSON in our modeling, if $J' = (n, \phi, g)$ then $n' = n$ and ϕ will just be a permutation of ϕ' (similarly g will be a permutation of g'). From Definition 9 we have that there must be $j \in [n']$ so that $\phi'(j) \notin \{\phi(i)\}_{i \in [n]}$ and $g(j) \notin \{g(i)\}_{i \in [n]}$. As a result, $S = \{\phi'(i), g'(i)\}_{i \in [n']} \not\subset \{\phi(i), g(i)\}_{i \in [n]}$ which is a contradiction.

Following we prove that $JCan$ is secure against Vulnerability 1 and 2 of our threat model, i.e., that it is "coalition" and "forgery resistant".

Lemma 3. *Let credentials* $C_1, C_2 \in \mathcal{CR}[K, V]$, *with* $C_1 \neq C_2$.

- $\nexists$ *credentials* $S_i \triangleleft C_1, i = 1, 2$ *with* $S_1 \neq S_2$ *and* $JCan_{C_1}(S_1) = JCan_{C_1}(S_2)$.
- $\nexists$ *credentials* $S_1 \triangleleft C_1$ *and* $S_2 \triangleleft C_2$ *with* $S_2 \ntriangleleft C_1$ *such that,* $JCan_{C_2}(S_2) \subset JCan_{C_1}(S_1)$

Proof. For the first property. Let $\psi_{C_1}(S_i) = S'_i = (n_{S_i}, \phi_{S'_i}, g_{S'_i}), i = 1, 2$. Since, $JCan_{C_1}(S_1) = JCan_{C_1}(S_2) \Rightarrow \{\phi_{S'_1}(i), g_{S'_1}(i)\}_{i \in [n_{S_1}]} = \{\phi_{S'_2}(i), g_{S'_2}(i)\}_{i \in [n_{S_2}]}$. From Lemma 1 we got that $\psi_{C_1}(S_1) = \psi_{C_1}(S_2)$ and from the construction of ψ_{C_1} that $S_1 = S_2$.

For the second property, let again $\psi_{C_i}(S_i) = S'_i = (n_{S_i}, \phi_{S'_i}, g_{S'_i})$, $i = 1, 2$. Let $m \subset JCan_{C_1}(S_1) = \{\phi_{S'_1}(i), g_{S'_1}\}_{i \in n_{S_1}}$ and $m = JCan_{C_2}(S_2)$. From Lemma 2, we get that $\psi_{C_2}(S_2) \triangleleft \psi_{C_1}(S_1) \Rightarrow S_2 \triangleleft S_1 \triangleleft C_1$ which is a contradiction.

For "hiding" (Definition 6), we cannot prove $JCan$ to be "total hiding", but we can prove it to be "values hiding". Intuitively, that is because we are considering the indexes of a list in a credential as keys which can give away some information of the credential's structure. For example, "*employees._lid#2: Jane*" reveals the information that likely there is a hidden message "*employees._lid#1: X*". The above problem has an easy solution, which is to transform every list in the credential to a mapping between a random key and the elements of the list (i.e., instead of _lid#i use _lid#r_i with r_i random). However, we deemed the gained simplicity of the algorithm to be warranted.

Lemma 4. *There is no PPT algorithm $\mathcal{A}^{\mathcal{O}^{Can}}$ that for credential C, and a sub credential $S \lhd C$ on input $(C, S, JCan_C(S))$ will return 1 with non negligible advantage over semantic interpretation. The advantage of $\mathcal{A}^{\mathcal{O}^{Can}}$ is defined in Eq. 1.*

Proof. From the definition of $\mathcal{A}^{\mathcal{O}^{Can}}$'s advantage for S of Eq. 1, we can see that essentially is the advantage that $\mathcal{A}^{\mathcal{O}^{Can}}$ has in distinguishing the distributions

$$\left\{ (C, S, JCan_C(S)) : C \in \mathcal{UP}(S) \right\} \text{ and } \left\{ (C', S, JCan_C(S)) : \begin{matrix} C, C' \in \mathcal{UP}(S) \\ C \neq C' \\ C' \xleftarrow{R_{val}} C/S \end{matrix} \right\}$$

Note also that we give $\mathcal{A}^{\mathcal{O}^{Can}}$ access to the $\mathcal{O}^{JCan}(\cdot, \cdot)$ oracle. Next we will construct a credential $C' \xleftarrow{R_{val}} C/S$ and prove that $\mathcal{O}^{JCan}(C, S) = \mathcal{O}^{JCan}(C', S)$. Let $C = (n, \phi, g)$ and $S \subset C$ with $S = (n_S, \phi_S, g_S)$. We create a random credential $C' = (n, \phi_{C'}, g_{C'})$ with $\phi_{C'} = \phi_C$ and,

$$g_{C'}(i) = \begin{cases} g_S(i) & i \in [n_S] \\ r_i & i \in [n] \setminus [n_S], r_i \text{ random value} \end{cases}$$

It is trivial to show that $S \lhd C'$ and that $\psi_C(S) = \psi_{C'}(S)$. For the last equality note that if $[a_1, a_2, ..., a_L]$ and $[b_1, b_2, ..., b_{L'}]$ are lists of C and C' correspondingly, if there is some indexes I_S for which the elements of those lists also appear in a list of S then

$$[a_i]_{i \in I_S} = [b_i]_{i \in I_S} \Rightarrow$$
$$\psi_C([a_i]_{i \in I_S}) = \{I_i : a_i\}_{i \in I_S} = \{I_i : b_i\}_{i \in I_S} = \psi_{C'}([b_i]_{i \in I_S})$$

All other elements of S (i.e., not lists) will remain constant. We can see that since $\psi_C(S) = \psi_{C'}(S) \Rightarrow JCan_C(S) = JCan_{C'}(S) \Rightarrow \mathcal{O}^{JCan}(C, S) = \mathcal{O}^{JCan}(C', S)$. Note that $\mathcal{A}^{\mathcal{O}^{Can}}$ can use only its internal state, coin flips or the random values of C' to decide on what other queries to send the Oracle, which means that those will not help distinguish the 2 distributions (since it will be the same in both cases). As a result $\mathcal{A}^{\mathcal{O}^{Can}}$ will have 0 advantage above semantic interpretation, in distinguish the two distributions above.

4.3   Real Life Example

In practice, as we mentioned, there will be only one algorithm and the Holder will send to the Verifier the necessary information to canonicalize the derived credential correctly. In effect, $Can_C(S)$ will be $Can(S, Info_C)$ or $Can(S_C)$, where the necessary information is directly encoded in the credentials. That said, all the security requirements defined in Sect. 3 (i.e., Definitions 4, 5 and 6) apply exactly, with the only difference that $Info_C$ should be passed as an input to the adversary $\mathcal{A}^{\mathcal{O}^{Can}}$ in Definition 6. Accordingly, we define $JCan$ to be Algorithm 2 without the transformation by $\psi_C(\cdot)$ in the first step (i.e., by replacing $\psi_C(\cdot)$ with the Identity function).

Consider the example of Fig. 3. The Issuer will start with the credential $C \in \mathcal{CR}[K, V]$. Then, they will transform that credential (using ψ) to the credential $C' \in \mathcal{SCR}[K, V]$ and finally they will canonicalize it to get the messages that they will sign. Next, they will send credential C' along with the signature to the Holder. The Holder will then choose the credential $S \lhd C'$ that they want to disclose and canonicalize it, using again $JCan$. From the messages returned from $JCan(S)$ and $JCan(C')$ (note that $JCan(S) \subseteq JCan(C')$) they will derive a proof (for example a zero-knowledge proof of knowledge of the signature and the rest of the messages) that they will send to the Verifier, together with the credential S. Finally, the Verifier will get the messages $JCan(S)$ and use them to validate the Holder's proof. Note from Fig. 3, that the messages returned from $JCan$ depend on the credential C (hence the reason we index $JCan$ with C in our modelling), but they do not reveal any information about the undisclosed values of C (as proven in Lemma 4).

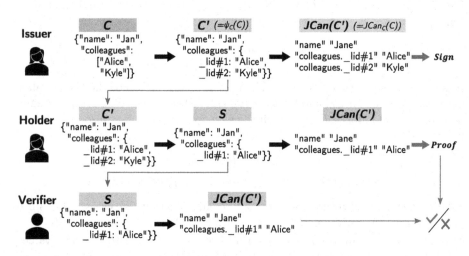

Fig. 3. Real life flow example for the signing, proof derivation and verification of a credential and sub-credential process.

5 Evaluation and Performance

We benchmarked and compared the URDNA canonicalization algorithm and the $JCan$ algorithm (Algorithm 2). The benchmarking procedure was executed on a personal computer using an Intel i5 with 3.2 GHz clock and 16 GBs of RAM. Also note that a JSON-LD credential before it is canonicalized it must first be expanded. The expansion process brings the credential to the proper form, so it can be correctly canonicalized. In the results below we do not include the expansion algorithm as part of the process of canonicalizing a credential, to get a more accurate performance measurement of just the URDNA algorithm.

5.1 Benchmarking Results

For the benchmarking procedure[5], we generated credentials of max depth (maximum number of continuously nested objects) 2, 4, 8 and 16. For each different JSON depth, we created credentials with 10, 20, 40 and 80 claims and benchmarked the 2 algorithms multiple times on each credential. Finally, we measured the mean canonicalization time of each algorithm, over the credentials with different number of claims, for each different JSON depth value. The results are shown in Fig. 4. Note that *JCan* runs 5× to 9× times faster than the URDNA algorithm. The examples for the benchmarks were generated purposefully to aid URDNA and hinder *JCan*, so we can get an accurate estimation of the performance differences.

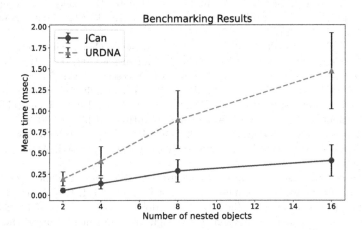

Fig. 4. Benchmarking results comparing the URDNA to *JCan* (Algorithm 2). The credentials used have only one chain of nested objects (i.e., max depth = number of nested objects). This creates a worst case scenario in favor of URDNA over *JCan*.

6   Conclusion

In this work we considered the use of anonymous credentials using W3C's credentials data model to preserve privacy in user-centric applications. We noted

---

[5] Code used: https://github.com/BasileiosKal/JCan.

that the cryptographic solutions developed do not consider what the interface with the higher layers will be (i.e., those of JSON and JSON-LD credentials etc.). We then proposed the key security properties that all canonicalization algorithms should possess for the serialization to be secure. We also presented a novel modelling of a JSON credential that we used to propose an efficient algorithm and formally analyse its security. For future work, we want to use our threat model and JSON modelling to analyse and construct security proofs for other canonicalization algorithms as well. We also plan to use those algorithms to construct a complete anonymous credentials system and formally analyse the security of all its aspects. Finally, we want to apply our model on canonicalization algorithms intended to be used by credentials systems supporting additional properties beyond selective disclosure (e.g., range proofs, etc.).

Acknowledgements. This work has been funded in part by subgrant *Securing Content Delivery and Provenance (SECOND)* of EU H2020 project *NGIatlantic.eu*, under grant agreement No 871582.

References

1. Alpár, G., van den Broek, F., Hampiholi, B., Jacobs, B., Lueks, W., Ringers, S.: IRMA: practical, decentralized and privacy-friendly identity management using smartphones. In: HotPETs 2017 (2017)
2. Arnold, R., Longley, D.: RDF Dataset Canonicalization (2020). https://lists.w3.org/Archives/Public/public-credentials/2021Mar/att-0220/RDFDatasetCanonicalization-2020-10-09.pdf, Accessed 06 Mar 2022
3. Bauer, D., Blough, D.M., Cash, D.: Minimal information disclosure with efficiently verifiable credentials. In: Proceedings of the 4th ACM Workshop on Digital Identity Management, pp. 15–24. Association for Computing Machinery (2008)
4. Brands, S.: The Problem(s) with OpenID. https://web.archive.org/web/20110516013258/, http://www.untrusted.ca/cache/openid.html. Accessed 15 Sep 2021
5. Camenisch, J., Lysyanskaya, A.: Signature schemes and anonymous credentials from bilinear maps. In: Franklin, M. (ed.) CRYPTO 2004. LNCS, vol. 3152, pp. 56–72. Springer, Heidelberg (2004). https://doi.org/10.1007/978-3-540-28628-8_4
6. Camenisch, J., Van Herreweghen, E.: Design and implementation of the idemix anonymous credential system. In: Proceedings of the 9th ACM Conference on Computer and Communications Security, pp. 21–30 (2002)
7. Chaum, D.: Blind signatures for untraceable payments. In: Chaum, D., Rivest, R.L., Sherman, A.T. (eds.) Advances in Cryptology, pp. 199–203. Springer, Boston, MA (1983). https://doi.org/10.1007/978-1-4757-0602-4_18
8. Chaum, D.: Security without identification: transaction systems to make big brother obsolete. Commun. ACM **28**(10), 1030–1044 (1985)
9. Goldwasser, S., Micali, S., Rackoff, C.: The knowledge complexity of interactive proof-systems. In: Proceedings of the Seventeenth Annual ACM Symposium on Theory of Computing, STOC 1985, pp. 291–304. ACM, New York (1985)
10. Hanzlik, L., Slamanig, D.: With a little help from my friends: constructing practical anonymous credentials. In: Proceedings of the 2021 ACM SIGSAC Conference on Computer and Communications Security, pp. 2004–2023 (2021)

11. Kalos, V., Polyzos, G.C.: Verifiable credentials selective disclosure: challenges and solutions, M.Sc CS Thesis (2021). https://mm.aueb.gr/master_theses/polyzos/2021-Kalos.pdf, Accessed 01 Feb 2022

12. Lagutin, D., Kortesniemi, Y., Fotiou, N., Siris, V.A.: Enabling decentralised identifiers and verifiable credentials for constrained IoT devices using OAuth-based delegation. In: Proceedings of the Workshop on Decentralized IoT Systems and Security (DISS 2019), in Conjunction with the NDSS Symposium, San Diego, CA, USA, vol. 24 (2019)

13. Neira, B., Queern, C.: Introduction to azure active directory verifiable credentials (2021). https://docs.microsoft.com/en-us/azure/active-directory/verifiable-credentials/decentralized-identifier-overview, Accessed 15 Sept 2021

14. Otto, N., Lee, S., Sletten, B., Burnett, D., Sporny, M., Ebert, K.: Verifiable Credentials Use Cases. Working Group Note, W3C (2019). https://www.w3.org/TR/vc-use-cases/

15. Paquin, C., Zaverucha, G.: U-Prove Cryptographic Specification V1.1. Revision 3. Technical Report, Microsoft Corporation (2013). https://www.microsoft.com/en-us/research/wp-content/uploads/2016/02/U-Prove20Cryptographic20Specification20V1.1.pdf

16. Sakimura, N., Bradley, J., Jones, M., Medeiros, B.D., Mortimore, C.: OpenID connect core 1.0 (2014). https://openid.net/specs/openid-connect-core-1_0.html, Accessed 01 Feb 2022

17. Sporny, M., Longley, D., Chadwick, D.: Verifiable Credentials Data Model 1.0. Recommendation, W3C (2021). https://www.w3.org/TR/vc-data-model/

18. Sporny, M., Longley, D., Kellogg, G., Lanthaler, M., Champin, P.A., Lindström, N.: A JSON-based Serialization for Linked Data. Recommendation, W3C (2020). https://www.w3.org/TR/json-ld11/

19. Zhiyi, Z., Michal, K., Alberto, S., Lixia, Z., Etienne, R.: EL PASSO: efficient and lightweight privacy-preserving single sign on. In: Proceedings on Privacy Enhancing Technologies, Sciendo, pp. 70–87 (2021)

Crypto-Based solutions

UP-MLE: Efficient and Practical Updatable Block-Level Message-Locked Encryption Scheme Based on Update Properties

Shaoqiang Wu[1,2], Chunfu Jia[1,2(✉)], and Ding Wang[1,2]

[1] College of Cyber Science, Nankai University, Tianjin 300350, China
cfjia@nankai.edu.cn
[2] Tianjin Key Laboratory of Network and Data Security Technology,
Nankai University, Tianjin 300350, China

Abstract. Deduplication is widely used to improve space efficiency in cloud storage. The Updatable block-level Message-Locked Encryption (UMLE) has been proposed to achieve efficient block-level updates for a deduplication system. However, the update design of the current UMLE instantiation adopts a static structure, which does not fit in with real update scenarios. This paper analyzes the File System and Storage Lab (FSL) Homes datasets that are widely used in deduplication research and reveals two interesting properties: i) Updated blocks are more likely to be updated again; ii) Updated blocks are always clustered in files. Based on these properties, we propose and implement an efficient and practical UMLE scheme. Experiments on real-world datasets show that our update algorithm is 24.85% more efficient than its foremost counterpart, increasing the space overhead by $\leq 0.39\%$.

Keywords: Deduplication · Message-locked encryption · Updatable

1 Introduction

Deduplication is an important technology that cloud providers adopt to enhance their space efficiency by removing redundant duplicates. For data privacy, users incline to encrypt their data before outsourcing. However, conventional encryption algorithms convert identical plaintexts into different ciphertexts, making it difficult for clouds to find duplicates for encrypted data. *Convergent Encryption* (CE) [5], where the hash of a message acts as the encryption key, ensures identical ciphertexts if the messages are identical. Therefore, CE is regarded as an appropriate method to implement encrypted deduplication. Bellare *et al.* [3] proved the security of CE and proposed a new cryptographic primitive named *message-locked encryption* (MLE) for secure deduplication.

Generally, there are two granularities for data deduplication [15]: File-level deduplication and block-level deduplication. File-level deduplication [23] directly

© IFIP International Federation for Information Processing 2022
Published by Springer Nature Switzerland AG 2022
W. Meng et al. (Eds.): SEC 2022, IFIP AICT 648, pp. 251–269, 2022.
https://doi.org/10.1007/978-3-031-06975-8_15

treats files as the basic units of deduplication. It is straightforward but cannot deduplicate redundant blocks across different files. While in block-level deduplication [4,9,12], files are divided into blocks as the deduplication units. Block-level deduplication is more fine-grained and has a better deduplication effect.

However, block-level deduplication generates a block-level MLE key[1] for each outsourced block, resulting in an enormous number of block keys for users to

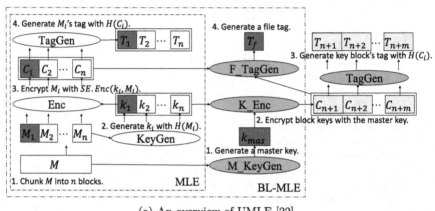

(a) An overview of UMLE [22].

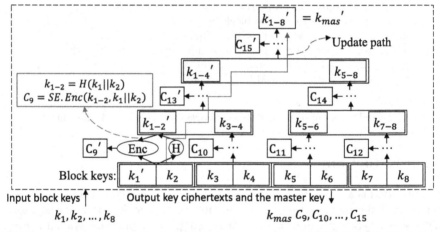

(b) The master key generation and block key encryption of UMLE19 [22]. Block keys are located in the leaf nodes ($k_{i,i\in[1,8]}$). UMLE19 recursively hashes (H) child nodes to derive the master key (k_{mas}) and uses the parent node to encrypt ($SE.Enc$) the child nodes in each recursive layer. Assuming the first file block is modified, UMLE19 only needs three hashes to update the master key (k'_{1-2}, k'_{1-4}, k'_{1-8}) and three re-encryptions to update the key ciphertexts (C'_9, C'_{13}, C'_{15}).

Fig. 1. Revisiting the updatable block-level message-locked encryption (UMLE). (Color figure online)

---

[1] We refer to the block-level MLE key as the block key for readability.

store and manage. As shown in the blue dashed box in Fig. 1(a), Chen *et al.* [4] proposed a *block-level MLE* (BL-MLE), which encrypts block keys with a master key, derived from the whole data. Then the encrypted block keys are outsourced to the cloud as well. In this encryption mechanism, the storage and management of numerous block keys are transparent to users, and they only need to hold one master key to access outsourced data.

However, BL-MLE [4] focuses on static files. To support efficient file updates, Zhao *et al.* [22] proposed the *"(Efficiently) Updatable (Block-Level) MLE"* (UMLE) based on BL-MLE. UMLE improves the master key generation and the block key encryption algorithms (M_KeyGen and K_Enc represented by the blue shaded ellipse in Fig. 1(a)) and introduces update algorithms. As shown in Fig. 1(b), the UMLE scheme in [22] (UMLE19[2]) iteratively executes MLEs for each node along the tree trunk and takes the root node as the master key. When a file block is modified, it needs to decrypt nodes along the path from the root to the to-be-modified leaf and re-execute iterative MLEs along the reverse path. For updating a block, its update cost is the logarithmic level of $|B| \log_{|B|}(|M|)$ (where $|B|$ and $|M|$ is the size of the block and the file, respectively).

We find that UMLE19 [22] can be improved to realize higher update efficiency. This improvement is motivated by our analysis of the block-level update property of the real-world datasets. Firstly, we explore the re-modification fraction, which means the percentage of modified blocks that are modified again. Our analysis result shows that the re-modification fraction is up to 80.82% (while the average modification fraction is just 8.60%). This indicates that modified blocks are more likely to be modified. Therefore, we say that the block-level update has temporal locality. Secondly, we find that the percentage of modified blocks does not increase linearly with the increase in the chunking size, indicating that the modified blocks are clustered. That is, the block-level update has spatial locality. Moreover, we find that many blocks remain unmodified for a long time and call them inactive blocks.

Based on the above update properties, we present an improved UMLE scheme (UP-MLE), in which updates of frequently updated active blocks go through a faster update path. Specifically, we set up a dynamic tree in which active blocks climb up along the tree path in each update, and even an enhanced dynamic tree in which the updated blocks are raised to the root node height in one step.

In addition, we discover the efficiency problem of updating the file tag of UMLE19 [22], which generates the file tag with IH.Hash of the Incremental Hash (*IH*). When updating a single block of a 1 GB file, its update algorithm IH.Update takes about ten milliseconds [22] for updating the file tag, which seems acceptable. However, the time cost of IH.Update is proportional to the number of updated blocks. Given our investigation into the real-world datasets, which show that the number of updated blocks at a time can be in thousands, UMLE19 [22] will take up to several minutes to update a file tag. The time cost is unacceptable when considering one server for the update calculation. We adopt a Merkle tree hash of the file ciphertext as the file tag to solve the problem. There are two

---

[2] In this paper, we term the UMLE scheme proposed in [22] as UMLE19.

advantages: 1) Block tags are ready-by as the leaf nodes of the Merkle tree, so that saves much computation overhead; 2) The update cost of the Merkle tree hash is a constant much smaller than that of IH.Update.

We make three main **contributions**:

- We find some block-level update properties of the FSL datasets, including: 1) Most modified blocks will be modified again next time; 2) Modified blocks are always clustered in files; 3) More than half of the file blocks always remain unmodified. These properties may be of independent interest.
- We propose an efficiently updatable block-level MLE scheme (UP-MLE) based on the above update properties. It improves the update algorithms by introducing a dynamic tree. In terms of file tags, we adopt a Merkle tree to generate file tags supporting efficient updates. Besides, we provide security proofs for our scheme in the random oracle model.
- We implement the prototype of UP-MLE and experiment on the real-world datasets providing comprehensive performance comparisons with UMLE19 [22]. The experimental results show that our update algorithms are more efficient than that of UMLE19 [22].

2   Preliminary

Notations. For $i, x, y \in \mathbb{N}$, $[x, y]$ denotes the set of all i, $x \leqslant i \leqslant y$. For $m, n \in \mathbb{N}$, $i \in [1, n]$, and the message $A = A_1 \| A_2 \| \cdots \| A_n$, A_i denotes the i-th block of A, $\{A_i\}$ denotes the set of all A_i, $\{A_i\}_{n'-n}$ denotes the set of A_i, $i \in [n+1, n']$, and $A_i \| A_{i+1}$ denotes the concatenation of A_i and $A_i + 1$. If S is a finite set, $|S|$ denotes the number of elements contained in S, and $e \leftarrow_\$ S$ means to randomly select an element from S and assign it to e. For $l \in \mathbb{N}$, by $y \leftarrow Alg(x_1, x_2, \cdots, x_l)$, we mean to run the algorithm Alg on inputs $x_1, x_2, \cdots, x_l$, with the output of y. λ is the security parameter.

Locality. Locality describes the tendency of repeated access to local data over a short period. It mainly includes temporal and spatial locality, which widely exist in the data access patterns [14,16,19]. The temporal locality refers to repeated access to specific data for a relatively short duration. Spatial locality refers to the access of data within relatively fixed locations. Studying a target system's temporal locality and spatial locality can provide guidelines for appropriate data management solutions. For example, iDedup [16] designed an efficient inline data deduplication scheme, which took advantage of the temporal and spatial localities of duplicated data. RapidCDC [14] dramatically reduced the chunking time by uniquely leveraging duplication locality and access history. We discover that block updates in deduplication systems are with locality by analyzing real-world datasets. Based on the update locality, we improve the UMLE scheme.

Merkle Tree Hash. A Merkle tree can generate a compact hash (the root hash) for a large file. Each leaf node of a Merkle tree is a cryptographic hash of a file block, and each non-leaf node is a cryptographic hash of its children. The calculation of a Merkle tree starts from the leaf nodes to the root node, and the calculation process is irreversible. The Merkle tree always generates an identical hash value for the data with the same contents. It can be used to ensure the integrity and correctness of cloud outsourced data [13] and provide efficient authentication [7]. We generate file tags based on the Merkle tree instead of the incremental hash of UMLE19 [22] with ready-made block tags as leaf nodes. The correctness of the Merkle hash as the file tag is obvious, and its security of the tag consistency is proved in Sect. 4.5.

3   Analysis of the FSL Homes Datasets

The FSL Homes datasets [1] are widely utilized in the field of deduplication research [8–11,20]. In most cases, the FSL dataset participates in the deduplication research as experimental data; on the other hand, there are studies [17,18] on its properties. For example, Tarasov et al. [18] studied the file-level update properties. They found that most files remain unchanged, and the probability of file re-modification is about 50%. Their analysis is at the file level, whereas our analysis is block-level and informative for block-level update schemes.

To the best of our knowledge, this is *the first analysis of block-level update properties for deduplication.*

Data Description. On a daily basis, FSL collects snapshots of the home directories of 33 people in the file-sharing system for 21 months. The dataset chunks files at seven chunking sizes (2, 4, 8, 16, 32, 128 KB) and records block information, including block metadata and md5-based hash values. The reasons why we choose the FSL dataset to explore block-level update properties are:

- It is a widely used dataset in deduplication. Our analysis based on the FSL dataset can provide more general guidance for other deduplication studies.
- It is collected for a sufficiently long period to meet the time-continuity requirement for exploring update properties.

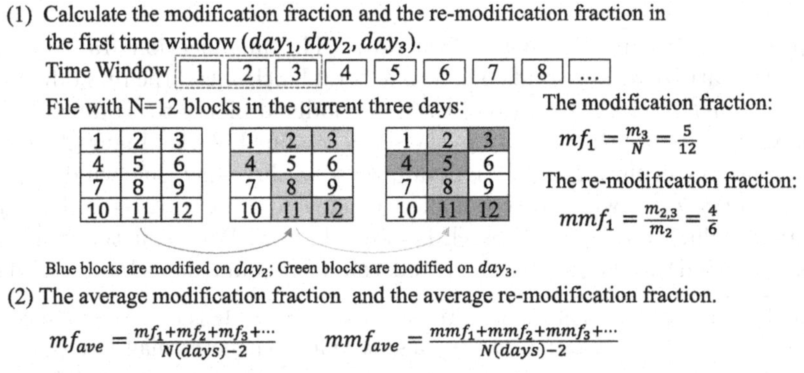

(1) Calculate the modification fraction and the re-modification fraction in the first time window (day_1, day_2, day_3).

Time Window [1][2][3][4][5][6][7][8][...]

File with N=12 blocks in the current three days: The modification fraction:

$$mf_1 = \frac{m_3}{N} = \frac{5}{12}$$

The re-modification fraction:

$$mmf_1 = \frac{m_{2,3}}{m_2} = \frac{4}{6}$$

Blue blocks are modified on day_2; Green blocks are modified on day_3.

(2) The average modification fraction and the average re-modification fraction.

$$mf_{ave} = \frac{mf_1+mf_2+mf_3+\cdots}{N(days)-2} \qquad mmf_{ave} = \frac{mmf_1+mmf_2+mmf_3+\cdots}{N(days)-2}$$

Fig. 2. Example of the calculation of the re-modification fraction (mmf) with the three-day time window.

Table 1. Features of the FSL Homes datasets for our analysis.

Item	Number/Size
Users	18
Snapshots	1448
Files	1.5×10^6
Unique chunks	3.9×10^9
Total size	130.33 TB

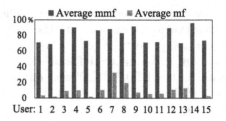

Fig. 3. Fractions of re-modification and modification of 15 users.

- It is collected under various chunking sizes, which helps to explore update properties at different block sizes and facilitates spatial locality analysis.

3.1 Methodology and Analysis Results

Before the update property analysis, we need to filter the FSL datasets. There are three criteria for filtering: large file, the existence of updates, and time continuity. Firstly, since only the block update for large files significantly impact the performance of the UMLE schemes, we select large files with a size larger than 1 MB from the FSL datasets. Secondly, since not all large files collected by the datasets have updates, we further filter the large files with updates. Finally, some daily snapshots in the FSL datasets were not collected daily, hindering our analysis since discontinuous data cannot directly reflect updates in each time unit. Therefore, we remove these intermittent snapshots as well. Through the above three-step filter, we obtain the datasets shown in Table 1.

Second, we perform block-level deduplication for each file to ensure that our summarised update properties are valid for the deduplicated data. Block-level deduplication of the FSL datasets is straightforward. We can deduplicate files by comparing the block hashes and deleting duplicates with identical hashes. The deduplication ratio of the filtered dataset is 14.09%[3].

Property 1. Re-modification Fraction. The modification fraction (mf) defines the ratio of to-be-modified blocks to total blocks. And the re-modification fraction (mmf) defines the ratio of to-be-re-modified blocks to modified blocks; Namely, mmf establishes the mf in the set of modified blocks. Figure 2 contains an example of calculating them. In detail, we set a three-day time window $(day_i, day_{i+1}, $ and $day_{i+2})$, which is the smallest window for observing re-modifications and under which the window search is most efficient. We count the number of blocks modified[4] on day_{i+1} as m_{i+1} and count the number of blocks modified

---

[3] The deduplication ratio of the FSL Home datasets actually is 61% [17]; in contrast, that of our filtered dataset is low because we filter out both small files (< 1 MB) with big deduplication ratios and inactive files occupying an immense total size.

[4] If the hash of a block in day_{i+1} is different from the hash of the block in day_i, we say that the block is modified on day_{i+1}.

both on day_{i+1} and day_{i+2} as $m_{i+1,i+2}$. The re-modification fraction in the i-th time window (mmf_i) is calculated by

$$mmf_i = (m_{i+1,i+2}/m_{i+1}) \times 100\%. \tag{1}$$

Figure 3 shows the re-modification fractions for different users, and their average re-modification fraction is 80.82%. The re-modification fraction is exceptionally high, being 9.40 times the average modification fraction (8.60%), which indicates that block modification is time-local. In other words, the modified blocks are more likely to be modified than other blocks.

Property 2. Spatial Distribution of Modified Blocks. We calculate the average modification fractions of datasets collected in various block sizes. We observe that with an increase in block size, the increase in modification fraction is slighter than the linear increase. This implies that modified blocks are clustered, indicating their distribution in file space is localized. With a similar method, iDedup [16] found that spatial locality exists in duplicated primary data.

Property 3. The Proportion of inactive blocks. We find that the modified blocks only account for a small part of the total blocks, between 4.50% and 13.10%. Moreover, we find that the distinction between active and inactive blocks is clear. Some blocks are frequently modified, while others remain unchanged for a long time. The average proportion of file blocks never been modified is 53.41%.

Summary. By analyzing the block updates of large files continuously recorded for a period in the FSL datasets, we reveal three update properties:

- Temporal locality. Modified blocks are more likely to be modified again than others. The fraction of to-be-modified blocks in modified blocks is 9.4 times that of to-be-modified blocks in all blocks.
- Spatial locality. Modified blocks in a file are always clustered.
- Inactive blocks constitute a significant percentage (53.41%), i.e., most blocks remain unchanged over an extended period.

4   Updatable Block-Level MLE Scheme

We briefly outline the UMLE at a high level in terms of encryption, decryption, and update. Firstly, a large file is divided into blocks, and these blocks are encrypted with MLE, with numerous block keys (B_KeyGen and B_Enc). Then, block keys are encrypted with the master key derived from the whole file (M_KeyGen and K_Enc). The encrypted keys are uploaded to the server along with encrypted blocks to facilitate block key management. The server generates a block tag for each block ciphertext and a file tag for all block ciphertexts (B_TagGen and F_TagGen), to support block-level and file-level deduplication.

Secondly, the encrypted data is downloaded from the server when the file owner with the master key accesses the outsourced file. The owner first uses the master key to decrypt the key ciphertexts to obtain all MLE block keys (K_Dec), and then uses decrypted block keys to decrypt the file block ciphertexts (B_Dec). Thirdly, when the file owner wants to modify a block of the file, the related block ciphertext and key ciphertexts are downloaded. After decrypting, modifying, and re-encrypting, the owner uploads the updated ciphertexts. And the server re-generates the block tag of the modified block and a new file tag.

We focus on improving the update algorithm of UMLE. An update is essentially a transition from one state to another. In UMLE, each state contains a master key, block ciphertexts, block key ciphertexts, block tags, and a file tag. The updates of the block ciphertext, the block key, and the block tag are fixed in an MLE-based encryption scheme. Therefore, *we focus on improving the update performance of the master key, block key ciphertext, and file tag.* To this end, we introduce a new UMLE scheme, termed UP-MLE, based on the update properties embodied in the real-world datasets and the idea of hierarchical processing. Specifically, UP-MLE shortens the update paths of active blocks (frequently updated blocks) by dynamically adjusting the tree structure of the UMLE scheme [22] to enhance update efficiency.

4.1 Definition

We follow the UMLE definitions [22], revisited in Appendix A, except for the Update. Instead, we re-divide the update algorithm to separate those parts of the irreducible algorithms and those that can be improved to facilitate scheme descriptions and performance analysis. Our Update algorithm is defined as $\{k_{mas}', C', T'\} \leftarrow Update(i, M_i', k_{mas}, C)$. It contains five sub-algorithms:

- $k_i \leftarrow K\_Return(k_{mas}, C_{key}, i)$. The block key decryption algorithm takes the master key k_{mas}, key ciphertexts C_{key} and a to-be-updated block index i as inputs and returns the block key k_i of the to-be-updated file block.
- $\{k_i', C_i'\} \leftarrow B\_Update(k_i, C_i, M_i')$. The block key and block ciphertext update algorithm takes the block key k_i, the block ciphertext C_i and a new file block M_i' as inputs and returns a new block key k_i' and a new block ciphertext C_i'.
- $\{k_{mas}', C_{key}'\} \leftarrow K\_Update(k_{mas}, k_i', \{k_i\}, i)$. The master key and key ciphertext update algorithm takes the old master key k_{mas}, the new block key k_i', old block keys $\{k_i\}$, and the index i as inputs and returns a new master key k_{mas}' and new key ciphertexts C_{key}'.
- $T_i' \leftarrow B\_UpdateTag(C_i')$. The block tag update algorithm returns a new block tag T_i', on input a new block ciphertext C_i'.
- $T_f' \leftarrow F\_UpdateTag(C')$. The file tag update algorithm takes new ciphertexts C' as inputs and returns a new file tag T_f'.

4.2 Partial Constructions of UP-MLE

Based on the definitions of UMLE and our Update definitions, we describes the details of partial constructions for our UP-MLE scheme directly:

- Setup: On input the security parameter λ, it returns $P = \{SE(Enc, Dec), H\}$, where SE is a symmetric encryption scheme, and H is a collision-resistant hash function, $H : \{0,1\}^{k(\lambda)} \leftarrow \{0,1\}^*$, where $k(\lambda)$ is the key length of the SE.
- KeyGen: On input $M = \{M_i\}_n$, it runs as follows and returns $K = \{\{k_i\}_n, k_{mas}\}$.
  - B_KeyGen: For each $i \in [1, n]$, $k_i = H(M_i)$;
  - * M_KeyGen: Generate k_{mas} with $\{k_i\}_n$.
- Enc: On inputs K and M, it runs as follows and returns $C = \{\{C_i\}_n, C_{key}\}$.
  - B_Enc: For each $i \in [1, n]$, $C_i = SE.Enc(k_i, M_i)$;
  - * K_Enc: Encrypt $\{k_i\}_n$ with k_{mas} and return C_{key}.
- Dec: On inputs K and C, it runs as follows and returns $M = \{M_i\}_n$.
  - * K_Dec: Decrypt C_{key} with k_{mas} and return $\{k_i\}_n$;
  - B_Dec: For each $i \in [1, n]$, $M_i = SE.Dec(k_i, C_i)$.
- TagGen: On input C, it runs as follows and returns $T = \{\{T_i\}_{n'}, T_f\}$.
  - B_TagGen: For each $i \in [1, n']$, $T_i = H(C_i)$, where $\{C_i\}$ ($i \in [n + 1, n']$) are blocks of the C_{key};
  - * F_TagGen: Generate T_f with C.
- Update: On inputs i, M_i', k_{mas}, and C, it runs as follows and returns k_{mas}', $C' = \{C_i', C_{key}'\}$, and $T' = \{T_i', T_f'\}$.
  - * K_Return: Decrypt C_{key} with k_{mas} and return k_i;
  - B_Update: $M_i = SE.Dec(k_i, C_i)$, modify M_i to M_i', $k_i' = H(M_i')$, and $C_i' = SE.Enc(k_i', M_i')$;
  - * K_Update: Generate k_{mas}' with $\{k_i\}_n$ and k_i' and encrypt $\{k_i\}_n$ and k_i' with k_{mas}' as C_{key}';
  - B_UpdateTag: $T_i' = H(C_i')$;
  - * F_UpdateTag: Generate T_f' with $\{C_i\}_n$ and C_i'.

Besides, some algorithm constructions marked with "*", such as M_KeyGen, K_Enc, K_Dec, F_TagGen, K_Return, K_Update, and F_UpdateTag, are at the core of our improvements, described in Sect. 4.3.

4.3   Designs of the Update Algorithms of UP-MLE

We find that updated blocks will be quickly updated again. In contrast, other blocks will never be updated for a long time. Based on the update property, we adopts a dynamic tree for the master key generation and update. *In the dynamic tree, the frequently updated block keys approach to the tree root in updates by replacing the parent node.* As shown in the left tree in Fig. 4, the updated block key k_1' moves one step along the leaf-to-root path and replaces the original k_{1-2} at its parent node. The new master key k_{mas}' is generated according to the dynamically adjusted tree by iteratively hashing children nodes as the parent node (i.e., $H(k_1'||k_2||k_{3-4}) \rightarrow k_{1-4}'$, $H(k_{1-4}'||k_{5-6}) \rightarrow k_{1-8}'$). In addition, the children nodes always are encrypted with their parent node. Since the closer the location to the root, the fewer re-encrypted blocks in the path during updates, the less expensive the updates are. In a future update, $k_1{}'$ intuitively will have a shorter update path than other block keys. Additionally, the block key k_2 in the same block with k_1 shortens the update path as well, considering the spatial locality. The dynamic tree *differentiates between handling frequently and infrequently updated blocks, providing a faster update approach for frequent ones.*

However, unlike the static tree structure, which sets the master key generation algorithm by default, the dynamic tree leads to the possibility that users generate different master keys for identical files with different tree structures. For this, we mark the current height of each key block and help users learn the current tree structure to generate the correct master key. We call the space *the height space*, in which we store the key block heights.

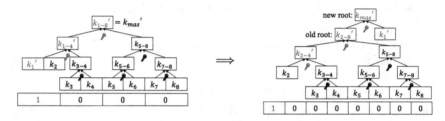

Fig. 4. The generation and update of the master key and block key ciphertexts of our UP-MLE scheme. For illustration, we assume an eight-block file, of which the first block will be updated. The key icons represent encryption and are in the middle of the keys in the same block. Child nodes are encrypted block-wise with their parent nodes. We assume that each key block contains two keys for the sake of brevity. Red nodes indicate the value to be recalculated. (Color figure online)

Considering that there is a clear boundary between active and inactive blocks, if a block is updated, it will be updated frequently and will reach the root node in a short duration. In the final UP-MLE scheme, we *elevate the updated block key outside the tree directly in one update,* and its concatenation with the root hash is encrypted with MLE, which is equivalent to adding a tree layer. The generated MLE key will be the new master key and the new root.

As shown in the right tree in Fig. 4, the block key k_1 is removed from the leaf node, and other block keys are iteratively hashed to generate the new root key $k_{2-8}{}'$ in the old tree. Then, its concatenation $(k_{2-8}{}'\|k_1{}')$ with the updated block key $k_1{}'$ is encrypted with MLE, and $H(k_{2-8}{}'\|k_1{}')$ is used as the new master key. In a future update of the first block, UP-MLE can decrypt and re-encrypt k_1' directly and efficiently. It is more efficient for UP-MLE to elevate the block directly to the old root height than to approach the root layer by layer. Besides, by moving updated blocks outside the tree, all nodes in the old tree will be stabilized, thereby avoiding recalculation of nodes in the old tree in future updates. Moreover, we allocate 1 bit height space for each key block ciphertext to mark whether the key block is raised outside the old tree.

New Generation and Update Algorithms of the File Tag. We generate a file tag with the Merkle tree with block tags as leaf nodes. As shown in Eq. (2), MT.Hash computes the hash of the concatenation of ready-made block tags as file tags. The advantage of the Merkle tree hash as a file tag is that when some blocks of the file are modified, we do not need to recompute the hash of the whole ciphertext, just that of block tags as MT.Update in Eq. (3). For good measure, the update cost of the file tag is independent of the number of updated blocks and is constant for files with a constant block number. The file tag generation and update algorithms are defined by

$$MT.Hash\,(C_1,\cdots,C_m) = H(H(C_1)\|\cdots\|H(C_m)) = H\,(T_1\|\cdots\|T_m)\,, \quad (2)$$

$$MT.Update\,(C_1{}',\cdots,C_m) = H(H(C_1{}')\|\cdots\|H(C_m)) = H\,(T_1{}'\|\cdots\|T_m)\,. \quad (3)$$

When any blocks are updated, the server only recalculates the hash of the concatenation of block tags as a new file tag with MT.Update.

4.4 Correctness and Efficiency

The correctness of the file tag is straightforwardly inherited from the correctness of the Merkle tree hash. The correctness of UP-MLE requires the correctness of symmetric encryption, which is straightforward, and the consistency of master keys, which is guaranteed by consistency of the tree structure. The correspondence of tree structure can be proved by the one-to-one correspondence of tree structure and leaf node heights, recorded in the height space.

With regard to efficiency, the dynamic tree structure may cause efficiency concerns, such as whether adjusting the tree structure will introduce an additional burden. However, it does not raise another cost because the impact of updates on the dynamic tree is limited to the leaf-to-root paths of the updated blocks. In UMLE19 [22], the blocks in the update path would all need to be re-encrypted, which gives us an upper bound. In addition, we note that the update cost of UP-MLE increases instead when the block keys moved outside the tree are more than the keys in the original update path. We effectively solve this problem by organizing keys outside the tree in a tree structure as well.

UP-MLE logs the current height for each key block to help users generate a consistent master key. Thus, the server needs to send these additional data to users involved in the deduplication of the same file. Practically speaking, the delivery of auxiliary data does not increase the communication rounds of the deduplication protocol because these data can be returned to the user together with the duplicate detection results. If the protocol contains ownership authentication, it can be returned together with the authentication result.

4.5 Security Definitions and Proofs

Privacy. Any MLE schemes can not achieve semantic security, nor can the MLE-based schemes [3], such as BL-MLE and UMLE. Indeed, they ask for semantic security when messages are unpredictable, with high min-entropy. Bellare *et al.* [3] formalized PRV$-CDA notion where the encryption of an unpredictable message must be indistinguishable from a random string of the same length. Based on PRV$-CDA, Zhao *et al.* [22] defined PRV$-CDA-B* for their updatable MLE (UMLE) scheme. Since our UMLE scheme introduces additional items (i.e., heights) compared with [22], we follow its spirit and define a new privacy model, denoted by PRV$-CDA-B**. We say that our UMLE scheme is secure under chosen distribution attacks if no probabilistic polynomial-time non-adaptive adversary $\mathcal{A}$ has a non-negligible advantage in the following PRV$-CDA-B** game:

- **Setup**: The adversary $\mathcal{A}$ sends the description of an unpredictable message source $\mathcal{M}$ to the Challenger. The Challenger generates the system parameter P and sends it to $\mathcal{A}$.
- **Challenge**: The Challenger selects randomly selects $b \leftarrow_\$ \{0,1\}$. If $b = 0$, it samples $M^{\{0\}}$ from $\mathcal{M}$. If $b = 1$, the Challenger chooses uniformly at random from $\{0,1\}^{|M^{\{0\}}|}$ as $M^{\{1\}}$. Then, set $M = M^{\{b\}}$ and suppose $n(\lambda)$ (n simply) is the block numbers of M. For each $i \in [1,n]$, the Challenger runs as follows for the file block encryption:
  - Compute $\hat{k}_i \leftarrow B\_KeyGen(M_i)$ as the block key of the i-th block of the message M.
  - Compute $\hat{C}_i \leftarrow B\_Enc(k_i, M_i)$ as the block ciphertext of M_i.

  Also run as follows for the key block encryption:
  - Compute $\hat{k_{mas}} \leftarrow M\_KeyGen(\{\hat{k_i}\}_n)$ as the master key of M and compute $\{\hat{C_{n+i}}\}_{n'-n} \leftarrow K\_Enc(\{\hat{k_i}\}_n)$ as the ciphertext of all block keys.

  And then run as follows for the tag generation:
  - Compute $\hat{T}_i \leftarrow B\_TagGen(C_i)$ as the block tag of the i-th ciphertext, for each $i \in [1,n']$.
  - Compute $\hat{T}_f \leftarrow F\_TagGen(\{\hat{C}_i\}_{n'})$ as the file tag.

  Then, the Challenger randomly picks $S \leftarrow_\$ \{\{\{0,1\}^{\lceil \log(n(\lambda))\rceil}\}_{\frac{n(\lambda)k(\lambda)}{B}}\}$.
  - Compute $\{\{C_i\}, \{T_i\}, T_f, k_{mas}\} \leftarrow Update(\{\hat{C}_i\}, \{\hat{T}_i\}, \hat{T}_f, \hat{k_{mas}}, S)$ as the updated data.

  Denote $\{C_i\}$ as C, $\{T_i\}$ and T_f as T, and the additional item S. Finally, Challenger sends $\{C, T, S\}$ to $\mathcal{A}$.
- **Output**: After receiving $\{C, T, S\}$, $\mathcal{A}$ guesses b' on b and outputs b'. If $b' = b$, the adversary $\mathcal{A}$ wins. Otherwise, the Challenger wins.

The above n' is the number of ciphertext blocks, and it can be calculated by

$$n' \leqslant n + \frac{((B/k(\lambda))^{\lceil \log_{B/k(\lambda)} n \rceil} - 1) \times k(\lambda)}{B - k(\lambda)}, \tag{4}$$

where $k(\lambda)$ is the key length, and B is the block size.

We define the advantage of the adversary $\mathcal{A}$ as:

$$Adv_{\text{PRV\$}-\text{CDA}-\text{B}^{**}}^{\mathcal{A},\mathcal{M}} = |Pr[b = b'] - \frac{1}{2}|. \tag{5}$$

Definition 1. *We say that our scheme is PRV\$-CDA-B**-secure if for any unpredictable source $\mathcal{M}$ and any probabilistic polynomial-time non-adaptive adversary $\mathcal{A}$, $Adv_{PRV\$-CDA-B^{**}}^{\mathcal{A},\mathcal{M}}$ is negligible.*

Theorem 1. *Let hash function H be a random oracle and let $SE = \{Enc, Dec\}$ is a symmetric encryption scheme with key length $k(\lambda)$. Suppose SE is both key recovery secure (KR-secure) and one-time real-or-random secure (ROR-secure). If there exists adversaries $\mathcal{B}'$ and $\mathcal{D}'$, for any adversary $\mathcal{A}$, his advantage is:*

$$Adv_{\text{PRV\$}-\text{CDA}-\text{B}^{**}}^{\mathcal{A},\mathcal{M}} \leqslant \frac{n^2}{2^{B-3}} + 2qn'Adv_{KR}^{\mathcal{B}'}(\lambda) + Adv_{ROR}^{\mathcal{D}'}(\lambda) + \frac{qn}{2^{\mu}}$$

$$\leqslant \mathcal{O}(qn)Adv_{KR}^{\mathcal{B}'}(\lambda) + Adv_{ROR}^{\mathcal{D}'}(\lambda) + \frac{n^2}{2^{B-3}} + \frac{qn}{2^{\mu}}, \quad (6)$$

where $\mu(\lambda)$ is the min-entropy of unpredictable source $\mathcal{M}$, $n(\lambda)$ (abbreviated as n) is the number of message blocks, n' is the number of ciphertext blocks, $q(\lambda)$ is the number of queries to the random oracle H by $\mathcal{A}$, $\mathcal{B}'$ and $\mathcal{D}'$ is adversaries in KR-game[5] and ROR-game[6] [3].

Proof. We prove the **Theorem** 1 by following the privacy proof of [22]. The proof introduces five games with the hidden bit b transition from 0 to 1 and proves that each transition is indistinguishable.

- **Game 0:** It has the hidden bit being 0.
- **Game 1:** It is identical to Game 0 except that the Challenger records query history to the random oracle H. If a random oracle query is a history query, the Challenger aborts. Otherwise, he does not abort, and Game 1 is identical to Game 0.
  All blocks of the deduplicated file are not identical. Since each block of message and each block of block key are hashed at most twice in KeyGen, Enc, and Update, the total number of random oracle queries is capped at twice the ciphertext block number, which can be calculated by Eq. (4). We conservatively assume $B > 2k(\lambda)$, and then $n \leqslant n' \leqslant (3n-3)$. Thus, Pr[Challenger aborting in Game 1] $< 2\sum_{i=n}^{3n-3} i/2^B < 2(4n^2 - 7n + 3)/2^B < n^2/2^{B-3}$. (We stress that $B/k(\lambda) \gg 2$ in practice.)
- **Game 2:** The adversary makes a history query, and the Challenger aborts. In addition, the adversary $\mathcal{A}$ breaks the KR-security with the negligible advantage of $Adv_{KR}^{\mathcal{A}}(\lambda)$.
  A block hash is as the key of the block in encryption. Suppose an adversary $\mathcal{B}$ of KR-game who makes q history queries with non-negligible probability. So we can build an adversary $\mathcal{B}'$ who can break the KR-security. In each block encryption, $\mathcal{B}'$ guesses the key (hash query). Thus, Pr[History hash query in Game 2] $\leqslant 2qn'Adv_{KR}^{\mathcal{B}'}(\lambda)$.

---

[5] The adversary $\mathcal{B}'$ can guess the random key K used by the oracle SE.Enc after obtaining the output C of the oracle SE.Enc on his specified input M.

[6] In ROR-game, the adversary $\mathcal{D}'$ can distinguish between a ciphertext generated by the oracle SE.Enc and a random string.

- **Game 3:** It replaces the ciphertexts of message M_i by ciphertexts of random messages with the same length. The adversary $\mathcal{A}$ breaks the KR-security with the negligible advantage of $Adv_{ROR}^{\mathcal{A}}(\lambda)$.

  Suppose an adversary $\mathcal{D}$ of ROR-game who can differentiate Game 3 from Game 2. So we can build an adversary $\mathcal{D}'$ who can break the ROR-security. $\mathcal{D}'$ queries the encryption oracle of the ROR-game and outputs the $\mathcal{D}$'s outputs. Thus, $Pr[\text{History hash query with differentiating random M in Game 3}] \leqslant Adv_{ROR}^{\mathcal{D}'}(\lambda)$.

- **Game 4:** The adversary queries $H(M_i)$ for i-th encryption, and the Challenger aborts. In Game 4, the hidden bit is 1 so that all returned ciphertexts are the ciphertexts of random messages. Each query is equivalent to randomly guessing M_i from a unpredictable message source $\mathcal{M}$. Thus, $Pr[\text{History hash query of completely random } M \text{ in Game 4}] \leqslant qn/2^{\mu}$.

Tag Consistency. Our block tag generation algorithm is the same as MLE and has the same strong tag consistency (STC). As for the file tag, $T_f = MT.Hash(C)$. It is known that *deterministic schemes are STC-secure when the tags are collision-resistant hashes of the ciphertext* [3], meaning an adversary cannot erase a user's file by creating (M, C). In addition, the collision resistance of Merkle trees [6] shows that MT.Hash is collision-resistant when $H(\cdot)$ is a collision-resistant hash. Thus, we state the **Theorem** 2. Its proof is obvious.

Theorem 2. *Suppose* $SE = \{Enc, Dec\}$ *is a symmetric encryption scheme and H is a collision-resistant hash, our schemes are STC-secure.*

Context Hiding. Context hiding ensures that privacy is not degraded during the update, defined by [22]. Zhao *et al.* proved that context hiding of a deterministic UMLE scheme only requires that the updated ciphertexts are indistinguishable from fresh ciphertexts. Our $SE = \{Enc, Dec\}$ is a deterministic symmetric encryption scheme, and H is a deterministic hash function. Therefore, the indistinguishability of ciphertexts, whether obtained by initial encryption or updated encryption, is not difficult to derive from the ROR-security. Thus, our scheme is context hiding.

Other Security Analysis. As proved in **Privacy**, with any height space as the returned parameter S by the Challenger in PRV\$-CDA-B**-game, our scheme is PRV\$-CDA-B**-secure. Thus, height space does not affect the privacy security.

5   Evaluation and Comparison

We implement UP-MLE with the C Programming Language and adopt the SHA256 as the cryptographic hash function and AES as the symmetric encryption function. The basic cryptographic functions are implemented based on the OpenSSL Library (Version 1.1.1h). We test the update performance on the real-world datasets, including the FSL datasets of user000 [1] and the Kernels datasets, which contains unpacked Linux kernel sources from Linux v5.0 to v5.2.8 [2]. All experiment results are the averages of 10 independent executions.

5.1 Update Performance on the Real-World Datasets

We collect the indexes of daily update blocks for the user000's files in the FSL datasets at block size of 4 KB. We use update block indexes as the input of the update algorithms to test the time cost required to complete all block updates. In addition, we treat each of the 100 Kernel sources as a file, and consider the changes between successive versions as updates, and then perform the same tests as the FSL dataset. The execution time of the update algorithms is shown in Table 2. We can see that our scheme has better performance than UMLE19. In the FSL test, UP-MLE's update cost sum of the K_Return and K_Update is only 83.40% of that of UMLE19, and in the Kernels test, it is only 66.89%.

Table 2. Execution time (ms) of the *Update* sub-algorithms.

		UMLE19 [22]	UP-MLE			UMLE19 [22]	UP-MLE
	K_Return	6.84	4.45		K_Return	69.18	28.51
FSL	K_Update	20.40	18.27	Kernels	K_Update	201.49	152.55
	Sum	27.24	22.72		Sum	270.67	181.06
	(%)	100.00	83.40		(%)	100.00	66.89

5.2 Performance of the Generation and Update of the File Tag

We can take the runtime of SHA256 as a reference to measure the performance of file tag algorithms. As shown in Table 3, the time cost of the IH.Hash is about 50 times that of the SHA256. However, the time cost of our file tag generation algorithm (MT.Hash) is 0.18%–0.24% as that of the SHA256. From Table 4, we

Table 3. F_TagGen execution time (ms) for various file sizes at 16 KB block size.

	File size (MB)	4	8	16	32	64
	IH.Hash	568.3	1138.5	2271.3	4545.2	9074.8
UMLE19 [22]	SHA256[†]	11.2	22.4	45	89.9	179.6
	%[‡]	5074	5083	5047	5056	5053
	MT.Hash	0.07	0.13	0.16	0.33	0.63
Ours	SHA256	28.61	59.44	86.90	147.98	262.70
	%[‡]	0.23	0.21	0.18	0.22	0.24

[†]Execution time of SHA256 is from the supplementary material of [22].
[‡]Percentage of execution time compared to SHA256.

can see that when updating a block, the time cost of the file tag update algorithm (IH.Update) of UMLE19 [22] is 20.09%–39.29% as that of the SHA256. The time cost of our file tag update algorithm (MT.Update) is 0.04%-0.68% as that of the SHA256. Therefore, our file tag generation and update algorithms are significantly better than UMLE19's, and the time cost of our algorithms is reduced by several orders of magnitude. Additionally, the incremental hash update algorithm used by UMLE19 is positively correlated with the number of updated blocks. In contrast, our Merkle tree-based update algorithm is independent of the number of updated blocks. We conclude that the more the number of update blocks, the greater the performance advantage of our file tag update algorithm.

Table 4. F_TagUpdate execution time (ms) for 8 MB files at different block sizes.

	Block size (KB)	4	8	16	32	64
UMLE19 [22]	IH.Update	8.8	8.8	4.5	4.6	4.7
	%†		39.29	39.29	20.09	20.54	20.98
Ours	MT.Update	0.40	0.26	0.12	0.06	0.02
	%‡	0.68	0.43	0.20	0.10	0.04

†Percentage compared to UMLE's SHA256, which costs 22.4 ms.
‡Percentage compared to our SHA256, which costs 59.44 ms.

5.3 Storage Efficiency

Table 5. Size of ciphertext expansion at different block sizes, for files of 1 GB.

Block size (KB)	2	4	8	16	32	64	128
UMLE19 [22]	16644.06	8256.50	4112.06	2052.00	1025.00	512.50	256.25
UP-MLE	16708.06	8288.50	4128.06	2060.00	1029.00	514.50	257.25

Considering a large file with a size of 1 GB, we calculate the ciphertext size when chunking with different block sizes in Table 5. We can see that the ciphertext expansion size of our scheme does not exceed 0.39% compared with UMLE19 [22]. It shows that the auxiliary data (i.e., height space) do not lead to an unacceptable storage expansion.

6 Conclusion

We study the block-level update properties of the FSL Homes datasets such as the temporal locality and the spatial locality. Considering these properties, we design and implement an efficient and practical updatable block-level MLE scheme. Our scheme optimizes the update algorithms through hierarchical processing frequently and infrequently updated blocks in the dynamic tree. We test our update algorithms on two real-world datasets. The experimental results show that our scheme has better update performance than the existing scheme. In future work, we will quantify the update localities and analyze the update performance of our scheme on datasets with various locality strengths, in order to provide general guidance for other workloads to adopt our scheme.

Other secure deduplication studies can migrate our dynamic tree design to help them expand the function of efficient updates, such as the password-protected deduplication scheme [21]. It uses the password secret to encrypt block keys. Our designs can be directly plugged into the deduplication scheme by replacing the key encryption method to support efficient updates. Furthermore, our update properties summarized from the real datasets have reference value for future deduplication research.

Acknowledgements. We sincerely thank the IFIP SEC 2022 anonymous reviewers for their valuable comments. Chunfu Jia is the corresponding author. This work was supported by the National Natural Science Foundation of China (62172238, 61972215, and 61972073) and the Natural Science Foundation of Tianjin (20JCZDJC00640).

A   Complete Definition of the UMLE

Zhao *et al.* [22] initiated the study of the updatable block-level message-locked encryption (UMLE) and defined it based on MLE [3] and BL-MLE [4]. We follow their UMLE definitions [22]:

- $P \leftarrow Setup(1^\lambda)$: It takes the security parameter λ as input and returns the system parameter P, which is public to all entities in the system.
- $K \leftarrow KeyGen(M)$: It takes a file M as input and returns a master key and all block keys of the file. It contains two sub-algorithms:
  - $k_{mas} \leftarrow M\_KeyGen(M)$: It takes M as input and returns a master key k_{mas}.
  - $k_i \leftarrow B\_KeyGen(M_i)$: It takes a file block M_i as input and returns a block key k_i.
- $C \leftarrow Enc(K, M)$: It takes a file, a master key, and block keys as inputs and returns ciphertexts. It contains two sub-algorithms:
  - $C_i \leftarrow B\_Enc(k_i, M_i)$: It takes a file block M_i and a block key k_i as inputs and returns a ciphertext C_i of the file block.
  - $C_{n+j} \leftarrow K\_Enc(k_{mas}, \{k_i\}_b)$: It takes a master key k_{mas} and all block key $\{k_i\}$ as inputs and returns ciphertexts $\{C_{n+j}\}_{n_k}$, where $j \in [1, n_k]$, n_k is the number of key blocks, and $C_{key} = \{C_{n+j}\}_{n_k}$.
- $M \leftarrow Dec(k_{mas}, C)$: It takes a master key and ciphertexts as inputs and returns the file in plaintext. It contains two sub-algorithms:
  - $\{k_i\} \leftarrow K\_Dec(k_{mas}, C_{key})$: It takes a master key k_{mas} and key ciphertexts C_{key} as inputs and returns block keys $\{k_i\}$.
  - $M_i \leftarrow B\_Dec(k_i, C_i)$: It takes a block key k_i and a ciphertext C_i as inputs and returns the file block M_i.

– $T \leftarrow TagGen(C)$: It takes ciphertexts as inputs and returns tags. It contains two sub-algorithms:

- $T_i \leftarrow B\_TagGen(C_i)$: It takes a ciphertext C_i of a block as input and returns a block tag T_i.
- $T_f \leftarrow F\_TagGen(C)$: It takes all ciphertexts C as inputs and returns a file tag T_f.

There are no Update algorithms, but we redefine them in Sect. 4.1.

References

1. Fsl traces and snapshots public archive (2014). http://tracer.filesystems.org/
2. The linux kernel archives (2021). https://www.kernel.org
3. Bellare, M., Keelveedhi, S., Ristenpart, T.: Message-locked encryption and secure deduplication. In: Johansson, T., Nguyen, P.Q. (eds.) EUROCRYPT 2013. LNCS, vol. 7881, pp. 296–312. Springer, Heidelberg (2013). https://doi.org/10.1007/978-3-642-38348-9_18
4. Chen, R., Mu, Y., Yang, G., Guo, F.: BL-MLE: block-level message-locked encryption for secure large file deduplication. IEEE Trans. Inf. Forensics Secur. **10**(12), 2643–2652 (2015)
5. Douceur, J.R., Adya, A., Bolosky, W.J., Simon, P., Theimer, M.: Reclaiming space from duplicate files in a serverless distributed file system. In: Proceedings of ICDCS, pp. 617–624 (2002)
6. Dowling, B., Günther, F., Herath, U., Stebila, D.: Secure logging schemes and certificate transparency. In: Askoxylakis, I., Ioannidis, S., Katsikas, S., Meadows, C. (eds.) ESORICS 2016. LNCS, vol. 9879, pp. 140–158. Springer, Cham (2016). https://doi.org/10.1007/978-3-319-45741-3_8
7. Li, H., Lu, R., Zhou, L., Yang, B., Shen, X.: An efficient Merkle-tree-based authentication scheme for smart grid. IEEE Syst. J. **8**(2), 655–663 (2013)
8. Li, J., Lee, P.P., Ren, Y., Zhang, X.: Metadedup: deduplicating metadata in encrypted deduplication via indirection. In: Proceedings of MSST, pp. 269–281 (2019)
9. Li, J., Qin, C., Lee, P.P., Li, J.: Rekeying for encrypted deduplication storage. In: Proceedings of IEEE/IFIP DSN, pp. 618–629 (2016)
10. Li, M., Qin, C., Lee, P.P.: Cdstore: toward reliable, secure, and cost-efficient cloud storage via convergent dispersal. In: Proceedings of USENIX ATC, pp. 111–124 (2015)
11. Lin, X., Douglis, F., Li, J., Li, X., Ricci, R., Smaldone, S., Wallace, G.: Metadata considered harmful... to deduplication. In: Proceedings of HotStorage (2015)
12. Liu, M., Yang, C., Jiang, Q., Chen, X., Ma, J., Ren, J.: Updatable block-level deduplication with dynamic ownership management on encrypted data. In: Proceedings of IEEE ICC, pp. 1–7 (2018)
13. Mao, J., Zhang, Y., Li, P., Li, T., Wu, Q., Liu, J.: A position-aware Merkle tree for dynamic cloud data integrity verification. Soft Comput. **21**(8), 2151–2164 (2015). https://doi.org/10.1007/s00500-015-1918-8
14. Ni, F., Jiang, S.: RapidCDC: leveraging duplicate locality to accelerate chunking in cdc-based deduplication systems. In: Proceedings of Cloud Computing, pp. 220–232 (2019)

15. Shin, Y., Koo, D., Hur, J.: A survey of secure data deduplication schemes for cloud storage systems. ACM CSUR **49**(4), 1–38 (2017)
16. Srinivasan, K., Bisson, T., Goodson, G.R., Voruganti, K.: iDedup: latency-aware, inline data deduplication for primary storage. In: Proceedings of USENIX FAST (2012)
17. Sun, Z., Kuenning, G., Mandal, S., Shilane, P., Tarasov, V., Xiao, N., et al.: A long-term user-centric analysis of deduplication patterns. In: Proceedings of MSST (2016)
18. Tarasov, V., Mudrankit, A., Buik, W., Shilane, P., et al.: Generating realistic datasets for deduplication analysis. In: Proceedings of USENIX ATC, pp. 261–272 (2012)
19. Weinberg, J., McCracken, M.O., Strohmaier, E., Snavely, A.: Quantifying locality in the memory access patterns of hpc applications. In: Proceedings of ACM/IEEE Conference on Supercomputing, pp. 50–50 (2005)
20. Yuan, H., Chen, X., Li, J., Jiang, T., Wang, J., Deng, R.: Secure cloud data deduplication with efficient re-encryption. IEEE Trans. Serv. Comput. **15**, 442–456 (2019)
21. Zhang, Y., Xu, C., Cheng, N., Shen, X.S.: Secure password-protected encryption key for deduplicated cloud storage systems. IEEE Trans. Depend. Secure Comput. (2021). https://doi.org/10.1109/TDSC.2021.3074146
22. Zhao, Y., Chow, S.S.: Updatable block-level message-locked encryption. IEEE Trans. Depend. Secure Comput. **18**(4), 1620–1631 (2021)
23. Zhou, Y., et al.: Secdep: a user-aware efficient fine-grained secure deduplication scheme with multi-level key management. In: Proceedings of MSST, pp. 1–14 (2015)

CryptKSP: A Kernel Stack Protection Model Based on AES-NI Hardware Feature

Bingnan Zhong[1,2(✉)], Zicheng Wang[1,2], Yinggang Guo[1,2], and Qingkai Zeng[1,2]

[1] State Key Laboratory for Novel Software Technology, Nanjing University, Nanjing, China
{zbnnjucsv9,wzc,gyg}@smail.nju.edu.cn, zqk@nju.edu.cn
[2] Department of Computer Science and Technology, Nanjing University, Nanjing 210023, China

Abstract. The kernel stack is an important data structure in the kernel. It stores the return address, local variables and a large amount of state information of the kernel and application. Therefore, the kernel stack is often a valuable target for the attackers. More seriously, some types of attacks, which could bypass existing protection mechanisms, such as "return-to-schedule" rootkit, have posed a serious security threat to the security of the kernel stack. Therefore, some defensive approaches have been proposed to protect the integrity of the kernel stack by setting it read-only, however, it does not protect the confidentiality of the key data in the kernel stack. In this paper, we propose a kernel stack protection model for both the confidentiality and integrity without relying on another higher privilege layer. It takes advantage of AES-NI to encrypt the kernel stacks of the threads that are not running, and decrypt the kernel stack of the thread which will be running. In order to improve the security and adaptability, we implement two AES algorithms with different key lengths. The experimental results show that the kernel stack protection model could provide effective protection for the integrity and confidentiality of the kernel stack and do not impose high performance overhead.

Keywords: Kernel stack protection · AES-NI · Kernel stack integrity · Kernel stack confidentiality · Memory isolation

1 Introduction

The kernel stack is a critical data structure in the kernel, which stores important information, including control data (such as the return addresses) and non-control data (such as local variables). The kernel stack is located in the direct mapping area [1, 2] of the kernel address space. Once the kernel is compromised, any kernel execution unit [3] (which is defined in KSP [3], it refers to a piece of code with its own stack) can easily steal the sensitive information or destroy the crucial data stored in the kernel stack by leveraging KOH [4], DKOH [5] and return-to-schedule rootkit [6] attacks.

Since the kernel stack is an untyped large memory area and is not easy to traverse, it is difficult to protect the data in the kernel stack. Therefore, many security protection mechanisms have been proposed to protect the integrity of the kernel stack. KCOFI [7] proposes a protection method for the control data in the kernel stack, thus ensuring

W. Meng et al. (Eds.): SEC 2022, IFIP AICT 648, pp. 270–286, 2022.
https://doi.org/10.1007/978-3-031-06975-8_16

the integrity of the kernel control flow. Fine-CFI [8] further implements fine-grained protection of the return address of the kernel stack. Silhouette [9] builds a shadow stack based on compiler technology, which effectively protects the return address of the embedded system. Some works [10, 11, 12] use encryption to check integrity of software to protect against computers virus. CCFI [13] uses cryptographic message authentication codes (MACs) to protect control flow information such as function pointers, return addresses, and vtable pointers.

Ret-to-sched is a serious threat to the return address in the kernel stack. The attacker can change the control flow by destroying the return address in the kernel stack to point to the rootkit. To address such threats, OSck [6] periodically checks that whether the return address in the kernel stack belongs to a valid kernel code region. However, it is an asynchronous event and only protects part not all data in the kernel stack. To protect the integrity of the entire kernel stack, KSP [3] introduces a higher privilege layer, and sets read-only protection on the kernel stack by clearing R/W bit in the corresponding page table entries. Similarly, methods such as ShadowMoniter [14] and xMP [15] that use hardware virtualization and EPT [16] to build a memory region protection mechanism can also be applied to the integrity protection of the kernel stack. SaVioR [17] uses randomization technology to protect the stack of application, and may be extended to protect the kernel stack.

However, the above methods have the following problems:

1) Lack of confidentiality protection. It is easy to ensure the integrity of the kernel stack by taking use of read-only protection mechanism. However, only read-only protection will still put the protected data stored in kernel stack at risk, the attacker is still able to collect enough information before launching the attack.

2) Memory granularity conflict. On the x86_64 architectures, the default size of the kernel stack is 16 KB. However, the page size is 4 KB, 2 MB or 1 GB. Therefore, there is a serious memory granularity conflict between the kernel stack and the page. The kernel stack is often allocated in the kernel direct mapping area (excludes the kernel stack of the initialization process). In order to improve the memory access performance, the page size of the direct mapping memory regions is 2 MB or 1 GB, which is inconsistent with the size of the kernel stack.

3) Switching across privilege layers. Some methods introduce hypervisor, which is executed on a higher privilege than the kernel, as the trusted computing base of the system and deploy the interception and verification mechanism for the kernel stack in the hypervisor. It will be trapped into the hypervisor when the interception and verification mechanism is triggered, which will result in large performance loss. What's more, the current mainstream commercial hypervisors (including Xen [18] and KVM [19]) have a large amount of code and a complex architecture, which leads to the expansion of the TCB (Trusted Computing Base) size of the overall system.

Aiming at the above problems, we propose an integrity and confidentiality protection model for the kernel stack based on AES-NI [20] hardware features, and implement a prototype system CryptKSP. CryptKSP builds two different views for the kernel stack of each thread or process (for the convenience of description, hereinafter collectively referred to as thread) by means of encryption. One is normal view, where the kernel stack is exposed to the kernel in plaintext. The other is an encrypted view, where the kernel stack is exposed to the kernel in ciphertext. When a thread is running normally, the corresponding kernel stack is the normal view, while when the thread is sleeping, the corresponding kernel stack is encrypted view. CryptKSP does not rely on higher privilege layers and read-only protection based on paging mechanism, and builds a trusted computing base (Intral-level kernel [21] or the same-privilege-layer trusted computing base [22], hereinafter referred to as the same-privilege-level TCB) at the same privilege level with the kernel. CryptKSP intercepts and verifies the key operations of the kernel stack, and implements the switching of different views of the kernel stack. To achieve fast view switching, CryptKSP implements the AES encryption algorithm by making use of AES-NI. In order to ensure the security of the cryptographic key, CryptKSP stores the cryptographic key in the DR register, and ensures that only the CryptKSP can access the DR register. CryptKSP configures different encryption keys for the kernel stack.

The contributions of this paper are as follows:

1) We implement a lightweight memory protection model to protect the confidentiality and integrity of the kernel stack based on the Nested Kernel [21] core architecture. It does not rely on higher privilege layers and does not need to maintain a large number of codes to support the corresponding virtualization functions, which effectively reduces the amount of code in the system and overall TCB size.
2) We use AES-NI feature to implement the encryption and decryption operations of the memory area of the kernel stack at the same privilege layer of the kernel. At the same time, we use the debug register to store the AES key and protect the AES key from being stolen or tampered by the compromised kernel.
3) We have implemented a simple prototype system of our model on Linux system and provided an evaluation for security and performance. The experiment results show that the model proposed in this paper can provide effective confidentiality and integrity protection for the kernel stack without incurring a large performance overhead.

The rest of this paper is organized as follows. Section 2 describes the background; Sect. 3 presents the threat model and assumptions; Sect. 4 and Sect. 5 describe the overall design and implementations of the CryptKSP prototype; Sect. 6 evaluates the security and performance of CryptKSP respectively; Sect. 7 presents the Related Work; Sect. 8 discuss the model and Sect. 9 describes the conclusion.

2   Background

Intral-Kernel TCB. EqualVisor [23] and Nested Kernel achieve a same-privilege-level TCB or intra-kernel TCB by leveraging the WP bit in the CR0 register and binary rewriting technology. When the kernel wants to operate the page table, it can only send a request to the same-privilege-level TCB. It eliminates the corresponding privileged instructions to prevent the untrusted kernel from destroying the memory protection. It can only make requests to the same-privilege-level TCB when the kernel wants to execute these privileged instructions. It is effective and efficient to deploy and implement kernel protection mechanism to provide kernel security services in the same-privilege-level TCB.

AES-NI. In order to increase the density of the AES encryption algorithm, Intel hardware chips have introduced a dedicated instruction set (Intel AES New Instructions, AES-NI for short). The AES-NI has six instructions to provide complete hardware support for AES. The instruction set mainly includes AESENC, AESENCLAST, AESDEC, AESDELAST, AESIMC and AESKEYGENASSIST. The AES instructions can flexibly support all encryption usages of AES, including standard key lengths (e.g. 128-bit key length), standard operating modes (e.g. ECB mode), and even some non-standard or future variants. AES-NI is turned on by default, and it can only be turned off by writing 11b to MSR_FEATURE_CONFIG MSR, but this operation will be invalid after system reset (restart).

Vector Register. In order to achieve media acceleration, Intel CPU provides vector instructions, including MMX [24], SSE [16], and AVX [25]. The registers of MMX are physically identical to floating point registers and are called MM registers. The SSE registers are called XMM registers, while the AVX registers are extensions of the XMM registers and are called YMM registers. The XMM register is the low 128-bit of the YMM register. On an x86_64 Intel CPU (such as Intel Haswell CPU), there are 16 64-bit GPRs, 8 64-bit MM registers, and 16 256-bit YMM registers.

Debug Register. To achieve hardware debug function, Intel hardware provides eight debug registers DR0–DR7. DR0–DR3 can be used to store the address of the debug point. DR6 is a status register and DR7 is a control register. DR4–DR5 are the aliases of DR6–DR7, respectively. In addition, the DR registers can only be accessed by privileged instructions, so the system can prevent the application being debugged from accessing these available registers [26].

3   Threat Model and Assumption

We assume that the kernel is untrusted, and the attacker can exploit the kernel vulnerabilities to attack the kernel or introduce untrusted kernel extensions. At present, according to the existing research, the attack methods against the kernel stack can be divided into two categories. Firstly, there are a large number of arbitrary read and write vulnerabilities in the kernel, and the attacker can use these vulnerabilities to arbitrarily read and write data in the kernel stack. Secondly, since main kernel and all kernel modules share the same address space, all kernel execution units [3] can access the address space of the kernel stack, and read and write data stored in the kernel stack arbitrarily. Since some existing research works [27–29] can effectively solve the first type of attack, therefore, we mainly consider the second type of attack.

CryptKSP ensures that the entire kernel boot process is trusted through the Trusted Boot hardware technologies (Intel TXT) [30]. As a module, CryptKSP will be loaded into the system during the kernel boot process and implement the corresponding initialization operation. We assume nested kernel architecture and the encryption and decryption module in CryptKSP are trusted. Moreover, the amount of code of CryptKSP is small, and it is possible to verify its security through formal verification methods as seL4 [31] does. In addition, the hardware is assumed to be trusted, and the denial of service attack is out of scope in this paper.

4   System Design

4.1   Basic Framework of CryptKSP

Figure 1 shows the basic model of CryptKSP. The encryption module is deployed in the same-privilege-level TCB (Trusted Computing Base, or referred to as intra-kernel TCB). CryptKSP intercepts all kernel stack operations, including kernel stack allocation, kernel stack deletion and kernel stack switching. CryptKSP encrypts the kernel stack switched out and decrypt the kernel stack switched in. As far as I know, KSP is currently the main method to protect kernel stack integrity based on hypervisor. Figure 2 shows the basic framework of hypervisor-based kernel stack integrity protection approach, which introduces a higher privilege layer and maintains the shadow page table in the hypervisor. KSP protects the kernel stack by setting kernel stack read-only. The hypervisor in the KSP intercepts the all kernel stack operations, and operates the corresponding page table entries to enable or disable read-only protection for kernel stack.

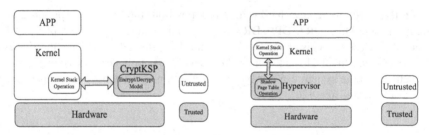

Fig. 1. CryptKSP architecture   **Fig. 2.** KSP basic architecture

Security Requirements and Challenges. Combined with the security purpose of the basic framework of CryptKSP and the security attributions of the same-privilege-level TCB described by NestedKernel, EqualVisor and other works, we will describe the basic security requirements and the challenges of CryptKSP. The security requirements are as following:

1) Security of the same-privilege-level TCB. CryptKSP should meet the three basic security attributes of the same-privilege-level TCB [22], including code and data integrity, control flow integrity and fixed entry points.
2) Interception and verification of kernel stack operation. CryptKSP should ensure that it can effectively intercept key operations of the kernel stack, as well as privileged operations in the kernel, and ensure the security of inserted hook points.
3) Cryptographic Key Protection. CryptKSP should ensure the security of the encryption module and the privacy and integrity of the cryptographic key.

When we achieve to protect the integrity and confidentiality of the kernel stack effectively and efficiently, we still need to solve the following challenges:

1) CryptKSP must make sure that the memory region of CryptKSP is isolated from the kernel. And CryptKSP must ensure that it can effectively intercept key operations of the kernel stack and.
2) CryptKSP needs to leverage the AES-NI hardware feature to build the encryption module in same-privilege-level TCB. CryptKSP should solve the problem to store the AES key and provide different cryptographic key for each thread.

The basic architecture of CryptKSP is consistent with Nested Kernel and EqualVisor, which both use the WP hardware mechanism in the CR0 register to implement the same-privilege-level TCB. Therefore, CryptKSP uses the WP hardware mechanism to build the same-privilege-level TCB in the same way, and intercepts and verifies the key operations of the kernel stack, and constructs different views for the kernel stack through the encryption module. CryptKSP uses debug register to store cryptographic key.

4.2 Interception and Verification of Kernel Stack Operation

The key operations of the kernel stack mainly include the kernel stack allocation, kernel stack deletion and the kernel stack switching. The kernel allocates a unique kernel stack to each thread, and maintains a one-to-one correspondence between threads and kernel stacks.

The structure of the kernel stack is shown in Fig. 3, which is a *union* data structure, including a *thread_info* and a 16 KB or 8 KB memory area.The default kernel stack size in x86 system is 8 KB (two page frames), and 16 KB for x86_64 systems. In our experiment, we use the x86_64 architectures, since the default kernel stack size is 16 KB in the rest of the paper. The bottom part of the stack is the *thread_info* data structure, while the top of the stack is area used to store the return address and local variables. The system allocates a data structure *task_struct* for each thread, and the *stack* field in the *task_struct* data structure points to the data structure *thread_info*.

CryptKSP can intercept key events in the kernel through Secure Gate [32]. To intercept the sensitive operations of the kernel stack, CryptKSP inserts appropriate hooks in the kernel. Once the hooks are triggered, the control flow is transferred to the CryptKSP. Then, CryptKSP can encrypt or decrypt part of the memory area where the kernel stack is located. At the same time, CryptKSP maintains two linked lists, one is used to maintain the base address pointer of the kernel stack (the address of the *thread_info* structure, hereafter named kernel stack address), the current macro shown in Fig. 3 can be used to obtain the kernel stack address. The other is used to maintain the stack pointer of the corresponding kernel stack (as the *rsp* in *thread_structure,* hereafter named kernel stack pointer). CryptKSP sets read-only protection for the above two linked lists. Next, this paper will detail the interception and verification of key operations of the kernel stack in CryptKSP.

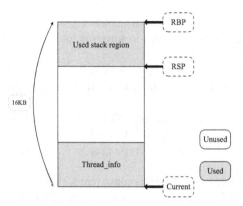

Fig. 3. Kernel stack framework

Kernel Stack Creation. During process creation, the system allocates a kernel stack for each thread, and initializes the *thread_info and task_struct* structure, which are mutually linked by means of the fields *task* and *stack*, respectively. Therefore, CryptKSP inserts the appropriate hooks in the function *dup_task_-struct*. The control flow will transfer to the CryptKSP after the thread has been created and initialized. At this time, the top of the stack does not load any execution information for the kernel. Therefore, CryptKSP only encrypts the memory area of bottom of the kernel stack, and constructs an encrypted view of the kernel stack. After the newly created kernel stack is initialized, the *thread_info* data structure at the bottom of the stack contains sensitive information such as the address of the thread's *task_struct* structure. Then CryptKSP update the newly created kernel stack address in the linked list of kernel stack addresses and kernel stack pointer in the linked list of kernel stack pointers.

Kernel Stack Deletion. When a thread exits, the kernel releases all the resources it occupies, including the memory resources occupied by the kernel stack. CryptKSP intercepts the kernel stack deletion operation, but does not need to decrypt the memory area of kernel stack. At this time, the data in the memory region of the kernel stack is in the state of ciphertext, and it will not affect the management and utilization of the physical memory page. Of course,there is also a way to clear the memory area of the kernel stack before the kernel stack is released. In addition, CryptKSP will delete the released kernel stack from the two linked lists of the kernel stack address and the kernel stack pointer.

Kernel Stack Switching. During thread switch, the scheduler will select a thread being activated and a thread being replaced. Again, prev thread is referred to as the thread being replaced and the next thread is referred to as the thread being activated.

When performing the thread switch, the scheduler needs to switch the kernel stack and the hardware context, which concludes all the information needed by the new thread being running on CPU. Even after switching the kernel stack, the scheduler still restores some more information for the thread being replaced. Therefore, CryptKSP inserts the hooks in the function *context_switch*. CryptKSP can decrypt the kernel stack of a thread being activated before reloading the kernel stack pointer into the *rsp* register. Before performing the decryption operation, CryptKSP will verify whether the value of rsp field in the *task_struct* structure of the next thread is legal.

CryptKSP encrypts the kernel stack being replaced at the end of the function *context_switch*. This means that there is a small attack surface during thread context switching, because the kernel stacks of two threads in the kernel are in the state of plaintext. The kernel execution unit that performs the context switch may be exploited by the compromised kernel to attack the kernel stack of the next thread. In order to eliminate the security threat here, CryptKSP ensures that the execution of the thread context switch is atomic. Firstly, CryptKSP applies the W $\oplus$ X mechanism to protect the integrity of kernel code. Secondly, CryptKSP ensures that the thread switch cannot be interrupted through the shadow IDT technology used by EqualVisor and NestedKernel.

Integrity Protection for Kernel Stack Pointer. An attacker can modify the kernel stack pointer maintained by the kernel and forge a kernel stack for a thread. To defend against such attacks, CryptKSP maintains a copy of the kernel stack pointer for each thread in the kernel stack pointer linked list. When the kernel performs the thread switch, CryptKSP can intercept the kernel stack switch and immediately check its legality. That is to say, CryptKSP can check that whether the stack pointer of the thread being activated is equal to the copy of kernel stack pointer maintained by the CryptKSP. If it is not equal, it means the stack pointer of the thread being activated has been tampered by the attacker. Therefore, CryptKSP stops thread switching and reports a serious warning. On the contrary, CryptKSP then decrypt the kernel stack of next thread and encrypt the kernel stack of prev thread. Afterwards, CryptKSP can update the kernel stack pointer linked list maintained in the CryptKSP for the next thread and prev thread.

Anti-bypass Interception for Kernel Stack Operation. CryptKSP applies the W $\oplus$ X mechanism to protect the integrity of the kernel code, then the hooks inserted into the kernel code cannot be destroyed. In addition, AES algorithm is public encryption algorithm, therefore, the secret key is most important for the system. CryptKSP is the only module which maintains the secret key in the kernel. Then, the kernel must send the encryption or decryption request to the CryptKSP when the kernel wants to select a sleeping thread to run. CryptKSP protects the secret key from damaging or disclosing. Then the attacker could not directly access the kernel stack protected by CryptKSP.

4.3 AES for Kernel Stack

CryptKSP uses the AES-NI hardware mechanism to implement the AES encryption algorithm instead of software, which can effectively improve the performance of the encryption algorithm. Since the data in the kernel are all shaped data, there may be frequent occurrences of shaped data with certain characteristics, such as zero. Therefore, in order to meet the security requirements in different scenarios, CryptKSP configures different cryptographic keys for each kernel stack. In addition, CryptKSP implements two AES algorithms with different key lengths, AES-128 and AES-256, in CBC mode. CryptKSP-128 means CryptKSP using AES-128 algorithm, and CryptKSP-256 means CryptKSP using AES-256 algorithm.

The key part of the encryption module in CryptKSP is cryptographic key generation, storage and protection.

Cryptographic Key Storage and Creation. CryptKSP adopts a similar method in PT_Rand [33], using the debug register to store critical information. CryptKSP only uses the DR2 and DR3 to store cryptographic key for AES. The debug registers are all 64 bits in the x86_64 architectures, and the values stored in the DR2 and DR3 registers can construct a 128-bit key for the AES-128 algorithm. Then, CryptKSP does not occupy all the registers, and the unoccupied DR0 and DR1 registers can still be used to support the hardware debugging function.

CryptKSP maintains two secret keys for each kernel stack, one is basic secret key and another is seed secret key. The basic secret key is only stored in debug registers and seed secret key is really used in AES algorithm. The seed secret key is generated by using the basic secret key and kernel stack address. CryptKSP can configure a different seed secret key for each kernel stack. CryptKSP uses the thread's kernel stack address (the address of *thread_info* structure) and the value stored in the DR2 and DR3 register to calculate the seed secret key for each thread. Because the address of kernel stack of each process is unique, CryptKSP can create a different seed secret key for each kernel stack. And the research shows that even if one bit of the secret key is different, about 50% of the bits in the ciphertext will change without changing the plaintext.

Although we can configure different seed secret key used in AES-128 for each kernel stack, the differences between the different seed secret keys are small. To increase the obfuscate of the seed secret key, we use the SHA-256 cryptographic hash algorithm to produce an output of fixed length, which is used as AES-256 key. The lengthen of output of SHA-256 is 256 bits. In order to calculate the 256-bit seed secret key quickly, CryptKSP-256 uses the kernel stack base address and value stored in DR3 register (referred to as DR3_value) to construct a 512-bit basic block, which is used as the input of SHA-256.CryptKSP first uses the kernel stack base address and DR3_value to construct the upper 384-bit data of the block, and the last 64 bits of the basic packet are used to store the initial length of the message. In Sect. 5.2, we detail how to construct the basic block by using the DR3_value and kernel stack address.

In order to improve the security of the AES algorithm, CryptKSP uses the YMM register to store the round keys. Then, it not only improves the performance of encryption, but also avoids exposing the secret key directly to memory. And after encryption or decryption operations have been finished, CryptKSP directly clears the YMM register that stores the round key.

XMM and other registers are directly used for encryption and decryption function in the kernel, which may result in affecting the normal running of applications that need to use these registers, CryptKSP uses the *kernel_fpu_end* and *kernel_fpu_begin* functions in the kernel to save and restore FPU hardware context.

Protection for Secret Key. Although storing the secret key in the debug register can effectively avoid exposing the secret key to the memory, the untrusted kernel can steal and modify the secret key stored in debug register through MOV-FROM/TO-DR0-DR7 instruction. In order to ensure the integrity and confidentiality of the basic cryptographic key stored in the debug register, we eliminate the MOV-FROM/TO-DR0-DR7 instructions in the kernel and only maintains MOV-FROM/TO-DR0-DR7 in the CryptKSP. Therefore, when the kernel wants to access the DR register, it must send the corresponding request to the CryptKSP. Then, CryptKSP can verify all the request and decide whether the request is legal. If the request is to access the DR register used to store the basic secret key, CryptKSP considers the request is illegal and does nothing. Thence, the attacker could not damage or disclose the critical information stored the DR registers.

The variables and memory areas that are used to store secret keys temporarily are cleared after the encryption or decryption has been finished. Meanwhile, such memory areas are set as non-cacheable.

Encryption/Decryption for Kernel Stack. In the x86_64 systems, the default size of the kernel stack is 16 KB. As shown in Fig. 3, only the *thread_info* data structure at the bottom of the kernel stack and the memory areas pointed to by rsp register at the top of the kernel stack are used. In most cases, there are large memory areas in the middle of the kernel stack are not used. To improve system performance, CryptKSP just only encrypts the *thread_info* data structure and the memory region pointed by the rsp register at the top of the kernel stack. The length of packet in AES algorithm is 16 bytes, however, the length of the *thread_info* structure is not aligned on a 16-byte.

Therefore, CryptKSP makes sure that the memory areas of *thread_info* data structure is aligned on a 16-byte when encrypting the *thread_info* data structure. Then, CryptKSP verifies the size of the memory area used at the top of the kernel stack. There is no need to encrypt or decrypt the memory area at the top of the kernel stack when the size of the memory area used at the top of the stack is 0. The *push* or *pop* operation of the kernel stack is aligned on an 8-byte, the address of memory areas at the top of the kernel stack should be moved forward 8 bytes from the current address when the size of the memory area used at the top of the stack is aligned on a 16-byte. The size of the memory area also needs to be increased by 8 bytes. It avoids that the encrypted memory areas go beyond scope of the kernel stack.

5 Implementation

5.1 Loading and Initialization of CryptKSP

To ensure the boot process of the kernel is trusted, trusted boot technology of Intel hardware [30] is used in the kernel boot process. CryptKSP is initialized during the kernel boot process. Therefore, the initialization process of CryptKSP is also trusted.

CryptKSP initializes the hardware context of the entire system, and the address space of the entire kernel page table. At the same time, CryptKSP will initialize the settings of shadow IDT and IOMMU, as well as the corresponding registers (including CR0, CR4, IA32_EFER, IA32_FMASK, IA32_FEATURE_CONFIG, IDTR and other registers). Then, CryptKSP implements the initialization work related to page table protection, deploys the $W \oplus X$ protection mechanism in the system, and starts to intercept and verify the page table update operation through the para-virtualized interface, and realizes the same-prvilege-level TCB with the kernel. The privileged instructions that need to be eliminated in the kernel are described in Table 1.

Table 1. Privileged instructions that require interception and verification.

Privileged instructions to be eliminated	Privileged instructions Opcodes
MOV_TO_CR0	0x 0f 22/1
MOV_TO_CR3	0x 0f 22/3
MOV_TO_CR4	0x 0f 22/4
lidt	0x 0f 01/3
lgdt	0x 0f 01/2
wrmsr	0x 0f 30
MOV_TO_DR0-DR7	0x 0f 21/r
MOV_FROM_DR0-DR7	0x 0f 23/r

5.2 Implementation of Encryption and Decryption Based on AES-NI

CryptKSP uses the AES-NI hardware mechanism to implement AES encryption algorithms with different cryptographic key lengths, such as 128-bit and 256-bit, which are called CryptKSP-128 and CryptKSP-256 respectively. We implement the encryption module in CryptKSP based on the source code provided by MemSentry [34]. However, MemSentry just realizes the AES-128 for the applications. In this article, we migrate it to the kernel layer. In addition, we extend it to AES-256 and apply it to CryptKSP-256. As MemSentry, both CryptKSP-128 and CryptKSP-256 use YMM registers to store the round keys, which not only improves the performance of encryption, but also does not expose the round keys to memory.

We prepare two secret keys in CryptKSP, one is basic secret key stored in debug register, and another is seed secret key which is really used in the AES algorithm. The seed secret key is calculated from the valued in debug register and the corresponding kernel stack address.

CryptKSP-128 performs a bit wise operation on the basic secret key stored in the DR3 register and the corresponding kernel stack address to ensure that each kernel stack has a different seed secret key. However, at the same time, the lower 14-bit of the basic secret key is retained. "|" means bitwise OR operation, "&" means bitwise AND operation, "$<\,<$" means bitwise left shift operation.

The pseudo calculation formula of the calculation is as follows:

$$High\_seed\_key = (DR3\_value\ \&\ 0x3fff) \mid (DR3\_value\ \&\ task\_struct-\,>\ stack)$$

$$(1)$$

The seed secret key consists of upper 64-bit High_seed_key and lower 64-bit Low_seed_key. The *task_struct- > stack* is the kernel stack address and the address of *thread_info* data structure.

In order to avoid the situation that two kernel stacks have the same seed secret key, CryptKSP sets all bit-15 to bit-42 of the DR3_value to 1. Therefore, the bit-15 to bit-42 of the High_seed_key value is determined by the value of the stack pointer in the *task_struct* data structure. The core difference of the kernel stack address of each thread is bit-15 to bit-42.

The secret key in CryptKSP-256 is calculated by hash function. The core of the calculation is to hash the basic secret key stored in the DR3 register and the kernel stack address. The pseudo calculation formula of the calculation is as follows:

$$Seed\_Key = SHA256((task\_struct-> stack << 448) \mid (DR3\_value << 384) \mid$$

$$(task\_struct-> stack << 320) \mid (DR3\_value << 256) \mid (DR3\_value << 192)$$

$$\mid (DR3\_value << 128) \mid (1 << 64) \mid (value\_length))$$

(2)

Among them, DR3_value is the basic secret key stored in the DR3 register, and task_struct-> stack is the kernel stack address allocated by the kernel for each thread. The value_length is length of the original message. Seed_Key is 256-bit data. Task_struct-> stack, DR3_value and value_length are all 64-bit data.

5.3 Interception and Verification of the Kernel Stack Operation

CryptKSP draws on the Secure Gate designed in SIM [32] and Nested Kernel, and inserts appropriate Secure Gate in the process of kernel stack creation, kernel deletion and kernel stack switching in the kernel.

CryptKSP maintain the copy of kernel stack address and current stack pointer for each kernel stack. CryptKSP will verify the legality of the kernel stack address and kernel stack pointer when intercept the kernel stack operations. Meanwhile, the IST mechanism is turned off during the system implementation to ensure that all interrupts use the same kernel stack.

6 Experimental Evaluation and Analysis

We will analyze the kernel stack model CryptKSP from two aspects: security and performance. The hardware environment used in this experiment is Intel Core i7-9700, 3.00 GHz, memory 8 GB DDR3, 1TB SATA hard disk. The operating system in the experiment is Ubuntu14.04 64-bit LTS, the kernel version is Linux 4.2.1, and the gcc version is 7.4.0.

6.1 Security Evaluation

1) Secret Key Security

In CryptKSP, the cryptographic key consists of two parts, one is the basic secret key stored in the DR3 register, and the other is the seed secret key actually used in the AES encryption algorithm. The relationship between the basic secret key and the seed secret key in CryptKSP-128 and CryptKSP-256 is described in detail in Sect. 5.3. The seed secret key in CryptKSP must be calculated by combining the basic secret key and kernel stack address.

CryptKSP eliminates all MOV-FROM/TO-DR0-DR7 instructions in the kernel by making use of the same method in Nested Kernel and EqualVisor, and only CryptKSP has corresponding instructions. When the kernel wants to access the DR register, it must send the request to the CryptKSP. Therefore, the untrusted kernel cannot tamper with the basic secret key to destroy the encryption module in CryptKSP, nor can steal the basic secret key maintained by CryptKSP through the MOV-FROM-DR0-DR7 privileged instruction. Since the kernel stack address of the thread stored in the process data structure *task_struct* is visible to the kernel, once the basic secret key is leaked, the attacker may deduce the seed secret key of thread. However, the attacker could not obtain the basic secret key protected by CryptKSP,so it is very difficult to deduce the seed secret key of the thread..

2)   Security Analysis of Protecting the Kernel Stack

Confidentiality. When a thread is in a sleeping state, its corresponding kernel stack is in ciphertext state. The attacker can read any data in the kernel stack of any other threads, but the contents are all ciphertext, so the attacker cannot steal any effective information. When the thread is scheduled, CryptKSP will verify the validity of kernel stack address and kernel stack pointer of the thread. Then, CryptKSP decrypted the kernel stack and load the kernel stack pointer stored in *task_struct* structure into rsp register when the verification is passed. As described in the Sect. 3, there are various techniques to protect the integrity of the kernel stack of the currently running process at this time, therefore, it is orthogonal to this paper.

Integrity. The attacker may try to modify the ciphertext information in the other kernel stacks. When the sleeping thread is scheduled to be executed, the data in the kernel stack may be invalid after decryption, which will eventually lead to a failure or error when the system is running. CryptKSP maintains the kernel stack address and kernel stack pointer of all threads and verifies its legality during the interception of kernel stack operations. Meanwhile, CryptKSP updates the maintained kernel stack address and kernel stack pointer synchronously. It can effectively prevent attackers from destroying the integrity of the kernel stack address and kernel stack pointer.

6.2   Performance Evaluation

To evaluate the performance overhead of CryptKSP. We have implemented three kinds of kernel stack protection model. Based on the basic idea of Nested Kernel and some implementation technologies in EqualVisor [23], we realize a simple model Nested-KSP, which protects the integrity of kernel stack by sets read-only protection for the kernel stack at the same-privilege-level TCB. We have implemented two kinds of AES encryption algorithm in CryptKSP, one is 128-bit cryptographic key for AES (referred to as AES-128) and another is 256-bit cryptographic key for AES (referred to as AES-256). The one using AES-128 in CryptKSP is called CryptKSP-128 and another using AES-256 in CryptKSP is called CryptKSP-256.

From the following two aspects, we will discuss the impact on performance. To measure the overhead different kernel operations, we adopt lmbench benchmarking suite [35] (v.3.0-a9). Table 2 shows the average experimental results based on three identical

Table 2. Latency on process-related kernel operation (in µs, smaller is better).

Benchmarks	Native	NestedKSP	CryptKSP-128	CryptKSP-256	NestedKSP slowdown	CryptKSP-128 slowdown	CryptKSP-256 slowdown
Null call	0.05	0.05	0.05	0.05	0.0%	0.0%	0.0%
Null I/O	0.12	0.12	0.12	0.12	0.0%	0.0%	0.0%
Stat	0.37	0.37	0.37	0.38	0.0%	0.0%	2.7%
Open/close	0.80	0.81	0.80	0.80	1.3%	0.0%	0.0%
Sig inst	0.13	0.14	0.14	0.14	7.7%	7.7%	7.7%
Sig hndl	0.80	0.84	0.83	0.83	5.0%	3.7%	3.7%
Fork+exit	68.63	155.90	155.57	159.23	127.2%	126.7%	132.0%
Fork+exec	228.00	415.70	414.93	420.53	82.3%	82.0%	84.4%
Fork+/bin/sh	546.40	906.00	904.77	916.27	65.8%	65.6%	67.7%
Protection fault	0.379	0.547	0.547	0.545	44.3%	44.3%	43.8%
Page fault	0.0330	0.1273	0.1278	0.1273	285.8%	287.3%	285.8%

runs. The overhead for foremost microbencmarks are basically the same. That is to say, CryptKSP cannot introduce high performance lost for foremost test cases.

Table 3 shows the corresponding communication bandwidth, the results presents the communication bandwidth of Native Kernel, NestedKSP, CryptKSP-128 and CryptKSP-256. For most benchmark, the results of CryptKSP-128 and CryptKSP-256 is close to that of NestedKSP. However, for CryptKSP the results of the benchmark Pipe, AF Unix and TCP are smaller than that of NestedKSP. What's more, the CryptKSP-128 is closer to the native kernel than the CryptKSP-256.

Table 3. Local-communication bandwidths (in MB/s, bigger is better)

Benchmarks	Native	NestedKSP	CryptKSP-128	CryptKSP-256	NestedKSP Ratio	CryptKSP-128 Ratio	CryptKSP-256 Ratio
Pipe	6681.67	5058.33	4169	3035.33	75.7%	62.4%	45.4%
AF UNIX	7983.67	7046.33	6268.67	5238.33	88.3%	78.5%	65.6%
TCP	6820	6301.33	5826.33	5199.33	92.4%	85.4%	76.2%
File reread	7818.63	7722.27	7796.73	7804.87	98.8%	99.7%	99.8%
Mmap	13.7K	13.7K	13.7K	13.7K	100.0%	100.0%	100.0%
Bcopy(libc)	8025.8	7934.20	7925.03	7951.87	98.9%	98.7%	99.1%
Bcopy(hand)	5786.67	5762.43	5765.30	5741.83	99.6%	99.6%	99.2%
Mem read	12K	12K	12K	12K	100.0%	100.0%	100.0%
Mem write	8022	8002.67	7976	7996.67	99.8%	99.4%	99.7%

7 Related Work

Hypervisor. OSck [6] protects the data in the kernel stack, but only part of the data is protected. KSP [3] uses virtualization and shadow page tables to set the entire kernel stack read-only. However, the read-only protection mechanism cannot effectively protect privacy of key information in the kernel stack. The attacker can still access relevant information. In addition, there is a conflict between the size of the stack and the granularity of the pages in the direct mapping area, which increases the overhead of memory access and consumes more memory resources. CryptKSP can not only protect the confidentiality and integrity of the entire kernel stack, but also does not rely on operating page tables to protect the kernel stack, so there is no memory granularity conflict.

Hardware Virtualization. ShadowMonitor [14] and xMP [15] utilize EPT to create memory isolation and data protection, which can also be applied to protect the kernel stack. However, they all rely on hardware virtualization support and need to trap into root mode when intercepting kernel stack operations, because the underlying EPT cannot be manipulated in non-root mode. The AES-NI hardware features is a widely supported hardware feature. It is also a typical method to use the WP bit in the CR0 register to construct the same-privilege-level TCB.

Encryption. CCFI [13] also uses AES-NI to encrypt the return address in the stack, which can also be applied to the return address in the kernel stack. However, it relies on modifying the compiler, which will result in higher overhead. CryptKSP do not need to modify the compiler.

8 Discussion

The SHA algorithm in CryptKSP is implemented by software. We will explore to realize the SHA-256 hash function with the help of the SHA-NI hardware feature to improve the performance. We just only consider the security of the kernel stack, but there is also a lot of kernel state information in the interrupt stack. Then, it is valuable for us to continue to discuss the protection for the interrupt stack in the future research.

9 Conclusion

In this paper, we propose a kernel stack integrity and confidentiality protection model using the AES-NI hardware feature at the same hardware privilege level with the kernel and have implemented the prototype system CryptKSP. Compared with other related kernel stack protection schemes, CryptKSP does not rely on higher privilege layer and effectively eliminates the performance lost caused by cross-privilege layer switching. Moreover, it has obtained better security for the kernel stack.

Acknowledgments. This work has been partly supported by National NSF of China under Grant No. 61772266, 61431008.

References

1. Love, R.: Linux Kernel Development. Pearson Educaiton, London (2010)
2. Bovet, D.P., Cesati, M.: Understanding the Linux Kernel: From I/O Ports to Process Management. O'Reilly Media Inc., Newton (2005)
3. Liu, W., Luo, S., Liu, Y., et al.: A kernel stack protection model against attacks from kernel execution units. Comput. Secur. **72**, 96–106 (2018)
4. KOH: Kernel object hooking rootkits (koh rootkits), March 2016. http://www.rootkit.com/newsread.ph-p?newsid=501
5. Butler, J., Hoglund, G.: Vice - catch the hookers! in Black Hat USA 2004 (2004)
6. Hofmann, O.S., Dunn, A.M., Kim, S., Roy, I., Witchel, E.: Ensuring operating system kernel integrity with OSck. In: 16th International Conference on Architectural Support for Programming Languages and Operating Systems (2011)
7. Criswell, J., Dautenhahn, N., Adve, V.: KCoFI: complete control-flow integrity for commodity operating system kernels. In: IEEE Symposium on Security and Privacy, pp. 292–307. IEEE (2014)
8. Ge, X., Talele, N., Payer, M., et al.: Fine-grained control-flow integrity for kernel software. In: IEEE European Symposium on Security and Privacy (EuroS&P), pp. 179–194. IEEE (2016)
9. Zhou, J., Du, Y., Shen, Z., Ma, L., Criswell, J., Walls, R.J.: Silhouette: efficient protected shadow stacks for embedded systems. In: USENIX Security Symposium 2020, pp. 1219–1236 (2020)
10. Popek, G.J., Kampe, M., Kline, C.S., Stoughton, A., Urban, M., Walton, E.J.: UCLA secure Unix. In: Proceedings of the AFIPS National Computer Conference, vol. 48, pp. 355–364 (1979)
11. Pozzo, M.M., Gray, T.E.: An approach to containing computer viruses. Comput. Secur. **6**(4), 321–331 (1987)
12. Davida, G.L., Desmedt, Y., Matt, B.J.: Defending systems against viruses through cryptographic authentication. In: IEEE Symposium on Security and Privacy, pp. 312–318 (1989)
13. Mashtizadeh, A.J., Bittau, A., Boneh, D., Mazières, D.: CCFI: Cryptographically enforced control flow integrity. In: CCS. ACM(2015)
14. Shi, B., Cui, L., Li, B., Liu, X.D., Hao, Z.Y., Shen, H.Y.: ShadowMonitor: an effective in-VM monitoring framework with hardware- enforced isolation. In: Bailey, M., Holz, T., Stamatogiannakis, M., Ioannidis, S. (eds.) Research in Attacks, Intrusions, and Defenses, vol. 11050, pp. 670–690. Springer, Berlin (2018). https://doi.org/10.1007/978-3-030-00470-5_31
15. Proskurin, S., Momeu, M., Ghavamnia, S., Kemerlis, V.P., Polychronakis, M.: xMP: selective memory protection for kernel and user space. In: Proceedings of the IEEE Symposium on Security and Privacy (S&P), pp. 233–247. IEEE (2020)
16. Intel Corporation. Intel 64 and IA-32 Architectures Software Developer's Manual. Intel Corporation (2019)
17. Lee, S., Kang, H., Jang, J., Kang, B.B.: SaVioR: thwarting stack-based memory safety violations by randomizing stack lay out. IEEE Trans. Dependable Secur. Comput. (2021)
18. Barham, P., et al.: Xen and the art of virtualization. In: Proceedings of the 19th ACM Symposium on Operating System Principles (SOSP), pp. 164–167. ACM (2003)
19. Kivity, A., Kamay, Y., Laor, D., Lublin, U., Liguori, A.: KVM: the Linux virtual machine monitor. In: Proceedings of the Linux Symposium, OLS, Ottawa, pp. 225–230 (2007)
20. Gueron, S.: Intel Advanced Encryption Standard (AES) New Instructions Set. Number 323641-001. Intel Corporation, May 2010

21. Dautenhahn, N., Kasampalis, T., Dietz, W., et al.: Nested kernel: an operating system architecture for intra-kernel privilege separation. In: Proceedings of the 20th International Conference on Architectural Support for Programming Languages and Operating Systems (ASPLOS). ACM (2015)
22. Deng, L.: Study on System Security Techniques in an Untrusted Kernel Environment Ph.D. Thesis. Nanjing University, Nanjing (2018). (in Chinese with English abstract)
23. Deng, L., Zeng, Q.K., Wang, W.G., Liu, Y.: EqualVisor: providing memory protection in an untrusted commodity hypervisor. In: Proceedings of the 13th IEEE International Conference on Trust, Security and Privacy in Computing and Communications (TrustCom), pp. 300–309. IEEE (2014)
24. DuLong, C., Gutman, M., Julier, M., et al.: Complete Guide to MMX Technology. McGraw-Hill Professional, New York (1997)
25. Lomont, C.: Introduction to Intel advanced vector extensions. Intel White Paper (2011)
26. Müller, T., Freiling, F.C., Dewald, A.: TRESOR runs encryption securely outside RAM. In: Proceedings of 20th USENIX Security Symposium (2011)
27. Li, J., Wang, Z., Jiang, X., Grace, M., Bahram, S.: Defeating return-oriented rootkits with "return-less" kernels. In: EuroSys, pp. 195–208 (2010)
28. Onarlioglu, K., Bilge, L., Lanzi, A., Balzarotti, D., Kirda, E.: G-free: defeating return-oriented programming through gadget-less binaries. In: ACSAC, pp. 49–58 (2010)
29. Wartell, R., Mohan, V., Hamlen, K.W., Lin, Z.: Binary stirring: selfrandomizing instruction addresses of legacy x86 binary code. In: CCS, pp. 157–168 (2012)
30. Intel. Intel Trusted Execution Technology Preliminary Architecture Specification (2006)
31. Klein, G., et al.: seL4: formal verification of an OS kernel. In: Proceedings of the 22nd ACM Symposium on Operating Systems Principles, pp. 207–220. ACM (2009)
32. Sharif, M.I., Lee, W., Cui, W., Lanzi, A.: Secure in-VM monitoring using hardware virtualization. In: 16th ACM Conference on Computer and Communications Security (CCS), pp. 477–487. ACM (2009)
33. Davi, L., Gens, D., Liebchen, C., Sadeghi, A.R.: PT-Rand: practical mitigation of data-only attacks against page tables. In. Proceedings of 24th Annual Network and Distributed System Security Symposium, NDSS 2017 (2017)
34. Koning, K., Chen, X., Bos, H., Giuffrida, C., Athanasopoulos, E.: No need to hide: protecting safe regions on commodity hardware. In: Proceedings of the 12th European Conf. on Computer Systems (EuroSys), pp. 437–452. ACM (2017)
35. McVoy, L., Staelin, C.: lmbench: portable tools for performance analysis. In: Proceedings of USENIX Annual Technical Conference (1996)

Usable Security

Usability Insights from Establishing TLS Connections

Lydia Kraus[1], Matěj Grabovský[2], Martin Ukrop[2], Katarína Galanská[2], and Vashek Matyáš[2(✉)]

[1] Institute of Computer Science, Masaryk University, Brno, Czechia
`lydia.kraus@mail.muni.cz`
[2] Centre for Research on Cryptography and Security, Masaryk University, Brno, Czechia
{`mgrabovsky,mukrop,galanska`}`@mail.muni.cz`, `matyas@fi.muni.cz`

Abstract. TLS is crucial to network security, but TLS-related APIs have been repeatedly shown to be misused. While existing usable security research focuses on cryptographic primitives, the specifics of TLS interfaces seem to be under-researched. We thus set out to investigate the usability of TLS-related APIs in multiple libraries with a focus on identifying the specifics of TLS. We conducted a three-fold exploratory study with altogether 60 graduate students comparing the APIs of three popular security libraries in establishing TLS connections: OpenSSL, GnuTLS, and mbed TLS. We qualitatively analyzed submitted reports commenting on API usability and tested created source code. User satisfaction emerged as an interesting, potentially under-researched theme as all APIs received both positive and negative reviews. Abstraction level, error handling, entity naming, and documentation emerged as the most salient usability themes. Regarding functionality, checking for revoked certificates was especially complicated and other basic security checks seemed not easy as well. In summary, although there were conflicting opinions on both the interface and documentation of the libraries, several usability issues were shared among participants, forming a target for closer inspection and subsequent improvement.

Keywords: API usability · TLS · User satisfaction · Usable security

1 Introduction

While the reliance on TLS for secure communications keeps growing [14], it has been repeatedly shown that real-world applications often contain vulnerabilities due to the misuse of TLS libraries [9,10,12,20]. Moreover, it has been demonstrated that current security and cryptographic interfaces are hard to use [1,11,17,23] and that writing code that is both secure and functional is difficult even for professional developers [4,12,19]. It is thus clear that the usability of security APIs is paramount in helping programmers develop secure applications.

© IFIP International Federation for Information Processing 2022
Published by Springer Nature Switzerland AG 2022
W. Meng et al. (Eds.): SEC 2022, IFIP AICT 648, pp. 289–305, 2022.
https://doi.org/10.1007/978-3-031-06975-8_17

The primary means of studying usability is conducting controlled experiments with the intended end users [27], i.e., application developers in our case of security interfaces. However, since recruiting IT professionals is labourious [3,4,8], we have chosen to perform our study with graduate students, that is, future professional developers. Recent research in usable security shows this subpopulation to be adequate for exploratory studies [2,4,24,25,31].

Although experimental developer studies in usable security tend to aim broadly at cryptographic libraries, few have, to our knowledge, focused specifically on TLS programming interfaces. We have decided to explore this important area using qualitative methods, which seem attractive in this respect, given their potential to generate interesting hypotheses from comparatively small samples. Moreover, the benefits of qualitative research for usable security have been recognized in several recent studies [16–19,24,25].

Our paper describes the design and results of an exploratory study, conducted in three rounds and investigating the usability of TLS-related APIs, specifically of three popular libraries: OpenSSL, GnuTLS, and mbed TLS.

2   Methodology

To investigate the usability of TLS interfaces, we conducted a programming experiment with IT security students, asking participants to establish a TLS connection using the OpenSSL, GnuTLS, and mbed TLS libraries. We designed the study in an open manner with no preset hypotheses in an attempt to capture the potentially unique and disparate issues arising from using TLS-related APIs. Due to the qualitative nature of the study and the so far little researched phenomenon of TLS API usability, we iteratively analyzed the data and increased our sample size until the data reached saturation.

2.1   Setting and Participants

The study was conducted at the Faculty of Informatics at Masaryk University within a small master-level course called *Secure Coding Principles and Practices*. The study ran in three subsequent runs of the course (autumn 2018/autumn 2019/spring 2021[1]). The course aims to explain typical security issues related to secure coding and help students design applications in a more secure way. Students enrolling in the course are required to have at least a basic knowledge in applied cryptography, IT security, and programming in C or C++. The course is compulsory for the master specialization of *Information Security*.

The experimental task was set as a homework in the week discussing usability of security APIs. The students were told that the submitted data will be anonymized and analyzed within local usable security research. Sharing their data (anonymously) for research purposes was advertised as optional (and not

---

[1] Note that the course was moved to spring in the academic year 2020/21 and did thus not run in autumn 2020.

influencing the grading in any way). If they chose to opt out, we would exclude their data after grading the homework. The instructor made sure to explain in the class what data will be used, how it will be used, and that opting out of the research will not have any consequences for this or any other course taken at the faculty. The instructor also explained that no one else except him would know who opted out and that the data processing will be done solely on anonymized data. There was no compensation for joining the research. The study was part of a project on TLS usability that received approval from the institutional ethics board.

The particular seminar on the usability of security APIs contained a short lecture-style introduction to usable security for both end-users and IT professionals (cca 60 min). It included multiple examples of (un)usability issues including TLS in non-browser software [12], deploying HTTPS on Apache servers [19] and ideas on developer-resistant cryptography [7]. This was followed by an in-lecture activity: In teams of 2–3, students were asked to design an intentionally *unusable* C-like API for encryption/decryption routines (to actively engage in the usability issues of APIs).

Altogether, there were 60 students participating in the study. In 2018, there were 13 students enrolled in the course. Nine completed the homework within the assigned week. Two of them were exchange students. In 2019, there were 32 students enrolled in the course. 26 completed the homework within the assigned week. Nine of them were exchange students. In 2021, there were 33 students enrolled in the course. 25 of them completed the homework within the assigned week. None of them was an exchange student. The 2021 sample was security-wise the most experienced one, with 18 out of 25 (72%) participants who had taken a related course which also handles OpenSSL – the *Laboratory of security and applied cryptography* – previously or in parallel, while this applied to 15 of 26 participants (57.7%) in 2019 and five out of nine participants (55.6%) in 2018. In all three years, none of the students who submitted the homework opted out of the research.

2.2   Experimental Task

In all three rounds of the experiment, the core of the task was to implement a simple TLS client in C using three different TLS libraries, in no predefined order: OpenSSL (v1.1.1 or above), GnuTLS (v3.5.6 or similar), and mbed TLS (v2.16.0 or similar). Apart from the implementation, we asked for a short written report comparing the differences of the APIs from the point of usability and usable security. Code skeletons with library initialization calls and working Makefiles were provided for each library to speed up the development.

We chose OpenSSL [28] as it is one of the most popular cryptographic libraries for generating keys and certificates [26]. GnuTLS [13], also quite widely used, was preferred to other alternatives since we cooperate with the maintainer and thus have a higher chance of incorporating improvements based on this research upstream. Lastly, mbed TLS [22] (formerly PolarSSL) was chosen as its API seems rather different from both OpenSSL and GnuTLS. All three libraries have a rather low-level TLS interface, especially in comparison with TLS libraries in higher-level languages such as Python[2], Java[3], Go[4], Javascript[5], or Rust[6].

The full task specification was to establish a TLS connection with the server www.example.com, check its certificate, enforce the minimal version of TLS 1.2 and gracefully close the connection. The certificate check was required to include at least the expiration date, server hostname match, the validity of the chain, and the revocation status (either by CRL or OCSP) using the default OS certificate store as the trust anchor. The participants were advised to use BadSSL [5] for debugging the implementation.

The report, conceived as a free-form written reflection to be submitted as a separate PDF file, was required to be at least one page long and contain five to ten specific points comparing the used libraries. We refrained from using existing scales for usability evaluation due to the exploratory nature of the study. Instead, participants were given a set of inspirational questions to illustrate the kind of reflection we sought. These were selected from an existing usability questionnaire for security APIs [32] based on their relevance to the task. The final set of questions can be seen at https://crocs.fi.muni.cz/public/papers/ifipsec2022.

2.3   Data Collection and Processing

For each participant, we collected the source code and the written report. Each implementation was then analyzed from the point of task compliance (functionality). We tested if the code compiled, if it succeeded in connecting to *example.com* and other valid domains, and how it handled selected invalid certificates on *badssl.com* subdomains [5]. The handling of revoked certificates was further checked on *revoked.grc.com*. If the program failed to compile, we first manually inspected the code and tried to identify the cause of the failure. In case of minor errors (such as a wrong set filepath), we fixed the error and continued. If the program still failed to compile or connect to one of the valid domains, we considered it failing and did not proceed with further tests. If it established a connection with any of the "defective" hosts without any errors, we considered it failing as well.

The submitted reports were analyzed using inductive coding. Firstly, two researchers processed the data of the first round (from the year 2018) using open coding [29]. Multiple codes naturally arose from the structure of the task (the questions given as inspiration). After the open coding, the researchers discussed the created codes, looked for reoccurring patterns in the data (axial coding), and consolidated a common codebook. To ensure analysis reliability and consistency, a third independent coder then coded all the reports using the codebook created by the first two researchers. We calculated interrater agreement (Cohen's

---

[2] https://docs.python.org/3/library/ssl.html.

[3] https://cr.openjdk.java.net/~iris/se/11/latestSpec/api/java.base/javax/net/ssl/SSLSocket.html.

[4] https://pkg.go.dev/crypto/tls.

[5] https://nodejs.org/api/tls.html.

[6] https://docs.rs/rustls/latest/rustls/.

$\kappa = 0.62$, $p < .001$), which showed to be substantial (according to Landis and Koch [21]). We then proceeded with coding the data from the second and third rounds (years 2019 and 2021). Few additional codes emerged in the second round. In the third round, no new codes emerged.

3   Results

In this section, we summarize the results of our analysis of the reports and functional testing of the submitted programs. Participants from the first round (year: 2018) were assigned three-digit numbers starting with *1*, while participants from the second round (year: 2019) were assigned numbers starting with *2*. Participants from the third round (year: 2021) were assigned numbers starting with *3*. Although we had provided the participants with a set of inspirational questions (see https://crocs.fi.muni.cz/public/papers/ifipsec2022), many of them preferred to give their own views on the libraries. In the following, we report the most salient themes of the reports: the diversity of library preferences and the most important usability factors with documentation and code snippets in a separate subsection due to the vast amount of comments concerning specifically this usability dimension.

3.1   Diverse Library Preferences

Following the analysis and coding of the submitted reports for all rounds (referring to altogether 60 participants), we set out to determine significant trends among the participants. Most surprisingly, no single favorite library emerged from the reports.

Although not explicitly asked to, several participants ordered the libraries in some order of preference. Each of the libraries was ranked first by the same amount of participants: four out of 60 participants ranked OpenSSL as their favorite library, while four participants preferred GnuTLS the most. Four other participants indicated that mbed TLS would be their library of choice. Apart from the rankings, participants also expressed positive and negative assessments of each library. For each of the libraries and each of the rounds, we will shortly provide an example of positive and negative quotes to illustrate the dichotomy of opinions that arose.

Note, however, that the composition of rankings and preferences differed between the rounds. In the third round, OpenSSL was neither ranked as a favorite library by any of the participants nor did it receive a positive overall assessment. On the contrary, GnuTLS did not receive a negative overall assessment in both, the second and the third round. Mbed TLS ranged between the other two libraries, with receiving both, positive and negative assessment in the first and second round, but not receiving an individual negative assessment in the third round. In round two and three, there were, however, participants who collectively assessed all three libraries negatively.

OpenSSL

"I found this API the easiest one to work with, but that might be just because I've experienced it before." (P101, OpenSSL)

"[OpenSSL] is very difficult to work with. The API is huge [...], many methods are generic and overall the API is quite low level. A lot of things have to be programmed manually [...]" (P104, OpenSSL)

"If I should choose just one library I'll use OpenSSL because of IMHO it's more common than others, a powerful command-line tool and there is good documentation as well." (P211, OpenSSL)

"Personally, this library [OpenSSL] had the worst API of these 3, considering mainly documentation and lack of examples." (P202, OpenSSL)

"The OpenSSL API was making me suicidal (like not really, but it is terrible)." (P308, OpenSSL)

GnuTLS

"The simplest library from given list. Fast development. Good documentation [...] Nice example programs in the package with sources." (P102, GnuTLS)

"The worst to work with was surely GnuTLS. It's required to create network connection manually before using it. Also most of the stuff has to be manually set, and documentation is not good." (P106, GnuTLS)

"In my opinion, the most successful approach was done in **gnutls**. The validity of the chain was checked by **gnutls** itself as well as the correctness of the hostname." (P212, GnuTLS)

"Maybe this [code length] is the main reason I liked the GnuTLS the most." (P303, GnuTLS)

mbed TLS

"I liked this one the most. It feels more "higher level" than OpenSSL [...] I also liked the documentation the most, I felt like I can find most of the answers quite quickly [...]" (P107, mbed TLS)

"Really hard to find example programs. Took lot of time to implement assignment. There is documentation, but for newbie really hard to find what required, short explanations for functions." (P102, mbed TLS)

"I have to point out that i found embed easiest to use and to setup" (P220, mbed TLS)

"I don't like EmbedTLS because there were no example in its documenta-tion, and I had to use example code because they have only auto-generated doxygen." (P222, mbed TLS)

"I kind of liked the MbedTLS mainly because of the tutorial for the TLS client." (P303, mbed TLS)

3.2 Considered Usability Factors

While a clear list of usability factors emerged from the qualitative coding of the reports, we encountered a wide range of reasons for favoring one library over another. For example, documentation was used to argue for both liking and disliking it by different participants. Other reasons reflect what has already been pointed to by related work (see Sect. 5): helpfulness and availability of code examples, ease of use and readability of the documentation, and the API's level of abstraction have a great impact on the overall usability. We describe these and other usability factors that were mentioned in the following paragraphs.

Abstraction Level: In the first and third round of the study, many partic-ipants generally commented on the abstraction level of the libraries (only few commented it in round 2). Opinions diverged with some participants finding the abstraction levels appropriate — *"well encapsulated, as expected"* (P105, GnuTLS), *"appropriate"* (P303, GnuTLS), *"more encapsulated than the oth-ers"* (P101, mbed TLS), *"appropriate"* (P305, mbed TLS), *"best abstraction and usage"* (P106, OpenSSL), *"not that bad, but also not great"* (P308, OpenSSL). Others criticized the abstraction level of single libraries— *"[GnuTLS] seems to be more lower level than the previous ones"* (P107, GnuTLS), *"lower level than what I would expect for such a library"* (P307, OpenSSL), *"lower but [...] under-standable if it is mainly for embedded devices"* (P303, mbed TLS), while even others were not satisfied with the abstraction level of all libraries— *"they mix low-level affairs (such as TCP sockets) with high-level interfaces (SNI, OCSP, certificate verification) and, most importantly, force the developer to write criti-cal code by hand"* (P103, all libraries), *"There is less abstraction in each of the APIs than I would desire, even for C. What seemed like a mainstream security task turned into having to manually request everything."* (P311, all libraries).

In all three rounds, several participants specifically criticized the fact that they had to handle the socket connection manually in GnuTLS: *"when you want to connect to the specific port, you need to use your own socket and you need to implement the connection by yourself, which is extremely annoying,"* (P101, GnuTLS); *"In this part, GnuTLS was the worst of these 3, considering I had to manually open socket, fill the structs with information like the type of the socket, hostname, port and then associate the created socket with my session"* (P202, GnuTLS); *"But in gnutls, I had to go all the way down in the abstraction to the system call level to create a socket, perform a lookup of the ip address and finally create a connection since it provided no builtin way of doing this (at least not one I could find)."* (P312, GnuTLS)

Similarly, in all three rounds, several participants were confused by the OpenSSL BIO system: *"I found some things confusing: for example the BIO and SSL structs"* (P107), *"Many times I had some confusions regarding the BIO or SSL structures and functions"* (P224), *"First time i saw this, I had no idea what BIO was"* (P308). Thereby, developers are obviously left alone to realize that they have *"to understand the whole BIO object machinery, in order to correctly communicate with a server"* (P225), while *"there was no information about the fact that I need to create an underlying BIO for the TSL connection (I had to deduce this from the fact that the SSL object has no setter for ports)"* (P307).

Error Handling and Return Values: While error reporting was mentioned multiple times, there was no consistent pattern in the reports. It included both positive comments: *"Thanks to the error handling, I could stop with implementation at any time and quickly verify that there's no problem so far."* (P101, OpenSSL), *"I found very helpful the error messages in gnutls."* (P215, GnuTLS); as well as negative ones: *"issue regarding not showing enough details about reasons for failing the verification was not resolved"* (P102, GnuTLS), *"this library was the worst thing to debug from the group"* (P310, OpenSSL).

In all three rounds of the study, OpenSSL was criticized for its inconsistent return values: *"Also, it does not match the typical bash/C convention for returned success/error code (usually 0 is success, but in OpenSSL 1 is success)"* (P104, OpenSSL); *"Semantics of return values is not consistent."* (P214, OpenSSL) *"For the whole process I had to keep looking up return values of functions in the documentation, because they differ for each call."* (P307, OpenSSL).

Entity Naming: Names of functions, parameters and constants were perceived by many positively across the libraries: *"[OpenSSL has] in the most of cases well named structures/types"* (P108, OpenSSL); *"very clear names for the functions"* (P219, GnuTLS); *"Usually the names are fine [...]"* (P302, all libraries).

Yet, for all of the libraries, several participants also criticized the naming and some of them pointed out concrete examples where naming is ambiguous and calls for improvement:

"Openssl - SSL_write + SSL_write_ex, SSL_read + SSL_read_ex felt a little too similar, the distinction is a little unclear" (P301, OpenSSL)

*"**Similar yet different** Another problem I found is with OpenSSL, where the usage of CTX is different between SSL_CTX and X509_STORE_CTX."* (P326, OpenSSL)

"Just looking at the list of the function gives stuff like:
– gnutls_pkcs11_privkey_generate
– gnutls_pkcs11_privkey_generate2
– gnutls_pkcs11_privkey_generate3

This pattern is present in different places and some others are a shame as well. With 1116 function beginning by gnutls... on my system, that's already complicated enough to find the one I need to put 3 times the same name with a number at the end." (P209, GnuTLS)

"Another thing was setting the minimal version of TLS to 1.2. Parameters for the function that provides this, which are MBEDTLS_SSL_MAJOR _VERSION_3 and MBEDTLS_SSL_MINOR_VERSION_3 are highly non intuitive." (P101, mbed TLS)

3.3   Documentation and Code Samples

In all three rounds of the study, many of the comments in the written report were concerning documentation and code samples in it. To keep the programming task as realistic as possible, we intentionally left it to the participants to search for appropriate documentation. They were thus free to use the sources available on the official API websites or any other sources available through the Internet. For each library, some participants positively assessed the found documentation, while others criticized it as a whole or in certain aspects.

OpenSSL: The OpenSSL website [28] provides under the menu point "Docs" a link to frequently asked questions, the manual pages of all releases, a link to the *OpenSSL Cookbook,* and historic information on the OpenSSL FIPS Object Module. Additionally, there is a wiki available[7], the link to which is, however, hidden in the "Community" section of the OpenSSL website. The "Download" section of the OpenSSL website further mentions the OpenSSL Github Repository[8].

Several participants criticized that the documentation is *"spread across whole openssl page"* (P204) that one *"had to click through several links"* (P312), or that while there is *"a lot of documentation for OpenSSL, both manuals, API description and examples, it seemed [...] very fragmented"* (P322). Mostly likely referring to the manual pages, some participants criticized that the documentation contains *"only [a] list of functions"* (P102), that it is *"just an index of every function and it's your job to sort everything"* (P224), or *"provided functions to be too tainted by deprecated features"* (P226). Some other comments wrapped these findings up: *"it is really hard to find something if you don't precisely know what you are looking for"* (P107) or *"finding [the] proper function always took me some time"* (P303).

These issues can be interpreted as a result of a dynamically growing development effort with a variety of contributors, however, the nature of the project also fosters a variety of contributions that help developers in different ways, as mentioned positively by our participants: *"Simplest to get into i found OPENSSL, mostly because of the community i would say and also because the level of the*

---

[7] https://wiki.openssl.org/index.php/Main_Page.

[8] https://github.com/openssl/openssl.

tutorials" (P220). Similarly, another participant pointed out: *"I find the documentation to be the best among all 3 libraries and there are lots of examples online"* (P207).

GnuTLS: The GnuTLS website [13] provides under the menu point "Documentation" links to the GnuTLS manual in several formats (HTML, PDF, EPUB), links to the GNU Guile bindings, and a link to frequently asked questions. The manual is a book-style document that does not only contain information on the API but also provides background on the TLS protocol and related matters (such as authentication and key management). It thus differs in style from the OpenSSL manual pages which only provide a list of functions. The project's Gitlab page[9] is linked under the "Development (gitlab)" menu point on the GnuTLS website.

Several participants criticized the manual and documentation as being *"hideous and hard to orient"* (P107), *"most confusing, because the tutorial website was difficult to read"* (P220), or simply mentioning that the *"tutorial was too much verbose and long and it was very hard to find here what you want"* (P317). Yet, other participants relativized these points, by noting that the documentation is *"at first very overwhelming (there is a LOT) but once you get into it it's nicely done"* (P301) or mentioning that *"At first, I was scared because it was just like a markdown file (just a single page) [...]. But I think in the end it was good."* (P303)

In general, it seemed that participants were more positive towards the GnuTLS documentation, for instance, considering it as *"pretty straightforward"* (P218) and as *"amazingly structured"* (P306), or – as wrapped up by this participant: *"With GnuTLS you can have an overview of everything and dig deeper from that"* (P224).

When it comes to code snippets, opinions were diverse with some participants praising the available examples – *"a couple somewhat helpful examples at the end of its manual"* (P103), *"beautiful commented example which had everything needed for homework"* (P204), *"In the documentation, I could find a nice example of a TLS client with an x509 certificate"* (P303) – and others being unable to find relevant ones *"[the documentation] doesn't provide any useful examples"* (P101), *"it took me ages to find some relevant examples"* (P309).

mbed TLS: The (now being deprecated) mbed TLS website [22] provides under the menu point "Dev corner" > "API reference" the Doxygen-generated API documentation. Moreover, under "Dev corner" > "High-level design", there is an overview of the API modules and their dependencies. Right on the homepage of the now being deprecated mbed TLS website, there is a link to the new website[10] where developers can find the link to the project's Github repository[11].

---

[9] https://gitlab.com/gnutls/gnutls/blob/master/README.md.

[10] https://www.trustedfirmware.org/projects/mbed-tls/.

[11] https://github.com/ARMmbed/mbedtls.

Several participants criticized the documentation as being *"not rich in details"* (P109), as containing only *"very brief descriptions and hardly any examples"* (P226), or simply as being *"difficult to navigate and also very few code examples"* (P301).

Participants pointed out several features that they are missing, such as man pages – *"lacking manpages"* (P203), *"that's a shame that mbedTLS does not provide man pages on my distribution (Arch Linux)"* (P209) – or an orientation help – *"where is the SEARCH feature on your website"* (P216), *"No real index"* (P204).

At the same time, participants also noted the features that they liked: *"their official web page provided detailed TLS tutorial where I found almost everything I needed"* (P109), *"nice dependency graphs on its website"* (P203), *"there are some git repositories linked on the websites to present some code examples"* (P220), *"I also like the visual part of the documentation"* (P303).

3.4 Functionality Analysis

To evaluate the functional correctness of the submitted solutions, we tested them as described in Sect. 2.3. Figure 1 summarizes the results of our testing.

| | | compilation | valid | | | expired | wrong host | self signed | untrusted root | revoked | | TLS 1.0* | TLS 1.1* | TLS 1.2 |
			example	google*	badssl*					badssl*	grc			
LIBRARY	OpenSSL	0.9	0.7	0.5	0.6	0.5	0.4	0.5	0.5	0.1	0.1	0.8	0.8	0.7
	GnuTLS	0.8	0.6	0.6	0.6	0.6	0.6	0.6	0.6	0.2	0.5	0.6	0.6	0.6
	mbed TLS	0.8	0.6	0.5	0.5	0.5	0.5	0.5	0.5	0.1	0.0	0.3	0.3	0.5
ROUND	YEAR 1	0.9	0.6	na	na	0.5	0.5	0.5	0.5	na	0.0	na	na	0.4
	YEAR 2	0.8	0.4	0.3	0.4	0.4	0.3	0.4	0.4	0.2	0.2	0.4	0.4	0.4
	YEAR 3	0.9	0.8	0.7	0.7	0.7	0.6	0.7	0.7	0.1	0.3	0.7	0.7	0.8

Fig. 1. Overview of the functionality analysis results. Numbers indicate the rounded fraction of all programs that succeeded in the given test category. Darkness indicates the severity of the issue. Valid domains were tested using *example.com*, *google.com*, and *badssl.com*. Certificate flaws and TLS version support were tested using *badssl.com*. Revoked certificates were tested using *badssl.com* and *revoked.grc.com*. Categories not tested in year 1 are marked with an asterisk (*).

A few clear patterns were observed. Out of the 180 total programs (3×60), most compiled. Several failed to connect even to the valid domains, indicating that getting the connection right with the given libraries can present a challenge. Handling flawed certificates turned out to be similarly hard in all three libraries with a medium amount of successful programs. Even worse, revocation checks were especially hard to implement—in all three libraries only a negligible minority succeeded.

For the enforcement of the correct TLS version, there seems to be a difference between the libraries with OpenSSL handling this task more easily than GnuTLS and mbed TLS.

While overall numbers are discouraging, participants in round three were generally more successful than in the other two rounds and this applied equally to all libraries (but not for revocation checks). Whether this difference is due to the higher experience of the participants or whether due to an increase in usability of all three libraries is to be investigated in future studies. As for now, the results of our qualitative analysis show that at least the perceived usability (as manifested in the user satisfaction) did not increase.

4   Discussion

The opinions on library usability appear to be diverse and sometimes conflicting: none of them was explicitly considered worst or best by a majority.

The most often mentioned usability factors include the quality of documentation and code samples, the abstraction level of the API, error handling and return values, and entity names. Properly checking for a revoked certificate turned out to be the most difficult part of the task and basic certificate checks were also not easy.

For all of the three libraries, there is space for improvement in different usability dimensions: OpenSSL should work on making developers aware of the BIO system and linking to suitable documentation. Moreover, return values showed to be confusing in this library (yet this is an issue that is hard to fix due to backward-compatibility reasons). Also, similar function names were sometimes perceived as confusing.

GnuTLS should support the developers in socket handling and explaining the differences between functions of similar naming. Apart from that, mixed comments on examples may hint towards a need to provide an easily accessible and unified resource for examples.

Similar to OpenSSL and GnuTLS, mbed TLS should address issues of hard-to-understand function names (e.g., from functions with similar names). When it comes to documentation, mbed TLS should work on navigability and additional resources (such as man pages).

While we discovered some options for improvement, API usability is most likely only one aspect that determines TLS client functionality and security. In real-world projects these factors may be further influenced by implementation constraints (such as compatibility with other systems, integration into legacy code, and library license models).

4.1 Study Limitations

As is the case with every study, various limitations may diminish the applicability of results. Our study was conducted in three rounds over the course of three years on real-world applications that might have changed during that time. While we could ensure in the task specification that students worked with similar versions of the API, we did not trace whether the (formal or informal) documentation changed. However, as we observed most of the themes appearing in all of the three rounds, we determine the possibility that the documentation sources underwent significant changes as small. The comparison of the libraries may have been biased by prior experience with some of them (this was mentioned by some participants, but there was no common pattern). Furthermore, library order may have played a role (since the task was the same, participants' background knowledge increased with each subsequent library). Although graduate students are future IT professionals and junior developers constitute a non-negligible share of the developer population (almost 40% with 4 years or less of professional coding experience [30]), our sample still deviates from the actual developer population, and generalizations should thus be made with caution.

5 Related Work

Multiple studies have looked into the security of applications using TLS. Georgiev et al. [12] analyzed a representative sample of non-browser software applications and libraries that use TLS for secure Internet connections. Multiple libraries and apps were found to be broken. Authors argue the causes are poor API design, too many options presented to the developers, and bad documentation.

Fahl et al. performed an automated analysis of more than 14,000 Android and iOS applications [10,11] focusing on TLS certificate verification and man-in-the-middle attack possibilities. Many applications were found exploitable. Common issues included not verifying certificates, not checking the hostname, and allowing mixed content. They suggested a couple of technical countermeasures and argued for more developer education and simpler, usable tools to write secure applications. Similarly, Egele et al. [9] in their analysis of 11,000 Android applications found 88% to be vulnerable. The main assumed reasons included poor documentation and inappropriate defaults of the Java APIs.

To summarize, we see that security APIs are frequently misused, despite their crucial function. Although there is a plethora of usability analyses based on automatic code analysis as mentioned above, only a few studies had inspected the usability of security APIs from the point of user satisfaction.

For instance, Naiakshina et al. [24] conducted a qualitative study asking why developers store user passwords incorrectly. Their results reveal, among other things, that more usable APIs are not sufficient if secure defaults are not in place and that security is often secondary to functionality. Satisfaction was studied only marginally, in terms of expected and actual difficulty of the task.

Acar et al. [1] conducted a study comparing the usability of five Python security libraries. Apart from the functional correctness ("usable" libraries resulting more often in secure code), they tried to assess user satisfaction using the System Usability Scale (SUS) [6] and their own usability scale. Although SUS is widely known and used, it is not diagnostic so no specific conclusions could be drawn. Their own scale is diagnostic and consists of 11 questions combining the *Cognitive Dimensions framework* [32] with usability suggestions from Nielsen [27] and from Green and Smith [15]. Similar to our results, their results indicate that documentation (and especially code examples in it) are of utmost importance and should be treated as a first-class requirement by library developers.

Nadi et al. [23] performed multiple separate usability studies in the context of Java's cryptographic APIs. One of the studies with developers identified several shortcomings replicated by later studies, as well as ours: lack of documentation and tutorials, unsatisfactory abstraction level, and lack of direct support for common tasks. User satisfaction was not considered explicitly. A different empirical study by Acar et al. [4] with GitHub users creating security-related code only included questions on self-reported success, task difficulty, solution security, previous experience, and demographics, not asking directly about user satisfaction with the API.

In summary, although TLS usually forms a crucial part of product security, misuse seems to be quite common. Previous research focused mainly on the effectiveness and efficiency components of usability, overwhelmingly in the context of cryptographic primitives. However, user satisfaction and specifics of TLS were usually understated—a gap which we intend to fill with our work.

6   Conclusion and Future Work

We conducted a three-fold exploratory study trying to identify usability issues of common TLS library APIs. 60 master-level students attempted to implement a simple TLS client using OpenSSL, GnuTLS, and mbed TLS.

We did not find evidence that any of the tested libraries was preferred by the participants, as they had multiple conflicting expectations. Common usability aspects mentioned by the participants included the quality of documentation (including the sample code snippets provided in it), the overall API abstraction level (especially complaining about network socket handling in GnuTLS and the BIO system in OpenSSL), return values consistency (especially in OpenSSL) and entity naming (where they found examples of similarly named functions in all three libraries).

Examining the effectiveness of the produced solutions, checking the revocation status of certificates turned out to be very difficult (with few successful participants) and basic certificate checks were also not overly easy.

The study suggests multiple directions for future work. Firstly, it may be beneficial for library developers to investigate the expectations of programmers using their interfaces. Secondly, user satisfaction with the APIs seems to be rather complex and a proper measuring methodology is still lacking. Key aspects of user satisfaction concerning APIs should be identified, synthesizing the existing API usability principles and user perceptions to answer questions such as: How do I write usable documentation? What error reporting is considered usable by the users? What is the right level of abstraction the users expect? Thirdly, further studies should be conducted to answer the question: "How can we teach developers to efficiently set up a TLS client in different libraries while taking into account diverse real-world constraints?".

Acknowledgments. This research was supported by the ERDF project *CyberSecurity, CyberCrime and Critical Information Infrastructures Center of Excellence* (No. CZ.02.1.01/0.0/0.0/16_019/0000822). We would like to thank Red Hat Czech for support and all students of the course for participating in this research. Thanks also go to Pavol Žáčik for helping to confirm different API functionality aspects.

References

1. Acar, Y., et al.: Comparing the usability of cryptographic APIs. In: 2017 IEEE Symposium on Security and Privacy (SP), pp. 154–171 (2017). https://doi.org/10.1109/sp.2017.52
2. Acar, Y., Backes, M., Fahl, S., Kim, D., Mazurek, M.L., Stransky, C.: You get where you're looking for: the impact of information sources on code security. In: 2016 IEEE Symposium on Security and Privacy (SP), pp. 289–305 (2016). https://doi.org/10.1109/sp.2016.25
3. Acar, Y., Fahl, S., Mazurek, M.L.: You are not your developer, either: a research agenda for usable security and privacy research beyond end users. In: 2016 IEEE Cybersecurity Development (SecDev), pp. 3–8. IEEE (2016)
4. Acar, Y., Stransky, C., Wermke, D., Mazurek, M.L., Fahl, S.: Security developer studies with GitHub users: exploring a convenience sample. In: Thirteenth Symposium on Usable Privacy and Security (SOUPS 2017), pp. 81–95. USENIX Association, Santa Clara (2017)
5. Memorable site for testing clients against bad SSL configs (2022). https://badssl.com/
6. Brooke, J.: SUS: a quick and dirty usability scale. In: Usability Evaluation in Industry, vol. 189, no. 194, pp. 4–7 (1996)
7. Cairns, K., Steel, G.: Developer-resistant cryptography. In: A W3C/IAB Workshop on Strengthening the Internet Against Pervasive Monitoring (STRINT) (2014)
8. Dietrich, C., Krombholz, K., Borgolte, K., Fiebig, T.: Investigating system operators' perspective on security misconfigurations. In: 25th ACM Conference on Computer and Communications Security. ACM, October 2018
9. Egele, M., Brumley, D., Fratantonio, Y., Kruegel, C.: An empirical study of cryptographic misuse in android applications. In: Proceedings of the 2013 ACM SIGSAC Conference on Computer and Communications Security, CCS 2013, pp. 73–84. ACM, New York (2013). https://doi.org/10.1145/2508859.2516693
10. Fahl, S., Harbach, M., Muders, T., Baumgärtner, L., Freisleben, B., Smith, M.: Why Eve and Mallory love android: an analysis of android SSL (in)security. In: Proceedings of the 2012 ACM Conference on Computer and Communications Security, pp. 50–61. ACM (2012). https://doi.org/10.1145/2382196.2382204

11. Fahl, S., Harbach, M., Perl, H., Koetter, M., Smith, M.: Rethinking SSL development in an appified world. In: Proceedings of the 2013 ACM SIGSAC Conference on Computer and Communications Security, CCS 2013, pp. 49–60. ACM, New York (2013). https://doi.org/10.1145/2508859.2516655

12. Georgiev, M., Iyengar, S., Jana, S., Anubhai, R., Boneh, D., Shmatikov, V.: The most dangerous code in the world: validating SSL certificates in non-browser software. In: Proceedings of the 2012 ACM conference on Computer and Communications Security, pp. 38–49. ACM (2012). https://doi.org/10.1145/2382196.2382204

13. GnuTLS: transport layer security library (2022). https://www.gnutls.org/

14. Google transparency report: HTTPS encryption on the web (2021). https://transparencyreport.google.com/

15. Green, M., Smith, M.: Developers are not the enemy!: the need for usable security APIs. IEEE Secur. Priv. 14, 40–46 (2016). https://doi.org/10.1109/msp.2016.111

16. Hazhirpasand, M., Ghafari, M., Krüger, S., Bodden, E., Nierstrasz, O.: The impact of developer experience in using Java cryptography (2019)

17. Iacono, L.L., Gorski, P.L.: I do and I understand. Not yet true for security APIs. So sad. In: Proceedings of the 2nd European Workshop on Usable Security. EuroUSEC 2017, Internet Security, Reston, VA (2017). https://doi.org/10.14722/eurousec.2017.23015

18. Krombholz, K., Busse, K., Pfeffer, K., Smith, M., von Zezschwitz, E.: "If https were secure, i wouldn't need 2FA" - end user and administrator mental models of https. In: S&P 2019, May 2019. https://publications.cispa.saarland/2788/

19. Krombholz, K., Mayer, W., Schmiedecker, M., Weippl, E.: "I have no idea what I'm doing" - on the usability of deploying HTTPS. In: 26th USENIX Security Symposium (USENIX Security 17), pp. 1339–1356 (2017)

20. Krüger, S., Späth, J., Ali, K., Bodden, E., Mezini, M.: CrySL: an extensible approach to validating the correct usage of cryptographic APIs. In: Millstein, T. (ed.) 32nd European Conference on Object-Oriented Programming (ECOOP 2018), Leibniz International Proceedings in Informatics (LIPIcs), vol. 109, pp. 10:1–10:27. Dagstuhl, Germany (2018). https://doi.org/10.4230/LIPIcs.ECOOP.2018.10

21. Landis, J.R., Koch, G.G.: The measurement of observer agreement for categorical data. Biometrics 33(1), 159–174 (1977). https://doi.org/10.2307/2529310

22. Mbed TLS (formerly known as PolarSSL) (2022). https://tls.mbed.org

23. Nadi, S., Krüger, S., Mezini, M., Bodden, E.: Jumping through hoops: why do Java developers struggle with cryptography APIs? In: Proceedings of the 38th International Conference on Software Engineering, pp. 935–946. ACM (2016)

24. Naiakshina, A., Danilova, A., Tiefenau, C., Herzog, M., Dechand, S., Smith, M.: Why do developers get password storage wrong? A qualitative usability study. In: Proceedings of the 2017 ACM SIGSAC Conference on Computer and Communications Security, CCS 2017, pp. 311–328. ACM, New York (2017). https://doi.org/10.1145/3133956.3134082

25. Naiakshina, A., Danilova, A., Tiefenau, C., Smith, M.: Deception task design in developer password studies: exploring a student sample. In: Fourteenth Symposium on Usable Privacy and Security (SOUPS 2018), pp. 297–313. USENIX Association, Baltimore, August 2018. https://www.usenix.org/conference/soups2018/presentation/naiakshina

26. Nemec, M., Klinec, D., Svenda, P., Sekan, P., Matyas, V.: Measuring popularity of cryptographic libraries in internet-wide scans. In: Proceedings of the 33rd Annual Computer Security Applications Conference (ACSAC), pp. 162–175. ACM Press, New York (2017). https://doi.org/10.1145/3134600.3134612

27. Nielsen, J.: Usability Engineering. Academic Press, Cambridge (1993)
28. OpenSSL: Cryptography and SSL/TLS toolkit (2022). https://www.openssl.org/
29. Saldaña, J.: The Coding Manual for Qualitative Researchers, 3rd edn. SAGE Publishing, Thousand Oaks (2015)
30. Stackoverflow developer survey (2021). https://insights.stackoverflow.com/survey/2021
31. Tahaei, M., Vaniea, K.: A survey on developer-centred security. In: 2019 IEEE European Symposium on Security and Privacy Workshops (EuroS&PW), pp. 129–138. IEEE (2019)
32. Wijayarathna, C., Arachchilage, N.A.G., Slay, J.: A generic cognitive dimensions questionnaire to evaluate the usability of security APIs. In: Tryfonas, T. (ed.) Human Aspects of Information Security, Privacy and Trust, HAS 2017. LNCS, vol. 10292, pp. 160–173. Springer, Cham (2017). https://doi.org/10.1007/978-3-319-58460-7_11

Usability of Antivirus Tools in a Threat Detection Scenario

Michael Körber, Anatoli Kalysch, Werner Massonne, and Zinaida Benenson[✉]

Friedrich-Alexander-Universität Erlangen-Nürnberg, Erlangen, Germany
{michael.koerber,anatoli.kalysch,werner.massonne,zinaida.benenson}@fau.de

Abstract. Usability of antivirus (AV) tools has not received much attention yet. We conducted a laboratory study with 34 German students to investigate how they experience notifications and interventions of their AV when a threat is detected. During the study, a specifically designed harmless file triggered AV on participants' laptops. Out of 34 participants, 19 users noticed AV messages, and 8 of them understood that the message communicated threat detection concerning a specific file. Moreover, only 6 users understood that this file was removed by the AV tool. Additionally, most participants were distracted by Windows OS messages that were unintelligible to them. We investigate reasons for incomprehension in our sample, and give recommendations for improved user interaction design of AV tools.

1 Introduction

Security-related media and security experts have multiple times declared that antivirus (AV) is dead, or should not be used [16,25,27]. Nevertheless, strong majority of non-expert users have reported using antivirus and consider AV usage to be a good and actionable security advice [8,18,28,30,38]. At the same time, most of the surveyed security experts do not rate using AV as a "top" security advice [8,18,31]. These contradictions raise a question: What makes AV a good security tool from the non-experts' point of view?

Ion et al. [18, p. 333] note that high acceptance of AV "might be due to the good usability of the install-once type of solution that antivirus software offers". Indeed, AV tools are usually not actively *used*. After installation, an AV tool is supposed to run in the background. However, when threats are detected, the AV tool has to interact with users and their systems: show the threat detection notifications and delete or quarantine infected or suspicious files.

A usable AV tool should provide users with enough information, such that they can react adequately. Which actions are adequate will depend on the situation and on the technical sophistication of the user. Non-expert users considered in this work may want to ask for help, and therefore, should be able to explain to other people what happened. Moreover, the users may want to warn other users about the threat, which at least requires them to understand which file is affected. Therefore, we consider the following main research questions in our study:

© IFIP International Federation for Information Processing 2022
Published by Springer Nature Switzerland AG 2022
W. Meng et al. (Eds.): SEC 2022, IFIP AICT 648, pp. 306–322, 2022.
https://doi.org/10.1007/978-3-031-06975-8_18

- RQ1: Which design and user interaction elements of AV notifications help users under real-life circumstances to understand that a particular file was removed by an AV tool, and that this file might be malicious?
- RQ2: What are users' attitudes to AV and their reasons for AV usage? Under which circumstances are users satisfied with their AV tools and feel well protected?

To answer the main research questions, we defined several subsequent questions that are presented in supplementary materials[1]. For example, in order for AV notifications to be helpful, at least the following steps are necessary: the users should be able to notice the notification, and understand why this notification was issued. Therefore, the corresponding subsequent questions are: Do the users notice the notifications of their AV tools? Can they explain that the notifications appeared because AV tool found a suspicious file?

We report the first (to our knowledge) laboratory study that investigates user experience when AV tools detect malware. The aim of this work is not to critique individual AV tools, but to show which notifications and user interaction elements support users well, and which need improvement.

Timeframe: The user study took place in 2017[2]. However, we tested in 2021 whether our results are still applicable: We used multiple Windows PCs with the AV tools considered in the study, and checked whether reactions of the AV tools changed over time. Whereas we registered changes in the notifications of some AV tools, we discuss in Sect. 5.2 that our results are still applicable and useful today, and represent a good starting point for further research.

2   Background and Related Work

2.1   Industrial AV Tests

To the best of our knowledge, no works on usability of AV tools have been published in academic research so far. However, some companies regularly publish AV tests, although these tests do not consider user interaction. For example, AV-TEST [5] measures usability as the number of false alarms using a system for automated deployment of programs from a large proprietary database of benign software samples [4]. However, an AV tool issues messages also when genuine threats are detected. Our study investigates whether these messages enable the users to understand what happened and to react adequately.

---

[1] https://www.cs1.tf.fau.de/research/human-factors-in-security-and-privacy-group/antivirus-usability.

[2] Due to a collision of several unfortunate circumstances, the research team found resources for writing up the results only in 2021.

2.2   Attitudes and Behavior Regarding Malware

Wash [37] investigated mental models of malware of US users through qualitative interviews. He found that various models (e.g., "viruses are buggy software") are connected to usage and non-usage of AV tools. Later, Wash and Rader [38] verified and extended these findings in a survey with a representative sample of the US population. Kauer et al. [20] replicated Wash's study in Germany, uncovering some additional mental models of malware.

Ion et al. [18] found in a survey that using AV is the most popular security measure for non-expert users in their sample. This result was later corroborated in a replication study by Busse et al. [8]. Whereas AV tools were much less popular among security experts in these studies, they still recommend AV usage to non-expert users [31]. Redmiles et al. investigated sources and acceptance of security advice qualitatively [29] as well as quantitatively [28]. AV is reportedly used by over 80% of US population, with family members' or media advice and negative experiences being important reasons for adopting AV. Overall, AV usage is considered actionable, effective and high priority security advice [30].

Lalonde Levesque et al. [23] investigated how devices get infected despite having an AV. The identified risk factors were high computer expertise, visiting many websites of particular categories, such as streaming, and installing a lot of software. Forget et al. [15] found that users with high engagement in security still get malware. Sharif et al. [33] investigated how customers of an AV company identify and describe virus incidents in customer support chats. They found that some users were surprised that they can get malware despite AV usage, and often could not precisely identify whether they got infected and how this happened. Overreliance on AV for protecting against a multitude of threats was reported by Krol et al. [21], and might be a likely factor of risky Internet behavior [9].

In contrast to the previous work, we consider how users interact with AV tools in a threat detection scenario.

2.3   Security Warnings

Security warnings inform users about possible dangers and offer a choice of at least two options on how to proceed, whereas notifications provide information about found and eliminated threats and usually offer either one option or none [6]. Design, wording and purpose of AV notifications is comparable to security warnings in many aspects. Reaction to security warnings and indicators, especially in web browsers, has been in focus of empirical studies for at least last 15 years [7,12,32,34,39]. These works considered existing warnings, made improvement suggestions and sometimes tested new warnings. Malware warnings in browsers and other tools have also been investigated [1,21,24].

Generally, a sizable amount of users consistently ignored warnings, did not trust them, and did not understand them across the studies. Ignoring warnings is tightly connected to the effects of habituation and generalization, especially if warnings have high false positive rates, or appear in non-critical situations [3,36]. Although some improvements in adherence could be reached through careful design and timing [14,19], warnings still remain an active research topic.

3   Method

3.1   Design and Usage of the 'Infected' File

We designed a harmless file that triggered AV tools of the participants. In the sequel, we refer to *'infected'* files using quotation marks to emphasize that these files were entirely harmless. This file was written in C and exhibited behavior typical for malware called *downloader*: It installs itself on the victim's PC and later downloads additional malicious files. Next, we uploaded this file from various IP addresses using the TOR network[3] to a malware detection service VirusTotal that automatically tests uploaded files against over 60 antivirus tools[4]. Uploads from different locations can indicate a malware campaign and prompt AV distributors to include the signature of the file into their databases. Whereas in the beginning only 10 out of 63 AV tools flagged our file as malicious, after two weeks of uploads 46 AV tools detected it.

To make the malicious file fit the cover story (usability study of Microsoft Word), we changed the file extension of the 'infected' file from .exe to .doc. This did not change its detection rate, because file extensions are not used for virus signature generation. The changed file could not be run anymore, but could be opened in Word as a binary file (i.e., it did not show any readable content).

Malware can be introduced via email attachments, file download (including drive-by downloads) and via USB drives or other portable media. We pretested all three scenarios using virtual machines and found that different email clients and browsers exhibit specific error messages that interact with AV notifications and actions, whereas USB drives only elicit error messages by Windows OS (as presented in Fig. 3 in Sect. 4.1). Therefore, we decided to use USB drives in this exploratory study, and leave other scenarios to future work. Otherwise, to make sure that the 'infected' files work as expected, we would have needed to test beforehand a variety of email clients or browsers used by the participants. When using USB drives, we only needed to test Windows OS without any additional software. Additionally, if the participants opened their emails during the study, we could not avoid observing at least some details of their emails, which has privacy implications. Moreover, if any emails unrelated to the study arrived shortly before or during the study, they would have distracted the participants.

3.2   Study Design and Procedure

We conducted an observational exploratory study, because nothing was known about user interaction with AV tools beforehand. For example, we were unable to predict from the literature on security warnings whether users would notice and understand AV notifications, and whether they would notice and understand that a suspicious file was removed by their AV tool. Therefore, it was necessary to observe user behavior under conditions that should be as natural

---

[3] https://www.torproject.org.

[4] https://support.virustotal.com/hc/en-us/articles/115002146809-Contributors.

as possible, with the aim to create a foundation for further research in this area. In our study design, we used the principles from the guideline by Krol et al. [22, p. 23] on conducting user studies in security: (1) Give participants a primary task; (2) Ensure participants experience realistic risk; and (3) Avoid priming the participants.

In order not to prime the participants, we recruited them for a usability study of Microsoft Word. Accordingly, their primary tasks in the study were concerned with text processing, e.g., copying a part of one text into another text, inserting an image or changing formatting. The participants used their own laptops, such that the risk to their data and system was made as realistic and salient as possible. Participants' laptops were connected to the laboratory computer via a remote access program TeamViewer[5] in order to use screen capture.

The overview of the study is presented in Fig. 1. After a short introduction, participants signed the informed consent form and received two envelopes, each containing a USB drive with 8 files (various Word documents, PDFs and figures) and a list of tasks. Both task lists first asked the users to copy files from the USB drive to the laptop, and then to execute some text processing tasks, as described above. The topic of texts and pictures in all tasks was German monetary policy.

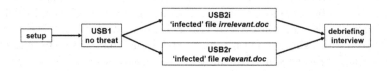

Fig. 1. Study design: participants first worked with USB1, which did not contain any 'infected' files. Their second task required them to copy files from USB2i or USB2r, where one file was 'infected'.

Participants first worked with USB1 that did not trigger their AV tool, such that they could familiarize themselves with the environment and the tasks. However, the USB drive in the second envelope (USB2r or USB2i) contained an 'infected' file. When the users inserted the second USB drive and started copying the files, their AV tool detected the threat and reacted by showing a threat detection message and moving the corresponding file into the quarantine.

Both second USB drives contained the same files, and one of these files was 'infected'. As all file names were in German, we call these files here *relevant.doc* and *irrelevant.doc* to improve readability. The tasks for both USB drives were the same. However, the 'infected' file on USB2r was *relevant.doc*, and it was relevant for the task: The participants were required to insert an image into it. In this case the participants would be unable to complete their tasks, because the file would be moved to quarantine. We were interested in how they would make sense of this situation. The 'infected' file on USB2i was *irrelevant.doc*, which was not needed for the tasks. In this case, we were interested whether the

---

[5] https://www.teamviewer.com.

participants would notice the removal of the file by their AV tool, and understand what happened. This condition emulates situations where a file is removed by the AV tool, but some time later the user needs this file, or receives a message from some program that this file was not found.

After task execution, the participants were interviewed about their experience during the study and debriefed about its real goal. We also showed to them screen capture of their task execution. Finally, we asked about their experience with viruses and attitudes to AV tools. The study took 37 min on average. The participants were reimbursed with a 10 EUR Amazon voucher. The interview guide is presented in the supplementary materials[6].

3.3   Ethics

The study protocol was reviewed by two usability experts who did not participate in study design and execution, and approved by the data protection office at our university. We also run four pretests and adjusted the study protocol accordingly.

To minimize the experimenter effect, the participants were left alone in the lab after the study setup. We were concerned that they might experience negative emotions during the unexpected threat detection, blame us for giving them an unsafe USB drive, or feel helpless if a file they need for the task is missing. Therefore, we told the participants that they can contact us anytime in the neighboring room. We also observed the participants through a one-way window of the lab (they were informed about this observation), such that we could interfere in case a participant remained helpless for too long or appeared frightened[7].

Participants were fully debriefed about the real goal of the study in the post-interview. A specific ethical issue arose because the USB drives were used multiple times in experimental runs. Thus, if any participant had undetected malware on their laptop, it could spread to other laptops. Therefore, we "disinfected" USB drives after every usage by securely erasing them under Mac OS.

3.4   Data Collection and Analysis

Two fixed team members were present at each study run. One of them was the main contact for the participant, handled the study setup and conducted the interview. The other observed the study through the one-way window and on a monitor in the lab and made structured notes in an Excel sheet that contained core observation points. Later both researchers independently watched screen capture videos and listened to audio recording of the interviews. They noted down their observations on user interaction and the answers of the participants, and additionally transcribed especially interesting or important phrases verbatim. They then compared and discussed their notes to validate the observations

---

[6] https://www.cs1.tf.fau.de/research/human-factors-in-security-and-privacy-group/
antivirus-usability.

[7] None of the participants felt frightened or blamed us for the unsafe USB drive. All participants called us if they could not proceed with the task.

and the interview data. Finally, core themes were extracted from the notes and categorized. Additional team members watched the videos and listened to the interviews, and wrote short summaries of the cases. These notes were subsequently used in several team meetings to complement the analysis.

3.5   Participants and Their AV Tools

Participants were recruited via student mailing lists of economics, social sciences and engineering departments at two German universities. They were invited to take part in a pre-screening questionnaire for a lab study concerning usability of Microsoft Word. To avoid priming, AV tools were not mentioned in the recruitment email. The goal of the pre-screening questionnaire was to find people who use AV, and to pretest their AV tools. To this end, the questionnaire asked whether the participants use a Windows laptop, would use it in the lab study and let us install TeamViewer on it, and which tools in general they use on their laptop, including word processing, web browsers, email programs, and AV tools. After this block of questions, the participants were asked multiple questions about their Internet usage, and also demographic questions. This disguise of the study goal was successful, as none of the participants in the lab study reported that they suspected the study to be connected to AV tools.

We received 91 completed questionnaires, of which 44 participants qualified for the invitation to the study. Of these 44 participants, 34 took part in the study. The rest either did not react to the invitation, or canceled their slot. To reach the intended aim of 40 participants, six additional users were recruited in the building where the study took place. AV tools that were mentioned by the participants in the recruiting survey were tested beforehand with default settings. We copied the 'infected' file from a USB drive to a laptop, and the tools reacted as expected: they showed notifications and removed the file into quarantine. Unfortunately, during the user study, all three recruited Avast users and two Avira users did not receive any notifications, and their 'infected' files were not removed. We could not find out why this happened, especially as AV tools of these users were able to recognize and remove the corresponding files through manual scan in all cases. Furthermore, one participant switched off Windows Defender on his laptop. Data of these six users were excluded from the analysis.

The remaining 34 participants were 23 years old on average, 25 identified as female, and 9 as male. Most of them studied economics (15) or social work (12), and the rest studied electrical engineering or design. They used the following AV tools: Windows Defender (9 participants), Avira (6), Sophos (6, with 4 using a fallback laptop[8]), AVG (3), Norton (3), Bitdefender (2), G Data (2), Microsoft Security Essentials (2), Kaspersky (1).

---

[8] If the participants could not use their own laptop (e.g., they forgot to bring it, or had technical issues), they used a "fallback" laptop with Windows 10 and the AV tool Sophos. Our university requires Sophos on university computers.

Table 1. User experience with AV tools; 34 users in total, 15 of them handled *irrelevant.doc* (*i* column), and 19 handled *relevant.doc* (*r* column)

	n	i	r	User experience: AV message
nn	15	6	9	Did not notice that an AV message appeared on the screen
nu	5	2	3	Did not understand that the message came from AV, but noticed it
pu	6	2	4	Remembers some parts of the message (e.g., that a threat was detected, or no action is needed), but cannot fully explain why the message appeared (e.g., does not connect the message to the disappearance of the 'infected' file, or thinks that the USB drive or a file is defect, or protected)
u	8	6	2	Explains that AV found a virus in a particular file and issued a message
	n	i	r	User experience: AV intervention
nu	21	8	13	Either appears to be completely lost, or says that something on the PC or on the USB is broken, or otherwise cannot be accessed or copied
pu	7	3	4	Explains that a virus was found, but does not fully understand the situation (e.g., does not know which file is affected, or says that "something" on the USB drive or on the PC is infected)
u	6	5	1	Explains that AV found a virus in a particular file and removed it

nn = not noticed; nu = not understood; pu = partially understood; u = understood

4 Results

4.1 User Experience with Threat Detection

Descriptions of observed user experience and cumulative statistics are presented in Table 1. Out of 34 participants, 15 users did not notice AV messages. Out of the remaining 19 users, 8 understood the messages. Moreover, only 6 users understood that the 'infected' file was removed by the AV tool. Although more users in the *irrelevant.doc* condition understood the situation, this occurred because the AV tools could not be balanced between conditions due to low number of participants for several AV tools. In the following, we first present three case studies to make clear how the combination of different factors shaped user experience. We then discuss each factor in more detail in Sect. 4.2.

Case Study 1: Windows Defender (9 Users). Notifications remained almost the same between 2017 and 2021 (Fig. 2). They are small (~3% of the screen), black and do not present any details about the found threat. They appear in the lower right corner of the screen, and disappear without user interaction after 3 s. The Windows OS notification Error (Fig. 3a) appears at roughly the same time in the center of the screen. Although this notification contains the word "virus" in the end of its second paragraph, only P20 noticed this fact, which led to his understanding the situation. All other participants either closed Error notification quickly, or clicked Try Again several times (the notification reappears in this case), and then closed it. During this time, the AV notification disappeared. P7 and P10 mentioned later that the `Error` message was too long.

Fig. 2. Windows Defender notifications: 2017 (to the left) and 2021 (to the right).

(a) `Error`: *An unexpected error is keeping you from copying this file.*

(b) `Adm`: *You'll need to provide administrator permission to copy this file.*

(c) `notF`: *Could not find this item.*

Fig. 3. Windows OS notifications (replicated in English). All messages named the affected file (called here *investment.doc*).

Combination of a long Windows OS notification in the middle of the screen with quick disappearance of the AV notification in the corner caused six users to overlook the AV notification. Additionally, two users noticed it, but thought that it belongs to other programs. As P9 remarked: *[AV notification] neither differs in size nor in anything else from all other Windows 10 messages.* This resulted in the extremely low understanding of the situation (1 out of 9). Later, when shown the AV notification on the screen capture, several users were dissatisfied with the absence of details about the virus: *It tells me that something has happened, but not in which program or where [...] the message also does not tell me due to which file this happened* (P3). They also commented that they would expect the AV notification to be red and appear in the center of the screen.

Case Study 2: Avira (6 Users). Notifications remained almost the same between 2017 and 2021 (Fig. 4). They are of middle size (∼8% of the screen), appear in the lower right corner, and users have to click on the red cross to close them. They show the name and path of the affected file, and the name of the mal-ware. Windows OS notification `Adm` (Fig. 3b) appeared simultaneously with the Avira notification, and if the users clicked `Continue`, the `notF` message (Fig. 3c) appeared. Four users did not notice the Avira notification at all, although it persisted till the end of their participation – they were too much distracted by the Windows OS notifications. When shown the screen capture video, they were surprised: *Oh, here it is! Oh my! I did not see it at all. Did it really appear?* (P21). Participants also reported habituation, as Avira seems to show a lot of information not connected to the threats: *I never look there [lower right corner], because Avira always shows ads there* (P21). Overall, only one user fully understood what happened.

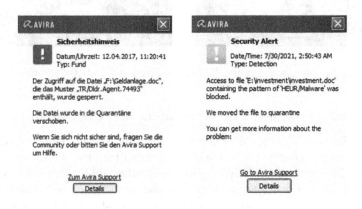

Fig. 4. Avira notifications: 2017 (to the left) and 2021 (to the right).

Opinions on the AV message differed. Thus, P21 wished the message to appear in the center, and P24 wished it was green, because she felt frightened by the red color. Generally, the information about file name and path was found very helpful. Still, some users found the message incomprehensible: *It does not tell me why this happened, and what should I do. And in "Details" it shows more things that I don't understand* (P11). Although P6 noticed the message and understood the situation well, she was unsure what happened to the file, and asked us to explain what is quarantine.

Case Study 3: AVG (3 Users). The notification is large and appears in the center of the screen (Fig. 5). It requires the user to choose an action: "Protect (recommended)" or "Ignore threat" (translated from German) and presents file name and path, as well as malware name. Two participants chose the "ignore" option, and one chose "protect". Even if the threat was "ignored", the file could not be accessed by users anymore. In all cases, participants were able to explain what happened, and understood the situation well. Two participants who ignored the threat explained that they would choose "protect" at home, but in the study, they trusted the lab environment. To summarize, the "ignore" option seemed to be unnecessary in 2017, as the file could not be accessed anyway, but the participants spent some time on the decision process. The change in 2021 (Fig. 5) seems to be positive: The message still appears in the middle of the screen, informs the users about the affected file, does not disappear without user interaction, but does not require taking a decision anymore.

Fig. 5. AVG notifications: 2017 (to the left) and 2021 (to the right).

4.2   Important Elements of Notifications and User Interaction

Position, Size and Colors. Most notifications appeared in the lower right corner of the screen. Several participants commented that the AV message should appear in the center. Especially Windows Defender and Sophos users, who saw small black AV notifications, wished that the notifications had a signal color. Central notifications were noticed and at least partially read by the users, and did not elicit any negative comments about their position, size or color.

Habituation and Generalization. Habituation refers to frequent appearances of notifications, whereas generalization transfers habituation from various non-essential notifications to important ones [36]. Avira users reported habituation (Sect. 4.1), and messages appearing in the lower right corner prompted several participants to comment on generalization. P25 (Sophos) said: *One is used to clicking away error messages. I thought it is connected to the USB drive, because it appeared when I inserted it.* P17 (Norton) explained: *If something appears at the bottom right, I pretend that it is not there. [...] I always click away everything at the bottom right, because things often appear there.*

Interaction with Windows OS Notifications. When AV notifications appeared at the lower right, some Windows OS notifications appeared around the same time in the center. This greatly distracted participants, such that they had difficulties to notice AV notifications, even if they did not disappear from the screen. Kaspersky, Security Essentials and Sophos exhibited a combination of a quickly disappearing AV message at the lower right with centrally placed Windows OS messages, similarly to Windows Defender, which resulted in confusion and low understanding rates. Central AV notifications appeared over the Windows OS messages, and thus did not distract the participants. Norton was the only AV tool where no Windows OS messages appeared for all three participants, showing that AV tools can work without evoking Windows OS notifications.

User Interaction and Decisions. As described in the AVG case, forcing users to decide what should happen to the 'infected' file was not helpful. However, AV notifications disappearing without any user interaction caused a lot of confusion. Most successful AV notifications were those that informed users about the threat detection and required user interaction to disappear.

Content. Notifications containing name of the 'infected' file greatly contributed to the understanding of the situation. Also path information was helpful, as the users could determine that the affected file comes from the USB drive. Malware name, on the other hand, did not help. P29 (Bitdefender) said: *There was this message that something somewhere was detected as malware.* Bitdefender presented only malware name, but no information about the file. Norton users received a succession of several messages. Some of these messages informed the users about "security risk Downloader", which was incomprehensible to them. However, some other messages referred to the name of the 'infected' file (without path), which helped them to partially understand what happened.

Terminology. Only G Data called the 'infected' file "virus". Other AV tools used terms "threat" (AVG, Bitdefender, Security Essentials, Sophos), "pattern" (Avira), "infected file" (Kaspersky), "security risk" (Norton), or "malware" (Windows Defender). Although previous work uncovered that "virus" is the most understandable term for non-experts [20,37], the terms used by participants' AV tools were understandable to them. However, some users commented that they don't know what is "quarantine".

4.3   AV Usage and Attitudes to AV Tools

When asked why they use AV, participants said that AV protects them from threats and provides a feeling of security. As many AV tools have extended functionality, some participants emphasized that their AV protects them from malicious websites: *My Norton also blocks some websites, then I don't go there* (P34). Users rely on the *expert function* of AV tools: *I find [using AV] sensible, because I cannot detect viruses by myself* (P33). However, several participants mentioned that AV cannot protect them from all threats, as one is never 100% secure. This effect is also reported by Wash and Rader [38]. 20 out of 34 users reported that they had a virus before (not necessarily on the same computer), and 11 of them lost data in consequence. 13 participants said that their present AV tool found threats previously, as it issued the corresponding notifications.

Participants expressed high satisfaction with their AV tools: they find them effective, trustworthy and usable, even if they were confused during the study. Many users think that paid AV tools offer better protection. Thus P15 (Avira) said: *It's for free, so I think it does not provide the best protection [...] On the other hand, I'm content with what I have.* P16 (Norton) commented: *I'm paying for it. Then they are taking care that it is okay.* Windows Defender is a special case, as five out of nine users were surprised that they have it on their laptops. They thought to have other AV tools: Avast, Avira, McAffee and Norton. P9 would like to return to Avira, but he has no idea how to do this. P20 and P31 seemed not to grasp at first that their previously installed AV tools were not active: *Windows Defender is not an antivirus program for me, I have Avira. I would have reacted to an Avira message* (P31).

When asked why they use this particular AV, 20 users said that a third person (parents, siblings, partners, computer shop) installed it, and 13 users installed their AV themselves. The latter performed better in the study: 9 out of 13 users at least partially understood the situation. Out of 17 users whose AV was installed by other people, only five at least partially understood the situation. Thus, it seems that past experience with the AV tool was helpful[9].

Parents were most often mentioned as a source of AV advice, which agrees with previous research [28,29]. Thus, P14 uses Kaspersky, because her mother uses it as well. P28 reports: *My father looked it all up [different AV tools] and recommended G Data.* P17 said (jokingly): *My parents have a Norton packet with four licenses, and forced me to install it, too.* Using AV seems to be a rule that parents convey to their children, just like rules of good behavior: *I know this from an early age* (P18).

5   Discussion

5.1   Preliminary Recommendations for AV Tool Design

To summarize our analysis, a helpful AV message should appear in the center of the screen and contain some signal colors, such as green or red. It should not require a decision about what should happen to the infected file, but it should also not disappear without user interaction. Name and path of the infected file should be communicated. Malware name, on the other hand, should not be presented in the threat detection notification (it can be presented in a more detailed view, which all AV tools offer). Furthermore, it is paramount that AV tools do not evoke Windows OS messages.

These findings are in line with the recommendations for design of security warnings [6]. A warning should present all important contextual information – for AV notification, this means file name and path. The warning should be concise, present information from users' viewpoint and offload expert information into "Details" – for AV notifications, this expert information is malware name. It is recommended to require user interaction in case of important events – a central AV notification that requires user interaction to disappear seems to be suitable.

Our recommendations are preliminary and should be systematically tested. Especially placing security notifications in the middle of the screen and requiring user action can be considered a controversial design decision, as it increases user effort [17]. However, confusion and incomprehension in case of threat detection also increases user effort and may be more disruptive to the users. This aspect needs further investigation.

---

[9] Four participants that used the fallback computer are excluded from these analyses.

5.2   Changes in AV Tools Over Time

According to Microsoft, Windows Defender was installed on 50% of Windows devices worldwide in 2019 [26,35], and its threat notification remained almost unchanged between 2017 and 2021. Thus, its poor performance in our study is likely to remain important in 2021. Also Avira and Norton notifications remained almost the same. These tools account for 17 out of 34 users in our study.

User interface and interaction of AVG, Bitdefender, Kaspersky and Sophos changed considerably from 2017 to 2021. Whereas changes in AVG seem to be positive according to our analysis, changes in other AV tools seem to be ambiguous. These tools present file name and path to the users in 2021, which is a positive change. On the other hand, all notifications appear in the lower right corner and have a black or dark blue background, which makes them similar to various Windows 10 notifications, implying danger of generalization. Whereas Sophos notifications now require user interaction to disappear (positive change), Kaspersky and Bitdefender notifications disappear without user interaction. On the whole, these changes make especially Kaspersky and Bitdefender notifications similar to the Windows Defender, which performed extremely poorly in our user study. We conclude that our study offers useful and novel insights irrespective of changes in AV tools over time.

5.3   Usability and User Acceptance of Security Tools

Our study shows that AV tools are not quite as usable as can be assumed from their popularity [18]. Nevertheless, participants considered AV to be usable and trustworthy, although not necessarily protecting them from all dangers. AV tools play the role of security experts that have knowledge and skills to recognize malicious files – which users would not be able to do on their own. Therefore, using AV seems to be a sensible protection measure. Returning to Microsoft's statement that more than 50% of Windows devices use Windows Defender [26], it is not quite clear whether this high usage rate is conscious, as some participants were not aware that they have Windows Defender. This raises a question of how *invisible* should a security tool be? Invisible, automated security has serious usability limitations [11], whereas visible security might offer better user experience, as is known for message encryption [13] and e-voting [10].

Recommendations for using particular AV tools usually refer to their malware detection rates, false positive rates and performance [2,4], but not to their usability. The key takeaway from this user study extends to all security tools with a user interface: Attention should be paid to the user experience and usability in cases where the tool detects an attack. These cases are most important for the users, and should be carefully tested.

5.4   Limitations

Conducting a lab study implies that participants might behave differently compared to their usual environment. To increase ecological validity, we gave the participants a task not related to security. Furthermore, 30 out of 34 participants used their own laptops, which accounted for realistic risk. We verified our realistic risk assumption by asking users which consequences a virus infection would have for their laptops, and 23 participants said that they would face serious problems. When we asked if participants would react differently at home, seven of them were unsure, and eight said "yes". They explained that they trusted the lab environment or wanted to complete the task, and therefore were less cautious. We used deception in recruitment to elicit most natural reactions of participants. In debriefing interviews, all participants said that they did not suspect that the study is concerned with AV tools.

We considered the scenario of inserting USB drives, but did not test drive-by downloads or email attachments. Therefore, these malware distribution scenarios need further investigation. Furthermore, as the user study was conducted several years ago, it is possible that users' reactions might have changed over time, as they learned more about their AV tools, and about the digital world generally.

Our sample was very young, well educated (university students) and skewed towards female participants. Therefore, our results may not generalize to older or less educated populations, and especially to those less knowledgeable about AV tools than our participants. Moreover, we could test only a limited number of AV tools, and most tools were tested only with a very small number of participants. Therefore, derived design guidelines should be further tested.

6   Conclusion and Future Work

We conducted a user study that observed user interactions with nine AV tools in a threat detection scenario, and uncovered serious user experience deficits. Our results, obtained in 2017, remain valid in 2021, as design of user interfaces and interactions of AV tools seems to lack evidence-based recommendations. Our study serves as a necessary starting point for further investigations. The next step is to validate our findings in a controlled experiment that systematically compares design elements from Sect. 4.2 with the goal of providing evidence-based recommendations for design of AV tools.

Acknowledgments. We thank Thilo Voigt for essential support in conducting the user study, Katrin Proschek for support in the usability lab and for the idea of the cover story, Martin Ortlieb and Stefan Brandenburg for help with study design, Stella Wohnig for assistance with data analysis, the anonymous reviewers for their valuable comments, and Simone Fischer-Hübner for shepherding.

References

1. Almuhimedi, H., Felt, A.P., Reeder, R.W., Consolvo, S.: Your reputation precedes you: History, reputation, and the chrome malware warning. In: Symposium on Usable Privacy and Security (2014)
2. Anti-Malware Testing Standards Organization (2021). https://www.amtso.org

3. Anderson, B.B., Kirwan, C.B., Jenkins, J.L., Eargle, D., Howard, S., Vance, A.: How polymorphic warnings reduce habituation in the brain: insights from an fMRI study. In: ACM Conference on Human Factors in Computing Systems (2015)

4. AV Test Modules (2021). https://www.av-test.org/en/about-the-institute/test-procedures/test-modules-under-windows-usability/

5. The best antivirus software for Windows Home User (2021). https://www.av-test.org/en/antivirus/home-windows

6. Bauer, L., Bravo-Lillo, C., Cranor, L., Fragkaki, E.: Warning design guidelines. Technical report CMU-CyLab-13-002 (2013)

7. Bravo-Lillo, C., Cranor, L.F., Downs, J., Komanduri, S.: Bridging the gap in computer security warnings: a mental model approach. IEEE Secur. Priv. **9**(2), 18–26 (2010)

8. Busse, K., Schäfer, J., Smith, M.: Replication: no one can hack my mind revisiting a study on expert and non-expert security practices and advice. In: Fifteenth Symposium on Usable Privacy and Security (2019)

9. Christin, N., Egelman, S., Vidas, T., Grossklags, J.: It's all about the benjamins: an empirical study on incentivizing users to ignore security advice. In: Danezis, G. (ed.) Financial Cryptography and Data Security, FC 2011. LNCS, vol. 7035, pp. 16–30. Springer, Heidelberg (2012). https://doi.org/10.1007/978-3-642-27576-0_2

10. Distler, V., Zollinger, M.L., Lallemand, C., Roenne, P.B., Ryan, P.Y., Koenig, V.: Security-visible, yet unseen? In: ACM Conference on Human Factors in Computing Systems (2019)

11. Edwards, W.K., Poole, E.S., Stoll, J.: Security automation considered harmful? In: Proceedings of the 2007 Workshop on New Security Paradigms (2008)

12. Egelman, S., Cranor, L.F., Hong, J.: You've been warned: an empirical study of the effectiveness of web browser phishing warnings. In: ACM Conference on Human Factors in Computing Systems (2008)

13. Fahl, S., Harbach, M., Muders, T., Smith, M., Sander, U.: Helping Johnny 2.0 to encrypt his Facebook conversations. In: Symposium on Usable Privacy and Security (2012)

14. Felt, A.P., et al.: Improving SSL warnings: comprehension and adherence. In: ACM Conference on Human Factors in Computing Systems (2015)

15. Forget, A., et al.: Do or do not, there is no try: user engagement may not improve security outcomes. In: Symposium on Usable Privacy and Security (2016)

16. Goodin, D.: Antivirus pioneer Symantec declares AV "dead" and "doomed to failure". Ars Technica (2014)

17. Herley, C.: More is not the answer. IEEE Secur. Priv. **12**(1), 14–19 (2013)

18. Ion, I., Reeder, R., Consolvo, S.: ...No one can hack my mind: comparing expert and non-expert security practices. In: Symposium on Usable Privacy and Security (2015)

19. Jenkins, J.L., Anderson, B.B., Vance, A., Kirwan, C.B., Eargle, D.: More harm than good? How messages that interrupt can make us vulnerable. Inf. Syst. Res. **27**(4), 880–896 (2016)

20. Kauer, M., Günther, S., Storck, D., Volkamer, M.: A comparison of American and German folk models of home computer security. In: Marinos, L., Askoxylakis, I. (eds.) Human Aspects of Information Security, Privacy, and Trust, HAS 2013. LNCS, vol. 8030, pp. 100–109. Springer, Heidelberg (2013). https://doi.org/10.1007/978-3-642-39345-7_11

21. Krol, K., Moroz, M., Sasse, M.A.: Don't work. can't work? Why it's time to rethink security warnings. In: International Conference on Risk and Security of Internet and Systems (CRiSIS) (2012)

22. Krol, K., Spring, J.M., Parkin, S., Sasse, M.A.: Towards robust experimental design for user studies in security and privacy. In: Learning from Authoritative Security Experiment Results (LASER) (2016)
23. Lalonde Levesque, F., Nsiempba, J., Fernandez, J.M., Chiasson, S., Somayaji, A.: A clinical study of risk factors related to malware infections. In: ACM SIGSAC Conference on Computer and Communications Cecurity (2013)
24. Modic, D., Anderson, R.: Reading this may harm your computer: the psychology of malware warnings. Comput. Hum. Behav. **41**, 71–79 (2014)
25. O'Callahan, R.: Disable Your Antivirus Software (Except Microsoft's) (2017). http://robert.ocallahan.org/2017/01/disable-your-antivirus-software-except.html
26. Popa, B.: Microsoft's Antivirus Defending More than Half of Windows PCs (2019). Softpedia
27. Purdy, K., Klosowski, T.: You Don't Need to Buy Antivirus Software. Wirecutter (2020). https://www.nytimes.com/wirecutter/blog/best-antivirus/
28. Redmiles, E.M., Kross, S., Mazurek, M.L.: How i learned to be secure: a census-representative survey of security advice sources and behavior. In: ACM SIGSAC Conference on Computer and Communications Security (2016)
29. Redmiles, E.M., Malone, A., Mazurek, M.L.: I think they're trying to tell me something: advice sources and selection for digital security. In: IEEE Symposium on Security and Privacy (2016)
30. Redmiles, E.M., et al.: A comprehensive quality evaluation of security and privacy advice on the web. In: USENIX Security (2020)
31. Reeder, R.W., Ion, I., Consolvo, S.: 152 simple steps to stay safe online: security advice for non-tech-savvy users. IEEE Secur. Priv. **15**(5), 55–64 (2017)
32. Schechter, S.E., Dhamija, R., Ozment, A., Fischer, I.: The emperor's new security indicators. In: IEEE Symposium on Security and Privacy (2007)
33. Sharif, M., et al.: A field study of computer-security perceptions using anti-virus customer-support chats. In: ACM Conference on Human Factors in Computing Systems (2019)
34. Sunshine, J., Egelman, S., Almuhimedi, H., Atri, N., Cranor, L.F.: Crying wolf: an empirical study of SSL warning effectiveness. In: USENIX Security (2009)
35. Tung, L.: Top Windows Defender expert: these are the threats security hasn't yet solved. ZDNet (2019)
36. Vance, A., Eargle, D., Jenkins, J.L., Kirwan, C.B., Anderson, B.B.: The fog of warnings: how non-essential notifications blur with security warnings. In: Symposium on Usable Privacy and Security (2019)
37. Wash, R.: Folk models of home computer security. In: Symposium on Usable Privacy and Security (2010)
38. Wash, R., Rader, E.: Too much knowledge? Security beliefs and protective behaviors among united states internet users. In: Symposium on Usable Privacy and Security (2015)
39. Wu, M., Miller, R.C., Garfinkel, S.L.: Do security toolbars actually prevent phishing attacks? In: ACM Conference on Human Factors in Computing Systems (2006)

Data Minimisation Potential for Timestamps in Git: An Empirical Analysis of User Configurations

Christian Burkert$^{(\boxtimes)}$, Johanna Ansohn McDougall , and Hannes Federrath

University of Hamburg, Hamburg, Germany
{christian.burkert,johanna.ansohn.mcdougall,
hannes.federrath}@uni-hamburg.de

Abstract. With the increasing digitisation, more and more of our activities leave digital traces. This is especially true for our work life. Data protection regulations demand the consideration of employees' right to privacy and that the recorded data is necessary and proportionate for the intended purpose. Prior work indicates that standard software commonly used in workplace environments records user activities in excessive detail. A major part of this are timestamps, whose temporal contextualisation facilitates monitoring. Applying data minimisation on timestamps is however dependent on an understanding of their necessity. We provide large-scale real-world evidence of user demand for timestamp precision. We analysed over 20 000 Git configuration files published on GitHub with regard to date-related customisation in output and filtering, and found that a large proportion of users choose customisations with lower or adaptive precision: almost 90% of chosen output formats for subcommand aliases use reduced or adaptive precision and about 75% of date filters use day precision or less. We believe that this is evidence for the viability of timestamp minimisation. We evaluate possible privacy gains and functionality losses and present a tool to reduce Git dates.

Keywords: Privacy · Data minimisation · Timestamps · Timestamp precision

1 Introduction

In increasingly digital work environments, employees' digital and non-digital work steps leave traces of their activities on computer systems. Employers, supervisors and analysts see such data as a resource and opportunity to gain intelligence for business optimisation. Without strong consideration of employees' right to privacy, such legitimate interests might easily lead to excessive and invasive monitoring, even without the employees noticing. Recent reports about mass lay-offs at the game design company Xsolla show that automatic monitoring of employee performance based on software activity logs is already done in

© IFIP International Federation for Information Processing 2022
Published by Springer Nature Switzerland AG 2022
W. Meng et al. (Eds.): SEC 2022, IFIP AICT 648, pp. 323–339, 2022.
https://doi.org/10.1007/978-3-031-06975-8_19

practice [7]. Such invasions of employee privacy are however restricted by data protection regulations like GDPR, which requires that the processing of personal data is necessary and proportionate for and limited to the intended purpose.

Software design can contribute to the protection of employee privacy by reducing the amount and detail of data that is stored about user interaction to such a necessary minimum. Prior work, however, indicates that software commonly used in workplaces records especially timestamps in excessive detail [2]. It shows that timestamps are not only often unused, but might otherwise also be of unnecessarily high precision. As timestamps allow an easy temporal profiling of employee activities, a reduction in precision could directly reduce the risk of profiling-related discrimination. For instance, a reduction can prevent the inference of intervals between successive work steps and thus mitigate the monitoring of speed and performance. Identifying the necessary level of precision is, of course, dependent on the domain and respective user demand. Nonetheless, similar precision demands can be expected for interactions of similar kind and frequency. In that sense, insights into which levels of timestamp precision are selected by workers if they have the choice, can inform the selection of more appropriate default precisions in software design. We argue that when users configure their tools to precisions that are lower than the default, this implies that the lower precision is still sufficient for them to fulfil their tasks. Therefore, user customisation is an indicator for users' demand for timestamp precision. With an informed understanding of users' demands, developers can then built software with demand-proportionate timestamping and privacy-friendly defaults.

To the best of our knowledge, we provide the first large-scale real-world analysis of user demand for timestamp precision. Our analysis is based on configuration files for the popular revision control system Git, that users have made publicly available on GitHub. Git is a standard tool for software development workers and its recording of worker activity in the form of commits, contributes significantly to the overall traces that developers leave during a workday. Commit dates have been used to infer privacy sensitive information like temporal work patterns [3] and coding times [17]. The analysed configurations can contain various preferences that customise the way Git presents dates, including their precision. For instance, using the date formats *iso* or *short* would indicate a high (second) or low (day) precision demand respectively. We also examined the precision of filters (e.g., *8 h ago*) used to limit the range of outputs. In total, we analysed over 20 000 configuration files. We make the following contributions:

- We compile and provide a comprehensive large-scale dataset of date-related usage features extracted from publicly available Git configs.
- We provide empirical evidence for the demand of date precision by users, as determined by the precision of user selected date formats.
- We discuss and evaluate privacy gain and functionality loss.
- We present a utility that allows users to redact their Git timestamps.

The remainder is structured as follows: Sect. 2 presents related work. Section 3 provides a necessary background on Git and its date handling. We describe the acquisition and analysis of our Git config dataset in Sect. 4 and Sect. 5, and discuss findings, issues and applications in Sect. 6. Section 7 concludes the paper.

2   Related Work

To the best of our knowledge, we are the first to gather empirical evidence for the potential of data minimisation in timestamps. In prior work, we inspected application source code in order to assess the programmatic use of timestamps in application data models [2]. The case study of the Mattermost application found that most user-related timestamps have *no* programmatic use and only a small fraction are displayed on the user interface. We addressed the potential to apply precision reduction to user-facing timestamps. However, the code analysis could not provide any indication of acceptable levels of reduction. More work has been done on the exploitation of Git timestamps and the potential privacy risks. Claes et al. [3] use commit dates to analyse temporal characteristics of contributors to software projects. Eyolfson et al. [6] use dates to find temporal factors for low-quality contributions. Wright and Ziegler [17] train probabilistic models on individual developers' committing habits in an effort to remove noise from coding time estimations. Traullé and Dalle [16] analyse the evolution of developers' work rhythms based on commit dates. Following a more general approach, Mavriki and Karyda [13] analyse privacy threats arising from the evaluation of big data and their impact on individuals, groups and society. Drakonakis et al. [4] evaluate privacy risks of meta data with a focus on online activity in social media and, e.g., try to infer location information from publicly available data. No work seems to exist that proposes or evaluates temporal performance metrics. Slagell et al. [15] proposes time unit annihilation, i.e., precision reduction, to make timestamps less distinct and sensitive. Looking at developer behaviour, Senarath and Arachchilage [14] found that while developers typically do not program in a way that fulfils data minimisation, being made aware of its necessity made them apply the principle across the whole data processing chain. With this paper, we also strive to raise the awareness for minimisation of temporal data.

3   Theoretical Background: Git and Date Handling

This section provides a background on Git's time and date configuration options. Experts in Git and its date and pretty formatting may jump directly to Sect. 4.

Git's command line interface exposes individual actions like creating a commit or listing the history via subcommands like `git commit` or `git log`. Their behaviour can be configured via command line arguments and—to some extent— via settings made in configuration files. Frequently used combinations of subcommands and arguments can be set as shortcuts via so-called *aliases*, similar to shell aliases. For example, the shortcut `git ly` set in Listing 1.1 configures the `log` subcommand to list all commits since yesterday.

In the following, we describe the role and creation of dates in Git and then explain the date-related features that will be empirically analysed later.

3.1   Dates in Git

Git associates two types of dates with each commit: the author date and the committer date. Both are usually automatically set to the current date and

Listing 1.1. Examplary Git config

```
[alias]
  ly = log --date=human --since=yesterday
[blame]
  date = short
[pretty]
  my = %h %an (%ai)
```

Table 1. Git's built-in date formats and their precision.

Name	Suffix	Precision	Example(s)
default	–	Second	Wed Sep 22 14:57:31 2021 +0200
human	–	Day to second	Sep 21 2021/7 s ago
iso	i/I	Second	2021-09-22 14:57:31 +0200
raw	–	Second	1632315451 +0200
relative	r	Year to second	7 years ago/7 s ago
rfc	D	Second	Wed, 22 Sep 2021 14:57:31 +0200
short	s	Day	2021-10-04
unix	t	Second	1632315451

time, except in case of operations that modify existing commits (e.g., rebases or cherry picks): Here, only the committer date will be updated, but the author date stays as is. Consequently, the author date reflects the time of an initial composition, while the committer date reflects the time of an insertion in the history. Both dates are recorded as seconds since the Unix epoch. Changes to the date precision are not supported by Git. For commit creation, users can provide custom dates through environment variables to use instead of the current. This interface could be used by users to manually set dates with reduced precision. This is however not supported for commands that modify commits in bulk. Here, precision reduction is only possible after the fact, by rewriting the history.

3.2   Features for Date Presentation and Filtering

Date Formatting. Date formatting is available for subcommands like log and show for commit history information, and also for commands that annotate the content of tracked files with commit metadata like blame or annotate. The formatting option customises how Git renders author and committer dates in the command outputs.

Git offers built-in date formats listed in Table 1 and the option for custom format strings which are passed to the system's strftime implementation. The chosen format influences the precision of the displayed date. Five of the eight built-in formats show the full second precision but in different styles like ISO 8601.

Table 2. Git offers predefined (built-in) pretty formats that vary in which dates they show and with what date format (Table 1) those are formatted by default. Some built-ins are fixed to that default and can not be changed by date options.

Built-in	full	oneline	short	medium	reference	email	mboxrd	fuller	raw
Dates used	None			Author				Both	
Date format	–	–	–	default	short	rfc	rfc	default	raw
Fixed format	–	–	–	–	–	✓	✓	–	✓

The others reduce the displayed date precision: *short* omits the time, and both *human* and *relative* use variable precisions that are exact (to the second) when the respective date is recent, and gradually less precise with growing temporal distance. Date formats can be set via the command line option `--date` or via config settings for the `log` and `blame` family of subcommands.

Pretty Formatting. Pretty formatting allows the customisation of commit metadata presentation by commands like `log` or `show`, including the names and email addresses of author and committer as well as the dates mentioned above. Like for date formatting, Git offers built-in formats as well as custom format strings with placeholders for each available piece of commit metadata.

Each built-in implies which dates are used (author, committer, or both) and a date format, that—with some exceptions—can be adapted via date options (see Table 2). In custom formats, the relevant placeholders are `%ad` for author dates and `%cd` for committer dates. The built-in date formats (cf. Sect. 3.2) are available as modifiers. For instance, `%cr` will set the committer date in the *relative* format. Hence, placeholders offer a way to adjust dates separately for each type and independently of other configurations. As shown in Listing 1.1, custom pretty formats can also be set as aliases in a config.

Date Filtering. Some Git subcommands offer limiting their output based on temporal constraints. By passing `--since` or `--until` to `log`, it will list only commits committed since or until the given reference. References can be given in a wide range of syntaxes and formats, as absolute points in time, time distances, and combinations thereof (e.g., *April 2020, 01/01 last year*, or *8 h ago*). Git understands a set of common temporal reference points like *midnight* or *yesterday*. We call those *points of reference*.

4   Dataset Acquisition

The basis for our analysis of timestamp precision demand are Git configuration files (configs). To the best of our knowledge, there was no previously available dataset of Git configs or derivations thereof. For that reason, we compiled a dataset based on configs that users published on GitHub. This section describes the identification of the relevant files, their extraction, de-duplication, and the subsequent feature extraction. We also discuss ethical and privacy concerns.

4.1 File Identification and Extraction

Git supports a multi-level hierarchy of configs from the individual repository level to the user and system level [9, git-config]. We limited our data acquisition to user-level configs, in which users typically set their personal preferences and customisations. These configs are located as `.gitconfig` in the user's home directory. GitHub recognises these files in repositories hosted on their service and assigns them the *Git Config* content language tag. To perform automatic searches, we used the code search endpoint of GitHub's REST API [11]. Due to strict rate limiting and the high load that large-scale code searches might induce on GitHub's servers, we added another condition to narrow down the search to configs that include alias definitions. The resulting search is `alias language:''Git Config"`. We ran the acquisition on Sep 17th, 2021. It yielded 23 691 matching files.

The code search API returns a paginated list including URLs to access the matching files. To obtain all files, we had to overcome GitHub's limitation to return at most 10 pages per query with 100 items each. To do so, we built a crawler that finds small enough sub-queries by using file size constraints. We found that result pages are not necessarily filled to their full 100 items, probably due to pre-emptive processing. We extracted 20 757 matches (88%).

4.2 De-duplication

Users might include the same config multiple times in the same or different repositories. To avoid an overrepresentation of users through duplicates, we compared the cryptographic hashes of each config: If a hash occurred more than once within the namespace of the same user, we included only one instance in our dataset. If namespaces differed, we included both instances. We argue that the latter does not constitute a duplicated representation, but a legitimate appropriation by another user and should therefore be counted. Also note that GitHub's Search API does not index forks unless their star count is higher than their parent's [11]. Forks do therefore not introduce unwanted duplicates to our dataset.

We identified and excluded 345 duplicates, i.e., configs that occurred repeatedly in the same namespace. We noticed 554 re-uses of configs in different namespaces. After de-duplication, our dataset comprised configs from 19 468 unique users. 695 users (3.6%) contributed multiple non-identical configs, which accumulate to 1637 configs (8.4%). We argue that those configs should not be excluded, as users might use different configs in different contexts to serve different use cases. Hence, we include them to capture as many use cases as possible.

4.3 Feature Extraction

Having extracted the content of matching configs from GitHub, we subsequently tried to parse each config and extract usage information about the date-related

Table 3. Support for date-related features in Git subcommands.

	annotate	blame	diff-tree	log	rev-list	shortlog	show	whatchanged
date	✓†	✓	✓*	✓	✓		✓*	✓
pretty			✓	✓	✓		✓	✓
since/until		✓		✓	✓	✓	✓*	✓

*=undocumented, †=disfunctional

features described in Sect. 3. In the following, we first describe our process of finding and verifying Git subcommands that support the features in question. After that, we briefly describe the extraction result.

To ensure that all relevant subcommands were regarded during extraction, we first searched and inspected the manual pages of each subcommand for the respective command line options. To compensate for any incompleteness or incorrectness in the manuals, we performed automatic tests to check whether any of the date-related options are accepted *and* make a difference to the resulting output. As a result, we identified discrepancies in terms of undocumented feature support as well as non-functioning documented support (in Git version 2.29.2), which we extracted nonetheless. The feature support is shown in Table 3.

We performed the feature extraction on all downloaded configs. 41 configs could not be parsed due to invalid syntax. The extraction result comprises usage counts for all options described above as well as derived precision information. We have made the dataset available on GitHub [1].

4.4   Potential Ethical and Privacy Concerns

Compiling a dataset of users' Git configurations might raise concerns about the ethics of data extraction or user privacy. We carefully designed our process to address potential concerns.

Code search queries cause a higher load for GitHub than other requests. However, using it enabled us to significantly reduce the total number of queries compared to alternative approaches like searching for repositories named `dotfiles` (about 150 000 matches). Conducting a pure filename based search is also only possible via code search and would have yielded more than three times as many results without the constraint of the `alias` keyword. We are therefore convinced that our approach minimised the load on GitHub compared to other approaches. In general, we followed GitHub's best practices [10].

Regarding user privacy, our dataset only includes configs that users made public on GitHub. The common practice of publishing *dotfile* repositories follows the spirit of sharing knowledge with the community and providing others with a resource of proven configurations. However, we cannot rule out that an unknown proportion of users uploaded their configuration accidentally or not knowing that it will be public. Our extraction is therefore designed to only extract feature usage counts and no free-form data. This ensures that *no* identifying information,

Table 4. Alias definitions and date-related feature usage in the dataset.

Aliases	Mean	Std.	Q_1	Q_2	Q_3	max
subcommand	15.49	22.35	4.00	9.00	19.00	334.00
- shell	3.52	8.64	0.00	1.00	4.00	258.00
- log-like	2.25	3.13	1.00	1.00	3.00	43.00
- blame-like	0.02	0.15	0.00	0.00	0.00	3.00
- filter capable	2.34	3.26	1.00	1.00	3.00	44.00
pretty format	0.03	0.29	0.00	0.00	0.00	12.00

(a) Descriptive statistics about the absolute frequencies of subcommand aliases with sub-types as well as pretty format aliases per config. (Q_i: i-th quartile)

in %	total	date	pretty	since
annotate	28	0.00	-	-
blame	396	2.02	-	0.00
diff-tree	169	0.00	0.00	-
log	41467	23.66	76.41	2.47
rev-list	194	0.00	5.67	0.52
shortlog	2202	-	-	4.77
show	3440	9.04	18.98	0.06
whatchanged	553	3.62	14.65	-

(b) Relative frequency of feature usage in aliases for subcommands (if supported).

sensitive data or unwanted disclosures like cryptographic secrets are included. We thus deemed it unnecessary to seek approval from the university ethics board.

5   Data Analysis

The extracted config features are the basis for our analysis described in this section. To put the findings into perspective, we first provide some basic statistics about the composition of our dataset, before we then analyse users' choices for formatting and filtering, and derive date precisions from them.

We extracted features from 20 369 files. Table 4a provides descriptive statistics about the per-config frequencies of subcommand and pretty format aliases. Overall, we extracted 315 520 definitions of subcommand aliases. On average, each config provided 15.5 such aliases. We identified and excluded in total 71 727 (23%) aliases with shell expressions. Table 4b provides relative occurrences of features accumulated per subcommand. We found that pretty formatting is very commonly used for `log` (76%), but less for other subcommands. Date formatting is used fairly often for `log` as well (24%), but far less for others.

5.1   Date Formatting

We analysed the usage of date formats in subcommand aliases and the two config settings for `log` and `blame`. The usage in subcommand aliases is dominated by aliases for `log` (see Fig. 1a), since almost a quarter of the more than 41 000 `log` aliases use date formatting. The prevalent formats are *relative* and *short*. Aliases for the `show` subcommand predominantly use the *short* option.

We saw a low use of the settings `log.date` and `blame.date`. Only 491 log and 68 blame date formats were set by users, less than 10% of which are custom format strings (see Fig. 1b). The *relative* format is again the most popular, but in contrast to command aliases, *short* is only forth after *iso* and *default*. Note that the high number for the *default* format is due to users having selected the

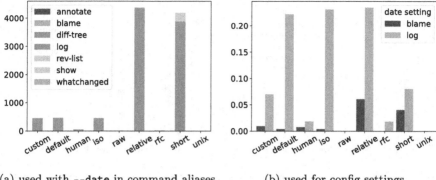

(a) used with --**date** in command aliases   (b) used for config settings

Fig. 1. Distribution of date formatting options used as arguments in subcommand aliases or as config settings. The most frequent options vary noticeably between those contexts: *short* is much less common in settings than in aliases.

Table 5. Date usage in pretty formats across all configuration options.

	Total	Built-in [%]				Custom [%]			
		None	Author	Committer	Both	None	Author	Committer	Both
Command aliases	32430	31.07	0.53	0.00	1.30	9.88	28.12	27.30	1.47
Pretty aliases	594	0.00	0.00	0.00	0.34	15.15	47.98	29.97	6.57
Format.pretty	603	9.95	1.99	0.00	6.63	1.33	48.59	29.35	2.16

default-local option. As localisation does not factor into date precision, we have counted all localised options for their non-localised correspondent.

Due to the overall low adoption of custom date format strings in conjunction with their comparatively complex and system/dependent interpretation, we omitted them from further analysis.

5.2 Pretty Formatting

Date Usage. We analysed which (if any) date types are used in pretty formats for command aliases, **pretty.*** aliases, and the **format.pretty** setting. For built-in formats, we classified the date use according to documentation [9, git-log], which we verified experimentally. For custom formats, we considered a date type as present if the corresponding placeholder (e.g., **%ad** for author) is contained and not escaped. If we encountered the use of a user-defined format alias, we resolved the alias and proceeded as if the resolved format was directly used. The results are shown in Table 5 and described in the following.

Pretty usage in **command aliases** is also dominated by **log**. Over three quarters of all **log** aliases use pretty formatting. The largest proportion of these formats use no dates at all. 31% are built-ins with no date and about 10% are date-less custom format strings. We found that **oneline** with over 90%

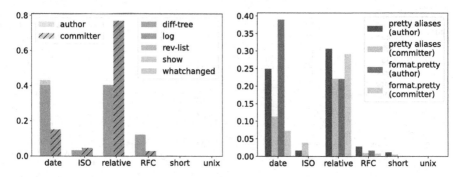

(a) custom formats in subcommand aliases   (b) format aliases and `format.pretty`

Fig. 2. Relative distribution of date modifier usage in pretty formatting. The *relative* and *date* modifiers are most commonly used across all config options. (Color figure online)

is the only built-in with frequent use in aliases. Custom formats with either author or committer date are used in around a quarter of formats each. Formats with both dates make up less than 3% combined. Regarding **pretty format aliases**, we extracted 594 uses, which are almost entirely user-defined formats. Their date usage varies significantly from subcommand aliases: Almost half the formats exclusively use author dates and 30% exclusively use committer dates. 15% contain no dates. Regarding **format.pretty settings**, we found 603 configs that use this feature. Here, most occurrences of built-in formats have no (10%) or both dates (7%). The usage of exclusive author and committer dates in custom formats closely corresponds to our observation for pretty aliases, with about 80% combined. However, only about 1% are custom formats with no date. It appears that demand for date-less formatting is satisfied by built-in formats.

Date Modifiers. As described in Sect. 3.2, custom pretty formats in addition to choosing the desired date type, also allow a rudimentary date formatting.

For **command aliases**, *date* and *relative* are the most common modifiers (see Fig. 2a). More than 75% of committer and 40% of author dates use the *relative* modifier. The *short* date format receives almost no usage. The *date* modifier, which makes the output dependent on `--date` and related settings, is used for about 40% of author dates and about 15% of committer dates. The modifier usage in **pretty format aliases** is illustrated in Fig. 2b (blue bars). Most used is the *relative* format with combined over 50%, followed by the adaptive *date* modifier with about 35%. The usage in **format.pretty settings** is depicted by the green bars in Fig. 2b. Similar to format aliases, *date* and *relative* are by far the most used modifiers with about 40 and 55% each.

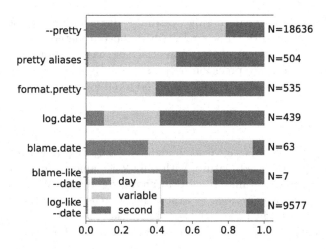

Fig. 3. Distributions of date output precision across the formatting options. Second precision is least common in alias definitions for log-like subcommands (regarding `--pretty` and `--date`) which also have the most frequent use.

5.3 Resulting Date Output Precisions

Based on the previous analysis, we could determine the precisions of dates displayed as a result of using the extracted configs. The precision directly follows from the used date format (see Table 1) and can be either *second*, *day*, or *variable*. The effective precision of variable formats depends on the recency of the event and ranges between day and second. As we cannot resolve this variability, we will leave it as a third precision in between. Formats with *no* dates are not considered in this section.

For **subcommand aliases** supplying explicit `--pretty` formats, we proceeded differently for built-in and custom formats: For built-ins a with fixed date format, the precision directly follows from the fixed format. For instance, `email` hard-codes the *rfc* format which has a precision of seconds. The precision of all other built-ins is determined by the `--date` option, or—if none is given— by the `log.date` setting or its default, the *default* date format. The same date format resolution applies, if custom pretty formats use the *date* modifier. Otherwise, the resulting precision directly follows from the used modifier. Note that the about 1.5% of custom pretty formats that use both date types could therefore use a different precision per type. In that case, we considered the higher precision of the two for our further analysis. For that purpose, we used the following sort sequence of precisions: day < variable < second. Figure 3 illustrates, e. g., that 60% of subcommands' pretty formatting that contains date information effectively display it with a variable precision. And over 90% of pretty-capable (log-like) aliases that supply `--date` options display with variable or day precision.

We applied the same evaluation to pretty formats set as **format aliases** and the **format.pretty** option. Since both settings are taken outside the context of a command invocation, considering possible --date options is not applicable. Otherwise, we followed the process described above to determine the applicable date format, including considering potential log.date options. In contrast to subcommand aliases, day precision outputs are negligible and second precision output is much more common with about 50 to 60% (see Fig. 3).

5.4 Date Filters

We found that date filter usage is again dominated by log. In general, it appears to be an infrequently used feature, with only 2.5% among log aliases. In relative terms, it is most commonly used in shortlog aliases. We also found that among the date filtering options, --since makes up for almost the entire feature usage, whereas --until is almost exclusively used in combination with since. All figures include the alternative names --after and --before.

Extraction Methodology. In contrast to date formatting, the precision of filters does not follow directly from a set of predefined options. Moreover, the leniency of the filter parser makes it difficult to cover all allowed inputs during precision classification. For that reason, we decided to directly use Git's parser code for our analysis. We sliced the responsible functionality from the official Git source code [8, v2.32.0-rc2] and linked the functions with our analysis tool. We instrumented Git's date parser at 25 locations to keep track of the smallest unit of time addressed by a filter. This is illustrated by the following two examples:

$$\underbrace{1\,\text{hour}}_{\text{hour}} \underbrace{30\,\text{minutes}}_{\text{minute}}\,\text{ago} \qquad \underbrace{\text{yesterday}}_{\text{day}} \underbrace{5\text{pm}}_{\text{hour}}$$

In the first example, the smallest unit is given in minutes, so we consider the filter to have minute precision. In the second example, the smallest unit is given by the full hour, thus we consider the filter to have hour precision. We excluded date filters containing shell command substitutions, of which we identified 26 (2.2%). Another 7 were rejected by Git as invalid, leaving 1156 valid filters.

Precision Classification. When classifying date filter precision, the question arises whether the hour 0 should be treated as hour precision like every other hour value, or as an indicator for the lower day precision. In order to not underestimate the demand for precision, we assumed the hour precision. This is also in concordance with the *midnight* point of reference (POR). The available precision levels are the date unit based precisions year to second (including week), supplemented by the *undefined* precision which is assigned if date filters use the PORs *now* or *never* which allow no classification. Figure 4 illustrates the resulting precisions. Most date filters are in the *day* precision (46%), followed by *hour* (23%) and *week* (18%). Precisions higher than *hour* make up less than 0.5%.

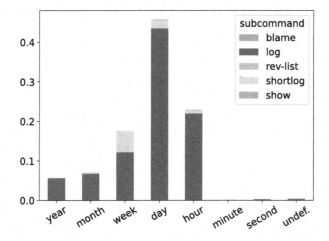

Fig. 4. Overall distribution of precisions that are implied by the date filters used for the `--since` or `--until` options in subcommand aliases. Day precision is by far the most common. Filters with precisions higher than hour have almost no use at all.

6 Discussion

In the following, we discuss the privacy gain and functionality loss related to precision reduction, as well as possible objections to the representativeness of our dataset. Additionally, we present options to reduce date precision in Git.

6.1 Privacy Gain and Functionality Loss

In principle, the GDPR mandates data minimisation regardless of achievable privacy gains. Legally, the necessity of data needs to be argued and not its harmfulness to privacy. Nonetheless, to evaluate technical minimisation approaches, some notion of privacy gain might be of interest. Benchmarking the effectiveness of timestamp precision reduction based on known inference techniques is however highly context specific and ignorant to future technical developments. Moreover, timestamp-specific inference techniques are scarce (cf. Sect. 2). Instead, we argue that a data-oriented evaluation of statistical properties like changes in distribution are more conclusive of discriminatory power and minimisation effects. For instance, the number of distinguishable activity points over a given period expresses an attacker's ability to observe intervals between actions, which might be used to monitor users' throughput. Following that method, we evaluated the effect of different precision reductions on real-world Git data. This provides additional empirical evidence on the question whether a reduction within the precision range of our previous demand analysis, i.e., no less than day precision, could meaningfully improve user privacy.

We obtained commits from a GitHub mirror curated by the GHTorrent project [12], which contains all public GitHub activity since 2012. Based on

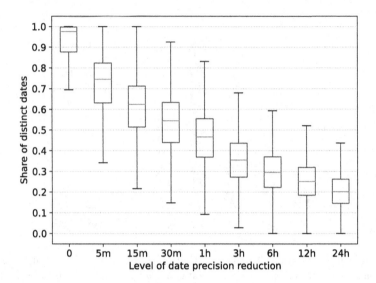

Fig. 5. The share of users' distinct Git dates decreases fast with increased precision reduction, as evaluated on a GitHub snapshot of 360 million commits. At a 1 h precision level, more than half of the median user's timestamps are indistinguishable from their chronological predecessors, thus preventing the inference of the temporal intervals between the respective activities.

a snapshot from April 1st, 2019, we extracted all commits from users with a total of one to ten thousand commits each, calculated over the full lifespan of the dataset. We argue that this sample of users adequately represents frequently active users without introducing much bias by bot-driven accounts that is expected to increase on more active accounts, given that ten thousand commits equates to almost four commits per day, for *every* day in the scope of the dataset. To nonetheless compare the findings, we also performed the analysis on the sample of users with between 10 and 100 thousand total commits. The expectation being, that the more commits a user has, the higher their activity density, and hence the higher the observed precision reduction effects. In total, we analysed 360 million commits by 160 thousand users in the range of one to ten thousand commits, and 100 million commits by 5000 users in the range of 10 to 100 thousand commits.

For each user, we counted the number of distinct activity points in time at various precision reduction levels from five minutes to one day. Activity points in time are given by the commit dates and are regarded as distinct, if—after applying the precision reduction—the remaining significant date information differs. The precision reduction is applied by rounding towards the next smaller integral multiple of the precision. As Fig. 5 shows, a 5 min reduction level already results in only 75% distinct dates (median), and less than 50% at 1 h. With the sample of very active users, we saw 54% and 28% for 5 min and 1 h respectively. This indicates that a moderate precision reduction already prevents monitoring of intervals for a significant share of activities.

Functionality loss on the other hand is relevant to evaluate the cost of minimisation techniques. Such loss could be caused to the minimised application itself or to attached processes and workflows. As Git itself does not programmatically use commit dates but only passes them on, there is no direct loss of functionality or integrity. Usability should only be effected in the sense that users get unexpected results, e. g., for filtering, if they were unaware of the precision reduction. For instance, if a commit occurred within the last minute but was reduced to hour precision, a filter for *until 30 min ago* would list this command, provided no further precautions where taken. Such precautions could be to show a notice if filters conflict with timestamp precision or to reject them. The extent to which precision reduction affects Git workflows is of course very subjective. Our empirical data on chosen display and filter precisions is one indicator for reduction impact. Any reduction within the range of those commonly chosen precisions would have limited loss for workflows based on our analysed features. In qualitative interviews with four DevOps workers of different seniority, their stated interest in timestamp precision varied from no interest to precise oversight of team activities. This underlines our assumption that workflow-related interest in precise timestamps might be more driven by individual mannerism than procedural necessities. As user privacy should not be left to individual discretion, tools like Git should support to enforce the precision levels agreed upon on a per-team basis.

6.2   Representativeness and Limitations

Configurations on GitHub might not be representative for the overall user base of Git. Only users that desire a behaviour different from the default even make certain settings like aliases. However, a motivation to define aliases in general, is to make frequently used commands and arguments more easily accessible. Such settings are therefore not necessarily motivated by a wish to change default behaviour. We argue that the subset of users that define aliases is therefore not necessarily biased towards a date-related behaviour that differs from the default. The analysed settings might require a more experienced Git user to discover and use them. In that sense our analyses might be biased towards such users. To assess whether experience influences precision demand, future research could correlate our precision analysis with, e.g., commit counts. We argue that experience certainly factors into the discoverability of options, but presumably less into their configuration. Whether or not users need second-precision dates in a log output is likely unrelated to their experience.

6.3   Timestamp Reduction Approaches and Tools

Timestamp reduction could be applied on the presentation level, but to hinder performance monitoring and not be easily circumventable, it should be applied during recording. Wherever precision demand is highly user-specific, the recorded precision should be customisable. Nonetheless, a privacy-friendly default should be chosen that reflects most needs. If Git users wish to reduce the precision with which their actions are timestamped, they find no support to do so in Git today. And as dates are included in the input to the hash function that determines the commit hash, retroactive reductions interfere with hash chaining and history keeping. As such, modification to the dates might cause diverging Git histories. To nonetheless provide users with the option to reduce their timestamp precision, we built `git-privacy` [5], a tool that uses Git hooks to reduce timestamps while avoiding conflict with previously distributed states. It uses a unit annihilation approach similar to the rounding down described in Sect. 6.1, where users can choose the most significant time unit that should remain precise. In systems like Git with integrity-protected timestamps, at least excluding higher-precision timestamp parts from the integrity protection would allow post-recording reduction policies to take effect without compromising the history.

7   Summary and Conclusion

Using Git config files that users published on GitHub, we have compiled and analysed a large-scale dataset of features related to users' demand for timestamp precision. Our analysis of the usage of date and pretty formatting as well as date filters indicates that Git's current behaviour of recording dates to the precise second might not be justified by user demand. In fact, we found that when users customise output of subcommand aliases, over 40% of formats omit dates entirely. And of the remaining formats, 80% display dates with a reduced variable or static day precision. As a result, a static full second precision is not utilised by nearly 90% of all subcommand pretty formats. Similarly, over 90% of date formatting in subcommand aliases uses variable or day precision. We saw a higher ratio of second precision output in pretty aliases as well as format and date settings, which could be due to users picking default date formats in pretty format stings, and due to a preference for ISO-style output. Our analysis of date filters found that only 0.5% of filters would require a precision of minute or second. In fact, 74% require a precision of day or less. All in all, we believe that our analysis provides strong empirical evidence, that user demand for precision can be met with less than second-precise timestamps. Our evaluation of possible privacy gains suggests that small precision reduction levels of a few minutes already have significant effects. As Git itself does not require any date precision, making it configurable would not only allow teams to define appropriate levels for their use case, but also facilitate a more GDPR-compliant use in companies. We encourage software engineers to employ reduced and adaptive precision timestamping for more proportionate solutions.

Acknowledgements. We would like to thank the anonymous reviewers and Vaclav Matyas for their constructive and very helpful suggestions to improve this paper. The work is supported by the German Federal Ministry of Education and Research (BMBF) as part of the project Employee Privacy in Development and Operations (EMPRI-DEVOPS) under grant 16KIS0922K.

References

1. Burkert, C.: gitconfig date study dataset (2022). https://github.com/EMPRIDEVOPS/gitconfig-study-dataset
2. Burkert, C., Federrath, H.: Towards minimising timestamp usage in application software. In: Pérez-Solà, C., Navarro-Arribas, G., Biryukov, A., Garcia-Alfaro, J. (eds.) Data Privacy Management, Cryptocurrencies and Blockchain Technology, DPM/CBT -2019. LNCS, vol. 11737, pp. 138–155. Springer, Cham (2019). https://doi.org/10.1007/978-3-030-31500-9_9
3. Claes, M., Mäntylä, M.V., Kuutila, M., Adams, B.: Do programmers work at night or during the weekend? In: ICSE. ACM (2018)
4. Drakonakis, K., Ilia, P., Ioannidis, S., Polakis, J.: Please forget where I was last summer: the privacy risks of public location (meta)data. In: NDSS (2019)
5. EMPRI-DEVOPS: git-privacy. https://github.com/EMPRI-DEVOPS/git-privacy
6. Eyolfson, J., Tan, L., Lam, P.: Do time of day and developer experience affect commit bugginess? In: MSR. ACM (2011)
7. Game World Observer: Xsolla cites growth rate slowdown as reason for layoffs, CEO's tweet causes further controversy (2021). https://gameworldobserver.com/?p=10949
8. Git: Git Source Code (2021). https://github.com/git/git
9. Git: Reference (2022). https://git-scm.com/docs. Accessed 28 March 2022
10. GitHub Docs: Best practices for integrators (2021). https://docs.github.com/en/rest/guides/best-practices-for-integrators. Accessed 24 Sep 2021
11. GitHub Docs: Search API (2021). https://docs.github.com/en/rest/reference/search. Accessed 24 Sep 2021
12. Gousios, G.: The GHTorrent dataset and tool suite. In: MSR 2013 (2013)
13. Mavriki, P., Karyda, M.: Profiling with big data: identifying privacy implications for individuals, groups and society. In: MCIS (2018)
14. Senarath, A., Arachchilage, N.A.G.: Understanding software developers' approach towards implementing data minimization (2018). https://arxiv.org/abs/1808.01479
15. Slagell, A.J., Lakkaraju, K., Luo, K.: FLAIM: a multi-level anonymization framework for computer and network logs. In: LISA, pp. 63–77. USENIX (2006)
16. Traullé, B., Dalle, J.-M.: The evolution of developer work rhythms. In: Staab, S., Koltsova, O., Ignatov, D.I. (eds.) Social Informatics, SocInfo 2018. LNCS, vol. 11185, pp. 420–438. Springer, Cham (2018). https://doi.org/10.1007/978-3-030-01129-1_26
17. Wright, I., Ziegler, A.: The standard coder: a machine learning approach to measuring the effort required to produce source code change. In: RAISE (2019)

Blockchain

Greedy Networking in Cryptocurrency Blockchain

Simeon Wuthier$^{(\boxtimes)}$, Pranav Chandramouli, Xiaobo Zhou,
and Sang-Yoon Chang

Department of Computer Science, University of Colorado,
Colorado, Colorado Springs, USA
{swuthier,pchandra,xzhou,schang2}@uccs.edu

Abstract. Proof of work (PoW) is a widely adopted distributed consensus protocol which enables cryptocurrency transaction processing without a trusted third party. The miners are financially incentivized to participate in the PoW consensus protocol, and PoW relies on the underlying peer-to-peer (P2P) networking for receiving and transmitting the transactions and the up-to-date blocks (which are the inputs for the PoW consensus protocol). We study the rational miner strategy but control an orthogonal parameter from those in the previous blockchain research, which has studied the control of the mining power or the timing of the block submissions (e.g., selfish mining or block withholding). More specifically, we study greedy networking, in which a miner node increases its connectivity beyond the default protocol to expedite the deliveries of blocks and transactions for an unfair mining advantage. While greedy networking has been actively studied in the general P2P networking, it has not been systematically studied in cryptocurrency and blockchain despite the alleged real-world instances by the Bitcoin community. We build an analytical framework for greedy networking and study how the networking control impacts the cryptocurrency application to quantify the benefits and costs of the networking control. To demonstrate the use of our framework, we implement a greedy networking prototype based on an active Bitcoin node connected to the Mainnet while simulating different miner capabilities by varying the computing backend of the miner. In contrast to the previous belief in blockchain and cryptocurrency, we discover that the optimal number of connections is bounded (limiting the greedy behavior) and depends on the hash computing capability of the miner.

Keywords: Blockchain · Bitcoin · Peer-to-peer networking · Proof of Work (pow) · Mining · Rational strategy · Greedy networking

1 Introduction

The rise of cryptocurrencies has sparked a new era where currency generation and financial transactions no longer depend on a centralized source but instead

© IFIP International Federation for Information Processing 2022
Published by Springer Nature Switzerland AG 2022
W. Meng et al. (Eds.): SEC 2022, IFIP AICT 648, pp. 343–359, 2022.
https://doi.org/10.1007/978-3-031-06975-8_20

rely on the cryptographic primitives that back the digital ownership of monetary quantities. Additionally, cryptocurrencies build on distributed computing and networking for further decentralization, including distributed storage (having the participating nodes locally store the ledger), distributed consensus protocol (deciding how financial transactions get processed), and distributed networking (to transmit and receive relevant information for cryptocurrency operations). In a decentralized peer-to-peer (P2P) system, having a healthy number of connections is important for the robustness of information delivery and synchronization in the network. The underlying principles that help to maintain the networking layer's operation include the reliability of information transmission, the latency/throughput per node, and the influence of peers in the selection process that is responsible for ensuring a strongly connected and efficient network topology.

Rational and incentive-driven optimization strategies are an active research field. In this study, we explore a new dimension of blockchain-based optimizations in which a miner node varies its connectivity (the number of P2P connections) for financial gain, unfair to the rest of the miners and potentially destructive to the network. We call this *greedy networking*. While greedy behaviors have been extensively studied in various P2P contexts (discussed in Sect. 7), we are the first work to study greedy networking in cryptocurrency. Greedy networking is rational (incentive compatible for the node's financial interest). Because the miners are incentivized to participate in the cryptocurrency network due to such financial interests, we systematically analyze the greedy networking incentives associated with the peer selection process and its impact on cryptocurrency mining applications. More specifically, we measure the benefits vs. costs of greedy networking based on our active cryptocurrency blockchain prototype in Bitcoin. We find that a self-interest-driven node/miner has a threshold at which the incentive to continue increasing peer connections eventually transforms into a disincentive. Thus, there exists an optimal number of peer connections dependent on a node's resource capabilities.

The rest of the paper is organized as follows. Section 2 builds the preliminary representation of PoW-based cryptocurrencies to serve as our baseline in Sect. 3 where we formulate the problem and build the motivations for our work. Our model and framework are introduced in Sect. 4. While we apply the framework to a limited number of variables, our general framework can support a greater number of parameters. Section 5 identifies and focuses on those parameters by formalizing their behavior and introducing our real-world experimental setup in Bitcoin. We quantify the framework into a utility function that is analyzed and optimized in Sect. 6. We then discuss related literature including the greedy strategies in blockchain and cryptocurrency in Sect. 7 followed by our discussions and future work in Sect. 8. Finally, we conclude our study in Sect. 9.

2   Background

Blockchain Networking. The distributed P2P networking is critical to blockchain as it provides the information for blockchain operations, e.g., the

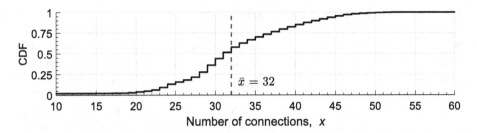

Fig. 1. Our empirical distribution of x, where x is the control variable in the number of peer connections while running a public Bitcoin node without artificial control (we later manually control x to study greedy networking). The dotted vertical line indicates the average number of peer connections, $\bar{x}$.

transaction propagation and up-to-date blocks for the distributed consensus protocol depend on the underlying network.

Bitcoin. Bitcoin was initially proposed by Satoshi Nakamoto in 2008 [19] and has achieved its first \$1 trillion market capitalization in February of 2021 [5]. Similarly, Bitcoin has served as the foundation for later cryptocurrency developments and blockchain-based consensus mechanisms. While our work can generalize across different cryptocurrencies, we focus on the most popular cryptocurrency, Bitcoin, to experimentally validate our work.

A Bitcoin Core (version 0.21.0) public node maintains 10 outbound peer connections that are initiated by the subject node, and between 0 to 118 inbound connections (initiated by other nodes). Thus, the default number of node connections varies between 10 and 128 with the average case being dependent on the subject node's resource capabilities. By default, nodes do not accept incoming connections and are therefore limited to $x = 10$. However, as shown in Fig. 1, using our active Bitcoin prototype and enabling incoming connections yields an empirical distribution of node connections that have an average of $\bar{x} = 32$. The networking/socket layer uses a distributed P2P system for information delivery that identifies nodes in one of three forms: IPv4, IPv6, or Tor, each of which holding different resource capabilities.

Mining Incentives. Cryptocurrencies and blockchain in general rely on the node processing the distributed consensus protocol to agree on the transactions that get recorded to the ledger. In PoW-based blockchains, nodes are called *miners* and they participate in the *mining process* involving finding the probabilistic proof-of-works (PoW) based on the hash computations that result in the creation of new blocks. The latest block is broadcasted to the other miners through networking and yields a financial reward (in newly-minted coins) to the miner who finds the block, and those paid by the cryptocurrency users/beneficiaries. Such financial rewards provide the incentive for the mining operations, e.g., mining is a popular investment to gain financial income. Because the miners are driven by their financial income, we study the rational strategy that increases this reward.

3   Our Motivations and Contributions

Bitcoin nodes are driven by their self-interests and financial gains. Thus, as discussed in the Bitcoin paper [20], the miner protocol is designed to be incentive-compatible. We however study the uncooperative and self-interest-driven behaviors in blockchain P2P networking.

In greedy networking, nodes deviate from the Bitcoin implementation specification/policy to increase the number of peer connections with the intention to expedite receiving blocks and transactions. By targeting the smallest block propagation time, miners can begin mining a block sooner for an increased chance of mining the next block. Likewise, miners that do not receive an expedited block delivery risk decreased probabilities in finding the next block, and, due to this probabilistic nature and race condition of PoW mining to mining cost estimation, the risk can be directly modeled into a loss of monetary value if the block propagation is delayed. Thus, the rational mining strategy holds the incentive to deviate from traditional blockchain networking protocols set by the cryptocurrency specification, e.g., Bitcoin Core. Consequently, increasing the peer connections scales the networking traffic of the node which impacts the processor/memory utilization, power consumption, and bandwidth (among other parameters). The trade-offs associated with mining rewards yield an optimal number of peer connections which the rational mining strategy can use to optimize its mining income.

The motivation for our work is in regards to [27] where a Bitcoin Core developer noted that increasing the number of connections can be detrimental to the health of the network, stating that *"connectable peers on the network are a scarce resource, and essential to the decentralization. If people go try connect to all of them like some sites do, we'll very quickly run out"*. The intention to increase peer connections for increased responsiveness is also mentioned in [9] stating that *"many of these services attempt to connect to a large portion of the listening network and gain insight into the chance of a transaction confirming"*. Our work largely corroborates with [27] and [9] but we make the following research contributions: i) we provide a general framework for greedy networking which can apply to PoW blockchains; ii) we systematically investigate the greedy networking on an active Bitcoin prototype, including the potential costs in an increased load on the broadcasting network and physical machine resources, which is in contrast to the previous research focusing only on the *benefits that discourage* greedy networking. Our results show that the optimal greedy networking strategy is not to keep increasing the peer connections but rather maintain an optimal number of connections, in contrast to the previous belief. We shed light on this greedy networking optimization problem in cryptocurrency to facilitate further research in aligning the incentives of the protocol to its design integrity and fairness.

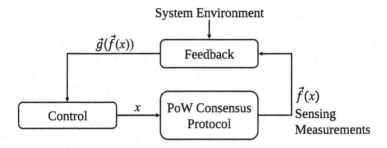

Fig. 2. Our greedy networking analytical framework. x is the control variable in the number of peer connections while $\vec{f}(x)$ are the sensing measurements dependent on x. The feedback $\vec{g}$ takes $\vec{f}(x)$ to normalize the sensing measurements.

4 Model and Framework

We describe our model and framework in this section for the general greedy networking framework, while Sect. 5 applies the framework to our Bitcoin prototype for a concrete instance including the sensing parameters (defined in Sect. 4.3) and the control processing (defined in Sect. 4.4).

4.1 Introduction to Our Model

Any node participating in the network for distributed consensus protocol and P2P communications can launch greedy networking. A greedy node controlling the number of peer connections impacts the financial outcomes in the consensus protocol, as it affects the delivery time of the consensus-relevant information and the mining operational costs. Because of its financial impact, any standard miner driven by its financial income would be incentivized to launch greedy networking.

4.2 Our General Framework

We begin by defining a general framework to enable the formal modeling of our novel greedy networking optimization problem. We later give a use case for this general framework (in Sect. 5) to show its instantiated function at the implementation level where we acquire a concrete value for x.

We build a protocol-independent utility function framework to measure the incentives and quantify the costs and benefits when using our framework. Figure 2 describes our framework for greedy networking. The number of connections, denoted by x, is the control parameter that affects the PoW consensus protocol and its resulting sensor measurements, denoted by $\vec{f}$. We define $\vec{f}$ to be comprised of elements that are dependent variables of x and involve those from not only ledger data but also the network sensing. This is used in the feedback processing to yield $\vec{g}(\vec{f}(x))$ which informs the control and selection of x. For validation, we implement concrete instances of our framework on an active Bitcoin node.

4.3 Sensing Measurements in $\vec{f}$

We define $\vec{f}$ for our sensing parameter measurements which are dependent on x, i.e., $\vec{f} = (\{f_i\}_i) = (f_1, f_2, ..., f_i)$ where f_i is the observed value for the i-th parameter. Because x affects not only the networking but also the cryptocurrency application, f_i are from those in networking (e.g., transmitted bytes/bandwidth and computing resources for networking), cryptocurrency application (e.g., block delay and computational power for mining), and hardware (e.g., processing and power consumption for mining execution). The relevant sensing parameters which are either increasing or decreasing with x affect the optimal selection of x, which we denote by $\hat{x}$.

4.4 Feedback Processing in $\vec{g}$

$\vec{g} = (\{g_i\}_i)$ transforms the sensor measurement values (f_i) to monetary values (g_i). Thus, g_i has a fixed monetary output in *coins earned per hour* for each parameter where coin is some unit of cryptocurrency, while its input, f_i, has a distinct measurement unit for each i. Thus, $g_i(f_i(x)) < 0$ yields that the i-th parameter is a *cost* parameter reducing the incentive for increasing x, and $g_i(f_i(x)) > 0$ yields a *benefit*/incentive for increasing x. To control x, the control algorithm processes $\vec{g} = (\{g_i\}_i)$, for example, our algorithm in Sect. 5 aggregates them with varying weights for a score.

5 Our Framework Implementation in Bitcoin

In this section, we build implementations for our framework in Sect. 4 by providing concrete values to the variables and functions. While this does introduce a concept of "design choice" in which there may exist many interpretations of the formal definition, we do so to show the existence of one instance that maps the formal definition to a proof-of-concept. Doing so allows us the ability to quantitatively optimize the greedy networking problem.

5.1 System-Dependent Control and Dynamic Environment

Our framework depends on the mining system and the underlying resources that the dynamic environment uses. For example, a miner's competitiveness (targeting their expected financial income) varies in its own capabilities while the others in the network aggregate their computing power to support the dynamic entries and exits of the participating miners. For example, in Bitcoin, a node in 2019 received 85.16% fewer transaction bytes and 66.44% fewer transactions when compared to 2021 [1]. While our framework in Sect. 4 sufficiently captures the dynamic and system-dependent nature of our modeling (using variables), this section provides a concrete implementation instance by constructing functions and assigning variable values based on our active Bitcoin implementations using multiple distinct mining hardwares.

5.2   Parameters for $\vec{f}$

Our Bitcoin prototype senses and monitors parameters as we will describe in
Sect. 6.3, including those we set a weight of zero to in $\vec{g}$ (i.e. zero effect on
controlling the number of connections). In this section, we identify the sensing
parameters we use for our greedy networking prototype in Bitcoin, where the
sensing parameters, $\vec{f}$, are still in their native unit of measurement.

Blockchain networking includes the delivery of new blocks and transactions
that are critical for mining. To decrease the **block propagation time**, denoted
with τ, and receive the block earlier motivates increasing x. The reason for this
is quite intuitive in that the more peer connections a network has, the more
connectivity there will be (which is expected to expedite information delivery).
In this regard, we consider τ to quantify how expedited the block deliveries
are (in the native unit of *seconds* since the block was mined), thus, we will be
referring to τ as a function dependent on x (being input parameter, i.e. $\tau(x)$).
The inclusion τ into the framework is possible since blocks contain timestamp
information, and subtracting this from the time that a block is received enables
the estimation of block propagation time; something that cannot be directly
computed by any other message in the protocol.

For transaction delivery, we denote the size of incoming transactions as β
bytes per second. We split this into two parts, 1) **number of redundant bytes**,
β^R (i.e. transactions that are received more than once in our subject node due
to our connections being oblivious to what transactions we have already seen),
and 2) **unique transaction bytes**, β^U (i.e. never-before-seen transactions that
are new and immediately added to the transaction memory pool upon being
received by our subject node). Therefore, $\beta = \beta^R + \beta^U$, and β^R increases as x
increases due to duplicate transmissions. At the time of writing, nodes from x
are unable to distinguish between seen/unseen transactions.

For mining, we denote a node's **hashrate** (i.e. number of hash computations per second) as α, which determines the expected probability of finding a
block and thus the expected financial reward amount given some mining time
interval. The mining process incurs **power consumption**, which we denote as
ρ kilowatt-hours. We additionally sense and measure processing-based metrics
such as CPU and memory utilization; however, power consumption, ρ, is dependent on both CPU, ϕ, and memory utilization, μ (in addition to every other
hardware component on the power supply) as ρ monotonically increases with
respect to x. For ρ, we use PowerTOP v2.14 [3] to derive the power output
estimation of the machine. Varying x, we observe that $\phi(x)$, $\mu(x)$, $\beta^R(x)$, and
$\beta^U(x)$ monotonically increase with $\tau(x)$ and $\beta^U(x)$ converging to values as x
grows large (diminishing return) and that $\tau(x)$ monotonically decreases with x.
Our framework uses $\vec{f} = \langle \alpha(x), \tau(x), \rho(x) \rangle$.

5.3   Transformation for $\vec{g}$

Since $\vec{f}$ has varying units of measurement specific to each parameter's native
unit, transforming from sensor measurements, $\vec{f}$, to a consistent unit of monetary

Table 1. Definition of all relevant variables.

Name	Definition	Name	Definition
x	Number of peer connections	ψ	Block solve interval (s)
α	Mining hashrate (hash/s)	D	Block difficulty
τ	Block propagation time (s)	$P(D)$	Probability a hash is a block
ρ	Power usage (kWh)	Γ	Block coinbase reward (satoshi)
β^U	Unique transaction rate (tx/s)	π	Block transaction reward (satoshi)
β^R	Redundant transaction rate (tx/s)	κ	Electric exchange rate (¢/kWh)
U	Utility function (satoshi/h)	ζ	Exchange rate (satoshi/$)

value, $\vec{g}$, depends on the Bitcoin mining system and environment. Thus, the definitions of each parameter in $\vec{g}$ must be explicit with regards to the application integrating the framework, e.g. τ is only relevant in blockchain applications where the monetary reward is proportional to block transmission time. The function that does this modeling is $\vec{g}$.

We identify those environmental parameters independent of x here, as well as list them in Table 1, including those from the Bitcoin protocol, for electricity use in general, and those for converting between the Bitcoin currency to fiat currency. In the Bitcoin protocol, we define the expected block arrival time, ψ, to be 600 s (10 min) which is fixed by adjusting Bitcoin's difficulty for mining a block, which we define to be D. In Bitcoin, this automatically adapts to the active miner network size (i.e. more nodes mining increases D to fix the average block arrival time to be $\psi = 600$). By design, the probability of finding a block depends on the block difficulty, D [2].

For the mining **hashrate** conversion, g_1, the power that gets utilized for mining is able to directly convert back to monetary value. The equation to estimate the mining reward income (coins earned per hour) for solo mining in a PoW scheme is as follows:

$$g_1 = \alpha \times \Gamma \times P \times 3600$$

Increasing **block propagation time** for g_1 results in a cost since mining on an outdated block wastes hash computations while using the outdated block before the new block arrives. For example, if the block propagation time is 30 s then that 30-s-transition to the new block can be seen as a loss. The number of hash computations wasted for the outdated block is the product of the hashrate (α) and block propagation time (τ) relative to its expected arrival time ($\frac{\tau}{\psi}$). The expected monetary compensation/income for each hash computation is the product of the reward amount Γ and the probability of finding a block per hash computation, P. Therefore, multiplying the two and using $-\tau$ (because τ monotonically decreases with x), the monetary loss on the outdated block for delayed block propagation in satoshi per hour is:

$$g_2 = -\frac{\tau \times \alpha \times \Gamma \times P \times 3600}{\psi}$$

Our standard unit for $\vec{g}$ is in the unit of hours, thus, since τ and α are based in seconds, multiplication by 3600 converts from satoshi per second to satoshi per hour. For Bitcoin, $P(D) = \frac{1}{D \times 2^{32}}$ [2]. At the time of writing, $D \approx 2^{44.19}$ and $\Gamma = (6.25 + \pi) \times 10^8$ satoshi, where π is the aggregate of the transaction fees selected by the block.

Outside of the Bitcoin protocol are system-dependent parameters such as **power**. For power in g_3, the monetary cost increases with power consumption in price per kilowatt-hour (kWh). We denote κ and ζ as environmental parameters independent of our control variable x. More specifically, κ is the cents per kWh in USD (where $\frac{\kappa}{100}$ is the dollars per kWh) with ζ being is the exchange rate for the coin. At the time of writing, $\frac{\kappa}{100} = \$0.1105$, and $\zeta = 6.325 \times 10^{-4}$. The equation to convert from power usage to satoshi per hour is as follows:

$$g_3 = -\frac{\frac{\kappa}{100} \times \rho \times 3600}{\zeta}$$

Putting them together for processing $\vec{g}$, we compute our utility function as the aggregation of $\vec{g}$. g_1 is the income-based mining incentive earned from mining and therefore $g_1 > 0$. g_2 is the lost income due to block propagation delay, $g_2 \leq 0$. Similarly, g_3 is the power cost to run such a node, so $g_3 < 0$, hence, the negations in g_2 and g_3 denote costs or disincentives, while g_1 is a benefit. Combining these parameters, we define our utility function, $U(x) = \sum_i g_i(f_i(x))$ where the optimal number of peer connections can be defined as:

$$\hat{x} = \mathrm{argmax}(U(x))$$

In the following sections, we discuss our implementation and experiment-based computation of $\hat{x}$ to derive the optimal greedy networking behavior.

6   Implementation and Analyses

Our framework models the rational strategy by analyzing multiple parameters for the dynamic environment (described in Sect. 5.1) that give us insight into greedy networking and connectivity optimization. We build our experimentation around 275 parameters that we log in our Bitcoin prototype and identify those that are the most relevant for greedy networking, which are α, τ, and ρ. The rest of this section discusses our implementation and the resulting analysis from the implementation.

6.1   Greedy Networking Implementation

To deviate from the default protocol and implementation limiting outbound peer connections, we modify the source code of Bitcoin Core (version 0.21.0), which involves minimal code change after identifying the relevant data parameters. For example, while Bitcoin Core already contains the *maxconnections* configuration parameter to enable peers to specify their own upper bound in peer connections,

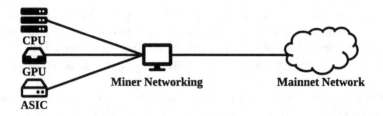

Fig. 3. Our experimental setup with varying computational capabilities. We test with two CPUs (🖥), one GPU (📷), and two ASICs (🗄), defined in Table 2.

these are inbound connections only (i.e. the subject node must wait for other nodes to connect to it). Consequently, this can only be used when the node chooses to be public and enables incoming connections. We add a new configuration, *minconnections*, to specify the lower bound for the number of outbound connections (i.e. a non-public node can define an arbitrary connection quantity that will be pro-actively achieved), which has previously been fixed to 10.

6.2 Experimental Setup and Reference Measurements Varying Mining Computing

Figure 3 provides a high-level overview of our experimental setup where we connect multiple miner types in processing units to a miner networking host machine. For this networking machine, our implementation makes use of a 4-core Intel Core i7 6700K processor with 8 threads and 16 GBs of RAM; for the networking machine, the operating system we use is Linux Mint 20, and the parameters are logged with our modified Bitcoin Core instance using C++17 and Python 3.7.

Varying the computational capabilities of the miner is important for analysis as it influences the optimal mining behavior due to its correlation with hashrate and mining income. Table 2 enumerates our experimental setup from Fig. 3 by defining the machine type and specifications, along with the hashrate of the device and total power consumption when maintaining the hashrate. We derive all values in Table 2 through our experimentation which is then used to derive the optimal behavior in the last column (introduced in Sect. 6.5).

6.3 Bitcoin Networking Sensor and Logging

The Bitcoin networking protocol has a protocol-defined set of 18 actively used signaling traffic message types [2]. The default Bitcoin Core keeps these messages private from the node operator with the exception of blocks, transactions, and ping/pong transmissions (for node latency). Therefore, we build and implement our message logger within Bitcoin's interface with the network and its corresponding RPC controller (*net_processing.cpp* and *net.cpp*, respectively). Upon a message transmission on the receiver's end, we log the number of bytes for

Table 2. The device resources and computational capabilities (in ascending order) used in our experimentation.

Type	Processor/Model	α (hash/s)	ρ (kWh)	Optimal strategy, $\hat{x}$
CPU (▤)	Intel Core i7-6700K, 4 GHz	$2^{19.07}$	0.08145	0.5997
CPU (▤)	Intel Core i7-11800H, 2.60 GHz	$2^{20.19}$	0.02978	0.6703
GPU (▭)	NVIDIA GeForce GTX 1660S	$2^{30.80}$	0.09385	16.87
ASIC (▤)	Rev 3 GekkoScience NewPac	$2^{36.20}$	0.1678	112
ASIC (▤)	MicroBT Whatsminer M32	$2^{45.70}$	75.48	3060

Table 3. Measurement values while varying the number of connections, x, from our experiment. The table shows the average and the 95% confidence intervals.

	$x = 1$	$x = 8$	$x = 64$	$x = 512$	Line of best fit
$\alpha(x)$	$2^{20.19} \pm 6909$	$2^{20.19} \pm 6352$	$2^{20.12} \pm 5760$	$2^{19.57} \pm 5874$	$-6.873 \times 10^5 \times x^{0.161} + 2.62 \times 10^6$
$\tau(x)$	30.94 ± 2.434	25.3 ± 1.667	22.84 ± 1.284	19.18 ± 0.3826	$1.818 \times 10^{-5} \times x^{0.3369} + 3.149 \times 10^{-5}$
$\rho(x)$	$5.165 \times 10^{-5} \pm 1.121$	$6.665 \times 10^{-5} \pm 1.15$	$11.74 \times 10^{-5} \pm 1.765$	$21.04 \times 10^{-5} \pm 2.138$	$324.7 \times x^{-1.802} + 22.72$
$\beta^U(x)$	3.3621 ± 0.09321	3.476 ± 0.09176	3.457 ± 0.0898	3.689 ± 0.09445	$0.01062 \times x^{0.5349} + 3.386 \times 10^4$
$\beta^R(x)$	0.009209 ± 0.002557	$0.066 + 0.01523$	0.4481 ± 0.1081	1.145 ± 0.7849	$0.09557 \times x^{0.4136} - 0.1122$

each message, the number of CPU clock cycles taken to process the message, and a counter to keep track of how many times each message has been received from the time that the node initially started, all of which can be accessed with our new RCP command, *getmsginfo*. For our experiment, we vary the number of peer connections, x, using the *minconnections* configuration parameter. Given x, the Bitcoin node selects its nodes randomly according to its random peer selection algorithm [14], and we periodically reset/restart the peer selections every 100 min (10 block arrivals on average) to sample and experiment with a new set of peer connections[1]. Our experimental measurements spanned 444 d with a resulting 88.8 GB of data.

6.4 Experimental Results

Figure 4a visualizes the block propagation time, $\tau(x)$. When x increases we see a decrease in the block propagation time due to a shorter path to the random block solver. The line of best-fit approximation based on minimizing the root mean squared error is in Table 3. Despite the long logging window, τ suffers great variation in block propagation time and as such, the confidence interval converges towards a range rather than a singular value. Figure 5a shows the individual distributions of $\tau(x)$ and we find that, for smaller values of x, the distribution of τ yields greater variance. Similarly, when $\tau = 512$, the top 95%

---

[1] For larger values of x, we modify/etc./security/limits.conf to increase the file limit. For our experiments, x is composed of outbound connections only. More concretely, we disable the random inbound connections and control the number of outbound connections for our experimental measurements.

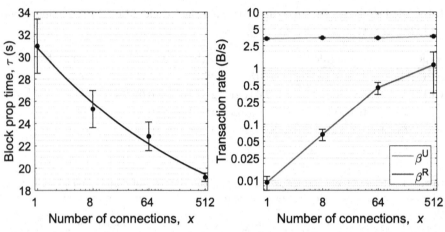

(a) Block propagation time delay with respect to x, alongside the 95% confidence interval and line of best fit.

(b) Rate of transaction unique/redundant bytes per second, $\beta^U(x)$ and $\beta^R(x)$, respectively.

Fig. 4. Block propagation time delay, τ, and transaction rates, β.

quantile is 25 s, and the lower 5% quantile is 13.08 s. Comparing this with $x = 1$, we find that the 95% and 5% quantiles are 98 and 14.5 s, respectively, thus, there is a more stable and faster block delivery time for larger x, as hypothesized in Sect. 5.2.

We also include the rate at which transactions are received (in bytes per second or B/s), β, by our subject node in Fig. 4b. Due to the increase in connectivity, new information is received faster and $\beta^U(x)$ quickly converges towards c, the rate of transaction submissions in the network. We find that $c \approx 3.496$ B/s. $\beta^R(x)$ continues to increase because the Bitcoin Core v0.21.0 protocol does not have a mechanism to distinguish between the transactions that have already been seen by our node and those which have not (unlike blocks that depend on the flooding of block headers). From these results, we discover that there exists a critical point in $U(x)$ where x loses incentive when it increases past this threshold.

6.5   Greedy Networking Analyses Results

Our experimental measurements are aggregated for the utility function as described in Sect. 5.3, i.e., $U = g_1 + g_2 + g_3$, which yields a polynomial line-of-best-fit approximation of:

$$U(x) = a_1 x^{b_1} + a_2 x^{b_2} + a_3 x^{b_3} + a_4 x^{b_4} + c$$

where $a_1 = 3.791 \times 10^{-8}$, $b_1 = -1.802$, $a_2 = 1.395 \times 10^{-11}$, $b_2 = -1.641$, $a_3 = -1.546 \times 10^{-9}$, $b_3 = 0.161$, $a_4 = -3.176 \times 10^{-11}$, $b_4 = 0.3369$, and

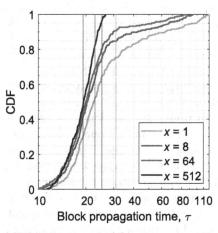

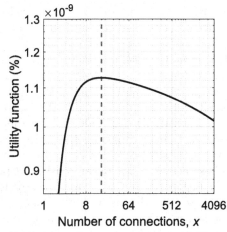

(a) Distributions of $\tau(x)$ in the real-world. The vertical lines are the average propagation times.

(b) Utility function difference from $U(1)$ when varying x for GPU ⊟. The vertical dotted line shows $\hat{x} = 16.87$.

Fig. 5. Distribution of block propagation time, τ, along with utility function U.

$c = 3258$. Figure 5b shows $\vec{g}(\vec{f}(x))$ when $\alpha = 2^{30.8}$ for the GPU, GeForce GTX 1660S as specified in Table 2, and shows that there is an optimal maximum, $\hat{x}$, at 16.87 peer connections (which can be rounded to 17, and is greater than Bitcoin's default value of 10 outbound connections). Using this mining device as our control with α being varied to change $\hat{x}$, we find that for lower hashrates, $\forall x, U(x) < 0$. This occurs when $\alpha \leq 2^{28.23} \approx 315$ MH/s using our experimental parameters. Thus, all the computing units we test would be more costly than beneficial, yielding a negative net income because Bitcoin mining has an increasingly competitive nature as there are a greater number of nodes participating in mining [8,26].

7 Related Work in Greedy Networking

7.1 Greedy Strategies in Cryptocurrency

Previous research in greedy/rational mining strategies (incentive-compatible but destructive to the network) controls the timing/conditions of the block submissions, e.g., selfish mining [12,13,21,23] or block withholding [6,7,13,17,22]. Other rational mining strategies include controlling the mining power and selectively turning off mining [8,25]. Our work is different since greedy networking controls an orthogonal parameter (the number of network connections).

7.2 Security Threats on Cryptocurrency Networking Connections

This paper is the first to study a node's greedy networking by increasing the number of its own networking connections in the cryptocurrency context (Sect. 7.3

describes greedy networking in general P2P networks beyond cryptocurrency). Other previous research studied threats based on compromising/occupying the other cryptocurrency node's connections (the victim node(s), distinct from the subject node launching the threat). Prominent studies include eclipse attack (to control the information to/from the victim node, enabling the attacker to reverse a block and launch a double-spending attack) [14,21] and partitioning attack (to partition the cryptocurrency network to prevent the network-wide block/ledger synchronization) [4,24]. Our work is different from these previous studies on the security threats attacking other cryptocurrency nodes in that our work considers the node's self strategy to improve its own unfair advantage. Furthermore, the eclipse attack is no longer considered practically feasible due to the measures and bug patches Bitcoin and cryptocurrency implementations took after the threat/exploit discovery [14,24], and partitioning attack is relatively difficult for the attacker to implement due to its requirement to compromise or manipulate the routing of the autonomous systems (AS). In contrast, greedy networking is currently applicable, incentivized, and requires only changes in the node's own implementation, as demonstrated by our proof-of-concept implementation from Sect. 6.1.

7.3   Greedy Networking in P2P Networks

Greedy networking has been studied in the general P2P community beyond cryptocurrency. In [28] the authors analyze the peer selection algorithm and probabilistic transmission in favor of Bitcoin information propagation time. They find that the optimal strategy exists in the NP-hard space, and instead propose a greedy probabilistic strategy to decrease the transaction propagation times in Bitcoin. While the authors propose a new information transmission protocol, our work utilizes the networking protocol of current PoW-based blockchains and does so with the inclusion of two additional parameters.

To further highlight the importance of greedy networking, [10,16,18], and [11] propose new incentive mechanisms designed to function on the information propagation layer of the subnet. These schemes increase the need to divert from the honest strategy in favor of a more financially rewarding strategy, however, [10,16], and [18] propose network-based optimization and incentive strategies that do not apply to blockchain and PoW. The authors in [11] consider blockchain-based networking overhead as the cost but do not apply them to greedy behaviors. Similarly, [15] proposes a mechanism for determining a node's connectivity to the network but does not analyze its influence on an incentive-based blockchain architecture, which we focus on.

8   Discussion About Security Relevance and Future Work

Greedy networking in blockchain and cryptocurrency is relevant to security because it provides an unfair advantage to the miners violating the integrity/fairness of the PoW consensus protocol design (the focus of this paper) and because it can have a negative impact on the network by causing excessive networking/broadcasting overhead impacting the network availability (beyond the scope of this paper).

Our work considers a node's own incentives to modify its peer connections. As stated by [27] and [9], described in Sect. 3, the concern lies in the nodes individually increasing their peer connections beyond the default protocol for an unfair networking advantage. We discover and highlight that continuing to increase the peer connections is not optimal for incentive-driven miners, in contrast to the previous belief in blockchain and cryptocurrency.

However, our work does not consider the networking impact of the greedy networking behavior beyond the individual node perspective. Many nodes practicing greedy networking can excessively increase the broadcasting repetition and overhead. Such greedy networking can be detrimental to the network by yielding congestion and thus disrupting the availability for other nodes [27]. We leave such network-level analyses, including greedy networking by multiple miner nodes and the Nash equilibrium, for future work.

9   Conclusion

Rational mining and incentivization are important in cryptocurrencies since the cryptocurrency integrity (for example, against revoking transactions and double-spending) relies on the networking node participation driven by the financial incentives/rewards. In this work, we propose a framework to study greedy networking and control the number of peer connections with respect to connectivity in the cryptocurrency application. We implement the framework on an active Bitcoin prototype connected to the Mainnet and vary the computing units. Our results show that a rational greedy networking miner will not continue to increase its peer connections, in contrast to the previous belief, and that the optimal number of connections depends on the hash computing capabilities of the miner. We shed light on the greedy networking behavior in cryptocurrency/PoW blockchains to facilitate further research in advancing and aligning the incentives for blockchain networking and consensus protocols.

Acknowledgment. This material is based upon work supported by the National Science Foundation under Grant No. 1922410.

References

1. Blockchain charts. https://www.blockchain.com/charts#network
2. Protocol documentation. https://en.bitcoin.it/wiki/Protocol_documentation
3. Powertop (2020). https://01.org/powertop
4. Apostolaki, M., Zohar, A., Vanbever, L.: Hijacking bitcoin: routing attacks on cryptocurrencies. In: 2017 IEEE Symposium on Security and Privacy (SP), pp. 375–392. IEEE (2017)
5. Cap, C.M.: Crypto-currency market capitalizations (2015). https://coinmarketcap.com

6. Chang, S.Y.: Share withholding in blockchain mining. In: Park, N., Sun, K., Foresti, S., Butler, K., Saxena, N. (eds.) Security and Privacy in Communication Networks, pp. 161–187. Springer International Publishing, Cham (2020). https://doi.org/10.1007/978-3-030-63095-9_9

7. Chang, S.-Y., Park, Y., Wuthier, S., Chen, C.-W.: Uncle-block attack: blockchain mining threat beyond block withholding for rational and uncooperative miners. In: Deng, R.H., Gauthier-Umaña, V., Ochoa, M., Yung, M. (eds.) ACNS 2019. LNCS, vol. 11464, pp. 241–258. Springer, Cham (2019). https://doi.org/10.1007/978-3-030-21568-2_12

8. Chang, S.Y., Wuthier, S.: Dynamic power control for rational cryptocurrency mining. In: Proceedings of the 3rd Workshop on Cryptocurrencies and Blockchains for Distributed Systems, pp. 47–52 (2020)

9. Claris: how do block explorers determine propagation through nodes/p2p protocol?. https://bitcoin.stackexchange.com/a/80877/128178

10. Drucker, F.A., Fleischer, L.K.: Simpler sybil-proof mechanisms for multi-level marketing. In: Proceedings of the 13th ACM conference on Electronic commerce, pp. 441–458 (2012)

11. Ersoy, O., Ren, Z., Erkin, Z., Lagendijk, R.L.: Transaction propagation on permissionless blockchains: incentive and routing mechanisms. In: 2018 Crypto Valley Conference on Blockchain Technology (CVCBT), pp. 20–30. IEEE (2018)

12. Eyal, I., Sirer, E.G.: Majority is not enough: bitcoin mining is vulnerable. In: Christin, N., Safavi-Naini, R. (eds.) FC 2014. LNCS, vol. 8437, pp. 436–454. Springer, Heidelberg (2014). https://doi.org/10.1007/978-3-662-45472-5_28

13. Gao, S., Li, Z., Peng, Z., Xiao, B.: Power adjusting and bribery racing: novel mining attacks in the bitcoin system. In: Proceedings of the 2019 ACM SIGSAC Conference on Computer and Communications Security, pp. 833–850. CCS '19, Association for Computing Machinery, New York (2019). https://doi.org/10.1145/3319535.3354203. https://doi.org/10.1145/3319535.3354203

14. Heilman, E., Kendler, A., Zohar, A., Goldberg, S.: Eclipse attacks on bitcoin's peer-to-peer network. In: 24th {USENIX} Security Symposium ({USENIX} Security 15), pp. 129–144 (2015)

15. Hong, H.J.,et al.: Robust p2p connectivity estimation for permissionless bitcoin network. In: 2021 IEEE/ACM 29th International Symposium on Quality of Service (IWQOS), pp. 1–6. IEEE (2021)

16. Kleinberg, J., Raghavan, P.: Query incentive networks. In: 46th Annual IEEE Symposium on Foundations of Computer Science (FOCS'05), pp. 132–141. IEEE (2005)

17. Kwon, Y., Kim, D., Son, Y., Vasserman, E., Kim, Y.: Be selfish and avoid dilemmas: fork after withholding (faw) attacks on bitcoin. In: Proceedings of the 2017 ACM SIGSAC Conference on Computer and Communications Security, pp. 195–209 (2017)

18. Li, C., Yu, B., Sycara, K.: An incentive mechanism for message relaying in unstructured peer-to-peer systems. Electron. Commer. Res. Appl. 8(6), 315–326 (2009)

19. Nakamoto, S.: Bitcoin: A Peer-to-peer Electronic Cash System. Tech. rep, Manubot (2019)

20. Nakamoto, S., Bitcoin, A.: A peer-to-peer electronic cash system. Bitcoin, 4 (2008). https://bitcoin.org/bitcoin.pdf

21. Nayak, K., Kumar, S., Miller, A., Shi, E.: Stubborn mining: Generalizing selfish mining and combining with an eclipse attack. In: 2016 IEEE European Symposium on Security and Privacy (EuroS P), pp. 305–320 (2016). https://doi.org/10.1109/EuroSP.2016.32

22. Rosenfeld, M.: Analysis of bitcoin pooled mining reward systems (2011). arXiv preprint arXiv:1112.4980
23. Sapirshtein, A., Sompolinsky, Y., Zohar, A.: Optimal selfish mining strategies in bitcoin. In: Grossklags, J., Preneel, B. (eds.) FC 2016. LNCS, vol. 9603, pp. 515–532. Springer, Heidelberg (2017). https://doi.org/10.1007/978-3-662-54970-4_30
24. Tran, M., Choi, I., Moon, G.J., Vu, A.V., Kang, M.S.: A stealthier partitioning attack against bitcoin peer-to-peer network. In: 2020 IEEE Symposium on Security and Privacy (SP), pp. 894–909 (2020). https://doi.org/10.1109/SP40000.2020.00027
25. Tsabary, I., Eyal, I.: The gap game. In: Proceedings of the 2018 ACM SIGSAC Conference on Computer and Communications Security, pp. 713–728. CCS '18, Association for Computing Machinery, New York (2018). https://doi.org/10.1145/3243734.3243737, https://doi.org/10.1145/3243734.3243737
26. Wuille, P.: Bitcoin network graphs. http://bitcoin.sipa.be
27. Wuille, P.: How does one attain 1,000+ connections like blockchain.info?. https://bitcoin.stackexchange.com/a/8140/128178
28. Zhang, H., Feng, C., Wang, X.: A greedy-based approach of fast transaction broadcasting in bitcoin networks. In: Proceedings of the ACM Turing Celebration Conference-China, pp. 1–5 (2019)

Towards Supporting Attribute-Based Access Control in Hyperledger Fabric Blockchain

Amshumaan Pericherla[1], Proteet Paul[1], Shamik Sural[1(✉)], Jaideep Vaidya[2], and Vijay Atluri[2]

[1] Indian Institute of Technology Kharagpur, Kharagpur, India
{amshumaan6pericherla,proteetpaul}@iitkgp.ac.in, shamik@cse.iitkgp.ac.in
[2] Rutgers University, Newark, USA
jsvaidya@business.rutgers.edu, atluri@rutgers.edu

Abstract. Hyperledger Fabric (HLF) is an open-source platform for deploying enterprise-level permissioned blockchains where users from multiple organizations can participate. Preventing unauthorized access to resources in such blockchains is of critical importance. Towards addressing this requirement, HLF supports different access control models. However, support for Attribute-Based Access Control (ABAC) in the current version of HLF is not comprehensive enough to address various requirements that arise when multiple organizations interact in an enterprise setting. To address those shortcomings, in this paper, we develop and present methods for providing full ABAC functionality in Hyperledger Fabric. Performance evaluation under different network configurations using the Hyperledger Caliper benchmarking tool shows that the proposed approach is quite efficient in practice.

Keywords: Hyperledger Fabric · Access control · ABAC · Blockchain · Smart contract · Chaincode

1 Introduction

A blockchain is a distributed ledger built on top of a decentralized peer-to-peer network, providing mechanisms for secure transfer of assets among its participants without the need for any intermediary. Transparency of the ledger combined with a secure execution platform provided by smart contracts has led to a widespread adoption of the blockchain technology across multiple industries. It has resulted in the development of novel applications in several domains like IoT, healthcare, supply chain, e-governance, etc.

There is no central authority in blockchains for monitoring user actions within the network. Hence, an access control mechanism needs to be exercised for preventing unauthorized access to the network resources, especially in enterprises. Some of the recent work [10, 14, 16, 23] propose enforcement of access control

© IFIP International Federation for Information Processing 2022
Published by Springer Nature Switzerland AG 2022
W. Meng et al. (Eds.): SEC 2022, IFIP AICT 648, pp. 360–376, 2022.
https://doi.org/10.1007/978-3-031-06975-8_21

models such as Role-Based Access Control (RBAC) and Attribute-Based Access Control (ABAC) for public blockchains like Ethereum. It may be noted that a public blockchain has no restriction on peers in joining the network. Any user can create a peer node on the network and access the data on the blockchain.

Hyperledger Fabric (HLF) [2], on the other hand, is an open-source tool for deploying enterprise-level permissioned blockchains. Unlike its public counterpart, a private blockchain introduces an additional authentication layer to control the users joining the network. Even though the users are authenticated, it is necessary to restrict access to the network resources for certain users, thus enforcing confidentiality and integrity policies. While other access control models are supported, HLF does not have any specific feature for aiding the implementation of ABAC. The only current feature of HLF that can be used is the concept of client certificates generated by certifying authorities. Most of the recent literature like [12] and [18] use the HLF network as an intermediary data store between off-chain users and resources for maintaining authorization related components. Some of the other work [9] considers only limited features of ABAC,

In contrast to such existing approaches, we propose a method for utilizing the full capabilities of ABAC in HLF. We targets the cases where clients on the network act as users and resource owners, and resources are stored directly on the blockchain. The key contributions of this paper are summarized below:

i We develop a novel approach for supporting attribute-based access control over the assets managed in any Hyperledger Fabric installation by appropriately designing its components on the decentralized network.
ii We build a complete Golang library for implementing the approach on a Hyperledger Fabric network. Performance tests are run on workloads under different configurations using the Hyperledger Caliper benchmarking tool.
iii We make both the library and the docker network for deploying an ABAC-enabled HLF instance publicly available through GitHub for reproducibility of our results and supporting the open source initiative.

The rest of the paper is organized as follows. Section 2 introduces the key concepts related to HLF and ABAC. In Sect. 3, we present our approach for supporting ABAC functionality in HLF along with the developed libraries and the workflow for system setup. The implementation details and experimental results are discussed in Sect. 4. Section 5 reviews related work in this field. Finally, Sect. 6 concludes the paper and provides directions for future research.

2   Preliminaries

In this section, we discuss some of the background concepts that would help in understanding our research contributions in the later part of the paper.

2.1   Hyperledger Fabric

Blockchain [22] is a distributed ledger spread over a completely decentralized peer-to-peer network without any hierarchy. As the name suggests, a blockchain

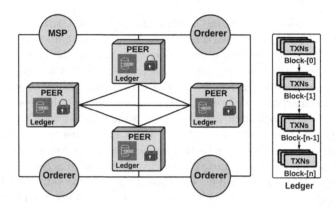

Fig. 1. Structure of a hyperledger fabric network

maintains a chain of blocks on the ledger recorded in chronological order linked using cryptographic techniques. Hyperledger Fabric[1] [2] is a framework for deploying permissioned blockchains with a modular structure with pluggable components for consensus mechanism, datastore, etc. HLF runs the component services in docker containers to isolate the application layer from physical resources. Any node needs to be authorized to enter the network. Figure 1 shows the overall structure of a typical HLF network. The main components are described below.

Chaincode - Chaincode is the HLF term for smart contracts originally introduced in the context of Ethereum. A smart contract refers to the business logic while a chaincode refers to the deployable entity enclosing this logic. Chaincodes are the only entry points for users or applications to access the ledger.

Peer - Peers are the client nodes on the network. They host the ledger, chaincodes, create/sign transactions and blocks.

Orderer - These are the special nodes that ensure block delivery across the network to all peers using a consensus protocol for ordering the transactions.

Organization (Org) - An HLF network can span multiple organizations, each controlling its peers on the network. Different organizations can contribute their resources to the network.

Membership Service Provider (MSP) - It uses certifying authorities (CAs) to create and manage identities for network members. An MSP generates necessary authentication material for all the participants to join the network that qualifies HLF as a permissioned network. Different Orgs can have independent MSPs.

Channel - It is a private subnet of communication among a collection of peers. A channel can include peers from multiple organizations. Every channel has an individual ledger which is replicated among all the peers on that channel.

Ledger - Ledger contains the data and transaction history in the HLF network. An HLF Ledger has two components - a) Blockchain, which contains blocks

---

[1] https://www.hyperledger.org/use/fabric.

with transactions chained to previous blocks by including their hash values, and b) World State, which is a ledger database describing the current ledger state. Any update to this state database is recorded on the blockchain.

Client - Clients belong to specific organizations and are registered using that organization's MSP to generate necessary certificates and key pairs for authorization to invoke the chaincodes on the network.

2.2 Attribute-Based Access Control

Attribute-based access control [4,8] is a fine-grained access control model that decides whether to give access based on the attributes (characteristics) of the user, object and environment, as well as the requested permission. Access granting decision is built upon the concept of an access control policy, which is a set of access rules that are comprised of logical combinations of the above-mentioned attributes and their values. When an access request is made, the rules are evaluated with respect to the pre-assigned attributes. ABAC subsumes several other access control models as they are considered to be special cases of ABAC with appropriately defined attribute sets. For example, RBAC [19] can be implemented by embedding user-role relations into a user attribute called role and role-permission relations into corresponding rules in the access control policy.

In its general form, an ABAC system consists of five components - *UA, RA, EA, OP, POL*, each of which is described below:

UA - Represents the attributes of users like identity, name, and other application specific attributes.

RA - Represents the attributes of a resource. It includes resource ID, owner, confidentiality level as well as other application specific attributes.

EA - Refers to environment attributes. It is used to capture context information like time of access, IP address of the requester, etc., which enables a fine level of control to be built in the access logic.

OP - Refers to the type of operation on the resource that a user is requesting. The operations can be resource-specific like read, update, delete, etc. This ensures different levels of user control on the resource.

POL - Refers to the access control policy of an organization. It is comprised of a set of rules, each defined in terms of the above-mentioned components. Based on the rules in *POL*, an incoming access request is either granted or denied.

An ABAC reference monitor intercepts every user request. It then retrieves the required attributes and matches them with the available policy. The request is further processed only if there is at least one rule in the policy that is satisfied.

3 Enabling ABAC in Hyperledger Fabric

While planning for ABAC support in HLF, having a traditional centralized reference monitor would defeat the very purpose of using blockchain technology, i.e., decentralized operation, trust independence, transparency and immutability. It would require a trusted third party to maintain and administer the reference monitor, making it susceptible to attacks, raising trust concerns and forming a source of single-point of failure in an otherwise distributed system. Hence, the access decision needs to be made in a distributed manner, involving all the network nodes and considering the majority decision. We take advantage of the inherent capabilities of HLF in obviating the above issues. It is felt that the blockchain ledger itself can be used to maintain necessary information related to access control including the complete history of access requests and their decisions. This is because the ledger is immutable and distributed across every peer, with consistency ensured by the consensus protocols. Such a design also provides a natural means for auditing, a desirable property of any reference monitor.

Besides designing the reference monitor, another major challenge from the perspective of supporting ABAC in HLF is how and where to securely configure the ABAC components, resources on the blockchain. After exploring various alternatives with their potential merits and demerits, we address this challenge by storing public attributes and policy on the ledger, while the sensitive-attributes and resources on certificates and private collections. It may be noted that directly implementing the policy logic in chaincodes would necessitate re-installation on all nodes for even a minor change in the policy. Instead, in the proposed design, a policy can be modified on the ledger without any overhead at other nodes.

Our approach focuses on designing a generalized access control framework for a set of organizations participating in the private blockchain. The users are all on-network peers and the resources are also stored on the network managed by owners internal to the network. A resource can be any type of asset supported by the blockchain. No external entity is involved at any step.

3.1   Configuring ABAC Components

We first explain how to configure and store different ABAC components on the HLF network. These can then be accessed and used for access decisions during a request. The proposed configuration for each component is described below.

Resource. A resource can be of any type that can be stored on the blockchain, e.g., a restricted URL, file data, images, etc. While registering a resource on the channel state, the transaction contains its key-value information along with the timestamp. If this transaction is packed into a block and stored on the ledger, any user on the network would then be able to query the ledger to get this transaction and hence, the resource. To guard against such disclosure, we use a feature of HLF called private data that enables us to securely store the resource.

Private Data Collection - It is a database maintained separately from the state database. This data is replicated through a *gossip* protocol only to the peers of respective organizations specified in the collection configuration. The ledger state at each peer for two representative organizations Org1 and Org2 is shown in Fig. 2. Any input data is stored in a transient storage at the anchor peers till it is successfully copied to all the peers. After replication, the hash value

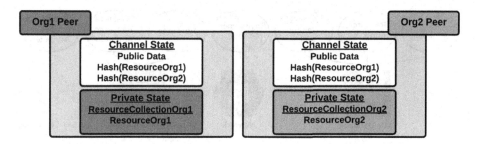

Fig. 2. Ledger states for multiple organizations

of the input data is written to the transaction on the ledger. This is useful while accessing actual data to validate that it is not tampered with. The resource data is available only to the peers of the respective organization. At least one node from the resource's organization should be available to retrieve the resource. These collections can be accessed using the STUB API of HLF.

A resource in the private collection is structured as a JSON object. When multiple MSPs are involved for different organizations, the same ID might get assigned to different clients across these MSPs. To circumvent the problem, we maintain the owner's public key in the resource for resolving any ambiguity.

User Attributes. We divide the user attributes (UA) into two subsets, namely (i) public attributes, denoted by UA_{pub}, that are shared among all the network users and (ii) sensitive attributes, denoted by UA_{priv}, that other network users cannot access. Attributes in UA_{priv} are stored on the client X.509 certificate generated by the MSP during enrollment. These X.509 certificates contain client ID, MSP ID, a public key and other subject related information. The generated client ID is unique within an MSP. We can also mention attribute-value pairs to be stored on the certificate during enrollment with MSP. These certificates are accessible to chaincodes through a CID library. In contrast, UA_{pub} attributes are stored on the channel state in the JSON format. They also have a pub-key field for resolving ambiguity when multiple MSPs are involved.

Resource Attributes. We divide the RA also into two subsets, namely, (i) public resource attributes, denoted by RA_{pub}, that consist of visible attributes and (ii) private resource attributes, denoted by RA_{priv}, that consist of sensitive attributes. Attributes in RA_{pub} are stored on the channel state in JSON format similar to UA_{pub}. RA_{pub} also has a pub-key field for the same reason as mentioned above. As an alternative, the client ID and MSP ID pair from the certificate can also be used for verification since the combination is unique for every client. RA_{priv} has a similar format but is stored on the Org private collection, similar to resources, instead of the channel state. This is to maintain the required additional privacy to keep them hidden to users on the network.

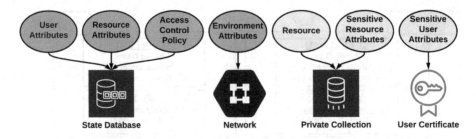

Fig. 3. Deployment locations of ABAC components

Environment Attributes. The environment attributes (*EA*) can be very specific to a use case. They typically need to be inferred from the context during an access request mediation. Chaincodes can be programmed accordingly to retrieve these attributes considering the requester details and the present context.

Access Control Policy. *POL*, the access policy, consists of several rules. At least one of these rules needs to be satisfied for a user to be granted the desired access when requested. These rules are stored on the ledger in JSON format and can be added/deleted/modified whenever necessary only by the Admin user. As the rules are attribute-based in ABAC, giving resource owners the right to add rules might result in inadvertently granting of unauthorized access to other resources having the same attribute values. Each rule is comprised of ID, necessary attributes and a set of access constraints on *UA*, *RA*, *EA* and *OP*. All these constraints need to be valid for the respective rule to be satisfied.

Decision Unit. It is mandatory for every user request to be intercepted by a decision unit (*DU*) for performing the access check. In an HLF network, interacting with the ledger is possible only through chaincodes. So having the *DU* as a chaincode with the resource access methods will require every user request for any resource to be made using this chaincode. This chaincode can then retrieve all the respective attributes, policies and validate the request.

Consider an HLF network for academic resource sharing within a university. Faculty (owners) can save classified data (resource) in a private collection on the network, registering attributes like ID, department, domain, etc., on the ledger based on sensitivity. Student (users) attributes like student id, department and year of study are registered on the certificates or ledger accordingly. When a student requests a resource, these attribute values are matched against the access constraints (e.g., same department, year of study $>= 3$, etc.), and the access decision is recorded on the ledger that can be audited if necessary.

3.2 Managing ABAC Components

To manage the ABAC components on the HLF network as proposed in Sect. 3.1, we have developed a Golang library and made it publicly available with detailed

Table 1. Golang library methods

ABAC component	Related methods
Resource	addResource(), updateResource(), getResource()
User attributes	registerUAPub(), updateUAPub(), getUAPub()
	getUAPriv()
Resource attributes	registerRAPriv(), updateRAPriv(), getRAPriv()
	registerRAPub(), updateRAPub(), getRAPub()
Access policies	registerPolicy(), updatePolicy(), getPolicy(), getPolicySet()
Decision unit	getContext(), validateAccess()

Algorithm 1. updateRAPriv() method

1: **procedure** UPDATERAPRIV(RID, $\overline{ownerID}$, ATTRIBUTES, COLLECTION)
2:      RA_{priv} = stub.GetPrivateData(COLLECTION, RID)
3:      **if** RA_{priv} = NULL **then**
4:          Res = getResource(RID, COLLECTION)
5:          **if** Res.ownerID $\neq$ Hash($\overline{ownerID}$, Res.ownerPubKey) **then**
6:              Return "Invalid Owner Credentials"
7:          RA_{priv} = [RID, Res.ownerID, Res.ownerPubKey, ATTRIBUTES]
8:          stub.PutPrivateData(COLLECTION, RID, RA_{priv})
9:          Return "Registered Private Resource Arrtibutes"
10:      **else if** RA_{priv}.ownerID $\neq$ Hash($\overline{ownerID}$, RA_{priv}.ownerPubKey) **then**
11:          Return "Invalid Owner Credentials"
12:      RA_{priv}^{new} = [RID, RA_{priv}.ownerID, RA_{priv}.ownerPubKey, ATTRIBUTES]
13:      stub.PutPrivateData(COLLECTION, RID, RA_{priv}^{new})
14:      Return "Updated Private Resource Arrtibutes"

---

documentation[2]. Table 1 lists all the available methods in this library. These methods can be used directly in the chaincodes by importing the library. To ensure that only an authorized client can carry out an activity, she has to digitally sign her identity in the request, which can be verified using her public key. Few methods are detailed in the following algorithms. The rest are also developed along similar lines and hence not repeated here for the sake of brevity.

Algorithm 1 takes resource ID, owner ID with digital signature ($\overline{ownerID}$ = Hash[owner ID, owner Private Key]), and updated private attributes (key-value pairs) for the resource as input and updates the RA_{priv} on the private collection. Here we refer to the client maintaining the resource as its owner. CID and STUB libraries are provided by HLF for retrieving user details and interacting with the ledger respectively. Steps 2 and 3 check if RA_{priv} for that resource is already registered. If not, it is added to the private collection in Steps 4 to 9. Steps 5 and 10 verify if the requester is the actual owner of the resource. In Steps 12 to 14, the RA_{priv} is updated with given input attributes and then written to the private collection. The transaction hash gets recorded on the ledger.

---

[2] Available at https://github.com/g4gekkouga/HLF_ABAC.

Algorithm 2. validateAccess() method

1: **procedure** VALIDATEACCESS($\overline{userID}$, RID, OP, COLLECTION)(ResourceData)
2:     userID = cid.GetClientIdentity().GetID()
3:     userCert = cid.GetClientIdentity().GetX509Certificate()
4:     UA_{priv} = userCert.GetAttributes()
5:     UA_{pub} = getUAPub(userID)
6:     **if** userID $\neq$ Hash($\overline{userID}$, UA_{pub}.userPubKey) **then**
7:         Return "Invalid User Credentials"
8:     $UA = [UA_{priv}, UA_{pub}]$
9:     RA_{priv} = getRAPriv(RID, COLLECTION)
10:     RA_{pub} = getRAPub(RID)
11:     $RA = [RA_{priv}, RA_{pub}]$
12:     EA = getContext()
13:     POL = getPolicy()
14:     **for** Rule in POL **do**
15:         **if** validate(Rule, UA, RA, EA, OP) = TRUE **then**
16:             Resource = getResource(RID, COLLECTION)
17:             Return Resource.ResourceData
18:     Return "Access Declined"

Algorithm 2 takes as input the resource ID, digitally signed user ID ($\overline{userID}$ = Hash[user ID, user Private Key]), operation on the resource and resource collection. Here, a client requesting the access is referred to as the user. All the required attributes and policies are retrieved in Steps 4 to 13. Step 6 verifies user credentials to ensure that UA_{pub} belongs to the invoking client. Steps 13 to 17 check if the attributes satisfy any of the rules. If so, the resource is obtained from the private collection and returned to the user. Else, access is denied.

3.3 Execution Workflow

We now describe the workflow of our proposed design of ABAC in Hyperledger Fabric from setup to access mediation using Fig. 4. The Step 0 mentioned in the figure for deploying the blockchain is detailed below:

i First, configure the CA and MSP for all the organizations to generate the certificates and identities. Next, configure the peer and the orderer nodes, and pack the respective certificates to enroll on MSP. Then, generate certificates for Admin using CA for each organization and enroll them on the MSP.

ii Define a private collection on each organization to store its resources. Configure the settings for these collections according to the requirement.

iii Create a channel for all the peers and orderers from different organizations to join. Next, install the chaincodes on the peers and approve them from necessary peers to commit the chaincodes to the channel.

While configuring peer nodes, we can use different services for the state database. By default, HLF provides two database services, both of which were

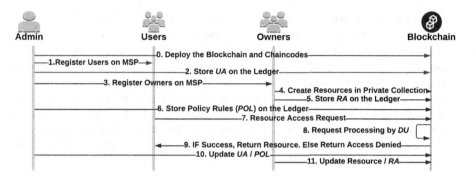

Admin   **Users**   **Owners**   **Blockchain**

————0. Deploy the Blockchain and Chaincodes————▶
——1.Register Users on MSP—▶
————————2. Store *UA* on the Ledger————————▶
——————3. Register Owners on MSP——————▶
————————4. Create Resources in Private Collection▶
——————————5. Store *RA* on the Ledger——————▶
——6. Store Policy Rules (*POL*) on the Ledger——▶
——————————7. Resource Access Request——————▶
8. Request Processing by *DU*
◀——9. IF Success, Return Resource. Else Return Access Denied——
————10. Update *UA* / *POL*——
————————11. Update Resource / *RA*————▶

Fig. 4. Proposed ABAC workflow

duly considered by us for their relative advantages and shortcomings. The first one is GoLevelDB, a simple key-value store database that is embedded into the peer process and runs on the same peer container. The other is CouchDB, an external database that runs alongside its peer on a separate container. CouchDB is also a key-value store and supports all the features of LevelDB. As a document object store, it can maintain data in JSON format and also support indexing. This facilitates execution of complex JSON queries on the value field apart from the key queries. Such a feature helps during the auditing and reporting process.

After the blockchain is deployed (Step 0), Steps 1 to 11 in Fig. 4 specify the subsequent tasks to be followed for exercising access mediation. The Admin enrolls required clients on the MSP and stores their public attributes on the blockchain. These clients can act as both users and resource owners. Owners now add resources to a private collection and store or update the resource attributes on the blockchain. Admin registers the access control rules on the blockchain. When the user makes a request, it is processed by the Decision Unit (a chain-code), and the requested resource is returned upon successful verification.

Our approach makes use of the security guarantees of the HLF itself. No additional security flaw is introduced. HLF architecture is natively secure in terms of design, confidentiality and privacy [3]. It also ensures secure storage and execution of any chaincode making HLF robust in preventing manipulation of business logic during execution. Peer-to-peer communications are secured using the transport layer security (TLS). The TLS certificates and key pairs issued by the CA for peers and orderers are included in their respective docker containers deployed on individual machines. When interacting with a peer container, these certificates are used for both client and server authentication during the TLS handshake, thus ensuring network integrity. Thus, security in terms of local enforcement depends on the security guarantees of Docker and in particular the isolation properties of Docker containers.

Note that the administration is responsible for issuing or modifying user attributes, policy rules, etc. Any change to these components requires invoking respective methods within *DU* chaincode. When a user makes an access request, it reaches all the nodes in the network. At each node, the access decision is made independently after processing the request using the DU chaincode. The orderer nodes use consensus protocols to create transactions on the ledger through a majority decision. Thus, even if an attacker modifies the DU on his own node to grant access, the consensus will still need to be reached for acceptance. Similarly, when an admin makes a register/modify request for attributes, policy, etc., it also reaches all the nodes and is processed individually. While these transactions are endorsed by all the peers by default considering the admin credentials, they are still recorded on the ledger simultaneously on all the peers and can be audited.

4   Implementation and Experimental Evaluation

In this section, we first present the implementation details of our proposed approach in Hyperledger Fabric followed by experimental results under different scenarios. The performance is measured with the help of the Hyperledger Caliper benchmarking tool.

4.1   Network Implementation

First, we deploy a custom HLF network to test our approach with the help of chaincodes. This docker network prototype is being made freely available by us to the research community along with the detailed steps for its deployment[3]. We use virtual instances on the Google Cloud Platform to deploy this HLF network and record the latency observed by an instance that functions as an individual node on the network. Hyperledger Explorer[4], an open-source web-based tool for visualizing the activities on the underlying blockchain, is used for tracking the deployed peers, channel state, and the recorded transactions on the network.

We initially deploy a vanilla smart contract (call it Reference Chaincode), which is a chaincode to store and return a resource without any access check. Next, we deploy a second smart contract (call it Proposed Chaincode), which has the full functionality of the workflow described in Fig. 4. It uses the developed Golang library to record the attributes, policy, resources, etc., and exercise access check before returning the desired resource. The Reference Chaincode acts as a baseline against which the actual ABAC enhanced chaincode (Proposed Chaincode) is benchmarked. This is to eliminate any idiosyncrasy in the network or system behavior due to the hardware or software configurations. It also lets us focus our study on the actual performance of the proposed access mechanism rather than the entire network itself. Both these chaincodes are included in the docker network being made openly available.

---

[3] Available at https://github.com/g4gekkouga/HLF_Custom_Network.

[4] https://www.hyperledger.org/use/explorer.

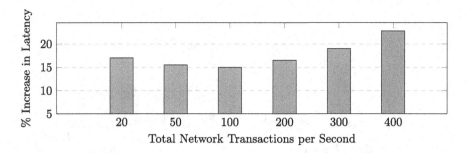

Fig. 5. Variation in latency with network traffic

4.2   Performance Evaluation

To evaluate our approach, we build a synthetic dataset for the ABAC system. This dataset contains randomly generated attributes for users, resources, environmental context, and rules defined on these attributes. To execute these transactions from the Proposed and Reference Chaincodes on the HLF network, we use the open-source benchmarking tool Hyperledger Caliper[5]. We use CouchDB for the state database and Raft consensus for the HLF network as default. We consider 100 users, 100 resources and 50 rules on the network by default.

Any access request is originated from a user as a transaction for operating on a system resource. These transactions call the validateAccess() method described in Algorithm 2. For an accurate estimation of the additional latency introduced due to the access check, we record the difference in latency between access transaction execution through the Proposed and the Reference Chaincodes.

Figure 5 shows the variation in ABAC-mediated access latency with increasing number of concurrent transactions in the entire network. The latency values are averaged over 10 transactions as recorded on one of the nodes. It is observed that there is an initial lowering of latency, which is due to an increase in the number of transactions being packed into a single block on the ledger, resulting in a decrease in the latency for each transaction. After the transaction count in a block reaches its limit, there is a need to add more than one block and hence, the latency starts slowly increasing due to higher network congestion.

The impact of the number of different ABAC components on latency is depicted in Figs. 6a and 6b. In these figures, cardinalities of the other components are set to default values except for the ones that were varied. It is observed that change in the number of rules in the policy (Fig. 6b) has a higher impact than the number of users or resources (Fig. 6a). This is because increasing the number of rules requires processing of more access constraints unlike for users and resources, which requires searching a larger state space. Also, an equal increase in the number of resources results in a slightly higher latency than for users as seen in Fig. 6a. This is because in the first case, two of the components, namely, resources and RA, are increased compared to only UA in the latter case.

---

[5] https://www.hyperledger.org/use/caliper.

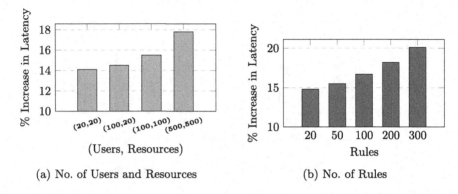

(a) No. of Users and Resources   (b) No. of Rules

Fig. 6. Variation in latency with the number of ABAC components

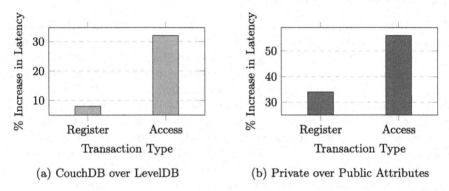

(a) CouchDB over LevelDB   (b) Private over Public Attributes

Fig. 7. Additional latency for different design choices

Overall, from Figs. 5 and 6, it is observed that there is not much increase in latency in any of the situations. This shows that the proposed authorization step using ABAC contributes very little additional processing time compared to the default network transmission and ledger interactions.

For studying the impact of alternative design choices as discussed in Sect. 3, we vary the database service used for both channel state and private collections as shown in Figs. 7(a) and (b). In each of these, the result of one choice is shown as a ratio of the other. From Fig. 7a, it observed that GoLevelDB outperforms CouchDB mainly for access transactions in a general use case. This is because LevelDB runs on a peer, unlike CouchDB that executes in a separate container. As a result, the rate of information transfer, which is greater in an access request, is higher. In general, if the entire policy is to be considered, LevelDB is a better choice since it has lower latency. But in specific cases where only a subset of rules need to be verified based on the attribute set, CouchDB can be effectively used since it is more robust, supports indexing, richer queries.

Figure 7b shows the performance comparison between the design choices of having all the attributes as public vs private. For keeping them as private, the

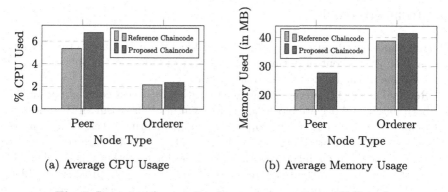

(a) Average CPU Usage   (b) Average Memory Usage

Fig. 8. Resource consumption for access requests at 200 Txns/s

Table 2. Comparison with the current state-of-the-art

Features	Our model	Iftekar et al. [9]	Liu at al. [12]	Stamatellis et al. [20]	Rouhani et al. [18]
Domain	General AC	IOT	IOT	Healthcare	General AC
UA	Private, Public	Private	Private	Private (only ID)	Private
RA	Private, Public	Private	Public	Private (only ID)	Private
EA	Supported	-	-	-	-
Pol	On ledger	In chaincode	In chaincode	-	On Ledger
Users	Network peers	External	External	External	External
Resources	Private collection	Off chain	Off chain	Off chain	Off chain
Benchmark	Caliper	Caliper	-	-	Caliper

access request latency is 56% higher compared to public. The same for register requests is 34%. This is due to relatively more interactions with the private space for access requests compared to the register requests.

Figure 8 depicts the resource consumption averaged over all the peer, orderer nodes. For both, there is a nominal difference in resource usage between the Proposed and the Reference Chaincodes, implying that the overhead of introducing ABAC is quite low. The difference is lower at the orderer node since only the consensus protocol runs at the orderer nodes and access control has no impact. As the actual access request is processed on the peer nodes, there is a minor increase in resource usage at peer nodee. Comparing Figs. 8a and 8b, it is observed that memory consumption is greater for orderers because they collect decisions from all the peers for running the consensus protocol. In contrast, access requests are handled at the peers, thus needing greater processing power.

In real-world applications, the networks are usually highly scaled-up with multiple organizations and peers. Hence, peer-to-peer communication would result for the major part of the depicted latency. As long as the network scales up with the cardinality of the ABAC components, the percentage of additional latency introduced due to access check over the default transaction latency will remain similar to that in the experimental results reported above.

5   Related Work

With a rapid proliferation of permissioned blockchains in large organizations, research on access control in this domain is also gaining pace. In this section, we review some of the related work in the literature.

Rouhani et al. [17] survey various state-of-the-art access control mechanisms for both public and private blockchains. Iftekhar et al. [9] detail an HLF network setup and chaincode installation process for implementing access control in IoT networks. Only user attributes from client X.509 certificates are considered to write access logic in chaincodes with no support for the other ABAC elements. Another secure data transmission method for IoT devices was proposed by Liang et al. [11] to test the private blockchain network communication performance and security factors for its compatibility in real-world use cases. Liu et al. [12] propose using HLF as an intermediary unit between the users and the IoT device resources. They use three chaincodes to manage policies, resource URLs and access control, respectively. Attributes are, however, not stored on the ledger. Instead, they are received with the request and verified using cryptographic techniques. We compare our work with other existing approaches in Table 2.

Stamatellis et al. [20] propose another similar healthcare framework using HLF where the user id from MSP is used for verification using Idemix to provide anonymity. However, these frameworks lack the ABAC logical access components. A chaincode based access control, specifically for RFID systems, was proposed by Figueroa et al. [7]. However, only UA from the MSP Certs are considered and RA are stored on the state database. Access logic is directly written in chaincode. Thus, any update to the access logic requires re-installing the access chaincode making it quite inflexible. There are also a few other domain-specific models for IoT [5,13], cloud federation [6], edge computing [21], etc., using HLF similar to the above solutions though with certain variations.

Akhtar et al. [1] develop a blockchain-based auditable access control mechanism for distributed business processes where the access policy is encoded within the smart contracts. Rouhani et al. [18] propose a distributed ABAC system using the HLF network. Users and resources are considered external to the network. Only their attributes and policies are stored on the ledger using chaincodes. An enforcement point intercepts the user requests and redirects them to HLF. There is, however, no support for user certificates as the requester is not a client on the network. Also, only the public attributes are considered. The HLF network is used merely as an intermediary for deciding access rights. Marcus et al. propose a decentralized ledger-based access control [15] tested using an HLF network. The owner stores hashed resource and its access policy containing the public keys of allowed users (similar to ACL) on the ledger. A ring signature scheme is used to verify the requester's id and reconstruct the resource upon access verification.

A critical review of related work highlights an evident lack of generalized and full ABAC support for Hyperledger Fabric. Most of the proposed solutions are either domain-specific or consider only limited ABAC features. Our work fills this gap and improves upon all the previous work by exercising a highly flexible, dynamic, and fully functional ABAC for Hyperledger Fabric.

6   Conclusions

In this paper, we have proposed a novel approach for supporting complete attribute-based access control functionality in a HLF network. We have detailed the underlying architecture and workflow for exercising access control through this method. An extensive evaluation using the Caliper benchmarking tool shows that the performance of this approach for different use cases is very promising. The additional overhead is within reasonable limits considering that security is significantly enhanced through ABAC. We also make the network prototype and the Golang library available to the research community through Github.

Future work in this area would include supporting verifiable credentials for providing ad hoc access for a requester external to the network by using her VCs as *UA* for policy evaluation. Besides, we plan to include support for more *EA* in the Golang library. We also aim to extend the library for other chaincode languages supported by HLF. This architecture is also generalized enough to support ABAC in any permissioned blockchain irrespective of the platform.

Acknowledgments. This research was supported by the National Institutes of Health under award R35GM134927, the Cisco University Research Program Fund under Silicon Valley Community Foundation award number 2020-220329 (3696), and by a research gift received from Cisco University Research. The content is solely the responsibility of the authors and doesn't necessarily represent the official views of agencies funding the research.

References

1. Akhtar, A., et al.: Blockchain based auditable access control for distributed business processes. In: 40th IEEE International Conference on Distributed Computing Systems, pp. 12–22 (2020)
2. Androulaki, E., et al.: Hyperledger fabric: a distributed operating system for permissioned blockchains. In: Proceedings of 13th EuroSys Conference, pp. 1–15 (2018)
3. Brotsis, S., et al.: On the security and privacy of hyperledger fabric: challenges and open issues. In: IEEE World Congress on Services, pp. 197–204 (2020)
4. Chung, T.H., et al.: Guide to attribute based access control (ABAC) definition and considerations. NIST Spec. Publ. **800**(162), 162–800 (2014)
5. Ding, S., et al.: A novel attribute-based access control scheme using blockchain for IOT. IEEE Access **7**, 38431–38441 (2019)
6. Ferdous, M.S.A.A.: Decentralised runtime monitoring for access control systems in cloud federations. In: IEEE 37th International Conference on Distributed Computing Systems, pp. 2632–2633 (2017)
7. Figueroa, S., et al.: An attribute-based access control using chaincode in RFID systems. In: 10th IFIP International Conference on New Technologies, Mobility and Security, pp. 1–5 (2019)

8. Hu, V.C., et al.: Attribute-based access control. Computer **48**(2), 85–88 (2015)
9. Iftekhar, A., et al.: Hyperledger fabric access control system for internet of things layer in blockchain-based applications. Entropy **23**(8), 1054 (2021)
10. Li, H., Han, D.: Edurss: a blockchain-based educational records secure storage and sharing scheme. IEEE Access **7**, 179273–179289 (2019)
11. Liang, W., et al.: A secure fabric blockchain-based data transmission technique for industrial internet-of-things. IEEE Trans. Ind. Inf. **15**(6), 3582–3592 (2019)
12. Liu, H., et al.: Fabric-iot: a blockchain-based access control system in IOT. IEEE Access **8**, 18207–18218 (2020)
13. Ma, M., et al.: Privacy-oriented blockchain-based distributed key management architecture for hierarchical access control in IoT scenario. IEEE Access **7**, 34045–34059 (2019)
14. Maesa, D., et al.: A blockchain based approach for the definition of auditable access control systems. Comput. Secur. **84**, 93–119 (2019)
15. Markus, I., et al.: Dacc: decentralized ledger based access control for enterprises. In: 2019 IEEE International Conference on Blockchain and Cryptocurrency, pp. 345–351 (2019)
16. Ouaddah, A., et al.: Fairaccess: a new blockchain-based access control framework for the internet of things. Secur. Commun. Netw. **9**(18), 5943–5964 (2017)
17. Rouhani, S., et al.: Blockchain based access control systems: state of the art and challenges. In: 2019 IEEE International Conference on Web Intelligence, pp. 423–428 (2019)
18. Rouhani, S., Belchior, R., Cruz, R.S., Deters, R.: Distributed attribute-based access control system using permissioned blockchain. World Wide Web **24**(5), 1617–1644 (2021). https://doi.org/10.1007/s11280-021-00874-7
19. Sandhu, R., et al.: Role-based access control models. Computer **29**(2), 38–47 (1996)
20. Stamatellis, C., et al.: A privacy-preserving healthcare framework using hyperledger fabric. Sensors **20**(22), 6587 (2020)
21. Stanciu, A.: Blockchain based control system for edge computing. In: 21st International Conference on Control Systems and Computer Science, pp. 667–671 (2017)
22. Xu, M., Chen, X., Kou, G.: A systematic review of blockchain. Financ. Innov. **5**(1), 1–14 (2019). https://doi.org/10.1186/s40854-019-0147-z
23. Zhang, Y., et al.: Attribute-based access control for smart cities: a smart-contract-driven framework. IEEE Internet Things J. **8**(8), 6372–6384 (2021)

Mobile Security and Privacy

AndroClonium: Bytecode-Level Code Clone Detection for Obfuscated Android Apps

Ardalan Foroughipour[1(✉)], Natalia Stakhanova[1(✉)], Farzaneh Abazari[1], and Bahman Sistany[2]

[1] University of Saskatchewan, Saskatoon, Canada
{arf027,faa851}@usask.ca, natalia@cs.usask.ca
[2] University of Ottawa, Ottawa, Canada
bsistany@uottawa.ca

Abstract. Detecting code clones is essential for many security tasks, e.g., vulnerability detection, malware analysis, legacy software patching. In many of these security scenarios, source code is not available, leaving binary code analysis as the only option. Yet, evaluation of binary code is often exacerbated by the wide use of obfuscation. In this work, we propose an approach for obfuscation-resistant fine-grained detection of code clones in Android apps at the bytecode level. To mitigate inherent constraints of static analysis and to achieve obfuscation resistance, we partially simulate the execution of Android code, and abstract the resulting execution traces. We validate our approach's ability to detect different types of code clones on a set of 20 injected clones and explore its resistance against obfuscation on a set of 1085 obfuscated apps.

Keywords: Code clone · Obfuscation · Android · Smali code

1 Introduction

Software applications are no longer built from scratch. They are assembled from open source and third party code components, this phenomenon is commonly known as *code reuse* or *code cloning*. While code reuse is typically associated with legitimate software development, malware writers are no exception and reuse existing code and third-party components to expedite malware development. Establishing the presence of third-party code at the binary code level may facilitate efficient triage of unknown samples, accurate detection and understanding of malicious functionality. Besides malware detection and analysis, identification of code clones in binary code is an essential task for other security applications, e.g., for code attribution, vulnerability search, legacy software patching.

In spite of significant research efforts focused on binary code similarity detection in the recent years, this is still non-trivial task mainly due to the diversity of hardware architectures, software platforms and the wide use of code obfuscation. Code obfuscation has become a common approach for both legitimate

© IFIP International Federation for Information Processing 2022
Published by Springer Nature Switzerland AG 2022
W. Meng et al. (Eds.): SEC 2022, IFIP AICT 648, pp. 379–397, 2022.
https://doi.org/10.1007/978-3-031-06975-8_22

and malicious software to disguise its appearance, intent, and to protect it from reverse engineering and analysis techniques. The majority of the existing studies that focus on binary code similarity leverage static analysis methods, e.g., extracting function features from assembly code [10] and analyzing the control flow graph (CFG) [13]. Static analysis methods are fast but often fail to cope with more sophisticated cases of code reuse, i.e., the instances of reused code that are broken into small and non-contiguous pieces, reordered, and intertwined with other pieces of code. The wide use of obfuscation techniques also renders most of these existing static-analysis based approaches ineffective. On the other hand, current solutions that rely on dynamic analysis are difficult to automate. They tend to analyze an app as a black-box, and hence are not well-suited for fine-grained code clone detection.

In this work, we address these challenges and propose AndroClonium: an approach for obfuscation-resistant fine-grained detection of code clones in obfuscated Android apps. Since in security setting, source code is rarely available, we focus on detection of code clones through the analysis of Android binary code. More specifically, we disassemble the Android bytecode to the Smali format, which can be considered as an equivalent of the assembly language for Android bytecode. Our approach first disassembles the bytecode of an app to the Smali format and then simulates the execution of the Smali code to extract possible app execution traces. To analyze these traces, we employ program backward slicing to extract data-dependent instructions that bear semantic significance. Code slices further produce smaller code segments which are then analyzed for the potential code similarity. This approach allows us, even in presence of code obfuscation, to recognize syntactically similar code clones, referred to as *Type-3* clones in addition to some cases of syntactically different but semantically equivalent code clones, referred to as *Type-4* code clones.

We validate our approach on 20 manually injected code clone samples and investigate its the obfuscation resistance on 1085 open-source Android apps. Our approach achieved between 78% to 87% similarity between its findings before and after obfuscation was applied on 1085 apps. We further perform code clone detection among 1603 non-obfuscated apps collected from F-Droid market[1]. We compare the performance of our approach to another method-level clone detection tool called Nicad [19]. Although our approach for the most part agrees with Nicad, we observe that we are able to find significantly more code clones missed by Nicad. Finally, we investigate the applicability of our approach in detecting Android malware variants through the analysis of their code clones. Through the analysis of the binary's code clones, we identify unique code clones between different samples of a malware family that can be further used for detecting other variants of the malware family. Our approach was able to detect correctly 88% of apps based on the presence of code clones in their binary code. Our contributions in this work can be summarized as follows:

- We introduce an approach for the detection of non-contiguous code clones that can be employed both at method level and code slice level in obfuscated

---

[1] https://www.f-droid.org/.

Android apps through analysis of their execution traces. To the best of our knowledge, this is the first work that offers detection of code clones in obfuscated Android apps.

- As an alternative to purely static or dynamic analysis approaches for analyzing Smali code, we have developed a Smali execution simulator to extract possible execution traces of an Android app. We offer our simulator and our dataset to the security community in an effort to facilitate research in this area[2].

2   Background and Literature Review

Android apps are packaged and distributed in the .apk file format. Each .apk file, when decompressed, includes one or multiple .dex files that contain the logic of an app in the form of Dalvik bytecode. Earlier Android versions executed apps using the *Dalvik Virtual Machine* (DalvikVM) but from Android 5.0, DalvikVM was replaced by *Android-Runtime* environment (ART). Dalvik bytecode standard contains a small, high-level and object oriented instruction set. As a result, Dalvik instructions can be easily understood, modified and even in some cases, decompiled back to the original Java code. Due to the security implications of these, code optimization and obfuscation are commonly adopted to make analysis of the Android apps more challenging.

Related Works: Code clone detection is a well-studied problem that has been examined both at the source code level, usually for program comprehension or plagiarism detection, and at the binary code level for vulnerability analysis and malware detection. In the literature, code clones have been categorized into four types [20]: *Type-1*: code pieces that are textually identical except for white spaces, comments, or layout characteristics, *Type-2*: code pieces that are syntactically identical except for identifier names or literal values, *Type-3*: syntactically similar code pieces with minor differences at statement level that may differ by addition, removal, or modification of some statements, and *Type-4*: syntactically different but semantically identical code clones. The majority of the existing studies on source code clone detection employ text-based [19], token-based [17,20,21], tree-based [15] or graph-based [18] heuristics. For example, *Nicad* [19] is a text-based approach that uses normalization and LCS algorithm to detect code clones. The approaches proposed by *Kamiya et al.* [17] and *Duric et al.* [21] employ tokenized sequences. *Duric et al.* [21] leverage Running Karp-Rabin Greedy String Tiling (RKR-GST) algorithm, which involves tiling a string with matching substrings of another string and Winnoing algorithm for similarity comparison. *Yang et al.* [26] uses token-sequences for clone detection but also considers features such as lambda expressions, and anonymous classes. Another token-based code clone detection, *SourcererCC* [20] uses inverted-index and heuristics to improve scalability. An abstract syntax tree (AST)-based analysis is employed by *DECKARD* [15]. *Komondoor et al.* [18]

---

[2] https://cyberlab.usask.ca/publications.html.

uses program dependence graphs (PDG) and the following program slicing to find isomorphic sub-graphs and consequently detect duplicated code.

Detection of code clones in binary or byte code level has also been studied by researchers. At the function level, *Eschweiler et al.* [13] employed numerical and structural features for detection of code clones. *Ding et al.* [11] represented assembly codes as control flow graphs and detected clones by finding similar sub-graphs between functions. *Yang et al.* [27] proposed *Asteria*, a deep learning-based approach that learns semantic representation of binary functions by first decompiling the binary to source code and then extracting the source codes AST to find semantically similar functions. At the block level, *Yu et al.*. [29] proposed a Java bytecode code clone detection tool based on instruction sequences and method calls as features to find code clones. Other studies have focused on finding semantically similar code in binaries. *Hu et al.* [14] proposed converting binaries to an intermediate representation and emulating selected codes with random values to extract semantic signatures. One major drawback of this approach is its limited code coverage since it relies on random values. To mitigate this problem, *Egele et al.* [12], proposed blanket execution, a dynamic analysis approach that performs repeated execution of binary functions using random values from the first un-executed instruction until every instruction has been executed at least once. Even though this solves the problem of code coverage, the approach still suffers from invalid executions.

In Android context, these approaches are not applicable since Android apps are developed in an event-oriented manner and rely heavily on user interactions which are major obstacle for efficient automated dynamic analysis. To detect code clones in Android apps, *Akram et al.* [2] proposed to analyze hashed n-grams extracted from the normalized decompiled code of .dex files. Other studies [3,9] explored code clone detection at application level and thus are not well suited for detection of fine-grade code clones between multiple applications. In this work, we address this concern and explore detection of code clones in a presence of obfuscation.

The categorization of obfuscation transformations were originally proposed in a seminal work by Collberg at el. [8]. *Balachandran et al.* [5] expanded this categorization by proposing several techniques specifically for Android apps, i.e., 1) packed-switch construct, 2) try-catch construct, and 3) combination of the last two techniques. Aonzo et al. [1] developed Obfuscapk, an obfuscation tool for Android which supports a variety of obfuscation techniques such as layout obfuscations, control-flow obfuscations, and string-encryption obfuscation.

While the obfuscation is common in legitimate and malicious apps, only a few studies attempted to address obfuscation in Android setting, yet, none of them focused specifically on clone detection. Wang et al. [23] and Bacci et al. [4] proposed a machine learning based approaches to detect the obfuscators used for obfuscating Android apps. Several studies explored deobfuscation of Android apps. *Bichsel et al.* [6] introduced DeGuard, an approach for reversing layout obfuscation of the program elements obfuscated with ProGuard. *Yoo et al.*. [28] introduced deobfuscation of string encryption, by dynamically execute Android

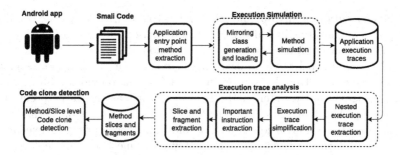

Fig. 1. The flow of the proposed approach

apps on a modified Dalvik VM which captures the executed Dalvik instructions and the corresponding metadata which is then used to find the original values of obfuscated strings. *Vos et al.*[22] proposed ASTANA, that reverts obfuscated string literals to their original value by executing the string deobfuscation logic inserted by the obfuscation tool.

In summary, none of the existing code clone detection approaches consider code obfuscation.

3   Methodology

In this work, we leverage partial code execution to overcome challenges of purely static or dynamic approaches. Approaches that rely on static analysis do not perform well with obfuscated code due to uncertainties of predicting the run-time code behaviour. Dynamic analysis techniques although less affected by obfuscation, due to the semantic-preserving nature of code obfuscation, require generation of a sufficient number of valid inputs to achieve high code coverage. These challenges make the pure dynamic analysis not suitable for large code bases. In Android apps, this is exacerbated by relying heavily on user interactions with GUI. Thus, we propose a hybrid approach that partially executes Android bytecode to extract possible app execution traces. We simulate the execution of an Android app at Smali code level and therefore refer to this approach as Smali simulation. These obtained traces are then further analyzed to extract semantically significant parts of the code for detection of code clones. Figure 1 summarizes the flow of the proposed approach that follows four main steps: (1) Entry Point Extraction, (2) Execution simulation, (3) Execution trace analysis, and (4) Code clone detection.

3.1   Entry Point Extraction

Android apps unlike traditional programs do not contain a main method and are compromised of multiple entry points which are invoked by ART. Separating the entry point methods is beneficial for efficient simulation code. This approach allows to select relevant portions of code that would have been invoked during an actual execution of an app, and effectively avoid unnecessary code simulation as Android apps often include residual and unused classes and APIs due to difference reasons such as obfuscation or inclusion of libraries.

Android apps consist of four key components as their building blocks, namely, Activities, Services, Broadcast receivers, and Content providers. These components can define and register methods that will act as the entry points to an Android app. We define app's *Entry Point Methods* as a set of methods in an Android app that are invoked by the Android framework during the execution of an app for performing a task. Android entry point methods can be categorized into 3 broad groups:

1. Methods defined by the Android app components, which are overridden by the developer and subsequently invoked by the Android system on certain events, e.g., the `Activity->onCreate(Bundle)` method.
2. Methods defined as event handlers which are registered into the system during execution of an application, e.g., `View.OnClickListener->onClick(View)`.
3. Methods declared as the click event handlers in layout files, XML files that define the structure of a user interface of an Activity. For example, the element "<Button>" in a layout file can declare an "android:onClick" property which should be invoked when an onClick event happens.

Extraction of the entry points from the group (1) is trivial as they correspond to an Activity or a Service declared in app's "AndroidManifest.xml" file. Yet, locating the entry points from groups (2) and (3) is challenging, since they represent callbacks that are dynamically registered by the code of an app. We design a heuristic to extract these entry points through a static analysis of the app's Smali code and the corresponding layout files. We use a list of Android methods that if overridden by an app may act as entry points. The list was compiled through an analysis of previous studies that have extracted some of these methods [7,24]. We parse Smali code to detect if any of the methods in our list are overridden. For the overridden methods from the group (1) entry points, we check if their declaring component is registered in the AndroidManifest.xml file. For groups (2) and (3), we take a more conservative approach. We include all methods that override methods from our list of entry point methods and methods defined as the onClick handlers in a layout file (if a method in an app matches it).

3.2 Execution Simulation

Once all app's entry points are obtained, the Smali simulation is performed for each entry-point method. Theoretically, any Smali instruction can be emulated at the application layer using the dynamic features of the ART such as reflection or method-handles. In practice, however, this requires correct values for the execution of these instructions. Yet, we observed that to determine code similarity, it is often unnecessary to know all precise values in real execution. Thus, we perform partial execution on Smali code by selectively executing instructions and leaving some unexecuted.

For modeling values corresponding to unexecuted instructions, we introduce the notion of *ambiguous value* which denotes any possible value in the execution. Our simulator takes a method's Smali code with its arguments as input and simulates its execution with the maximum threshold of 10 executions per method. In our currently implemented prototype, we use ambiguous values for all the input values needed to execute a method. While this may reduce the accuracy of simulation in some cases, we show empirically that this is sufficient to detect code clones. To realize our vision of such Smali simulator two challenges have to be addressed: 1) creating and loading a class into the ART, mirroring the types defined in the Smali files. 2) separating the methods that our simulator is allowed to execute from the methods that should not be invoked during the execution.

Mirror Class Generation and Loading. One major challenge in Smali code simulation is modelling user-defined classes. These classes declared in the .smali files need to be loaded into the ART as if they were loaded during an actual execution of an application. To solve this issue, we use the ByteBuddy framework [25], a dynamic Java class generator. With the help of ByteBuddy framework, we can dynamically create a class to ART that mirrors the Smali class. With this approach, the Smali class is loaded to the ART engine which is then treated as a regular Java class.

Selecting Methods for Partial Execution. The logic of partial execution is simple, if any method invocation that can return an unpredictable or invalid result should not be executed. For example, `Context->getPackageName()` API if executed in our custom execution environment, incorrectly returns the name of the simulator and not the package name of an app under analysis. Similarly, method invocations that perform I/O operations may produce unexpected results. To support partial execution, we separate methods bundled with ART into *safe* and *unsafe*. A method that can be correctly executed in the context of the simulator is considered to be *safe*. Similarly, we define a class as safe if it only includes safe methods. When an unsafe method is invoked, its return value is modelled using an ambiguous value. Furthermore, all mutable objects passed to this unsafe method are also replaced with ambiguous values.

To reduce the propagation of ambiguous values in our simulation, we also differentiate *pure* methods, methods that are functionally pure and do not change the state of passed arguments, i.e., do not assign a new value to any field or invoke methods which would change state of an object such as ArrayList.add() method. Hence, any invocation of a pure method with ambiguous value stops its propagation on mutable passed arguments. Other instruction that operates on an ambiguous value also usually results in an ambiguous value. If an instruction needs to branch on an ambiguous value, an execution branch path is chosen at random.

To separate safe and unsafe classes and methods from classes bundled with the ART, we create an initial set of safe classes manually. Based on this initial set, we automatically extracts all other safe classes/methods bundled in Android Runtime that only use methods that previously have been marked as safe. To account for inheritance and overridden methods, we divide safe methods into two groups:

1) *static-safe methods*, i.e., static methods where all arguments are either from a static-safe class or an instance-safe class and all the invoked methods inside the method body are safe.
2) *instance-safe methods* i.e., methods with arguments including its reference object coming from an instance-safe class and with only all safe method invocations inside its body. In this definition, we include constructors as methods. Furthermore, a class is considered instance-safe if all of the methods it defines are safe, its super class is instance-safe and all of its child types are also instance-safe.

For extracting pure methods, similar to the safe methods, we start by manually creating a set of pure methods, and then recursively traverse Android Runtime code to extract other pure methods.

3.3   Execution Trace Analysis

For a given app, the simulator generates its possible execution traces (as an example see Fig. 2). These raw execution traces are further analyzed to extract semantically significant parts of code for detection of clones. This analysis consists of the following steps:

Nested Execution Trace Extraction. During simulation stage, all callee's invocations (and their corresponding instructions) are embedded in the caller execution trace. Hence, as we perform execution trace flattening in the next steps, it appears as if all instructions were executed by caller. In order to perform code clone detection on each method, we need to separate all the nested execution traces.

Execution Trace Simplification. The next step is to normalize and simplify the execution trace to purge any side effects obfuscation might have had on the execution trace. The simplification transformations we perform are as follows. 1) *Execution trace flattening*: an execution trace is modified so that the instructions in nested traces can be treated as if they were executed in their parent executions. To achieve this the register number used by nested execution traces has to be updated to new unused register numbers. Furthermore, the invocation call in the parent execution trace and the return instruction in the nested trace are substituted by new move instructions to connect the data dependency between nested and parent execution trace. 2) *Removing register aliasing*: register aliasing refers to cases when a single value is referenced by multiple registers. For backward slicing at a later stage, we need to remove any register aliasing in our execution

```
// App: com.gabm.fancyplaces:9        const/4 v1 1 &0
package com.gabm.fancyplaces.functional;   const/4 v2 0 &1
                                       if-nez v9 @6 &2
class LocationHandler {                new-instance v0 Landroid/text/format/Time; &6
                                       invoke-direct v0 Landroid/text/format/Time;-><init>()V &7
...                                    invoke-virtual v0 Landroid/text/format/Time;->setToNow()V &8
protected Boolean                      invoke-virtual v0 v1 Landroid/text/format/Time;->toMillis(Z)J &9
isValidLocation(Location location){    move-result-wide v4 &10
    if (location == null) {            invoke-virtual v9 Landroid/location/Location;->getTime()J &11
        return false;                  move-result-wide v6 &12
    }                                  sub-long/2addr v4 v6 &13
    Time now = new Time();             const-wide/32 v6 120000 &14
    now.setToNow();                    cmp-long v3 v4 v6 &15
    return (now.toMillis(true) -       if-gtz v3 @20 &16
location.getTime()) <= TWO_MINUTES;    invoke-static v1 Ljava/lang/Boolean;->valueOf(Z)Ljava/lang/Boolean; &17
}                                      move-result-object v1 &18
                                       goto @5 &19
...                                    return-object v1 &5

}
```

Fig. 2. An example source code of an app and a possible execution trace

traces. 3) *Reflection normalization*: replaces any method invocation done using reflection with a normal method invocation. This transformation is not trivial since it requires to use new registers and add new instructions to with the correct data dependency relationship. 4) *Constant transformation simplification*: locates any method invocation that takes constant primitive values or strings as inputs and computes a new primitive value or string based on the inputs. After finding such methods, we replace the consequent Smali "move-result" instructions in the parent execution with the "const" Smali instructions.

Important Instruction Extraction. An important step in analyzing execution traces is to find semantically significant parts of it. Knowing that not all instructions bear the same significance, one key task is to define what instructions we consider semantically important. We consider instructions important if they can affect the system outside of the method's scope. From all Smali instructions, only few are capable of causing side effects outside of a method scope. Such instructions include 1) a method's return instruction which is not void, 2) invocation of Java or Android API methods that change global state such as reading from 'input' or writing to 'output', 3) invocations of methods that change the state of an object not created in local method scope, 4) changing the value of a static field of classes, 5) changing the value of an instance field of an object. Figure 2 shows the important instruction in execution trace.

Separating the return instruction or instructions that assign a new value to a field is straightforward, however, separating method invocations that can generate side effects is much more difficult. To find ART API invocations that change the global state of an application, e.g., printing or writing a value, we reuse our list of safe and pure methods. Essentially in our current implementation, any method invocation on unsafe methods is considered to potentially cause a side effect. For method invocations that change the state of a non-local object, we reuse our list of pure methods. In this case, any non-pure method invocation on

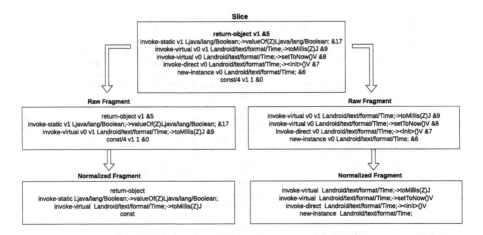

Fig. 3. Extracted slices and the corresponding fragments

a non-local object is also considered to change its state. For example, adding a new value to an ArrayList object that has not been instantiated inside a method.

Slice and Fragment Extraction. Each important instruction usually depends on multiple instructions executed before it. We therefore need to discover and extract all data dependencies for each important instruction. We use *backward slicing* approach to partition execution traces into smaller and meaningful chunks of code. We denote a *slice* of a code with respect to an important instruction *in* and a single data value *x* involved in this instruction as a set of all preceding instructions that might affect the value of *x*. In essence, each slice corresponds to instructions that perform one semantically significant task in code.

We use *backward slicing* approach for two reasons: 1) control-flow can be modified by obfuscation and therefore might be difficult to simplify using only execution traces; 2) due to the fact that Smali is an object oriented instruction set, data-dependency between instructions includes significant semantic information.

Our next step is to break the slices into smaller pieces in order to capture small but semantically important code segments that can be shared between different methods. Given that instructions of a slice usually work with multiple objects and primitive values, we partition them into smaller sets of instructions each of which follows a single variable value. We refer to these partitions as *fragments*.

Finally, after separating fragments, we normalize them to remove minor differences caused by different literal values, user-defined type names, register numbers, and repeated instructions caused by loops and recursion. We keep instruction mnemonics and type identifiers only if they are not user-defined types. Figure 3 depicts extracted slices and the corresponding fragments for the example shown in Fig. 2.

3.4   Code Clone Detection

The last step is to detect code clones based on the partitioned fragments. In this work, we measure the similarity of two code pieces by calculating the Jaccard Index on two sets of fragments A and B. This similarity comparison can be both performed at the method level or the slice level which also makes our approach capable of finding smaller code clones.

$$JaccardIndex = \frac{|A \cap B|}{|A \cup B|}$$

4   Validation and Experiments

Our simulator is implemented as an Android application for the Android version 26 or above. After installation, the simulator exposes APIs over the network which can be used to interact with it and perform Smali simulation. For our experiments, we installed our simulator on multiple emulated Android devices with 2 CPU cores and 4 GB of memory.

4.1   Dataset Creation

Due to the lack of labelled datasets containing Android code clones at bytecode level (with or without obfuscation), we ventured to create our set. We collected all available apps with multiple versions in the F-droid Android market. The resulting set had 5,045 Android app source projects for 1814 unique apps. From this set, we filtered apps containing code written in Kotlin, as our current implementation does not support Kotlin programming language, and removed apps that do not use the Gradle build tool as they cannot be compiled automatically. For the remaining projects we tried compiling them and those that did not produce any errors during build time were used in further analysis.

The total of 1751 projects from 685 unique apps were successfully compiled and comprise our non-obfuscated apps set. To generate obfuscated versions of these apps, we employed Obfuscapk [1], a free and open-source Android tool that includes a range of obfuscation techniques including some advanced approaches such as reflection and control flow obfuscation. To explore the obfuscation resiliency of our code clone detection approach, we obfuscate our compiled apps with various obfuscation techniques creating four different sets of obfuscated apps. Unfortunately, Obfuscapk failed to successfully obfuscate some of the apps with some obfuscation transformations. To ensure a proper comparison, for the further evaluation experiments, we used 1085 apps in the intersection of all these sets that all were successfully obfuscated. The summary of our created dataset is shown in Table 1.

Table 1. The summary of the employed datasets

Dataset	Num. of apps
Downloaded source code projects	5045
Successfully compiled projects	1751
Successfully simulated applications	1603
Successfully obfuscated applications:	
Control-flow obfuscations	1320
Reflection obfuscations	1741
String encryption obfuscations	1740
All obfuscations (set used for evaluation)	1085
Banking malware applications	1076

4.2   Code Clone Detection Validation

In the first experiment, we examined the effectiveness of our approach in finding different types of code clones. We manually created 4 code clones samples for 5 different code snippets at source code level and injected them into an Android app. This resulted in 20 code clones which were then compiled to Smali code. Note that some differences in source code such as variable names are not present in the Smali code, and hence once compiled become a different types of code clones. Since our code clone analysis is based on the Smali code, we further modified some of the compiled Smali code to retain the types of code clones initially created in source code. Our modifications included removing the debugging information (for type-1 clones) and changing the register numbers (for type-2 clones). For type-3 and type-4 clones, no further changes were done since the differences in the source code were enough for creating type-3 and type-4 clones at the Smali code level. Table 2 shows our detection results for the injected code clone samples. The similarity results show that our approach is successful in finding type-1 to type-3 clones and also can detect some of the type-4 clones. The difference in results when detecting type-4 clones stems from the fact that our approach leverages data dependency between instructions and analyzes only semantically significant instructions for code clone detection. However, since the relationship between different types and APIs in Android Runtime is not captured, our approach can potentially miss some type-4 code clones. For example, our approach would not consider two code snippets that use different APIs for performing a file operation to be similar.

Table 2. Detection of injected code clones

Code clone Name	Type-1	Type-2	Type-3	Type-4
appendTextToFile	100%	100%	100%	44%
isTreeFull	100%	100%	100%	100%
removeDuplicatedInIntegerArrayList	100%	100%	100%	0%
reverseNumber	100%	100%	100%	26%
removeMiddleNodeInLinkedList	100%	100%	100%	100%

Table 3. Obfuscation resistancy validation

Obfuscation set	Applied transformations	Num. apps	Num. methods	Avg. Sim.
Control-flow obf.	CallIndirection, MethodOverload, ArithmeticBranch, Reorder, Goto, Nop	989	72638	84%
Reflection obf.	Reflection, AdvancedReflection	1017	7613	81%
String encryption obf.	ConstStringEncryption	1035	13836	87%
All obfuscations	All control-flow obf., All reflection obfuscations, ConstStringEncryption	846	53564	78%

4.3 Obfuscation Resistance Validation

To evaluate the obfuscation resistance of our approach against different obfuscation techniques, we use our four obfuscated datasets. In order to perform a valid and uniform comparison we discarded any apps with methods that failed to simulate properly. We manually analyzed the errors for such failures and noticed that most of the failures are caused by the ByteBuddy framework failing to dynamically create classes in cases when classes refer to types that do not exist in the apps .dex files. This however does not prevent an app from working in Android since the ART engine load classes lazily and the methods or fields with non-existent types are not invoked during execution. However, in our current implementation, classes are created and loaded eagerly, and thus, loading classes referring to non-existent types results in an error. When performing this experiment we also noticed that some transformations such as reflection do not affect all methods. Thus we base our evaluation on a set of methods that have been affected by the corresponding obfuscations. In this analysis, we consider the original set of non-obfuscated apps as a ground truth and evaluate our approach resiliency to obfuscation by comparing an obfuscated version of each app to its non-obfuscated coun

The results of these comparisons are shown in Table 3. As the results show, string encryption has the highest similarity (87%), meaning 87% of fragments from non-obfuscated sets are found to be similar to the apps' set obfuscated with String encryption. The set with all obfuscations applied generated the largest number of methods (53,564) from 846 apps, and showed the minimum similarity (78%) which is expected due to complexity of obfuscation techniques. It should be noted though that after obfuscating apps with the control-flow and reflection transformations, our approach achieves 84% and 81% similarity with the non-obfuscated apps, respectively. In other words, our approach can detect code clones even in the presence of advanced obfuscation techniques, i.e., control-flow and reflection.

Table 4. Code clone detection among all non-obfuscated apps.

Total	Similarity range					
Code clone clusters between different versions of apps						
All clones	100%	96%—100%	92%—96%	88%—92%	84%—88%	80%—84%
29,744 (66%)	14,076 (47.32%)	1,802 (6.06%)	2,895 (9.73%)	3,504 (11.78%)	3,447 (11.59%)	4,020 (13.52%)
Code clone clusters between different apps						
All clones	100%	96%:100%	92%:96%	88%:92%	84%:88%	80%:84%
15,032 (34%)	3,562 (23.7%)	343 (2.28%)	1087 (7.23%)	2,122 (14.12%)	2,678 (17.82%)	5,240 (34.86%)

4.4   Inter-App Code Clone Detection

In this experiment, we investigate the presence of method-level code clones among all of our 1603 successfully simulated apps from our non-obfuscated set. To perform such comparison effectively, instead of performing computationally intensive pair-wise comparison, we grouped similar methods into clone clusters. We define a code clone cluster as a group of methods that were detected as identical to each other or similar (with similarity > 80%).

In this experiment, we discard very small methods, i.e., any methods that have less than four fragments. For Android apps, it is very common to include a group of libraries called support libraries in their build process to improve compatibility. After extracting code clone clusters, we also filtered the clusters that have been detected as the Android support library classes. In essence, in our analysis, we investigate the code clones appearing in user-defined code or any common library code that the developer has used. The results of our code clone analysis among all apps without Android support libraries are shown in Table 4. Out of 44,776 code clones, 29,744 code clones (66%) are associated with different versions of the same apps, while 15,032 (34%) are seen between different apps. Among 29,744 code clones, 47% are identical clones (100% similarity). This is expected as different versions of the same app typically contain a significant portion of identical code. The rest of the identified code clones show different code similarity as these are the modified code chunks. In the case of code clones found between different apps, we see that presence of identical code clones is less significant (23.7%) This also shows that code clones are a common phenomenon in Android applications and thus can be an effective way for analyzing and profiling Android applications.

To further investigate the extracted code clones, we randomly selected 15 clusters with different similarity degree and analyzed them manually. From the selected clusters, 12 clusters indeed contained correctly identified code clones, and 3 clusters contained methods that were not code clones. The code samples that were not correctly identified, shared one problem related to low code coverage for apps that use the Android support library classes.

The methods defined in support library classes perform many checks to validate the state of the device and if one of the checks fails, the method throws an exception. In the current implementation of our approach as we lack input generation and Ambiguous value is used as the reference object of each method,

Table 5. The comparison results with Nicad.

	Reported results
Agreed clones	15,865 (81%)
Disagreed clones	3,565 (19%)
Not detected as clone by Nicad	312,906
Not detected as clone by AndroClonium	455,624
Not detected as clone by AndroClonium due to code coverage	443,393 (97.3%)

at each check a random path is taken which in most cases causes an exception to be thrown and thus the user defined code rarely is executed. This problem in the execution path causes many methods to be detected as clones since all of them show a similar execution trace leading to the throw exception.

4.5 Comparative Analysis

We further compare the code clone detection capabilities of our approach with the source code Nicad. Since Nicad was not designed for obfuscated code analysis, in this experiment we use non-obfuscated dataset. For fair comparison, we use pairs of different versions of apps as they are expected to contain code clones. Nicad leverages a threshold for declaring similar code pieces as clones, hence, in this analysis we set the threshold to 70% for both approaches.

The source code of 1,555 app-version pairs were analyzed by both approaches at the method level. Next, the findings of our approach on the Smali code that originated from source code files were compared with the findings of Nicad. When comparing two approaches, any method-clone pair with the difference of similarity degree less than 15% was marked as "Agreed clones", if the difference in similarity was greater than 15% we marked it as "Disagreed clones". For any clones that were detected by one tool, but not both we marked them as "Not detected" by the corresponding tool. In essence, these two groups include code clones that either of the tools failed to analyze or their similarity degree was <70% threshold. Table 5 shows our findings after comparing our approach with Nicad.

From 19,430 code clones found by both tools, 15,865 (81%) of code clones are clones that both tools agree on (similarity ≥ 70%) and 3,565 (19%) of clones were marked as disagreed clones. However, a vast difference between the clones detected by our approach and Nicad is also clear. Our approach found 312,906 clones not detected by Nicad. On the other hand, our approach missed 455,624 clones, more than 97% of them are due to code coverage problem. Another difference in the detected clones stems from the definition of code clones. Our approach when analyzing a method, considers the behaviour of all invoked nested methods as the behaviour of method under analysis, whereas most of the existing code clone detection tools do not. This is the design choice that we had to make since method in-lining or out-lining are common obfuscation techniques.

Table 6. Detection of malware apps

Malware family	Num. of samples	Num of identical clones	Num. of similar clones	Detected samples (only identical clones)	Detected samples (only similar clones)	Missed samples
BankBot	136	224	581	90 (66.2%)	15 (11%)	31(22.8%)
Binv	2	8	5	2 (100%)	0 (0%)	0 (0%)
Citmo	3	42	10	3 (100%)	0 (0%)	0 (0%)
FakeBank	151	1216	1887	105 (69.5%)	18 (12%)	28 (18.5%)
SMSspy	131	1458	27540	130 (99.2%)	1 (0.8%)	0 (0%)
Sandroid	61	830	5620	60 (98.3%)	1 (1.7%)	0 (0%)
Spitmo	191	55	704	142 (74.3%)	44 (23%)	5 (2.7%)
Wroba	152	344	1004	106 (69.7%)	12 (7.9%)	34 (22.4%)
ZertSecurity	4	2	7	2 (50%)	1 (25%)	1 (25%)
Zitmo	142	531	837	116 (81.7%)	10 (7%)	16(11.3%)
Total	973	4710	38195	756 (77.5%)	102 (10.5%)	115 (12%)

4.6   Malware Detection Using Code Clone Fragments

We look at one of the practical applications of code clone detection. We investigate an ability of our approach to detect malware variants using code clones. In this experiment, we use a set of Android banking malware collected by [16]. The dataset consists of 973 malicious Android banking apps distributed across 10 malware families: BankBot, Binv, Citmo, FakeBank, Sandroid, SMSspy, Spitmo, Wroba, ZertSecurity and Zitmo.

Similar to our previous experiments, we extract code clones from banking binary samples and then cluster them based on their similarity. We define a code clone cluster as a group of methods that were detected as identical to each other or similar with similarity > 75%. We discard small methods with less than 3 fragments to highlight longer and more meaningful methods. Our analysis produces 47,149 code clone clusters among 973 apps. To further analyze detected code clone clusters, we first separate clusters with clones that are unique to one malware family and clones that have been seen among multiple families or benign apps. We leverage unique clones for malware detection. In our experiment, 91% of code clone clusters are unique and 9% of clusters contain code clones from apps in different malware families. To better explore the effectiveness of code clones for malware detection, we further divided the unique clones into identical clones (similarity = 100%) and similar clones (75% < similarity < 100%). For each malware sample, we then checked if it shares any unique clones with any other samples of its family and if so we marked it as *detected*. If no unique clones were found between the malware samples, we marked a sample as *missed*.

Table 6 shows our approach effectiveness in detection of malware samples. 77.5% of binary samples were correctly detected based on only identical code clones within their code. 10.5% were detected solely based on similar code clones. The total of 88% of apps were detected correctly based on the presence of code clones in their binary code.

5   Conclusion

In this paper, we introduced an approach for obfuscation-resistant fine-grained detection of code clones in obfuscated Android apps. Our approach uses program backward slicing on execution traces to extract semantically significant instructions based on data-dependency to overcome the challenges of purely static and dynamic approaches. We validated our approach, by comparing the results of our approach in presence and absence of obfuscation. We achieved 84%, 81%, 87%, 78% similarity when analyzing four obfuscated sets of Android apps. We compare the performance of our approach with Nicad in finding method-level code clone. We observe that both approaches agree on most of the code clones detected with high degree of similarity. Yet, our approach is able to find a significantly more code clones not detected by Nicad approach. e user-defined code in order to be semantic preserving.

The proposed approach is resistant to code obfuscation and is effective in finding different types of code clones at the binary level. We also have identified few limitations that our current prototype implementation has: limited code coverage and scalability. The code coverage problem mostly stems from the fact that our current implementation uses ambiguous values for all inputs and thus traverses undesired paths. While further differentiating inputs can produce higher code coverage, we leave it as future work. The scalability of our approach is another challenge as our current implementation needs to compare fragments for pairs of code for measuring code similarity. This can be also potentially improved by using heuristics based on the size of code for more efficient code clone detection. These implementation improvements would not fundamentally change the approach and would result in marginal gains.

References

1. Obfuscapk: an open-source black-box obfuscation tool for android apps. SoftwareX, **11**, 100403 (2020)
2. Akram, J., Shi, Z., Mumtaz, M., Luo, P.: DroidCC: a scalable clone detection approach for android applications to detect similarity at source code level. In: 2018 IEEE 42nd Annual Computer Software and Applications Conference (COMPSAC), vol. 1, pp. 100–105. IEEE (2018)
3. Alam, S., Riley, R., Sogukpinar, I., Carkaci, N.: Droidclone: detecting android malware variants by exposing code clones. In: 2016 Sixth International Conference on Digital Information and Communication Technology and its Applications (DICTAP), pp. 79–84. IEEE (2016)
4. Bacci, A., Bartoli, A., Martinelli, F., Medvet, E., Mercaldo, F.: Detection of obfuscation techniques in Android applications. In: Proceedings of the 13th International Conference on Availability, Reliability and Security, pp. 1–9 (2018)
5. Balachandran, V., Tan, D.J., Thing, V.L., et al.: Control flow obfuscation for android applications. Comput. Secur. **61**, 72–93 (2016)
6. Bichsel, B., Raychev, V., Tsankov, P., Vechev, M.: Statistical deobfuscation of android applications. In: Proceedings of the 2016 ACM SIGSAC Conference on Computer and Communications Security, pp. 343–355 (2016)

7. Calzavara, S., Grishchenko, I., Maffei, M.: Horndroid: practical and sound static analysis of android applications by SMT solving. In: 2016 IEEE European Symposium on Security and Privacy (EuroS&P), pp. 47–62. IEEE (2016)
8. Collberg, C., Thomborson, C., Low, D.: A Taxonomy of Obfuscating Transformations. Department of Computer Science, The University of Auckland, New Zealand, Technical report (1997)
9. Crussell, J., Gibler, C., Chen, H.: Scalable semantics-based detection of similar android applications. In: ESORICS, pp. 182–199 (2013)
10. David, Y., Yahav, E.: Tracelet-based code search in executables. Sigplan Not. **49**(6), 349–360 (2014)
11. Ding, S.H., Fung, B.C., Charland, P.: Kam1n0: MapReduce-based assembly clone search for reverse engineering. In: Proceedings of the 22nd ACM SIGKDD International Conference on Knowledge Discovery and Data Mining, pp. 461–470 (2016)
12. Egele, M., Woo, M., Chapman, P., Brumley, D.: Blanket execution: dynamic similarity testing for program binaries and components. In: 23rd USENIX Security Symposium (USENIX Security 14), San Diego, pp. 303–317. USENIX Association (2014)
13. Eschweiler, S., Yakdan, K., Gerhards-Padilla, E.: Discovre: efficient cross-architecture identification of bugs in binary code. In: NDSS, vol. 52, pp. 58–79 (2016)
14. Hu, Y., Zhang, Y., Li, J., Wang, H., Li, B., Gu, D.: Binmatch: a semantics-based hybrid approach on binary code clone analysis. In: 2018 IEEE International Conference on Software Maintenance and Evolution (ICSME), pp. 104–114. IEEE (2018)
15. Jiang, L., Misherghi, G., Su, Z., Glondu, S.: Deckard: scalable and accurate tree-based detection of code clones. In: 29th International Conference on Software Engineering ICSE 2007, pp. 96–105. IEEE (2007)
16. Kadir, A.F.A., Stakhanova, N., Ghorbani, A.A.: An empirical analysis of android banking malware. Protecting Mobile Networks and Devices: Challenges and Solutions, 209 (2016)
17. Kamiya, T., Kusumoto, S., Inoue, K.: CCfinder: a multilinguistic token-based code clone detection system for large scale source code. IEEE Trans. Softw. Eng. **28**(7), 654–670 (2002). https://doi.org/10.1109/TSE.2002.1019480
18. Komondoor, R., Horwitz, S.: Using slicing to identify duplication in source code. In: Cousot, P. (ed.) SAS 2001. LNCS, vol. 2126, pp. 40–56. Springer, Heidelberg (2001). https://doi.org/10.1007/3-540-47764-0_3
19. Roy, C.K., Cordy, J.R.: NICAD: accurate detection of near-miss intentional clones using flexible pretty-printing and code normalization. In: 2008 16th IEEE International Conference on Program Comprehension, pp. 172–181 (2008). DOI: https://doi.org/10.1109/ICPC.2008.41
20. Sajnani, H., Saini, V., Svajlenko, J., Roy, C.K., Lopes, C.V.: SourcererCC: scaling code clone detection to big-code. In: Proceedings of the 38th International Conference on Software Engineering, pp. 1157–1168 (2016)
21. Đurić, Z., Gašević, D.: A source code similarity system for plagiarism detection. Comput. J. **56**(1), 70–86 (2013)
22. de Vos, M., Pouwelse, J.: Astana: practical string deobfuscation for android applications using program slicing. arXiv preprint arXiv:2104.02612 (2021)
23. Wang, Y., Rountev, A.: Who changed you? Obfuscator identification for Android. In: 2017 IEEE/ACM 4th International Conference on Mobile Software Engineering and Systems (MOBILESoft), pp. 154–164. IEEE (2017)

24. Wei, F., Roy, S., Ou, X.: Amandroid: a precise and general inter-component data flow analysis framework for security vetting of android apps. ACM Trans. Priv. Secur. (TOPS) **21**(3), 1–32 (2018)
25. Winterhalte, R.: Byte buddy - runtime code generation for the java virtual machine. https://bytebuddy.net/
26. Yang, J., Xiong, Y., Ma, J.: A function level java code clone detection method. In: 2019 IEEE 4th Advanced Information Technology, Electronic and Automation Control Conference (IAEAC), vol. 1, pp. 2128–2134. IEEE (2019)
27. Yang, S., Cheng, L., Zeng, Y., Lang, Z., Zhu, H., Shi, Z.: Asteria: deep learning-based ast-encoding for cross-platform binary code similarity detection. In: 2021 51st Annual IEEE/IFIP International Conference on Dependable Systems and Networks (DSN) (2021)
28. Yoo, W., Ji, M., Kang, M., Yi, J.H.: String deobfuscation scheme based on dynamic code extraction for mobile malwares. IT Convergence Pract. **4**(2), 1–8 (2016)
29. Yu, D., et al.: Detecting java code clones with multi-granularities based on byte-code. In: 2017 IEEE 41st Annual Computer Software and Applications Conference (COMPSAC), vol. 1, pp. 317–326. IEEE (2017)

One Light, One App: Tackling a Common Misperception Causing Breach of User Privacy

Efi Siapiti, Ioanna Dionysiou[✉] [iD], and Harald Gjermundrød[iD]

Department of Computer Science, School of Sciences and Engineering,
University of Nicosia, Nicosia, Cyprus
{siapiti,dionysiou.i,gjermundrod.h}@unic.ac.cy

Abstract. Built-in and computer-connected web cameras can be hacked with malware that aim in activating the camera without setting on the green led indicator (in systems that support this feature). A simple countermeasure to at least preserve the user privacy, until the security incident is contained, is to cover the camera up when not in use. One could also argue that there is a sense of security when an application (e.g. zoom, WebEx, Skype) is using the web camera and the light is on. The user trusts that there is one-to-one relationship between the web-camera (and its light indicator) and an application. In this paper, we tackle this common misperception by demonstrating that the aforementioned relationship could be one-to-many, allowing many applications accessing the web camera stream simultaneously, posing a serious privacy threat that could go undetected.

Keywords: Privacy · Simultaneous access · Web camera · macOS

1 Introduction

One could argue that a user is not entirely oblivious to the fact that cybercriminals could spy on us through the web-cameras. Numerous articles, news reports, even posts on social media, communicate to the general public that there is a risk of unauthorized access to the web-camera, either built-in or externally connected, that could be gained without turning the camera light on (in systems that support this feature). This is undoubtedly troublesome as the camera light is viewed as a privacy safeguard, notifying the user that data is being collected. In order to preserve one's privacy from this threat a variety of countermeasures are deployed, ranging from simple solutions such as dark-colored tape and sticky notes to more sophisticated accessories such as sliding camera covers. Needless to say, these approaches do not address the cause of the privacy compromise (i.e. detect and/or recover from the malware deployment); they merely provide, at some level, guarantees for the user privacy.

Suppose we were to formulate the user perception of the web-camera with regards to his/her privacy (see Table 1). We claim that this perception is linked

W. Meng et al. (Eds.): SEC 2022, IFIP AICT 648, pp. 398–411, 2022.
https://doi.org/10.1007/978-3-031-06975-8_23

to the technical background of the user. A user with no technical background
is likely to only think about the concept of on and off; presumes that the web
camera is on as long as the application that is using it is active and off otherwise.
The camera is viewed as an integral part of the application and subsequently its
overall functionality. A user with no technical knowledge but informed on security threats could consider the possibility of unwanted surveillance via malware
installed on his/her machine, something that compromises his/her privacy. On
the other hand, technically-oriented users are aware of the surveillance threat
and its impact on privacy.

Table 1. User perception of his/her privacy related to a computer web camera

User profile	Perception
No technical background	No privacy concerns
No technical background, but security-informed	Privacy compromise possible via unauthorized access

This paper addresses the common misperception of a mutex-based camera
by demonstrating that the aforementioned relationship could be one-to-many.
Consider the macOS operating system and its camera access policy. Its current
configuration allows for simultaneous access of the camera resource by multiple
processes originating from different programs. For example, whilst a web browser
is accessing the camera stream, a video chat service may request and be granted
access to the same stream. Table 2 displays the findings of a simple experiment
conducted to investigate the simultaneous access policy to the camera resource
in various operating system environments. Six applications that required the
use of camera started execution in a sequential order. It was observed that
for macOS and Windows operating systems, all six applications were granted
access to the camera stream simultaneously. iOS and Android systems locked
the camera resource when used by an application that had access to it, denying
access requests to the camera resource until it was released by the application.

Table 2. Operating systems simultaneous camera access policy

Operating system	Simultaneous camera access	Documented
macOS, versions 11.0 - 12.1 (Intel CPU)	Yes	Yes
macOS, version 12.1 (M1 CPU)	Yes	Yes
Windows 10, version 20H2	Yes	Not explicitly mentioned
iOS	No	yes
Android	No	Yes

The camera led light acting as a privacy measure is only meaningful in the
case of exclusive camera access by applications, a policy enforced in the iOS
operating system. The simultaneous access to the camera stream poses a privacy

threat yielding to either accidental or deliberate breach of privacy. In the former case, one could be caught in a *hot camera*[1] situation (similar to *hot mic*) whereas in the latter the camera stream could be unauthorized accessed and stored for a later replay by a malicious agent. The privacy threat that stems from allowing simultaneous access to the camera stream is further amplified by the absence of visible notifications informing the user that a new process is granted access to the camera feed. The default access control notification pops up only the first time when an application attempts access to the camera, essentially asking the user to grant access to the camera resource. Once the access control privilege is set, any new processes spawned for running the application are assigned the access right without informing the user about it. Figure 1 shows the expanded *control center* on macOS obtained during the experiment, listing the applications currently using the microphone but omitting details for the camera resource.

Fig. 1. *Control center* in macOS BigSur

The objective of this paper is to demonstrate the breach of privacy caused by the simultaneous camera resource access. Thus, the paper contributions are twofold:

– Implementation of a proof-of-concept application that eavesdrops and stores the camera stream currently accessed by a legitimate application, causing privacy incident. To be more specific, an application is implemented using Swift v.5 that detects when the camera is currently used by a legitimate application, requests and gets granted camera access as well, and stores the camera stream in a file that could be replayed at a later stage. The application detects when the legitimate application halts its camera access and does the same as not to be detected.
– Demonstration that current notification policies are not adequate to protect the average user privacy. It will be shown that the eavesdropping application does not appear on the *control center* due to the fact that it does not use the microphone.

---

[1] The camera is on but the user is unaware of it. As an example, consider having a multi-user Zoom meeting where one participant needs to leave the meeting. Instead of leaving the meeting, the user minimizes the window and starts his/her next Webex meeting. Both applications have access to the camera feed.

The rest of the paper is organized as follows: Sect. 2 gives a brief overview of privacy issues related to the use of cameras. Section 3 discusses the design and implementation details of the eavesdropping application. Experiments are presented in Sect. 4. Section 5 concludes the paper.

2   Camera-Related Privacy Issues and Challenges

Traditionally, the privacy concerns related to the data collected by cameras focused on surveillance cameras. Private organizations use surveillance cameras for physical security, organizational, and/or operational reasons. Several live-feed cameras located inside and also outside the premises capture and store everything within their view. Needless to say, the collected data includes sensitive information like license plates of cars, identification cards of customers, patient files in hospitals, personal financial information in banks, to just name a few [10]. Clearly, there is an elevated risk for violating the privacy of individuals who did not give their consent to the collection of data involving them.

Similarly, using a mobile device to take a picture in a public place could also pose a threat to one's privacy. Not only it is common to take publicly a personal photo or a video that also contains bystanders who did not consent to be included in that picture/video, but quite often these photos/videos are posted on social media and made public [4]. With the use of a simple facial recognition software, which is easy to obtain, one could track an individual's whereabouts by performing a scan on publicly available photos.

The above privacy concerns are related to the breach of user privacy based on the actual photo/video content and could be alleviated with machine-learning based countermeasures, such as automatic obfuscation of sensitive information and bystanders [4,6,10]. In the case of sensitive information, a running list of items considered to be sensitive is maintained. Using object recognition technology, those items are identified in the live feed and obfuscated [10]. In the case of bystanders, the identification of who is the target of the picture and who is the bystander is done by either training a model with already existing images, or with mathematical evaluation of parameters like where an individual's head is turned, and how close an individual is to the camera. The people who are deemed to be bystanders by the software, have their faces obfuscated to preserve their privacy [4,6]. A complicating factor in the deployment of the above solutions is the need to have access to a large number of training data, including a plethora of images of personal information and faces.

User privacy could also be violated if one could correlate a photo/video to a specific camera using the photo response non-uniformity (PRNU) fingerprint. The privacy threat is related to how the contents were rendered rather than the contents themselves. PRNU fingerprints are caused from imperfections in the image sensors, something that is unavoidable due to the camera manufacture process. To be more specific, imperfections are created due to the different light sensitivity of each individual pixel, making the photos taken by a specific camera traceable to the specific camera they were taken from. This method of identification is also applicable to videos generated by web cameras [7]. In this case, the fingerprint is extracted by having several pictures taken by a specific camera, collecting noise parameters, and using a mathematical formula to derive the camera-specific fingerprint. As a matter of fact, this is a technique used by law enforcement to identify perpetrators for serious crimes such as child pornography and terrorist propaganda.

The privacy threats are similar to those of biometric identification. There is the risk of unauthorized disclosure of the PRNU fingerprint. If any PRNU fingerprint is leaked, even an anonymous one, it could be matched to the PRNU fingerprints of publicly available photos on social media. It is trivial to determine the fingerprint as only a couple of photos are required to get a good estimate of the camera fingerprint. As aforementioned, this is a technique used in serious crimes where a fingerprint could be matched to several potential suspects (biometric identification is not a binary operation). Unauthorized disclosure of the suspect list would undoubtedly have serious life altering implications to the innocent ones [8]. Furthermore, a malicious individual could determine one's camera fingerprint from images posted on his/her social media accounts, superimpose it into images with incriminating material, essentially framing an innocent person for these criminal activities [5].

Several approaches were suggested to overcome the privacy concerns that the PRNU fingerprint poses. One rather straightforward approach is encrypting both the fingerprint and the noise. The computation of the fingerprint is done in unencrypted form but in a trusted environment, then saved in an e-PRNU form (encrypted) that can only be accessed by authorized users having the appropriate decryption key. A significant overhead due to the encryption process and the key management [8] is added, and as a result hybrid solutions of keeping part of the data unencrypted and adding equalization (a mathematical model) to prevent leakages were also proposed [9].

Rather than focusing on the confidentiality of the PRNU fingerprint, other solutions targeted its integrity. This is a countermeasure to forging the PRNU of a photo and incriminating an innocent individual. This is the *triangle test* where the victim cross checks and identifies the images that were forged using the original images and thus proving his/her innocence [5].

3   Eavesdropping Application Design and Implementation Specifics

The privacy issues described in Sect. 2 are linked to the disclosure of one's identity without his/her consent. There are also privacy compromises that do not target an individual's identity but his/her actions. Consider the virtual meetings. The confidentiality of a virtual meeting is taken for granted as end-to-end encryption is used among the participating parties, providing guarantees that eavesdropping the communication stream is not feasible. This is partially accurate; it is indeed impractical to hijack a secure connection and in-transit flow. However, locally this is possible.

The web-camera is a shared resource to an operating system, with all its implications. Popular operating systems allow multiple access to resources to support multi-tasking and multi-user environments. The trade-off though, in the case of the web-camera, is at the expense of privacy, as it will be demonstrated. An eavesdropping application, once it is granted access to the web camera, can proceed with accessing the camera feed without any further explicit authorization. It is highly unlikely that a user with no technical background would detect that his/her current virtual meeting is eavesdropped by another application running locally.

In this section, the design and implementation details of an eavesdropping application, which monitors in real time the camera stream used by a legitimate application and replays it a later time, are given. Detailed information about the application can be found in [11].

3.1 Eavesdropping Application Overview

Figure 2 illustrates the dataflow diagram of the developed application. As shown, the external entities are the user, who initiates the functions to start, the authorization center in the macOS, and the physical camera. The data storage is the folder that stores all the captured streams. For brevity reasons, the functions included are the ones considered to be the primary building blocks of the application framework. *CameraOn()* is a function that runs in a loop and detects if the camera is on or not. *findCamId()* retrieves the camera ID assigned to the camera by the operating system. If the status of the camera resource is set to *on* the *setupStartCamera()* function is called that creates two objects: *AVCaptureSession* and *AVCaptureMovieFile*. The former is used to initiate a session with the camera and access the camera stream. The latter is used to create a file and copy the stream in that file. When the camera status is detected to be *off*, both objects are deleted and *setupStartCamera()* terminates. Last, but not least, *resetAuthorization* uses CLI to reset all camera authorizations. This

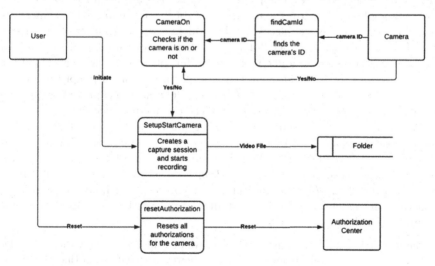

Fig. 2. Dataflow diagram of the eavesdropping application

is done in order to grant camera access rights to the eavesdropping application. More details on this are given below.

3.2   API Library Details

The application development framework is based on two media libraries: *Core-MediaIO* and *AVFoundation*.

CoreMediaIO[2] is a low-level C-based framework that publishes the Device Abstraction Layer (DAL) plug-in API. It allows access to media hardware through a kernel extension (KEXT), capture video, and capture audio with video[1]. The application utilizes *CMIOObjectPropertyAddress* to find the address of the physical camera and uses one of its parameters (the *property selector*) as input to the the *kCMIOHardwarePropertyDevices* to determine that a physical device is the target. *CMIOObjectGetPropertyDataSize* and *CMIOObjectGetPropertyData* are queries on *CMIOObjects* (e.g. camera resource) to detect data passing through it. The response for both queries is an OS status indicating success or failure.

AVFoundation is a high-level framework that manages audio and visual information, controls device cameras, processes audio and video, and is used to configure sessions with both audio files and video files. The specific subsystem of *AVFoundation* that was used is the *capture* subsystem that allows users to customize and build camera interfaces for photos and videos. Additionally, it gives users control over the camera capture to adjust the focus, exposure, and/or stabilization. Another important feature is the direct access to audio data streaming from a capture device, something that is utilized by the application to access the camera stream and store it to a file [2]. To be more specific, *AVCaptureSession* is the object that establishes the connection with the camera and manages capture activity and data flow from camera input devices or audio input devices to output such as a file or a window. The particular object has a central role in the eavesdropping application as it is the means to establish connection to the camera and proceed with unauthorized access to the camera stream. Another object used is the *AVCaptureDevice*, an object for a device that supports input, video or audio. It is used in capture sessions and offers controls for software specific features of capture. *AVCaptureDeviceInput* defines the specific input from any capture device to a capture session whereas *AVCaptureMovieFileOutput* is a captured output that specifically records video or audio in a QuickTime media video file.

An auxiliary library used by the application is the *RunLoop*[3]. A *RunLoop* object behaves as an event manager, has inputs for sources like window system, port objects and mouse or keyboard events. This object also processes timer events. Each thread has its own *RunLoop* object and thus it is not thread-safe. However, if the *RunLoop* object was not implemented, the changes in the camera would not have been detected after each loop. It is also used as a timer to implement delays after each loop.

---

[2] There is little documentation on this framework, which is possibly due to the fact that this is a low-level framework. There is however no indication that this library is deprecated.

3.3   Implementation Challenges

Two main challenges were encountered during the development of the application. The first one was detecting when the legitimate stream was turned off. The issue was experienced due to the fact that when the camera is detected to be on (i.e. used by a legitimate application), the eavesdropping application establishes connection to the camera itself. Thus, even though the legitimate application terminates, the camera status is still detected as on.

The first attempt to fix the problem was to have the eavesdropping application pausing its connection to the camera stream after a predefined time interval, checking if the camera was still on, and resuming the connection to the stream if the camera was on or stopping it if the camera was off. This approach was not successful as pausing the connection does not release the resource; it just stops the recording to the output file. Thus, the camera is still in an active status.

This observation led to the second approach that resolved the issue. When the camera is detected as on, a new session is created, a new file is created and the stream is saved in that file. After a predefined time interval, the capture session is terminated and the camera status is inquired. An *on* status will only be returned if it is still used by the legitimate application. In the case of a positive status, a new session is established and a new file is created. The files are numbered in an incremental order. Once the camera is detected as *off*, no further session is established. A few-seconds delay could be observed, i.e. the legitimate application was terminated but the capturing of the camera stream still continues until the eavesdropping application detects the *off* status of the camera. The application keeps checking periodically the camera status to start capturing the next legitimate camera stream. All the files created for a specific camera stream could be assembled together to reconstruct the original stream, with short gaps at regular intervals due to the time switching between terminating the session and reinitiating a new one.

It is worth noting that the time delay variables could be adjusted depending on the balance between the timing accuracy in starting/ending the stream capturing and the acceptable amount of loss of stream. A longer delay would mean less loss of stream but worse accuracy in starting/ending the stream, whereas shorter delay entails a very good accuracy, but more seconds lost from the stream.

The second challenge encountered was the fact that the eavesdropping application does not operate correctly on a MacBook with an M1 processor and macOS Big Sur (Version 11); the result of the queries that detect if the camera is *on* or *off* is always true. It is believed that this was due to a bug in the used framework, as the application works as expected under macOS Monterey (version 12) when using the same MacBook with the M1 processor.

4   Experimental Analysis and Findings

The experimental objectives were twofold: (a) demonstrate the workflow of an attack that compromises the victim's privacy using the developed eavesdropping application and (b) assess the performance of the eavesdropping application in

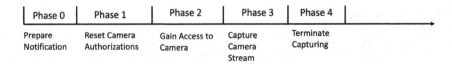

Fig. 3. Attack timeline and phases

terms of CPU, memory, and disk usage and compare it against the legitimate application's performance to deduce any discrepancies that could alert the victim to suspect the unauthorized access to the camera. The experiment configuration settings are as follows: 2015 MacBook air (1.6 GHz Dual Core Inter Core i5, with 8 GB of RAM) running macOS Big Sur (version 11.5.1).

4.1 Attack Workflow

Without any loss of generality, it is assumed that the malicious payload is already downloaded on the victim's system and the user (attacker) had established remote access to it. The attack timeline is shown in Fig. 3 and details of the attack phases are given below.

Pre-Attack Phase 0: Preparing the Notification Window. The goal of the pre-attack Phase 0 and Attack Phase 1 is to assign camera access rights to the eavesdropping application. This is accomplished by manipulating the victim into clicking the pop-up notification window asking permission to access the camera by the eavesdropping application. Thus, prior the attack, the eavesdropping application file is renamed to resemble the legitimate application and the description of the access control notification is also changed to be the exact same as the one observed for the legitimate application (see Fig. 4). The notification text is partly modifiable and can be changed to impersonate another application that is not malicious. One could even change the application name and the icon to completely impersonate a legitimate app.

Fig. 4. Modifiable notification description

Attack Phase 1: Resetting Camera Access Authorizations. Once the eavesdropping application is initiated, the first step is to reset all authorizations to the camera resource. This is a *social engineering attack* step; Resetting the authorization to the camera for **all** applications will require all applications to explicitly request camera access from the user again. The OS does indeed provide the necessary API to reset the permissions for all applications via a single function call.

Attack Phase 2: Establishing Connection to Legitimate Camera Stream. The camera detection sequence is initiated next, which checks whether or not the camera is on (i.e. used by the legitimate application). Once the victim starts a legitimate application that needs access to the camera resource,

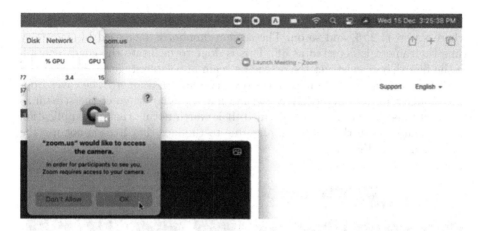

Fig. 5. Legitimate application authorization notification

the authorization notification pops-up (Fig. 5) because of the *social engineering attack* performed in Phase 1. Granting the access results in activating the camera, something that is detected by the eavesdropping application. An opportunity window is created to assign camera access rights to the eavesdropping application by displaying an almost identical authorization notification (Fig. 6). The second notification is displayed just one second after the first one. Due to the similarities, it is anticipated that the average user will click on the second notification, thus granting authorization to the camera resource.

Fig. 6. Eavesdropping application authorization notification

Attack Phases 3 and 4: Capturing Camera Stream and Terminating Connection. After the successful outcome of Attack Phase 2, the eavesdropping application captures the camera stream and copies it to multiple output files.

These output files are sequentially numbered in the format of *session x, file y.mov* where x,y = 1, 2, 3, and so on. The session number is increased by one every time the camera is detected as off. This is done to facilitate the concatenation of the files that reconstruct the original stream at a later stage.

When the legitimate application stops accessing the camera, the eavesdropping application also immediately (within few seconds) let go of the stream as well and thus the victim is not alarmed. It is worth noting that the application does not appear on the *control center* due to the fact that it does not use the microphone (see Fig. 7).

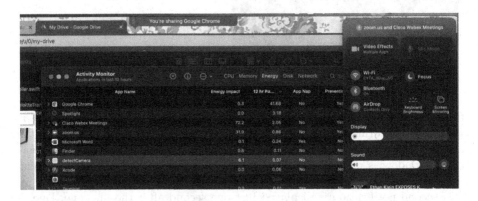

Fig. 7. Eavesdropping application not appearing on the control center

4.2   Experimental Findings

Performance Metrics. It was observed that the overall resource usage of the eavesdropping application was lower than the one of the legitimate application (Fig. 8 and Fig. 9 respectively). Thus, it could be asserted that the victim will not be alerted to the privacy compromise incident as the resource consumption is not significant.

More specifically, the values for the eavesdropping application were fluctuating due to time switching between the connection and the termination of the camera stream. The CPU usage was in the range 0% to 13%, the memory increased from 17 MB to 23.4 MB and the disk usage was in the range 0 to 396 KB/s. On the other hand, the values for the legitimate application were stable. The CPU usage was around 35%-50%, the memory at 110.7 MB and the disk at 340 KB. The average approximate values are summarized in Table 3.

Fidelity of the Captured Stream. As it was mentioned earlier, in order for the eavesdropping application to go unnoticed by the end-user, it must release access to the camera at regular intervals. This is done to check if the legitimate application has ended its usage of the camera. A short interval entails that the fidelity of the captured stream will be low, however the camera will stay on for

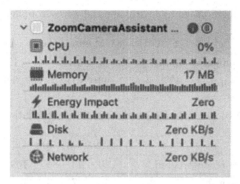

Fig. 8. Eavesdropping application resource usage

Fig. 9. Legitimate application resource usage

a very short time (high accuracy) after the legitimate application released its access to the camera. On the other hand, a long interval will increase the fidelity of the captured stream at the cost of having the camera be on for a longer time (low accuracy) after the legitimate application has ended.

Thus, there is a compromise to be considered between the required fidelity of the captured stream vs. the time interval that the camera still remains on once the legitimate application releases its access to the camera. If the time interval is long, that increases the risk that user may suspect the privacy breach. However, the *usefulness* of the captured stream depends on its fidelity (i.e. fewer gaps in the recording result in a higher-quality video). Configuring the accuracy depends on the usage scenario.

An experiment was conducted in order to benchmark the fidelity of the captured stream with varying accuracy levels. The findings could be used as guidelines for setting the minimum accuracy value that yields the desired fidelity of the captured stream. The experiment was based on having a legitimate application using the camera for 120 s. Five different runs were conducted, where in each run the eavesdropping application was using the accuracy values of 2 s, 5 s, 10 s, 20 s, and 30 s respectively. The results are summarized in Table 4. As it can be seen, very high accuracy approximately captures 12 % of the video stream while at a very relaxed accuracy of 30 s approximately 93 % of the stream is captured. Furthermore, there is a substantial delay in restarting the recording as well a high variance in the restart delay recorded for these specific experience. This delay can be attributed to the releasing of a resource (i.e. the camera) and then determining if the camera is still in use followed by a request to access the camera resource again. As each deployment scenario will have different requirements (both with respect to accuracy and fidelity) any general recommendation is difficult to recommend. However, as this is a proof-of-concept application, better approaches are possible and will be investigated as future work.

Table 3. Resource usage by legitimate and eavesdropping applications

	CPU Usage	Memory Usage	Disk Usage
Eavesdropping app	6.5%	20.5 MB	185 KB/s
Legitimate app	42%	110 MB	340 KB/s

Table 4. Accuracy and stream loss correlation

	2 s	5 s	10 s	20 s	30 s
Seconds reconstructed	13	43	84	109	112
Seconds lost	107	77	36	11	8
Video files created	30	12	9	5	4
Avg. delay to restart capture	3.7	2.8	4.5	7	2.7

5   Concluding Remarks and Future Directions

User privacy in a distributed collaborative networked environment has been given more attention the last few years. The privacy policy of the European Commission related to personal data protection (widely known as the GDPR), the support of private browsing mode as well as privacy policies in popular social networking media are initiatives that aim in cultivating a privacy culture not just at the work place but in all aspects of one's life. The unprecedented hike in the video conferencing due to the exponential growth of remote working and teaching forced users to reconsider their privacy during virtual meetings. Background blurring features using proximity and movement as classifiers of what should be blurred and disabling the video stream if it is not required are measures taken by the participants to protect their privacy.

One could claim that a user without technical background, when it comes to the web camera, mainly associates his/her privacy with the data collected by the camera resource. The user most likely is unaware of the fact that in certain systems multiple applications could access the camera stream, giving him/her a false sense of privacy. A camera is considered to be a resource to an operating system, similar to files, disks, and printers, to just name a few. Simultaneous access is permitted, especially for read-only access, allowing concurrent sharing of system resources among users or processes acting on behalf of users.

In this paper, an application that eavesdrops and stores the camera stream currently accessed by a legitimate application was presented. The experimental findings demonstrated that the eavesdropping application does not consume system resources at a rate that the user will be alerted to the privacy incident.

A thorough investigation is currently underway for other desktop operating systems like Microsoft Windows (different versions will be evaluated) and different GNU/Linux distributions. This comprehensive view could allow us to determine whether this is a platform-dependent feature or a multiplatform one. Regarding future directions, there are several enhancements that could leverage the functionality of the current application. First, there are extensions to the application that could be integrated, such as microphone audio capturing. Second, devising a more effective way of detecting when the legitimate camera application is releasing the camera, as this will greatly improve the quality of the captured stream and minimize the probability that the victim will become suspicious as the eavesdropping application will release the camera almost immediately. Third, lab experiments could be conducted with users to assess the user awareness/realization of the privacy incident while varying the accuracy levels.

References

1. Apple: Mac technology overview (2015). https://developer.apple.com/library/archive/documentation/MacOSX/Conceptual/OSX_Technology_Overview/SystemTechnology/SystemTechnology.html. Accessed 20 Jan 2022
2. Apple: Documentation of AVFoundation (2022). https://developer.apple.com/documentation/avfoundation. Accessed 20 Jan 2022
3. Apple: Documentation of runloop (2022). https://developer.apple.com/documentation/foundation/runloop/ Accessed 20 Jan 2022
4. Darling, D., Li, A., Li, Q.: Identification of subjects and bystanders in photos with feature-based machine learning. In: IEEE INFOCOM 2019 - IEEE Conference on Computer Communications Workshops (INFOCOM WKSHPS), pp. 1–6 (2019)
5. Goljan, M., Fridrich, J., Chen, M.: Defending against fingerprint-copy attack in sensor-based camera identification. IEEE Trans. Inf. Forensics Secur. 6(1), 227–236 (2011). https://doi.org/10.1109/TIFS.2010.2099220
6. Li, A.: Privacy-preserving photo taking and accessing for mobile phones. Ph.D. thesis, University of Arkansas (2018). https://doi.org/10.13140/RG.2.2.28953.88166
7. Martin-Rodriguez, F.: PRNU based source camera identification for webcam videos (2021)
8. Mohanty, M., Zhang, M., Asghar, M., Russello, G.: e-PRNU: encrypted domain PRNU-based camera attribution for preserving privacy. IEEE Trans. Dependable Secure Comput. 18(01), 426–437 (2021). https://doi.org/10.1109/TDSC.2019.2892448
9. Pérez-González, F., Fernández-Menduiña, S.: PRNU-leaks: facts and remedies. In: 2020 28th European Signal Processing Conference (EUSIPCO), pp. 720–724 (2021). https://doi.org/10.23919/Eusipco47968.2020.9287451
10. Ramajayam, G., Sun, T., Tan, C.C., Luo, L., Ling, H.: Deep learning approach protecting privacy in camera-based critical applications. CoRR abs/2110.01676 (2021). https://arxiv.org/abs/2110.01676
11. Siapiti, E.: Camera privacy analysis. Technical report, University of Nicosia (2022). BSc Final Year Project

Double-X: Towards Double-Cross-Based Unlock Mechanism on Smartphones

Wenjuan Li[1(✉)], Jiao Tan[2], and Nan Zhu[2]

[1] Department of Electronic and Information Engineering, The Hong Kong
Polytechnic University, Hong Kong, China
wenjuan.li@polyu.edu.hk
[2] KOTO Research Center, Macao, China

Abstract. Thanks to the convenience and the increasing functionalities, mobile devices especially smartphones are becoming an essential electronic device in people's daily lives. Users can take the smartphone for online shopping and payment, as well as chatting with friends. However, with more private and sensitive information stored on such devices, how to secure the phone data becomes an open challenge. To protect a smartphone from unauthorized access, a direct and intuitive approach is to deploy an unlock mechanism, which requires users to input a correct pattern and unlock the phone. In the literature, combining behavioral biometrics can further enhance the security of unlock mechanisms, e.g., Android unlock patterns. In this work, we develop Double-X, a double-cross-based unlock scheme that requires users to unlock the phone by inputting two cross shapes on the selected dots. To authenticate the user, Double-X has to check the selected dots and the behavioral features when drawing the cross shapes. To examine the scheme performance, we perform two user studies with 80 participants with several typical supervised algorithms. The results indicate that participants can achieve a good success rate (e.g., 95%) under our scheme compared with two similar schemes.

Keywords: User authentication · Double cross · Behavioral authentication · Unlock mechanism · Touch dynamics

1 Introduction

Smartphone is a portable device that integrates various functions such as mobile telephone and computing resources into one unit. A recent survey from IDC [1] indicated that phone vendors shipped a total of 362.4 million smartphones during the last quarter (4Q21) in 2021, resulting in a 5.7% increase in shipments (i.e., with a number of 1.35 billion smartphones shipped). According to Statista [2], the number of smartphone users around the world in 2021 is 6.648 billion, and this means 83.89% of the world's population owns a smartphone.

Currently, smartphones have become much popular and competent with many fancy features. For example, a smartphone allows users to access webpages and browse the web, operate on documents, play music and games, take

W. Meng et al. (Eds.): SEC 2022, IFIP AICT 648, pp. 412–428, 2022.
https://doi.org/10.1007/978-3-031-06975-8_24

photos and record videos. In this case, smartphones may collect and store a large number of personal and private data/information, while how to safeguard the stored data is a big challenge. Hence user authentication is a necessary security mechanism to enforce access control against unauthorized users.

For user authentication, password-based authentication (e.g., textual passwords, unlock patterns) is still the most widely adopted method, while it suffers from known security and usability limitations. In the aspect of usability, common users are hard to remember complicated and multiple passwords for a long time for the sake of the long-term memory limitation and multiple password interference [29,30]. In this case, most users would like to select an easy-to-remember password, which is often a weak password in practice [5,46]. On the other hand regarding security, password-based authentication could be easily captured and recorded by attackers, i.e., recording attack [34] and charging attack [27,28], where cyber attackers can monitor and record users' input on the phone screen and then exfiltrate required data and information.

In addition to textual passwords, graphical password (GP) is another alternative that requires users to unlock their smartphones by inputting a correct pattern. Currently, Android unlock patterns are the most popular GP, which allows users to create a pattern within a grid of 3×3 [25,26]. Previous research has proved that people can usually remember images better than textual information [35], which motivates the development of GP. However, GP may encounter similar security limitations the same as traditional textual passwords, such as recording attacks and charging attacks. Moreover, with only 9 dots on the grid of 3×3, brute force attack is still feasible as Android unlock patterns can only have 389,112 possible patterns. Also, cyber attackers can further decrease the password space by conducting a smudge attack to recover the touch trails remained on the touch screen [3]. In the aspect of usability, GP may also increase the memory burden according to specific design methods, i.e., *PassPoints* [45] allows users to create credentials by selecting some locations on an image, whereas it may cause a high error rate for some users.

To enhance the security of GP like Android unlock patterns, there are two general directions in the literature. One is to increase the pattern complexity, for example, Forman and Aviv [10] introduced a method to increase the security of Android unlock patterns, called Double Patterns, allowing users to choose two sequential, superimposed patterns as their unlock pattern. Another direction is to combine unlock patterns with behavioral biometrics, for example, De Luca et al. [6] introduced a method by combining Android unlock patterns with behavioral features (e.g., touch coordinates) by means of dynamic time warping (DTW). In this way, the authentication process needs to verify not only the input patterns, but also how users input the pattern. Similarly, Li et al. [17,18] introduced SwipeVlock, an unlock mechanism that verifies users based on the unlock patterns and their swipe actions.

Motivated by this developing trend, in this work, we advocate the merit of designing a phone unlock mechanism by combining behavioral biometrics. We particularly develop a double-cross-based unlock mechanism (called *Double-X*) to enhance Android unlock patterns, whereby a user can draw two cross shapes by selecting two dots on a 3 × 3 grid. For authentication, Double-X has to verify the selected dots and how users input the cross shapes, namely the touch behavioral features. The contributions can be summarized as below.

– We develop Double-X, a double-cross-based unlock scheme on smartphones, which can verify users based on their selected dots and the touch behavioral features. For registration, users have to select two dots on the 3 × 3 grid and input two cross shapes on the pre-selected dots. A successful authentication trial requires both correct inputs. The scheme design is considered as transparent and easy-to-use.
– For our current scheme, we allow users to select the same dot and input two cross shapes. To model a user's touch behavior, we actually need to verify users' touch movement. In this work, we extract a set of behavioral features such as touch movement speed & direction, touch pressure, time difference, and acceleration.
– In the evaluation, we involve a total of 80 common phone users to explore the classifier selection and the performance of Double-X. Based on the collected data and users' feedback, our results indicate the viability and usability of our scheme as compared with two similar unlock schemes.

The rest of this work is structured as follows. Section 2 introduces related work on unlock mechanisms and behavioral authentication. Section 3 introduces our developed Double-X in detail, and Sect. 4 presents two approved user studies with 80 participants as compared with two similar unlock schemes. We conclude our work in Sect. 5.

2   Related Work

2.1   Phone Unlock Mechanism

To design an unlock scheme is a basic and important security solution to defeat unauthorized access to mobile platforms, especially smartphones. For example, Android unlock patters are a typical and popular unlock mechanism on Android phones, which requires users to unlock the screen by drawing a correct pattern [6, 26]. In the literature, Android unlock patterns were indeed extended from an authentication scheme called *Pass-Go* [41], whereby a user needs to authenticate by generating a pattern on an image.

Due to the easy-to-use characteristic, various phone unlock schemes have been proposed in the literature. For instance, a Face Unlock system was proposed by Findling and Mayrhofer [8], which could verify both frontal and profile face information during a pan shot around the user's head. This scheme relied on a camera and movement sensor to capture the features and could provide a success rate at roughly 90.5%. DeLucaUnLock scheme [6] combined the original Android unlock patterns with touch dynamics, by considering behavioral features and performing a match through dynamic time warping (DTW). Guo *et al.* [12]

introduced an unlock mechanism called OpenSesame, which could authenticate a user in terms of shaking behavior. Their study found support vector machine (SVM) was a fit to their scheme. In the evaluation, OpenSesame could provide a false negative rate of 11% (with a deviation of 2%) and a false positive rate of 15% (with a deviation of 2.5%). With the development of phone sensors, accelerometer and pressure features can be considered. Izuta et al. [13] developed an unlock scheme by verifying the behavioral features when a user takes a phone from the pocket and the pressure distribution when the user grips the phone. In the study, this scheme could provide a false acceptance rate of 0.43 with only 18 training instances. Meng et al. [26] designed a touch movement-based solution to enhance the security of Android unlock patterns, which requires users to draw the correct pattern and behave soundly.

Then Yi et al. [47] designed an unlock scheme called WearLock, which relies on the signal detection through preamble identification, time synchronization using preamble and cyclic prefix, channel estimation, etc. In the study with 5 users, their scheme provided a success rate of around 90%. Wang et al. [43] presented an unlock scheme based on the heartbeat vibration that can be captured by built-in accelerometer. Users could unlock the phone by pressing the device on their chest for seconds, as the scheme can collect heartbeat signals and verify the user with several heartbeats. They involved 35 participants in the study, and gathered more than 110,000 heartbeat samples. When using 5 heartbeat cycles, their scheme could achieve an Equal Error Rate (EER) of 3.51%. Then a swipe-based unlock scheme was proposed by Li et al. [17,18] called SwipeVLock, whereby a user can be authenticated by selecting a location on an image and performing a swiping action. A success rate of 98% could be achieved in the best scenario. Forman and Aviv [10] introduced a method to increase the security of Android unlock patterns, called Double Patterns, allowing users to choose two sequential, superimposed patterns as their unlock pattern.

Intuitively, phone unlock schemes are a kind of pure graphical password [39], or a hybrid GP scheme (e.g., map-based GP [31,36]). Many research studies are attempting to enhance the security of unlock schemes by considering a background image, for instance, *RouteMap* [24] needs a user to select a region on a world map and create a route based on their prior experience. Similarly, *PassMap* [40] requires a user to choose two location points on a world map, and *GeoPass* [42] then reduces the location number to only one.

2.2 Touch Behavioral Authentication

With the touchscreen being popular, user authentication based on touch dynamics becomes an important topic. To investigate the feasibility, Fen et al. [7] designed an authentication scheme by verifying the finger gesture. With a random forest algorithm, their scheme could achieve a false acceptance rate of 4.66% and a false rejection rate of 0.13%. Meanwhile, Meng et al. [21] focused on the same challenge, and developed a touch dynamics-based authentication scheme with 21 features. With a hybrid classifier of PSO-RBFN, their scheme could reach an average error rate of 3%. Frank et al. [9] then introduced a similar behavioral authentication scheme with 30 features, which could reach a median equal error rate of around 4%.

With the increasing capability of touchscreen, multi-touch actions receive more attention. Meng *et al.* [22] developed a scheme called CD-GPS, which combined multi-touch actions in graphical password creation. It is found that multi-touch behavior could benefit the authentication process and increase the cracking difficulty. Zheng *et al.* [48] then combined tapping actions with passcode input. In the study, they considered the one-class classifier and achieved an averaged equal error rate of nearly 3.65%. Sharma and Enbody [38] studied users' touch behavior when playing with applications. With an ensemble classifier based on SVM, their scheme could provide a mean equal error rate of 7%. Li *et al.* [19] developed a type of simple shape-based behavioral authentication, where a user needs to draw different shapes during the verification. Five common shapes were considered: circle, square, rectangle, triangle and diamond. In the evaluation, they explored the performance between one-shape, two-shape and three-shape schemes, and found that two-shape scheme could be adopted by majority of participants. Shahzad *et al.* [37] presented an authentication scheme by studying how a user inputs a gesture in terms of velocity, device acceleration, and stroke time. They found that these features could be used for verifying a user. How to protect a password input is also an interesting question. Li et al. [15,16] focused on this question and presented three practical anti-eavesdropping password entry schemes on stand-alone smart glasses, named gTapper, gRotator and gTalker. Some more behavioral authentication schemes can be referred to [20,32,33] and several surveys [11,23].

3   Our Proposed Scheme

In the literature, many research studies are working on the security enhancement of phone unlock schemes, especially Android unlock patterns, by integrating with touch behavioral authentication. Motivated by this trend, in this work, we focus on improving the security of Android unlock patterns and introduce a double-cross-based unlock scheme (called Double-X), which allows phone users to input two cross shapes on two dots within the 3×3 grid. Figure 1 describes the scheme design with two steps: 1) selecting the first dot and drawing the cross shape, and 2) selecting the second dot and inputting the second cross shape.

- **Double-X registration.** As shown in Fig. 1, in order to register a credential, users have to follow the two steps to select two dots and draw two cross shapes. It is worth noting that our current scheme allows users to select the same dot and draw two cross shapes. The motivation behind is that our scheme can enhance the security by verifying the touch behavioral features. It is believed that users can draw the cross shapes in different ways, even on the same dot location.
- **Double-X authentication.** To unlock the phone, users need to select the same dots and draw the cross shapes in the same way when they create the

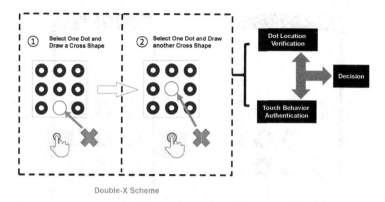

Double-X Scheme

Fig. 1. Double-X unlock scheme: (1) Step 1: select one dot from the grid and draw a cross shape; and (2) Step 2: choose another dot from the grid and draw another cross shape.

credential. A successful trial requires to verify both the dot location and how users draw the cross shapes, e.g., behavioral features. An algorithm then can be used to judge whether the current input is authenticated.

Scheme Implementation. Figure 2 depicts an implementation of our designed Double-X scheme. In the first step, users will be guided to select one dot from the grid and draw the first cross shape. Then in the second step, users will be asked to choose the second dot and draw another cross shape. For usability, we set the error tolerance to a 21×21 pixel box around the dot location, where the tolerance value is selected based on the previous work [17,31]. As shown in Fig. 3(b), there are many ways to draw a cross shape, i.e., from top to bottom or versus, and the cross angles can be distinct among users. All these behavioral differences can be utilized to differentiate phone users.

To determine whether the current user is legitimate, our scheme has to verify the dot selection and the touch behavior when drawing the two cross shapes. For dot location, we can compare the current dot with the stored location by considering the error tolerance. To verify touch behavior, our current scheme uses machine learning techniques to help model the touch dynamics and make a decision. Several typical machine learning algorithms are considered in our scheme, such as support vector machine (SVM), decision tree, K-Nearest Neighbors (KNN) and neural networks.

Feature Selection for Double-X. Touch behavioral verification is the key for our unlock scheme. To draw a cross shape, users have to perform touch movement on their phone touchscreen. In this case, our current scheme considers some typical and popular behavioral features regarding touch movement. As shown in Fig. 3(a), we separate a 2D plane into four directions: up, down, left and right. Then we can use an angle value of d to describe the direction of a touch movement.

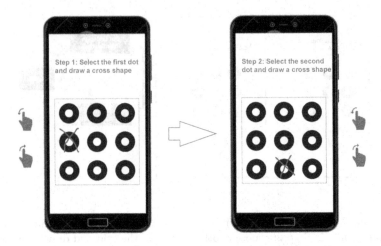

Fig. 2. An implementation of our designed Double-X scheme in the user study.

Similar to the former study [26], we mainly consider two features to represent a touch movement: touch movement speed (TMS) and touch movement angle (TMA). If a touch movement starts at coordinate (x1, y1) and ends at coordinate (x2, y2), suppose the event system time is $S1$ and $S2$, then we can use the following equations to calculate the speed ($TMS1 - TMS4$) and the angle ($TMA1 - TMA4$) of four touch-movement inputs.

$$TMS = \frac{\sqrt{(x2 - x1)^2 + (y2 - y1)^2}}{S2 - S1} \tag{1}$$

$$TMA \ (d) = \arctan \frac{y2 - y1}{x2 - x1}, \theta \in [0, 360^\circ] \tag{2}$$

Moreover, our scheme also considers some more features such as the time difference between two touch movement actions when drawing a cross shape, touch pressure, and touch acceleration. The coordinates of touches would be examined by location matching process.

– *Time difference between two touch movement actions within a cross shape.* Our scheme records the time difference between the first touch movement and the second touch movement. Intuitively, the time difference should be varied among users.
– *Touch pressure.* Most smartphones are able to record touch pressure values, which can be utilized to model a user's touch behavior.
– *Touch acceleration.* Similar to the previous work [48], our work also considers touch acceleration with three vectors, such as the magnitude of acceleration when the touch is pressed down; the magnitude of acceleration when the touch is released; and the average value of magnitude of acceleration during touch-press to touch-release.

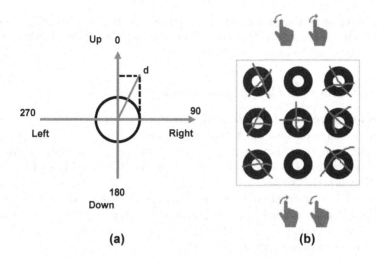

Fig. 3. (a) The directions on a 2D plane, and (b) several examples of drawing different cross shapes on a dot.

4   User Study

In this section, in order to investigate the performance of Double-X, we conduct two IRB-approved user studies with a total of 80 common phone users, including 80% Android phone users and 20% iPhone & Android phone users (currently using both types of phones). Android phone (Samsung Galaxy Note) was used in our study. In the first study, we randomly selected 20 students to evaluate the classifier performance under Double-X, and the second user study aims to evaluate our scheme performance compared with similar unlock schemes.

Table 1 summarizes the information of occupation and age for all participants. In particular, we have 43 males and 37 females who aged from 19 to 55, including bachelor/master students, business people, university staff and faculty members. Each participant can get a $50 gift voucher after the user study.

Table 1. Participants' information in the user study.

Information	Male	Female	Occupation	Male	Female
Age <25	30	25	Bachelor & master students	36	29
Age 25–35	10	8	University faculty & staff	5	5
Age 35–50	3	4	Business people	2	3

For the performance comparison, we select two similar schemes: *DeLucaUn-Lock scheme* [6] and *Double Patterns* [10]. The selection is due to their popularity and reported performance. As introduced earlier, DeLucaUnLock scheme combines the original Android unlock patterns with touch dynamics, by considering behavioral features and performing a match via dynamic time warping (DTW). Double Patterns scheme [10] allows a user to choose two patterns entered one-after-the-other on the same 3×3 grid.

4.1   First Study on Classifier Performance

Supervised Machine Learning. Similar to previous research [17,19], in this study, we mainly consider five typical supervised learning algorithms that have been realized on smartphones, such as Decision tree (J48), Naive Bayes, support vector machine (SVM), K-nearest neighbours (IBK) and Back Propagation Neural Network (BPNN).

To avoid implementation bias, all the algorithms were extracted from the WEKA platform [44], which is an open-source machine learning platform written in Java. For performance evaluation, we selected the default settings for all classifiers and adopted two common metrics as follows.

- False Acceptance Rate (FAR) indicates the rate of how many intruders are classified as legitimate users.
- False Rejection Rate (FRR) indicates the rate of how many legitimate users are classified as intruders.

Classifier Evaluation. To explore the classifier performance for our designed Double-X, we first randomly selected 20 students to create their credentials and then authenticate themselves with 400 trials (20 trials per student). Similar to several research studies, e.g., [17], we used 60% of trials as training data and the rest as testing data. Table 2 indicates the performance of different classifiers with a 10-fold cross-validation mode.

It is found that SVM could outperform other classifiers, i.e., it could achieve an average error rate (AER) of 4.35%, as compared with J48 8.35%, NBayes 12.65%, IBK 8.3%, and BPNN 8.05%. Therefore, our unlock scheme of Double-X would use SVM for user authentication in the second study.

Table 2. The authentication performance of different classifiers.

Metric	J48	NBayes	SVM	IBK (k = 3)	BPNN
FAR (%)	7.8	12.1	4.1	8.4	8.2
FRR (%)	8.9	13.2	4.6	8.2	7.9
AER (%)	8.35	12.65	4.35	8.30	8.05

4.2   The Second Study on Scheme Performance

Study Steps. Excluding 20 students in the first study, we randomly separated the remaining participants into two groups (30 participants per group): Group-1 focuses on DeLucaUnLock scheme and our scheme of Double-X, while Group-2

Table 3. Success rate in the confirmation, login and retention phase for Group-1.

Phase	DeLucaUnLock scheme	Double-X scheme
Confirmation	282/300 (94.0%)	283/300 (94.3%)
Login	288/300 (96.0%)	286/300 (95.3%)
Retention	277/300 (92.3%)	281/300 (93.7%)

focuses on Double Patterns and our scheme of Double-X. For each group, the starting sequence would be random, which means participants may start from either DeLucaUnLock scheme, Double Patterns or Double-X.

Before the study, we provided an explanation about our objectives and what kind of data would be collected and stored. We also prepared a set of guidelines for all participants to follow and a consent form would be collected as well. In addition, each participant would have three trials to get familiar with the scheme and address any confusion. All participants then would perform the study in our lab environment. The detailed study steps are shown as below.

- Step 1. Creation phase: participants need to register their credentials according to the respective scheme (e.g., DeLucaUnLock, Double Patterns and Double-X).
- Step 2. Confirmation phase: participants have to confirm the credentials by verifying dot location and touch behavior for 10 times. Participants can change their credentials if they fail or want to create a new one.
- Step 3. Distributed memory: participants are given one paper-based finding task to distract them for 15 min.
- Step 4. Login phase: participants should unlock the phone with their credentials for 10 trials.
- Step 5. Feedback form: participants are provided with a set of questions (*feedback from*) regarding the scheme usage.
- Step 6. Retention. After three days, participants are invited to unlock the phone for 10 times in our lab.
- Step 7. Participants are provided with another *feedback from* regarding the scheme usage.

Study Results. During the study, we could collect 300 trials in the confirmation, the login and the retention phase. It is the same that we used 60% of trials as training data and the rest as testing data. We adopted Chi-square tests to judge whether the results are statistically significant between two conditions. Table 3 and Table 4 describe the success rate for confirmation, login and retention phase under two groups, respectively.

- *Confirmation phase.* For Group-1, participants could reach a success rate of 94% vs. 94.3% under DeLucaUnLock Scheme and Double-X, respectively. The errors for both schemes were mainly caused during the verification of behavioral features: 1) a touch movement action is faster or slower than the pre-built normal profile, and 2) for Double-X, the touch direction was not

Table 4. Success rate in the confirmation, login and retention phase for Group-2.

Phase	Double patterns	Double-X scheme
Confirmation	277/300 (92.3%)	281/300 (93.7%)
Login	289/300 (96.3%)	287/300 (95.6%)
Retention	271/300 (90.3%)	283/300 (94.3%)

Table 5. Time consumption in the login for different groups.

Unlock scheme	DeLucaUnLock	Double-X	Double patterns
Time consumption (s)	3.8	4.2	5.1
Standard deviation (s)	1.5	2.1	3.4

matched. For Group-2, participants could achieve a success rate of 92.3% and 93.7% for Double Patterns and Double-X, respectively. The errors made under Double-X were similar to Group-1, while the errors made under Double Patterns were mainly caused by inputting a wrong pattern, especially for the second pattern. Overall, there is no statistically significant difference regarding the success rate for two groups.

- *Login phase.* In this phase, for Group-1, participants could perform well with a success rate of 96% and 95.3% under DeLucaUnLock Scheme and Double-X. While participants in Group-2 could provide a success rate of 96.3% and 95.6% for Double Patterns and Double-X. The errors made were similar to the confirmation phase. There is no statistically significant difference regarding the success rate for two groups.

- *Retention phase.* After Step 5, we invited all participants to come back to our lab in three days, and only 5 of them were failed. For retention phase, participants could achieve a success rate of 92.3% and 93.7% under DeLucaUnLock Scheme and Double-X for Group-1, and 90.3% and 94.3% under Double Patterns and Double-X for Group-2. The authentication rate is positive as there is only a small decrease as compared with the rates in the login phase. It is interesting to identify that Double-X can provide a much better success rate than Double Patterns, and there is a statistically significant difference.

The above success rates indicate that all these unlock schemes are usable. To further explore the scheme usage, Table 5 shows the time consumption for each scheme. It is seen that DeLucaUnLock scheme required less time than the other schemes. This result is very easy to understand because it is a one-step scheme. For two-step scheme between Double Patterns and Double-X, it is found that participants only need around 4.2 s for Double-X, but required 5.1 s for Double Patterns. This is because participants have to recall the patterns they created under Double Patterns, whereas it is much easily to remember a cross shape. It is the same to the standard deviation, whereby Double-X could have a smaller deviation than Double Patterns.

Table 6. Major questions and average scores from the participants.

Questions (Group-1)	Average scores
1. I could easily create a password under DeLucaUnLock scheme	9.1
2. I could easily create a password under Double-X scheme	9.2
3. The time consumption for DeLucaUnLock scheme is acceptable	9.2
4. The time consumption for Double-X scheme is acceptable	9.1
5. I could easily login to DeLucaUnLock scheme	8.8
6. I could easily login to Double-X scheme	8.7
7. I could remember DeLucaUnLock credentials easily	8.6
8. I could remember Double-X credentials easily	8.8
9. I think DeLucaUnLock scheme is more secure than Double-X scheme	3.8
Questions (Group-2)	Average scores
1. I could easily create a password under Double Patterns scheme	8.6
2. I could easily create a password under Double-X scheme	9.0
3. The time consumption for Double Patterns scheme is acceptable	8.3
4. The time consumption for Double-X scheme is acceptable	8.9
5. I could easily login to Double Patterns scheme	8.8
6. I could easily login to Double-X scheme	9.0
7. I could remember Double Patterns credentials easily	8.2
8. I could remember Double-X credentials easily	9.0
9. I think Double Patterns scheme is more secure than Double-X scheme	4.3

User Feedback. In the user study, two feedback forms were provided to each participant regarding the scheme usage, in the aspects of both security and usability. Ten-point Likert scales were used for each question, where 1-score indicates strong disagreement and 10-score indicates strong agreement. The major questions and scores are shown in Table 6.

- *Group-1.* For the credential creation, most participants believed that both DeLucaUnLock and Double-X are easy to use, with an average score of 9.1 vs. 9.2, respectively. For the time consumption, both schemes were satisfied with most participants. For login process, most participants advocated the easy usage for both schemes with 8.8 and 8.7 each. For memory capability, Double-X received a higher score of 8.8 compared with 8.6 for DeLucaUnLock scheme. For the security aspect, most participants believed that our scheme of Double-X is more secure, as it is a two-step unlock scheme, which should be able to increase the cracking difficulty.
- *Group-2.* Regarding the credential creation, Double-X received a higher score of 9.0 than the score of 8.6 from Double Patterns. This is because participants have to remember two patterns under Double Patterns, but the memory load is much lower under Double-X. This is the main reason why most participants considered it is easier to remember Double-X credentials, i.e., Double-X: 9.0 vs. Double Patterns: 8.2. For the time consumption, Double-X also received a

higher score of 8.9 versus 8.3 for Double Patterns, where the result is in-line with Table 5. For login process, both schemes were considered to be usable with a score of 8.8 and 9.0 for Double Patterns and Double-X. For the security aspect, most participants considered Double-X is more secure due to the involvement of behavior verification.

According to the collected feedback, most participants in Group-1 believed that DeLucaUnLock and Double-X scheme can have similar usability, but Double-X is more secure by selecting two dots and drawing two cross shapes. In Group-2, most participants considered Double-X is more usable and secure than Double Patterns. The main reason is that Double Patterns scheme requires users to remember two patterns while Double-X can ease the memory burden and integrate touch behavioral features. Overall, our results indicate the viability and positive performance of Double-X.

4.3   Limitation and Discussion

In the evaluation, we performed two user studies to explore the classifier selection and the scheme performance. The results are positive, indicating the viability and usability of Double-X. As the scheme is still developing at an early stage, below are some challenges and limitations that could be investigated in future.

- *The number of participants.* In this study, we involved 20 participants for evaluating the classifier performance, and 60 participants for exploring the scheme performance. To verify the results, we plan to recruit more participants with diverse background.
- *Classifier selection.* In this work, we mainly consider some typical supervised algorithms, which can be deployed in a smart device. Intuitively, there are many other algorithms, and our future work plans to consider more advanced learning algorithms like deep learning.
- *Security and attacks.* Based on the feedback, most participants believed that Double-X is more secure than DeLucaUnLock scheme and Double Patterns, but we did not evaluate the scheme under adversarial scenarios and attacks. In our next work, we plan to focus on the security aspect and explore the scheme performance under some typical attacks, e.g., mimic attack.
- *Dot selection.* In our current scheme, we allow users to select the same dot for inputting the cross shapes. It is an interesting topic to explore the scheme performance if we only allow users to select different dots. In addition, it is also an interesting and important topic to study whether there is a dot-selection bias.

5   Conclusion

Phone unlock mechanisms are a basic and important security solution to protect smartphones from unauthorized access and authenticate legitimate users.

Android unlock patterns are a typical and popular unlock mechanism on Android phones, allowing users to draw a pattern on the 3×3 grid. However, such unlock mechanism is still vulnerable to various attacks. In this work, we advocate the integration of touch behavioral features, and design Double-X, a double-cross-based unlock mechanism that requires users to draw two cross shapes by selecting two dots. For evaluation, we performed two user studies: the first one explored the classifier performance and selected SVM to be deployed in Double-X; and the second one investigated the scheme performance of Double-X, compared with two similar unlock schemes of DeLucaUnLock and Double Patterns. It is found that participants under Double-X could provide a success rate of around 95% in login and retention phase. In addition, most participants believed that Double-X is more secure than the other two schemes.

Acknowledgments. We would like to thank all the participants for their hard work in the user study.

References

1. Smartphone Shipments Declined in the Fourth Quarter But 2021 Was Still a Growth Year with a 5.7% Increase in Shipments. https://www.idc.com/getdoc.jsp?containerId=prUS48830822
2. February 2022 Mobile User Statistics. https://www.bankmycell.com/blog/how-many-phones-are-in-the-world
3. Aviv, A.J., Gibson, K., Mossop, E., Blaze, M., Smith, J. M.: Smudge attacks on smartphone touch screens. In: Proceedings of the 4th USENIX Conference on Offensive Technologies, pp. 1–7, USENIX Association (2010)
4. Al-Sudani, A.R., Gao, S., Wen, S., Al-Khiza'ay, M.: Checking an authentication of person depends on RFID with thermal image. In: Wang, G., Chen, J., Yang, L.T. (eds.) SpaCCS 2018. LNCS, vol. 11342, pp. 371–380. Springer, Cham (2018). https://doi.org/10.1007/978-3-030-05345-1_32
5. Bonneau, J.: The science of guessing: analyzing an anonymized corpus of 70 million passwords. In: Proceedings of the 2012 IEEE Symposium on Security and Privacy, pp. 538–552 (2012)
6. De Luca, A., Hang, A., Brudy, F., Lindner, C., Hussmann, H.: Touch me once and i know it's you!: implicit authentication based on touch screen patterns. In: Proceedings of CHI (ACM), pp. 987–996 (2012)
7. Feng, T., et al.: Continuous mobile authentication using touchscreen gestures. In: Proceedings of the 2012 IEEE Conference on Technologies for Homeland Security (HST), pp. 451–456. IEEE (2012)
8. Findling, R.D., Mayrhofer, R.: Towards face unlock: on the difficulty of reliably detecting faces on mobile phones. MoMM, pp. 275–280 (2012)
9. Frank, M., Biedert, R., Ma, E., Martinovic, I., Song, D.: Touchalytics: on the applicability of touchscreen input as a behavioral biometric for continuous authentication. IEEE Trans. Inf. Forensics Secur. **8**(1), 136–148 (2013)
10. Forman, T., Aviv, A.: Double patterns: a usable solution to increase the security of android unlock patterns. ACSAC, pp. 219–233 (2020)

11. Gomez-Barrero, M., Galbally, J.: Reversing the irreversible: a survey on inverse biometrics. Comput. Secur. **90**, 101700 (2020)

12. Guo, Y., Yang, L., Ding, X., Han, J., Liu, Y.: OpenSesame: unlocking smart phone through handshaking biometrics. INFOCOM, pp. 365–369 (2013)

13. Izuta, R., Murao, K., Terada, T., Iso, T., Inamura, H., Tsukamoto, M.: Screen unlocking method using behavioral characteristics when taking mobile phone from pocket. MoMM, pp. 110–114 (2016)

14. Larrucea, X., Moffie, M., Asaf, S., Santamaria, I.: Towards a GDPR compliant way to secure European cross border healthcare industry 4.0. Comput. Stand. Interfaces **69**, 103408 (2020)

15. Li, Y., et al.: A closer look tells more: a facial distortion based liveness detection for face authentication. AsiaCCS, pp. 241–246 (2019)

16. Li, Y., Cheng, Y., Meng, W., Li, Y., Deng, R.H.: Designing leakage-resilient password entry on head-mounted smart wearable glass devices. IEEE Trans. Inf. Forensics Secur. **16**, 307–321 (2021)

17. Li, W., Tan, J., Meng, W., Wang, Yu., Li, J.: SwipeVLock: a supervised unlocking mechanism based on swipe behavior on smartphones. In: Chen, X., Huang, X., Zhang, J. (eds.) ML4CS 2019. LNCS, vol. 11806, pp. 140–153. Springer, Cham (2019). https://doi.org/10.1007/978-3-030-30619-9_11

18. Li, W., Tan, J., Meng, W., Wang, Y.: A swipe-based unlocking mechanism with supervised learning on smartphones: design and evaluation. J. Netw. Comput. Appl. **165**, 102687 (2020)

19. Li, W., Wang, Y., Li, J., Xiang, Y.: Towards supervised shape-based behavioral authentication on smartphones. J. Inf. Secur. Appl. **55**, 102591 (2020)

20. Liang, Y., Samtani, S., Guo, B., Yu, Z.: Behavioral biometrics for continuous authentication in the internet-of-things era: an artificial intelligence perspective. IEEE Internet Things J. **7**(9), 9128–9143 (2020)

21. Meng, Y.: Designing click-draw based graphical password scheme for better authentication. In: Proceedings of the 7th IEEE International Conference on Networking, Architecture, and Storage (NAS), pp. 39–48 (2012)

22. Meng, Y., Li, W., Kwok, L.-F.: Enhancing click-draw based graphical passwords using multi-touch on mobile phones. In: Janczewski, L.J., Wolfe, H.B., Shenoi, S. (eds.) SEC 2013. IAICT, vol. 405, pp. 55–68. Springer, Heidelberg (2013). https://doi.org/10.1007/978-3-642-39218-4_5

23. Meng, W., Wong, D.S., Furnell, S., Zhou, J.: Surveying the development of biometric user authentication on mobile phones. IEEE Commun. Surv. Tutor. **17**(3), 1268–1293 (2015)

24. Meng, W.: RouteMap: a route and map based graphical password scheme for better multiple password memory. In: NSS 2015. LNCS, vol. 9408, pp. 147–161. Springer, Cham (2015). https://doi.org/10.1007/978-3-319-25645-0_10

25. Meng, W.: Evaluating the effect of multi-touch behaviours on android unlock patterns. Inf. Comput. Secur. **24**(3), 277–287 (2016)

26. Meng, W., Li, W., Wong, D.S., Zhou, J.: TMGuard: a touch movement-based security mechanism for screen unlock patterns on smartphones. In: Manulis, M., Sadeghi, A.-R., Schneider, S. (eds.) ACNS 2016. LNCS, vol. 9696, pp. 629–647. Springer, Cham (2016). https://doi.org/10.1007/978-3-319-39555-5_34

27. Meng, W., Lee, W.H., Liu, Z., Su, C., Li, Y.: Evaluating the impact of juice filming charging attack in practical environments. In: Kim, H., Kim, D.-C. (eds.) ICISC 2017. LNCS, vol. 10779, pp. 327–338. Springer, Cham (2018). https://doi.org/10.1007/978-3-319-78556-1_18

28. Meng, W., Fei, F., Li, W., Au, M.H.: Harvesting smartphone privacy through enhanced juice filming charging attacks. In: Nguyen, P., Zhou, J. (eds.) Information Security. ISC 2017. LNCS, vol. 10599. Springer, Cham (2017). https://doi.org/10.1007/978-3-319-69659-1_16

29. Meng, W., Li, W., Kwok, L.-F., Choo, K.-K.R.: Towards enhancing click-draw based graphical passwords using multi-touch behaviours on smartphones. Comput. Secur. **65**, 213–229 (2017)

30. Meng, W., Li, W., Lee, W.H., Jiang, L., Zhou, J.: A pilot study of multiple password interference between text and map-based passwords. In: Gollmann, D., Miyaji, A., Kikuchi, H. (eds.) ACNS 2017. LNCS, vol. 10355, pp. 145–162. Springer, Cham (2017). https://doi.org/10.1007/978-3-319-61204-1_8

31. Meng, W., Lee, W.H., Au, M.H., Liu, Z.: Exploring effect of location number on map-based graphical password authentication. In: Pieprzyk, J., Suriadi, S. (eds.) ACISP 2017. LNCS, vol. 10343, pp. 301–313. Springer, Cham (2017). https://doi.org/10.1007/978-3-319-59870-3_17

32. Meng, W., Li, W., Wong, D.S.: Enhancing touch behavioral authentication via cost-based intelligent mechanism on smartphones. Multimed. Tools Appl. **77**(23), 30167–30185 (2018). https://doi.org/10.1007/s11042-018-6094-2

33. Meng, W., Wang, Y., Wong, D.S., Wen, S., Xiang, Y.: TouchWB: touch behavioral user authentication based on web browsing on smartphones. J. Netw. Comput. Appl. **117**, 1–9 (2018)

34. Nyang, D., et al.: Two-Thumbs-Up: physical protection for PIN entry secure against recording attacks. Comput. Secur. **78**, 1–15 (2018)

35. Shepard, R.N.: Recognition memory for words, sentences, and pictures. J. Verbal Learn. Verbal Behav. **6**(1), 156–163 (1967)

36. Spitzer, J., Singh, C., Schweitzer, D.: A security class project in graphical passwords. J. Comput. Sci. Coll. **26**(2), 7–13 (2010)

37. Shahzad, M., Liu, A.X., Samuel, A.: Behavior based human authentication on touch screen devices using gestures and signatures. IEEE Trans. Mob. Comput. **16**(10), 2726–2741 (2017)

38. Sharma, V., Enbody, R.: User authentication and identification from user interface interactions on touch-enabled devices. In: Proceedings of the 10th ACM Conference on Security and Privacy in Wireless and Mobile Networks (WiSec), pp. 1–11 (2017)

39. Suo, X., Zhu, Y., Owen, G.S.: Graphical passwords: a survey. In: Proceedings of the 21st Annual Computer Security Applications Conference (ACSAC), pp. 463–472. IEEE (2005)

40. Sun, H., Chen, Y., Fang, C., Chang, S.: PassMap: a map based graphical-password authentication system. In: Proceedings of AsiaCCS, pp. 99–100 (2012)

41. Tao, H., Adams, C.: Pass-Go: a proposal to improve the usability of graphical passwords. Int. J. Netw. Secur. **2**(7), 273–292 (2008)

42. Thorpe, J., MacRae, B., Salehi-Abari, A.: Usability and security evaluation of GeoPass: a geographic location-password scheme. In: Proceedings of the 9th Symposium on Usable Privacy and Security (SOUPS), pp. 1–14 (2013)

43. Wang, L., et al.: Unlock with your heart: heartbeat-based authentication on commercial mobile phones. Proc. ACM Interact. Mob. Wearable Ubiquitous Technol. **2**(3), 140:1–140:22 (2018)

44. WEKA: machine learning software in Java. https://www.cs.waikato.ac.nz/ml/weka/

45. Wiedenbeck, S., Waters, J., Birget, J.-C., Brodskiy, A., Memon, N.: PassPoints: design and longitudinal evaluation of a graphical password system. Int. J. Hum Comput Stud. **63**(1–2), 102–127 (2005)

46. Weir, M., Aggarwal, S., Collins, M., Stern, H.: Testing metrics for password creation policies by attacking large sets of revealed passwords. In: Proceedings of CCS, pp. 162–175 (2010)
47. Yi, S., Qin, Z., Carter, N., Li, Q.: WearLock: unlocking your phone via acoustics using smartwatch. ICDCS, pp. 469–479 (2017)
48. Zheng, N., Bai, K., Huang, H., Wang, H.: You are how you touch: user verification on smartphones via tapping behaviors. In: Proceedings of the 2014 International Conference on Network Protocols (ICNP), pp. 221–232 (2014)

PETs and Crypto

Post-Quantum Cheating Detectable Private Information Retrieval

Lin Zhu[1], Changlu Lin[2], Fuchun Lin[3(✉)], and Liang Feng Zhang[1]

[1] ShanghaiTech University, Shanghai, China
[2] Fujian Normal University, Fujian, China
[3] Imperial College London, London, UK
`flin@ic.ac.uk`

Abstract. Private Information Retrieval (PIR) allows a user to privately retrieve any item from a database such that the server(s) holding the database cannot learn any information about the user's choice. Most existing PIR protocols focus on minimizing the communication cost for retrieving one bit from the database, in an honest-but-curious server model. Dishonest servers were studied in an ad-hoc fashion including the robust PIR and verifiable PIR for cheater identification, where the former further guarantees error correction but only works when the number of dishonest servers are bounded and the latter works for any number of dishonest servers but has to rely on the intractability assumption of certain computational hard problems and a tag published by the honest data owner. We initiate a systematic study of the fundamental problem of cheating detection for PIR (cd-PIR). We first show a theoretic result that rules out the possibility of information-theoretically secure cd-PIR against arbitrary number of cheaters (even allowing the data owner to publish a tag and lifting cheater identification), which justifies our study of computational cd-PIR. On the positive side, we show that computational cd-PIR against arbitrary number of cheaters can be achieved much more efficiently than all previous constructions and with weaker cryptography hardness assumptions. In particular, we obtain efficient cheating detection for PIR with more than one server that resists quantum algorithm for the first time.

Keywords: PIR · Cheating detection · Merkle tree · Verifiability

1 Introduction

Private information retrieval (PIR) allows a user to retrieve an item x_i from a database $x = (x_0, x_1, \ldots, x_{n-1})$ such that the server/servers storing the database cannot gain any information about the user's choice of $\{0, 1, \ldots, n-1\}$. It is a fundamental privacy-preserving primitive in cryptography and has applications in many systems such as friend discovery [23], publish-subscribe [6], private media browsing [14], private messaging [3,25], privacy preserving ad targeting [12,17], certificate transparency [21], online anonymity [20,22], and location-based services for smartphones [18,31].

© IFIP International Federation for Information Processing 2022
Published by Springer Nature Switzerland AG 2022
W. Meng et al. (Eds.): SEC 2022, IFIP AICT 648, pp. 431–448, 2022.
https://doi.org/10.1007/978-3-031-06975-8_25

The notion of PIR was introduced by Chor, Goldreich, Kushilevitz and Sudan [7]. In a trivial PIR protocol, the user may simply download the entire database and then locally extract the item of his/her interest. Although the protocol achieves perfect secrecy, it incurs a prohibitive communication complexity of $O(n)$. In general, the communication complexity of a PIR protocol is the total number of bits that have to be exchanged by the user, for the sake of retrieving one bit from the database. Reducing the communication complexity has been the most challenging problem in PIR-related research. Chor et al. [7] showed that if there is only one server and perfect secrecy is needed, then $O(n)$ communication is unavoidable. In order to have a protocol with $o(n)$ communication complexity, we have to work in a *multi-server* information-theoretic setting [9,10,32], where the user's index i is still perfectly secret as long as the servers do not collude, or in a single-server *computational* setting [5,19], where the secrecy of i is based on cryptographic assumptions. In particular, the communication complexity of the best protocols in both settings can be as small as $\exp(O(\sqrt{\log n \log \log n}))$ (using two servers) [9] and $O(\log n)$, respectively.

Most of the existing PIR protocols consider only honest-but-curious servers, which strictly follow the protocols' specifications. A dishonest server may arbitrarily deviate from the protocols and thus cause the user to output a wrong value of the retrieved database item. In fact, it has been an interesting and challenging problem to design PIR protocols that allow the user to detect a wrong output. Such protocols have particular interest in the modern age of cloud computing because they allow the PIR servers to be implemented by the untrustworthy cloud services, i.e., outsource the PIR servers' computations to the cloud. The multi-server *robust* PIR (RPIR) protocols of [4,8,11] allow the user to reconstruct the correct value of x_i, even if some of the Byzantine servers (called cheaters) [8] provide wrong answers. These protocols provide *information-theoretic* security of error correction and cheater identification (so that cheaters can be avoided in the future) by using error-correcting techniques, but the number of cheaters tolerated must be bounded. For a "t-private τ-Byzantine robust k-out-of-ℓ PIR", there exists a protocol that will always output to the client the unique correct block (called unique decoding) if $\tau \leq t < k/3$; and there exists a protocol that will always output to the client a small number of blocks including the correct block (called list decoding) if $t < k$ and $\tau < k - t - 1$.

The *verifiable* PIR (VPIR) protocols of [29,33] are constructed either in the multi-server model or the single-server model such that any number of servers providing wrong answers will be detected and identified (but there is no guarantee of recovering the correct block, or even a small list containing it). These protocols have communication complexities that are comparable to the best known protocols in an honest-but-curious server model and allow all servers to be Byzantine. Different from RPIR, where the robustness does not rely on computational assumptions, the VPIR assumes the hardness of certain computational problems, and more importantly, the data owner who is supposed to be honest must publish a short tag (similar as in the PIR-Tor [20]) that can be used by the user for verifying the servers.

Allowing all the servers to be Byzantine make the model one big step closer to being practical and cheater identification seems no much weaker than error correction (one could exclude the cheaters and run a basic PIR with remaining honest servers if there are enough number of honest servers). Nevertheless, the multi-server VPIR constructed in [33] relies on the strong Bilinear Diffie-Hellman (SBDH) assumption, which is no longer true in front of quantum attacks [16,24], and it is not known if SBDH can be replaced by any post-quantum assumptions. On the other hand, the VPIR protocol of [29] is based on latticed-related cryptographic assumptions, which is post-quantum secure. But it is not clear if the construction can be efficiently extended to more than one party. Another drawback of these protocols is that to facilitate cheater identification, both the user and servers in these protocols have to do a lot of public-key operations such as pairing computations and lattice-related computations. For example, in the VPIR protocols of [29,33], the user has to take thousands of seconds to retrieve an item from a database of 1G bits.

It can be argued that identification of cheating servers may be overly strong in many scenarios, such as private media browsing [14], where a large database of movies is stored on several non-Byzantine servers and the client hides its media diet by using PIR to retrieve a movie. In such scenarios, it may suffice for the client to detect the existence of wrong responses (or cheating servers) and then refuse to pay for the browsing. It is then an interesting problem to consider the relaxed security requirement of detecting the existence of wrong responses (or cheating servers) in exchange for obtain significant improvements of efficiency and weaker hardness assumptions. Given the recent trend of reducing the computational cost of PIR, it may be more appealing to obtain PIR protocols that have both relaxed security and better efficiency than the protocols that have overly strong security but very poor efficiency. On the other hand, given that the quantum computing is making great strides [15,26], the rule of thumb in designing cryptographic protocol is to avoid basing the security on assumptions that are vulnerable in the face of a quantum computer. There have been two well-performed quantum algorithms that can solve the problem of integer factorization (by Shor's algorithm [28]) and elliptic curve encryption algorithm (by Grover's algorithm [13]), respectively. Note that cheating detection is equivalent to cheater identification in single server special case and hence [29] already gives a post-quantum tampering detection protocol. It is not known if one can realize post-quantum tampering detection for the high-performing PIR protocols for more than one server.

1.1 Our Contributions

We initiate a systematic study of the fundamental problem of cheating detection for PIR. In this work, we aim at providing practical solutions that assumes the existence of dishonest servers, which captures real-life adversary. We note that investigating what is the minimum number of honest servers required for enabling cheating detection in a t-private τ-Byzantine robust k-out-of-ℓ PIR is an interesting theoretic open question.

We begin with showing negative results on cheating detection for PIR against arbitrary number of Byzantine servers. Our negative results consist of two arguments of different flavours (see the beginning of Sect. 3 for details).

The first negative result rules out the possibility of cheating detection for PIR against arbitrary number of Byzantine servers in the setting without the involvement of the data owner, who is supposed to be honest and publishes a tag of the database for verification. This is shown by relating PIR to secure Multi-Party Computation (MPC) (PIR can be seen as a weaker form of MPC where only the privacy of the user is required). In the case that no tag of the database is published by the data owner, we can consider a variant that we dub *data-private PIR*, where the privacy of the database of the servers are also required instead of only the privacy of the input of the user. It can be observed that data-private PIR is equivalent to secure MPC against passive adversary (no information is revealed to a participant in the computation beyond that can be inferred from the participant's input and output). We then argue that the robustness of secure MPC against active adversary (by definition must allow input substitution of corrupt servers) renders cheating detection for data-private PIR against arbitrary number of Byzantine servers impossible. The impossibility result holds for both information-theoretic security and computational security, which makes it necessary for one to involve the data owner and his/her tag.

Our second negative result only holds when one imposes information-theoretic security. We argue that if the mapping from database to its tag is not injective, then there exist two distinct databases that are mapped to the same tag value. In this case, when one of the two databases is the database of the data owner, the servers can replace it with the other database and execute the protocol honestly after the substitution of the database. Since the correctness of the protocol guarantees that for any choice of database, honest execution should always lead to acceptance of the retrieved block by the user, we conclude that this substitution attack is not detectable at least for one block index. This argument leaves us with the only possible information-theoretic cheating detection PIR, whose tag must be as long as the database. But in that case, the user could as well download the original database (locally retrieve the desired block) and circumvent running the protocol by downloading the tag and communicate with the servers before verifying against the tag.

The above two negative results justify our following cheating detectable PIR (cd-PIR) model. Intuitively, we want to achieve cheating detection that is resistant to quantum attacks at the cost of communicating a small amount of verification information (logarithmic in n, the number of items) and conducting an efficient verification taking no more time than the query. Moreover, it is of practical importance that the protocol should come with a communicational low-cost update algorithm that allows the data owner to modify a specific item while maintaining the cheating detection capability.

cd-PIR Model. For any integer $k \geq 1$, our k-server cd-PIR model consists of a *database owner* who has a database $x = (x_0, x_1, \ldots, x_{n-1})$ of n items, a *user* who wants to retrieve an item x_i of the database, and k *servers* $\mathcal{S}_1, \mathcal{S}_2, \ldots, \mathcal{S}_k$.

The database owner prepares both a public encoding X of the database and a public tag Tag for verification. Each server keeps an identical copy of the encoding X. To retrieve x_i, the user may use Tag to convert its retrieval index $i \in \mathbb{Z}_n$ to k queries $\{q_j\}_{j=1}^k$ and possibly a private auxiliary information aux for reconstruction. For every $j \in [k]$, the server $\mathcal{S}_j$ uses (X, q_j) to generate an answer a_j to the user. Finally, the user makes use of $(\mathsf{Tag}, i, \mathsf{aux}, \{a_j\}_{j=1}^k)$ to locally reconstruct and verify the value of x_i. As a useful extension, we also include an update algorithm in the model that allows the database owner to dynamically update the value of any database item with (Tag, X). A cd-PIR protocol is said to be t-$private$ if any t of the k servers cannot learn the user's index i. For $k > 1$ and $k = 1$, we consider information-theoretic and computational privacy, respectively. A cd-PIR protocol is said to be $secure$ (i.e., cheating detectable) against active adversary if the user is able to detect the existence of wrong server answers, even when all servers are Byzantine servers.

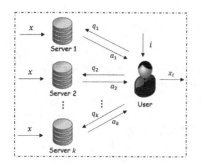 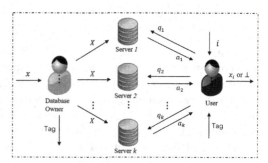

Fig. 1. PIR model   **Fig. 2.** cd-PIR model

The PIR model and cd-PIR model can be depicted by the Fig. 1 and Fig. 2. Following the standard PIR literature, the communication complexity $\mathsf{CC}_\Gamma(n)$ of a cd-PIR protocol Γ will be defined as $\sum_{j=1}^k (|q_j| + |a_j|)$, maximized over all possible choices of x, i and underlying randomness.

Merkle Tree-Based Transformation. In this paper, we propose a method of using Merkle tree to transform PIR into cd-PIR. Specifically, if we are given a k-server PIR protocol Π with communication complexity $\mathsf{CC}_\Pi(n)$, then the transformation will give a k-server cd-PIR protocol Γ with $\mathsf{CC}_\Gamma(n) = 2\mathsf{CC}_\Pi(n) + \sum_{\ell=1}^{\log n - 1} \mathsf{CC}_\Pi(n/2^\ell)$, where w is the length of the digests under a hash H and H is used for constructing a Merkle tree encoding of the database x. If the underlying PIR protocol Π is t-private, then the cd-PIR protocol will be t-private as well. As long as H is collision-resistant, the cd-PIR protocol Γ will be secure such that a user will never output a wrong value (see Definition 4 for details). As cryptographic hash functions are believed better immune to quantum attacks [1], our protocols are post-quantum secure.

By instantiating with the SHA-256 and applying the Merkle tree-based transformation to [2,30], we obtain both a 2-server cd-PIR protocol Γ_{WY} with communication complexity $O(n^{1/3})$ and a single-server cd-PIR protocol Γ_{SL} with communication complexity $O(Nd\lceil \sqrt[d]{n}/N\rceil)$. See the following Table 1 for a comparison between VPIR and our cd-PIR protocols in terms of quantum resistance and communication complexity.

Table 1. Comparison between VPIR and cd-PIR protocols

Protocol		Post-quantum	Communication complexity
Multi-server	Γ_{WY}^a	✓	$O(2^{\lceil \log n\rceil/\lfloor \frac{2k-1}{t}\rfloor})$
	Γ_{ZSN} [33]	✗	$O(2^{\lceil \log n\rceil/\lfloor \frac{2k-1}{t}\rfloor})$
Single-server	Γ_{SL}	✓	$O(Nd\lceil \sqrt[d]{n}/N\rceil)$
	Γ_{WZ} [29]	✓	$\Theta(c\cdot \mathsf{poly}(n)\cdot \log n)$

^{a} Set $(k,t)=(2,1)$ in Γ_{WY}

The 2-server protocol Γ_{ZSN} in [33] achieves the unconditional 1-privacy and computational security, under the strong Bilinear Diffie-Hellman (SBDH) assumption. Our 2-server protocol has comparable communication cost with [33] and is computationally much more efficient. In the cd-PIR protocol Γ_{WY}, the user spends less than 1.2 s to retrieve an item from a 1G bits database, which gains significant practical improvement compared with [33].

The single-server protocol Γ_{WZ} in [29] is based on the LWE with binary errors. It is computationally private and secure, and the communication complexity is $\mathsf{CC}_{\Gamma_{WZ}}(n)=\Theta(c\cdot \mathsf{poly}(n)\cdot \log n)$. Our single-server cd-PIR protocol Γ_{SL} requires strictly less communication than that. The user in Γ_{SL} only spends about 0.044 s retrieving the data from a 1G bits database, more than 28000 times less than Γ_{WZ}. Furthermore, the computation time of user of increases very slightly, whereas that in Γ_{WZ} grows almost twice as fast. The computer time of the server of Γ_{SL} is also very small, but as the computation time of the server in Γ_{WZ} is too long to show, we do not make more comparisons.

1.2 Our Techniques

A Merkle tree (see Fig. 3) is a binary tree such that the value of every internal node is the hash value of its two children. It allows a prover to convince a verifier of the value of any leaf node i. In particular, the prover only needs to provide the values of the nodes along the *authentication path* of i, where the authentication path consists of the siblings of all nodes on the path from i to the root. In our transformation, a collision-resistant hash function $\mathsf{H}:\{0,1\}^*\to\{0,1\}^w$ will be chosen, which maps two siblings to their parent (e.g., $\mathsf{H}(\cdot\|\cdot)\in\{0,1\}^w$). The owner of a database $x=(x_0,x_1,\ldots,x_{n-1})$ will construct a Merkle tree X out of (H,x) such that the n data items $x_0, x_1, \ldots, x_{n-1}$ are sequentially taken as n leaf nodes of X and values of other $\lceil \log n\rceil$ levels are hash values. The value of the root of X is defined as the Tag. Note that X has exactly $\lceil \log n \rceil + 1$ levels with the root being level 0.

The $\lceil \log n \rceil$-th level is the original database for a k-server PIR. For $\ell = \lceil \log n \rceil - 1, \lceil \log n \rceil - 2, \ldots, 1$, the ℓ-th level is considered as a database for a distinct k-server PIR (of different database size). For the purpose of retrieving the value of a leaf node i, the user firstly simply runs the $\lceil \log n \rceil$-th PIR to retrieve x_i. Secondly, in order to check the correctness of this invocation, the user needs to retrieve the authentication path of i, which is indicated by an integer sequence of the form $(v_{\lceil \log n \rceil}, v_{\lceil \log n \rceil - 1}, \ldots, v_1)$. For every $\ell \in \{\lceil \log n \rceil, \lceil \log n \rceil - 1, \ldots, 1\}$, invoke the ℓ-th PIR to retrieve v_ℓ-th data. Finally, the user may determine the correctness of the retrieved database item (i.e., x_i), by simply re-computing the root of X with that item and the $\lceil \log n \rceil$ path values on the authentication path, and then compare with the Tag (i.e., the Merkle root published by the database owner). Note that in the re-computation of the root of X, it is computationally infeasible to use an authentication path for $i' \neq i$ to replace the authentication path for i, even when i and i' are siblings (in this case, the same collection of values are retrieved). This is because the re-computation of the root from the i-th item and $\lceil \log n \rceil$ path values uses an ordering specific to i, which is a $\lceil \log n \rceil$-bit string, each bit indicating on either "left" or "right" side, the path value appears in the two inputs to the hash function.

Merkle tree also allows one to efficiently update the value of every leaf node, yielding an updatable cd-PIR. An update algorithm for the data owner to modify a specific item can be realized by updating the corresponding path, which only cost $\log n$ times of computing of hash function. The cost for update is much less than a naive approach of making the data owner signing each data item and publish the public key of the signature scheme, and the user privately retrieving the a data item together with the corresponding signature. To avoid the servers reusing an old data item and corresponding signature to fool the user, a new pair of public key and secret key must be used, rendering the data owner replacing all the signatures.

1.3   Organization

In Sect. 2, we give explanations for some symbols, and introduce the basics about Merkle trees; In Sect. 3, we formally define the model of cd-PIR. In Sect. 4, we show the Merkle tree based transformation from PIR protocol to cd-PIR protocol; In Sect. 5, we instantiate the transformation to obtain two concrete cd-PIR protocols, implement them to show their performance by experimental results; Finally, Sect. 6 contains our concluding remarks.

2   Preliminaries

2.1   Notation

For any integer $m > 0$, we denote with $\mathbb{Z}_m = \{0, 1, \ldots, m-1\}$ the ring of integers modulo m and denote $[m] = \{1, 2, \ldots, m\}$. For any integer $n > 0$, we denote with $\lceil n \rceil$ the least integer $\geq n$ and denote with $\log n$ the logarithm of n to the base

2. For any integers $i \geq 0$ and $\ell \geq \lceil \log i \rceil$, the ℓ-bit binary representation of i is an ℓ-bit string $\langle i \rangle_\ell = i_1 \| i_2 \| \cdots \| i_\ell \in \{0,1\}^\ell$ such that $i = \sum_{j=1}^\ell i_j \cdot 2^{\ell-j}$. We say that a function $\epsilon(\lambda)$ is *negligible* in λ and denote $\epsilon(\lambda) = \mathsf{negl}(\lambda)$, if for any $c > 0$, there exists $\lambda_c > 0$ such that $\epsilon(\lambda) < \lambda^{-c}$ for all $\lambda \geq \lambda_c$.

2.2   Merkle Tree

A *Merkle tree* is a complete binary tree where the value of every internal node is the hash value of its two children's values. Let $n = 2^m$ and $x = (x_0, x_1, \ldots, x_{n-1})$. Let H be a cryptographic hash function. The *labels* and *values* of the nodes in a Merkle tree $\mathsf{MT}_{x,\mathsf{H}}$ of depth m can be defined as follows:

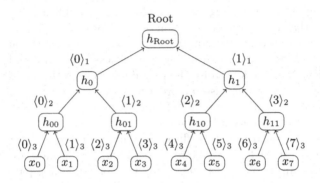

Fig. 3. Merkle tree for a database of length 8

Labels. Nodes of $\mathsf{MT}_{x,\mathsf{H}}$ (see Fig. 3 for an example) are labeled such that:

- For $1 \leq \ell \leq m$, the 2^ℓ nodes at depth ℓ are labeled (from left to right) with $\langle 0 \rangle_\ell, \langle 1 \rangle_\ell, \ldots, \langle 2^\ell - 1 \rangle_\ell$, respectively. The node at depth 0 is labeled as Root.
- For $1 < \ell \leq m$ and $0 \leq j < 2^\ell$, the parent of $\langle j \rangle_\ell$ is $j_1 \| j_2 \| \cdots \| j_{\ell-1}$. The parent of the nodes at the depth 1 is Root;
- For $1 \leq \ell < m$ and $0 \leq j < 2^\ell$, the left child of $\langle j \rangle_\ell$ is $\langle 2j \rangle_{\ell+1}$, and the right child of $\langle j \rangle_\ell$ is $\langle 2j+1 \rangle_{\ell+1}$. The left and right child of Root are $\langle 0 \rangle_1$ and $\langle 1 \rangle_1$, respectively.
- For $1 \leq \ell \leq m$ and $0 \leq j < 2^\ell$, the sibling of $\langle j \rangle_\ell$ is $j_1 \| j_2 \| \cdots \| (j_\ell \oplus 1)$.

Values. Every node $\langle j \rangle_\ell$ in $\mathsf{MT}_{x,\mathsf{H}}$ is assigned a value $h_{\langle j \rangle_\ell}$ such that:

- $h_{\langle j \rangle_m} = x_j$ for $0 \leq j < 2^\ell$;
- $h_{\langle j \rangle_\ell} = \mathsf{H}\left(h_{\langle 2j \rangle_{\ell+1}} \| h_{\langle 2j+1 \rangle_{\ell+1}}\right)$ for $1 \leq \ell < m$ and $0 \leq j < 2^\ell$;
- $h_{\mathsf{Root}} = \mathsf{H}(h_0 \| h_1)$.

In our definition, values of the n leaf nodes are $x_0, x_1, \ldots, x_{n-1}$ sequentially. This is slightly different from the traditional definition of Merkle trees where the values of leaves are defined as the hash values of $x_0, x_1, \ldots, x_{n-1}$. This change is made to obtain a more efficient transformation (see Sect. 4 for details).

Verification. Merkle tree allows a prover to convince a verifier of the value of any leaf node. For any $i \in \mathbb{Z}_n$, the nodes on the path from Root to $\langle i \rangle_m$ are

$$(\text{Root}, i_1, i_1 \| i_2, \ldots, i_1 \| i_2 \| \cdots \| i_m). \tag{1}$$

The *authentication path* for the leaf node $\langle i \rangle_m$ is defined as $\varrho(i) = (v_1, v_2, \ldots, v_m)$, where $v_\ell = i_1 \| i_2 \| \cdots \| i_{\ell-1} \| (i_\ell \oplus 1)$ for all $\ell \in [m]$. The *proof* π for the value of $\langle i \rangle_m$ consists of the values of the nodes on its authentication path. In order to verify $h_{\langle i \rangle_m} = \alpha$, the verifier simply recomputes the root value with α and the proof. The verification algorithm $\mathsf{MTVer}(h_{\text{Root}}, i, \alpha, \pi)$ outputs 1 if the re-computed value equals h_{Root}; otherwise it outputs 0.

Update. Merkle tree also allows one to update the value of any leaf node. In the cause of changing $h_{\langle i \rangle_m}$ to α, the update algorithm $\mathsf{MTUpd}(i, \alpha, \mathsf{MT}_{x,\mathsf{H}})$ only needs to recompute the values of the nodes on path (1) with the new leaf value α. The output of this algorithm consists of the new Merkle tree and the new root value.

3   The cd-PIR Model

Negative Result 1. Assume the user only receive information about the database x from the servers (in the form of answers to his/her queries) as indicated in Fig. 1. Then the servers can replace x with some prefixed x_0 and execute the rest of the protocol honestly. According to the correctness of the protocol, which says that for any given database if all parties execute the protocol honestly, the user will output the correct ith data item, this *substitution attack* succeeds in replacing the ith data item of x with ith data item of x_0. In the case $x = x_0$, this attack is vacuous. For all $x \neq x_0$, this attack is effective and renders cheating detection impossible. Note that in this attack, the servers are not required to do extra computation, as the substitution x_0 is prefixed. This means that the negative result is true for both computationally limited and unlimited servers.

Negative Result 2. Assume the user also receives a Tag containing information about the database x, which is published by the database owner, on top of receiving information about the database x from the servers (in the form of answers to his/her queries) as indicated in Fig. 2. Assume the servers have unlimited computation power. We argue that the tag size has to be at least as big as the database, which undermines the motivation of using a PIR protocol (if the user were to download a tag as big as the database itself, he/she could just as well download the database and locally retrieve the desired data item). Indeed, assume by contradiction that the map from the databases to tags is not injective. Then there exist at least two databases x and x' that are mapped to the same tag. The servers can compute such a pair of databases x and x', then launch a substitution attack using, e.g. the database x'. Similarly to negative result 1, in the case $x = x'$, this attack is vacuous. For all $x \neq x'$, this attack is effective and renders cheating detection impossible. Unlike in negative result 1, this attack requires the servers to be capable of finding a pair of *collision* x and

x'. In particular, this negative result does not hold in the case when the map from databases to tags is defined by a *collision-resistant hash function*.

Definition 1 (cd-PIR). *A t-private k-server cd-PIR protocol* $\Gamma = (\mathcal{G}, \mathcal{Q}, \mathcal{A}, \mathcal{R}, \mathcal{U})$ *consists of five polynomial-time algorithms as follows:*

- $(\mathsf{Tag}, X) \leftarrow \mathcal{G}(x, \lambda)$: *It is a deterministic algorithm. The inputs are a database* x *and a security parameter* λ, *and the outputs are a database encoding* X *and a public tag* Tag.
- $(q_1, q_2, \ldots, q_k, \mathsf{aux}) \leftarrow \mathcal{Q}(i)$: *It is a probabilistic algorithm. It takes a retrieval index* $i \in \{0, 1, \ldots, n-1\}$ *as input, and outputs the query* q_j *to the j-th server. It also computes an auxiliary information* aux.
- $a_j \leftarrow \mathcal{A}(X, q_j)$: *It is a deterministic algorithm. For every* $j \in [k]$, *it takes the database encoding* X *and the query* q_j *as input, and outputs an answer* a_j *as a response to the user.*
- $\{x_i, \bot\} \leftarrow \mathcal{R}(\mathsf{Tag}, i, \mathsf{aux}, (a_1, a_2, \ldots, a_k))$: *It is a deterministic algorithm. The user uses* $\mathsf{Tag}, i, \mathsf{aux}$ *and* $(a_1, a_2, \ldots, a_k)$ *to do reconstruction and verification. It outputs either the correct value of* x_i *or a rejection symbol* $\bot$.
- $(\mathsf{Tag}', X') \leftarrow \mathcal{U}(x', X)$: *It is a deterministic algorithm. With* X *and the new database* x' *being the input, it outputs a new tag* Tag' *and the new encoded database* X'.

Definition 2 (Correctness). *The protocol* Γ *is said to be* correct *if for any* $k, n \in \mathbb{N}$, *any* $x \in (0, 1)^n$, *any* λ, *any* $i \in \mathbb{Z}_n$, *any* $(q_1, q_2, \ldots, q_k, \mathsf{aux}) \leftarrow \mathcal{Q}(i)$ *and any* $\{a_j \leftarrow \mathcal{A}(X, q_j)\}_{j=1}^k$, *it always holds that* $\mathcal{R}(\mathsf{Tag}, i, \mathsf{aux}, (a_1, a_2, \ldots, a_k)) = x_i$.

Definition 3 (t-Privacy). *Any t servers cannot learn information about the user's input. Formally, the protocol* Γ *is* information-theoretically (resp. computationally) *t-private if for any* $k, n, i, i' \in \mathbb{Z}_n$, *and any set* $T \subseteq [k]$ *of cardinality* $\leq t$, *the random variables* $\mathcal{Q}_T(i)$ *and* $\mathcal{Q}_T(i')$ *are identically distributed (resp. computationally indistinguishable), where* $\mathcal{Q}_T$ *denotes the concatenation of j-th outputs of* $\mathcal{Q}$ *for* $j \in T$.

Definition 4 (τ-Security). *The protocol* Γ *is* τ-secure *if for any* $T \subseteq [k]$ *of cardinality* τ, *for all probabilistic polynomial-time adversaries* $\mathcal{B}$, *there is a negligible function* negl *such that* $\Pr[\mathsf{EXP}_{\mathcal{B}, \Gamma}^{\mathrm{Ver}}(T, \lambda) = 1] \leq \mathsf{negl}(\lambda)$, *where* $\mathsf{EXP}_{\mathcal{B}, \Gamma}^{\mathrm{Ver}}(T, \lambda)$ *is performed between* $\mathcal{B}$ *and its challenger, as defined in Fig. 4.*

4   A Merkle Tree Based Construction

In this section, we describe a transformation from PIR protocols to cd-PIR protocols. For all $\ell \in [m]$, let $V_\ell = \{\langle 0 \rangle_\ell, \ldots, \langle 2^\ell - 1 \rangle_\ell\}$ and $H_\ell = \{(h_{\langle 0 \rangle_\ell}, \ldots, h_{\langle 2^\ell - 1 \rangle_\ell})\}$. Let $V_{(0)} = \{\mathsf{Root}\}$ and $H_0 = \{h_{\mathsf{Root}}\}$. In our construction, we denote $\mathsf{MT}_{x, \mathsf{H}} = (V, H)$ with $V = \bigcup_{\ell=0}^m V_\ell$ and $H = \bigcup_{\ell=0}^m H_\ell$. Any t-private k-server PIR protocol $\Pi = (\mathcal{Q}, \mathcal{A}, \mathcal{R})$, can be transformed into a cd-PIR protocol $\Gamma = (\mathcal{G}, \mathcal{Q}, \mathcal{A}, \mathcal{R}, \mathcal{U})$ as follows:

1. The adversary $\mathcal{B}$ chooses a database x and an index i, and outputs (x, i).
2. The challenger computes $(\mathsf{Tag}, X) \leftarrow \mathcal{G}(x, \lambda)$ and $(q_1, q_2, \ldots, q_k, \mathsf{aux}) \leftarrow \mathcal{Q}(i)$. It gives $(X, \{q_j\}_{j \in T})$ to the adversary $\mathcal{B}$.
3. The adversary $\mathcal{B}$ chooses t answers $\{\breve{a}_j\}_{j \in T}$ to the challenger.
4. The challenger computes $\breve{a}_j \leftarrow \mathcal{A}(X, q_j)$ for every $j \in [k] \setminus T$. It executes the algorithm $\mathcal{R}(\mathsf{Tag}, i, \mathsf{aux}, (\breve{a}_1, \breve{a}_2, \ldots, \breve{a}_k))$ and learns its output y.
5. If $y \notin \{x_i, \bot\}$, then $\mathsf{EXP}_{\mathcal{B}, \Gamma}^{\mathsf{Ver}}(T, \lambda)$ is defined as 1; $\mathsf{EXP}_{\mathcal{B}, \Gamma}^{\mathsf{Ver}}(T, \lambda) = 0$ otherwise.

Fig. 4. Experiment $\mathsf{EXP}_{\mathcal{B}, \Gamma}^{\mathsf{Ver}}(T, \lambda)$

– $(\mathsf{Tag}, X) \leftarrow \mathcal{G}(x, \lambda)$: Let $m = \lceil \log n \rceil$. (If $\log n < m$, fill the empty leaf nodes with 0.) The database owner constructs $\mathsf{MT}_{x, \mathsf{H}} = (V, H)$. It outputs a public tag $\mathsf{Tag} = h_{\mathsf{Root}}$ and the database encoding $X = \mathsf{MT}_{x, \mathsf{H}}$.
– $(q_1, q_2, \ldots, q_k, \mathsf{aux}) \leftarrow \mathcal{Q}(i)$: The user computes the authentication path

$$\varrho(i) = (v_1, v_2, \ldots, v_m) \in V_1 \times V_2 \times \cdots \times V_m \qquad (2)$$

with $v_\ell = i_1 \| i_2 \| \cdots \| i_{\ell-1} \| (i_\ell \oplus 1)$, for all $\ell \in [m]$, where $i_j \in \{0, 1\}$ for all $j \in [m]$ and $i = \sum_{j=1}^m i_j \cdot 2^{m+1-j}$. It then generates $(q_1^\ell, q_2^\ell, \ldots, q_k^\ell, \mathsf{aux}_\ell) \leftarrow \Pi.\mathcal{Q}(v_\ell)$, for every $\ell \in [m]$, and $(\zeta_1, \zeta_2, \ldots, \zeta_k, \mathsf{a\bar{u}x}) \leftarrow \Pi.\mathcal{Q}(i)$. The outputs are $\{q_j = (q_j^1, q_j^2, \ldots, q_j^m, \zeta_j)\}_{j=1}^k$ and $\mathsf{aux} = (\{\mathsf{aux}_j\}_{j=1}^m, \mathsf{a\bar{u}x}, \varrho(i))$.
– $a_j \leftarrow \mathcal{A}(X, q_j)$: This j-th server computes $\alpha_j = \Pi.\mathcal{A}(x, \zeta_j)$ and $a_j^\ell = \Pi.\mathcal{A}(H_\ell, q_j^\ell), \forall \ell \in [m]$. It responds with $a_j = (a_j^1, a_j^2, \ldots, a_j^m, \alpha_j)$.
– $\{x_i, \bot\} \leftarrow \mathcal{R}(\mathsf{Tag}, i, \mathsf{aux}, (a_1, a_2, \ldots, a_k))$: The user computes $\alpha = \Pi.\mathcal{R}(i, \mathsf{a\bar{u}x}, (\alpha_1, \alpha_2, \ldots, \alpha_k))$ and $z_\ell = \Pi.\mathcal{R}(v_\ell, \mathsf{aux}_\ell, (a_1^\ell, a_2^\ell, \ldots, a_k^\ell))$ for all $\ell \in [m]$. If the verification algorithm $\mathsf{MTVer}(h_{\mathsf{Root}}, i, \alpha, (z_1, z_2, \ldots, z_m)) = 1$ (as discussed in Sect. 2), it outputs α; o.w., it outputs $\bot$.
– $(\mathsf{Tag}', X') \leftarrow \mathcal{U}(j, x_j', X)$: It runs $\mathsf{MTUpd}(j, x_j', X)$ with X and then outputs both a new tag Tag' and the updated encoded database X'. In particular, X' is identical to X except that the values of the nodes on the path from the root to the j-th leaf are recomputed with x_j'. The Tag' is essentially the value of the root of the new Merkle tree X'.

Remark 1. For the sake of reduction of both communication and computation, if v_m is on the right of $\langle n-1 \rangle_m$, that is the value of the node v_m is 0 by default according to the construction, we substitute the original database x for H_ℓ in the PIR invocation during the cd-PIR execution, then the user randomly chooses $v_m \in \{\langle 0 \rangle_m, \langle 1 \rangle_m, \ldots, \langle n-1 \rangle_m\}$ to run the query algorithm. Therefore, in the reconstruction phase, the user can write $z_m = 0$ directly, which circumvents dealing with the related answers and saves some computation.

Remark 2. Besides x_i, the value of x_i's sibling in the Merkle tree could be revealed to the user as a part of the proof. Revealing more information than x_i to the user is allowed in PIR (including the cd-PIR of this paper), because what the PIR protocols protect is the user's privacy rather than the server's privacy.

Communication Complexity. In the execution of cd-PIR Γ, the underlying PIR protocol will be invoked for $\lceil \log n \rceil + 1$ times with database of different size. If the communication complexity of the PIR protocol Π is $CC_\Pi(w, n)$ for any database $x \in ((0, 1)^w)^n$ and the outputs of the hash function H are w-bit long, then the communication complexity of our protocol Γ will be $CC_\Gamma(w, n) = 2CC_\Pi(w, n) + \sum_{\ell=1}^{m-1} CC_\Pi(w, 2^{\lceil \log n \rceil - \ell})$.

Theorem 1. *Our cd-PIR protocol Γ satisfies the following:*

- **Correctness:** Γ *is correct if the PIR protocol $\Pi = (\mathcal{Q}, \mathcal{A}, \mathcal{R})$ is correct.*
- **t-Privacy:** Γ *is information-theoretically t-private (resp. computationally private) if the PIR protocol $\Pi = (\mathcal{Q}, \mathcal{A}, \mathcal{R})$ is information-theoretically t-private (resp. computationally private).*
- **k-Security:** Γ *is k-secure if the hash function H is collision-resistant.*

The output of our cd-PIR protocol will always be true due to the correctness of the underlying PIR protocol. The privacy, inherited from the PIR protocol, guarantees that any k honest-but-curious servers are not able to learn i. The security of our cd-PIR protocol comes from the collision resistance of the hash function. The properties of correctness and privacy can be easily proved and omitted from this version. Below we only prove the k-security.

Proof. Because H is collision-resistant, for any PPT adversary $\mathcal{D}$, there is a negligible function $\mathsf{negl}(\lambda)$ such that

$$\Pr\left[(\delta, \delta') \leftarrow \mathcal{D}(H) : \delta \neq \delta', H(\delta) = H(\delta')\right] \leq \mathsf{negl}(\lambda). \tag{3}$$

Let $T = [k]$. For any Probabilistic Polynomial Time (PPT) adversary $\mathcal{B}$, we consider the experiment $\mathsf{EXP}_{\mathcal{B},\Gamma}^{\mathrm{Ver}}(T, \lambda)$ between $\mathcal{B}$ and its challenger, which is shown in Fig. 5. We need to show that

$$\epsilon(\lambda) := \Pr[\mathsf{EXP}_{\mathcal{B},\Gamma}^{\mathrm{Ver}}(T, \lambda) = 1]$$

is negligible. Assume for contradiction that $\epsilon(\lambda)$ is non-negligible.
When $\mathsf{EXP}_{\mathcal{B},\Gamma}^{\mathrm{Ver}}(T, \lambda) = 1$, we have that $\breve{y} \notin \{x_i, \bot\}$. Let $\breve{z}_\ell = \Pi.\mathcal{R}(v_\ell, \mathsf{aux}_\ell, (\breve{a}_1^\ell, \breve{a}_2^\ell, \ldots, \breve{a}_k^\ell))$ for all $\ell \in [m]$ and let $\breve{\alpha} = \Pi.\mathcal{R}(i, \bar{\mathsf{aux}}, (\breve{\alpha}_1, \breve{\alpha}_2, \ldots, \breve{\alpha}_k))$. Due to the specification of $\Gamma.\mathcal{R}$, the event $\breve{y} \notin \{x_i, \bot\}$ occurs if and only if $\breve{\alpha} \neq x_i$ but

$$\mathsf{MTVer}\left(h_{\mathrm{Root}}, i, \breve{\alpha}, (\breve{z}_1, \breve{z}_2, \ldots, \breve{z}_m)\right) = 1. \tag{4}$$

For every $j \in [k]$, let $a_j = (a_j^1, a_j^2, \ldots, a_j^m, \alpha_j) \leftarrow \Gamma.\mathcal{A}(X, q_j)$ be the correct answer. Let $z_\ell = \Pi.\mathcal{R}(v_\ell, \mathsf{aux}_\ell, (a_1^\ell, a_2^\ell, \ldots, a_k^\ell))$ for all $\ell \in [m]$ and let $\alpha = \Pi.\mathcal{R}(i, \bar{\mathsf{aux}}, (\alpha_1, \alpha_2, \ldots, \alpha_k))$. We have $\alpha = x_i$ since Π is correct. The correctness of Γ implies that

$$\mathsf{MTVer}\left(h_{\mathrm{Root}}, i, \alpha, (z_1, z_2, \ldots, z_m)\right) = 1. \tag{5}$$

1. The adversary $\mathcal{B}$ chooses a database x and an index i, then outputs (x, i).
2. The challenger computes $(\mathsf{Tag}, X) \leftarrow \Gamma.\mathcal{G}(x, \lambda)$ and $(q_1, q_2, \ldots, q_k, \mathsf{aux}) \leftarrow \Gamma.\mathcal{Q}(i)$, where $\mathsf{Tag} = h_{\mathsf{Root}}$ and $\mathsf{aux} = (\{\mathsf{aux}_\ell\}_{\ell=1}^m, \bar{\mathsf{aux}}, \varrho(i))$. For all $\ell \in [m], v_\ell$ is the ℓ-th element of $v(i)$. It gives $(X, \{q_j\}_{j=1}^k)$ to $\mathcal{B}$.
3. The adversary $\mathcal{B}$ chooses k answers $\{\breve{a}_j\}_{j=1}^k$, where $\breve{a}_j = (\breve{a}_j^1, \breve{a}_j^2, \ldots, \breve{a}_j^m, \breve{\alpha}_j)$ for all $j \in [k]$, and gives them to the challenger.
4. The challenger executes $\Gamma.\mathcal{R}(\mathsf{Tag}, i, \mathsf{aux}, (\breve{a}_1, \breve{a}_2, \ldots, \breve{a}_k))$ and learns its output $\breve{y}$.
5. If $\breve{y} \notin \{x_i, \bot\}$, then $\mathsf{EXP}_{\mathcal{B},\Gamma}^{\mathsf{Ver}}(T, \lambda)$ is defined as 1; $\mathsf{EXP}_{\mathcal{B},\Gamma}^{\mathsf{Ver}}(T, \lambda) = 0$ otherwise.

Fig. 5. Experiment $\mathsf{EXP}_{\mathcal{B},\Gamma}^{\mathsf{Ver}}(T, \lambda)$

For all $\ell \in [m]$, let $\breve{\gamma}_\ell$ (resp. γ_ℓ) be the value of the ℓ-th node on the path from the root to the i-th leaf that is computed with (4) (resp. (5)), then

$$\begin{cases} \gamma_\ell = \mathsf{H}(z_{m+1-\ell} \| \gamma_{\ell-1}), \\ \breve{\gamma}_\ell = \mathsf{H}(\breve{z}_{m+1-\ell} \| \breve{\gamma}_{\ell-1}), \end{cases} \text{ or } \begin{cases} \gamma_\ell = \mathsf{H}(\gamma_{\ell-1} \| z_{m+1-\ell}), \\ \breve{\gamma}_\ell = \mathsf{H}(\breve{\gamma}_{\ell-1} \| \breve{z}_{m+1-\ell}), \end{cases} \quad (6)$$

for every $\ell \in [m]$. It follows that $\breve{\gamma}_m = h_{\mathsf{Root}} = \gamma_m$. If $(\breve{z}_1, \breve{\gamma}_{m-1}) \neq (z_1, \gamma_{m-1})$, then (6) indicates that either $(\breve{z}_1 \| \breve{\gamma}_{m-1}, z_1 \| \gamma_{m-1})$ or $(\breve{\gamma}_{m-1} \| \breve{z}_1, \gamma_{m-1} \| z_1)$ will be a collision of H. Otherwise, $\breve{\gamma}_{m-1} = \gamma_{m-1}$. With a similar argument, a collision of H of the form $(\breve{z}_2 \| \breve{\gamma}_{m-2}, z_2 \| \gamma_{m-2})$ or $(\breve{\gamma}_{m-2} \| \breve{z}_2, \gamma_{m-2} \| z_2)$, or $\breve{\gamma}_{m-2} = \gamma_{m-2}$ will be found. In general, we may find an index $1 < \ell' \leq m$ such that H has a collision being $(\breve{z}_{m+1-\ell'} \| \breve{\gamma}_{\ell'-1}, z_{m+1-\ell'} \| \gamma_{\ell'-1})$ or $(\breve{\gamma}_{\ell'-1} \| \breve{z}_{m+1-\ell'}, \gamma_{\ell'-1} \| z_{m+1-\ell'})$, or $\breve{\gamma}_1 = \Gamma_1$. If $\breve{\gamma}_1 = \Gamma_1$, then here comes $\mathsf{H}(\breve{z}_m \| \breve{\alpha}) = \mathsf{H}(z_m \| x_i)$ or $\mathsf{H}(\breve{\alpha} \| \breve{z}_m) = \mathsf{H}(x_i \| z_m)$. Either $(\breve{z}_m \| \breve{\alpha}, z_m \| x_i)$ or $(\breve{\alpha} \| \breve{z}_m, x_i \| z_m)$ will be a collision of H, as $\breve{\alpha} \neq x_i$.

The above process shows that when $\mathsf{EXP}_{\mathcal{B},\Gamma}^{\mathsf{Ver}}(T, \lambda) = 1$, we can always find a collision of H. That is, there is a PPT algorithm that uses $\mathcal{B}$ to find a collision with probability $\geq \Pr[\mathsf{EXP}_{\mathcal{B},\Gamma}^{\mathsf{Ver}}(T, \lambda) = 1] = \epsilon(\lambda)$, which is non-negligible in λ. Therefore, the assumption is incorrect and the cd-PIR protocol Γ is k-secure when H is collision-resistant. □

5   Performance Evaluation

In this section, we instantiate the transformation of Sect. 4 with both multi-server PIR and single-server PIR protocols from the literature, and evaluate the obtained cd-PIR protocols with implementations in C++ with the FLINT library. We measure the computational performance of these protocols on the Ubuntu 20.04 with 64GB RAM and 6-cores 4.00GHz Intel(R) Xeon(R) E-2286G CPU made by GenuineIntel. The hash function H is chosen as SHA-256.

5.1   Multi-Server cd-PIR Protocol Γ_{WY}

By applying the transformation of Sect. 4 to the t-private k-server PIR protocol $\Pi_{\mathsf{WY}} = (\mathcal{Q}_{\mathsf{WY}}, \mathcal{A}_{\mathsf{WY}}, \mathcal{R}_{\mathsf{WY}})$ in [30], we obtain a cd-PIR protocol $\Gamma_{\mathsf{WY}} =$

$(\mathcal{G}, \mathcal{Q}, \mathcal{A}, \mathcal{R}, \mathcal{U})$. As the communication complexity of Π_{WY} is $O(\frac{k^2}{t} \log k \, n^{\lfloor \frac{2k-1}{t} \rfloor})$ for a database $x \in (0,1)^n$. For the database $x \in ((0,1)^w)^n$, the communication complexity of using our cd-PIR protocol to retrieve a w-bit block from x is

$$\mathsf{CC}_{\Gamma_{WY}}(n) = O(2n^{1/\lfloor \frac{2k-1}{t} \rfloor}) + \sum_{\ell=1}^{m-1} O(2^{(m-\ell)/\lfloor \frac{2k-1}{t} \rfloor}) = O(2^{\lceil \log n \rceil / \lfloor \frac{2k-1}{t} \rfloor}).$$

Experimental Results. In the experiment, the database $x \in ((0,1)^w)^n$ consists of n blocks, each having w bits, and we set $(k,t) = (2,1)$ as an example to demonstrate the efficiency. We execute each protocol for 100 times and fetch the average results as the final results and the user chooses the private index randomly in each of the 100 iterations to avoid occasionality.

The Fig. 6 shows the comparison of computation time of the cd-PIR protocol Γ_{WY} and the PIR protocol Π_{WY}. In order to achieve the verification compared with the underlying PIR protocol, the cd-PIR protocol needs to spend some extra time, even so, the computation time should not be too large, and it should be almost linear with the computation time of the underlying PIR protocol. The experimental results show that the server's computation time in Γ_{WY} is no more than 3 times of that in the PIR protocol Π_{WY}, and the user's computation time in Γ_{WY} is about 6 to 7 times longer than that of Π_{WY}, which are in good agreement with our analysis.

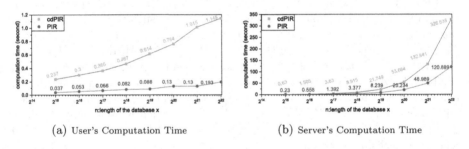

(a) User's Computation Time   (b) Server's Computation Time

Fig. 6. Comparison of Computation Time between Γ_{WY} and Π_{WY}

5.2 Single-Server cd-PIR Protocol Γ_{SL}

The single-server PIR protocol [2] $\Pi_{SL} = (\mathcal{Q}_{SL}, \mathcal{A}_{SL}, \mathcal{R}_{SL})$ uses the Microsoft SEAL homomorphic library [27], based on the Fan-Vercauteren(FV) cryptosystem. The user sends d ciphertexts containing the information of the desired index as queries, the server expands them into ciphertext vectors by a homomorphic method to work out the answer.

By applying the PIR protocol Π_{SL}, we get a single-server cd-PIR protocol $\Gamma_{SL} = (\mathcal{G}, \mathcal{Q}, \mathcal{A}, \mathcal{R}, \mathcal{U})$. The communication complexity of Π_{SL} is $O(Nd\lceil \sqrt[d]{n}/N \rceil)$ for a database $x \in (0,1)^n$, where d is the number of the ciphertext tuple and N decides size of the ciphertexts, as ciphertexts consist of polynomials in $R_q = $

$\mathbb{Z}_q[x] \setminus (x^N + 1)$. So the communication complexity of retrieving any w-bit block from $x \in ((0,1)^w)^n$ is computed as

$$\mathsf{CC}_{\Gamma_{\mathrm{SL}}}(n) = 2O(Nd\lceil \sqrt[d]{n}/N \rceil) + \sum_{\ell=1}^{m-1} O(Nd\lceil 2^{\lceil \log n \rceil / d}/N \rceil) = O(Nd\lceil \sqrt[d]{n}/N \rceil).$$

Experimental Results. In the experiment, the database $x \in ((0,1)^w)^n$ consists of n blocks, each having w bits. We execute each protocol for 100 times and fetch the average results as the final results and the user chooses the private index randomly in each of the 100 iterations to avoid occasionality.

The Fig. 7 shows the comparison of computation time of the cd-PIR protocol Γ_{SL} and the PIR protocol Π_{SL}. In order to achieve the verification compared with the underlying PIR protocol, the cd-PIR protocol needs to spend some extra time, even so, the computation time should not be too large, and it should be almost linear with the computation time of the underlying PIR protocol. The experimental results show that the server's computation time in Γ_{SL} is around 3 times of that in the PIR protocol Π_{SL}, and the user's computation time in Γ_{SL} is around 15 times longer than that of Π_{SL}, which meets our expected analysis.

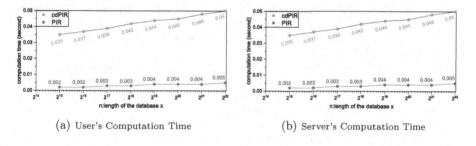

(a) User's Computation Time   (b) Server's Computation Time

Fig. 7. Comparison of Computation Time between Γ_{SL} and Π_{SL}

6   Conclusion

This paper initiated the fundamental problem of cheating detection for PIR protocol and introduced a new variant of PIR, *cheating detection* for PIR (cd-PIR). It also demonstrated the impossibility of the information-theoretic cd-PIR protocol and the inevitability of the database owner in the computational cd-PIR protocol, to justify the cd-PIR model.

With the Merkle tree, we proposed a construction that enables any PIR protocol to be transformed into a cd-PIR protocol. Moreover, our proposed cd-PIR protocol can be resistant to quantum attacks, as the security is derived from the collision resistance of the hash function. We further implemented two cd-PIR protocols obtained by the transformation. For the multi-server setting, the experiment results display the efficient computation and the practicality compared with the existing multi-server VPIR protocol. For the single-server setting, the cd-PIR protocol can be viewed as a VPIR protocol, the experiment results show a large scale improvements compared with the latest VPIR protocol. In addition, we pose an open question about the PIR with Byzantine servers.

Acknowledgments. The authors would like to thank the anonymous referees for helpful comments to improve the presentation of this paper.

Liang Feng Zhang's research was supported by Natural Science Foundation of Shanghai under grant 21ZR1443000 and Singapore Ministry of Education under grant RG12/19. Changlu Lin's research was supported in part by National Natural Science Foundation of China under grant U1705264. Fuchun Lin's research was supported by EPSRC grant EP/S021043/1.

References

1. Aaronson, S., Shi, Y.: Quantum lower bounds for the collision and the element distinctness problems. J. ACM **51**(4), 595–605 (2004)
2. Angel, S., Chen, H., Laine, K., Setty, S.: PIR with compressed queries and amortized query processing. In: 2018 IEEE Symposium on Security and Privacy (SP), pp. 962–979 (2018)
3. Angel, S., Setty, S.: Unobservable communication over fully untrusted infrastructure. In: 12th USENIX Symposium on Operating Systems Design and Implementation (OSDI 2016), pp. 551–569 (2016)
4. Beimel, A., Stahl, Y.: Robust information-theoretic private information retrieval. J. Cryptol. **20**(3), 295–321 (2007)
5. Cachin, C., Micali, S., Stadler, M.: Computationally private information retrieval with polylogarithmic communication. In: Stern, J. (ed.) EUROCRYPT 1999. LNCS, vol. 1592, pp. 402–414. Springer, Heidelberg (1999). https://doi.org/10.1007/3-540-48910-X_28
6. Cheng, R., et al.: Talek: private group messaging with hidden access patterns. In: Annual Computer Security Applications Conference, pp. 84–99 (2020)
7. Chor, B., Goldreich, O., Kushilevitz, E., Sudan, M.: Private information retrieval. In: Proceedings of IEEE 36th Annual Foundations of Computer Science, pp. 41–50 (1995)
8. Devet, C., Goldberg, I., Heninger, N.: Optimally robust private information retrieval. In: Presented as part of the 21st USENIX Security Symposium (USENIX Security 2012), pp. 269–283 (2012)
9. Dvir, Z., Gopi, S.: 2-server PIR with subpolynomial communication. J. ACM **63**(4), 1–15 (2016)
10. Efremenko, K.: 3-query locally decodable codes of subexponential length. SIAM J. Comput. **41**(6), 1694–1703 (2012)
11. Goldberg, I.: Improving the robustness of private information retrieval. In: 2007 IEEE Symposium on Security and Privacy (SP 2007), pp. 131–148 (2007)
12. Green, M., Ladd, W., Miers, I.: A protocol for privately reporting ad impressions at scale. In: Proceedings of the 2016 ACM SIGSAC Conference on Computer and Communications Security, pp. 1591–1601 (2016)
13. Grover, L.K.: A fast quantum mechanical algorithm for database search. In: Proceedings of the Twenty-Eighth Annual ACM Symposium on Theory of Computing. STOC 1996, Association for Computing Machinery, pp. 212–219 (1996)

14. Gupta, T., Crooks, N., Mulhern, W., Setty, S., Alvisi, L., Walfish, M.: Scalable and private media consumption with popcorn. In: 13th USENIX Symposium on Networked Systems Design and Implementation (NSDI 2016), pp. 91–107 (2016)
15. Gyongyosi, L., Imre, S.: A survey on quantum computing technology. Comput. Sci. Rev. **31**, 51–71 (2019)
16. Häner, T., Jaques, S., Naehrig, M., Roetteler, M., Soeken, M.: Improved quantum circuits for elliptic curve discrete logarithms. In: Ding, J., Tillich, J.-P. (eds.) PQCrypto 2020. LNCS, vol. 12100, pp. 425–444. Springer, Cham (2020). https://doi.org/10.1007/978-3-030-44223-1_23
17. Juels, A.: Targeted advertising ... and privacy too. In: Naccache, D. (ed.) CT-RSA 2001. LNCS, vol. 2020, pp. 408–424. Springer, Heidelberg (2001). https://doi.org/10.1007/3-540-45353-9_30
18. Khoshgozaran, A., Shahabi, C.: Private information retrieval techniques for enabling location privacy in location-based services. In: Bettini, C., Jajodia, S., Samarati, P., Wang, X.S. (eds.) Privacy in Location-Based Applications. LNCS, vol. 5599, pp. 59–83. Springer, Heidelberg (2009). https://doi.org/10.1007/978-3-642-03511-1_3
19. Kushilevitz, E., Ostrovsky, R.: Replication is not needed: single database, computationally-private information retrieval. In: Proceedings 38th Annual Symposium on Foundations of Computer Science, pp. 364–373 (1997)
20. Kwon, A., Lazar, D., Devadas, S., Ford, B.: Riffle: an efficient communication system with strong anonymity. Proc. Priv. Enhancing Technol. **2016**(2), 115–134 (2016)
21. Lueks, W., Goldberg, I.: Sublinear scaling for multi-client private information retrieval. In: Böhme, R., Okamoto, T. (eds.) FC 2015. LNCS, vol. 8975, pp. 168–186. Springer, Heidelberg (2015). https://doi.org/10.1007/978-3-662-47854-7_10
22. Mittal, P., Olumofin, F., Troncoso, C., Borisov, N., Goldberg, I.: PIR-Tor: scalable anonymous communication using private information retrieval. In: Proceedings of the 20th USENIX Conference on Security (SEC 2011), p. 31 (2011)
23. Borisov, N., Danezis, G., Goldberg, I.: Dp5: a private presence service. Proc. Priv. Enhancing Technol. **2015**(2), 4–24 (2015)
24. Roetteler, M., Naehrig, M., Svore, K.M., Lauter, K.: Quantum resource estimates for computing elliptic curve discrete logarithms. In: Takagi, T., Peyrin, T. (eds.) ASIACRYPT 2017. LNCS, vol. 10625, pp. 241–270. Springer, Cham (2017). https://doi.org/10.1007/978-3-319-70697-9_9
25. Sassaman, L., Cohen, B., Mathewson, N.: The pynchon gate: a secure method of pseudonymous mail retrieval. In: Proceedings of the 2005 ACM Workshop on Privacy in the Electronic Society, pp. 1–9 (2005)
26. National Academies of Sciences, Engineering, and Medicine: Quantum computing: progress and prospects. National Academies Press, Washington, DC (2019)
27. Microsoft SEAL (release 3.2) Microsoft Research, Redmond (2019). https://github.com/microsoft/SEAL
28. Shor, P.W.: Polynomial-time algorithms for prime factorization and discrete logarithms on a quantum computer. SIAM J. Comput. **26**(5), 1484–1509 (1997)
29. Wang, X., Zhao, L.: Verifiable single-server private information retrieval. In: Naccache, D., Xu, S., Qing, S., Samarati, P., Blanc, G., Lu, R., Zhang, Z., Meddahi, A. (eds.) ICICS 2018. LNCS, vol. 11149, pp. 478–493. Springer, Cham (2018). https://doi.org/10.1007/978-3-030-01950-1_28
30. Woodruff, D., Yekhanin, S.: A geometric approach to information-theoretic private information retrieval. In: 20th Annual IEEE Conference on Computational Complexity (CCC 2005), pp. 275–284 (2005)

31. Yannuzzi, M., Milito, R.A., Serral-Graciá, R., Montero, D., Nemirovsky, M.: Key ingredients in an IoT recipe: Fog computing, Cloud computing, and more Fog computing. In: 2014 IEEE 19th International Workshop on Computer Aided Modeling and Design of Communication Links and Networks (CAMAD), pp. 325–329 (2014)
32. Yekhanin, S.: Towards 3-query locally decodable codes of subexponential length. J. ACM **55**(1), 1–16 (2008)
33. Zhang, L.F., Safavi-Naini, R.: Verifiable multi-server private information retrieval. In: Boureanu, I., Owesarski, P., Vaudenay, S. (eds.) ACNS 2014. LNCS, vol. 8479, pp. 62–79. Springer, Cham (2014). https://doi.org/10.1007/978-3-319-07536-5_5

Anonymous Trusted Data Relocation
for TEEs

Vasco Guita, Daniel Andrade, João Nuno Silva, and Miguel Correia[✉]

INESC-ID, Instituto Superior Técnico, Universidade de Lisboa, Lisbon, Portugal
{vasco.guita,daniel.andrade,joao.n.silva,
miguel.p.correia}@tecnico.ulisboa.pt

Abstract. Trusted Execution Environment (TEE) technology like ARM TrustZone allows protecting confidential data using cryptographic keys that are bound to a specific TEE and device. However, there are good reasons to allow relocating such data from a TEE to another TEE in another device, often in a non-interactive (offline) and anonymous manner. We propose the Trusted Relocation Extension (TRX), a TrustZone-based trusted storage service enabling backup/recovery and sharing of data between TEEs in different devices. TRX works offline, without previous key exchange, and ensures the anonymity of the sender and the receiver. We present an implementation of TRX compatible with OP-TEE and its evaluation with Raspberry Pi 3 B+ devices.

1 Introduction

Trusted Execution Environment (TEE) technology has the important role of reducing the Trusted Computing Base (TCB) and the attack surface of services or functions that run inside the TEE itself [26]. The technology of this type we consider in the paper is ARM TrustZone, a security extension of ARM processors that supports two separate environments: the normal world, that runs the Rich Execution Environment (REE) software stack; and the secure world, that runs the TEE software. TrustZone provides hardware-enforced isolation to the secure world, guaranteeing that the REE has no access to the memory and resources of the REE. Something similar is offered by the Intel Software Guard Extensions (SGX) [24] and Sanctum [11], among others.

A service that can be provided by a TEE is *trusted storage*, used for storing private and confidential data, since TEEs can isolate data from the REE [17]. This protection is enforced with *cryptographic keys bound to the specific TEE and device that stores the data*. Current TrustZone trusted storage systems depend on the Hardware Unique Key (HUK) for deterministically deriving the Secure Storage Key (SSK) to protect their data. The HUK is a Root of Trust (RoT) element that is written by the manufacturer on the device's One Time Programmable (OTP) memory guaranteeing that trusted storage data is bound to the device that encrypts it. Although positive from the security angle, this binding can also be seen as a limitation.

© IFIP International Federation for Information Processing 2022
Published by Springer Nature Switzerland AG 2022
W. Meng et al. (Eds.): SEC 2022, IFIP AICT 648, pp. 449–466, 2022.
https://doi.org/10.1007/978-3-031-06975-8_26

There are good reasons to allow the *relocation of encrypted data from a TEE to a different TEE in another device*. One is when applications require sharing data with another person or system. Another is performing data backups inside the TEE and recover them later in another device, as the devices can be stolen or get broken. In both cases, data transfer is often done *offline*, i.e., in a non-interactive manner. For example, data is transferred first to a flash drive or an external disk, and only then, and when needed, to the destination device. This avoids the constraint of having the destination device connected and available when the data is transferred, which is desirable when doing backups. In addition, in several applications there is a requirement of anonymity of the sender and/or the receiver. For example, during a data transfer from a clinic to a patient, we may not want the clinic specialized in cancer to reveal that it is the source of a personal health report and who is the receiver.

The paper presents the design of the *Trusted Relocation Extension (TRX)*, a TrustZone-based trusted storage service that allows sharing and backing-up/recovering data between/in TEEs in different devices. The design goals of TRX are: (1) *DG1 Non-interactivity* – data can be transferred offline, i.e., without the need of an online handshake between source and destination TEEs, either as part of the transfer or at some initial point in time for key exchange; (2) *DG2 Anonymity* – the identities of the sender and the receiver are not disclosed in the transference; (3) *DG3 Confidentiality* – no entity other than the sender and the receiver can read the data; (4) *DG4 Integrity* – the receiver can verify if the data transferred was modified in the transference.

A few classical solutions to this problem come immediately to mind: (1) to encrypt and export the SSK using public-key cryptography (e.g., RSA or ECC) and use this key to ensure confidentiality (DG3) and integrity (DG4), but this requires the distribution of public keys in certificates, breaking non-interactivity (DG1) and possibly anonymity (DG2); (2) to encrypt and export the SSK with a password-derived key, but this requires users to memorize and share passwords, which is inconvenient and breaks non-interactivity (DG1) and anonymity (DG2); (3) to display a QR code with the SSK in a TEE-controlled display and scan it with a TEE-controlled camera, but this would bloat the TCB with much image handling software and break non-interactivity (DG1) and anonymity (DG2).

With the TRX service, each data bundle, called Trusted Volume (TV), is protected with its own secret key, the Trusted Volume Key (TVK). TRX uses a very recent cryptographic scheme, *Matchmaking Encryption* [5], to encrypt the TVK when relocating a TV. Matchmaking Encryption allows protecting non-interactive communication between two entities. It allows the sender and the receiver to impose policies that the other party has to satisfy in order to reveal the message, TVK in our case.

We implemented a prototype of the TRX service for OP-TEE that runs as a companion to Linux on a Raspberry Pi (RPI) 3 Model B+.[1] Our work is one of the first to use Matchmaking Encryption [9,33] and the first to use Matchmaking Encryption with ARM TrustZone. We implemented our own version of

---

[1] All software available at: https://github.com/vascoguita/trx.

Identitybased Matchmaking Encryption (IB-ME) as a C library (the first IB-ME library) to avoid bloating the TCB of TRX with the dependencies of the existing IB-ME prototype [5] which is implemented in Python. Our evaluation shows that the TCB overhead and time costs involved are small.

The main contributions of our work are: (1) TRX, a new solution to relocate encrypted data from a TEE in a device to another TEE in a different device, with non-interactivity (DG1), anonymity (DG2), confidentiality (DG3), and integrity (DG4), which is also one of the first schemes to leverage IB-ME; (2) the conceptual instantiation of TRX in OP-TEE and TrustZone; (3) the experimental evaluation of TRX in Raspberry Pi 3 Model B+ devices; (4) the first IB-ME library (in C); (5) a prototype of the TRX service, and a Proof of Concept (PoC) Trusted Authority that supports this mechanism.

2   Background

2.1   ARM TrustZone

A physical core of a TrustZone-enabled processor is divided into two virtual cores [2]: the normal world that hosts the REE, where the main Operating System (OS)and the untrusted applications run; the secure world that hosts the TEE, where the trusted software runs. These worlds are isolated from each other, with independent memory address spaces and different privileges, in such a way that applications running in the secure world can access memory regions associated with the normal world, but not the opposite [26]. The context switch between worlds is handled by the *Secure Monitor* (that runs in Monitor Mode) that is responsible for preserving the state of the current world and restoring the state of the world being switched to; and the processor that switchs from the normal world to the secure world when some process calls the Secure Monitor Call (SMC) instruction or a hardware exception is raised.

In a TrustZone-enabled device, the DRAM is partitioned into *Secure* and *Non-Secure* regions, with the assistance of the TrustZone Address Space Controller (TZASC). Peripherals can be reserved for exclusive secure world use by the TrustZone Protection Controller (TZPC). This feature can be used to implement a Trusted User Interface (TUI) [21] to allow users to interact directy with the TEE.

Trusted Applications (TAs), also called truslets [26,28], are programs that perform sensitive operations in the TEE, therefore isolated from the REE. REE applications perform requests to a TA using the TEE Client API. This API puts the request in a message buffer and calls the SMC instruction, which passes the control to the secure world. Then, the trusted kernel invokes the requested TA, which takes the request from the message buffer. After executing the requested operation, the TA responds to the REE application using the same buffer.

The trustworthiness of a TrustZone-based TEE software stack depends on its Chain of Trust (CoT) [4]. The CoT starts with two implicitly trusted components of the Trusted Board Boot (TBB) sequence [3]: (1) The hash of the Root of Trust Public Key (ROTPK), stored on the System-on-a-Chip (SoC)'s OTP memory.

The Root of Trust Private Key (ROTRK) is property of the Original Equipment Manufacturer (OEM); and (2) the AP ROM Bootloader (BL1) image stored on the Application Processor (AP) Trusted ROM. At power on, BL1 executes and validates Trusted Boot Firmware (BL2) that does the same with three Third Stage Bootloader (BL3x) images.

The HUK is another important RoT element. The HUK is a per-device unique symmetric key generated by the OEM and written to the SoC's OTP memory [4]. The HUK is accessible only inside the secure world and is used to derive other keys, providing the TEE with seal and unseal primitives [35]. The Unique SoC Identifier (SoC_ID) [3] is calculated from the HUK and the ROTPK with:

$$SoC\_ID = SHA\text{-}256(ROTPK \parallel AES_{HUK}(Fixed\ Pattern))$$

2.2 Cryptographic Schemes

In *Matchmaking Encryption* [5], there is a sender that sends a message to a receiver. The sender and the receiver agree on policies the other must satisfy to reveal the message. A message is revealed when a *match* occurs, i.e., when the sender's attributes satisfy the policies established by the receiver and the receiver's attributes satisfy the policies established by the sender.

Matchmaking Encryption assures that during message decryption no information about the parties' policies is leaked beyond the fact that a match did or did not occur, namely which policy failed when there is a mismatch, therefore preserving sender and receiver anonymity (DG2). Furthermore, Matchmaking Encryption is non-interactive (DG1), meaning that the communicating parties do not need to be online at the same time to authenticate to each other or to exchange data.

In TRX we use a construction of Matchmaking Encryption called Identity-based Matchmaking Encryption. In IB-ME access policies are simply bit-strings that represent identities. Therefore, an attribute $x \in \{0,1\}^*$ only satisfies the access policy $\mathbb{A}$ if $\mathbb{A} = x$, i.e., the sender s and the receiver r just specify a single identity in place of general policies.

In relation to Matchmaking Encryption, the decryption algorithm of IB-ME does not require a decryption key $DK_{\mathbb{S}}$ associated with a policy $\mathbb{S}$ chosen by the receiver and satisfied by the sender's attributes. This not only simplifies this Matchmaking Encryption construction, but also makes it more scalable since a receiver does not have to request different $DK_{\mathbb{S}}$, from the Trusted Authority, for different senders. Notice that this does not ensure the anonymity of the sender to the receiver after the ciphertext has been decrypted, since a successful decryption implies that the receiver specified the sender's identity string; however, this is not a requirement of our anonymity property (see the definition of DG2).

IB-ME relies on a Trusted Authority that yields a Master Public Key (MPK) and a Master Secret Key (MSK) generated by a *Setup* function on input 1^λ, where $\lambda \in \mathbb{N}$ is the security parameter: $(MPK, MSK) \leftarrow Setup(1^\lambda)$. The MPK is published, and both the sender and the receiver have access to it.

The encryption key EK_s, associated with the sender identity s, is generated by the Trusted Authority with an *SKGen* function: $EncryptionKey(EK)_s \leftarrow$

$SKGen(SKGen(MSK, s)$. Afterwards, EK_s is sent to the sender s. In a similar manner, the decryption key DK_r, associated with the receiver identity r, is generated by the Trusted Authority with a $RKGen$ function: $DecryptionKey(DK_r \leftarrow RKGen(MPK, MSK, r)$. The DK_r key is sent to the receiver r, e.g., by the Trusted Authority.

Having the encryption key EK_s, the sender s can encrypt a message m specifying the receiver identity r' as an access policy resulting in a ciphertext c: $c \leftarrow Enc_{\text{IB-ME}}(MPK, EK_s, r', m)$. Upon receiving the ciphertext c, the receiver r can try to decrypt it with the decryption key DK_r and specifying the sender identity s': $m' \leftarrow Dec_{\text{IB-ME}}(MPK, DK_r, s', c)$. If a match occurs $(r = r' \wedge s = s')$, the message is revealed $(m' = m)$. In case of a mismatch $(r \neq r' \vee s \neq s')$, the decryption function returns an error $(m' = \bot)$.

Another cryptographic scheme, *Authenticated Encryption with Associated Data (AEAD)* [27], is used to ensure confidentiality and integrity (DG3, DG4). Specifically, TRX encrypts the Trusted Volume data with AEAD. AEAD has operations $Enc_{AEAD}(K, N, P, A) \rightarrow (C, T)$ for authenticated encryption and $Dec_{AEAD}(K, N, C, A, T) \rightarrow P'$ for authenticated decryption. Enc_{AEAD} has four inputs: a secret key K, a nonce N, plaintext P and Additional Authenticated Data (AAD) A. The output consists of a ciphertext C and a tag T. P is encrypted, producing C, but A is not encrypted. T authenticates P and A. Dec_{AEAD} has five inputs: K, N, C, A and T, as above. If all inputs are authentic, P is revealed $(P' = P)$, otherwise an error is returned $(P' = \bot)$.

3   TRX: A Data Relocation Service

3.1   TRX Service

TRX is a trusted storage service for TrustZone TEEs that supports transferring TVs with Persistent Objects (POs) to the TrustZone TEEs of other devices. IB-ME is used to share and import the POs with the four properties DG1-DG4. All TRX sensitive operations are performed within the TEE; on the contrary, the REE is entrusted only with confidentiality-and-integrity-protected data. A TUI is assumed to exist for the user to grant/deny authorization.

Figure 1 shows how TRX can be used to *transfer data* (a TV with several POs) between two devices. TRX organizes POs in shareable bundles called TVs (one TV is a set of POs). Each TV is protected with a master key (TVK), then stored in a directory on the REE File System (FS). TRX shares a TV with another device by sharing both the cryptographically protected TV and its TVK. Each device has a Unique Device Identifier (UDID). The sender encrypts the TVK using the Enc_{IB-ME} function and specifying the receiver UDID. TRX imports a foreign TV by decrypting its TVK. The receiver decrypts the TVK using the Dec_{IB-ME} function and specifying the sender UDID. The transfer itself is made offline using some storage device, e.g., a flash drive.

TRX also supports the *backup and recovery* of TVs. The process is similar to the one shown in the figure with two changes. First, the receiver device is the same as the sender device. Second, the storage device is not used to transfer

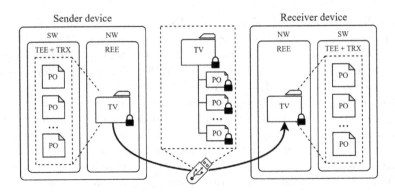

Fig. 1. Sharing a TV with TRX

the TV to the receiver device but to/from the backup device (or it can be the backup device itself).

3.2   IB-ME Use in TRX

In Identity-Based Encryption (IBE), entities obtain private keys associated with their identities from a Trusted Authority; the public key is the identity/identifier that has an application-dependent format, e.g., an e-mail address. This process involves no direct communication between potential sender and receiver participants: they only interact once with the Trusted Authority, during setup.

IB-ME, used by TRX, also allows expressing the policies necessary to decrypt the message (TVK) in terms of the identities of the sender and the receiver. With this scheme, the TVK is revealed only if the specified identities match those of the participants; otherwise, nothing is leaked, namely, the identity of the participants, so anonymity (DG2) is satisfied. The data inside a TV is encrypted with AEAD, which provides confidentiality (DG3) and integrity (DG4) [27].

In TRX, the IB-ME keys of each participant are kept protected inside its TEE, and the relocation of data between TEEs is carried out by encrypting a TVK and specifying the receiver identity. A relocated TV is imported by decrypting the TVK. Relocating and importing TVs requires no interaction between the sender and receiver devices, i.e., it can be carried out in a non-interactive way (DG1), e.g., using a flash drive or a dead drop. TRX provides an API that allows applications running in the secure world to write and read persistent data objects, and to share and import TVs.

Before sharing a TV, the system requests user authorization using a TUI (e.g., a touchscreen) such as those that extend TrustZone [7]. A TUI is a user interface controlled by the TEE and isolated from the REE [13] and provides: (1) Secure Display – information displayed to the user cannot be observed, modified or removed by REE software. TZASC and TZPC are used to switch the control of the display to the secure world and protect the display data [21]. (2) Secure Input – information entered by the user cannot be observed or modified by

REE software. The Generic Interrupt Controller (GIC) is used to register TEE interrupt handlers for the input device and isolate the control of the device from the normal world [19]. (3) Secure Indicator (optional) – indication that the displayed screen can be considered trusted by the user. An LED under exclusive control of the TEE can be used to indicate when the screen is controlled by the TEE [34].

3.3   Threat Model and Trust Assumptions

We trust the device's hardware, including the TrustZone extensions, the SoC's OTP memory and trusted ROM. We trust the OEM for securing the ROTRK, the software vendors of the TBB images for securing the secure world private key and the BL3x private keys, and the TEE software vendor for securing the TEE private key (Sect. 2.1).

The Secure Monitor and the secure world software stack are trusted. The normal world software stack, including the OS, device drivers and libraries, is not trusted. The network is also not trusted. Denial of Service (DoS) attacks issued by the REE OS or any individual with physical access to the device or its peripherals are not considered. Side-channel attacks [20] and other physical attacks that fall outside the defense capabilities of ARM TrustZone are also not considered.

The Trusted Authority is also trusted, similarly to the Attestation Service used in all SGX solutions [18], or a Certificate Authority in a PKI. We assume the assumptions of the cryptographic schemes are held, so they work as expected.

3.4   System Architecture

Figure 2 shows the architecture of a device with TRX, where grayed boxes represent new TRX components or original TrustZone components that were modified for TRX. The original TrustZone system has the following components: (1) *Trusted Kernel*: a program that provides run-time support for TAs: cross-world and cross-TA communication management, TUI management and a Kernel Managed Trusted Storage (KTS) service. The KTS implements a *hybrid setting* in which data is encrypted inside the TEE and then stored in the file system of the REE, and a *master hash* that protects this data is stored in the TEE. The trusted kernel has a driver for controlling the User Interface (UI) device leveraged for TUI; (2) TAs: TEE user-level applications. Each TA has a Unique Trusted Application Identifier (TA_ID). TAs are signed with the TEE software vendor private key and the signature covers the TA_ID. The TEE software vendor public key is embedded into the trusted kernel for authenticating the TAs; (3) Storage device: a storage device with support for rollback-protection, such as an embedded Multi-Media Controller (eMMC) device. This storage device backs the REE FS and has a rollback-protected region, such as a Replay Protected Memory Block (RPMB) partition, that is controlled by the TEE; (4) *Internal API*: an interface that exposes the core services of the trusted kernel to the TAs.

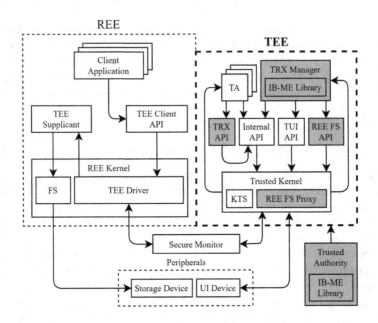

Fig. 2. Architecture of a device with TRX, plus a trusted authority

The Internal API provides functions for cross-world communication and cross-TA communication, and for accessing the KTS; (5) *TUI API*: allows the secure display of information to the user and the secure input of information from the user. The UI wields a *Secure Indicator* such as a LED, under exclusive control of the TEE; (6) *TEE Supplicant*: user-level service running in the REE that listens to requests from the TEE and performs operations on the REE FS on its behalf; (7) *TEE Client API*: allows REE applications to perform requests to TAs; (8) REE Driver: driver used by the REE kernel to handle low-level interactions with the TEE.

TRX extends the base TrustZone architecture with the following components: (1) *TRX API*: an interface that exposes the TRX *write, read, share* and *mount* functions to TAs (see Table 1); (2) *TRX Manager*: a TA responsible for managing TRX key materials, handling data encryption and decryption, and enforcing access control of TRX resources and operations; (3) *Trusted Authority*: an entity that issues IB-ME keys; (4) *IB-ME Library*: provides the IB-ME functions: *Setup, SKGen, RKGen, Enc$_{IB\text{-}ME}$* and *Dec$_{IB\text{-}ME}$*. The library also defines the IB-ME key types: *MPK, MSK, EK* and *DK*. (5) REE FS Proxy: a trusted kernel service which allows TAs to access the REE FS by forwarding FS operation requests to the TEE Supplicant; (6) *REE FS API* exposes REE FS file operation functions to the TAs.

TRX protects the POs in a device with the following types of keys: (1) TVK – a randomly generated per-TV key, used to derive the Trusted Storage Space Key. Each TVK is stored on the TV record of the TV it protects; (2)

Table 1. The trusted API of TRX

Function	Description
write (*path*, *data*)	Write data into PO
read (*path*) → *data*	Read data from PO
share (*UDID*, *mountpoint*, *label*) → (*C*, *dir*)	Share TV
mount (*UDID*, *mountpoint*, *C*, *dir*)	Mount shared TV

Trusted Storage Space Key (TSSK) – a key derived from a TVK and a TA_ID. A TSSK protects a Trusted Storage Space (TSS) within one TV. The TSSK is not persistently stored as it can be deterministically derived from the TVK; (3) Persistent Object Key (POK)—a randomly generated key for protecting a PO. PO data is encrypted with the POK and stored in the body of the PO file. The POK is encrypted with the TSSK and stored in the header of the PO file.

3.5 Workflow

TAs use the TRX API to perform the TRX operations: *write*, *read*, *share* and *mount*. The TRX Manager has an entry point for each operation. The TRX API uses the Internal API to request the trusted kernel for a *session* with the TRX Manager and to call a TRX Manager's entry point. The trusted kernel establishes the session and provides the TRX Manager with a set of client properties. This set of properties includes the client type, which may be a REE application or a TA, and the TA_ID, if the client is a TA. The TRX Manager filters each request and enforces the following access policies: (1) Only TA clients are granted access to the TRX operations; (2) The *write* and *read* entry points select the client's TSS based on its TA_ID; (3) The *share* and *mount* entry points require user authorization via TUI.

The TRX Manager persistently stores data using the KTS and the REE FS Proxy. The Internal API interacts with the KTS, whereas the REE FS API interacts with the REE FS Proxy. Each function of the REE FS API calls an Supervisor Call (SVC) function implemented in the REE FS Proxy. The REE FS Proxy sends REE file operation commands to the TEE Supplicant through a series of Remote Procedure Call (RPC) requests [29]. The TEE Supplicant performs the requested operations on the REE FS and responds. The TRX Manager encrypts the plaintext data before using the REE FS Proxy to store it to REE FS files. The KTS stores the Trusted Volume Table (TVT) which contains key materials for protecting the REE FS files. The KTS implements the *hybrid setting* (cf. Sect. 3.4), so a *master hash* of the KTS is stored to the TEE-controlled storage region. When the TRX Manager updates the TVT, the KTS updates the *master hash*, providing integrity (DG4) and rollback-protection to the TVT.

When a TA requests the *share* and *mount* operations to the TRX Manager, the TRX Manager uses the TUI API to request user authorization for the operation. The TUI API calls the SVC functions implemented in the TUI management

---

Algorithm 1. TRX Write Operation

1: **function** $write(path, data)$
2:    Get $(M, PO\_ID) \leftarrow path$
3:    Get UDID
4:    Read TVT from KTS
5:    **if** TVT has record of TV mounted on M **then**
6:       Get $(TVK, V_{TSST}, UDID_{TSST}, d) \leftarrow$ TV record
7:       Read C_{TSST} from d/f_{TSST}
8:       $TSST \leftarrow Dec_{TRX}(TVK, TA\_ID_{MGR}, V_{TSST}, UDID_{TSST}, PO\_ID_{TSST}, C_{TSST})$
9:    **else**
10:       Generate d and random TVK
11:       Initialize TSST and set $V_{TSST} \leftarrow 0$
12:       Add TV record $\leftarrow (M, TVK, V_{TSST}, UDID, d)$
13:    **end if**
14:    Get $TA\_ID_{CLI} \leftarrow$ client properties
15:    **if** TSST has TSS record for TA_ID_{CLI} **then**
16:       Get POT $\leftarrow$ TSS record
17:    **else**
18:       Initialize POT
19:       Add TSS record $\leftarrow (TA\_ID_{CLI}, POT)$
20:    **end if**
21:    **if** POT has PO record for PO_ID **then**
22:       Get $(V_{PO}, f_{PO}) \leftarrow$ PO record
23:    **else**
24:       Generate f_{PO} and set $V_{PO} \leftarrow 0$
25:       Add PO record $\leftarrow (PO\_ID, V_{PO}, UDID, f_{PO})$
26:    **end if**
27:    Increment V_{PO}
28:    $C_{PO} \leftarrow Enc_{TRX}(TVK, TA\_ID_{CLI}, V_{PO}, UDID, PO\_ID, data)$
29:    Write C_{po} to d/f_{po}
30:    Update PO record with V_{po} and UDID
31:    Increment V_{TSST}
32:    $C_{TSST} \leftarrow Enc_{TRX}(TVK, TA\_ID_{MGR}, V_{TSST}, UDID, PO\_ID_{TSST}, TSST)$
33:    Write C_{TSST} to d/f_{TSST}
34:    Update TV record with V_{TSST} and UDID
35:    Write TVT to KTS
36: **end function**

---

service of the trusted kernel. The TUI management service uses a device driver to handle low-level interactions with a UI device, such as a touchscreen.

The Trusted Authority uses the IB-ME library to generate IB-ME keys. The TRX Manager uses the IB-ME library and the IB-ME keys to encrypt a TVK when a TV is being shared, and to decrypt a TVK when a TV is being mounted.

Write is the TRX operation for inserting data in a PO. Algorithm 1 shows the procedure of the *write* operation, which has two inputs: the PO path and the plaintext data. On lines 2 to 4, the mount point M and the PO Identifier (PO_ID) are parsed from the PO path ($path = M/PO\_ID$), UDID is fetched and the TVT is read from the KTS using the Internal API.

If the TVT has a record of a TV mounted on M (lines 5 to 8), the TVK, the Trusted Storage Space Table (TSST) version V_{TSST}, the UDID of the device which wrote the TSST $UDID_{TSST}$ and the REE directory path d of the TV are read from the TV record. Then, the encrypted TSST C_{TSST} is read from the KTS file of d using the REE FS API. The filename of a TSST file f_{TSST} is a fixed string defined in the TRX Manager (e.g., *tsst.trx*). Then, C_{TSST} is decrypted with Dec_{TRX}. Dec_{TRX} receives the TVK, the TA_ID of the TRX Manager TA_ID_{MGR}, V_{TSST}, $UDID_{TSST}$, the PO_ID of the TSST PO_ID_{TSST} and

C_{TSST} as input and outputs the TSST. PO_ID_{TSST} is a fixed string defined in the TRX Manager (e.g., *"TSST"*). If the TVT has a record of a TV mounted on M (lines 9 to 12), a new TV is created and mounted on M. To create a new TV, the TRX Manager randomly generates a TVK, selects a new d, initializes an empty TSST and sets V_{TSST} to zero. Then, the new TV is mounted on M by creating a new TV record on the TVT with M, TVK, V_{TSST}, UDID and d.

Once the TSST of the TV is mounted on M, the TRX Manager uses the client's TA_ID, TA_ID_{CLI}, to find the TSS record of the client. The Internal API is used to fetch the TA_ID_{CLI} from the set of client properties provided by the trusted kernel. If the TSST has a TSS record for the client (lines 15 to 16), the Persistent Object Table (POT) of the client's TSS is read from the TSS record. Otherwise, a TSS for the client is created on the TV mounted on M. To create a TSS for the client, an empty POT is initialized and a new TSS record is created on the TSST with the TA_ID_{CLI} the new POT. Having the POT of the client's TSS, the TRX Manager queries the record of the PO with the specified PO_ID. If the POT has a record of the PO with the specified PO_ID (lines 21 to 22), the PO version V_{PO} and the filename of the PO file f_{PO} are read from the record. Otherwise, a new is created on the TSST of the client (lines 23 to 25). To create a new PO, the TRX Manager generates a new f_{PO} and sets V_{PO} to zero. Then, a new PO record containing the PO_ID, V_{PO}, UDID and f_{PO} is added to the POT.

Finally, having V_{PO} and f_{PO}, the TRX Manager encrypts the PO with TRX encryption mechanism and stores it to the REE FS (lines 27 to 29). Before encrypting the PO, V_{PO} is incremented. Then, the PO plaintext data is encrypted with Enc_{TRX}. Enc_{TRX} receives the TVK, the TA_ID_{CLI}, the V_{PO}, the UDID, the PO_ID and the plaintext data as input and outputs the encrypted PO C_{PO}. C_{PO} is written to the PO file d/f_{PO} with the REE FS API. After persistently storing the PO to the REE FS, the TSST is updated and persistently stored as well (lines 30 to 33). First, the PO record is updated with the incremented V_{PO} and the UDID. Note that the TSST contains the POT which in turn contains the PO record. Before encrypting the TSST, V_{TSST} is incremented as well. Then, the TSST is encrypted with Enc_{TRX}. Enc_{TRX} receives the TVK, the TA_ID_{MGR}, the V_{TSST}, the UDID, the PO_ID_{TSST} and the TSST as input and outputs C_{TSST}. C_{TSST} is written to the TSST file of d using the REE FS API. After persistently storing the PO to the REE FS, the TSST is updated and persistently stored as well (lines 30 to 33). First, the PO record is updated with the incremented V_{TSST} and theUDID. Note that the TVT contains the TV record. Finally, the updated TVT is stored to the KTS using the Internal API.

We omit a similar explanation for the other three operations for lack of space.

4   Evaluation

We implemented the TRX prototype as an extension to OP-TEE [30], a TEE implementation for ARM TrustZone (and Linux as REE) compliant with the GlobalPlatform specifications [14]. We extended OP-TEE with the TRX Manager TA, the TRX API, the REE FS API, the IB-ME library and the REE FS

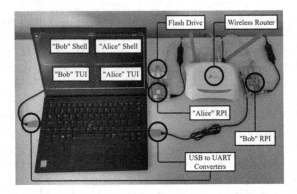

Fig. 3. TRX prototype

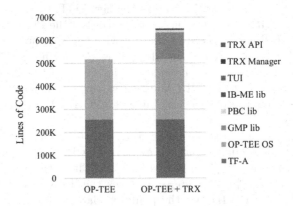

Fig. 4. Impact of TRX on the TCB size

proxy. As Secure Monitor, the Trusted Firmware-A (TF-A) implementation is used [31]. TRX was deployed on RPI 3 Model B+ boards. This is a single-board computer with a BroadCom SoC, a quad-core ARM Cortex-A53 with TrustZone, and 1 GB of RAM. The experimental setting is shown in Fig. 3.

We evaluated experimentally the impact of TRX on the TCB, the performance of IB-ME library, and the performance of the main operations.

4.1   Impact on the Trusted Computing Base

This section assesses the impact of TRX on the TCB of a TrustZone-enabled system by comparing the TCB size before and after adding our extension to a system with OP-TEE. Figure 4 shows the TCB size of the system with OP-TEE and without/with our implementation of TRX. Before adding TRX, the TCB was composed of TF-A and OP-TEE OS. After adding TRX, the TCB was composed of TF-A, our fork of OP-TEE OS (which includes the REE FS Proxy and the REE FS API), the ports of the GNU Multiple Precision Arithmetic (GMP) and Pairing-Based Cryptography (PBC) libraries, the OP-TEE IB-ME library,

Table 2. Execution time of the IB-ME functions

	Mainstream (Core i5)		OP-TEE (BCM2837B)	
Function	μ (ms)	σ (ms)	μ (ms)	σ (ms)
$Setup$	2.32	0.55	40.26	0.49
$SKGen$	3.41	0.96	67.48	0.50
$RKGen$	4.80	1.57	87.66	0.48
$Enc_{IB\text{-}ME}$	6.38	1.09	173.44	0.67
$Dec_{IB\text{-}ME}$	3.90	0.42	146.18	0.48

the TUI simulator, the TRX Manager and the TRX API. TRX increased the TCB size in 25.49%. The GMP library port is the component which increased the TCB the most (+22.38%). This last result was not unexpected as the port of this library was not optimized. A lower impact on the TCB can be achieved by shrinking our port of the GMP library, which was left for future work. Note that originally the PBC library had 65130 lines of code (LoC) and that shrinking reduced the PBC library to 9700 LoC – a reduction of 85.11%. A similar reduction might be achieved with the GMP library, reducing the impact on the TCB size from 22.38% to less than 4%. We estimate that shrinking the GMP library would drop the impact of TRX on the TCB size to less than 8%.

4.2 IB-ME Library Performance

This experiment compares the performance of the IB-ME C library, that we developed for TRX, in two environments: one with an Intel Core i5-8265U CPU and a mainstream Linux system (mainstream version); and another with a Broadcom BCM2837B0 SoC adapted for OP-TEE (OP-TEE version). The Trusted Authority uses the mainstream version and the TRX Manager uses the OPTEE version.

Table 2 shows the average execution time μ and standard deviation σ of the of the IB-ME functions for both versions of our IB-ME library. The observed timings suggest that both versions are practical for data encryption and decryption, and for key generation. The OP-TEE version takes, in average, 173.44 ms to encrypt data, thus being responsible for 98.60% of the *share* function average execution time, which is 175.90 ms. To decrypt data, the OP-TEE version takes, in average, 146.18 ms, being responsible for 39.96% of the *mount* function average execution time, which is 368.86 ms. There is a performance discrepancy between the mainstream version and the OP-TEE versions because the Intel CPU is faster. In addition, the OP-TEE version is executed on OP-TEE on a system scheduled by Linux; although the world switch is controlled by the Secure Monitor, the REE determines when the TEE is executed and when it is paused. Therefore, the IB-ME operations of the OP-TEE library take longer to finish.

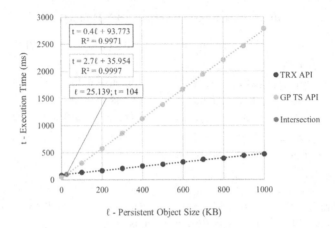

Fig. 5. Write operation benchmark

4.3 Write and Read Operations Performance

This experiment benchmarks the TRX API against the OP-TEE implementation of the GlobalPlatform trusted storage API for Data and Keys to evaluate the relative performance of TRX *write* and *read* operations.

Figure 5 shows the average time t, in milliseconds, required to write a PO of size ℓ, in kilobytes. The performance of writing POs with the TRX API and GlobalPlatform trusted storage API for Data and Keys was modeled with the linear regressions t_{TRX} and t_{OPTEE}, respectively: $t_{TRX} = 0.4\ell + 93.773$ and $t_{OPTEE} = 2.7\ell + 35.954$. The correlation coefficient R^2 of t_{TRX} equals 0.9971 and the correlation coefficient of t_{OPTEE} equals 0.9997. t_{OPTEE} has a bigger gradient than t_{TRX}, meaning that the execution time t required to write a PO of an increasing size ℓ increases at a higher rate with the GlobalPlatform trusted storage API than with the TRX API. The two lines intersect when $\ell = 25.139$, meaning that the GlobalPlatform trusted storage API for Data and Keys is faster than TRX for writing POs smaller than 25 KB and the TRX API is faster for POs larger than 25 KB.

Figure 6 shows the average execution time t, in milliseconds, required to read a PO of size ℓ, in kilobytes. The performance of reading POs with the TRX API and GlobalPlatform trusted storage API for Data and Keys was modeled with the linear regressions t_{TRX} and t_{OPTEE}, respectively: $t_{TRX} = 0.3\ell + 3.5354$ and $t_{OPTEE} = 0.3\ell + 16.175$. The correlation coefficients R^2 of both regressions equals 1 – a perfect positive correlation. Both regressions have the same gradient, meaning that the execution time t required to read a PO of an increasing size ℓ increases at the same rate with both Application Programming Interfaces (APIs). However, the TRX API is, in average, 9 ms faster to read a PO than the GlobalPlatform trusted storage API for Data and Keys.

The results show that TRX outperforms the OP-TEE trusted storage to write POs larger than 25 KB. However, the OP-TEE trusted storage duplicates

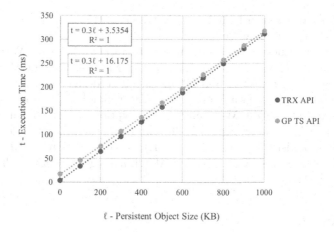

$t = 0.3\ell + 3.5354$
$R^2 = 1$

$t = 0.3\ell + 16.175$
$R^2 = 1$

Fig. 6. Read operation benchmark

all fields of its PO system to ensure atomicity while writing a PO and the TRX prototype does not ensure atomicity, which gives TRX a performance advantage over OP-TEE. Implementing a mechanism to ensure the atomicity of the TRX operations is left for future work.

TRX outperforms OP-TEE in reading POs since the OP-TEE trusted storage mechanism reads and decrypts the *dirf.db* file, which lists all files in trusted storage as well as their versions and MAC tags, before reading and decrypting a PO file whereas TRX only needs to read and decrypt the PO file itself due to optimizations in TVT and TSST.

5   Related Work

This section briefly presents the work related to TRX. The section is necessarily brief due to lack of space; many other works exist. Although several considered the use of TrustZone or TEEs for data storage [15,17,28], to the best of our knowledge, none focused on the transfer, backup, and recovery of TrustZone-protected data providing properties DG1-DG4.

Intel SGX TEEs, called enclaves, can seal data, i.e., to encrypt enclave data for persistent storage. Sealing keys are derived from a key burned into on-chip OTP memory, thus the sealed data is bound to the device [10]; therefore, Intel Software Guard Extensions (SGX) shares with TrustZone the challenge of accessing sealed data in a different device. Several enclave migration solutions for SGX use a variation of the first alternative presented in the introduction, with its limitations in terms of non-interactivity (DG1) and anonymity (DG2) [1,22,25].

There is a large literature on anonymization of communications, but unrelated to TEEs, such as Chaum's Mix-Net that hides the match between sender and receiver by wrapping messages in layers of public-key cryptography, relaying them through mixes [8]. The Tor network does something similar but with better performance and a large practical adoption [12]. Babel is a proposal for anonymity (DG2) in e-mail communications [16].

Matchmaking Encryption is a recent cryptographic scheme [5]. We only found four other works on Matchmaking Encryption: Xu et al. present Matchmaking Attribute-based Encryption (MABE) and use it to design a secure fine-grained bilateral access control data sharing system for cloud-fog computing [32]; Xu et al. present Lightweight Matchmaking Encryption (LME) and use it in the domain of distributed access control [33]; Lin et al. provide a Functional Encryption for Deterministic Functionalities (FE) [6] construction for Matchmaking Encryption [23]; recently, Certificateless Matchmaking Encryption (CL-ME) was introduced IB-ME [9].

6   Conclusion

We introduce TRX, a trusted storage mechanism that enables TrustZone-TEEs to relocate data to other TEEs with confidentiality, integrity and anonymity guarantees in a non-interactive way. TRX is one of the first systems based on Matchmaking Encryption. We implemented TRX for Raspberry Pi, obtaining a small TCB increase and a delay that is practical.

Acknowledgments. This work was supported by the European Commission through contract 870635 (DE4A) and by national funds through Fundação para a Ciência e a Tecnologia (FCT) with reference UIDB/50021/2020 (INESC-ID).

References

1. Alder, F., et al.: Migrating SGX enclaves with persistent state. In: 2018 48th Annual IEEE/IFIP International Conference on Dependable Systems and Networks, pp. 195–206 (2018)
2. ARM. ARM security technology: building a secure system using TrustZone technology (2009)
3. ARM. Trusted board boot requirements client (TBBR-CLIENT) Armv8-A. Document number: ARM DEN0006D (2018)
4. ARM. TrustZone for Armv8-A. Version 1.0 (2020)
5. Ateniese, G., Francati, D., Nuñez, D., Venturi, D.: Match me if you can: matchmaking encryption and its applications. J. Cryptology **34**(3), 1–50 (2021). https://doi.org/10.1007/s00145-021-09381-4
6. Boneh, D., Sahai, A., Waters, B.: Functional encryption: definitions and challenges. In: Ishai, Y. (ed.) TCC 2011. LNCS, vol. 6597, pp. 253–273. Springer, Heidelberg (2011). https://doi.org/10.1007/978-3-642-19571-6_16
7. Cai, Y., et al.: SuiT: secure user interface based on TrustZone. In: 2019 IEEE International Conference on Communications (ICC), pp. 1–7 (2019)
8. Chaum, D.L.: Untraceable electronic mail, return addresses, and digital pseudonyms. Commun. ACM **24**(2), 84–90 (1981)
9. Chen, B., et al.: CL-ME: efficient certificateless matchmaking encryption for internet of things. IEEE Internet Things J. **8**(19), 15010–15023 (2021)

10. Costan, V., Devadas, S.: Intel SGX explained. IACR Cryptology ePrint Arch. **2016**(086), 1–118 (2016)
11. Costan, V., Lebedev, I., Devadas, S.: Sanctum: minimal hardware extensions for strong software isolation. In: 25th USENIX Security Symposium, pp. 857–874 (2016)
12. Dingledine, R., Mathewson, N., Syverson, P.: Tor: the second-generation onion router. In: Proceedings of the 13th Conference on USENIX Security Symposium (2004)
13. GlobalPlatform, Inc. Trusted user interface API version 1.0. Document Reference: GPD_SPE_020, June 2013
14. GlobalPlatform, Inc. TEE internal core API specification version 1.1.2.50 (target v1.2). Document Reference: GPD_SPE_010, June 2018
15. González, J., Bonnet, P.: TEE-based trusted storage. Technical report, IT University Technical Report Series (2014)
16. Gulcu, C., Tsudik, G.: Mixing E-mail with Babel. In: Proceedings of the Symposium on Network and Distributed Systems Security, pp. 2–16 (1996)
17. Huang, S., Liu, C., Su, Z.: Secure storage model based on TrustZone. In: IOP Conference Series: Materials Science and Engineering (2019)
18. Intel. Attestation service for Intel software guard extensions: API documentation. Intel Corporation. Revision 6.0 (2020)
19. Lentz, M., et al.: SeCloak: ARM trustZone-based mobile peripheral control. In: Proceedings of the 16th Annual International Conference on Mobile Systems, Applications, and Services (2018)
20. Lerman, L., Bontempi, G., Markowitch, O.: Side channel attack: an approach based on machine learning. Center for Advanced Security Research Darmstadt, pp. 29–41 (2011)
21. Li, W., et al.: Building trusted path on untrusted device drivers for mobile devices. In: Proceedings of 5th ACM Asia-Pacific Workshop on Systems (2014)
22. Liang, H., Zhang, Q., Li, M., Li, J.: Toward migration of SGX-enabled containers. In: 2019 IEEE Symposium on Computers and Communications, pp. 1–6 (2019)
23. Lin, X.-J., Sun, L.: Matchmaking encryption from functional encryption for deterministic functionalities (2020). https://www.researchgate.net/
24. McKeen, F., et al.: Innovative instructions and software model for isolated execution. In: Proceedings of the 2nd International Workshop on Hardware and Architectural Support for Security and Privacy, June 2013
25. Park, J., Park, S., Kang, B.B., Kim, K.: eMotion: an SGX extension for migrating enclaves. Comput. Secur. **80**, 173–185 (2019)
26. Pinto, S., Santos, N.: Demystifying Arm TrustZone: a comprehensive survey. ACM Comput. Surv. **51**(6), 130 (2019)
27. Rogaway, P.: Authenticated-encryption with associated-data. In: Proceedings of the 9th ACM Conference on Computer and Communications Security, pp. 98–107 (2002)
28. Santos, N., Raj, H., Saroiu, S., Wolman, A.: Using ARM TrustZone to build a trusted language runtime for mobile applications. In: Proceedings of the 19th International Conference on Architectural Support for Programming Languages and Operating Systems (2014)
29. Thurlow, R.: RPC: remote procedure call protocol specification version 2. RFC 5531, RFC Editor, May 2009
30. TrustedFirmware. OP-TEE documentation (2021). https://optee.readthedocs.io/
31. TrustedFirmware. Trusted firmware-a documentation (2021). https://trustedfirmware-a.readthedocs.io/

32. Xu, S., et al.: Match in my way: fine-grained bilateral access control for secure cloud-fog computing. IEEE Trans. Dependable Secure Comput. **19**(2), 1064–1077 (2020)
33. Xu, S., et al.: Expressive bilateral access control for internet-of-things in cloud-fog computing. In: Proceedings of the 26th ACM Symposium on Access Control Models and Technologies, pp. 143–154 (2021)
34. Ying, K., Thavai, P., Du, W.: Truz-view: developing TrustZone user interface for mobile os using delegation integration model. In: Proceedings of the 9th ACM Conference on Data and Application Security and Privacy, pp. 1–12 (2019)
35. Zhao, S., et al.: Providing root of trust for ARM TrustZone using on-chip SRAM. In: Proceedings of the 4th International Workshop on Trustworthy Embedded Devices (2014)

Efficient Volume-Hiding Encrypted Multi-Maps with Support for Conjunctive Queries

Tianci Li, Jiaojiao Wu, and Jianfeng Wang$^{(\boxtimes)}$

State Key Laboratory of Integrated Service Networks (ISN), Xidian University,
Xi'an 710071, China
{tcli_134,jiaojiaowujj}@stu.xidian.edu.cn, jfwang@xidian.edu.cn

Abstract. Structured Encryption (STE), introduced by Chase and Kamara (ASIACRYPT 2010), enables to perform efficient private queries over an encrypted data structure. Very recently, Kamara and Moataz (EUROCRYPT 2019) formalized the notion of volume-hiding STE to mitigate the volume attack, and presented the first concrete volume-hiding encrypted multi-map (EMM) scheme with densest subgraph transform, which can ensure that the volume of values associated with the queried key is hidden to the adversary. To achieve better performance, Patel et al. (CCS 2019) designed a volume-hiding EMM scheme from cuckoo hash dubbed dprfMM. However, we observe that all the existing volume-hiding EMMs focus only on queries over a single key. Although the state-of-the-art conjunctive queries scheme OXT (CRYPTO 2013) can achieve sub-linear search complexity for conjunctive queries, it reveals the real volumes of the queried keys. Therefore, it is desirable to explore the volume-hiding encrypted multi-maps supporting conjunctive queries. In this paper, we initiate the study of volume-hiding EMM supporting conjunctive queries. We present, to our best knowledge, the first volume-hiding conjunctive EMM scheme OXTMM. Compared with the state-of-the-art volume-hiding single-key EMM scheme dprfMM, our proposed OXTMM can guarantee that the real volume of each key is hidden while supporting efficient conjunctive queries, the query communication overhead is 2ℓ encrypted key/value pairs together with a succinct data structure Bloom filter, where ℓ is the maximum volume of all keys. In addition, we prove the security of our proposed OXTMM and give a thorough efficiency analysis between our proposal and the existing constructions. Finally we implement OXTMM and compare it with the most efficient scheme OXT. Experiments result demonstrates that OXTMM can achieve volume-hiding conjunctive queries with a moderate efficiency loss.

Keywords: Encrypted search · Volume-hiding · Conjunctive queries

1 Introduction

Structured Encryption (STE), introduced by Chase and Karama [7], enables the data owner to outsource an encrypted data structure to an untrusted party, e.g.,

© IFIP International Federation for Information Processing 2022
Published by Springer Nature Switzerland AG 2022
W. Meng et al. (Eds.): SEC 2022, IFIP AICT 648, pp. 467–485, 2022.
https://doi.org/10.1007/978-3-031-06975-8_27

the cloud server, while maintaining the ability to access it. An STE scheme is secure if it reveals nothing about the structure and queried key beyond the pre-defined leakage. Encrypted multi-map (EMM) is a classic instance of structured encryption, which is utilized to achieve optimal search over encrypted data [2,3,5].

Searchable Symmetric Encryption (SSE), a special case of STE, is initialed by Song et al. [29] and well studied in the past two decades [2,3,6,8,18,22,30]. Among that, a line of work has focused on the attack caused by some leakages [4,14,25]. Very recently, Kellaris et al. [19] introduced a new data recovery attack via communication volume (i.e., the number of the matched documents for a query). Since then, some volume-based attacks on SSE has been presented [1,11,12,27]. To suppress the volume leakage, Kamara and Moataz [16] initialed the study on volume-hiding STE and presented the first volume-hiding EMM scheme with densest subgraph transform. To further reduce the query and storage overhead, Patel et al. [26] introduced an efficient volume-hiding EMM scheme from cuckoo hash. The main idea is to assign each key/value pair to one of the two possible positions associated with two tables of cuckoo hash and pad all remaining empty positions with dummy strings. As a result, the total storage overhead is very close to $2 \cdot (1 + \alpha)n$ while the query overhead is 2ℓ, where n and ℓ refer to the total number of key/value pairs and the maximum volume length of all keys respectively, and $\alpha > 0$. However, we observe that both the mentioned solutions focus only on a single key search.

To achieve volume-hiding EMM supporting conjunctive queries, a naive way is to perform multiple-round single-key queries in a volume-hiding EMM and obtain the intersection of queries. However, as indicated by [6], it results in too much search overhead (i.e. all the matched values associated with each queried key) and leakages (i.e. the encrypted key/value pairs associated with all the queried keys). Note that, in an ideal volume-hiding conjunctive EMM, the client always receives ℓ matched results for each query, and learns the intersection values that are satisfied with query criteria. Intuitively, we can obtain volume-hiding EMM supporting conjunctive queries from secure conjunctive keyword search SSE. To clarify our technical overview, we provide a brief sketch of the state-of-the-art conjunctive SSE OXT by Cash et al. [6]. The basic framework of OXT relies on two new data structures, i.e. TSet and XSet. TSet is responsible to retrieve all the documents matching with the least frequent keyword of a conjunctive query, while XSet is used to check whether the retrieved documents from TSet satisfy the query condition. For example, given conjunctive keys $\{key_1, key_2, ..., key_s\}$, the client will send a search token for the least frequent key (named tok_{key_1}) along with a set of intersection tokens (named $xtraps$) for the remaining keys to the server. Then, the server will retrieve the values $MM[key_1]$ associated with key_1 by tok_{key_1} in TSet. After that, the server will obtain $xtag$ by $xtraps$ and check the existence of $xtag$ in XSet to filter $MM[key_1]$ and obtain the intersection values $MM[key_1] \cap MM[key_2] \cap ... \cap MM[key_s]$. Finally, the client can receive the final matching results for the conjunctive query. Nevertheless, we argue that OXT leaks some response pattern such as the intersection of all the queried keys and the real volume of key_1, which may suffer from volume-based attacks. Thus, a natural question arises as follows:

Is there an efficient volume-hiding EMM scheme supporting conjunctive queries?

In this paper, we initiate the study on volume-hiding EMM supporting conjunctive queries. That is, the client sends a conjunctive query to the server and receives the matching results satisfying the search criterion, while the server will not learn the real volume for any key.

Our Contributions. We present, to our best knowledge, the first volume-hiding conjunctive EMM scheme OXTMM from OXT [6], which eliminates the corresponding volume leakages in OXT. More specifically, we built TSet for all keys in the style of volume-hiding to suppress the volume leakage of the least-frequent key. Note that the server in OXT can check whether the matched documents from TSet contain the remaining keys. It reveals the result pattern (i.e., the number of retrieved documents). To address this issue, we transfer the *checkability* of XSet from the server to the client. That is, the server is to only generate all the tags *xtag* for the remaining keys in a conjunctive query and send the encrypted message which contains whether the tags *xtag* exist in XSet to the client. To optimize the communication overhead, we adopt the Bloom filter, a succinct data structure, to store all the corresponding message.

To ensure the security of our scheme OXTMM, we introduce its leakage functions and then prove that the STE scheme OXTMM is volume-hiding and adaptively secure, which refers to [6,22,26]. Note that there are additional leakages from *xtrap* and *xtag*, different from [26]. Finally, we implement our proposed scheme OXTMM and OXT [6]. Compared with OXT, OXTMM can achieve volume-hiding conjunctive queries with a moderate efficiency loss.

1.1 Related Work

Structured Encryption [7], introduced by Chase and Kamara, can be widely used in outsourced encrypted data structures, such as encrypted graph [23], encrypted relational database [15]. As a special case of structured encryption, searchable encryption was intialized by Song et al. [29] and has been well-studied in terms of security [2,8,30], functionality [6,18], and performance [24].

Golle et al. [10] proposed the first conjunctive SSE scheme with linear search complexity. To achieve sub-linear SSE schemes with supporting conjunctive queries, Cash et al. [6] designed a new conjunctive SSE protocol named OXT with sub-linear search complexity, where they introduced an additional data structure XSet to store all the pairs of keywords and identifiers of documents containing them. As a result, its search complexity is only depended on the number of results matching the least frequent queried keyword. Subsequently, Lai et al.[22] proposed a primitive, called hidden vector encryption, to construct a new conjunctive SSE scheme with result pattern hiding. To further improve security in the malicious server, Wang et al. [32] developed the verifiable SSE-conjunctions scheme, which is based on the accumulator.

Another line of structured encryption is to disclose as few leakages as possible due that some "reasonable" leakages may be used to launch some leakage-abuse attacks [4,14,25]. In these years, Kellaris et al. [19] developed a novel attack for range queries by exploiting volume leakages, called volume attack. To deal with volume leakages, Kamara et al. [16] firstly discussed the volume-hiding property and then introduced the volume-hiding schemes for multi-maps. Their scheme can achieve the storage overhead $\Theta(n)$ and search overhead $\ell \cdot \log n$ by planted densest subgraph, where ℓ is the maximum volume length and n is the total number of key/value pairs in a multi-map. To reduce the storage and search overhead, Patel et al. [26] considered the volume-hiding encrypted multi-map schemes based on cuckoo hash with a stash [21] and delegatable PRF [20]. Their scheme, named dprfMM, can achieve the storage overhead $2(1+\alpha)n$ and search overhead $2 \cdot \ell$, where $\alpha > 0$ is a constant number. To enrich functionality, Ren et al. [28] introduced a volume-hiding scheme with support for range queries based on trusted hardware. After that, more and more works focus on the volume-hiding property [9,13,31].

2   Preliminaries

In this section, we briefly review the volume-hiding scheme and then introduce the detailed security definition for volume-hiding EMM.

2.1   Volume-Hiding Encrypted Multi-Maps

Patel et al. [26] presented an efficient volume-hiding EMM scheme from delegatable PRF and cuckoo hash, dubbed dprfMM, which can support asymptotically optimal storage as well as query complexity. We here recall the detailed description of dprfMM as follows:

- dprfMM.Setup(1^λ, MM): The client adopts the security parameter λ to generate private keys $K_E, K_D \in \{0,1\}^\lambda$ for IND-CPA encryption function and delegatable PRF (dPRF), $F = (F.GenTok, F.Eval)$ [20] respectively. Two cuckoo hash tables T_1, T_2 of size $(1+\alpha)n$ and a local stash are initialized, where n is the total number of key/value pairs in the multi-map and α is a constant number. After that, each key/value pair in the multi-map MM is inserted into one of two tables by cuckoo hash with a stash, and delegatable PRF is used to determine the location associated with the key/value pair (cf. Line 5–28). Note that the key/value pairs which cannot be inserted into the cuckoo hash tables after $d \log n$ evictions, are placed into the local stash. After that, each empty location in two tables will be filled with the dummy and then encrypted, while others will be encrypted. Finally, the encrypted cuckoo hash tables will be sent to the server. The private keys $K \leftarrow (K_E, K_D, Stash)$ are held in the client.
- dprfMM.Query(K, key): To perform a single-key query on key, the client generates the search token tok_{key} by the private key K and the delegatable PRF, then send it to the server.

Algorithm 1. The Construction of dprfMM

Setup$(1^\lambda, \mathrm{MM})$

1: $K_D, K_E \leftarrow \{0,1\}^\lambda$
2: $\mathrm{MM} = \{(key_i, \vec{v}_i)\}$, where $i \in [m]$
3: $T_1, T_2 \leftarrow \phi$, where $|T_1| = |T_2| = (1+\alpha)n$ and $n = \Sigma_{i \in [m]} |\vec{v}_i|$
4: $Stash \leftarrow \phi$
5: **for** $i \in [m]$ and $j \in [|\vec{v}_i|]$ **do**
6:    $count \leftarrow 0, tmp \leftarrow false$
7:    **while** $count < d\log n$ **do**
8:       **for** $t \in [1,2]$ **do**
9:          $pos \leftarrow F_{K_D}(key_i||j||t)$
10:          **if** $T_t[pos] = null$ **then**
11:             $T_t[pos] \leftarrow (i,j)$
12:             $tmp \leftarrow true$
13:             $Break$
14:          **else**
15:             $(i',j') \leftarrow T_t[pos]$
16:             $T_t[pos] \leftarrow (i,j)$
17:             $(i,j) \leftarrow (i',j')$
18:             $count \leftarrow count + 1$
19:          **end if**
20:       **end for**
21:       **if** $tmp = true$ **then**
22:          $Break$
23:       **end if**
24:    **end while**
25:    **if** $count = d\log n$ **then**
26:       $Stash \leftarrow (key_i, \vec{v}_i[j])$
27:    **end if**
28: **end for**
29: **if** $|Stash| > f(n)$ **then**
30:    $Abort$
31: **end if**
32: **for** $t \in [1,2]$ and $u \in [|T_t|]$ **do**
33:    **if** $T_t[u] = null$ **then**
34:       $T_t[u] \leftarrow Enc(K_E, \perp)$
35:    **else**
36:       $(i,j) \leftarrow T_t[u]$
37:       $T_t[u] \leftarrow Enc(K_E, key_i||\vec{v}_i[j])$
38:    **end if**
39: **end for**
40: $K \leftarrow (K_D, K_E, Stash)$
41: $\mathrm{EMM} \leftarrow (T_1, T_2)$
42: **return** $(K; \mathrm{EMM})$

Query(K, key)

1: $(K_E, K_D, Stash) \leftarrow K$
2: $tok_{key} \leftarrow F.GenTok(K_D, key)$
3: **return** tok_{key}

Reply$(tok_{key}, \mathrm{EMM})$

1: $CT_{key} \leftarrow \phi$
2: **for** $j \in [\ell]$ and $t \in [1,2]$ **do**
3:    $F_{K_D}(key||j||t) \leftarrow F.Eval(tok_{key}, j||t)$
4:    $CT_{key}[j][t] \leftarrow \mathrm{EMM}[F_{K_D}(key||j||t)]$
5: **end for**
6: **return** CT_{key}

Result(K, key, CT_{key})

1: $(K_E, K_D, Stash) \leftarrow K$
2: $R_{key} \leftarrow \phi$
3: **for** $j \in [\ell]$ and $t \in [1,2]$ **do**
4:    $(key', val') \leftarrow Dec(K_E, CT_{key}[j][t])$
5:    **if** $key' = key$ **then**
6:       $R_{key} \leftarrow val'$
7:    **end if**
8: **end for**
9: **for** $(key', val') \in Stash$ **do**
10:    **if** $key' = key$ **then**
11:       $R_{key} \leftarrow val'$
12:    **end if**
13: **end for**
14: **return** R_{key}

- dprfMM.Reply$(tok_{key}, \mathrm{EMM})$: After receiving the token tok_{key}, the server generates 2ℓ locations by delegatable PRF and then returns results (i.e. CT_{key}) associated with these locations.
- dprfMM.Result(K, key, CT_{key}): Upon receiving CT_{key}, the client uses the private key K_E to decrypt each encrypted key/value pair in CT_{key} and puts the values associated with key into R_{key}. Except that, client also needs to query key in the local stash and put the values associated with key to R_{key}. Finally, the client obtains the values R_{key} associated with the queried key.

2.2 Structured Encryption

In this section, we review definitions of structured encryption [17,26] to analyze the security of our scheme. The aim of designing an STE scheme is to protect the security of the data owner to perform operations in the third untrusted party without leaking any information about data structure beyond what we define.

Definition 1 *(non-interactive, STE for MMs). A non-interactive STE scheme $\sum_{STE} = $ (Setup, Query) is defined as following algorithms:*

- $(K, \mathrm{EMM}) \leftarrow Setup(1^\lambda, \mathrm{MM})$: *It inputs the security parameter λ as well as a multi-map MM. It outputs a private key K for the client, and an encrypted multi-map EMM for the server.*
- $\mathrm{MM}[\psi(\mathbf{key})] \leftarrow Query(K, \psi(\mathbf{key}), \mathrm{EMM})$: *It inputs the private key K, a query $\psi(\mathbf{key})$ as well as an encrypted multi-map EMM. The output is $\mathrm{MM}[\psi(\mathbf{key})]$ matching the query $\psi(\mathbf{key})$.*

In STE, the security of a structured encryption scheme is determined by two leakage functions, $\mathcal{L}_{Setup}$ and $\mathcal{L}_{Query}$. In Setup phase, a structured encryption scheme for multi-maps leaks no information about its construction beyond the leakage information $\mathcal{L}_{Setup}$. In Query protocol, the communication between the client and server leaks no information about the structure and the queries beyond the leakage information $\mathcal{L}_{Query}$. Then we move on to formally introduce the security notion.

Definition 2 *Let $\Sigma = $ (Setup, Query) be the non-interactive structured encryption scheme for multi-maps. And we consider the following experiments that $\mathcal{A}$ is a stateful semi-honest PPT adversary and $\mathcal{S}$ is a stateful PPT simulator, $\mathcal{L}_{Setup}$ and $\mathcal{L}_{Query}$ are leakage functions.*
In the real game $\mathbf{Real}_{\Sigma,\mathcal{A}}(1^\lambda)$, there are two PPT players, i.e. an adversary $\mathcal{A}$ and a challenger $\mathcal{C}$, as follow:

1. *The adversary $\mathcal{A}$ chooses a multi-map MM to send to the challenger $\mathcal{C}$.*
2. *Upon receiving the multi-map MM, $\mathcal{C}$ executes $(K, \mathrm{EMM}) \leftarrow Setup(1^\lambda, \mathrm{MM})$ to get private key K and returns the encrypted multi-map EMM to $\mathcal{A}$.*
3. *The adversary $\mathcal{A}$ adaptively chooses a polynomial number of queries $(q_0, ..., q_{ploy(\lambda)})$ to send to $\mathcal{C}$.*
4. *For each query q_i, the challenger $\mathcal{C}$ interacts with the adversary $\mathcal{A}$ by Query protocol.*
5. *After the experiment, $\mathcal{A}$ outputs a bit.*

In the ideal game $\mathbf{Ideal}_{\Sigma,\mathcal{A},\mathcal{S}}(1^\lambda)$, there are two PPT players, i.e. an adversary $\mathcal{A}$ and a simulator $\mathcal{S}$, as follow:

1. *The adversary $\mathcal{A}$ chooses a multi-map MM.*
2. *By receiving $\mathcal{L}_{Setup}(\mathrm{MM})$, the simulator $\mathcal{S}$ returns an encrypted multi-map EMM to $\mathcal{A}$.*

3. The adversary $\mathcal{A}$ adaptively chooses a polynomial number of queries $(q_0, ..., q_{ploy(\lambda)})$.
4. For each query q_i, the simulator $\mathcal{S}$ interacts with the adversary $\mathcal{A}$ by using $\mathcal{L}_{Query}(MM, q_0, ..., q_{i-1})$.
5. After the experiment, $\mathcal{A}$ outputs a bit.

The non-interactive STE scheme is adaptively $(\mathcal{L}_{Setup}, \mathcal{L}_{Query})$-secure for all PPT adversaries $\mathcal{A}$ if there is a PPT simulator $\mathcal{S}$:

$$|Pr[\textbf{Real}_{\Sigma,\mathcal{A}}(1^\lambda) = 1] - Pr[\textbf{Ideal}_{\Sigma,\mathcal{A},\mathcal{S}}(1^\lambda) = 1]| < negl(\lambda)$$

2.3 Leakage Functions for Conjunctive Queries

In this section, we review typical leakage functions for conjunctive queries schemes [6,22]. Note that a conjunctive query $\psi(\textbf{key})$ for structured encryption consists of a set of search keys, i.e. $\textbf{key} = (key_1, ..., key_s)$, where ψ is a boolean formula. Without loss of generality, we consider that each conjunctive query consists of s search keys. And we call that sterm is the first search key and xterm is the other search key in the conjunctive query. For a set of conjunctive queries $\textbf{q} = (fk, xk_2, ..., xk_s)$, there are a sequence of sterms fk as well as a list of xterms $(xk_2, ..., xk_s)$.

- **Domain Size (dsize)** : it reports the number of total key/value pairs in a multi-map MM. That is $dsize(MM) = n$.
- **Query Equality (qeq)** : it reports whether the same sterm is performed in two queries. That is a two-dimensional table M for given a set of keys, where $M[i][j] = 1$ if and only if $fk[i] = fk[j]$.
- **Response Length (rlen)** : it reports the number of values for the queried sterm in a multi-map MM. That is $rlen(MM, fk[i]) = |MM(fk[i])|$.
- **Maximum Response Length (mrlen)** : it reports the maximum number of values for a key in a multi-map MM. That is $mrlen(MM) = \ell$.
- **Result Pattern (rp)** : it reports the intersection of all the search keys in a conjunctive query. That is an array R, where $R[i] = MM(fk[i]) \cap_{j=2}^s MM(xk_j[i])$.
- **Conditional Intersection Pattern (ip)** : it reports the intersection of two different conjunctive queries. That is a four-dimensional table IM where $IM[i, j, p, q] = MM(fk[i]) \cap MM(fk[j])$ if $i \neq j, p \neq q$ and $xk_p[i] = xk_q[j]$.

Thus, the aim of our volume-hiding STE-conjunctions scheme is to eliminate the leakage of response length and result pattern.

2.4 Volume-Hiding Leakage Functions

In this section, we recall the volume-hiding leakage function, which is defined in [26]. Note that we modify the query protocol to adapt to our volume-hiding scheme with support for conjunctive queries.

Definition 3 *We consider the game* $\mathbf{VHG}_\eta^{\mathcal{A},\mathcal{L}}$ *which consists of the leakage* $\mathcal{L} = (\mathcal{L}_{Setup}, \mathcal{L}_{Query})$, *the adversary* $\mathcal{A}$, *the challenger* C *as well as a constant* $\eta \in \{0, 1\}$.

- *Given the number of total key/value pairs* n *and maximum volume length* ℓ, *the adversary* $\mathcal{A}$ *can produce two different signatures* $S_0 = \{(key_i, \ell_0(key_i))\}_{i \in [m]}$ *and* $S_1 = \{(key_i, \ell_1(key_i))\}_{i \in [m]}$ *with the same* n *and* ℓ.
- *Given two signatures* S_0 *and* S_1, *the challenger* C *randomly selects* S_η *to generate a multi-map* MM_η, *which is filled with randomly chosen key/value pairs. And then an encrypted multi-map is obtained by* MM_η. *After that, the challenger* C *sends* $\mathcal{L}_{Setup}$ *to* $\mathcal{A}$.
- *The adversary* $\mathcal{A}$ *chooses different conjunctive keys* $(\psi(\mathbf{key_1}), ..., \psi(\mathbf{key_p}))$ *for queries. And then, the challenger* C *will return* $\mathcal{L}_{Query}$ *to* $\mathcal{A}$.
- *Eventually,* $\mathcal{A}$ *outputs a bit* $b \in \{0, 1\}$.

The leakage function $\mathcal{L} = (\mathcal{L}_{Setup}, \mathcal{L}_{Query})$ *is volume-hiding when it can satisfy*

$$p_0^{\mathcal{A},\mathcal{L}}(n, \ell) = p_1^{\mathcal{A},\mathcal{L}}(n, \ell)$$

for all adversaries $\mathcal{A}$ *and* $n \geqslant \ell \geqslant 1$, *where* $p_\eta^{\mathcal{A},\mathcal{L}}(n, \ell)$ *denotes the probability that the adversary* $\mathcal{A}$ *outputs '1' during the game* $\mathbf{VHG}_\eta^{\mathcal{A},\mathcal{L}}$. *Note that the adversary can only choose the queried keys and obtain the response in the query phase.*

3   Volume-Hiding EMM Supporting Conjunctive Queries

In this section, we first give a high-level idea of our volume-hiding EMM scheme supporting conjunctive queries OXTMM. In the following, we further present it in detail.

3.1   High-Level Idea

To design volume-hiding EMM supporting conjunctive queries, our starting point is to suppress volume-related leakages information from the state-of-the-art conjunctive SSE scheme OXT. More concretely, we first need to hiding the *real* volume of the least frequent key (i.e., key_1) in a conjunctive query. To this end, what we need to do is insert a multi-map $\mathrm{MM} = \{(key, \vec{v})\}$ into the cuckoo hash tables (i.e., TSet) while padding all the remaining locations with dummies. As a result, all queries over either single or conjunctive keys will return 2ℓ search results. Furthermore, we focus on how to obfuscate the exact number of the documents that satisfy the conjunctive query condition. Specifically, recalling that the server in OXT builds an additional data structure called XSet and stores all $(key, \vec{v}[j])_{j \in |\mathrm{MM}[key]|}$ for all document identities (i.e., $\vec{v}[j]$) and key contained in $\vec{v}[j]$. By this way, the server can retrieve the final result for conjunctive query condition by checking whether $(key_i, \vec{v}[j])_{i \in [2,s]}$ in XSet. We argue that it is necessary to avoid the mentioned leakage in volume-hiding conjunctive queries setting. For this purpose, we store all $\mathrm{Hash}(K_H, key||\vec{v}[j])$ with K_H to cuckoo hash table. As a result, the server will no longer distinguish the real hash value from dummies and send all the $4\ell(s-1)$ hash values to the client. In addition, we insert all the hash values into the bloom filter to optimize the response overhead.

3.2   The Concrete Construction

Our proposed OXTMM adopts (1) the cuckoo hash with a stash, where α, d are the constants for table size and the maximum number of evictions respectively, (2) a bloom filter which consists of an array BF as well as c hash functions $\{H_q\}_{q \in [c]}$, (3) a group G with prime order p as well as the generator g, (4) hash functions h that outputs values in range $[(1+\alpha)n]$ and Hash that outputs values in $\mathcal{Y}$, (5) the PRF F_p with range Z_p^*, (6) a volume-hiding single-key scheme dprfMM [26], depicted in Sect. 2.1.

Algorithm 2. The Setup of OXTMM

Setup$(1^\lambda, \text{MM})$

1: $K_I, K_Z, K_X, K_H \leftarrow \{0,1\}^\lambda$
2: $\text{MM} = \{(key_i, \vec{v}_i)\}$, where $i \in [m]$
3: $T_1, T_2 \leftarrow \phi$, where $|T_1| = |T_2| = (1+\alpha)n$ and $n = \Sigma_{i \in [m]}|\vec{v}_i|$
4: $Stash, xlist, \text{YMM} \leftarrow \phi$
5: **for** $i \in [m]$ and $j \in [|\vec{v}_i|]$ **do**
6:     $xv \leftarrow F_p(K_I, \vec{v}_i[j])$
7:     $z_k \leftarrow F_p(K_Z, key_i||j)$
8:     $y \leftarrow xv \cdot z_k^{-1}$
9:     $xlist[i][j] \leftarrow g^{xv \cdot F_p(K_X, key_i)}$
10:     $\text{YMM} \leftarrow (key_i, \vec{v}_i[j], y)$
11: **end for**
12: $(K, \text{EMM}) \leftarrow \text{dprfMM.Setup}(1^\lambda, \text{YMM})$
13: **for** $i \in [m]$ and $j \in [|\vec{v}_i|]$ **do**
14:     $count \leftarrow 0, tmp \leftarrow false$
15:     **while** $count < d\log n$ **do**
16:         **for** $t \in [1, 2]$ **do**
17:             $pos \leftarrow h(xlist[i][j]||t)$
18:             **if** $T_t[pos] = null$ **then**
19:                 $T_t[pos] \leftarrow (i, j)$
20:                 $tmp \leftarrow true$
21:                 $Break$
22:             **else**
23:                 $(i', j') \leftarrow T_t[pos]$
24:                 $T_t[pos] \leftarrow (i, j)$
25:                 $(i, j) \leftarrow (i', j')$

26:                 $count \leftarrow count + 1$
27:             **end if**
28:         **end for**
29:         **if** $tmp = true$ **then**
30:             $Break$
31:         **end if**
32:     **end while**
33:     **if** $count = d\log n$ **then**
34:         $Stash \leftarrow (key_i, \vec{v}_i[j])$
35:     **end if**
36: **end for**
37: **if** $|Stash| > f(n)$ **then**
38:     $Abort$
39: **end if**
40: **for** $t \in [1, 2]$ and $u \in [|T_t|]$ **do**
41:     **if** $T_t[u] = null$ **then**
42:         $T_t[u] \xleftarrow{\$} \{0,1\}^{|\mathcal{Y}|}$
43:     **else**
44:         $(i, j) \leftarrow T_t[u]$
45:         $T_t[u] \leftarrow \text{Hash}(K_H, key_i||\vec{v}_i[j])$
46:     **end if**
47: **end for**
48: $K_T \leftarrow (K, K_I, K_Z, K_X, K_H, Stash)$
49: $\text{XMM} \leftarrow (T_1, T_2)$
50: $\text{EXMM} \leftarrow (\text{EMM}, \text{XMM})$
51: **return** $(K_T; \text{EXMM})$

Setup$(1^\lambda, \text{MM})$: The client takes as input the security parameter λ, and generates the private keys (K_I, K_Z, K_X, K_H). Then two cuckoo tables T_1, T_2 with size $(1+\alpha)n$ as well as a stash $Stash$ are initialized, where n refers to the total number of key/value pairs in a multi-map. Similar to the construction of OXT, the blinded value y and the tag $xtag$ will be computed and then pushed into

YMM $\leftarrow (key_i, \vec{v}_i[j], y)$ and $xlist \leftarrow xtag$ (cf. Line 5–11), respectively. Then, the client generates an encrypted multi-map EMM and a private key K by invoking dprfMM.Setup for the multi-map YMM. Note that the blinded value y is not encrypted and only stored with its relevant encrypted key/value pair in dprfMM.Setup. And each key/value pair should be put into the EMM while not in the local stash to ensure the integrity of search results for the first search key. Thus, we need to replace the way of storing into a stash with randomly reselecting dPRFs after $d \log n$ evictions in dprfMM.Setup. After that, similar to the construction of dprfMM, each key/value pair will be inserted into a location in two cuckoo tables or the local stash (cf. Line 13–36). However, the different point is that each location is determined by the $xtag$ (i.e. $xlist[i][j]$), which is constructed as in OXT. And then, each empty location in two tables will be filled with dummies, while others are hashed. Finally, the client holds the private key $K_T \leftarrow (K, K_I, K_Z, K_X, K_H, Stash)$ and sends the encrypted multi-map EXMM $\leftarrow (T_1, T_2, EMM)$.

Algorithm 3. The Query of OXTMM

Query$(K_T, \psi(\text{key}), EXMM)$

Client :

1: $(K, K_I, K_Z, K_X, K_H, Stash) \leftarrow K_T$
2: $(key_1, key_2, ..., key_s) \leftarrow \psi(\text{key})$
3: $tok_{key_1} \leftarrow \mathsf{dprfMM.Query}(K, key_1)$
4: $xtoken \leftarrow \phi$
5: **for** $j \in [\ell]$ **do**
6: $\quad \eta_{key_1} \leftarrow F_p(K_Z, key_1 \| j)$
7: $\quad$ **for** $k \in [2, s]$ **do**
8: $\quad\quad xtoken[j][k] \leftarrow g^{\eta_{key_1} \cdot F_p(K_X, key_k)}$
9: $\quad$ **end for**
10: **end for**
11: **return** $(tok_{key_1}, xtoken)$

Server :

12: $EY_{key_1}, CV_{key_1} \leftarrow \phi$
13: $(K, K_I, K_Z, K_X, K_H, Stash) \leftarrow K_T$
14: $(EMM, XMM) \leftarrow EXMM$
15: $(key_1, key_2, ..., key_s) \leftarrow \psi(\text{key})$
16: $BF \leftarrow 0^b, \{H_q\}_{q \in [c]} : \{0,1\}^{\mathcal{Y}} \rightarrow [b]$
17: $EY_{key_1} \leftarrow \mathsf{dprfMM.Reply}(tok_{key_1}, EMM)$
18: **for** $j \in [\ell]$ and $t \in [1, 2]$ **do**
19: $\quad (e, y) \leftarrow EY_{key_1}[j][t]$
20: $\quad CV_{key_1} \leftarrow e$
21: $\quad$ **for** $k \in [2, s]$ and $t' \in [1, 2]$ **do**
22: $\quad\quad xtag \leftarrow xtoken[j][k]^y$
23: $\quad\quad pos_{t'} \leftarrow h(xtag \| t')$
24: $\quad\quad$ **for** $q \in [c]$ **do**
25: $\quad\quad\quad BF[H_q(XMM[pos_{t'}])] \leftarrow 1$
26: $\quad\quad$ **end for**
27: $\quad$ **end for**
28: **end for**
29: **return** $(CV_{key_1}, BF, \{H_q\}_{q \in [c]})$

Client :

30: $(K, K_I, K_Z, K_X, K_H, Stash) \leftarrow K_T$
31: $(key_1, key_2, ..., key_s) \leftarrow \psi(\text{key})$
32: $R_{key_1}, MR_{key} \leftarrow \phi$
33: $R_{key_1} \leftarrow \mathsf{dprfMM.Result}(K, CV_{key_1})$
34: **for** $val \in R_{key_1}$ **do**
35: $\quad tmp \leftarrow true$
36: $\quad$ **for** $k \in [2, s]$ and $q \in [c]$ **do**
37: $\quad\quad xkv \leftarrow Hash(K_H, key_k \| val)$
38: $\quad\quad$ **if** $BF[H_q(xkv)] \neq 1$ **then**
39: $\quad\quad\quad$ **if** $(key_k, val) \notin Stash$ **then**
40: $\quad\quad\quad\quad tmp \leftarrow false$
41: $\quad\quad\quad\quad$ *Break*
42: $\quad\quad\quad$ **end if**
43: $\quad\quad$ **end if**
44: $\quad$ **end for**
45: $\quad$ **if** $tmp = true$ **then**
46: $\quad\quad MR_{key} \leftarrow val$
47: $\quad$ **end if**
48: **end for**
49: **return** MR_{key}

Query$(K_T, \psi(\textbf{key}), \text{EXMM})$: To perform a conjunctive query on $\psi(\textbf{key})$, the client starts to generate the token tok_{key_1} associated with the first key by invoking dprfMM.Query, and intersection tokens $xtoken$ which are constructed as in OXT. And then, the client sends $(tok_{key_1}, xtoken)$ to the server. Upon receiving search tokens $(tok_{key_1}, xtoken)$, the server randomly chooses hash functions and initializes a bloom filter of size $b = 1.44 \log_2(1/P_e) \cdot (4\ell \cdot (s-1))$, where P_e is the false probability. After that, in EMM, 2ℓ tuples (e, y) are obtained by 2ℓ locations, which are calculated by tok_{key_1} with dprfMM.Reply. In these tuples, the encrypted key/value pairs e are stored into CV_{key_1} and blinded values y are used to get $xtag$ with $xtoken$, similar to OXT. Subsequently, each $xtag$ is mapped into two locations in XMM and its corresponding hash values $\text{XMM}[h(xtag\|t')]_{t' \in [1,2]}$ are obtained. Note that the server cannot determine which hash values can meet the requirement for search keys in our volume-hiding scheme. Thus, all the hash values should be sent back to the client. In order to reduce communication cost, each hash value will be inserted into the bloom filter BF. Finally, the encrypted key/value pairs CV_{key_1} and the bloom filter BF with its hash functions $\{H_q\}_{q \in [c]}$ will be sent to the client. After receiving search results for the conjunctive query, the client will get values val associated with the first search key in CV_{key_1} by invoking dprfMM.Result. Next, the client will generate hash values for the value val with the other search keys. Finally, its all hash values will be tested whether they exist in the bloom filter BF or their key/value pairs exist in the local stash $Stash$. If they can satisfy either of these two requirements, val will be put into MR_{key}. And the client obtains intersection results MR_{key} for all queried keys.

3.3 Security Analysis

To analyze the security of our scheme OXTMM, we depict its leakage $\mathcal{L} = (\mathcal{L}_{Setup}, \mathcal{L}_{Query})$. In the setup phase, it reveals the number of total key/value pairs because of $2(1 + \alpha)n$ encrypted key/value pairs and blinded values as well as hash values respectively, i.e. $\mathcal{L}_{Setup} = dsize(\text{MM}) = n$. For queries in an encrypted multi-map, it reveals the query equality and maximum volume length because of observing the search token and search results. Except that, conditional intersection pattern is also leaked, i.e. $\mathcal{L}_{Query} = (qeq, mrlen, ip)$.

To show the security of OXTMM, it requires to prove that our scheme OXTMM is adaptively $\mathcal{L}$-secure and has the volume-hiding property, where $\mathcal{L} = (\mathcal{L}_{Setup}, \mathcal{L}_{Query})$ is the leakage function for setup and query phases. Thus, there are two parts for the security proof, described below:

Theorem 1 *For constants $\alpha > 0$ and $f(n) = \omega(1)$, the STE scheme OXTMM is adaptively $\mathcal{L}$-secure for multi-maps, where $\mathcal{L} = (dsize, (qeq, mrlen, ip))$.*

Proof. To prove that OXTMM is adaptively secure, we construct a simulator which consists of Setup and Query, shown in Algorithm.4. For all adversaries $\mathcal{A}$, we prove that the probability the real game $\textbf{Real}_{\Sigma, \mathcal{A}}(1^\lambda)$ outputs '1' can be negligibly different from the probability the ideal game $\textbf{Ideal}_{\Sigma, \mathcal{A}, \mathcal{S}}(1^\lambda)$ outputs '1', where Σ is the OXTMM scheme and $\mathcal{S}$ is a simulator. Because our scheme

Algorithm 4. Simulator of OXTMM

$\mathcal{S}.\text{SimSetup}(1^{\lambda}, dsize)$

1: $n \leftarrow dsize$
2: $t_s = 2 \cdot (1 + \alpha) \cdot n$
3: $\text{EMM}, \text{XMM} \leftarrow \phi$, with the same size t_s
4: **for** $i = 0$ **to** t_s **do**
5:     $e \xleftarrow{\$} \{0,1\}^{\lambda}$
6:     $y \xleftarrow{\$} Z_p^*$
7:     $\text{EMM}[i] \leftarrow (e, y)$
8:     $\text{XMM}[i] \xleftarrow{\$} \{0,1\}^{\lambda}$
9: **end for**
10: $\text{EXMM} \leftarrow (\text{EMM}, \text{XMM})$
11: **return** $(\perp, \text{EXMM})$

$\mathcal{S}.\text{SimQuery}(1^{\lambda}, qeq, mrlen, ip)$

1: $Using\ qeq(\psi(\textbf{key}_1), ..., \psi(\textbf{key}_j))\ to\ analyze$
    $\psi(\textbf{key}_j)$
2: $key_{j,1}, ..., key_{j,s} \leftarrow \psi(\textbf{key}_j)$
3: **for** $i = 1$ **to** $j - 1$ **do**
4:     $key_{i,1}, ..., key_{i,s} \leftarrow \psi(\textbf{key}_i)$
5:     **if** $key_{i,1} = key_{j,1}$ **then**
6:         $State[\psi(\textbf{key}_j)][key_{j,1}]$ $\leftarrow$
    $State[\psi(\textbf{key}_i)][key_{i,1}]$
7:         **for** $k = 2$ **to** s **do**
8:             **if** $key_{j,k} \in \psi(\textbf{key}_i)$ **then**
9:                 $State[\psi(\textbf{key}_j)][key_{j,k}]$ $\leftarrow$
    $State[\psi(\textbf{key}_i)][key_{j,k}]$
10:            **end if**
11:        **end for**
12:    **end if**
13: **end for**
14: **if** $State[\psi(\textbf{key}_j)][key_{j,1}] = null$ **then**
15:    $State[\psi(\textbf{key}_j)][key_{j,1}] \xleftarrow{\$} \{0,1\}^{\lambda}$
16: **end if**
17: **for** $k = 2$ **to** s **do**
18:    **if** $State[\psi(\textbf{key}_j)][key_{j,k}] = \phi$ **then**
19:        $(r_1, ..., r_\ell) \xleftarrow{\$} G$
20:        $State[\psi(\textbf{key}_j)][key_{j,k}] \leftarrow (r_1, ..., r_\ell)$
21:    **end if**
22: **end for**
23: **return** $(State, State[\psi(\textbf{key}_j)])$

OXTMM is based on dprfMM, the security proof of OXTMM is similar to that of dprfMM [26]. Details can be found as below:

– $Game_0$ is identical to $\textbf{\textit{Real}}_{\Sigma,\mathcal{A}}(1^{\lambda})$.
– $Game_1$ replaces the PRF with a random function.
– $Game_2$ replaces the blinded values and tags with random values.
– $Game_3$ removes the cuckoo hash algorithm from OXTMM.Setup.
– $Game_4$ replaces the hash functions with random functions.
– $Game_5$ replaces the encryption function Enc in dprfMM.Setup with a random function.
– $Game_6$ replaces the outputs of random functions with uniformly picked random values.
– $Game_7$ replaces the dPRF in dprfMM with a random function.

Note that $Game_0$ and $Game_1$ are hardly distinguished by the security of PRFs. $Game_1$ and $Game_2$ are based on Diffie-Hellman assumption. $Game_2$ and $Game_3$ can be distinguished with negligible probability when $f(n) = \omega(1)$ in cuckoo hash with a stash. $Game_3$ and $Game_4$ are indistinguishable, based on the security of hash functions. $Game_4$ and $Game_5$ are computed indistinguishable by the security of encryption schemes. $Game_5$ and $Game_6$ are distinguished with negligible probability because of the outputs of identical distributions. $Game_6$ and $Game_7$ are computed indistinguishable by the security of dPRF [20]. Finally, we can obtain $Game_7$, which is identical to $\textbf{\textit{Ideal}}_{\Sigma,\mathcal{A},\mathcal{S}}(1^{\lambda})$.

Theorem 2 *The leakage function* $\mathcal{L} = (dsize, (qeq, mrlen, ip))$ *for the STE scheme OXTMM is volume-hiding.*

Proof. To prove that the leakage function $\mathcal{L} = (dsize, (qeq, mrlen, ip))$ for OXTMM is volume-hiding, the adversary constructs two multi-map signatures of the same size n and maximum volume length ℓ to the challenger. And the challenger randomly chooses a multi-map signature to generate an encrypted multi-map as well as a hashed multi-map and then interacts with the adversary. In OXTMM scheme, the setup leakage $\mathcal{L}_{Setup}$ consists of data size $dsize(\text{MM}) = n$. As for the query leakage $\mathcal{L}_{Query}$, it consists of the maximum volume length $mrlen(\text{MM}) = \ell$ as well as query equality qeq and conditional intersection pattern ip . Note that the leakage of data size $dsize$ as well as maximum volume length $mrlen$ are identical in two multi-map signatures, and query equality qeq is independent of the construction of a multi-map. As for conditional intersection pattern, it is only leaked to the challenger but not to the adversary. For a conjunctive query, there are two kinds of tokens to send to the challenger. The one is a token associated with the first search key, which is used to retrieve 2ℓ encrypted key/value pairs to realize volume-hiding. It is identical to dprfMM [26]. And the others are $\ell \cdot (s-1)$ intersection tokens, which are used to retrieve a bloom filter. And the bloom filter always contains $4(s-1)\ell$ values which are independent of the volume of any key for hiding result pattern. Thus, the volume of all the queried keys can be hidden. Consequently, we can obtain that OXTMM is a volume-hiding scheme.

3.4   Efficiency Analysis

In this section, we theoretically compare our scheme OXTMM with the traditional conjunctive queries scheme (i.e. OXT) and volume-hiding scheme (i.e. dprfMM) in terms of server storage, token complexity, query complexity and functionality.

Table 1. Efficiency and functionality comparison

STE scheme	Server storage	Token complexity	Response complexity	Volume-hiding	Conjunctive queries
OXT [6]	$st \cdot m + (ev + y + x)n$	$tk + (s-1)\ell(key)xt$	$\ell(\psi(\mathbf{key}))ev$	✗	✓
dprfMM [26]	$2ekv(1+\alpha)n$	tk	$2\ell \cdot ekv$	✓	✗
OXTMM	$2(ekv+y+h)(1+\alpha)n$	$tk + (s-1)\ell \cdot xt$	$2\ell \cdot ekv + BF(s,\ell)$	✓	✓

st: the stag in TSet; ev: an encrypted value; ekv: an encrypted key/value pair; y: the blinded value; x: the xtag in XSet; h: the hash value; m: the number of total keys; n: the number of total key/value pairs; tk: a search token; xt: the intersection tokens; s: the number of conjunctive keys; ℓ: the maximum volume length; $\ell(key)$: the volume length associated with the key; $\psi(\mathbf{key})$: conjunctive search keys; α: a constant for cuckoo hash, where $\alpha > 0$; $BF(s,\ell)$: a bloom filter which contains $4\ell(s-1)$ values.

For server storage, it exists the extra values to perform auxiliary calculations in an STE-conjunctions scheme while the dummy values to pad in a volume-hiding scheme. Thus, in a volume-hiding scheme with support for conjunctive queries, it is necessary to add some extra and dummy values, which leads to much storage overhead but is indispensable. For token complexity, there is only one token in a volume-hiding single-key query while some additional intersection tokens for maintaining the privacy of other search keys in a conjunctive query. To perform conjunctive queries, our scheme also needs intersection tokens which are similar to an SSE-conjunctions scheme. The difference is that the volume length of the first search key should be hidden, which causes many tokens in our scheme. For response complexity, it only returns the intersection values associated with all search keys in a conjunctive query while 2ℓ values in a volume-hiding single-key query. To achieve the volume-hiding property, it is inevitable to pad dummy values to maintain the same length in each query, which leads to more query overhead than previous SSE-conjunctions schemes. And to suppress result pattern, auxiliary values will be sent to the client to filter out the real values for all search keys in a conjunctive query, which results in some expenses for response complexity. In our scheme, there is some extra overhead, which is needed for achieving volume-hiding and conjunctive queries.

4   Performance Evaluation

In this section, we compare the performance of our proposed scheme OXTMM with the SSE-conjunctions scheme OXT [6]. We firstly describe the setup for two experiments and then evaluate the overhead of setup and query phase.

4.1   Experiment Setup

We evaluate the performance of our scheme by adopting the same machine for the players, i.e. the client and the server. The experimental machine is equipped with Ubuntu PC operating system, Core(TM) i9-11900K and 3.50 GHz.

Parameters. In both experiments, we adopt multi-maps of size $n \in \{2^{13}, 2^{14}, 2^{15}, 2^{16}, 2^{17}\}$ with the maximum volume length $\ell \in \{2^5, 2^6, 2^7, 2^8, 2^9\}$, and the number of conjunctive search keys $s \in \{2, 3, 4, 5, 6\}$. To construct our proposed scheme, similar to [26], we choose the parameter $\alpha = 0.3$ for cuckoo hash with a stash. That is, cuckoo hash tables are filled with $2.6n$ entries. And for each insert operation, the entry will be stored into the local stash after $5 \log n$ evictions. To reach negligible false probability for the bloom filter, we choose 20 hash functions to map an entry to the filter.

Primitives. In two experiments, we implement the PRFs and hash functions by SHA-256. And we implement delegatable PRFs by constructing GGM tree [20]. For each key/value pair, it will be encrypted by AES and then a 32-byte ciphertext is obtained. For a single value, it only outputs a 16-byte ciphertext.

4.2   Evaluation and Comparison

Setup Cost: We start to evaluate the overhead of Setup phase in two schemes, which consists of storage and time overhead, shown in Fig. 1 and Fig. 2.

In OXT scheme, the storage overhead consists of two parts, i.e. TSet and XSet. Similar to OXT, the storage overhead of OXTMM is also composed of

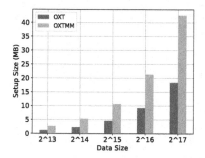

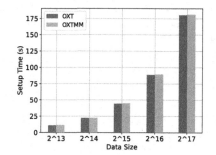

Fig. 1. Setup storage comparison   **Fig. 2.** Setup time comparison

two parts, i.e. EMM and XMM. However, the different point is that two parts in OXTMM are constructed by the idea of the volume-hiding scheme dprfMM, while TSet is constructed by inverted index and XSet is a collection in OXT. For a multi-map of size n, an encrypted multi-map of size $2.6n$ will be generated in dprfMM. Thus, our proposed scheme OXTMM needs more storage space than OXT does, shown in Fig. 1. And in the aspect of time overhead, OXTMM is slightly more than OXT, shown in Fig. 2. The reason is that, compared with OXT, the extra elements in OXTMM are constructed by SHA-256 or AES, which is much more efficient than exponential operation in both schemes.

Query Cost: In a volume-hiding STE scheme supporting conjunctive queries, there are two factors to affect the query overhead, i.e. the maximum volume length and the number of search keys. Thus, we then evaluate the overhead of query phase in these two schemes from the above two aspects, shown in Fig. 3, 4, 5 and 6.

To evaluate the impact of the maximum volume length, we select the first search key in a conjunctive query as the key with the maximum volume length and maintain the number of search keys as well as the same intersection results. Due to the increase of maximum volume length associated with the first search key, it leads to much more search token overhead in both schemes. Except for the increase of search token, it also causes much more search results and the size of the bloom filter in our volume-hiding scheme OXTMM, while not in OXT. In a volume-hiding scheme, it needs to return search results of the same volume length to avoid the volume attack. In a static multi-map, the server only returns search results of the maximum volume length. And we construct OXTMM by the volume-hiding scheme dprfMM. Thus, for query size overhead, the increase of volume length does a more impact in OXTMM than that in OXT, shown in Fig. 3. In the volume-hiding scheme dprfMM, for each single key query, it returns 2ℓ search results. Thus it needs 2ℓ blinded values y to obtain $xtags$ by exponential operations in OXTMM while ℓ blinded values y in OXT. And it can be seen that the query time overhead in OXTMM is much more than that in OXT, shown in Fig. 4.

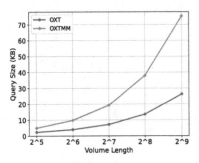

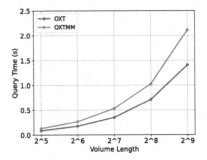

Fig. 3. Query size with volume length   **Fig. 4.** Query time with volume length

To evaluate the impact of the number of search keys, we choose the first search key as the key with the maximum volume length and maintain the intersection results. Due to the increase of the number of search keys, it also leads to the increase of search token while not affects the search results in both schemes. However, except for search results, it also returns the bloom filter which is filled with hash values associated with *xtag* in OXTMM. And *xtags* are generated by the search token *xtoken* with the blinded values y. Thus, the bloom filter is also influenced by the number of search keys. As shown in Fig. 5, the number of search keys is much more influential in OXTMM than that in OXT. As the increase of search token, it needs much more time to calculate more *xtag* by exponential operations in both schemes. Since OXTMM is based on dprfMM, it needs 2ℓ blinded values y to obtain 2ℓ *xtags* while ℓ *xtags* in OXT. Except for the time overhead of exponential operations, it also needs time to obtain $4\ell(s-1)$ hash values and insert them into the bloom filter, which does not exist in OXT. Therefore, it takes more time to perform a conjunctive query in OXTMM than that in OXT, shown in Fig. 6.

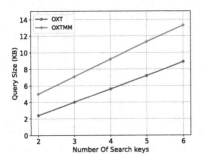

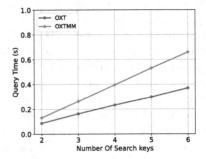

Fig. 5. Query size with the number of keys   **Fig. 6.** Query time with the number of keys

5   Conclusions

In this paper, we propose an efficient volume-hiding scheme with support for conjunctive queries, dubbed OXTMM. We start from OXT [6] and suppress leakages which may lead to volume attacks. We first replace TSet with dprfMM [26] and then return 2ℓ search results with a bloom filter which contains the corresponding intersection values. Our proposed scheme OXTMM is the first to achieve volume-hiding supporting conjunctive queries at the expense of some reasonable overhead. However, OXTMM is just suitable for static database, so how to design dynamic volume-hiding EMM supporting conjunctive queries remains a challenging problem.

Acknowledgements. This work is supported by the National Nature Science Foundation of China (No. 62072357), the Key Research and Development Program of Shaanxi (No. 2022KWZ-01) and the Fundamental Research Funds for the Central Universities (No. JB211503).

References

1. Blackstone, L., Kamara, S., Moataz, T.: Revisiting leakage abuse attacks. In: NDSS 2020, San Diego, California, USA, 23–26 February 2020, p. 1175. The Internet Society (2020). https://www.ndss-symposium.org/ndss-paper/revisiting-leakage-abuse-attacks/
2. Bost, R.: $\sum o\varphi o\varsigma$: Forward secure searchable encryption. In: Weippl, E.R., Katzenbeisser, S., Kruegel, C., Myers, A.C., Halevi, S. (eds.) CCS 2016, Vienna, Austria, 24–28 October 2016, pp. 1143–1154. ACM (2016). https://doi.org/10.1145/2976749.2978303
3. Bost, R., Minaud, B., Ohrimenko, O.: Forward and backward private searchable encryption from constrained cryptographic primitives. In: CCS 2017, Dallas, TX, USA, 30 October - 03 November 2017, pp. 1465–1482. ACM (2017). https://doi.org/10.1145/3133956.3133980
4. Cash, D., Grubbs, P., Perry, J., Ristenpart, T.: Leakage-abuse attacks against searchable encryption. In: CCS 2015, Denver, CO, USA, 12–16 October 2015. pp. 668–679. ACM (2015). https://doi.org/10.1145/2810103.2813700
5. Cash, D., Jaeger, J., Jarecki, S., Jutla, C.S., Krawczyk, H., Rosu, M., Steiner, M.: Dynamic searchable encryption in very-large databases: Data structures and implementation. In: NDSS 2014, San Diego, California, USA, 23–26 February 2014. The Internet Society (2014). https://www.ndss-symposium.org/ndss2014/dynamic-searchable-encryption-very-large-databases-data-structures-and-implementation
6. Cash, D., Jarecki, S., Jutla, C., Krawczyk, H., Roşu, M.-C., Steiner, M.: Highly-scalable searchable symmetric encryption with support for boolean queries. In: Canetti, R., Garay, J.A. (eds.) CRYPTO 2013. LNCS, vol. 8042, pp. 353–373. Springer, Heidelberg (2013). https://doi.org/10.1007/978-3-642-40041-4_20
7. Chase, M., Kamara, S.: Structured encryption and controlled disclosure. In: Abe, M. (ed.) ASIACRYPT 2010. LNCS, vol. 6477, pp. 577–594. Springer, Heidelberg (2010). https://doi.org/10.1007/978-3-642-17373-8_33

8. Curtmola, R., Garay, J.A., Kamara, S., Ostrovsky, R.: Searchable symmetric encryption: improved definitions and efficient constructions. In: CCS 2006, Alexandria, VA, USA, 30 October - 3 November 2006, pp. 79–88. ACM (2006). https://doi.org/10.1145/1180405.1180417

9. Demertzis, I., Papadopoulos, D., Papamanthou, C., Shintre, S.: SEAL: attack mitigation for encrypted databases via adjustable leakage. In: USENIX Security 2020, 12–14 August 2020, pp. 2433–2450. USENIX Association (2020). https://www.usenix.org/conference/usenixsecurity20/presentation/demertzis

10. Golle, P., Staddon, J., Waters, B.: Secure conjunctive keyword search over encrypted data. In: Jakobsson, M., Yung, M., Zhou, J. (eds.) ACNS 2004. LNCS, vol. 3089, pp. 31–45. Springer, Heidelberg (2004). https://doi.org/10.1007/978-3-540-24852-1_3

11. Grubbs, P., Lacharité, M., Minaud, B., Paterson, K.G.: Pump up the volume: practical database reconstruction from volume leakage on range queries. In: CCS 2018, Toronto, ON, Canada, 15–19 October 2018, pp. 315–331. ACM (2018). https://doi.org/10.1145/3243734.3243864

12. Gui, Z., Johnson, O., Warinschi, B.: Encrypted databases: new volume attacks against range queries. In: CCS 2019, London, UK, 11–15 November 2019, pp. 361–378. ACM (2019). https://doi.org/10.1145/3319535.3363210

13. Gui, Z., Paterson, K.G., Patranabis, S., Warinschi, B.: Swissse: system-wide security for searchable symmetric encryption. IACR Cryptol. ePrint Arch., p. 1328 (2020). https://eprint.iacr.org/2020/1328

14. Islam, M.S., Kuzu, M., Kantarcioglu, M.: Access pattern disclosure on searchable encryption: ramification, attack and mitigation. In: NDSS 2012, San Diego, California, USA, 5–8 February 2012. The Internet Society (2012). https://www.ndss-symposium.org/ndss2012

15. Kamara, S., Moataz, T.: SQL on structurally-encrypted databases. In: Peyrin, T., Galbraith, S. (eds.) ASIACRYPT 2018. LNCS, vol. 11272, pp. 149–180. Springer, Cham (2018). https://doi.org/10.1007/978-3-030-03326-2_6

16. Kamara, S., Moataz, T.: Computationally volume-hiding structured encryption. In: Ishai, Y., Rijmen, V. (eds.) EUROCRYPT 2019. LNCS, vol. 11477, pp. 183–213. Springer, Cham (2019). https://doi.org/10.1007/978-3-030-17656-3_7

17. Kamara, S., Moataz, T., Ohrimenko, O.: Structured encryption and leakage suppression. In: Shacham, H., Boldyreva, A. (eds.) CRYPTO 2018. LNCS, vol. 10991, pp. 339–370. Springer, Cham (2018). https://doi.org/10.1007/978-3-319-96884-1_12

18. Kamara, S., Papamanthou, C., Roeder, T.: Dynamic searchable symmetric encryption. In: CCS 2012, Raleigh, NC, USA, 16–18 October 2012, pp. 965–976. ACM (2012). https://doi.org/10.1145/2382196.2382298

19. Kellaris, G., Kollios, G., Nissim, K., O'Neill, A.: Generic attacks on secure outsourced databases. In: CCS 2016, Vienna, Austria, 24–28 October 2016, pp. 1329–1340. ACM (2016). https://doi.org/10.1145/2976749.2978386

20. Kiayias, A., Papadopoulos, S., Triandopoulos, N., Zacharias, T.: Delegatable pseudorandom functions and applications. In: CCS 2013, Berlin, Germany, 4–8 November 2013, pp. 669–684. ACM (2013). https://doi.org/10.1145/2508859.2516668

21. Kirsch, A., Mitzenmacher, M., Wieder, U.: More robust hashing: Cuckoo hashing with a stash. SIAM J. Comput. 39(4), 1543–1561 (2009). https://doi.org/10.1137/080728743

22. Lai, S., et al.: Result pattern hiding searchable encryption for conjunctive queries. In: CCS 2018, Toronto, ON, Canada, 15–19 October 2018, pp. 745–762. ACM (2018). https://doi.org/10.1145/3243734.3243753

23. Meng, X., Kamara, S., Nissim, K., Kollios, G.: GRECS: graph encryption for approximate shortest distance queries. In: Ray, I., Li, N., Kruegel, C. (eds.) CCS 2015, Denver, CO, USA, 12–16 October 2015, pp. 504–517. ACM (2015). https://doi.org/10.1145/2810103.2813672

24. Miers, I., Mohassel, P.: IO-DSSE: scaling dynamic searchable encryption to millions of indexes by improving locality. In: NDSS 2017, San Diego, California, USA, 26 February - 1 March 2017. The Internet Society (2017). https://www.ndss-symposium.org/ndss2017/ndss-2017-programme/io-dsse-scaling-dynamic-searchable-encryption-millions-indexes-improving-locality/

25. Naveed, M., Kamara, S., Wright, C.V.: Inference attacks on property-preserving encrypted databases. In: CCS 2015, Denver, CO, USA, 12–16 October 2015, pp. 644–655. ACM (2015). https://doi.org/10.1145/2810103.2813651

26. Patel, S., Persiano, G., Yeo, K., Yung, M.: Mitigating leakage in secure cloud-hosted data structures: volume-hiding for multi-maps via hashing. In: CCS 2019, London, UK, 11–15 November 2019, pp. 79–93. ACM (2019). https://doi.org/10.1145/3319535.3354213

27. Poddar, R., Wang, S., Lu, J., Popa, R.A.: Practical volume-based attacks on encrypted databases. In: EuroS&P 2020, Genoa, Italy, 7–11 September 2020, pp. 354–369. IEEE (2020). https://doi.org/10.1109/EuroSP48549.2020.00030

28. Ren, K., et al.: Hybridx: new hybrid index for volume-hiding range queries in data outsourcing services. In: ICDCS 2020, Singapore, 29 November - 1 December 2020, pp. 23–33. IEEE (2020). https://doi.org/10.1109/ICDCS47774.2020.00014

29. Song, D.X., Wagner, D.A., Perrig, A.: Practical techniques for searches on encrypted data. In: SP 2000, Berkeley, California, USA, 14–17 May 2000, pp. 44–55. IEEE Computer Society (2000). https://doi.org/10.1109/SECPRI.2000.848445

30. Sun, S., et al.: Practical backward-secure searchable encryption from symmetric puncturable encryption. In: CCS 2018, Toronto, ON, Canada, 15–19 October 2018, pp. 763–780. ACM (2018). https://doi.org/10.1145/3243734.3243782

31. Wang, J., Chow, S.S.M.: Simple storage-saving structure for volume-hiding encrypted multi-maps. In: Barker, K., Ghazinour, K. (eds.) DBSec 2021. LNCS, vol. 12840, pp. 63–83. Springer, Cham (2021). https://doi.org/10.1007/978-3-030-81242-3_4

32. Wang, J., Chen, X., Sun, S.-F., Liu, J.K., Au, M.H., Zhan, Z.-H.: Towards efficient verifiable conjunctive keyword search for large encrypted database. In: Lopez, J., Zhou, J., Soriano, M. (eds.) ESORICS 2018. LNCS, vol. 11099, pp. 83–100. Springer, Cham (2018). https://doi.org/10.1007/978-3-319-98989-1_5

Vulnerabilities

Upside Down: Exploring the Ecosystem of Dark Web Data Markets

Bogdan Covrig[1]([✉]), Enrique Barrueco Mikelarena[1], Constanta Rosca[1], Catalina Goanta[2], Gerasimos Spanakis[1], and Apostolis Zarras[3]

[1] Maastricht University, Maastricht, The Netherlands
b.covrig@maastrichtuniversity.nl
[2] Utrecht University, Utrecht, The Netherlands
[3] Delft University of Technology, Delft, The Netherlands

Abstract. Large-scale dark web marketplaces have been around for more than a decade. So far, academic research has mainly focused on drug and hacking-related offers. However, data markets remain under-studied, especially given their volatile nature and distinct characteristics based on shifting iterations. In this paper, we perform a large-scale study on dark web data markets. We first characterize data markets by using an innovative theoretical legal taxonomy based on the Council of Europe's Cybercrime Convention and its implementation in Dutch law. The recent Covid-19 pandemic showed that cybercrime has become more prevalent with the increase of digitalization in society. In this context, important questions arise regarding how cybercrime harms are determined, measured, and prioritized. We propose a determination of harm based on criminal law qualifications and sanctions. We also address the empirical question of what the economic activity on data markets looks like nowadays by performing a comprehensive measurement of digital goods based on an original dataset scraped from twelve marketplaces consisting of approximately 28,000 offers from 642 vendors. The resulting analysis combines insights from the theoretical legal framework and the results of the measurement study. To our knowledge, this is the first study to combine these two elements systematically.

1 Introduction

The rise of cryptocurrencies led to a flourishing marketplace environment on the dark web [5]. Since the first pioneering marketplace (i.e., Silkroad) has started using a technological customer infrastructure involving Tor, Escrow payments, and Bitcoin, hundreds of other platforms have followed suit. Once infamous for the drug trade, dark web marketplaces have also gradually become ecosystems to monetize unlawfully obtained data, ranging from stolen data to data dumps or blatant scams. The value of data traded like this is estimated to be USD 1.5 trillion annually, and it includes personal, corporate, and financial data [26]. While law enforcement has been increasingly active in taking down markets and vendors offering for sale drugs, guns, and other traditionally illicit goods, data markets remain underexplored.

© IFIP International Federation for Information Processing 2022
Published by Springer Nature Switzerland AG 2022
W. Meng et al. (Eds.): SEC 2022, IFIP AICT 648, pp. 489–506, 2022.
https://doi.org/10.1007/978-3-031-06975-8_28

Given their volatile nature and scale, dark web marketplaces are inherently challenging to investigate [3]. The adversarial ecosystem of dark marketplaces forces these environments to adapt constantly. This means business models, infrastructure, and market features (e.g., reputation systems) often do not have time to mature, and that new market iterations mushroom at a breakneck pace, often with different characteristics. Each year of activity may shape a different picture in this space, so it is essential to constantly generate new datasets, as most studies in this field often rely on older data. However, using empirical methods for automated data collection makes it easier to compare activity across marketplaces and understand how market structures evolve.

Data markets are hard to define, as the variety of things available for sale makes it difficult to categorize what *data* may be. For instance, data can range from personal information, aggregated public information, and software to online services. Simultaneously, while certain practices may develop around the virtual spaces where data is offered for sale, a vast spectrum of environments is used by vendors or providers, including dark web marketplaces, Tor forums, or private conversations. So far, most investigations on data markets are either tech journalism reports addressing individual incidents or investigations by cybersecurity companies, which often lack transparent and reproducible methodologies [10]; it is often unclear how these studies calculate their estimations, as they typically use sources from the web and not analyses of original data obtained from *.onion* pages. In addition, scientific studies focus on classifying hacking products [15] or the commoditization of cybercrime with particular emphasis on *Business-to-Business* (B2B) and *Business-to-Consumer* (B2C) transactions [22].

In this paper, we contribute to the existing literature on dark web measurement in two significant ways. First, we answer the question of how cybercrime harms on dark web data markets can be classified according to international standards of criminal law, as well as their incorporation in the Dutch legal system. Second, we explore data market economic activity by performing a comprehensive measurement of digital goods sold on twelve marketplaces.

In summary, we make the following main contributions:

- We build on earlier research and critically reflect on the criteria used to define and categorize data offers available on dark web marketplaces, including those proposed on the marketplaces we investigate.
- We propose a novel legal theoretical framework for the criminal qualification of economic activities on dark web data markets, including their punishment, as the foundation of further comparative law research that can complement web measurement methodologies.
- We report on economic indicators relating to offers, commissions, and vendors to describe the economic activity of the data markets in our original large-scale dataset, and we compare these results to earlier findings of studies focused on the commoditization of cybercrime.
- We discuss potential new features of dark web marketplaces based on their current iteration (e.g., the platformization or standardization of dark web marketplaces).

2 Crimes on Data Markets: A Legal Framework

The interest in dark web marketplaces, in general, and in data-related transactions, in particular, has been on the rise. However, even when zooming into the latter, the vast majority of these studies have a particular economic focus [11,14]. Such markets rely on and amplify the intermediation of cybercrime, and given the complex web of applicable rules and resulting legal uncertainty [18], expert legal analyses have not been used so far to classify dark web marketplace activities for the purpose of measurement studies. In this section, we endeavor to define data markets and qualify data products and services as crimes under international and Dutch law.

2.1 Defining Data Markets

Web marketplaces are virtual spaces connecting vendors with buyers. On the dark web, transactional environments are formed (*i*) randomly or structurally around communication networks such as forums (e.g., threads designed explicitly for transactions), or (*ii*) structurally around platforms that systematize transactions both for vendors and buyers (e.g., e-commerce platforms).

Data markets on the regular web are often categorized based on the object of the transaction (e.g., goods versus services) or based on the parties involved in the transaction (e.g., consumers or traders). This classification can affect the applicable legal regime, i.e., whether one can have ownership rights over data can distinguish goods from services. However, these criteria do not capture the legal harms arising on such markets. First, although the business models and industries formed around data are becoming complex [29], they are not often linked to legal qualifications under applicable legal regimes. Second, given the features of dark markets, such as pseudonymity and cybercriminality, it is often difficult to distinguish between consumers and traders. Other classifications focus on the type of data transacted and acknowledge personal, corporate, and financial data [26]. Still, as neither the law (e.g., personal data as defined by the GDPR is a highly interpretable concept) nor business practice led to harmonized criteria of cataloging data, such concepts remain vague.

The most popular approach to categorizing data-related transactions on the dark web focuses on the functional description of listings, which is the starting point of the categories employed by the marketplaces themselves. Dark web marketplaces as data markets can be thus said to have three essential characteristics:

- *From the perspective of the object of the transactions*, they are inherently illegal and, in consequence, operate in an adversarial setting for the purpose of which typical legal classifications of data goods and services are irrelevant.
- *From the perspective of the transacting parties*, pseudonymity makes it challenging to specify the nature of the actors in a transaction (B2B/B2C/C2C).
- *From the perspective of the nature of the listings*, while some items can be identified based on their functions (e.g., malware, tutorials, or guides), this clustering may sometimes result in overlaps (e.g., selling access to a cash-out bank account is very similar to selling access to a porn or a Netflix account).

2.2   Dark Web Marketplaces and Criminal Qualifications

Legal criminal qualifications of activities on dark web data marketplaces reflect a considerable research gap due to at least the following factors:

Lack of Legal Harmonization. Criminal rules governing cybercrime are inherently national. In other words, how cybercrime is regulated, interpreted, and enforced is left to the discretion of sovereign states [18]. Translating these standards into computational frameworks entails mapping national rules to create annotation taxonomies, which requires considerable interdisciplinary efforts involving computational methodologies and comparative law.

Regulatory Debt. With fast-evolving business models leading to new iterations of dark web marketplaces, the law is often criticized for lagging behind, as new technologies may render existing legal frameworks obsolete [2]. For criminal law, this may result in a constant need to generate new interpretations for existing legal standards or draft regulation in a future-proof manner.

Prioritizing Legal Practice. As cybercrime often leads to harm of real people, the literature on the dark web aims to assist law enforcement authorities optimize compliance with criminal rules [2]. Thus, theoretical frameworks based on expert knowledge are essential in making legal standards computational.

As such, we propose an exploratory legal taxonomy that aims to classify listings on dark web data marketplaces. Such a taxonomy makes two main contributions: (i) it complements existing academic research on measurement, economics, and criminology by systematically mapping a legal regime applicable to cybercrime, and (ii) it offers an approach to assessing cybercrime harms by highlighting maximum penalties imposed at the national level in the Netherlands. This theoretical framework shows the potential of exploring cybercrime from a comparative law and computational perspective, as further research can explore additional jurisdictions so that comparisons between legal regimes can be made.

Cybercrimes can be qualified according to general and special rules. To provide insights into criminal qualifications systematically, we depart from the Council of Europe's Convention on Cybercrime. The Convention governs a wide range of cybercrimes, ranging from hacking to interfering with computer systems. It also criminalizes certain Internet activities, but it does not harmonize the level of the sanctions imposed on these crimes since that is left to the discretion of the ratifying countries. This is why it is essential to map further the implementation of the Convention in a national legal system. To this end, we chose to report on the Netherlands, a jurisdiction where law enforcement has been actively pursuing the reduction of cybercrime through international and European coordinated actions. Dutch courts have also been increasingly dealing with cases relating to phishing and hacking. A complete overview of the Dutch implementation of the Convention can be found in Table 1, where the sanctions applicable to the cybercrimes comprised therein can also be consulted. It must be noted that this overview reflects legal statutes and thus constitutes a theoretical and descriptive rendition of the legal regime applicable in the Netherlands as a result of the ratification of the Cybercrime Convention.

Table 1. Legal qualifications of cybercrime according to the Cybercrime Convention and Dutch criminal law

Convention	Dutch Criminal Code	Maximum Jail Sentence (NL)
Illegal Access	Hacking	Max. 4 years
Illegal Interception	Tapping over Telecoms	Max. 2 years
	Placing of Tapping	Max. 4 years
Data Manipulation	Intentional Interference	Max. 4 years
Systems Interference	Intentional Sabotage	Max. 15 years
Misuse of Devices	Placing of Tapping	Max. 15 years
Computer-Related Forgery	Forgery	Max. 6 years
	Skimming	Max. 6 years
Computer-Related Fraud	Fraud	Max. 4 years

2.3   The Challenges of Mapping Legal Regimes

Mapping the criminal legal regime applicable to dark web data markets has several limitations. First, as the Cybercrime Convention pre-dates dark web marketplaces operating at scale, crimes such as illegal access and interception, data manipulation, systems interference, misuse of devices as well as computer-related fraud and forgery, reflect a criminal landscape with less intermediation than the supply chains amplified by the dark web. Courts, though, may interpret that in providing the tools with which additional crimes are perpetrated, for instance, sellers of malware can be held accountable for the crimes of their buyers.

Second, criminal courts' application of any legal rules will entail a level of discretion that goes hand in hand with the evidence presented in a criminal indictment, based on procedural safeguards. Evidence is also used to prove a perpetrator's criminal intent, essential in sentencing. Two provisions relevant to the Convention's implementation on Dutch law have not been integrated (see Table 1) since they deal with negligent interference and negligent sabotage, and they go beyond the seller-buyer relationship this paper focuses on.

Third, theoretical insights from Dutch law cannot be extrapolated to other legal systems with potentially different criminal public policies. While we do not tackle the problem of applicable law in this exploratory framework, it is worth noting that determining what criminal law applies to cyberspace is in itself a fascinating albeit highly complex question. Therefore, the location and nationality of sellers on the dark web may play a role in applying different or even diverging rules. This is why harmonization is necessary for this field.

Finally, other criminal rules are also applicable. Most prominently, these rules include criminalizing the making, distribution, or possession of child pornography, copyright-protected content, or other forms of illegal content. Interestingly, all the markets included in this paper have provisions excluding the sale of child pornography, and some prohibit even certain cybercrimes covered by the Convention. Dark web marketplaces can be seen as private legal orders which make their own rules regarding the conduct allowed on the platform. Most platforms draw up general terms and conditions to deal with rights and obligations for both vendors and buyers, ranging from contractual to moral standards. These terms also touch upon digital goods/services, such as government data.

3   Measuring Activity on Data Markets

3.1   Data Collection

To compile a list of marketplaces to crawl, we monitored the active marketplaces listed in the #Markets category on *Onion.Live*, a clearnet Tor Network directory created to monitor and study popular .onion hidden services. Having excluded marketplaces with niche specializations such as guns, drugs and/or cannabis, as well as local marketplaces (with the exception of Hydra, which is reportedly one of the largest and most resilient markets, having been in existence since 2015), we selected twelve omnibus marketplaces: *Asean, Big Blue, Darkfox, Dark Market, Deepsea, Empire, Hydra, Icarus, Neptune, Torrez, Versus*, and *White House*. After an initial exploration of these marketplaces, we targeted our collection of data to the offers listed under the *"Digital products"* and *"Fraud"* (where available) marketplace categories only, as these categories were most likely to contain offers of interest, essential for our study.

Since the available offers in the marketplaces continuously alter (i.e., new offers appear and the old ones get removed), we periodically crawled each marketplace to generate a more representative corpus of these offers. Our crawler was based on Selenium, a software-testing framework for web applications that can programmatically control a real web browser (Google Chrome connected to Tor in our experiments). This approach allowed us to retrieve the entire content of a rendered offer, which may not be possible if we used a simple command-line tool like wget. We scraped the content included in the categories mentioned above in a period of four months (June – September 2020). It must be noted that during this time, two of the markets (Empire and Icarus) were taken down, and thus we were able to crawl only a portion of these two markets. Another important fact is that all of the markets were available in English, except for Hydra, which was available in Russian.

Most of these marketplaces attempt to keep their activities away from prying eyes, especially those of automated bots designed to extract information of the marketplaces' activities. As such, they have deployed CAPTCHA mechanisms to protect themselves. To overcome this hurdle, we initiated the crawling process by logging in into the markets, manually solving any necessary CAPTCHAs, and storing the login and CAPTCHA cookies. The crawler then used these cookies to collect the data from the marketplaces without any barriers. Someone could claim that the process could become entirely automated, using machine learning techniques able to solve CAPTCHA challenges [27]. We did not try this approach because it requires long training periods, and the number of images needed to model each type of CAPTCHA made it unfeasible for us, given the number of markets we scraped, most of which used a different kind of CAPTCHA challenge. In addition, human intervention would still be needed when solving logical puzzles present in many markets as anti-DDoS measures. However, we found ways to minimize the amount of human intervention necessary by taking advantage of blind spots in these markets' bot detection algorithms or by exploiting bugs in the sites' implementation. These include:

1. Switch the onion circuit through which the crawler accesses the market.
2. Rotate trough different mirrors of the same market before or when getting blocked by the market.
3. Log out and log back in before reaching the threshold and flagged as a bot.
4. Go through the search results of a category and save the links that are then accessed randomly to avoid sequential scraping of the products.
5. Wait random times between visits.

For markets where we could not avoid being flagged as a bot, either we made the crawler notify us and wait until we would intervene if graphical puzzles were present, or in the case of markets that only required regular CAPTCHAs to be solved, an email was sent, and the solved CAPTCHA was read and submitted to the market to resume the scraping.

3.2 Data Preprocessing

Our crawler exfiltrated all the data available when visiting an offer from a marketplace. However, as the various marketplaces differ from each other, so do their data representation, which can produce misleading results. Therefore, the quality of data and their representation is considered the most critical step before running any analysis. As such, we have to bring the data to such a state that our algorithms can easily parse and interpret it.

Duplicates: The dataset duplicates were identified and removed. The reposts of the offers (e.g., exact title match but different price, date, or description) were kept for correlations and future analysis.

Prices: The offers' prices are displayed in different currencies depending on the market preferences. To have a more accurate view regarding the offers' prices, we normalized them by exchanging the displayed value to USD using the exchange rate recorded on 31 August 2020. From the price analysis, we dismissed the prices equal to zero (free offers) and higher than USD 1,000,000. After that, we discarded the outliers identified as prices lower/higher than two times the standard deviation below/above the average value for each market.

Vendors: Due to the pseudonymized nature of the scraped markets and the lack of vendor identification upon their registration, the vendors' cross-market identity cannot be fully recognized. We considered *unique vendors* by matching their exact username across markets. In addition, we anonymized the usernames of the vendors in the presented results. We attributed common first names to the vendors, keeping them consistent cross-table.

Categories: The available offers were categorized, and 15,377 of them were also sub-categorized. Given that many of the categories and sub-categories on

Table 2. Keywords assigned to categories

Category	Keywords
General data	*Account, database, plaintext, leads, accounts, streaming, hacked, voter, vpn, mobile, hacking, email, voters, cracked, crack, records, record, porn, clone, access, config, mba, checker, emails, dtabase, sentry, numbers, buffered*
Banking & tokens	*Card, carding, balance, credit, money, bank, cvv, cashout, gift, egift, carded, cards*
E-learning	*Method, tutorial, guide, hack, amazon, make, get*
PII	*psd, template, license, statement, passport, ssn, dob, fullz, utility*
Other	*Fraud, snapshot, month, mac, pack, android, paypal, market, login, live, bitcoin, generator, btc, usa*

the markets were relatively generic and not always comparable for the selected markets, we categorized the offer titles ourselves. We explored topic modeling and strategies deployed in previous studies, such as human labeling of the complete dataset. Natural language processing techniques, such as topic modeling yielded poor results. Instead of a labor-intensive human labeling process that would be difficult to apply in other contexts, we opted for a simple heuristic. We categorized the offers by selecting the most prevalent terms (or unigrams) in the offer titles across the platforms. We grouped the most prevalent and relevant unigrams (e.g., cvv, passport, porn) after discarding irrelevant terms (e.g., premium, lifetime, or other descriptors in the titles), the removal of which would not affect the nature of the offer. To do so, we manually scanned through the complete titles for each of the 100 most prevalent and relevant unigrams.

3.3   Economic Activity on Data Markets: Strange Facts

We explored various metrics that shed light on the economic activity taking place on the scraped marketplaces by showcasing relevant descriptive statistics. Based on the generated keywords and the categories previously found on the markets, the following categories were produced: (*i*) *General Data*, (*ii*) *Banking & tokens*, (*iii*) *E-learning*, (*iv*) *Personal Identifiable Information (PII)*, and (*v*) *Other*. Each offer was placed under categories based on its title containing at least one keyword from Table 2. This resulted in a coverage of 85,58%, meaning that almost nine out of ten offers could be categorized based on the selected unigrams, and some titles were considered in more than one category.

We compared the categorization results of the unigram method to those 11,261 product titles that had sub-category information from the labels used on the scraped markets. To do so, we manually grouped all different sub-categories present in the data and derived from the different markets (in total, there are 45, some overlapping) into the five categories that we constructed when using the unigram method. This way, we could compare for which of these products there is an agreement in the categorization. The method we applied finds that

Table 3. Overview of markets. Some vendors participate in more than one market; this is why the total number of vendors differs from the expected one.

Market	No. of offers	No. of vendors	Sum of offers ($)
Asean	4,043	36	30,663.95
Big Blue	1,669	78	31,381.80
Darkfox	1,300	34	21,446.80
Dark Market	3,629	127	73,956.12
Deepsea	4,210	111	46,757.14
Empire	2,690	135	38,176.93
Hydra	204	204	11,434.43
Icarus	4,091	37	28,961.87
Neptune	2,352	23	16,187.55
Torrez	615	14	5,399.99
Versus	901	25	5,330.83
White House	2,842	88	145,977.37
Total	**28,546**	**642**	**455,674.78**

Table 4. Overview of categories

Category	No. of offers	No. of vendors	Sum of offers ($)	Max. jail time (years)
General data	15,219	277	248,603.16	**2–15**
Banking & tokens	5,673	269	125,888.12	**2–6**
E-learning	3,821	181	27,920.27	**4**
PII	2,689	150	42,996.53	**6**
Other	10,410	573	186,039.71	**n/a**

there is a perfect match for only 46.70% of the titles. That percentage rises to 69.87% when considering products that the unigram assigns to two categories. By manually inspecting some of the titles where there was a disagreement, we observed that our method is superior in classifying many titles more accurately. Similarly, many sub-categories of markets that have broad titles (e.g., *Other*) are more accurately classified by our method (e.g., into *E-learning* or *PII*).

We subsequently looked at the sum of all offers on the twelve marketplaces. This represents the total offers (goods and services) advertised on the platforms (Table 3), which is one way of estimating the value of the total supply of data economy in the scraped categories (Table 4). However, prior research has shown the problems with such estimates [20]. These offers sometimes do no reflect real prices but are rather scam (i.e., meant to deceive buyers), spam, or may employ techniques such as *"holding price"* (i.e., raising the price so much that no one can afford to buy it), in an attempt to keep the offer listing open, while having the (temporary) intention of not selling, or marking the offer as not in stock.

An extreme example of holding price found in our dataset for the offers *"out of stock Wowcher accounts with balance Auto Delivery & Lifetime Warranty"*, as

Table 5. Top 10 spam offers

Offer	# Posts	Market	Vendor	# Sold	Price ($)
Credit Cards #1	25	Dark Market	Barb	189	20.00
Carding Software Setup	16	Dark Market	Barb	65	5.00
E-Gift Cards	14	Icarus	Connie	n/a	1.00
Debit Cards	13	Dark Market	Scott	16	20.00
Spotify Account	13	Neptune	Phil	0	1.92
RealityKings Account	11	Neptune	Phil	0	7.23
Credit Cards #2	10	Dark Market	Barb	44	15.00
TeamSkeet Account	10	Neptune	Phil	0	7.23
Torrent Accounts	10	Big Blue	Karen	n/a	20.52
Credit Cards #3	9	Dark Market	Holly	60	15.00

Table 6. Sum of Offers (with and without outliers)

Market	Sum of offers ($) with outliers	Sum of offers ($) without outliers	Difference
Asean	51,948.35	30,663.95	21,284.40
Big Blue	390,481.80	31,381.80	359,100.00
Darkfox	35,099.62	21,446.80	13,652.82
Dark Market	118,516.85	73,956.12	44,560.73
Deepsea	82,374.17	46,757.14	35,617.03
Empire	638,176.93	38,176.93	600,000.00
Hydra	18,511.24	11,434.43	7,076.81
Icarus	35,507.87	28,961.87	6,546.00
Neptune	31,184.52	16,187.55	14,996.97
Torrez	7,344.94	5,399.99	1,944.95
Versus	7,564.39	5,330.83	2,233.56
White House	486,177.37	145,977.37	340,200.00
Total	**1,902,888.05**	**455,674.78**	**1,447,213.27**

well as for *"not working Auto Delivery & Warranty"*, both listed at the skyrocketing value of USD 11,111,100,000.00. As the titles indicate, they are listed as *"out of stock"* and respectively *"not working"*. Particular attention can be paid to spam offers (Table 5). It seems that certain vendors list the same offer on the same market up to 25 times. Perhaps, this may be a marketing strategy aimed at making an offer more visible when browsing through listings to increase the number of sold items. However, what works for one vendor on one market (e.g., vendor *"Barb"* on *"Dark Market"*), might not apply to other vendors on other markets (e.g., vendor *"Phil"* on *"Neptune"*). Additional attention needs to be paid to 17 free offers in our dataset (USD 0.00): 10x *virtual camwhore* (offered by the same vendor), 1x *porn tutorial*, 2x *porn accounts* (offered by the same vendor), 1x *Spotify*, and 2x *bitcoin exchange accounts*.

Table 7. Top 10 vendors and offers by the number of sold units

Vendor	# Units	Offer	Market	Category	Price ($)	# Units
Eleven	13,838	Netflix Account #1	Empire	General data	3.35	4,712
Erica	9,211	Doordash USA Account	Empire	General data	2.99	2,354
Steve	5,523	Grubhub Account	Empire	General data	0.99	1,501
Billy	4,712	TryCaviar Account	Empire	General data	0.75	1,493
Jim	4,572	Get a free iPhone	Empire	E-learning	4.99	1,491
Bob	4,475	Make 2500$ a day on Bet365	Empire	E-learning	4.99	1,425
Robin	3,920	Tip Jar	Versus	Other	1.00	1,409
Sam	3,603	2 Brazzers Accounts	Empire	General data	1.95	1,338
Will	3,336	Netflix Account #2	Empire	General data	0.80	1,327
Murray	3,269	Deep Web Onion Links List	Empire	General data	1.30	1,280

Table 8. Top 10 vendors and offers by the number of markets

Vendor	# Markets	# Offers	Sum of offers ($)	Offer	# Markets	Category	Vendor	Price ($)
Will	9	3,120	30,312.86	Atlas Quantum Database	9	General data	Will	9.99
Jim	8	789	4,850.62	JobStreet Database	9	General data	Will	9.99
Robin	8	4,058	16,836.61	Money Bookers Database	9	Banking & tokens	Will	9.99
Mike	7	172	4,098.12	United Kingdom Mobile Numbers	9	General data	Will	9.99
Dustin	7	264	4,181.57	Australia Mobile Numbers	9	General data	Will	9.99
Lucas	6	81	1,440.39	Germany Mobile Numbers	9	General data	Will	9.99
Nancy	6	116	4,017.56	Italy Mobile Numbers	9	General data	Will	9.99
Jonathan	6	364	1,990.92	Oregon Voter Database	9	General data	Will	9.99
Karen	6	1,545	24,533.33	Canadian Business Database	8	General data	Will	4.50–65.00
Max	6	328	5,643.88	Canadian Residential Database	8	General data	Robin	9.00–65.95

There is no way of identifying holding prices that are not outliers. Thus, we decided to remove listings that were two standard deviations above and below the mean when calculating the sum of offers. Since we report the sum of offers rather than means of price listings, there was no need to remove zero-price listings. The results suggest that removing the outliers does not only have a significant impact on the sum of offers, but it also substantially reduces the differences between the sum of offers of the markets Table 6.

We continued the analysis by inspecting the distribution of vendors across multiple markets (Fig. 1). While the majority of vendors are present on one market (78.63%), vendors with the same name are present on anywhere between two and five markets (19,97%), and a few are present on up to six and nine markets (1,4%). Similarly, offers are also posted on multiple markets, albeit by different vendors. Table 7 and Table 8 provide more insights into which vendors and offers can be mostly found across the markets we inquired into.

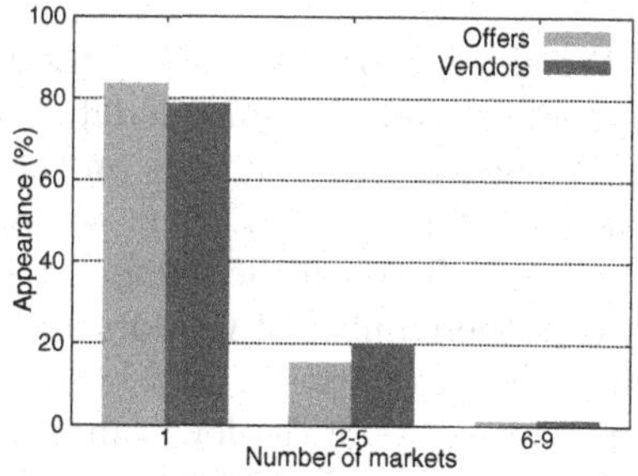

Fig. 1. Offers and vendors that appear in multiple markets

Table 9. Fees and commission rates

Market	Vendor fee (%)	Buyer fee (%)	Vendor bond ($)
Asean	3	n/a	400
Big Blue	1.5–3.5	0.5–2	250
Darkfox	4–5	n/a	150
Dark Market	n/a	5	750
Deepsea	2–4	n/a	150
Empire	n/a	n/a	n/a
Hydra	1.5–5	no fee	300
Icarus	n/a	n/a	n/a
Neptune	n/a	4	125
Torrez	4–5	no fee	250
Versus	n/a	n/a	n/a
White House	5	no fee	400

Table 10. Estimated marketplace turnover

Market	Maximum Bond ($)	Maximum Commission ($)	Estimated Turnover ($)
Asean	1,617,200.00	n/a	1,617,200.00
Big Blue	417,250.00	n/a	417,250.00
Darkfox	195,000.00	54.40	195,054.40
Dark Market	2,721,750.00	5,864.17	2,727,614.17
Deepsea	631,500.00	4,826.68	636,326.68
Hydra	61,200.00	n/a	61,200.00
Neptune	294,000.00	2.03	294,002.03
Torrez	153,750.00	n/a	153,750.00
White House	1,136,800.00	n/a	1,136,800.00
Total	**7,228,450.00**	**10,747.28**	**7,239,197.28**

We also explored the associations between the number of offers, the number of vendors, and the sum of offers on the various marketplaces. For this, we ran Pearson correlation tests on the elements mentioned above. The correlation between the number of offers and vendors is close to zero ($r = -.03, ns$). The correlations between the number of offers and the sum of offers ($r = .44, ns$) and between the number of vendors and the sum of offers ($r = .25, ns$) are moderate and weak, respectively, but both not statistically significant, which does not surprise because of the low sample size.

Finally, we looked at how much markets make based on their commissions (Table 9). For this purpose, we investigated what commission rates platforms apply by manually checking the general terms, FAQ sections, and other descriptive materials markets make available to their users. Some markets seem to be more buyer-friendly by only charging lump percentage fees to vendors, others only charge buyers, and some markets charge both vendors and buyers. A few markets have set up progressive commission rates, so they charge vendors depending on, for instance, the transaction price bracket they can be found in. The commission information was not available for all markets. Wherever it was available, we were able to estimate the maximum commission turnover. This is based on the maximum commission calculated on reported sales, which could be accounted for. As it can be observed in Table 10, the commission turnover varies across markets (e.g., Neptune's turnover resulted in a mere USD 2.03), and it can highlight whether data transactions are profitable for marketplaces.

Additionally, most markets also have rules on vendor bonds, namely a one-time fee that users need to pay to obtain vendor status. Not all markets charge bonds, and some deem them refundable. If marketplaces apply bonds to all vendors equally and if the bonds are non-refundable, they can make a considerable turnover based on this business model. However, many markets indicate in their terms and conditions or FAQs that bonds may be waived for various reasons (e.g., if vendors can prove their legitimate activity on other marketplaces). It is, therefore, problematic to make more accurate estimates of the marketplace turnover. In Table 10, we estimate the turnover based on the maximum turnover based on bonds and commissions. Overall, for the markets where this data was available, we could estimate that across six marketplaces, the overall bond and commission turnover amounts to USD 7,239,197.28. This does not account for additional business models such as the monthly rent which Hydra charges its vendors, as we have incomplete information regarding whether this fee is charged to all vendors, or only active vendors. If applicable to all vendors, this fee (USD 100.00) would generate an additional monthly turnover of USD 20,400.00 for the 204 vendors identified in our snapshot. Moreover, Hydra also refers to a commission charged for disputes started, meaning that economic incentives may be linked to reputation costs even more directly, as disputes can end up costing money in commissions paid, and not only sales lost as a reputation cost.

4 Discussion

4.1 Main Findings

Dark web data markets prove difficult to operationalize empirically. The field lacks methodologies for measuring basic characteristics such as the classification of data products. We explored topic modeling and strategies deployed in previous studies, such as human labeling of the complete dataset. Topic modeling yielded poor results. Instead of a labor-intensive and dataset-dependent process of human labeling, we opted for a simple heuristic. This approach successfully allowed us to identify offers for three categories: *Banking & tokens*, *E-learning*, and *PII*. Yet, most offers were assigned to the *General data* and *Other* categories.

These categories were then used to understand the legal risks according to the Cybercrime Convention implementation in the Netherlands. *General data*, the category featuring most listings and vendors, may reflect crimes sanctionable with incarceration where the maximum punishment ranges from 2 to 15 years. The high ceiling of this range is driven by the crime of intentional sabotage, which certainly includes the use and distribution of worms, viruses, trojans, and ransomware. However, punishments may only go beyond 6 years if lives are in danger or lost due to intentional sabotage. This may be the case when ransomware is used to take hospitals or other essential service operators hostage. This category of harms arising from dark web data marketplaces may deserve more individual attention or categorization in further research. What is interesting is that after setting aside the most harmful malware listings as described by the crime of systems interference (Convention) or intentional sabotage (Dutch Criminal Code), the category of *General data*, which includes the sale of data dumps affecting millions of individuals, leads to less severe punishments (max. 4 years) for the category of *PII*, which entails forging individual documents based on sold templates (max. 6 years). Similarly, the crime of skimming, associated with the category of *Banking & tokens*, leads to a higher punishment (6 years) than the crime of hacking (4 years). In the light of the measurement we completed, as *General data* is the most popular listing category, it is worth asking whether the current hierarchy of punishments in Dutch law is fit to tackle the realities of the dark web. Further research should explore the role of knowledge relating to criminal punishments on the activity of dark web markets.

The economic activity on the selected markets was examined in terms of the offers listed, activity across the 12 markets, best-performing products, and marketplace turnover. It was found that markets differ significantly in terms of the number of offers, vendors, and the sum of offers, with no weak and moderate correlations among them, meaning that there are markets with relatively few vendors but with a large number of offers and vice versa, but also there are markets with a large number of vendors, a large number of offers, and a large sum of offers. Consequently, the question arises whether it is possible to speak about **the dark web data marketplace** or it is more accurate to see this marketplace as a collection of markets with significant differences among them.

Interestingly, the sum of offers of around USD 455,000 is overwhelmingly lower than figures that are floating around in market research (e.g., USD 1.5 trillion annually [26]). Even when looking at the most popular ten offers (Table 7), there is a massive difference between how many units of the first and tenth most popular offers were sold (4,712 vs. 1,280), based on reported sales of one of the largest marketplaces in our dataset (Empire). The fact that not all marketplaces list sales is an interesting finding in itself. On earlier marketplaces such as the Silk Road, sale reports reflected a vendor's reputation [5]. However, reputation building takes time and maintenance (e.g., dealing with fake sales, fake reviews), and more volatile markets may not have sufficient resources to develop these systems under the adversarial circumstances they need to operate.

Furthermore, we find several similar listings and vendor names across different platforms. This finding is important because, in its early days, the dark web had a handful of markets that invested many resources into devising original solutions to improve their resilience. Nowadays, with ±20% of vendors operating on up to five marketplaces, this is reminiscent of developments on the regular web due to the platformization of digital transactions by intermediaries. Platforms simplify economic activity and reduce the necessary literacy skills and transaction costs. While the Internet's first dark web marketplaces had to be built from scratch, current marketplaces may take the form of Platform-as-a-Service, which may explain the proliferation of both marketplaces as well as the business models they support. This proliferation can signify a variety of marketing techniques in getting more business out of data transactions.

The cross-posting of items likely inflates estimates of cybercrime revenues, at least with respect to dark web data markets. Of course, we only included twelve markets, and our data collection is a snapshot rather than a longitudinally collected dataset. Nevertheless, our findings do question how much value should be attached to popular estimates of how the value is associated with data on the dark web. More generally, one may wonder how accurate any predictions about dark web data markets are, considering the difficulty of defining which product categories should fall under the umbrella of *dark web data markets*.

4.2   Limitations of the Study

For two of the markets (Empire and Icarus), we only have partial data, as they were taken down during our scraping. We also acknowledge that these statistics do not reflect longitudinal data but are a snapshot of the economic activity at the time of scraping. Like any online market, dark web data markets may be subject to constant changes. However, longitudinal of continuous scraping is difficult considering the technical measures (e.g., CAPTCHA) taken by markets. Moreover, certain variables of interest are difficult or impossible to capture. Closed transactions, and consequently, the actual number of sales, revenue, and profit, are not reported and are impossible to retrieve. Furthermore, categorization, or natural language processing tasks, prove difficult due to spelling mistakes, jargon, and abbreviations. Addressing these limitations might reveal additional characteristics and patterns compared to the ones presented in this paper.

4.3   Future Research

Future research should further compare and develop the categorization of titles of dark web data markets as well as address how to collect data over an extended period so that results across different studies can be more directly comparable. While academic literature on dark web marketplaces is growing, studies remain disparate and use complementary yet uncoordinated approaches from the perspective of a vast array of disciplines to investigate what is happening on dark web marketplaces. Yet, the nature of these marketplaces and the business models behind some of the offers (e.g., data markets) are highly volatile, so coordination may lead to more clarity regarding dark web marketplaces as objects of study.

This is not to say that further angles cannot be added to this already vast body of knowledge. A comparative analysis of cybercrimes in different legal systems (e.g., all EU countries or EU countries and the United States) could support additional or alternative computational measures of the activities offered on the dark web market to design public policy on this matter. Research may also include exploring relationships between what is offered on the markets by whom and against which price on the one hand and the governance structure of the platforms, including the terms of service. More generally, research into the trust mechanisms developed and applied on dark web markets and comparisons with offline equivalents could contribute to understanding the role of contracts and trust.

Finally, the platformization of dark web marketplaces warrants further investigation. While exploring and contextualizing dark web data markets, we encountered services offered for the creation of markets. Similarly to creating a WordPress website, one can create a dark web marketplace. It is interesting to discover the business models behind such platformization on dark web data markets, and dark web marketplaces in general, and how the platformization interacts with the economic activity in those places.

5   Related Work

Exploring the specifics of dark web activity has attracted the interest of many computer science studies. Research has explored anonymity and privacy regarding the use of the dark web [1] and tried to answer the questions about which actors can be found therein [23]. Trust and engagement in dark web forums have also been studied widely. In particular, there have been studies exploring the popularity of listings either by looking at trust mechanisms [25] or predicting demands for drugs (on such markets) using Wikipedia views [16]. Similarly, there has been research that explores the connection of dark web markets with the global drug supply chain [4]. Researchers have also been trying to provide forensic frameworks for assisting with the investigation of dark web markets [6]. Previous works have also attempted to automatically identify drug traffickers based on writing and photography styles [28], or detect multiple identities of the same vendor over different dark markets, again using photography style [24].

Researchers have looked into the factors that contribute to criminal performance and which influence the advertised price for offers like dumps and account credentials [8], the signals of trust used by vendors to indicate trustworthiness within their advertisements for stolen data [9], the structure and organisation of underground forums [7], and the type of interventions that can be applied [10]. Researchers have also developed tools for the automated analysis of cybercrime markets operating on underground forums [17], for profiling their member users and identifying top vendors in these communities [13].

Researchers have also studied the cybercrime and stolen dark web data markets by comparing the distribution of victim nations in stolen data markets and examining variations between Open and Dark Web operations [19], evaluating the factors influencing pricing for stolen identities [21], and categorizing products offered on marketplaces specializing in malicious hacking products [15]. A few classifications and measurement studies draw insights from legal scholarship, but expert legal analyses are generally lacking from this work [12].

To the best of our knowledge, this paper presents the first systematic study at the intersection of expert legal knowledge and web measurement approaches. It explores the characteristics of twelve dark web marketplaces focusing on the data economy in particular, instead of dark web markets in their entirety (e.g., including drugs) or on a sub-category of cybercrimes (e.g., malware economy).

6   Conclusion

This paper set out to understand and describe the criminal and economic activity on dark web data markets by focusing on two research questions: how to use criminal law insights from international and Dutch law to sketch an exploratory legal framework applicable to dark web data markets and how to measure such markets using an original large-scale dataset of twelve scraped marketplaces.

References

1. Beshiri, A.S., Susuri, A., et al.: Dark web and its impact in online anonymity and privacy: a critical analysis and review. J. Comput. Commun. **7**(3), 30–43 (2019)
2. Chertoff, M.: A public policy perspective of the dark web. J. Cyber Policy **2**(1), 26–38 (2017)
3. Christin, N.: Traveling the silk road: a measurement analysis of a large anonymous online marketplace. In: The Web Conference (2013)
4. Dittus, M., Wright, J., Graham, M.: Platform criminalism: the last-mile geography of the darknet market supply chain. In: Proceedings of The Web Conference (2018)
5. Goanta, C.: The private governance of identity on the silk road. Front. Blockchain **3** (2020)
6. Hayes, D.R., Cappa, F., Cardon, J.: A framework for more effective dark web marketplace investigations. Information **9**(8) (2018)
7. Holt, T.J.: Exploring the social organisation and structure of stolen data markets. Glob. Crime **14**(2–3), 155–174 (2013)
8. Holt, T.J., Chua, Y.T., Smirnova, O.: An exploration of the factors affecting the advertised price for stolen data. In: eCrime Researchers Summit (2013)
9. Holt, T.J., Smirnova, O., Hutchings, A.: Examining signals of trust in criminal markets online. J. Cybersecur. **2**(2), 137–145 (2016)
10. Hutchings, A., Holt, T.J.: The online stolen data market: disruption and intervention approaches. Glob. Crime **18**(1), 11–30 (2017)
11. Hyslip, T.S., Holt, T.J.: Assessing the capacity of DRDoS-for-hire services in cybercrime markets. Deviant Behav. **40**(12), 1609–1625 (2019)
12. Kaur, S., Randhawa, S.: Dark web: a web of crimes. Wirel. Pers. Commun. **112**(4), 2131–2158 (2020). https://doi.org/10.1007/s11277-020-07143-2
13. Li, W., Chen, H.: Identifying top sellers in underground economy using deep learning-based sentiment analysis. In: IEEE Joint Intelligence and Security Informatics Conference (2014)
14. Macdonald, M., Frank, R.: Shuffle up and deal: use of a capture-recapture method to estimate the size of stolen data markets. Am. Behav. Sci. **61**(11), 1313–1340 (2017)
15. Marin, E., Diab, A., Shakarian, P.: Product offerings in malicious hacker markets. In: IEEE Conference on Intelligence and Security Informatics (ISI) (2016)

16. Miller, S., El-Bahrawy, A., Dittus, M., Graham, M., Wright, J.: Predicting drug demand with wikipedia views: evidence from darknet markets. In: The Web Conference (2020)
17. Portnoff, R.S., et al.: Tools for automated analysis of cybercriminal markets. In: The Web Conference (2017)
18. Shillito, M.: Untangling the dark web: an emerging technological challenge for the criminal law. Inf. Commun. Technol. Law **28**(2) (2019)
19. Smirnova, O., Holt, T.J.: Examining the geographic distribution of victim nations in stolen data markets. Am. Behav. Sci. **61**(11) (2017)
20. Soska, K., Christin, N.: Measuring the longitudinal evolution of the online anonymous marketplace ecosystem. In: USENIX Security Symposium (2015)
21. Steel, C.M.: Stolen identity valuation and market evolution on the dark web. Int. J. Cyber Criminol. **13**(1), 70–83 (2019)
22. Van Wegberg, R., et al.: Plug and prey? Measuring the commoditization of cybercrime via online anonymous markets. In: USENIX Security Symposium (2018)
23. Wang, M., et al.: Who are in the darknet? Measurement and analysis of darknet person attributes. In: Proceedings of the International Conference on Data Science in Cyberspace (DSC) (2018)
24. Wang, X., Peng, P., Wang, C., Wang, G.: You are your photographs: detecting multiple identities of vendors in the darknet marketplaces. In: Asia Conference on Computer and Communications Security (2018)
25. Wehinger, F.: The dark net: self-regulation dynamics of illegal online markets for identities and related services. In: European Intelligence and Security Informatics Conference (2011)
26. Wilson, E.: Disrupting dark web supply chains to protect precious data. Comput. Fraud Secur. **2019**(4), 6–9 (2019)
27. Zarras, A., Gerostathopoulos, I., Fernández, D.M.: Can today's machine learning pass image-based turing tests? In: Lin, Z., Papamanthou, C., Polychronakis, M. (eds.) ISC 2019. LNCS, vol. 11723, pp. 129–148. Springer, Cham (2019). https://doi.org/10.1007/978-3-030-30215-3_7
28. Zhang, Y., et al.: Your style your identity: leveraging writing and photography styles for drug trafficker identification in darknet markets over attributed heterogeneous information network. In: Proceedings of The Web Conference (2019)
29. Zheng, Z., Zhu, J., Lyu, M.R.: Service-generated big data and big data-as-a-service: an overview. In: Proceedings of the IEEE International Congress on Big Data (2013)

An Efficient Use-after-Free Mitigation Approach via Static Dangling Pointer Nullification

Yue Yu[1,2], Xiaoqi Jia[1,2(✉)], Xun An[1,2], and Shengzhi Zhang[3]

[1] CAS-KLONAT (Key Laboratory of Network Assessment Technology, CAS),
BKLONSPT (Beijing Key Laboratory of Network Security and Protection
Technology), Institute of Information Engineering, Chinese Academy of Sciences,
Beijing, China
`jiaxiaoqi@iie.ac.cn`
[2] School of Cyber Security, University of Chinese Academy of Sciences,
Beijing, China
[3] Metropolitan College, Boston University, Boston, USA

Abstract. UAF (use-after-free) is one of the most severe program vulnerabilities, caused by dangling pointers. Existing vulnerability mitigation approaches either attempt to block possible exploitation without fixing the root cause problem, or identify and remove dangling pointers with huge runtime overhead. In this paper, we present SDPN (Static Dangling Pointer Nullification) to defeat use-after-free vulnerability by eliminating dangling pointers filtered in multiple stages during compilation time. We implement a prototype of SDPN and evaluate it using real-world CVE vulnerabilities, and the results show that SDPN can effectively protect programs from use-after-free vulnerability. We also test SDPN using SPEC 2006 and the experimental results demonstrate that the time overhead introduced by SDPN is almost negligible, i.e., <1%.

Keywords: Use-after-free vulnerability · Vulnerability mitigation · Alias analysis · Dangling pointer

1 Introduction

Use-after-Free (UAF) Vulnerability is widely used by attackers to remotely execute arbitrary code and escalate privileges. Such a vulnerability exists when dereferencing a dangling pointer, i.e., a pointer that points to a freed memory object. It is challenging to eliminate dangling pointers in the program due to at least the following two reasons. On one hand, the memory allocation/de-allocation, pointer nullification/re-initialization operations are usually handled in different functions, even different files, leaving opportunities for dangling pointers between the memory de-allocation in one function and the pointer nullification/re-initialization in another function. On the other hand, during program runtime, complicated pointer operations may lead to a number of alias

© IFIP International Federation for Information Processing 2022
Published by Springer Nature Switzerland AG 2022
W. Meng et al. (Eds.): SEC 2022, IFIP AICT 648, pp. 507–523, 2022.
https://doi.org/10.1007/978-3-031-06975-8_29

pointers that point to the same memory object. Hence, a memory de-allocation may produce lots of dangling pointers, which are nontrivial to be completely identified.

Existing works [5,6,14,17] use dynamic dangling pointer nullification to defeat UAF vulnerability. Such kind of nullification eliminates dangling pointers by implementing a pointing information management structure into the program, tracking point-to information and inserting nullify instructions after free operations. However, it introduces complex synchronization issues, and cannot handle memory allocation or release operation intensive applications. In addition, such an approach requires the program to maintain additional data structures during runtime, which will expand the original program's code space. Moreover, heavy instrumentation and extra address operations of this approach often involve some clear operations on function stack frames, which increases the risk of crashing the program. Finally, such a dynamic approach highly depends on the amount and diversity of testing inputs to the program to improve code coverage, but sufficient testing inputs are hard to obtain in reality.

In this paper, we view identifying dangling pointers as a demand-driven alias analysis problem and propose a novel mitigation approach against use-after-free vulnerability, Static Dangling Pointer Nullification (SDPN). SDPN involves two stages, namely analysis stage and dangling pointer repair stage. During the analysis stage, SDPN utilizes our alias analysis algorithm to collect potential dangling pointers, filters them according to the definition of the alias pointer, and classifies them into global dangling pointers, dangling pointers in the same function and dangling pointers in different functions. During the dangling pointer repair stage, SDPN directly repairs global dangling pointers and dangling pointers in the same function, and repairs the dangling pointers in different functions in the proper program location. We implement a prototype of SDPN, and demonstrate its effectiveness against real-world UAF vulnerabilities. We also evaluate it using SPEC CPU2006 benchmarks, and obtain negligible runtime overhead, i.e., less than 1%.

Our contributions are summarized as below:

- To the best of our knowledge, we are the first to use static analysis to eliminate dangling pointers.
- We generalize identifying dangling pointers as a special alias analysis problem and devise a novel algorithm to solve it.
- We implement a prototype of SDPN and evaluate it against real-world CVE vulnerabilities. The experimental results demonstrate its effectiveness against UAF, incurring negligible runtime overhead.

2   Background and Related Works

2.1   Background

Use-after-free and Dangling Pointers. A memory chunk allocated by a memory allocator can be pointed to by many pointers during the runtime of a program. When the memory chunk is freed, those pointers become dangling pointers. Essentially, the use-after-free vulnerability refers to the use of those dangling pointers. The root cause of the UAF vulnerability is that the memory chunk release does not destroy the pointers that dereference the memory chunk. Hence, using those dangling pointers may be exploited to escalate privileges or remote code execution.

In order to perform efficiency and defragment memory management, modern memory allocators, such as ptmalloc, usually put freed chunks into a well-designed linked list. If there exists any suitable freed chunk when the program requests memory next time, the chunk will be directly removed from the linked list to satisfy memory request. Attackers use the elaborate memory request to occupy the previously released chunk, then use a dangling pointer to access the memory. Therefore, use-after-free exploitation is to create a memory chunk that can be interpreted in different program semantics: in a certain period of program running, the memory units are interpreted as writable data; however, in another period of program running, the memory may be interpreted as control flow data, such as function pointers.

Dangling Pointer Analysis and Alias Analysis. Pointer operations in the program can be classified into create, use and release, corresponding to the three sets $\mathcal{C}$, $\mathcal{U}$ and $\mathcal{F}$ respectively. Program location of a pointer p is represented as l_p. $\forall p \in \mathcal{F}, \forall q \in \mathcal{U}$, the UAF vulnerability demands that p and q point to the same memory object spatially and there are one or more execution paths from l_p to l_q temporally [16]. In contrast, dangling pointers only require p and q point to the same memory object, so they are a pair of alias pointers spatially. Dangling pointer analysis basically is alias analysis starting from pointers in free memory statements.

Alias analysis [11,15,20] attempts to examine whether memory references point to the same memory, thus concluding alias:

$$Alias(p, q) = \begin{cases} true \ , \ if PointTo(p) == PointTo(q) \\ false \ , \ else \end{cases}$$

where $PointTo(p)$ is defined as a set consisting of variables or storage locations pointed to by a pointer p. $PointTo(p)$ can be obtained using point-to analysis, one of the most fundamental static program analysis techniques that analyze variables or storage locations that pointers point to [2].

Alias analysis can be regarded as the path reachability problem of the context-free grammar on the graph. [9] proposed four variants of alias analysis problems: the all-pairs L-path problem, the single-source L-path problem, the single target L-path problem and the single-source-single-target L-path problem. A variety of current studies mainly focus on solving the single-source-single-target alias problem [15,20] and the all-pairs L-path problem [18,19]. In fact, the dangling pointer problem should be viewed as the single-target L-path problem or the single-source L-path problem, that is, there must be at least one L-path for each dangling pointer to reach the memory release statement either forward or backward. For clarity, we define the set of dangling pointers associated with a pointer p as $DP(p) = \{q_0, q_1, ..., q_n\}$: $\forall q \in DP(p), Alias(p, q) = true$.

2.2   Related Works

Recently, many UAF mitigation measures have been proposed, e.g., Cling [1], Diehard [3], Dieharder [8], etc., which try to avoid unsafe memory reuse by reconstructing a new memory allocator. For example, Cling improves the memory safety by only allowing memory reuse of objects of the same type and alignment, but it still leaves the opportunity for attackers to exploit UAF vulnerability on objects of the same type. In addition, the approach of reconstructing the memory allocator highly depends on the actual deployment/operating environment. If the program is deployed in a non-secure allocator environment, such an approach will almost completely fail.

Reference counting approach [10] prevents recycling memory objects that still have dangling pointers point to, by keeping reference count values to the memory chunks in the program, and only reuses memory objects that have zero reference counts. However, this approach will delay the memory reuse in the program, and can still cause severe memory leakage if the to-be-reused memory is not properly cleaned up. In addition, such an approach requires strict and accurate instrumentation. Otherwise, the reference count value can be recorded incorrectly, leading to memory leakage and other security issues.

Runtime check, i.e., dynamic analysis, has been proposed to solve the problem of dangling pointers [4,7]. This approach identifies dangling pointers and prevents dangling pointer dereference by maintaining additional metadata for each pointer and precisely tracking its semantics. However, accurate pointer semantic tracking during runtime is a complicated and challenging problem, and may generate a huge amount of pointer-related data during runtime, thus incurring significant performance downgrade.

3   Overview

3.1   A Motivating Example

The method SDPN uses to identify dangling pointers is inspired by equipotentiality which refers to a region in space where every point in it is at the same potential in mathematics and physics. We found that alias properties are similar to equipotentiality, and this feature can simplify some program analysis.

There is an example to describe our idea as shown in Fig. 1. The left of Fig. 1 is a piece of code that goes through complex pointer assignments and finally releases the pointer p. For ease of expression, this code does not show the memory allocations and variable declarations. The right of Fig. 1 is the PEG (Program Expression Graph) converted from the code. The nodes labeled with numbers, such as $7, 8, 9$, on the PEG are temporary nodes generated by '*' (dereference), and the nodes labeled with letters, such as u, o, p, correspond to variables in the code. Horizontal arrows represent assignment edges (A) and vertical arrows represent dereference edges (D).

The code finally releases the memory pointed to by p, resulting in dangling pointers. For the safety of the program, we should nullify these dangling pointers.

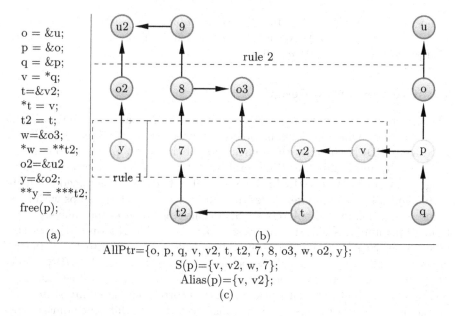

```
o = &u;
p = &o;
q = &p;
v = *q;
t=&v2;
*t = v;
t2 = t;
w=&o3;
*w = **t2;
o2=&u2
y=&o2;
**y = ***t2;
free(p);
```

(a)

(b)

AllPtr={o, p, q, v, v2, t, t2, 7, 8, o3, w, o2, y};
S(p)={v, v2, w, 7};
Alias(p)={v, v2};

(c)

Fig. 1. Example: Node p is the pointer in the free statement selected in the program. Horizontal arrows represent assignment edges (A) and vertical arrows represent dereference edges (D).

Nullifying the pointer p is obvious and easy to do. The other dangling pointers are supposed to be aliases for the pointer p, but it's hard to find out. In the process of finding these dangling pointers, we found that the alias correlation of pointers with p forms an equipotential layer with the combination of assignment and dereference operations. For example, other pointers after some assignments would necessarily be an alias. It seems that their layers have not changed. The dereferencing operation is like lowering the level, and the address taking operation (reverse dereferencing) is similar to raising the level. After the rise and fall of the level, it is possible to make alias when the pointer returns to the alias level. We found that aliases must be in the equipotential layer, but the aliases in the equipotential layer are not necessarily aliases. This feature does not accurately determine aliases, but can be used to narrow down the range of pointers that are considered when looking for aliases. The layer are discussed further in Sect. 4.1 and Sect. 4.4. The relationship between equipotential layers and aliases is summarized as Rule 1 and Rule 2.

Following this intuition, we introduce a new parameter *level* to the PEG graph to roughly measure the relationship between pointers. *Level* will propagate and change with the edges on the graph. Equipotential surfaces based on level values can be used to filter pointers. We can filter out nodes with the same level value such as $\{v, v2, w, 7, y\}$. Next, we can make more accurate judgments about the pointers in the set. Node 7 is actually the variable $v2$, because t and $t2$ are aliases with each other and both point to $v2$. After pointer analysis, we found that, $PointTo(v) = PointTo(v2) = PointTo(p) = \{o\}, PointTo(w) = \{o3\}, PointTo(y) = \{o2\}$. According to the definition of alias, $v, v2$ are alias with pointer p and should be nullify.

3.2 Overview of the Design

This paper designs and implements a prototype SDPN that uses a multi-step filtering method to find out dangling pointers. The whole process is shown in Fig. 2. In Stage 0, SDPN compiles the source code of the target program to generate the llvm IR, and builds the PEG graph with the *level* parameter of the target program according to the IR. In Stage 1, SDPN finds free pointer nodes in the graph, and collects all pointer nodes that may have alias relationships with these pointers to form selected pointers set $S(p)$. This stage reduces the analysis target from all pointers to selected pointers set. In Stage 2, SDPN reduces the selected pointers set $S(p)$ to remained pointers set $DP(p)$ according to the definition of the alias and the validity of the pointers in $S(p)$. In Stage 3, SDPN divides $DP(p)$ into global pointers, local pointers of the same function stack and local pointers of different function stacks, generates corresponding nullify statements and finds corresponding insertion locations according to different pointer types to complete the repair. Finally, SDPN will generate the repaired executable.

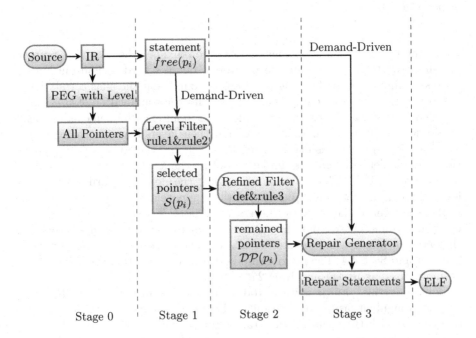

Fig. 2. Overview

4   Design

4.1   Stage 0: Generate PEG with Level

This section describes the program information that needs to be obtained during the SDPN analysis phase.

PEG (Pointer Expression Graphs) [19,20] $G = (N, E)$ is a bidirected graph extracted by program statements. N is set of nodes and E is set of edges. The nodes of PEG represent variables in the program, and there are two types of edges: pointer dereference edges (D) and pointer assignment edges (A). Edge D represents the dereference relationship between variables. For example, the expression *p in the C language will produce two nodes $*p$ and p, and an edge here to express that *p can be obtained by dereferencing p, $p \xrightarrow{D} *p$. Edge A represents the assignment relationship between variables. For example, the expression $p = q$ means that the value of q is assigned to p, so there is an edge A, $p \xleftarrow{A} q$. In PEG, there is a reverse edge for every edge, i.e., $\forall p \xrightarrow{D} *p \in E$, so $p \xleftarrow{\overline{D}} *p \in E$; $\forall p \xleftarrow{A} q \in E$, so $p \xrightarrow{\overline{A}} q \in E$.

Previous research used a detailed context-free grammar path reachability method in order to analyze all aliases as accurately as possible. The productions of the context-free grammar for alias analysis on a PEG graph is as follows [20]:

$$M \quad ::= \quad \overline{D} \, V \, D \tag{1}$$

$$V \quad ::= \quad (M?\overline{A})^* \, M? \, (AM?)^* \tag{2}$$

There are two types of aliases here: memory aliases, M, represents two pointers point to the same memory; value aliases, V, represents two pointers evaluate to the same pointer value. In the grammar, '?' indicates 0 or 1 repetition; '*' indicates any repetition. If the labels on the edges in the connection path between two pointers can be reduced to the above formula, then the two pointers are aliases to each other. However, SDPN adopts a method of producing candidate aliases first, and then gradually screening to make the results more precise. SDPN can use some non-essential and sufficient conditions derived from the above formula to select candidate pointers.

In order to deduce the filter rules, SDPN extends the traditional PEG nodes with a new parameter *level*. Mark the pointer p in each free statement as $level = 1$, and start the graph traversal from this node. The traversal process passes through the A and $\overline{A}$ edges, and the level remains unchanged; after the $\overline{D}$ edges, the level increases by 1; after the D edges, the level decreases by 1.

$$
\begin{array}{lll}
p = \&o & lv_p = lv_o + 1 & \text{[ADDR]} \\
p = q & lv_p = lv_q & \text{[COPY]} \\
p = *q & lv_p = lv_q - 1 & \text{[LOAD]} \\
*p = q & lv_p = lv_q + 1 & \text{[STORE]}
\end{array}
$$

Fig. 3. Interpretation of expressions on extended PEG graphs

As Fig. 3, the calculation of level is equivalent to interpreting the expressions in the program as follows: the ADDR expression is translated into $\overline{D}$ edge on the PEG graph, so the level value increases by 1 along the direction of the edges; the COPY expression is translated into A edge on the PEG graph, so the level value remains unchanged; the LOAD expression is translated into a combination of D edge and A edge on the PEG graph, so the level value should be decremented by 1; the STORE expression is translated into a combination of A and $\overline{D}$ edge on the PEG graph, so the level value should be incremented by 1.

4.2   Stage 1: Level Filter

Now, SDPN has extended PEG. Next, we will show how SDPN implements the filtering of candidate alias pointers through the new level attribute.

SDPN introduces a $lv()$ function:

$$lv(x) = \begin{cases} x.level, \ x \in N; \\ |n_1.level - n_2.level|, \ x \ is \ (n_1 \to n_2) \in E; \\ lv(e_1) + ... + lv(e_n), \ x \ is \ (e_1 \to ... \to e_n) \in Path \end{cases}$$

For $lv(x)$, if x is a node, return the level value of the node x; if x is an edge, return the absolute value of the level difference between the start node and the end node of this edge; if x is a path, return the absolute value of the level difference between the start node and the end node of this path.

For the context-free grammar (1)(2) on PEG mentioned above for alias analysis,

$$lv(M) = lv(\overline{D} \ V \ D)$$
$$= lv(\overline{D}) + lv(V) + lv(D)$$
$$= 0$$
$$lv(V) = lv((M?\overline{A})^* \ M?(AM?)^*)$$
$$= (lv(M)? + lv(\overline{A}))^* + lv(M)? + (lv(A) + lv(M)?)^*$$
$$= 0$$

According to the definition above, $lv(A) = lv(\overline{A}) = 0, lv(D) = -1, lv(\overline{D}) = 1$. Here '?' is interpreted as (0 or 1). Two '*' are take any natural number, suppose take m and n. Bringing in the above two formulas, we know that $lv(M) = lv(V) = 0$.

That is to say, both memory alias and value alias require that the level difference of the traversed path is 0. But conversely, the two endpoints of a path with a level difference of 0 are not necessarily aliases to each other. For example, $\overline{D}AD\overline{A}$ has a path level difference of 0, but it does not belong to the grammar of aliases.

SDPN uses two filtering rules based on the above conclusions to obtain alias pointers related to free pointers from all pointers in the program.

Rule 1: For any node p, the level value of its alias node is the same as it, but the node with the same level value as it is not necessarily its alias.

This is a necessary but not sufficient condition. Although we cannot use it to accurately determine the alias, we can use it to do the first screening. With this simple condition, the number of candidate nodes with a size of $|\mathcal{C} \cup \mathcal{U} \cup \mathcal{F}|$ drops drastically.

Rule 2: Starting from node p, the nodes reachable by the path through nodes with $lv(o) < 0$ will not be aliases of p.

If $lv(o) >= 1$, it is possible to reach node m through a path, $lv(m) = 1$.

If $lv(o) = 0$, it means that the level of node o needs to be reached by dereference of node p. Then when the node o takes the address and assigns it to another pointer q, then q returns to the $lv(q) = 1$ layer. It is possible for q and p to become aliases.

If $lv(o) = -1$, it means that the level of node o is reached by dereference twice of node p. Suppose this dereference chain is $p \xrightarrow{*} m \xrightarrow{*} o$. If the level wants to rise, it must go through the $ADDR$ or $STORE$ instructions. That is, only the address of the o node can be stored in the new memory address node n and n is stored in q, so an address chain $q \xleftarrow{\&} n \xleftarrow{\&} o$ is generated. It is possible that node m and node n are aliases because they may both point to node o. But p and q cannot be aliases, because the new node q can only point to the new node n, and cannot point to the old node m. The aliases of p should, all point to node m, not a new node, even though the pointer n represented by the new node is equal to m.

The deeper reason is that the pointer can be used to obtain the object it points to, but the pointer cannot be obtained routinely according to the object. It can then be inferred that a node cannot affect the alias relationship between nodes that are more than two layers higher than itself. In the example of Fig. 1, the level of node p is 1, then the level value of node 9 becomes -1, and the node y reached through node 9 can be filtered out in advance.

SDPN generates the initial alias candidate nodes by starting a demand-driven graph traversal process from pointer in every free statement while calculating the level value with these two rules and combines these nodes into set $\mathcal{S}(p)$.

4.3   Stage 2: Refined Filter

$\mathcal{S}(p)$ is a set of aliases selected according to necessary conditions, many of which are false positives. This section discusses how to use the definition of alias and variable scope to filter those aliases that are not true.

Definition of Alias Analysis. SDPN combines the elements of $S(p)$ one by one with the release pointer p for more precise filtering. There are two ways to determine whether two pointers are aliases: single-source-single-target alias analysis or alias definition. Since the single-source-single-target alias analysis is similar to the stage 1 analysis, SDPN selects the definition for further analysis:

def: Aliased pointers represent two pointers point to the same memory.

It just find the *PointTo* set of dangling pointer dp and free pointer p, separately and then determine the relationship between the two sets by definition of alias. If $PointTo(dp)$ and $PointTo(p)$ are completely equal, the relationship between dp and p can be considered as must alias. If these two sets have intersection but are not necessarily equal, the relationship between these two pointers can be considered as may alias. If the intersection of these two sets is $\emptyset$, the relationship between these two pointers can be considered as no alias. When repairing the dangling pointers in the Sect. 4.4, SDPN will also insert dynamic judgment code, so in order to reduce the false negative rate, we select may alias as the filtering result.

Useless Alias Filter. SDPN divides $S(p)$ into three categories according to the positional relationship between the dangling pointers and the pointers in free statements: global dangling pointers, dangling pointers in same function with free statements and potentially dangerous dangling pointers not in same function with free statement. The scope of a stack pointer is limited to the function this pointer belongs to. One of the more complicated cases is when a dangling pointer and a pointer in free statement come from different functions.

The life cycle of a global pointer has gone through two stages: the normal pointer stage before the free expression, and the dangling pointer stage after the free expression. It is throughout the entire program, so once a dangling pointer is formed, it will pose a potential threat until the end of the program. Not every dangling pointer will cause use-after-free vulnerabilities, but dangling pointers are the prerequisite for most use-after-free vulnerabilities. These global dangling pointers will all be nullify at the appropriate locations in Sect. 4.4.

The life cycle of the stack pointer is too short, so some methods of dynamically clearing dangling pointers directly ignore all stack pointers. Most of the dangling pointers in different functions with a released pointer have been destructed when the program executes to the free statement. However, Some dangling pointers still on the function stack are not discussed by other papers. They are not destructed when the free statement is executed. So stack pointers also risk serious vulnerabilities.

SDPN uses relative call paths to solve the problem. The relative call string $rcs = [f_1...f_n]$ is used to represent the function call relationship from the function, f_1, where a dangling pointer dp is located to the function, f_n, where release statement $free$ is located. If such a path exists, it means that there is a runtime state where the dangling pointer is still in the function stack, and the program will re-enter the scope of dp in the future. If such a path does not exist, the dangling pointer dp can be ignored. This is filter Rule 3:

Rule 3: A dangling pointer will be filtered if there is no call path from the function containing the dangling pointer to the free statement.

SDPN combines Rule 3 and stack pointer repair localization implemented in Algorithm 1 discussed in Sect. 4.4. SDPN utilizes these strategy to eliminate a large number of meaningless stack pointers in $S(p)$ and produce a new set $DP(p)$. Now the remaining dangling pointers in $DP(p)$ are either risky or meaningful.

4.4   Stage 3: Repair Generator

Dangling pointers in $DP(p)$ have to be repaired now, including global dangling pointers, dangling pointers in same function with free statements and potentially dangerous dangling pointers not in same function with free statement. In this section, we design their own repair schemes for the two dangling pointers.

Global Dangling Pointers Repair. Generally, the global dangling pointer has the longest life cycle, so it has the greatest probability of being converted into a use-after-free vulnerability. Global dangling pointers can be accessed in most locations in the program, so they can be all nullified directly after the appropriate free statements like g_bzf in Fig. 4. Nullified dangling pointers cannot completely prevent the occurrence of vulnerabilities, but they can downgrade high-threat vulnerabilities to null pointer dereferences that are basically useless. In view of the existence of false positives in the analysis results, a conditional statement should be inserted before the nullification code in the program. This conditional statement will determine whether each global pointer actually points to the memory location pointed to by bzf when the program has just executed the $free(bzf)$ expression.

Stack Dangling Pointers Repair. It is more difficult to nullify the stack dangling pointers. The life cycle of a stack variable is very short, and the scope of the variable is the function which the variable belongs to. However, dangling pointers are often located in different functions with the $free$ statement, so it may not be possible to access some dangling pointers immediately after the $free$ statement. If the stack dangling pointers in $DP(p)$ are in the same function stack frame with statement $free$, they can be nullified in accordance with the global pointer method. In other cases, the stack dangling pointers can only be accessed or nullified in its function. Therefore, the specific nullification statement should be inserted after a statement in its function that can be called deeply into the $free$ statement like Fig. 4.

For dangling pointers in different function with its free statements, this paper proposes Algorithm 1 to find the appropriate nullification statement insertion locations. These pointers can not be cleared immediately after the free statement, and the use operation of the use-after-free vulnerability can not occur.

```
'bzip2/bzip2.c'
    BZFILE* g_bzf;
    void compressStream ( FILE *stream, FILE *zStream )
    {
        BZFILE* bzf = NULL;
        ...
        bzf = BZ2_bzWriteOpen ( &bzerr, zStream,
                                blockSize100k, verbosity, workFactor );
        g_bzf = bzf;
        ...
        BZ2_bzWriteClose64 ( &bzerr, bzf, 0,
                             &nbytes_in_lo32, &nbytes_in_hi32,
                             &nbytes_out_lo32, &nbytes_out_hi32 );
++++    bzf = NULL; // dangling pointer in different func
        ...
    }
```

```
'bzip2/bzlib.c'
    void BZ2_bzWriteClose64
                    ( int*            bzerror,
                      BZFILE*        b,
                      ...)
    {
        bzFile* bzf = (bzFile*)b;
        ...
        free ( bzf );
++++    if( b == bzf )
++++        b = NULL;   // dangling pointer in the same function
++++    if( g_bzf == bzf )
++++        g_bzf = NULL; // global dangling pointer
++++    bzf = NULL;
    }
```

Fig. 4. Repair Example: g_bzf was added for demonstration purposes. The b and bzf in the function $BZ2_bzWriteClose64$, the bzf in the function compressStream and the global variable g_bzf are the dangling pointers formed by the free statement in the function $BZ2_bzWriteClose64$.

Dangerous execution regions are the remaining unexecuted statements in the function which the dangling pointer was born in. The algorithm is to find all positions in the function where the dangling pointer is located that can reach the free statement in the Call-Graph. The function $isReachable$ is use a common graph traversal algorithm. In addition, there may be multiple caller functions in the same function that can execute to the free statement. So the output of the algorithm is a set containing all the locations to be inserted.

Algorithm 1: Stack-pointer repair location search

Data: The function which the dangling pointer dp belongs to, fun_{dp}.
The function which the $free$ statement belongs to, fun_f.
The array of instructions in function dp_{dp}, $InstArray$.
Function $CallGraph = <N, E>$
Result: $InstSet$, Nullification statement will insert after $inst \in InstSet$.

```
 1  Function LocationSearch(InstArray, funf):
 2      for inst : InstArray do
 3          if inst is call Instruction then
 4              node ← CallGraph.getNode(fundp);
 5              sinkNode ← CallGraph.getNode(funf);
 6              edgeSet ← inst.getOutEdgeSet();
 7              for edge : edgeSet do
 8                  srcNode ← edge.getDstNode();
 9                  if isReachable(srcNode, sinkNode) then
10                      InstSet ← InstSet ∪ inst;
11                      break ;
12                  end
13              end
14          end
15      end
16  end
17  Function isReachable(src, sink):
18      worklist ← src;
19      visited(src);
20      while worklist is not empty do
21          node ← worklist.pop() if node = dst then
22              return true;
23          end
24          edgeSet ← inst.getOutEdgeSet();
25          for edge : edgeSet do
26              temp ← edge.getDstNode();
27              if not isVisited(temp) then
28                  worklist.push(temp);
29                  visited(temp);
30              end
31          end
32      end
33      return false;
34  end
```

---

5   Evaluation

In this section, we compare the performance of SDPN-protected program and the original program. First, we test how effective SDPN mitigate UAF exploits. Next, we measured the overhead of analysis phase and runtime phase. All experiments are carried out on Ubuntu 20.04.3 LTS system (Linux Kernel 5.11.0-44-generic) with a quad-core 3.90 GHz CPU (Intel Xeon E3-1240 v5), 48 GB RAM, 1TB SSD-base hard disk.

5.1   Implementation

We implement a prototype SDPN that statically clears dangling pointers on top of the llvm 12.0.0 compiler framework. SDPN uses the bytecode file composed of llvm IR as input, and dumps the repaired IR to another bytecode file ending in '_dpn.bc'. SDPN uses SVF [12] to extract CFG, PAG, SVFG and other intermediate graph structures from llvm IR. SDPN combines the instruction traversal api of CFG and llvm to obtain the order of execution of the instructions. The PAG in the SVF project is converted into PEG with *level* by SDPN for pointer selection and filtering. SDPN utilizes SUPA [13] as pointer analysis, a demand-driven and strongly updated pointer analysis performed on the SVFG. SDPN uses c++ to implement various pointers filtering and verification rules , and repair location and generation on llvm and SVFG.

5.2   Security

To test the effectiveness of our method, we choose five real word UAF vulnerability in two software. We select programs that are open source programs and with available pocs. As list in Table 1.

Table 1. Security evaluation against real world vulnerabilities

CVE ID	Affected Program	Dangling pointer type	Result
CVE-2018-20623	Binutils 2.31.1	Same function pointer	Protected
CVE-2018-5747	Lrzip 0.631	Global pointer	Protected
CVE-2018-11496	Lrzip 0.631	Global pointer	Protected
CVE-2018-10685	Lrzip 0.631	Different function pointer	Protected
CVE-2017-8846	Lrzip 0.631	Different function pointer	Protected

5.3   Runtime Overhead

As SDPN employs static analysis and static instrumentation to clear potential dangling pointers, the main overhead of this method lies in the static analysis phase and its runtime overhead is very little. The statically inserted instructions are just simple like if instruction, empty operation, and adding some global variables. Since the dangling pointer corresponding to the object is relatively limited, the inserted instructions are relatively few, instead of blindly tracing pointers in a dynamic way. Therefore, after inserting instructions, the size of the file should not change much compared with its original state. According

Table 2. Statistics for SPEC CPU2006.

Name	Lan.	Alloc	Free	Pointers	Stage1	Stage2	Stage3	Insert-inst	Analysis	Overhead
bzip2	C	5	5	21589	142	129	20	35	1 s	0
mcf	C	3	3	3486	9	8	6	9	0	0
milc	C	54	37	31762	296	233	76	115	2 s	0.85%
namd	C++	0	0	90866	0	0	0	0	6 s	0
soplex	C++	16	16	82814	4721	2563	422	828	87 s	0
hmmer	C	37	297	80828	297	297	297	297	626 s	0
sjeng	C	10	18	33614	291	105	18	18	3 s	0
libquantum	C	14	9	8898	13	13	8	8	0	0.90%
lbm	C	1	1	4724	4	2	0	0	0	0
astar	C++	22	19	11439	654	505	107	195	2 s	0.11%

to the data in Table 2, it can also be found that the size of the file has not changed much. Intuitively, this method should bring extremely small, or almost no additional memory overhead. And according to the experimental results, the additional memory overhead is very little indeed.

The overhead of SDPN running SPEC CPU2006 is shown in Table 2. It can be found that the runtime overhead of SDPN is little, with the maximum additional runtime overhead less than 1%. In fact, the impact of the three different types of pointers on the program overhead is also very different. Global dangling pointers and dangling pointers of the same function contain many pointers used by free statements. For these dangling pointers, we only add clearing operations; while the remaining dangling pointers will add safe clearing judgments. The branch statement will bring more overhead to the program.

6   Discussion

Loops and pointer arithmetic are what make a lot of static analysis inaccurate. The loop will continuously increase the node level value calculated by SDPN. If the level of the freed pointer node is 1, we guess that the greater the difference with the node level, the less likely it will become a dangling pointer. SDPN adopts the method of dynamic loop unrolling by setting the maximum level value: if the level value is higher when entering the loop, the number of loop unrolling becomes less; if the level value is lower when entering the loop, the number of loop unrolling is greater. In llvm, pointer computation and address dereference operations are separated. Therefore, SDPN interprets computation instructions as level-invariant propagation instructions. Although we considered these two situations in the pointer filtering, the pointer analysis method selected in the subsequent stage did not consider it. So the final result ignores both cases.

7   Conclusion

Now there are several dynamic dangling pointer elimination methods available, but no programmer is willing to deploy them to eliminate dangling pointers because of their high runtime overheads. Based on the static program analysis, SDPN has low runtime overhead and slightly changes the original program. We applied it to the UAF vulnerability in the real world, which shows the effectiveness and compatibility of SDPN. Through a series of evaluation experiments, we proved that SDPN has very low runtime overhead and hardly changes the program. We believe SDPN will be applied to real-world applications to eliminate dangling pointers.

Acknowledgement. We would like to thank all of our participants for taking part in the study. This work is supported in part by Program of Key Laboratory of Network Assessment Technology of Chinese Academy of Sciences, Program of Beijing Key Laboratory of Network Security and Protection Technology, National Key Research and Development Program of China (No. 2019YFB1005201), Strategic Priority Research Program of Chinese Academy of Sciences, Grant No. XDC02010900.

References

1. Akritidis, P., et al.: Cling: a memory allocator to mitigate dangling pointers. In: USENIX Security Symposium, pp. 177–192. Washington DC (2010)
2. Andersen, L.O.: Program analysis and specialization for the C programming language. Ph.D. thesis (1994)
3. Berger, E.D., Zorn, B.G.: Diehard: probabilistic memory safety for unsafe languages. **41**, 158–168. ACM New York, NY, USA (2006)
4. Caballero, J., Grieco, G., Marron, M., Nappa, A.: Undangle: early detection of dangling pointers in use-after-free and double-free vulnerabilities. In: Proceedings of the 2012 International Symposium on Software Testing and Analysis, pp. 133–143 (2012)
5. Lee, B., et al.: Preventing use-after-free with dangling pointers nullification. In: NDSS (2015)
6. Liu, D., Zhang, M., Wang, H.: A robust and efficient defense against use-after-free exploits via concurrent pointer sweeping. In: Proceedings of the 2018 ACM SIGSAC Conference on Computer and Communications Security, pp. 1635–1648 (2018)
7. Nagarakatte, S., Zhao, J., Martin, M.M., Zdancewic, S.: CETS: compiler enforced temporal safety for c. In: Proceedings of the 2010 International Symposium on Memory Management, pp. 31–40 (2010)
8. Novark, G., Berger, E.D.: Dieharder: securing the heap. In: Proceedings of the 17th ACM Conference on Computer and Communications Security, pp. 573–584 (2010)
9. Reps, T.: Program analysis via graph reachability. Inf. Softw. Technol. **40**(11–12), 701–726 (1998)
10. Shin, J., Kwon, D., Seo, J., Cho, Y., Paek, Y.: CRCount: Pointer invalidation with reference counting to mitigate use-after-free in legacy c/c++. In: NDSS (2019)
11. Sridharan, M., Bodík, R.: Refinement-based context-sensitive points-to analysis for java. ACM SIGPLAN Not. **41**(6), 387–400 (2006)
12. Sui, Y., Xue, J.: SVF: interprocedural static value-flow analysis in llvm. In: Proceedings of the 25th International Conference on Compiler Construction, pp. 265–266. ACM (2016)
13. Sui, Y., Xue, J.: Value-flow-based demand-driven pointer analysis for c and c++. IEEE Trans. Softw. Eng. **46**(8), 812–835 (2018)

14. Van Der Kouwe, E., Nigade, V., Giuffrida, C.: Dangsan: scalable use-after-free detection. In: Proceedings of the Twelfth European Conference on Computer Systems, pp. 405–419 (2017)
15. Yan, D., Xu, G., Rountev, A.: Demand-driven context-sensitive alias analysis for java. In: Proceedings of the 2011 International Symposium on Software Testing and Analysis, pp. 155–165 (2011)
16. Yan, H., Sui, Y., Chen, S., Xue, J.: Spatio-temporal context reduction: a pointer-analysis-based static approach for detecting use-after-free vulnerabilities. In: 2018 IEEE/ACM 40th International Conference on Software Engineering (ICSE), pp. 327–337. IEEE (2018)
17. Younan, Y.: FreeSentry: protecting against use-after-free vulnerabilities due to dangling pointers. In: NDSS (2015)
18. Zhang, Q., Lyu, M.R., Yuan, H., Su, Z.: Fast algorithms for dyck-cfl-reachability with applications to alias analysis. In: Proceedings of the 34th ACM SIGPLAN Conference on Programming Language Design and Implementation, pp. 435–446 (2013)
19. Zhang, Q., Xiao, X., Zhang, C., Yuan, H., Su, Z.: Efficient subcubic alias analysis for c. In: Proceedings of the 2014 ACM International Conference on Object Oriented Programming Systems Languages & Applications, pp. 829–845 (2014)
20. Zheng, X., Rugina, R.: Demand-driven alias analysis for c. In: Proceedings of the 35th Annual ACM SIGPLAN-SIGACT Symposium on Principles of Programming Languages, pp. 197–208 (2008)

Author Index

Printed in the United States
by Baker & Taylor Publisher Services